CONQUESTS AND CULTURES

CONQUESTS
AND
CULTURES

AN
INTERNATIONAL
HISTORY

THOMAS SOWELL

Basic Books
A Member of Perseus Books, L.L.C.

First edition.

Library of Congress Cataloging-in-Publication Data
Sowell, Thomas, 1930–
Conquests and cultures / Thomas Sewell.
p.   cm.
Includes bibliographical references and index.
ISBN 0-465-01399-6
1. War and civilization. 2. Conquerors—History.
3. Imperialism—History. 4. Ethnology. I. Title.
CB481.S58   1998
325'.32—dc21   97-50290
CIP

1   3   5   7   9   10   8   6   4   2
98   00   01   99

Now, if there be a fact to which all experience testifies, it is that when a country holds another in subjection, the individuals of the ruling people . . . think the people of the country mere dirt under their feet . . .

JOHN STUART MILL

CONTENTS

	Preface	*ix*
	Acknowledgments	*xiii*
Chapter 1	Conquests and Cultures	3
Chapter 2	The British	22
Chapter 3	The Africans	99
Chapter 4	The Slavs	174
Chapter 5	Western Hemisphere Indians	249
Chapter 6	An Overview	329
	Notes	381
	Index	477

PREFACE

This book completes a trilogy that began with *Race and Culture* in 1994 and continued with *Migrations and Cultures* in 1996. All three were initially parts of a single huge manuscript that I began writing in 1982. Over the next decade, it grew to a size that militated against its becoming the one book that it was initially conceived to be. Parts of that original manuscript were removed over the years. Other material from the original manuscript was incorporated into a fourth book, an international study of affirmative action programs titled *Preferential Policies: An International Perspective*, published in 1991, before any of the books in this trilogy. The remaining material was not simply split into three parts but also continued to grow and develop as I read new scholarly studies that were being published during the long incubation period of this trilogy.

The underlying theme of all these books has been that racial, ethnic, and national groups have their own respective cultures, without which their economic and social histories cannot be understood. Modest as this claim may seem, it collides head-on with more widely accepted visions in which the fates of minority groups are determined by "society" around them, which society is therefore both causally and morally responsible for the misfortunes peculiar to the less fortunate of these groups—though apparently not responsible for the good fortune of the more successful minority groups. This trilogy also collides head-on with prevailing doctrines about "celebrating" and preserving cultural differences. Cultures are not museum-pieces. They are the working machinery of everyday life. Unlike objects of aesthetic contemplation, working machinery is judged by how well it works, compared to the alternatives. The judgment that matters is not the judgment of observers and theorists, but the judgment implicit in millions of individual decisions to retain or abandon particular cultural practices, decisions made by those who personally benefit or who personally pay the price of inefficiency and obsolescence. That price is not always paid in money but may range from inconveniences to death.

On a broad international canvas, the role of culture reaches beyond particular racial and ethnic groups to encompass the differing economic and social fates of nations and of civilizations. That is particularly true of the present volume, which deals with the cultural consequences of conquests. Like migrations, conquests have changed the cultural landscape of the world. Indeed, the great mass migrations which have had such historic impact in the Western Hemisphere, Australia and New Zealand, and to a striking though lesser extent in Southeast Asia and Africa, have often been fostered by prior conquests. Those who resettled in these regions have not been simply members of the conquering nation or race, but have also included those who migrated from other lands with different cultures and races—the overseas Chinese in Southeast Asia, emigrants from India in East Africa and Lebanese immigrants in West Africa—settling under the protection of a colonial system of law and government in which they had greater confidence than in the laws and governments of the indigenous peoples. Among the indigenous peoples themselves, greater local or regional mobility became feasible under foreign hegemony than when different indigenous groups controlled different regions and jealously guarded them against outsiders. The negative aspects of conquest, ranging from routine oppressions to wanton slaughters and atrocities, are of course not to be overlooked either.

The history of conquests, like the history of international migrations, extends to a broader canvas many racial, ethnic, and cultural issues usually discussed within the restricted confines of a given nation. The histories of conquests in the chapters that follow also cover a wider time dimension than the histories of migrations, simply because the age of mass migrations across the oceans of the world began much later than the age of conquests, which encompasses all of recorded history. Thus, while most of the group histories in *Migrations and Cultures* begin no earlier than the eighteenth century, the history of the British in this volume begins in the days of Roman Empire, when the intrusion of a more advanced culture began a long process of transformation of an island and a people.

Nor was this peculiar to Britain. The long shadow of Rome still falls over much of Europe—and the absence of the Roman cultural contributions has left other parts of Europe economically and socially in arrears for centuries, as the history of the Slavs illustrates. In still earlier times, the civilizations developing in the Middle East and in China likewise had cultural consequences that reached thousands of miles beyond the countries in which these civilizations developed. The current cultural impact of the Western world on non-Western societies is neither a new nor a unique phenomenon, and has lasted thus far nothing like the many centuries in which cultural advances radiated outward from China or from the nations clustered around the eastern end of the Mediterranean.

What matters ultimately is not what themes or conclusions are proposed here, but the facts behind those themes and conclusions. That is why recourse must be had to history, rather than to abstract models. That history also has the incidental effect of offering an opportunity to appreciate how much more fortunate we are than peoples who lived through much poorer times, with far more limited options, and often suffered enormously in the process of producing the advancements we take so much for granted today.

Explosive issues of racial differences can be assessed more rationally on an international scale and over many centuries of history, viewing other times and peoples more dispassionately than we can our own, and drawing on a wider variety of evidence produced under a wider range of circumstances than in the contemporary world around us. The enormous changes in the relative positions of peoples—and of nations and civilizations—over the centuries not only undermines theories which may seem more plausible within narrower confines of a given time and space, it provides far more variables to consider. Here, as elsewhere, what matters are not so much the particular conclusions reached but the knowledge and understanding acquired in the process of reaching them—which knowledge and understanding are equally available to those who read this evidence differently.

Those who yearn for the certainties of doctrine or the elegance of abstract theoretical models will not find them here. As a noted economic historian has aptly said, "perhaps an inelegant analysis of a central problem would be more valuable than a rigorous analysis of a peripheral issue."[1] The purpose of this trilogy is not to say the last word on the vast subject of peoples and cultures but, on the contrary, to open a wider door for exploration by others. Certain kinds of historical writings have been characterized as "works which may be visibly more than ephemeral and still considerably less than definitive."[2] That is the honorable role to which this series of books aspires.

THOMAS SOWELL
Rose and Milton Friedman Senior Fellow for Public Policy
The Hoover Institution

ACKNOWLEDGMENTS

A work of the scope of these three volumes could not have been written without the help of many other people, in many roles, in countries around the world. A full acknowledgement of my indebtedness to others whose scholarly studies, logistical support, analytical foundations, or financial underwriting made these books possible would be a book in itself. The fifteen years during which my synthesis evolved were enriched and inspired by many specialized studies from both earlier and contemporary times. Victor Purcell's monumental study of *The Chinese in Southeast Asia*[1] first turned me toward the international study of ethnic groups in general. Charles Price's model of painstaking scholarship, *Southern Europeans in Australia*,[2] as a further inspiration and source of insights which applied to many other groups in many other countries. Fernand Braudel's beautifully blended combination of geographical, historical, and cultural analysis of the Mediterranean world of the sixteenth century,[3] Bernard Lewis' masterful writings on the history of the Islamic world,[4] and the works of many others in many fields contributed invaluable knowledge and perspectives. These authors were among the giants on whose shoulders I have tried to stand. However, gratitude, like charity, must begin at home—in this case, with the Hoover Institution and with my research assistant, Na Liu, and my secretary during most of the years when these volumes were being written, Agnes Page.

The freedom to go my own way, for years on end, with minimal accounting and no real monitoring, was the greatest gift of the Hoover Institution. Without this, none of the rest of it—not even the generous financing of extensive international travel, including two trips completely around the world—could have enabled a study of this scope and magnitude to evolve at its own pace, modified by reconsiderations, tempered by new insights from a variety of sources published while this work was in progress, and rewritten innumerable times for clarity and readability. Na Liu's research went beyond looking up things I needed and included contributing insights and suggestions of her own about things I had not thought of. Both she and my secretary, Agnes Page, also formed a protective ring around me, preventing my work from being interrupted and my time from being frittered away by numerous people, whose requests and desires were in most cases quite reasonable individually, though collectively impossible. Ruth Alben, my agent for speaking engagements, also spared me and my office from having to deal with many requests to give talks, thereby allowing us to put more time into this study. A note of appreciation is also due to Nancy Wright, who has filled in as secretary and research assistant from time to time over the years, doing excellent work in a job that is demanding, even for those who do it regularly, since I am almost never on hand to help with knotty problems that arise.

Among those whose financial support enabled this study to take place, in addition to the Hoover Institution itself, were the Institute for Educational Affairs and the Earhart Foundation. Decades earlier, a generous grant from the Earhart Foundation—at the request of the late and great George J. Stigler—enabled me to complete the studies that led to my receiving a Ph.D. at the University of Chicago, and to having a career as an economist.

After the manuscript was ready for publication, my wife Mary then gave it its last and most critical reading, leading me to make some changes, argue about others but, in the end, produce a better book on a vast subject whose challenges required much help.

Among the other people whose help deserves to be acknowledged individually, there will undoubtedly be some inadvertently omitted through the vagaries of memory and to those I can only offer my apologies. Those whose contributions are remembered are, in alphabetical order, Dr. Bernard E. Anderson, Assistant Secretary of Labor, Professor

Reginald Appleyard of the University of Western Australia (Perth), Dr. H. Avakian, Australian Institute of Multicultural Affairs (Melbourne), Dr. Alexandre Bennigsen of the École des Hautes Études en Sciences Sociales (Paris), Dr. André Bétéille, University of Delhi, Dr. Marie Bennigsen Broxup, editor of *Central Asian Survey*, Professor Rondo Cameron of Emory University, Dr. Suma Chitnis of the Tata Institute of Social Science (Bombay), Professor Gregory Clark of Stanford University, Professor Walker Connor, Trinity College (Connecticut), Professor John B. Cornell, University of Texas, Mr. Suman Dubey of *India Today* (New Delhi), Dr. Peter Duignan of the Hoover Institution (Stanford), Professor James Fawcett, Director of the East-West Center, University of Hawaii, Professor James R. Flynn of the University of Otago (New Zealand), Dr. Lewis Gann of the Hoover Institution (Stanford), Mr. Hu Gentles of the Private Sector Organisation of Jamaica, Mr. Petro Georgiou of the Australian Institute of Multicultural Affairs (Melbourne), Professor Margaret A. Gibson of California State University (Sacramento), Mr. Harvey Ginsberg of William Morrow Publishers, Professor Nathan Glazer of Harvard University, Professor Anthony G. Hopkins of Oxford University, Professor Donald L. Horowitz of Duke University, Professor James Jupp, Australian National University (Canberra), Professor Wolfgang Kasper of the Australian Defence Force Academy (Campbell), Professor Robert Klitgaard of the University of Natal (South Africa), Mr. Leslie Lenkowsky of the Hudson Institute, Mr. Greg Lindsay of the Centre for Independent Studies (Sydney), Professor Seymour Martin Lipset of Stanford University, Professor John McKay, Monash University (Australia), Dr. Ratna Murdia of the Tata Institute of Social Science (Bombay), Professor Charles A. Price of the Australian National University (Canberra), Dr. Alvin Rabushka of the Hoover Institution (Stanford), Mr. Sohindar S. Rana of the U.S. Information Service (New Delhi), Professor Peter I. Rose of Smith College (Massachusetts), Miss Claudia Rosett of the *Asian Wall Street Journal* (Hong Kong), Dr. Dominique Schnapper of the École des Hautes Études en Sciences Sociales (Paris), Dr. Sharon Siddique and Dr. Kernial Sandhu Singh of the Institute for Southeast Asian Studies (Singapore), Professor Sammy Smooha of the University of Haifa (Israel), Professor Leo Suryadinata of the National University of Singapore, Professor Malcolm Todd, University of Exeter (England), Mrs. Mary Lynn Tuck, American Historical Society of Germans from Russia (Nebraska), Professor

Philip E. Vernon of the University of Calgary (Canada), Professor Myron Weiner and Mr. Steven Wilkinson of the Massachusetts Institute of Technology, and Dr. S. Enders Wimbush of the Strategic Applications Intelligence Corporation (Virginia).

CONQUESTS AND CULTURES

CHAPTER 1

CONQUESTS AND CULTURES

"We do not live in the past, but the past in us."[1] Conquest is a major part of that past and a major shaper of the cultures of the world today. Wars of conquest have changed the language, the economy, and the moral universe of whole peoples. As a result of conquests, the Western Hemisphere is today a larger region of European civilization than Europe itself. Even those in the Western Hemisphere who hate European civilization express that hatred in a European language and denounce it as immoral by European standards of morality. The history of conquests is not just about the past, it is very much about the present and about how we came to be where we are economically, intellectually, and morally.

While migrations have transferred knowledge, skills, technology, and economically valuable aptitudes around the world, conquests have played a more varied and ambiguous role. Where a technologically or organizationally more advanced people have conquered a people lagging behind in these respects, then conquest—like migration—has been a way of spreading the existing human capital of mankind and promoting the development of more human capital among more peoples. But, where conquerors are clearly less economically or intellectually developed than those they conquer—a common situation for centuries, during which ancient civilizations in the Middle East were prey to mounted nomadic warriors from the steppes of Central Asia[2]—

3

then conquest has not promoted the spread of human capital, but instead has destroyed much of it where it existed and prevented civilization from spreading to militarily vulnerable areas. Ancient and irreplaceable manuscripts went up in flames when illiterate barbarian invaders or marauders set fire to libraries for the sheer pleasure of destruction.

Roman conquerors spread a more advanced civilization from the Mediterranean to Western Europe, with momentous impact on the history of the world, but the destruction of the Roman Empire by invading barbarians produced one of the most catastrophic retrogressions of whole peoples ever seen. Scholars may debate how many centuries it took medieval Europe to recover the standard of living it had once enjoyed in Roman times, but what is not debatable is that it took centuries—and, in some respects, more than a thousand years.[3] The Moors' conquest of medieval Spain brought with it an Islamic culture that was, at that juncture in history, more advanced than Europe's in such fields as mathematics, science, medicine, and philosophy. In Asia, ancient Chinese culture likewise spread by conquest.

At one period of history or another, conquest has encompassed virtually all peoples, either as conquerors or as victims, and the consequences have been wide-ranging as well. Some conquests have been followed by systematic exterminations of the vanquished, as in Rome's conquest of Carthage. Nor have such draconian policies been limited to major conquerors of historic dimensions. The massacres of the Tutsi by the Hutu, and vice versa, in late twentieth century Africa and "ethnic cleansing" in the Balkan wars of the same era clearly show that it does not take a great power to create great human tragedies. Nor have the much idealized Polynesians been immune:

> On the Chatham Islands, 500 miles east of New Zealand, centuries of independence came to a brutal end for the Moriori people in December 1835. On November 19 of that year, a ship carrying 500 Maori armed with guns, clubs, and axes arrived, followed on December 5 by a shipload of 400 more Maori. Groups of Maori began to walk through Moriori settlements, announcing that the Moriori were now their slaves, and killing those who objected. . . . A maori conqueror explained, "We took possession . . . in accordance with our customs and

we caught all the people. Not one escaped. Some ran away
from us, these we killed, and others we killed—but what of
that? It was in accordance with our customs."[4]

Spontaneous atrocities and deliberate, systematic terror have long
marked the path of the conqueror. The Mongol hordes who swept
across vast reaches of Central Asia, Eastern Europe, and the Middle
East, cultivated an image of ruthless barbarities, as a calculated strategy to demoralize future victims.[5] But, although the Mongols excelled
in such practices, they had no monopoly of them. The Normans did the
same.[6] Emperor Basil II of the Byzantine Empire in the eleventh century ordered the blinding of 99 of every 100 Bulgarian captives, leaving each 100th man with only one eye to lead the others back home, so
as to provide graphic evidence of the emperor's treatment of his enemies.[7] It was a common practice in the Ottoman Empire to present the
sultan with pyramids of severed heads of enemy soldiers, usually
defenseless prisoners, sometimes numbering in the thousands.[8]

Twentieth century conquests have been equally hideous. The
Japanese conquest of the Chinese capital of Nanking in 1937 was followed by an orgy of rapes of thousands of women living there, the use
of Chinese soldiers and civilians for bayonet practice, and a general
wanton slaughter of civilians.[9] Similar atrocities marked Japanese
conquests throughout Southeast Asia during the Second World War.
Their allies, the Nazis in Germany, set new lows for brutality and
dehumanization, of which the Holocaust against the Jews was only the
worst example.

While conquest has often produced horrifying tragedies, its consequences have extended far beyond those tragedies. In some cases,
where whole ways of life have changed in the wake of conquest, later
generations of the conquered peoples have been born into an enlarged
world of ideas, of technology, and of possibilities undreamed of by
their ancestors. It is both unnecessary and impossible to determine the
net advantages or disadvantages of conquest. Often the benefits and
the losses have each been of staggering dimensions and long dura-
tions, with consequences that have been cultural, institutional, and
biological.

CAUSES AND CONSEQUENCES OF CONQUESTS

Conquests often have not only cultural consequences but also cultural antecedents. While one culture may be more effective militarily and another culture more effective economically, in many cases the two things interact. For example, more efficient methods of agriculture or industry, capable of supporting higher population densities on a given amount of land, can give one side decisive military advantages in launching attacks with larger armies, whose conquests then spread more effective economic methods to new lands or peoples.

In ancient times, sedentary agriculture was an epoch-making advance beyond seeking food by hunting or gathering the spontaneous products of nature, or by transient slash-and-burn planting methods. Because sedentary agriculture supported much higher population concentrations, it spread and transformed the world, not only by example but also by conquest. Those groups still practicing slash-and-burn methods of cultivation, which usually support only thin population densities, were often forced off their lands and up into the hills or out into the hinterlands and backwaters by people from regions with more dense populations, made possible by sedentary agriculture. Hunter-gatherers, who had not yet achieved even primitive forms of agriculture, were of course even more thinly spread and therefore even more vulnerable. Rice cultivation supports especially heavy population densities, so it is not surprising that the irrigation systems crucial to rice cultivation in many parts of Asia were spread by conquests in China, India, and the southeastern regions of the continent.[10]

Cultural Consequences of Conquests

In Europe, a thousand years after the Roman Empire had come and gone, those parts of the continent once conquered by the Romans remained culturally different—and more advanced—than those regions which had not been. The Christian religion and Latin letters long remained symbols of this cultural demarcation between Western Europe and Eastern Europe, though other cultural differences persisted for centuries after Eastern Europe adopted Christianity and parts of it began to use the Latin alphabet.[11] Similarly, in Southeast Asia, those regions conquered by the ancient Chinese dynasties continued to incorporate aspects of the Chinese culture into their own ways of life, centuries after they became independent nations and China ceased to be an empire.

Cultures in prolonged contact with one another usually influence one another, whether that contact is due to conquest, migration, or commerce. At the most elementary level, material things are interchanged, whether these be products of industry or of nature. Sugar, cocoa, maize, and rubber were just some of the products of the Western Hemisphere that became known throughout Europe, Asia, and Africa as a result of conquest, while horses, guns, liquor, and literacy all became familiar to the indigenous peoples of the Western Hemisphere by the same process. Particular skills are often also interchanged between conquerors and conquered, and these too can range widely, from agricultural skills to such intellectual skills as mathematics, philosophy, and astronomy.

The Slavic and Baltic peoples whose lands were overrun by German conquerors during the Middle Ages and the early modern era were exposed to, and to some extent incorporated into, German culture. Later, Polish immigrants to the United States from Prussia brought artisan and industrial skills largely lacking in Polish immigrants from outside the German cultural orbit. These Prussian Poles were more often literate, Lutheran, and familiar with the world of modern commercial and industrial societies. Among the relatively few Polish immigrants who became machinists, shoemakers, weavers, tailors, or cabinet makers in the United States, most came from Prussia, while the majority of other Polish immigrants were unskilled laborers, many of whom ended up in the coal mines of Pennsylvania.[12] Not all these skills among Prussian Poles were absorbed within Prussia itself. Hundreds of thousands of Poles migrated westward to the industrial heartland of Germany in the Ruhr valley to work in the industries there.[13]

It was much the same story halfway around the world in India. Among the millions of Telugu-speaking people in eastern India during the colonial era, some lived under the direct rule of the British conquerors while others lived under Indian princes. When these peoples were united, years after India's independence, into a newly created state of Andhra Pradesh, the Andhras who had lived under British rule proved to be overwhelming competition for the Telanganans who had lived under Indian princes. Andhras not only bested the Telanganans on civil service examinations, taking over great numbers of government jobs as a result, but also outperformed them in agriculture, where they were able to buy out Telanganan farmers and make their farms much more productive and more profitable.[14]

Cultural dissemination among the conquered peoples is neither automatic nor uniform, however, and the consequences of uneven dissemination may be momentous and long-lasting. As will be seen in the chapter on the British, the technological and entrepreneurial achievements of the English did not inspire similar achievements among the Welsh or the Irish whom they conquered, though among the Scots such achievements not only inspired imitation, but also further developments, which ultimately enabled the Scots to surpass the achievements of the English themselves in some fields, such as medicine and engineering.

Where the spread of skills from the conquerors to the conquered proceeds unevenly among different groups of the conquered people, sometimes due to varying proximity to the cultural centers of the conquerors and sometimes due simply to different receptivities to the conqueror's culture, this can also create greater economic inequality among the conquered. Even more explosively, it can create a reshuffling of the relative positions of different groups in the society, so that historically poorer and lower-ranked groups rise above their erstwhile superiors and remain above them after the conquerors have withdrawn and the country has become independent. Thus the rise of the Ibos in Nigeria and the rise of the Tamils in Sri Lanka during the colonial era set off bitter social reactions that lasted into the era of independence, ultimately leading to civil war in both countries.

Different groups in the same conquered nation may also react differently in terms of resistance to or collaboration with the conqueror. Thus, during World War II, the Serbs in Nazi-occupied Yugoslavia formed a guerilla movement while many of the Croats collaborated with the Nazi puppet regime. (Halfway around the world, at the same time, the resistance movement against the Japanese occupation of Malaya was overwhelmingly Chinese, while the collaborators were more often Malays.) Such differences left legacies of intergroup bitterness, long after the war itself was over and the conquerors were gone. In earlier centuries, some of the Balkan peoples conquered by the Ottoman Empire converted to Islam and became part of the privileged or ruling classes in that region, while others were subordinated to Moslem overlords—again, adding another legacy of lasting intergroup bitterness among the already fragmented peoples of that region.

Sometimes the differences among the conquered peoples were not ethnic but varied by social class. Often the higher classes among the conquered people have adopted the language and the ways of the conqueror, in order to gain a share in the wealth and power of the new order, while the masses (lacking such tempting opportunities) have clung to the native language and the old ways. This cleavage may reach such an extreme that the very laws and business of government are carried on in a language foreign to the majority of the population subjected to those laws and that government, as in Norman England or in twentieth-century Ceylon.

Not all conquests involve a culturally more advanced conqueror, as these conquerors themselves have clearly understood where they adopted part—or most—of the culture of the conquered peoples. Thus the Ottoman Turks became Moslems after conquering Islamic nations, as the Slavs became Christians after invading Christian Europe, as the Manchus adopted Chinese culture wholesale even before conquering China, and as the ancient Romans absorbed the culture of the Greeks whom they conquered. Other conquerors have neither sought to acquire the culture of the conquered nor to impose their own culture on them, but simply to collect tribute or acquire booty. This latter kind of conquest has shaded off into simple predation—forays for both material booty and the carrying off of people as slaves to be sold or used later. Such predations remained a major activity of various peoples around the world until the rise of nation-states with armies, navies, and fortified towns made such forays too risky and too seldom successful.[15] Part of the reason for this historic change was the changing technology of military conquests.

Military Technology

The ever-changing technology of warfare has been no more evenly spread among the peoples of the world than other cultural advantages. Mastery of fighting on horseback made Central Asians the greatest conquerors in the world for centuries on end, winning victories and empires from China to Eastern Europe. Only after the development of more formidable fortifications and the invention and perfection of handguns and cannon was the cavalry charge drastically reduced in its effectiveness, changing the balance of power among peoples and giving rise to new nations and empires, based on the new technology. The rise of gunpowder weapons in particular marked the rise of Europeans as conquerors on the world stage, whereas before then Europe had had difficulties even defending itself against the invasions of Mongols, Turks, and Moors. It was symbolic of this dramatic turnaround that the year the Spaniards finally liberated the last of their country from Moorish rule was the same year when Columbus set sail across the Atlantic, marking the beginning of the age of European worldwide empires.

The very nature of European dominance evolved in step with the evolution of guns and cannon. Early, crude, inaccurate, and slow-loading firearms had no decisive advantage against fast-charging horsemen and fast-shooting archers. Although Europeans began making cannons in the first half of the fourteenth century, it was two centuries later before military battles began to be won by field artillery.[16] The immobility of heavy early cannons, which limited their usefulness on land, was not as much of a handicap at sea, however, where the warship itself provided the mobility for its cannon, leading to European dominance on the oceans of the world, long before the mass territorial conquests which created European land empires overseas.[17]

The technology of shipbuilding and the science of navigation were crucial in determining which European powers would become the militarily predominant ones, both in Europe itself and overseas, raising some to new heights and reducing others from their former pre-eminence. Venice, for example, was the leading sea power of the continent for centuries before the era of sail and cannon, but later had to be protected from Spanish naval attack by the warships of their British and Dutch allies in the early seventeenth century.[18] With the development of lighter, more mobile, more accurate and faster-firing artillery, as well as corresponding advances in pistols and rifles, the balance of military power shifted decisively to the Europeans on land as well as at sea.

Environmental Factors

Patterns of conquest have not been determined solely by technology or even by culture in general. Geography, including disease environments, has played a major role in the history of conquest, as it has in the history of cultural evolution in general.

The steppes of Central Asia and the plains of Eastern Europe have been far better settings for cavalry charges than the mountainous terrain of the Balkans or the heavily forested parts of Central Europe, while island nations such as Britain and Japan have of course been wholly immune. China tried to create the effects of natural barriers with its Great Wall, as Hadrian's wall in Britain and the Maginot Line in prewar France attempted the same thing on a smaller scale. Geographic barriers have spared some peoples from conquest or delayed its coming. Mountainous terrain has permitted independence to persist in some places, long after the adjoining lowlands have been overrun by invaders. Morocco, Ceylon, Abyssinia, Scotland, and Tibet are just some of the places in which this has been so. However, geographical barriers have been a mixed blessing, as technological and cultural backwardness have likewise been the fates of many of these isolated regions. Moreover, the relative poverty of such regions has also been one of the deterrents to conquest, along with the fighting abilities of mountain men, for there was little or no profit to be had from the conquest of many such areas.

Differential resistance to one another's diseases, which played a key role in the conquest of the Western Hemisphere, retarded the conquest of Africa until much later in history, because it was the indigenous peoples who succumbed to new, mixed disease environments in the Americas while it was the Europeans who were fatally vulnerable to the diseases of tropical Africa, until quinine and other modern medical and public health measures made it possible for them to survive amid the tropical diseases that flourished south of the Sahara.

The Atlantic and Pacific oceans long protected the indigenous peoples of the Western Hemisphere from the conquerors of the rest of the world and, even as late as the first half of the twentieth century, these oceans made isolationism a viable option for the United States, as it was not for most of the nations of Europe or Asia. However, smaller bodies of water may facilitate, rather than impede, military attacks, for huge differences between the high cost of land transport and the low cost of water transport can be as important militarily as it has been economically. During the Crimean war, for example, the British and the French attacking forces were supplied by water, while the Russian defenders at Sevastopol had to be supplied by land, since the waters were controlled by British and French warships. Even with approximately 125,000 peasant carts requisitioned to supply the defenders from their own adjacent homeland, their limited supplies of ammunition did not permit them to reply in kind to the barrages fired at them from the sea.[19] Nor was this simply a matter of conditions favoring attackers or defenders in general. Both in Spain and in Russia, Napoleon's attacking armies met disaster when they had to be supplied over land, while the opposing armies were supplied across water.[20]

The inaccessibility of African rivers to ocean-going warships made this continent less vulnerable to European naval power than much of the Western Hemisphere was. The Dutch, for example, could send ocean-going vessels more than a hundred miles up the Hudson River to establish an outpost at what would later become the city of Albany. No river in Africa was that accessible, whether due to insufficient water levels or—more commonly—sandbars, cascades and waterfalls. The shallow coastal waters in many parts of sub-Saharan Africa meant that large European warships often could not even get close to the shore in many places, necessitating the loading of European troops into smaller boats, which could in many places be effectively opposed by Africans in similar-sized boats, particularly in the early centuries before European firearms had developed the accuracy and speed of firing that they would have in later eras.[21]

Forms of Subjugation

Ultimately it is not simply territory that is conquered, it is people, and their subjugation can take the form not only of political subordination but also of enslavement, whether in their own homelands or in other lands to which they are transported. Here too, environmental factors have been major influences—moreso than race, for example— in determining who would and would not be enslaved.

While slavery existed around the world for thousands of years, and has been abolished generally only within the past two centuries, it tended to decline with the rise of many powerful nation-states, whose armies and navies stood between their own people and marauders from outside who might attempt to capture and enslave them. Thus the consolidation of nation-states around the world reduced the number of peoples who remained vulnerable to enslavement.

The regions of the world which continued to be subjected to mass enslavement had much more in common geographically than racially. Typically, these were regions where internal geographical barriers made it more difficult to consolidate political control over areas large enough to produce powerful nation-states, able to protect their populations from marauding outsiders. The Balkan mountains, which fragmented peoples culturally and isolated them from the economic and intellectual advances of the outside world made this region a major supplier of slaves for centuries before Europeans turned to Africa as a source of slaves for the Western Hemisphere.[22] Such geographical handicaps had other counterparts which kept the peoples of sub-Saharan Africa isolated from one another, as that whole region remained insulated from the outside world by the vast Sahara Desert to the north and three oceans on its other sides. In Asia as well, geographical isolation and the technological backwardness which so often went with it left many vulnerable people in stateless societies like those of Bali, which was raided for tens of thousands of slaves by peoples from more fortunate places. Other stateless peoples, or peoples only nominally part of states which lacked effective control of remote regions, continued to be victimized by marauders who captured and enslaved them. Hill tribes, slash-and-burn agriculturalists, scattered bands of nomads, and others living in the remote backwaters of Asia continued to be raided and enslaved, on into the twentieth century.[23]

In short, what successively removed various peoples of the world from the ranks of those vulnerable to being enslaved was the long process of consolidation of state power, whether their own or that of European imperialist nations. Thus slavery was ended in the Philippines, for example, only after the American conquest of the islands,[24] which did not simply replace the pre-existing authorities with new ones, but replaced them with a more powerful government in firmer control. In the Indonesian islands as well, the advance of Dutch power marked the retreat of slavery.[25] More generally, the spread of Western imperialism in Asia during the nineteenth century was the principal factor in the decline of slavery there.[26] In Africa, slavery remained resistant on into the twentieth century, but here too it was the consolidation of European power that forced back the frontiers of slavery,

whether it was the consolidation of French power in Morocco or Senegal, British power in many parts of Africa, or other European power in
other regions of the continent.[27]

What was crucial to this development was the emergence in Western civilization of a general revulsion against slavery in the late eighteenth and early nineteenth century. This anti-slavery movement
became and remained politically powerful enough to force political
leaders and colonial officials into opposition to slavery, regardless of
whether they personally felt such revulsion or not. The other crucial
factor was that the West had such overwhelming military superiority at
the time as to be able to enforce anti-slavery policies around the
world, as it imposed its will in other matters.

RELATIONS BETWEEN
CONQUERORS AND CONQUERED

Sometimes the conquerors have simply established themselves as a
ruling class whose members all take precedence over all members of
the conquered peoples. In principle, this was the situation of Moslems
in the lands of the Islamic conquests, where Christians and Jews were
explicitly placed on a lower plane in the law itself and dared not
defend themselves, even when struck by Moslem adults or stoned by
Moslem children. Similarly, blacks in South Africa long remained in a
sweeping legal subordination to whites, compounded by a degree of
poverty not usually experienced by Christians or Jews in the Ottoman
Empire, where both were often more prosperous than the Moslem population to whom they were legally subordinated. Other conquerors
have co-opted either the existing aristocracy among the conquered
peoples or particular talented individuals, of whatever social origins,
who were permitted to rise to wealth and power when those individuals
served the interests of the conquerors.

In the Roman Empire, non-Romans could rise to high command in
the Roman legions, become governors of provinces, or even emperor.
In principle, such was also the situation in the Soviet Union, though in
practice Slavs in general and Russians in particular dominated the
strategic heights of power, just as they had under the czars, when the
country was more candidly referred to as the Russian Empire.

Sometimes conquerors have settled concentrations of their own people in strategic places in the conquered lands, in order to secure themselves militarily against external or internal enemies. Both the Roman Empire in ancient times and the Ottoman Empire during the Middle Ages settled their soldiers or military veterans in strategic locations.[28] At other times conquerors have granted land and other privileges to particular foreigners, chosen for their fighting qualities, to serve the same purpose of securing an otherwise vulnerable conquered region. Thus, in medieval times, Hungarian fighting men became petty nobles in the border region of Poland, and both Hungarian and German nobles were settled in parts of Croatia,[29] while Anglo-Norman nobility were similarity settled in parts of Scotland.[30] Where the concern has been with internal unrest, rather than with external military threats, politically reliable elements of the conqueror's existing population have been resettled into newly conquered territories, as both Turks and Jews were resettled into parts of the Balkans conquered by the Ottoman Empire.[31] Later, as the Habsburg Empire pushed the Ottomans back in the Balkans, they settled Croats, Serbs, and Germans in the frontier zones for the sake of security.[32] The Aztecs followed similar policies in their empire in the Western Hemisphere.[33]

The culture of the conquered peoples has sometimes been targeted for extermination, even where the people themselves are not, but are urged or forced toward adoption of the conqueror's language, technology, and way of life. Attempts to turn the peoples of France's African empire into "black Frenchmen," Russification campaigns among the conquered subjects of the czars, and the spread of Islamic culture in the wake of Moslem conquests across North Africa and the Middle East are just some examples of this pattern. Other conquerors balanced many considerations as they sought to preserve their hegemony at minimal cost to themselves, which in many circumstances meant allowing cultural autonomy to the conquered. "Indirect rule" in much of the British Empire often involved such cultural accommodation for the sake of maintaining political control at low cost, and a similar pattern was common among the Aztecs in pre-Columbian times.[34] However, even a given conquering nation could follow very different policies in different places at the same time. The British, for example, followed a policy of cultural extermination where their goal was colonization in the strict sense of establishing new settlements of transplanted members of the imperial race, whether in North America,

Australia, or closer to home in Ireland in the seventeenth century.

Racial differences between the conqueror and the conquered have been sometimes sharp, sometimes not, and have sometimes been submerged under other differences that mattered more at the time, such as differences in religion. The degree to which physical differences between the rulers and the subjugated mattered to each is an empirical question, rather than a foregone conclusion. Racism has scarred and bloodied the histories of lands around the world, but Northern Ireland, India, and the Middle East are contemporary reminders of the enduring and lethal hatreds that have revolved around religion. History's Crusades, pogroms, Jihads, and Inquisitions underscore the point. Secular religions or ideologies have likewise claimed their millions of victims, from the "killing fields" of Kampuchea to the Soviet Gulags. (Race has been a major enduring factor in some conquests, but can claim no monopoly as a cause of man's inhumanity to man.)

The material things and the intellectual and moral concepts spread by conquest do not all originate within the conquering peoples themselves. Much of the cultural advances in mathematics, science, philosophy, and other fields spread by Arab conquests and absorbed into medieval European civilization originated with peoples who were not Arabs but Persians, Hindus, and others.[35] The fact that Europeans used the term "Arabic numerals" to refer to numbers which in fact originated among Hindus in India was symptomatic of this role of conquest in spreading cultural features originating elsewhere, either from among the conquered in the case of so-called Arabic numerals or from other independent nations in other parts of the world. The Islamic empires, for example, also transmitted to Europeans such things as paper and printing from China, which the Islamic conquests in Asia made them aware of before the Europeans penetrated that part of the world.

While migrations compete with conquest as methods of spreading cultures over vast distances, conquest has in many cases facilitated migration, not only among the conquering peoples themselves but also among others who become more willing to move to new areas now made more secure under the conquerors' hegemony. Thus Jewish peddlers and merchants followed in the wake of the Roman legions,[36] as Lebanese peddlers and merchants would in later centuries follow in the wake of European conquerors in West Africa, and people from

India and China would migrate to colonial Malaya after British hegemony had been established there. Neither racial nor cultural affinities with the conquerors are necessary for this to happen. All that is necessary is for the conqueror to establish a degree of law and order under which others can feel secure.

This law and order need not be equal or just for all—and seldom is. What is crucial is its dependability, which involves not only the physical power to enforce its edicts but also a legal and political system whose predictability has not been fatally undermined by corruption or caprice. Where weak, corrupt and capricious indigenous governments have been supplanted by stronger and more dependable colonial governments, immigration has often increased, even when those who immigrated were never accorded the same rights as the imperial race or even the conquered native population. The Chinese, for example, prospered economically in much of colonial Southeast Asia, where they were legally third-class citizens. So did emigrants from India, who went to live under various European colonial governments in East Africa, Fiji, and the Carribbean.

NATIONAL INDEPENDENCE AND
SELF-DETERMINATION OF PEOPLES

However profound the effects of conquests, and however long lasting, nevertheless empires fall and—even before that—particular peoples break free of their conquerors. Just as the Spaniards spent centuries driving out their Moorish conquerors, so the Russians drove out their Mongol overlords, and much of Europe and the Middle East erupted again and again in revolt against Ottoman, Habsburg, and other empires. In more recent times, post–World War II uprisings in Indonesia, Algeria, Kenya, and Rhodesia brought independence to these countries and undoubtedly influenced imperial authorities to grant independence to other colonies in the less developed world before overt resistance reached similar proportions.

At one time, the struggle between conquered and conquerors was largely a matter between those directly concerned. However, just as slavery became a general moral and political issue in Western civilization in the nineteenth century, so "the right of self-determination of peoples" became a general moral and political issue in the twentieth century. In both cases, the overwhelming military power of the West stood behind these moral and political imperatives. For example, the victorious allies of the First World War carved up the defeated Habsburg and Ottoman empires into smaller states run by formerly subjugated peoples, such as the Poles, Czechs, and Hungarians, and the various southern Slavs who were then lumped together in a newly created Yugoslavia.

President Woodrow Wilson's championing "the right of self-determination of peoples" was a landmark in this development, though his own Secretary of State confided in his diary the misgivings he had about the president's words:

> These phrases will certainly come home to roost and cause much vexation. The President is a phrase-maker par excellence. He admires trite sayings and revels in formulating them. But when he comes to their practical application he is so vague that their worth may well be doubted. He apparently never thought out in advance where they would lead or how they would be interpreted by others. In fact he does not seem to care so that his words sound well. The gift of clever phrasing may be a curse unless the phrases are put to the test of sound, practical application before being uttered.[37]

Just ten days later, Secretary Lansing returned to the issue of "self-determination" and wrote in his diary:

> The phrase is simply loaded with dynamite. It will raise hopes which can never be realized. It will, I fear, cost thousands of lives . . . What a calamity that the phrase was ever uttered! What misery will it cause! Think of the feelings of the author when he counts the dead who died because he coined a phrase![38]

The military and political viability of the newly created states, and the dangers to the peace of Europe as a whole when the international balance of power was made fragile by the existence of so many small and vulnerable countries, were considerations lost in the euphoria of victory and the heady process of "nation-building"—or, more accurately, empire dismemberment. But the importance of these factors was painfully revealed by the subsequent breakdown of the balance of power in Europe, as Hitler was able to pick off—one by one—countries that would have been much more difficult to conquer when they were part of a consolidated empire, thus enabling Nazi Germany to begin shifting the military balance of power in its own favor, even before the onset of the Second World War. Nor did the damage end with the end of the war that this fragmentation of Europe had helped foster. Even in the last decade of the twentieth century, there were still consequences from the artificial creation of new states after the First World War. Czechoslovakia and Yugoslavia both came apart in the 1990s, peacefully in the first case and amid hideous atrocities in the second. At the same time, the breakup of another multi-national empire—the Soviet Union—likewise unleashed civil wars within the newly independent republics. The "right of self-determination" has had a high cost. Whether or not it was ultimately worth that cost is another question. Unfortunately, it is a question seldom asked by those who have repeated the phrase, any more than it was asked by Woodrow Wilson.

Nor is this issue confined to Europe. The breakup of empires seldom, if ever, restores the world that existed before conquest. The practical question is therefore not how the conquest should be viewed—either morally or politically—but what options now exist in a world irretrievably changed by the conquests of the past.

THE CHAPTERS THAT FOLLOW

In seeking to assess the role of conquest in the cultural evolution of peoples, it is of course impossible to present conquest in isolation from the many other influences that interweave with it to determine cultural and other outcomes. Thus the history of conquered peoples cannot be understood if it is limited to the era of conquest or even to the role of conquest alone, since our subject is as much cultural evolution as it is conquests. The history of the peoples covered here—the British, the Slavs, the Africans, and the Western Hemisphere Indians—includes strong influences of both.

The antecedents and the long-run consequences of conquest are integral parts of the story. This is especially so for nations or peoples that have played the roles both of conquered and conqueror at different periods of history, for what happened in between is a major part of

the story of the cultural evolution that reversed their roles. The differing physical settings in which peoples and their cultures evolved facilitated some things and limited others, so these geographical influences
are examined in each of these chapters. One of the most important
things influenced by geography is the size and diversity of the area
over which economic and cultural interactions can take place, for this
strongly affects not only the economic well-being of the people but,
even more fundamentally, their own development of the skills, knowledge, and wider cultural exposure that can be summarized as human
capital. Whether people are united by navigable waterways or cut off
by rugged mountains or other geographical barriers has enormous cultural as well as economic and political significance. The geographical
differences between Eastern and Western Europe, or between Europe
and Africa, for example, are major influences on the economic and
cultural evolution of the peoples living in these regions of the world.
Moreover, these cultural differences persist after these peoples emigrate to other countries and continents.

Merely to say that there is cultural evolution—and in particular that
this evolution has dramatically changed the relative position of peoples, nations, and whole civilizations—moves us beyond the narrow
confines of our own times to look at the broader tapestry of human
events. This vast historical scene also has implications for the world
around us today, and especially for reconsidering the beliefs and theories that might seem plausible within the narrower confines of the contemporary world, but which do not hold up when a more sweeping
array of evidence from other times and places is examined.

Our first history of a conquered people begins in the time of the
Roman Empire. By then, other great civilizations had already arisen
(and some fallen) in China, in India, in Persia, and in ancient Greece.
But much of the world that would later be considered civilized had by
no means achieved that status yet. The greatest of the civilizations of
Europe were still those on the Mediterranean, those most accessible to
the great non-European civilizations of that era. Parts of Europe farther away—Scandinavia, the British Isles, or what would later become
Russia—were centuries or millennia behind the level of civilization
already developed in ancient Greece and Rome.[39] Agriculture had by
no means reached all parts of these outer regions yet and nothing like
the literature of the Greeks and Romans existed in such places, many

of which did not even have written languages. Nations and governments, much less empires, were as yet unknown in these regions.

Our story opens in an island not yet part of the civilization of its
time, among illiterate tribal peoples, far removed in distance and culture from the glories of Rome. It begins in Britain.

CHAPTER 2

THE BRITISH

*How, in the first place, did a peripheral island rise
from primitive squalor to world domination?*

Luigi Barzini[1]

For about one-fifth of its recorded history, Britain was a conquered country, a province of the Roman Empire—and one of the more backward provinces at that. Men from other provinces ruled over Britain, but Britons did not rule other provinces.[2] One measure of the backwardness of pre-Roman Britain was the ease with which it was conquered by greatly outnumbered Roman soldiers and held in subjugation, despite a massive and desperate uprising in 61 A.D. The Romans were simply far better equipped and far better organized.[3] In many other ways as well, the Romans represented a much more advanced civilization than existed in Britain at that point in history. Indeed, after the Romans withdrew from Britain four centuries later, the Britons began to retrogress, and in many respects it was centuries after that before Britain regained the economic, social, or cultural levels it had reached as a province of the Roman Empire.

The history of the British Isles shows the cultural effects of conquest and imperialism in many ways. What is now England was at first the object of conquest and, much later in history, itself a conqueror—first within the British Isles and then in such widely scattered regions of the world that it was possible to say, "The sun never sets on the British Empire." There was little inkling of such historic potential in the land and people that Julius Caesar encountered in a raiding expedition on the British coast in 55 B.C. Indeed, not a single Briton's name had entered the pages of history before that time.[4]

THE BRITISH ISLES

There was no *nation* of England or Britain before the Roman invasions. The island was divided among thirty tribes,[5] who fought fiercely among themselves. Their military equipment was obsolete by continental European standards, however,[6] and their agriculture likewise lagged behind that in the Roman world.[7] Geographically, Britain was just beyond the boundaries of the Roman Empire, which dominated continental Western Europe. Culturally, Britain was also on the fringes of Roman civilization, though using many of the cultural artifacts of that civilization, acquired in trade. Britons, however, remained a predominantly Celtic-speaking people in a Celtic culture, much like that found among the conquered peoples just across the channel.[8] To the Romans, Britons were simply "barbarians." However, these Britons were by no means merely primitive hunters and gatherers of the spontaneous produce of nature. They had agriculture, weaving, craftsmen who could work in iron, and economic transactions utilizing coins, often derivative in style from coins originating on the channel coast of northern Europe.[9] Nevertheless, the Britons that Julius Caesar saw were to him primitive exotics with long hair, dyed bodies, and living in a society of shared wives.[10]

During Caesar's raiding expedition in 55 B.C., his fleet met disastrous weather in unfamiliar waters off the British coast and his cavalry was unable to get ashore.[11] Nevertheless, the discipline and armor of the Romans prevailed and the expedition returned in triumph to Rome with captured British slaves marching behind them in the procession.[12] Disunity among the British tribes contributed to the Roman victory.[13] A century later, under the emperor Claudius, the Romans returned as full-scale invaders. Claudius subdued a large part of the island and was back in Rome in six months.[14] Yet the battle for the remainder of Britain continued on for decades. The British tribes took up arms "with savage fierceness," in Gibbon's words, but they also "laid them down, or turned them against each other with wild inconstancy."[15] The Romans, by contrast, proceeded methodically with a divide-and-conquer strategy politically, and sustained and disciplined military operations. It was a difference that would distinguish the conquerors from the conquered, in many parts of the world, for many centuries to come.

Roman Britain

Among the other common characteristics of conquerors that marked the Roman subjugation of Britain were arrogance, greed, and brutality. In southeastern Britain, for example, the king of the Iceni died in 59 A.D., leaving half of his estate to the Roman emperor, in hopes that this gesture would enable his heirs to enjoy the remainder in peace and the realm to remain undisturbed. But the Roman authorities in Britain confiscated the entire estate, flogged the widowed queen, Boudicca, for resisting and raped her daughters.[16] The oppressions and atrocities of the Romans provoked a massive revolt of the Iceni, led by Boudicca, and joined by other tribes with grievances against their Roman overlords.[17] The rebellious Britons rampaged through the southern part of the island, spreading death and destruction to Romans, Roman sympathizers, and Roman structures and symbols.[18] Eventually, however, enough Roman military units were assembled to confront the Britons, who nevertheless had great numerical superiority. After see-saw battles in which neither side showed mercy or took prisoners, once again the superior discipline, organization, and armaments of the Romans prevailed. They then slaughtered the old as well as the young—men, women, children, and animals, throwing human and animal bodies on a common pile of corpses.[19]

The Roman authorities in Britain who provoked the Boudiccan revolt were replaced by men who could maintain Rome's rule without such ruinous costs. In the centuries that followed, the Romans conquered Britain culturally as well as militarily. Well-to-do Britons began to wear the Roman toga, speak Latin, and have arcades, baths, and sumptuous banquets.[20] However, this Romanization spread unevenly down the social scale, with most Britons continuing to speak in a Celtic tongue, for example.[21] As with other conquered peoples, it was the higher classes among the Britons who had the greatest tendency to adopt the language and culture of the conquerors, thereby acquiring some of the prestige of the dominant culture and such opportunities as existed to achieve favored positions within the new order. To the poorer masses below, working primarily in agriculture, such considerations had little weight, certainly not enough for them to take on the burden of learning a new language and a whole new way of life, though various products and practices of Roman civilization might be accepted. In short, conquest created language differences and accentuated cultural differences among the conquered people. It was a pattern that would recur in later centuries, after later conquests, both within the British Isles and in other societies around the world.

Under the Romans, towns developed, roads were built, and trade flourished.[22] The more efficient Roman plow was used for farming,[23] pottery and metal work were imported,[24] and new building methods were used and taught.[25] Window panes were introduced by the Romans.[26] So were such mundane things as latrines.[27] Architecture made its first real appearance, as the Britons, used to huts, now for the first time saw buildings.[28] Sculpture and representational art in general were also introduced into a country where art before had meant Celtic designs.[29] Roman capital helped develop the British economy.[30] Like other less developed regions, Britain was an exporter of raw materials.[31]

The period from 96 A.D. to 180 has often been regarded as the golden age of the Roman Empire.[32] It was the era of the *Pax Romana*, the peace secured by the overwhelming superiority of Roman military power over any possible challenger—and by an awareness in Rome that little remained to be conquered that would be worth the cost of conquest.[33] Symptomatic of this era was a wall built to the north of Roman Britain, to secure it against marauders from the unconquered northern region of the island—present day Scotland. Roman Britain thrived during this era of peace, when Rome was invincible and its culture spread among the Britons. The enduring Roman contributions to the country included the building of a major port on the Thames. In Winston Churchill's words: "We owe London to Rome."[34]

The importance of the Roman cultural contribution to the development of Britain was demonstrated, not only by the progress that took place while they were there, but also by the retrogression that took place after they left. Both covered sweeping areas of British life. The Roman legions withdrew from the British Isles early in the fifth century A.D., to meet growing military threats to the declining Empire on the continent. By the beginning of the sixth century, British towns were crumbling, with buildings and statues in ruins, and the forests were beginning to reclaim some human settlements.[35] Increasingly, Britain was raided, and then invaded, by fierce continental tribes, notably the Angles and the Saxons, two Germanic peoples from what is now southern Denmark and the northwest coastal plains of Germany. These were illiterate, pre-Christian tribes who helped contribute to the destruction of much of Roman civilization in Britain, as well as eventually changing the racial composition of the British people.

England

Germanic tribes settled in what is now England in a number of ways. Some were immigrant settlers during Roman times. Some were invited in during the fifth century A.D. as military allies to help repel attacks from other British tribes, the Picts and the Scots (ancestors, respectively, of today's Scots and Irish). In the centuries that followed, still more Germanic invaders arrived, pushing many of the original Britons westward toward what is now Wales,[36] and subjugating or annihilating those who remained. These Germanic conquests were neither as swift nor as coordinated as those of the Romans had been. Various tribes—the Angles, Saxons, and Jutes, for example—independently conquered different areas, and there were periods of territorial stability before new expansions of these conquests began. Archaeological evidence suggests that most of these realms contained peoples of differing tribal backgrounds, including the original Britons.[37] The widespread illiteracy of this age meant a lack of written records, so that less is known today about many aspects of the emerging English people, as they now began to be called, than is known about the earlier era of Roman Britain.

There is much archaeological evidence that the Germanic invaders did not simply conquer and assume control over a viable Roman-British society, but rather that the existing economy and society—rural as well as urban—was largely devastated and abandoned before new barbarian communities took shape, largely independently of the locations or functions of pre-existing communities.[38] Much of this collapse took place within half a century of the withdrawal of the Romans, which is to say, much of Roman Britain was in ruins before the dawn of the sixth century. It is questionable whether even London maintained a continuity of existence during this period. Not all the devastation of the times was due to war. Much of it represented the collapse of a culture too advanced and too complex, too economically interdependent, as well as too militarily indefensible, without the Romans who created it.

As the central governmental structure of the Romans collapsed into fragmented local powers, Britons struggled to maintain some semblance of Roman culture as they retreated before the invading Germanic peoples. Many of these Romanized Britons fled to France, to what is now called Brittany. In Britain itself, Christianity, Latin scholarship, and the remnants of Roman civilization in general, survived among those Britons who retreated westward and northward before the Germanic invaders. One of these Britons, St. Patrick, has been credited with transplanting this Christian civilization to Ireland. As of the end of the sixth century A.D., the emerging English world was a backwater of Western civilization, an enclave of illiterate pagans in Christianized Western Europe.

Markets disappeared and population declined.[39] The economy of Britain was in general less sophisticated in the sixth century than it had been in Roman times.[40] This economic retrogression was manifested in many ways. The market agriculture of Roman times gave way to smaller farms and subsistence farming.[41] Imitations of Roman mass-produced goods began to be crudely hand-made.[42] The use of coins declined. Pottery ceased to be mass produced.[43] Roads and waterways fell into disrepair.[44] Central heating and hot baths disappeared for many centuries.[45] So did bricks, which the Romans used, but which did not reappear in Britain until the fourteenth century, when they were imported from the continent.[46] Glass bottles, which had been produced in Roman times, disappeared from England and did not reappear until Elizabethan times, when bottles began to be imported from Venice, and it was the seventeenth century before glass-blowing was re-established in the British Isles.[47] These post-Roman retrogressions pervaded both the lives and deaths of the times. The barbarian invaders practiced cremation of the dead but, among the Christian Britons, people were now buried more crudely, in shallower graves, and increasingly without coffins.[48]

The military vulnerability of fragmented, post-Roman Britain was illustrated by the variety of raiders and invaders who struck various parts of the island. Although many of these invaders were referred to generically at the time as "Saxons," they included, besides people from Saxony, Danes who settled in the east midlands and Norwegians who settled in the northwest of England.[49] The degree to which England was altered by the invasions of Angles, Saxons, Jutes, and others, and by the later Norman invasions, may be indicated by the fact that the present-day English language contains very few words from the language of the Britons in pre-Roman times,[50] though it contains many words of Latin, Germanic, and French origin. The Germanic conquerors—some from what is now Germany and others from Scandinavia—brought with them some of the skills that the Romans had, but not all. They could not build in stone, for example. Only after centuries of religious missionary work did the English become part of the Christian tradition of the West.[51]

The Norman invasion and conquest of England in 1066 marked the last of the great cultural and racial additions to British society from continental Europe. A people of Norse origins, the Normans had become culturally French after their conquests in France during the century and a half preceding their invasion of England. Concurrently, individual bands of Normans launched campaigns of conquest in southern Italy and Sicily and, still later, Normans would also be involved as individuals in the Spanish reconquest of the Iberian peninsula from its Islamic rulers.

In addition to being renowned warriors, the Normans were also effective as rulers, creating a reign of law and order under which economic development flourished in Normandy. They were also active in building and patronizing churches and schools, both of which were outstanding by the standards of the times.[52] That the Normans came from France was not incidental, for France was in the forefront of European civilization, while England still lagged behind. The decisive battle of Hastings which settled the fate of England in 1066 was fought by about 7,000 men on each side[53]—large numbers for their day, though very small compared to the armies of a later era of the industrial revolution and its accompanying advances in transportation. Thus the Normans came to put their stamp on England and eventually on Britain as a whole.

The Norman conquest meant not simply the replacement of one king with another but a widespread takeover of land and power by Normans, a cultural revolution among the upper classes of the country,

a strengthening of the power of the monarchy, an architectural revolution, and an infusion of new racial strains into an already mixed population.[54] To the original Britons of pre-historic times had been added,
over the centuries, the Celtic invaders of the fifth century B.C., the
Roman invaders of the first century A.D., the Angles, Saxons, and Jutes
of the fifth century, Scandinavians in the ninth century, and now the
Normans in the eleventh century—a mixture of peoples and cultures
today very loosely characterized as "Anglo-Saxon." The role of these
successive conquests over the ages may be assessed to some extent by
the relative development of England, which (being nearest to the continent) received their fullest impact, as compared to the development
of Wales, which was much less affected, or of Scotland or Ireland,
which escaped conquest for centuries, largely through the accident of
geography.

In the wake of the Norman conquest came the French language and
culture, which became dominant in the political and elite social life of
England. The English people were excluded from the top secular and
religious posts. Parliamentary proceedings and the law were in
French, as was social discourse among the aristocracy, while Latin was
the language of religious and scholarly work. The English language
and culture remained largely that of the masses and the lesser gentry.
The fact that the Normans held territory on the continent of Europe as
well as in England—that the early kings of England were also dukes
of Normandy—made the ruling class especially distinct from the English society that they ruled. King Edward III, whose reign began more
than two and a half centuries after the Norman conquest, was perhaps
the first king of England who spoke more than a few words of the English language.[55]

Eventually, however, both the Norman rulers and those English who
came in contact with them tended to become bilingual. The Normans
were noted for their adaptability—one of the secrets of their success—
but, over the centuries, they were said to "adapt themselves out of existence."[56] Intermarriage began early at the lower social levels and then
proceeded up the scale, until eventually even kings began to marry
women of English ancestry.[57] The English language and culture correspondingly rose up the social scale over the generations and centuries.
In the middle of the thirteenth century, an important state document
was circulated in English, though this was unusual at that time. In the

fourteenth century, Chaucer's *Canterbury Tales* marked the beginning of an epoch in the use of English in literature. By the early fifteenth century, parliamentary records and official correspondence were written in English.[58] This was also the first century in which members of the upper classes began to correspond with one another in English.[59]

The social and cultural absorption of the Norman elite into English society was aided by the loss of the Norman connections with France, as a series of wars led ultimately to the loss of their continental territories. This loss of the continental empire was accompanied by further conquests within the British Isles. The English invaded Ireland in 1169, conquered Wales by 1284, and invaded Scotland in 1296. Individual members of the Anglo-Norman aristocracy typically had multiple landholdings over which they ruled in various parts of the British Isles so that, despite their local attachments, they were to varying extents a national ruling class, rather than simply regional barons. It has been estimated that nearly a third of all English earls in the thirteenth century also held land in Scotland, while most Scottish earls held land in England.[60] All these tendencies toward a more consolidated and inward-looking Britain, developing separately from continental Europe, were accentuated by Henry VIII's rupture with the Roman Catholic Church in the sixteenth century.

England at this juncture was not yet on a par with the leading continental European powers, either militarily or economically. It was backward in mining and in the production of metals, and much of its international commerce was carried in foreign ships. It was still an exporter of raw materials, such as wool and agricultural products.[61] Flanders, for example, became a major textile center in continental Europe by importing British wool for centuries, before the British themselves finally began to process their own wool into cloth.[62] Italian shipbuilders contributed to the development of the British navy during the reign of Henry VIII, while imported German miners contributed to the development of the British mining industry, and Dutch engineers contributed to land clearance and to the development of waterworks.[63]

As medieval England began to become transformed into a money economy, finances were at first handled primarily by Jews and Lombards, with foreigners in general conducting financial transactions that Englishmen were not yet capable of handling.[64] After the expulsion of the Jews near the end of the thirteenth century, the Lombards then conducted virtually all the major financial transactions of the kingdom until they too fell into disfavor and were subjected to restrictions and predations which drove them out of the English financial markets in the fourteenth century.[65] Again, however, it was foreigners from the continent of Europe who took over money-lending, tax-collection, and other financial transactions that produced both wealth and unpopularity. However, by the time that these latter-day financiers also fell into disfavor, there were now Englishmen able to handle financial markets, often using methods introduced by successive waves of foreigners.[66] One relic of the era of foreign domination of English financial markets is the name of Lombard Street in modern London's financial district.

In industry, as in commerce and finance, England's early economic development owed much to foreigners—and to its own stability of government and dependability of laws which attracted foreigners. The Dutch, the Walloons, and the Flemings were among the many foreigners who brought their skills to England with them. As of 1618, there were 10,000 skilled foreign workers in London alone. Refugee groups such as Jews, Huguenots, and Flemings—all seeking respite from persecution on the continent—played key roles in England's emergence from being a backward part of Europe's economy to becoming one of its economic leaders. Between 50,000 and 100,000 Huguenots fled to Britain from France in the seventeenth century, particularly after revocation of the Edict of Nantes, which had previously guaranteed religious freedom to Protestants.[67] Even earlier, however, Huguenot watchmakers had turned London from a city where no watches were manufactured to one of the leading watch-producing centers of the world.[68] The British woolen, linen, cotton, silk, paper, and glass industries were likewise revolutionized by foreign workers and foreign entrepreneurs.[69] Moreover, as these immigrants settled and were absorbed into the English population, their skills diffused and influenced Englishmen, who now began to make their own contributions to the process.

The fourteenth and fifteenth centuries marked a turning point in England's evolution from an exporter of raw materials to a producer of finished products. The country's leading export ceased to be wool and became woolen cloth. During the second half of the fourteenth century, England's exports of raw wool dropped by half and its export of cloth increased more than sevenfold.[70] In production processes in general, however, England was still importing technological advances from

continental Europe until the late seventeenth century, when the tide
began to turn in this respect as well. By the early eighteenth century,
the net flow of technological advances was from the British Isles to the
continent[71]—and thereafter Europe and the world continued copying
and adapting British technology for most of the next two centuries.

Profound and sweeping changes in technology, in the economy, and
in the society were all inter-related with one another. The first great
industry to emerge in Britain was the textile industry. Initially a cot-
tage industry, cloth production in later centuries became a pioneering
sector in the industrial revolution. The machines invented and developed in this industry—the spinning jenny, the mule, the flying shut-
tle—pioneered machine-building in general, creating a whole class of
mechanics and inventors, whose skills and examples would prove
valuable to heavier industry later on. The use of water wheels to tap
the power of rivers and streams for turning factory machinery set the
stage for applying the power of the epoch-making steam engine that
would revolutionize factories, mines, railroads, and ships. While the
use of water power attracted industry and workmen to places where
rivers and streams could be tapped, so the later emergence of coal-
fired steam engines attracted industry and workmen to places where
coal deposits were found. The escalating importance of coal was
reflected in the dramatic rise in the amount of coal extracted from the
earth—2 million tons at the beginning of the eighteenth century, 10
million tons before the end of that century, and more than 64 million
tons by the middle of the nineteenth century.[72]

Why Britain became the first industrial nation and retained its pre-
eminence for a century is one of the great questions of history—which
is to say, one to which no definitive answer has been found. However,
Britain had some unique combinations of influences. What the British
had earlier than many other peoples was a framework of law and government that facilitated economic transactions. The arbitrariness of
despotic government gave way in Britain to a de facto separation of
powers, first between lords and king and then between king and parliament. None of this developed in a simple progression, however.
Nevertheless, the evolution of the rule of law in the British Isles not
only helped promote the internal economic development of Britain
itself, it helped attract to Britain—and more particularly to London—
much of the commerce of Europe.

Complex and time-consuming international economic transactions, including long-term investments, are particularly dependent on a reliable framework of law, so that changes of government policy or of individuals in power, do not create large uncertainties as to whether commitments will be honored or foreigners treated on an equal plane with the natives involved in commercial and financial transactions. Over the centuries, British law acquired a reputation for such fairness that merchants and financiers preferred London to alternative ports and financial centers in Europe, thereby attracting vast amounts of foreign capital to supplement Britain's own capital.[73] The fact that sovereignty in Britain was not vested solely in the person of the king meant that British kings could not repudiate national debts—and this in turn made Britain a more attractive country for lenders.[74]

While a dependable framework of law was crucial for economic development, its evolution and elaboration were accompanied by an erosion of government control over the specific terms and conditions of economic transactions, which may have been equally crucial. In Britain, as elsewhere in medieval Europe, a "market" meant a specifically authorized gathering place for selling on days specified by the authorities, in places specified by the authorities, and at prices specified and monitored by the authorities. Farmers would bring their produce to these officially scheduled markets or fairs, as would producers or importers of various other products, all with the presence and supervision of officials. However, the rapid growth of towns and cities, and the changing locations, organization, and technology of production created innumerable economic producers, consumers, and middlemen operating outside this carefully devised framework.[75] As large, scheduled markets and fairs gave way to innumerable, smaller, scattered, and continuously-operating shops and stores, official control of prices and conditions became much more tenuous as a practical matter. Nor could such developments simply be forbidden, without jeopardizing the growth of more and larger towns and cities, and the spread of economic progress, on which the authorities themselves were dependent for the growing taxes which financed their own military and other activities.

Attempts at economic controls were not abandoned in principle, and they continued to be imposed in practice wherever they could be. It was just that the effectiveness of these controls eroded with the growth, and public acceptance, of smuggling and other illegal or otherwise unauthorized ways of doing business beyond the reach of government officials. It was in the wake of these erosions of economic controls that intellectual challenges were then made to the role of government in the economy, first by the Physiocrats in France, who coined the term "laissez-faire," and then by Adam Smith in Britain, who became its leading champion. By the mid-nineteenth century, widespread support of "free trade" internationally, and of freeing the domestic economy from many political controls, were in the ascendancy in Britain.

In addition to having an economy less subject to governmental controls than in most other countries, the British people and British institutions had centuries of experience as a *commercial* nation before it became the first *industrial* nation. What Napoleon disdainfully referred to as "a nation of shopkeepers" was a nation with vast accumulations of experience in economic transactions, as well as a wide range of other "human capital" in the form of specific skills that would all contribute to its later industrial growth. Britain also underwent a transportation revolution which preceded the industrial revolution. Long before it was a country of factories and railroads, Britain in general and England in particular was a country of improved highways that greatly facilitated the movement of people, goods, and raw materials, even though they were moving by nothing more revolutionary than horse-drawn vehicles. The building of turnpikes in England began in the latter half of the seventeenth century and, by the mid-eighteenth century, a substantial highway network had been created. Thanks to a continued rapid spread of turnpikes, the travel time from London to many parts of England by stagecoach in 1821 was half of what it was in 1750. By 1830, movement between the larger towns was four or five times as fast as in 1750—and all of this before the age of the railroad.[76]

The coming of the modern railroad—the first in the world being constructed in Britain in 1830—further revolutionized travel, both in terms of the numbers of passengers and in the rapidly falling cost of transporting people, goods, and raw materials. Railroads did not simply carry the same people who were previously using stagecoaches. Early in the history of the railroad, the rule of thumb developed that the rails carried twice as many people as had previously walked, taken stagecoaches, or travelled in other ways.[77] Moreover, the cost advantages of railroads continued to improve with the technological and organization development of the rail industry, leading to ever-growing usage of the new technology. While there were 10 million stagecoach journeys in 1835, there were 30 million rail journeys by 1845 and more than 330 million by 1870.[78]

The cost reductions which made this greater expansion of trade economically possible for people who had previously been unable to afford travel also applied to freight, which included the raw materials needed by industry and their finished products to be taken to markets. The fact that these economic advantages developed first in Britain gave British commerce and industry striking advantages over those of other nations. Thirty years after its beginning in 1830, the British railroad network had created the basic infrastructure that the country would use on into the twentieth century.

While freight traffic did not shift to railroads as early as passenger traffic, nevertheless the change was substantial and dramatic, once it got underway. In 1840, for example, virtually all the coal shipped to London came by sea but, fifteen years later, about one-fourth came by rail—and, fifteen years after that, more than half came by rail.[79] Ironically, while the railroad substituted for horses in many cases, the generally larger volume of transportation and the growing prosperity of people and of industry led to an absolute increase in the number of horses in Britain up till the end of the nineteenth century.[80] These horses served many purposes, including some directly connected with the railroads, such as pulling carriages that took people to and from railroad stations, or from towns without railroad stations to towns that had them, or from one rail line to another, when they did not intersect. A sharp downturn in the number of horses began only in the early twentieth century, when the automobile and its offshoots such as trucks and mechanical farm vehicles appeared on the scene.

In addition to the economic advantages Britain received from its technological pioneering, the country's geography was another favorable influence on its economic progress. Britain's iron ore and coal deposits were located near to one another and both were located near the sea[81]—an enormous advantage over most continental European countries, where even a distance of 10 miles between the two minerals was a formidable obstacle to early German industrial development,[82] for example, in an era before railroads reduced the high cost of land transport. In Britain, however, coal could be shipped by water to Scottish ports located far from the coalfields at prices only negligibly different from the cost at nearer ports, while a shipment of coal on land was said to double in price in just 10 miles during the pre-railroad era. In those parts of the British Isles without the advantage of coal deposits or ports, industrialization was as handicapped as in other countries.

Coal arriving at a Scottish port in the eighteenth century could sell for about £1 per ton, but the price rose 50 to 100 percent by the time it reached the interior highlands, where only the wealthy could afford to buy it for heating their homes.[83] More important, the highlands could not participate in the industrialization which turned the lowlands into a predominantly urban society during the nineteenth century, since the highlands lacked their own coal[84] and it was prohibitively expensive to transport coal there from other parts of Britain. Thus highland Scots could participate in the modernization process only be moving down to the lowlands, to other parts of the British Isles, or overseas. In doing so, however, they would arrive at their destinations without the kinds of skills, experience, and orientation—the human capital—in demand in industrial societies.

The rise of a British iron and steel industry was intertwined with the development of coal mining. The steam engine was first applied to pumping ground water out of coal mines, to enable digging to proceed deeper into the earth, thereby promoting not only the extraction of coal, but with it the production of iron and steel. Then, as the steam engine itself was improved to the point of being a practical alternative to water power for driving machies in factories, the greater stresses on the machinery created by powerful steam engines created a rising demand for iron and steel that could take such stresses better than the wooden machine parts used to transmit water power. Later, as steam engines were further developed to serve as power for railroad locomotives, coal replaced wood as fuel, and iron and steel rails replaced wooden rails.

By 1870, the largest number of steam engines were being used in manufacturing, but the largest amount of horsepower supplied by steam engines was in mining—about one fourth of the total horsepower produced by steam in the country—with textiles next, using nearly one fifth of the nation's horsepower supplied by steam.[85] The declining demand for wood as fuel and as an industrial material—due to the rise of coal and iron, respectively—freed land from timber-

growing for agricultural production[86] or allowed it to revert to woodlands. Woodlands in Britain increased in area by more than one-fourth
between 1873 and 1911.[87]

It was not merely things that developed. People developed. Textile
mills began to locate in the vicinity of iron works because there one
could find skilled mechanics familiar with machinery and able to
repair and maintain textile machinery, as well as the other machines
they dealt with.[88] Engineers and mechanics were as much products of
the industrialization process as the material goods and the machinery
by which those goods were produced. So were inventors. More patents
were issued in the quarter-century after 1760 than in the preceding
one hundred and fifty years.[89]

British mechanics and engineers were in demand around the world.
Many made repeated trips to the new United States of America,[90]
where their skills and knowledge were in great demand during the late
eighteenth and early nineteenth centuries, while others went to various countries in continental Europe or even to Japan. As late as 1876,
there were more than a hundred foreign industrial workers in the
Japanese railroad industry alone and, of these, 94 were British.[91] In
Russia, more than a hundred Scottish industrial workers arrived in St.
Petersburg on a single vessel.[92] The movement of skilled artisans was
especially important during the early phases of British industrialization, when the predominant form of human capital consisted of individual experience, personal knacks, and trial-and-error methods,
rather than the application of science, which would come later. Not
only did Britons travel abroad to spread industrial knowledge, other
countries sent mechanics and engineers to Britain to learn the most
advanced information in their fields. These included Americans, Germans, Japanese, and Norwegians, among others.[93]

Over time, however, machines made individually by the knack of
particular craftsmen began to be replaced during the 1820s to the
1840s by machines made in a standardized manner by machine
tools.[94] Using machines to make other machines allowed finer toler-
ances to be maintained—sometimes down to a thousandth of an
inch[95]—and this in turn meant that parts could be made interchange-
able. Standardized and systematized production of machines also promoted the rise of engineering as a profession for which people could
be trained. The export of British technology and the emigration of the

people who understood that technology was on such a scale as to cause laws to be passed forbidding both, so as to maintain British pre-eminence, but such laws proved to be very ineffective. However, it was 1825 before these laws were repealed.[96]

None of these developments occurred with the kind of suddenness or pervasiveness suggested by the phrase "industrial revolution," but the profound depth and eventually far-reaching scope of these incremental changes certainly deserved that title. Life would never be the same again, either for Britain or for the world. For example, Englishmen introduced railroads to the rest of the world, not only by the example of railroad building in their own country, but also by themselves building and manning the first railroads in Germany, Argentina, India, Russia, Uganda, Kenya and Malaya,[97] as well as financing the building of railroads in the United States, France, and elsewhere. Railroads, in turn, were revolutionary in their social consequences. The concentrations of the world's populations along coasts and near rivers was reduced, as land transport into interior hinterlands became cheaper. This was even more of a factor in countries with large, landlocked interiors, such as Germany, the United States, and Russia, than in England itself. It has been said that the characteristic feature of nineteenth century economic development was "the development of continents instead of coast lines."[98]

Germany, in particular, was freed from its dependence on North Sea ports, which could freeze over in the winter, and became instead a hub of railroad networks that stretched across Europe. As a nation located in the center of the continent, Germany could, for example, ship its own and other countries' goods in all directions, establishing rail links that ultimately reached the Mediterranean and through it the Middle East. Inside Germany, railroads made it economically feasible to bring the iron ore of Lorraine to the coal fields of Westphalia, enabling Germans to become major producers of steel and with it one of the leading industrial powers of the world.[99] One indication of the historic role of the British in bringing railroads to Germany is that, of the 240 locomotives in Germany in 1840, 166 came from England.[100] In the United States as well, the coming of the railroad age permitted separate deposits of iron ore and of coal to be brought together for the production of iron and steel, the ore from the vicinity of Lake Superior, for example, being transported by rail to the coal deposits near Pittsburgh, which became one of the great iron and steel producing centers of the world.[101]

The British role in the world's shipping was no less dramatic. In addition to inventing the steam engine that facilitated massive international emigration and made possible the international shipment of bulky and relatively low-valued commodities such as wheat, the British built many of the world's transoceanic ships, in addition to carrying much of the world's international commerce in British ships, for other countries as well as for themselves. As late as 1912, Britain carried more than half the goods shipped across the seas of the world.[102] In addition, British ship-yards built more than half the tonnage of steamships used by France, Russia, Spain, Holland, Italy, and Belgium.[103]

The revolution in transportation created by the railroad and the steamship affected not only industry and commerce, but also the lives of millions of ordinary people. As late as the mid-nineteenth century, only the affluent could afford such things as tea, coffee, sugar, raisins, oranges, and cocoa, but cheap transportation made all these things available to the masses.[104] Perishable commodities like fish could now be sold internationally, when swift and cheap transportation on the high seas was combined with refrigeration en route. Thus English fish was sold in Switzerland and even Canadian salmon was sold on the European continent.[105]

Not only things but people moved more readily, some for permanent settlement abroad, but many to work just for a season in agriculture or in the building trades before returning home. Thousands of Russians went to Germany when it was time to harvest crops there, just as Italian agricultural workers went to Argentina for their harvest and Italian buildings trades workers travelled seasonally to the United States.[106] Transatlantic travel became quicker, cheaper, and safer. The horrendous death rates from crossing the Atlantic in the era of wind-driven ships were drastically reduced,[107] partly because steel steamships did not sink as often as wooden sailing ships and partly because the much shorter times spent on the water subjected people to fewer dangers of debilitation and illness. Steamships also largely rid the seas of the centuries-old, worldwide scourge of piracy, for steamships were too expensive for freebooters to finance and sailing ships could no longer suffice to enable pirates to catch steamers. Moreover, steamships required ports where they could refuel with coal, and pirates could hardly expect to obtain this service from their potential victims.

At the heart of the industrialization process was iron and steel, and Britain was pre-eminent in their production. As of 1830, the production of pig iron in Great Britain was nearly double that in Germany and France combined.[108] As of 1871, the British produced more steel than Germany, France, Sweden and Austria combined.[109] British agriculture was also acknowledged to be the best in the world.[110] Britain likewise spearheaded the development of the modern textile industry, supplying not only the major inventions, but also initially the managers and skilled labor needed to train foreign workmen to operate British-made machinery in Russia, China, India, Mexico, and Brazil.[111] British firms also dominated the production of mining and other heavy equipment in late nineteenth and early twentieth century Chile.[112] In short, British technology and British capital were transplanted and took root around the world—in Africa, Asia, and Latin America, as well as in such offshoots of British civilization as the United States, Canada, and Australia. Partly as a result of a massive shipment of capital goods, British exports in the early 1870s exceeded the exports of the United States and Germany combined.[113]

The effect of early nineteenth-century industrialization on the standard of living of ordinary working people in Britain is a question long shrouded in controversy. However, what is clear is that industrial regions of Britain attracted large numbers of people from the countryside and from smaller towns, that the wage rates paid in industrial centers were higher than in rural areas, and that consumption patterns indicate that these higher wages were not simply dissipated in meeting higher costs of living in the cities, but represented a real increase in what people could afford to buy.[114] High death rates in large industrial centers were a sobering reminder of the negative aspect of industrialization, as accidents, overcrowding (with accompanying vulnerability to endemic and epidemic diseases), and perhaps the congregation of people from different disease environments with different levels of resistance to one another's disease, all added to the hazards. Nevertheless these hazards were known at the time to the people who moved to the cities, so their choices to move there suggested what their trade-offs were. Moreover, the over-all death rate in Britain changed very little from 1820 to 1870, because increasing lifespans in the rural areas offset the higher death rates in urban areas.[115] The rising wealth of the country, deriving from industrialization, may well have contributed to the increasing life expectancy outside the urban industrial centers themselves. The longer-run effects of industrialization on living standards in Britain were even more clearly positive. Even Karl Marx, who spent more than three decades living in Victorian England, acknowledged the rise in British workers' living standards between the 1840s and the 1860s.[116]

Although the question as to why England became the standard-bearer in the advancement of human economic and technological achievements in the world may never be fully answered, its location, institutions, and social practices were all conducive to this result—though clearly not determinative, as shown by the long centuries during which Britain lagged behind continental Europe and other parts of the world. However, during the era when European civilization emerged as the most economically and technologically advanced in the world, Britain had the advantage of being able to share in that civilization, while being an island nation spared the country the direct ravages of the wars that repeatedly disrupted and devastated the continent. Even when the British took part in these wars, they fought on other people's territory or at sea.

Internally, both the political system and social practices were also favorable to economic development. Stability of government and laws, and security of property, made it possible to raise vast aggregations of capital from the public at low interest rates for projects that took decades to complete, such as canals and railroads. The long-term interest rate in Britain was 6 percent at the beginning of the eighteenth century—and fell to 3½ percent by mid-century.[117] Social factors were also favorable in England, where the prosperous and educated classes were a functional factor in commerce and industry, as well as in agriculture, letters, law, and politics.[118] In Scotland as well, land ownership might be crucial for entry into the upper classes, but did not preclude careers in law or commerce.[119] For all the snobbishness of British society, its aristocracy was not sealed off from the mundane, practical, economic concerns of the nation, as were those of many other societies, where an hereditary aristocracy hindered or stifled the spirit of enterprise,[120] thereby holding back national economic development. Moreover, the rise of the gentry and the decline of the nobility in Tudor times, and the intermingling of these gentry with people of the commercial class, meant that "gentlemen" in Britain could also be businessmen and vice versa,[121] making not only the wealth but the talents of the more fortunate classes available for the economic development of the country:

> The younger son of the Tudor gentleman was not permitted to hang idle about the manor-house, a drain on the family income like the impoverished nobles of the Continent who were too proud to work. He was away making money in trade or in law.[122]

Among those of the landed gentry who remained on the land, the enterprising spirit of improvement was also apparent. New crops, new agricultural methods, and new techniques in animal husbandry were widely introduced by landowners in England. As new methods of raising feed for animals made it easier to keep them alive over the winter, the widespread and almost automatic slaughter of animals in the autumn ceased, leading to a year-around supply of fresh meat that changed the English diet, greatly reducing diseases growing out of the heavy salting of meat that had formerly been necessary when far more meat was slaughtered than was needed at one time and had to be stored.[123]

By the eighteenth century, England was one of the leading nations of Europe in agricultural technique and in the commercial development of farming, as distinguished from the feudal serfdom of Eastern Europe or the small peasant farming of much of continental Western Europe.[124] At the lower end of the social scale, as well as among the gentry, enterprise and social mobility were part of the pattern in England. Most hired farm hands, for example, did not live out their entire lives in that role but usually moved on to other occupations after marriage.[125] Moreover, people in a wide variety of roles on the land—great landlords, small owners, tenants, and hired hands—all produced for the marketplace. The number of people in the agricultural population grew absolutely with the growth of population in general, though their proportions declined as the country industrialized. Around the middle of the nineteenth century, the total number of people working in British agriculture reached its peak at 2 million, constituting just under one-fifth of the total population of the nation. As the number of farmers began to decline, total agricultural output continued to rise for some time, due to increased productivity, but the share of agriculture in Britain's total output declined to just 6 percent by the first decade of the twentieth century. By this time, however, Britain was importing more than half of its beef, mutton, and lamb, and three-quarters of its wheat.[126]

Other nations had some of the advantages of England but none combined them all. Germany had large iron ore and coal deposits, but not as close together as in England, and the numerous tariff barriers between the disunited German states and principalities, before the formation of their customs union in the early nineteenth century, were economically crippling. France was lacking in iron ore and, like Germany, had no such advanced financial institutions as England's to finance industrialization. Even a French entrepreneur who developed the first successful machine for spinning linen yarn in the late eighteenth century went to England to get financing for his venture because he could not raise the needed capital in France.[127] Scottish inventors, including James Watt, likewise sought financing in England to produce their inventions commercially. France had the intellectual foundations for modern industry without the commercial and financial complements. French chemists, such as Lavoisier, Berthollet, and Leblanc, made fundamental contributions to the development of modern chemistry but, here too, what they contributed was then commercially applied first in England.[128]

With its take-off into the industrial age, England emerged from centuries in the shadow of continental European powers and left a lasting imprint on the world, greater than that of any other nation since the days of the Roman Empire. Indeed, the worldwide scope of the British impact was far beyond anything possible in Roman times. However, having set in motion the industrial revolution and spread its technology world wide, Britain in the last decades of the nineteenth century was faced with the international competition of rapidly growing industrial rivals. As of 1870, Britain produced 32 percent of all the manufactured goods in the world, followed by the United States at 23 percent and Germany at 13 percent. By 1913, however, Britain's relative share of the world's growing supply of manufactured goods was down to 14 percent—exceeded by Germany at 16 percent and by the United States at 36 percent.[129]

This loss of world leadership in industrial output was perhaps inevitable, given that Germany, the United States and other industrializing nations had much larger populations than Britain. However,

Britain was overtaken not only in gross output but also in output per worker. It lost its lead in technological innovation.

After producing more than 40 percent of all the major inventions, discoveries and innovations in the world from 1750 through 1825, Britain found its relative share declining and ultimately being surpassed by the shares of Germany and the United States. By 1950, Britain's share was down to 3 percent and that of the United States was 82 percent.[130] In short, British inventiveness and efficiency did not keep pace.

One factor in the loss of British economic pre-eminence in the world was Britain's earlier development of strong and widespread labor unions, which were able to restrict the application of new technology, both directly and by appropriating a sufficient share of technology's economic benefits to reduce the incentives for further technological investment. In the United States, by contrast, industrial labor unions did not become dominant in the major industries until the late 1930s. An ironic consequence of this difference in industrial unionization was that much British labor and British capital moved to the United States, where both were more productive than they were at home.[131] Other factors in Britain's relinquishing its economic and technological lead include a failure to standardize its products to the extent that German, American, or Canadian firms did, and a neglect of technical education. Despite Britain's dependence on exports, it often failed to adapt its products to foreign tastes, or their marketing to foreign languages, or even to quote export prices in foreign currencies, rather than in the complex system of British shillings, pence, and pounds sterling that existed before British money was put on the decimal system in the late twentieth century.[132]

Wales

Wales, as a rugged mountainous region, was for many centuries a refuge for peoples fleeing those with greater power, who could not be confronted on the plains of England or on the continent of Europe. Wales could be fled to by land or by sea, or via rivers from England. Innumerable peoples settled in what is now Wales and eventually intermingled. Cultures, like peoples, survived in Wales after vanishing from other parts of Britain.[133]

The rugged geography of Wales made it not only a refuge but also a land internally divided by natural barriers, which in turn became cultural barriers among its peoples. Like many such geographically divided areas in various parts of the world, Wales was fragmented politically as well as culturally. Over the centuries, major outside political forces—the Romans, the Normans, and then the English—were able to penetrate Wales, especially along the coastal lowlands and in the central river valleys,[134] while other parts of Wales remained less affected by the invaders' influence. The region that is today Wales resisted Roman conquest longer than the southeastern portion of Britain that is now England. The Roman expedition dispatched to conquer Wales in 61 A.D. had to be recalled to put down the revolt of Boudicca. Nevertheless, toward the end of the first century of the Christian era, Wales was conquered and became part of the Roman Empire. However, archaeological evidence suggests that Wales was not as culturally Romanized as England, but remained instead a militarily secured frontier area.[135]

Just as the Romans took possession of what is now Wales some years after taking possession of what is now England, so they abandoned Wales some years before abandoning Roman England.[136] In short, Wales felt the impact of Roman civilization to a lesser degree, and for less time, than did England. Welsh speech remained Celtic rather than Latin, for example.[137] The progress of the Welsh during the centuries of Roman rule has been characterized as "negligible."[138] The southeastern part of Wales was unique in having a significant number of Roman villas,[139] but the region as a whole was never fully incorporated culturally into Roman civilization.

When later centuries brought invasions of southeastern Britain by Angles, Saxons, and others, some of the Britons there amalgamated with the conquerors, some fled west to be absorbed by (or to absorb) the population already living in the Welsh region, while others crossed the channel to settle on the northern coast of France. Many others may have perished in the wars and epidemics of that era. The numbers and proportions of these historic re-arrangements of races remain obscured in the mists of time.[140] Usually history is written by the conquerors, but the Anglo-Saxon conquerors of Britain were illiterate. One scholar has called this era "the shadowy phase of British history"[141] and another has more bluntly said, "informed guesswork must make do for history"[142] for much of this period that was decisive for the social transformation of Britain. Even the great figure of King Arthur is not known for certain to have existed historically. What is known is that remnants of the culture of Roman Britain survived in Wales, both in material things and in Christianity.

The next great wave of conquests, those of the Normans, are much more fully documented. The Normans, like the Romans a thousand years earlier, conquered England more quickly and decisively than they conquered Wales. The struggles and revolts of the Welsh over the centuries gave them enduring traditions as a people separate from the English, who ultimately established political and economic dominance. Ironically, it was a British king of Welsh ancestry—Henry VIII—who attempted to abolish Wales as a separate cultural and political entity. However, the Act of Union with England in 1536 by no means led to the cultural or biological absorption of the Welsh, despite efforts to fasten English culture and institutions on Wales. That Act made English the official language of Wales and decreed that those who spoke Welsh could hold no official office. This had much more impact on the Welsh gentry, who subsequently became Anglicized, than on the mass of the Welsh people,[143] who had no realistic prospects of such advancement in any case. By 1640, the Welsh gentry was well on its way to being Anglicized and many of its children attended Jesus College at Oxford, a college established in the previous century, largely for Welsh students.[144]

Just as the English language became the official language of Wales in 1536, so the Anglican Church became its officially established church, supported at the expense of the Welsh, most of whom did not belong to it. It was centuries later, after long political struggles, before the Anglican Church was finally disestablished in Wales in 1920. Religious grievances were among many sources of Welsh separatism and resentment of the English. Medieval Wales, though not as economically advanced as most of contemporary Europe, had nevertheless a more complex agriculture than that of a simple subsistence economy. There were estates, tenants, slaves, and property rights.[145] Wales also had England as a market for its agricultural and meat products. The relatively backward agriculture in Wales became a more progressive agriculture after exposure to more advanced English practices. Still, the agricultural revolutions that transformed England and

Scotland came later and more slowly in Wales. Welsh landlords lacked the capital for carrying out some of the more ambitious reorganizations of agriculture that took place elsewhere and a lack of good roads limited the marketability of Welsh produce.[146]

Sharp class differences and class hostilities have long marked the history of Wales—Welsh landlords, for example, being predominantly Anglicized in culture, English-speaking, political Tories, and of the Anglican religion, while their tenants were predominantly Welsh in culture, Welsh-speaking, political Whigs, and belonged to various religions outside the established Anglican church. Before the secret ballot was introduced in 1872, landlords sometimes retaliated with rent increases or evictions against tenants who did not vote as the landlord demanded.[147]

Similar differences of culture, language, religion, and politics existed between the urban industrial employers—whether English or Welsh—and their workers.[148] The poverty and vulnerability of the Welsh masses further embittered class relations. Like the Scots in earlier times, the rural Welshmen of the eighteenth century wore home-made clothing and typically lived in crude dwellings containing little that could be called furniture. Their thatched roof cottages also served as home for pigs and poultry as well. An absence of soap and a meager diet usually meant poor health.[149] Such diseases as smallpox, typhus, scarlet fever, and even cholera ravaged the Welsh as late as the first half of the nineteenth century.[150] The passing generations brought economic improvements but poverty and a periodically precarious existence remained grim facts of life for many in Wales.

Wales was among the first regions of Europe to industrialize, due largely to its huge deposits of coal and the availability of English capital, technology, and entrepreneurship to develop coal-related industries. The copper smelting industry, for example, began in Wales in 1584 and became a world center of this activity. At various times, Wales also had the largest iron-making town in the world, was dominant in world production of tinplate, and became a major supplier of coal in the era of international steamships. However, outside the realm of primary metals processing, Wales had little manufacturing.[151] Still, as early as the mid-nineteenth century, more than 60 percent of the Welsh labor force worked in non-agrarian occupations.[152] The urbanization of Wales was so rapid that its population went from 80 percent rural in the early nineteenth century to 80 percent urban by the early twentieth century.[153] Welsh miners were central figures in the country's economic and social history. As of 1914, the coal mines in Wales employed more than a quarter of a million people and supplied approximately one third of the world's coal exports.[154]

The thrust of modern industrialization in Wales came not primarily from the Welsh themselves but from foreigners—and continued to do so even in the late twentieth century. Great iron mills in Wales were created by English capitalists,[155] as were many other businesses there, some of which also attracted workers from England and Ireland, though mostly from rural Wales.[156] Prosperous foreigners employing Welshmen in hard, dangerous, and dirty occupations in mining and metals industries promoted a resentful nationalism already rich in historical fuel. Limited upward movement may also have contributed to Welsh labor militancy. In the middle of the nineteenth century, a government investigator said, "the Welsh workman never finds his way into the office. He never becomes a clerk or agent. He may become an overseer or contractor, but this does not take him out of the labouring and into the administring class."[157]

Language long remained a cultural barrier between the Welsh and the English, and a symbol of Welsh identity—much longer than in Scotland or Ireland.[158] Industrialization did not change that. The Welsh language remained dominant in most industrial areas of Wales until at least the beginning of the twentieth century.[159] However, the official British policy of teaching only English in the schools, beginning in 1870—with punishment for children caught speaking Welsh—eventually eroded the indigenous language among succeeding generations. Only half the population of Wales still spoke Welsh in 1901, fewer than 40 percent in 1921, and fewer than 20 percent by 1981. This decline was especially pronounced among the young.[160] Wales' most famous writer, Dylan Thomas, spoke no Welsh.

More than sheer coercion was involved, however, for this would not explain the great *variation* in the survival of Welsh in different geographical regions.[161] The English language became dominant in southern and eastern Wales, where the majority of the Welsh population lived,[162] and where the industrial and commercial incursions from England came earliest and most transformed the life of the Welsh people, while the Welsh language remained dominant in the northern and western hinterlands. In those parts of Wales where the English created a modern commercial and industrial economy, the English language was a means of upward mobility, a chance to escape the coal mines and the drudgery of the mills and factories. This incentive meant much less in those parts of Wales where farming and livestock were the principal means of livelihood.

While, in centuries past, the masses of the people in Wales clung to their native tongue as the more fortunate classes chose English, in the twentieth century a small resurgence of the Welsh language, led by the Welsh intelligentsia, became a nationalistic political symbol. Their key successes were produced in the British political arena, rather than by persuading the Welsh people to re-adopt their ancient language. The Welsh Nationalist Party (Plaid Cymru) won an occasional Parliamentary seat or two in the heart of the Welsh-speaking region,[163] and various demonstrations, vandalism of signs in English, and other factors have provided leverage with which to gain concessions from London. The Welsh Language Act of 1967 accepted the principle of "equal validity" of the English and Welsh languages in Wales. Some schools were established teaching in the Welsh language, reversing the decline of the language among the young—the bulk of whom still spoke only English, however. A Welsh-speaking television channel was also established by the British government—pleasing not only the Welsh-speaking population but also the English-speaking population of Wales, which before resented having their viewing interrupted by programs in Welsh.[164]

The political activities of Welsh nationalism have not been simply a matter of the Welsh people versus the English people. Within Wales itself, nationalism in general and the language issue in particular have been divisive. A referendum on greater home rule in Wales was overwhelmingly rejected in 1979 by the Welsh themselves, out of the mutual fears of different factions.[165] Ambivalence toward identity and acculturation has long marked the history of the Welsh.

The development of new steel-making processes in Britain was especially a boon to Wales, where much iron and steel were produced. By 1911, more than 22,000 men were employed in steel production in southwest Wales. As of 1913, coal, steel, and tinplate production in Wales were at an all-time high. Moreover, the First World War created a still greater demand for such products. However, the wartime boom was followed by a drastic reduction in world demand for these products from Wales, not only because the wartime uses were no longer sustained but also because alternative sources of supply developed elsewhere in the world. By the 1920s, the demand for coal, steel, and tinplate from Wales were at a new low. Unemployment rates among Welsh workers remained consistently above 20 percent from the mid 1920s to the late 1930s, sometimes rising as high as the 37 percent.[166] Not all Welsh industry declined in tandem—the copper industry began its decline in the 1860s, for example[167]—and some had rebounds. But the role of Wales as a major industrial center of the world was gone by the second half of the twentieth century.

By the late twentieth century, Wales was economically and socially transformed by the decline of its historic industries—coal, iron, steel, non-ferrous metals, and textiles. Coal mines which once employed more than a quarter of a million people now employed less than one-tenth that number. Employment in the steel industry of Wales was, by 1988, less than one-third what it was at its peak in 1970. Altogether, unemployment in Wales was even higher than in England, as both rates more than doubled in less than a decade.[168] There was still no entrepreneurial tradition among the Welsh, their educated classes typically seeking teaching or political careers and their universities having a strong anti-business outlook.

Many of the ablest young people in Wales went away to England, often to study at Oxford or Cambridge.[169] Major Welsh-owned businesses—with the notable exception of Laura Ashley—tended to be located outside Wales. In the late twentieth century, Wales had the lowest per capita output of any region of mainland Britain,[170] and was still handicapped by poor roads and poor rail transportation, as well as by the natural geographic barriers of this rugged land.[171] Moreover, the Welsh have been regarded by businessmen as poor credit risks.[172] Much of Wales' economic activity—agricultural as well as industrial—now survived on heavy subsidies by the British government.[173]

While Wales developed a sizeable tourist industry, especially along the southern coast, it has been in general regarded as an unattractive place to live. Ancient and declining industrial cities, slag heaps, and the vandalism of nationalistic extremists made it still less attractive. Nevertheless, there were some new industries being created in the late twentieth century. In fact, nearly one-fourth of all direct foreign investment in Britain in 1983–1984 went to Wales.[174] The largest concentration of Japanese-owned industry in Britain was in Wales[175] and a South Korean electronics company made an investment in Wales that was the largest overseas investment in Europe.[176] A large pool of available labor seems to have been Wales' major attraction, especially now that hard times had muted the Welsh labor unions' historic militant radicalism and brought more pragmatic cooperation with management. With the new industries as with the old, however, Welsh labor was used more to produce parts rather than finished products, to do low-skill work even in high-tech industries.[177]

The history of Wales as a conquered country shows patterns common elsewhere, not only in the British Isles but also in Africa, Asia, and the Western Hemisphere. Where the conqueror has been more organizationally or technologically advanced, those portions of the conquered country which were subjugated earliest and most thoroughly have tended to become—and remain—the most advanced regions, even in countries which later regained their independence. Another pattern has been that internal divisions created or accentuated by different levels of exposure to the culture of the conquerors have complicated and impeded political or cultural unification among the conquered.

While labor unions developed somewhat later in Wales than in England, Welsh unions became noted for their militancy and the Welsh voters for their support of the Labour Party. The only competition for the Welsh vote, after the decline of the Liberal Party led by the Welsh Prime Minister of Britain, David Lloyd George, was the Communist Party.[178] Monumental strikes and lockouts marked labor relations in Wales, where the interaction of ethnic and class differences made for particularly embittered industrial strife. One of the most militant left-wing British Labour Party figures in the mid-twentieth century was Welsh Member of Parliament Aneurin Bevan.

The history of Wales illustrates the great difficulty of creating an entrepreneurial tradition where none has existed before, even after centuries of exposure to the entrepreneurial activities of outsiders. The creation or expansion of an indigenous educated class in these circumstances tends not to supply entrepreneurship but, on the contrary, to create a class with a vested interest in promoting intergroup resentment and strife, using the symbols of identity and of historic oppression to gain current political ends, even at the expense of creating a climate unfavorable to either indigenous or foreign entrepreneurship. Bitter economic consequences may sometimes mute these tendencies, however, as they did in late twentieth century Wales.

Scotland

The northernmost portion of Britain—what is now Scotland—was never subdued by the Romans, nor was a conquest of Ireland attempted by the Romans, though it was contemplated as a relatively easy task.[179] That Scotland was not conquered was due to the poverty of the land as well as to the fierceness of its tribes. The Romans decided that it was simply not worth the trouble.[180] Eventually, around 122 A.D., the emperor Hadrian had a wall constructed across a narrow isthmus south of Scotland, to protect Rome's British province from marauders. Scotland thus remained largely cut off for centuries from developments in England. A comparison of the two countries provides at least some rough indication of the impact of Roman civilization and of Anglo-Saxon and Norman influences, all of which filtered only belatedly into Scotland from England.

Scotland long remained what all of Britain had been before the Roman invasion—a country on the fringes of European civilization, not only geographically but culturally, economically, and politically as well. Scottish agriculture, as late as the beginning of the seventeenth century, still used farming implements as primitive as those of ancient Mesopotamia.[181] Houses lacked furniture, people went barefoot or sometimes wore crude shoes made of hides that might be tanned or not.[182] It was common for animals and humans to share unventilated, shanty-like homes—leading to an abundance of vermin.[183] The demand for soap was so small that no one manufactured it.[184]

Politically, Scotland for centuries lacked a national framework of law and order. Each local baron was virtually a law unto himself and murderous feuds among the clans kept the country in an uproar internally, while wars and skirmishes with England made the border regions insecure. These border regions were plagued not only by the recurrent wars between the English and the Scots, but were more continuously rendered lawless by murderous marauders who flouted the authorities of both countries and paid little heed to kings or clans.[185]

Scots regularly raided settlements in northern England, carrying off livestock and people as slaves, among other booty.[186]

Neither towns nor industry could flourish in these circumstances.[187] Even some of the leading towns in Scotland in the thirteenth century numbered their inhabitants in the hundreds rather than the thousands.[188] The total population of the country apparently remained below one million as late as the sixteenth century.[189] Even in the seventeenth century, the largest city in Scotland—Edinburgh—had only 16,000 people.[190] Roads were much worse in Scotland than in England and most could not accommodate a horse-drawn carriage.[191] In medieval Scotland, trade was usually by barter,[192] and such coins as circulated were usually foreign.[193] The Scots were unable to manufacture even the arms they used in their incessant battles. Spears, armor, and bows and arrows were imported.[194] Skilled labor was virtually unknown.[195] Scotland was primarily a supplier of raw material—salt, fish, coal, wool, skins and hides, for example.[196] Ignorance and superstition were widespread. There was said to be no fourteenth-century Scottish baron who could write his own name.[197]

A succession of medieval Scottish kings tried to establish law and order, and to move the country forward economically and culturally— in the direction of England, which represented a more advanced European civilization. These Scottish kings, where possible, replaced the tribal basis of power in kinship with the feudal basis of power in territory. This often involved making grants of land to new Anglo-Norman noble families and establishing royal burghs, whose urban residents were typically English-speakers rather than the indigenous Gaelic-speaking Celts. These burghers, possessing craft skills and commercial experience still lacking among the Celts, were able to prosper, and these many enclaves have been regarded as one possible reason for the spread of the English language, which eventually replaced Gaelic as the language of the Scottish lowlands during the Middle Ages.[198] In the countryside as well, Scots landlords brought in English farmers and plowmen to teach their tenants the agricultural methods used in England.[199]

None of this was accomplished quickly, fully, or uniformly, and all of it encountered resistance—often bloody and sometimes successful—by the indigenous clans and nobles. Royal power was unevenly effective at different times and places. It was least effective in the

rugged highlands, which maintained their freedom from the conqueror—and their isolation from European civilization. The Scottish
highlands were able to hold out for centuries, maintaining a Gaelic-
speaking society with older, indigenous traditions, as the lowlands
blended the indigenous culture with Anglicized practices and adopted
a Scottish dialect of the English language. Newcomers to Scotland
from England, Scandinavia, and the continent began to blend in with
the lowland Scots, leading to a new cultural gulf between lowland and
highland Scots that persisted for centuries.[200] The highland Scots
derived much of their livelihood from plundering the farms and towns
of the lowland Scots.[201] It was said of these highland raiders that their
greatest pleasure was stealing and their next greatest pleasure was
destruction.[202] A fourteenth century writer described the lowland Scots
as people "of domestic and civilized habits" and the highland Scots as
"a savage and untamed nation, rude and independent, given to rap-
ine," and "exceedingly cruel."[203]

Scandinavians and Normans, as well as lowlanders and highlanders, contended for various parts of medieval Scotland, and Scottish kings battled their own nobles as well as the English. In addition,
many local kings of both British and Scandinavian ancestry had
realms in various parts of the British Isles, including Scotland, until a
consolidation over the centuries reduced the realms to those of the
Scottish and the English kings.[204] Only the advent of gunpowder and
cannons swung the balance of power decisively in the royal direction,
enabling European kings in general—who maintained a monopoly of
this new and expensive weaponry—to batter down the castle walls of
recalcitrant nobles[205] and establish a unified order.

England launched an invasion of Scotland in the late thirteenth
century. In the fourteenth century the English captured the Scottish
town of Berwick, subjecting it to what Winston Churchill called "a
sack and slaughter which shocked even those barbaric times,"[206] for
the inhabitants were not simply killed but tortured to death and the
king himself set fire to their homes. For centuries thereafter, Scottish
soldiers fighting the English used the cry, "Remember Berwick!" and
they skinned alive captured English officers, setting off new rounds of
atrocities and counter-atrocities.[207]

During those centuries of strife, the contested borderlands were not
simply a region of battles between opposing armies during intermittent

warfare, they were a continuously lawless frontier where feuding
clans, marauders, vigilantes, and "protection" racket extortionists
flourished. In short, these were not loyal followers of either English or
Scottish kings, but freebooters who were said to be "Scottish when
they will, and English at their pleasure."[208] Among the enduring consequences of these centuries of borderland disorder was the development of a culture of disregarding the law and settling disputes by
personal violence, whether violence between individuals or between
families. Rustling, squatting on land without legal title, abductions of
women, and ruthless brutality in general became some of the hallmarks of lawlessness among these frontier people, whether on the
frontiers of Britain or, later, on the frontiers of America.[209] Border people were also prominent among the Scots who settled in Ulster County,
Ireland,[210] contributing to the enduring turbulence there as well.

Along with the internal pacification of Scotland, over a period of
centuries, came an easing of military hostilities between Scotland and
England, over an even longer span of time. The uniting of Scotland
with England was to be the work of centuries of war and political
intrigue. When Scottish King James VI inherited the English throne
and became King James I of England, the two countries were partially
united politically in 1603 with one king, but still maintained separate
parliaments and separate political institutions in general. Just over a
century later, they were fully united, with one Parliament in London,
in 1707. This marked not only a political but also an economic, social,
and cultural turning point in the history of Scotland.

As with the earlier Roman conquest of Britain, the first economic
and social fruits of unification were law and order. With the pacification of the borders, trade grew between England and Scotland after
four centuries.[211] England was, at this point, far ahead of Scotland economically, as well as in population and power,[212] so that resumption of
trade represented an exposing of Scots to a more advanced society, as
well as to the immediate benefits of trade. Scottish cities grew rapidly
in the eighteenth century.[213] There were improvements in industry and
agriculture.[214] Trade was now open not only with England itself but
also with the British Empire as a whole. The export of Scottish linen
doubled in the decade between 1728 and 1738.[215] The population of
Scotland grew rapidly as the death rate declined sharply.[216] By the
middle of the eighteenth century, Scotland had about a million and a

quarter people and, over the next three-quarters of a century, that population nearly doubled.[217]

The economic and cultural evolution of Scotland was complicated by religious, dynastic and military struggles, growing ultimately out of the historic Protestant-Catholic split that convulsed much of Europe. The last, desperate uprising in the Scottish highlands in 1745, designed to restore the Catholic Stuarts to the throne in the person of "Bonnie Prince Charlie," marked a cultural turning point in the history of the highlands. Despite some initial successes, including the capture of Perth and Edinburgh, the forces of the Pretender were ultimately routed by a combination of English and loyalist Scottish troops from the lowlands. Bitter reprisals and a punitive peace followed, breaking the power of the highland clans and their chiefs, both militarily and politically. For a time, even the wearing of kilts and clan tartans was forbidden.

With much of the foundation of highland culture destroyed in the wake of the abortive 1745 uprising, the highlands began to be absorbed culturally, as well as politically, into the life of Scotland and of Great Britain. The Gaelic language, which still dominated the highlands in the mid-eighteenth century, began to give way to English. Roads brought into the highlands the religion, the schools, the law and order, the agricultural practices, and the general way of life of the lowlands. The Gaelic language and culture were stigmatized as barbaric, even among the highlanders themselves, and highland chiefs began to send their sons to be educated among the lowlanders.[218] Over time, the Scottish population in general tended to concentrate more and more in the lowlands.[219]

Among the lowland Scots, anglicization had begun much earlier, particularly among the wealthier and more educated classes. This acculturation extended well beyond use of the English language to domestic lifestyles, agricultural practices, and sometimes religious observances—most of the Scottish elite belonging to the Church of England, rather than to the Scottish denominations. A sense of the cultural inferiority of Scotland was found even among leading Scots.[220] In their zeal to imitate English agricultural methods themselves, and to promote these methods among Scots in general, the Anglicized Scottish elite seldom inquired into the suitability of English farming practices to the different climate and soil of Scotland. A widely introduced English plow, for example, ended up being widely abandoned after it was found to be less effective in the rocky Scottish soil. On the whole, however, the reorganization of Scottish agriculture along the lines of English agriculture improved output, even though this reorganization often displaced tenants and sub-tenants.[221]

As of the middle of the eighteenth century, most highlanders spoke little English,[222] and even in the early nineteenth century, Gaelic had still not died out in the highlands[223] but, when the Scottish highlanders changed from speaking Gaelic to speaking English during the nineteenth century, they put themselves in touch with more people and a more advanced culture among their contemporaries, as well as now having available to them a vast literature in English, reaching back through centuries of intellectual development in many fields, and a literature reaching back two thousand years through English translations of ancient writers. By contrast, Gaelic was largely a spoken language with very little literature and those who spoke it could seldom read it.[224] In short, what was involved was not simply a change of language but acquiring a whole new intellectual universe, which expanded enormously beyond the essentially non-literate Gaelic folk culture. This did not mean that the average highlander was reading the ancient classics, but the Scottish intellectual classes could not avoid being affected by the ideas of other times and places, as well as the ideas of English-speaking contemporaries around the world, if only through an awareness of how much more there was to the human experience than the highlands, and this awareness could not help filtering down to erode the insularity of centuries past.

The cultural progress of Scotland, especially in the lowlands, was by no means all imported from England. Even before the union of crowns with England in 1603, Scotland had made remarkable progress on its own. The change from Catholicism to Protestantism, promoted by John Knox in the sixteenth century, led to a Presbyterian church of wide popularity, which used its great influence and resources to create schools and promote education on a massive scale. Initially, this was education in a narrow orthodoxy,[225] and none of the leading scientific, literary, or artistic figures of Europe made an impact on Scotland.[226] But, in a country where even the nobility had been ignorant, now even the commoners became educated. By the late eighteenth century, the lowlands of Scotland had developed the most extensive system of education in Europe.[227] Moreover, education was now a vehicle of upward mobility, especially within the church. With the passage of time and the rapid spread of education to all levels of Scottish society, there developed for the first time an intellectual class in Scotland. It was not only the quantity, but also the quality, of this intellectual class which contrasted sharply with the previous condition of Scotland.

As historian Henry Buckle put it, "in every branch of knowledge this once poor and ignorant people produced original and successful thinkers."[228] These included not only the great philosopher David Hume, but also men who pioneered in shaping whole new fields of intellectual endeavor, such as economics (Adam Smith), chemistry (Joseph Black), and sociology (John Millar). In literature, there was the poetry of Robert Burns and the novels of Sir Walter Scott. Scots were among the leading architects of the age, notably Robert Adam, whose work had international repercussions on the design of everything from palaces to book bindings.[229] In applied science, James Watt's steam engine made possible not only manufacturing industries and railroads, but also revolutionized travel on rivers and oceans, with global consequences for the migrations of peoples and the transport of goods.

In medicine, as in other fields, Scotland was a late starter but quickly moved to the forefront. The Edinburgh University medical faculty was established in 1726, using as its model the Leiden medical school in the Netherlands, where all of its original professors had studied. By the second half of the eighteenth century, however, Edinburgh itself was considered the leading medical school in Europe. It both attracted an international student body and sent its Scottish doctors overseas.[230] Between 1720 and 1790, about 12,800 men passed through the Edinburgh medical school.[231] Dozens of these doctors settled in Virginia alone and many others were scattered throughout the American colonies.[232] Graduates of the Edinburgh medical school established the first American medical school in Philadelphia in 1765 and, three years later, another graduate of Edinburgh founded the medical school at King's College, later renamed Columbia University. The medical school established at Dartmouth in 1798 was likewise founded by graduates of Edinburgh.[233] Scottish physicians also became common in eighteenth century Russia, and included the court physician to Catherine the Great. Another Scot became head of the Medical Chancery at St. Petersburg.[234]

From the mid-eighteenth to the mid-nineteenth century, a disproportionate share of the leading British intellectual figures were either
from Scotland or of Scottish ancestry, including—in addition to those
already mentioned—Francis Hutcheson and Thomas Reid in philosophy, James Mill and John Stuart Mill in economics and political science, and Thomas Carlyle in history. Scotland also produced Britain's
leading intellectual journal, the *Edinburgh Review*. The dominance of
the Scots in British intellectual life was akin to that of the Jews in
other countries—with the important difference that the Scots had no
such centuries of intellectual tradition to draw upon. Moreover, the
Scots were not merely pre-eminent in Britain. In their golden age, during the last half of the eighteenth century, Scottish intellectuals as a
group were among the leading intellectuals in European civilization.

The social origins of these outstanding intellects were by no means
random. Virtually all were from the Scottish lowlands, and neither the
poor nor the aristocracy were well represented. Most of the leading
Scottish intellectuals came from middle class backgrounds.[235] The
Scottish aristocracy played a role as patrons of this talent, and in some
cases as its discoverers and financial supporters[236]—the classic example being James Mill, who was sponsored by Sir John Stuart, and in
gratitude named his first-born after him. That the rich, though well-
educated during this period, should be so little represented at the
intellectual peaks may seem to be an anomaly, but perhaps the com-
placency of assured social position dulled the incentives necessary for
the arduous task of developing native talents to the fullest.

The achievements of the Scottish enlightenment were all the more
remarkable for originating in a small country—smaller than either
Portugal or Guatemala, or the American state of Florida—with a population less than half that of present-day New York City or Tokyo. Moreover, these leading intellects were not drawn from this whole
population, small as it was, since the rich, the poor, and the highlanders (except for philosopher Adam Ferguson[237]) were not included.

Another peculiarity of the golden age of Scottish intellectuals was
its concentration in time and in fields. There had been few Scottish
intellects of international renown before—exceptions being Duns Scotus in the Middle Ages and the seventeenth-century mathematician
John Napier, who created logarithms and introduced the decimal
point—but nothing like the golden age of the eighteenth century

occurred before or since. Moreover, even within this era, the Scots made little or no impact as playwrights or in the field of music.[238] That the Scots did not reach these peaks before has been explained, first, by their lack of education, and then by the oppressive control of education by the Scottish church in an earlier period, but that this intellectual predominance did not continue remains largely unexplained.

At a more mundane level, the highlands as well as the lowlands were drawn into the economic and cultural progress of Scotland, after the union with England in 1707, though with a lag that kept the highlanders long in arrears. Standards of social behavior tended to be cruder in the highlands.[239] Education spread more rapidly in the lowlands than in the highlands[240] and the potato was introduced into the lowlands about 15 years before it was introduced into the highlands.[241] Both lowlanders and highlanders long considered themselves behind the people of England in manners, polish, and sophistication. The highlanders tended to copy the lowlanders and the lowlanders to copy the English.[242] Educated Scots sought to purge their speech of Scotticisms.[243]

This was not simply a matter of subjective perceptions. Many Scottish practices, particularly as regards sanitation, lagged behind what was acceptable in England. The legendary lack of cleanliness of the rural Scots became even more dangerous as they migrated to the city. A visitor to Edinburgh in the late eighteenth century found it worthy of note that its inhabitants no longer threw sewage out their windows into the street. Passersby had long had to be on the alert to avoid having this sewage fall on them.[244] Improvements in this respect were parallelled by numerous other improvements in manners, dress, household furnishings, and cultural activities—much of it financed by a growing prosperity in Scotland, beginning in the middle of the eighteenth century.

The wages of Scottish day laborers rose faster than the cost of living between 1760 and 1790.[245] In the wake of rising income came rising standards of living over time, though this happened gradually and unevenly across the social spectrum. While glass window panes began to appear in the windows of some of the larger farmhouses and churches in the early eighteenth century, many Scots at mid-century still lived in hovels that could be constructed in a day, measuring about 12 feet square, with roofs of straw and turf laid over rough branches.[246] As late as 1861, more than one-fourth of the population of Scotland still lived in one-room houses, but fewer than one-tenth did so half a century later.[247]

The rising prosperity of the Scots was associated with a shift of the working population from agriculture into industry. As late as the middle of the nineteenth century, one-fourth of all employed Scots worked in agriculture, but that was down to 11 percent half a century later, and to 4 percent in 1971. In the highlands, however, more than 40 percent of its working population worked in agriculture as late as 1911. For Scotland as a whole, the shift from agriculture to industry was paralleled by a shift to larger and larger communities. As of 1861, 28 percent of the Scottish population lived in communities of 50,000 or more people and none in communities of half a million but, half a century later, 42 percent were living in communities of 50,000 or more, including 20 percent in communities of half a million or more. Per capita income in Scotland was nearly as high as that of the United Kingdom as a whole by 1911, though the dependence of this prosperity on heavy industry made Scotland particularly vulnerable to changing world markets and the rise of competing industrial regions around the world. Thus unemployment in Scotland was higher than in England from the late 1920s through the late 1930s.[248]

In some respects, Scotland did not merely catch up with England, but overtook it. This was especially striking in education. As early as the eighteenth century, some of the English aristocracy were sending their sons to Scotland for an education in universities that were considered outstanding, at a time when Oxford and Cambridge were considered stagnant.[249] Among American colonists who studied at British universities, more went to Edinburgh than to either Oxford or Cambridge.[250] In addition to the primacy of Scottish medical and engineering education, at the more mundane levels the Scots also came to compare favorably with the English. Thus primary school education became compulsory in Scotland in 1872, seventeen years before it became compulsory in England, and became free in 1889, two years before it became free in England. While the number of university students in Scotland was never as large as the number in England, due to the disparities in populations of the two countries, in proportion to its population Scotland had far more university students than England as early as 1830 and as late as 1950.[251] While illiteracy in Scotland in 1750 was 22 percent for men and 77 percent for women,[252] a century later this was down to 11 percent among bridegrooms and 23 percent among brides, though the regional variations ranged from 1 percent for both sexes in lowland Berkwickshire to 37 percent of men and 49 percent of women in some highland communities. By 1917, illiteracy was down to 1 percent for both sexes in Scotland as a whole, and less than 3 percent even in those highland communities where it had been so high in the mid-nineteenth century.[253]

Unlike Ireland or Wales, Scotland developed its own class of entrepreneurs, industrialists, and financiers. As with England, Scotland had a commercial class long before it had an industrial class.[254] Many Scots rose from modest beginnings to become business magnates of national or even international stature.[255] Engineering, steelmaking, ship building, textiles, and chemicals were just some of the industries in which the Scots excelled.[256] Most of these industries developed from small beginnings in the early nineteenth century. As of 1805, Scotland produced just 5 percent of the pig iron made in the United Kingdom; by 1835 it produced nearly 30 percent.[257] In 1831, the shipyards on the Clyde River employed 3 percent of the British ship-building labor force but by 1871 they employed 21 percent and launched 48 percent of the ships built in Great Britain.[258]

Many technological innovations of the industrial age originated with Scots. For example, a boiler developed by a Glasgow engineer powered about three fourths of the British merchant marine fleet by 1876.[259] The world's first university chair in engineering was founded in Glasgow in 1840.[260] Scottish universities forged ahead of English universities in science, pure and applied[261] while traditional classical education prevailed among the English.[262] Japan, newly emerging on the world scene in the late nineteenth century, sought its science and engineering in Scotland.[263] In agriculture as well, Scotland began the eighteenth century behind the English but, after copying and applying English methods of farming, then surpassed the English in agricultural technique.[264]

Scottish agriculture underwent a far-reaching transformation from long-traditional methods to modern farming practices that greatly increased output per acre, raised the real wages of farm workers and increased the average size of landowners' holdings. Between the mid-eighteenth century and the early nineteenth century, this economic revolution was accompanied by large, and not always welcome, changes in social patterns, reducing the class of tenant farmers and increasing the number of landless agricultural laborers, as well as

replacing stable traditional roles and expectations with the fluidity
and uncertainty inherent in a changing market economy.[265] One consequence was greater geographical movement within Scotland, as those
displaced from ancestral lands and occupations wandered in search of
work elsewhere. One third of all Scots in the mid-nineteenth century
moved from one county to another and, for some, there was emigration
to other lands around the world.[266]

The enduring importance of these historic developments may be
indicated by comparing two groups of Scots—one of whom experienced their full influence, and one of whom did not. In 1610, the
British opened Ulster County in Ireland to settlement by Englishmen
and Scotsmen. The opportunity was especially attractive to people
from then poverty-stricken Scotland, who predominated numerically
among those who migrated to Ireland, though the English settlers were
financially better off.[267] The Scots who began to settle in Ulster left
their homeland when it was still a very backward country on the
fringes of European civilization. These Scots lived as frontier settlers
and colonizers in a hostile land where the dispossessed and embittered Irish continued armed resistance for years—in a sporadic sense,
for centuries.

The historic ferocity and clannishness of the Scots enabled them to
survive in this hostile environment. Three decades after the project
began, there were 40,000 Scots in Ulster.[268] Others continued to join
them over the years, now coming from a more advanced Scotland, so
that not all Ulster Scots (or "Scotch-Irish" as they later came to be
called) were either poor or uneducated by any means. Nevertheless
their lag behind other Scots could be seen both in the British Isles
and, later, overseas in the United States and Australia.

Ireland

A common characteristic of Celtic peoples, both on the continent of
Europe and in the British Isles, was their inability to unite into forces
of national dimensions, even though they covered vast areas that today
constitute several nations. Julius Caesar's victories in Gaul were in significant part a result of the disunity of the Celts there, and of his ability
to divide and conquer, both politically and militarily.[269] The Celtic
tribes that dominated pre-Roman Britain were conquered for the same

reasons a century later. A thousand years after that, a similar internal disunity made Ireland vulnerable to conquest by a united Britain.

While the fragmented Irish resistance was unable to drive out the British invaders, neither could the British score a decisive victory for centuries. There was no central government whose surrender or collapse would be recognized by the Irish as marking the end of the war. Although the invasion of Ireland began in the thirteenth century, as late as the fifteenth century effective British control did not extend beyond some walled towns and a coastal strip of land around Dublin.[270] Even after later centuries brought complete British military conquest of Ireland, underground resistance groups rose and fell, sporadically spreading terrorism, or launching mass uprisings that were bloodily suppressed.

The most spectacular—and embittering—of the British suppressions of the Irish was Oliver Cromwell's punitive expedition of 1649, ostensibly to avenge Protestants killed in a Catholic uprising in 1641. Cromwell, who hated Catholics in general and priests in particular, was merciless in battle and vengeful after victory, killing defenseless prisoners and confiscating vast areas of land from Irish owners to award to British settlers. As of 1641, the indigenous Irish Catholics owned an estimated three-fifths of the land of Ireland but, just 24 years later, this proportion was down to one-fifth. By 1709, the Irish owned only 14 percent of the land in their own country.[271]

Cromwell's punitive expedition marked a watershed in Irish history. An estimated 40 percent of the Irish population died either in the war or in the famine which accompanied the devastation.[272] In the aftermath of Cromwell's subjugation, the Irish became a people without many basic rights in their own land. Under the Penal Laws imposed on Ireland, they could neither vote nor hold office, nor receive military commissions. They could not freely practice the Catholic religion, nor receive any education but Protestant education, and they were taxed to support the Anglican Church. While these and other Penal Laws were not consistently carried out to the letter in all cases, the Irish suffered other disabilities imposed without the sanction of law. Many British landlords, for example, maintained their own private jails to punish the Irish—and while this was illegal, grand juries repeatedly refused to indict landlords found practicing this particular form of oppression in Ireland.[273]

Underground Catholic education and underground terrorist groups were among the Irish responses. Brutal guerrilla warfare was directed not only at the British overlords but also against Irish collaborators. The British were equally implacable in suppressing such movements and hanging their leaders.[274] Eventually, however, a non-violent political movement emerged as the Penal Laws were relaxed, leading to agitation for their complete repeal. This finally happened in 1829, in what has been called Catholic Emancipation.

The dire poverty of the early nineteenth century Irish may be indicated by their average life expectancy of 19 years—compared to 36 years for contemporary American slaves—and the fact that slaves in the United States typically lived in houses a little larger than the unventilated huts of the Irish and slept on mattresses, while the Irish slept in piles of straw.[275] Slaves also ate a wider variety of foods, including low grades of meat, while an Irishman, subsisting on potatoes and occasionally fish, might not see meat from one year to the next.[276] Bad as these "normal" conditions were among the Irish masses in the early nineteenth century, worse conditions followed in the 1840s, when potato blight destroyed the crop that provided their basic nutrition.

In the great famine that ensued, about a million people died of starvation and diseases related to malnutrition.[277] Close to two million emigrated between the mid 1840s and the mid 1850s.[278] The poorest tended to settle in nearby Britain while others went to the United States, usually in the cheapest, most crowded, and most stark and dirty accommodations on passenger or cargo ships.[279] Upon arrival, whether in England or the United States, the Irish typically lived in the worst slums, amid the greatest filth, and worked in the least skilled, lowest paid, and most dangerous occupations.[280] Such massive outflows of population from Ireland went to Britain and the United States that, by 1891, nearly two-fifths of all living people born in Ireland were living outside Ireland.[281] Ireland's population of 8 million people in 1841 fell to only half of that by 1926.[282] Even in the late twentieth century, there were more people of Irish ancestry in the United States than in Ireland.[283] The Irish were one-third of the population of Great Britain at the beginning of the nineteenth century and less than 10 percent of the British population by the middle of the twentieth century.[284]

Culturally, the Irish were drawn into the orbit of the English in language but not in religion or politically. By the mid-nineteenth century, the indigenous language was still being spoken by only about a fifth of the people of Ireland. Yet nine-tenths of the people in Irish counties were Roman Catholic.[285] Industrially, the Irish lagged far behind the English. Unlike Scotland, Ireland did not become more industrialized after its Act of Union with England. On the contrary, Irish industry, with the exception of linens, declined after the union with England in 1801 because it could not compete with English industry.[286] Nor was Irish agriculture as advanced as that in England, which had resident landlords overseeing farming techniques, while Irish landlords were more often absentees living in England on the rents of their property in Ireland. Scotland was also well ahead of Ireland in economic development. While the Scots established themselves as bankers, both at home and overseas, not one private bank was opened in Dublin in the quarter century before 1793.[287] In the early twentieth century, Scottish industrial workers produced about 20 percent more output per capita than Ireland's industrial workers and Scotland's industries as a whole produced nearly four times the output of Ireland's industries, even though the two countries had very similar sized populations at that point.[288]

Politically, the struggle for independence from Britain reached a climax in 1922, when the Irish Free State was formed, making most of the island independent, except for predominantly Protestant Ulster County. Although the majority and minority in Ulster are conventionally described with religious labels as Protestants and Catholics, they are in fact different ethnic groups, and their continuing bitter differences are not religious, as such. Independent Ireland escaped the social strife and terrorism which continued to plague Ulster, but independence did not solve Ireland's historic economic and social problems. High unemployment, one of the heaviest tax burdens in Europe and a national debt exceeding the annual gross national product were some of the grim indicators of Ireland's economic condition at the end of the 1980s. With an annual emigration of 46,000 people, Ireland's population of 3.5 million was still declining, despite one of the highest birth rates in Europe.[289]

Although the Irish Free State's standard of living was significantly lower than that in Ulster, the latter's standard of living was in turn below that in the United Kingdom as a whole, despite being subsidized by the British taxpayers, since Ulster received more from the British government than it paid in taxes.

Within Ulster, the Catholic population has tended to be poorer than the Protestant and less represented in higher-level occupations, as well as more represented in public housing projects. All this points toward differences in human capital, such as have marked the Irish, compared to the Scots or the English, in other countries around the world. The preferred explanation among the Irish in Ulster, however, has been discrimination, even though the evidence for such discrimination consists largely of statistical disparities, rather than actual individual examples. Among students, the Irish Catholics tended to study science and technology less often than Ulster Protestants did.[290]

BRITAIN IN THE WORLD

British history is by no mean confined to Britain, for no other nation has had such a large and enduring role in shaping events, institutions, and the fates of other peoples around the world. Much of the world today, including the United States, is still living in the social, cultural, and political aftermath of Britain's cultural achievements, its industrial revolution, its government of checks and balances, and its conquests around the world. Many fundamental concepts of law and government, and the traditions that make them viable, originated in Britain, as did much of the technology that made the modern world possible.

While the technological influence of the British in leading the world into the industrial age has reached every corner of the globe, and the legal and political example of the British system of government has influenced countries on all continents, the more direct transplantation of Britons has been concentrated in a relatively few places, mostly offshoot societies such as the United States, Canada, Australia, and New Zealand. Here there has been transferred not a single British culture so much as a collection of British cultures, varying not only among such ethnic groups as the English, Welsh, Scots, and Irish, but also among groups bearing the same ethnic label but coming from different parts of the British Isles with contrasting cultural backgrounds.

The social impact of these groups in other countries not only reflected their initial differences in Britain but also helped shape the history of the countries in which they settled.

Britons Overseas

The British people may be divided along many lines other than purely ethnic lines. Nor are these other divisions any less sharply contrasting. Just as the Irish, the Scots, the Welsh, and the English have had different histories at home and overseas, so have different people from contrasting regions of England, contrasting regions of Scotland, or the peoples of what has been loosely called "the Celtic fringe" as a whole, as compared to those from the more Anglicized parts of the British Isles.

Like other culturally distinctive groups, the Irish have taken their way of life with them around the world. Whether at home or abroad, the distinctive behavior patterns of the Irish have been striking, though not all these patterns remained unchanged over the generations. The Irish immigrant generations of the nineteenth century, whether in Britain or the United States, were largely an unskilled urban proletariat, settling in large cities but living a way of life more suited to the rural world from which they came. For example, nineteenth century Irish city-dwellers kept pigs and fowl, and disposed of their garbage in the streets, whether in America or England. Not surprisingly, in both countries cholera and other filth-related diseases struck Irish neighborhoods particularly hard.[291]

Fighting and widespread alcoholism were also hallmarks of the Irish abroad, as in Ireland itself.[292] The occupational distribution of the Irish living in nineteenth-century Philadelphia was very similar that of the Irish living in London at the same time.[293] Much the same story could be told of the Irish in Australia, though here a significant number settled in rural areas.[294] The great majority of Irish men in Australia were laborers and the great majority of Irish women were servants.[295] As late as the 1880s and 1890s, more than 95 percent of Irish women working in Australia were domestic servants, as were a similar proportion of Irish women working in the United States at that time.[296]

In Argentina, however, the availability of land grants drew many of the Irish immigrants away from their initial settlement in Buenos Aires. The Irish who left the city often formed communities where Irish names continued to predominate even in the twentieth century.[297] Surviving initially very difficult conditions as shepherds on a sharecropping basis with the sheep owners in the early nineteenth century, the Irish prospered as international demand for Argentine wool and sheep increased.[298]

The Catholic Church was a central feature of Irish life, at home and abroad. The Church played a major role in the social development of Irish immigrants and their assimilation to higher standards of education and behavior, so that the Irish of later generations became much more socially accepted in the larger societies in which they lived in Britain, Australia and the United States. In Argentina, however, Irish Catholic organizations kept the immigrants a separate community, fearing that they might otherwise degenerate to the level of the surrounding Argentines, even though the latter were also Catholic. Arriving Irish immigrants were met at the dock, the men steered toward jobs with Irish employers and the women toward marriage with established Irish immigrants who had arrived before them, and the children of these marriages were educated in English-speaking Irish Catholic parochial schools.[299] The newspapers the immigrants read in Argentina were English-language papers dealing with news from the particular counties from which they had come in Ireland.[300] These cultural enclaves began to be broken up only after the rise to power of Juan Perón, near the middle of the twentieth century, leading to the end of specifically Irish schools.[301]

Around the world, the Irish have been especially successful in fields requiring insights into human relations—politics, writing, law, labor union leadership—rather than fields requiring mathematical, scientific, or entrepreneurial aptitudes. The organizational skills of the Irish, developed while maintaining their own underground religious and secular institutions in Ireland, proved to be a major factor in their advancement to leadership positions in labor unions and in politics in urban communities, whether in Britain, the United States, Australia, or Canada. Of 110 labor union presidents in the American Federation of Labor in 1900, more than 50 were Irish.[302] Irish control of American big city political machines in the nineteenth century was scattered literally from coast to coast.[303]

Whether in the U.S., Britain, or Australia, Irish politicians tended to be concentrated on the left—but the pragmatic left, concerned with obtaining immediate, tangible benefits for their working class constituencies, rather than an eventual reconstitution of society along ideologically-defined lines.[304] In Britain, the Irish have been concentrated in the Labour Party, in the U.S. in the Democratic Party, and in Australia in the Australian Labour Party. There were four second-generation Irish Prime Ministers of Australia who dominated politics in that country during the era from 1929 to 1949.[305] Britain and Canada have also had Irish Prime Ministers. The United States elected its first Irish President in 1960 and its second in 1980.

The Welsh have likewise had their own distinctive patterns, at home and abroad. One of their differences from the Irish, for example, has been in the far lesser tendency of the Welsh to emigrate at all. In proportion to their respective populations, the Irish have immigrated to the United States more than twenty times as much as the Welsh.[306] Those Welsh who did go overseas took their cultural patterns with them, including not only such things as being miners in both Australia and the United States,[307] but also their language, their religion, and their ambivalence about their ethnic identity. An isolated Welsh colony was established in nineteenth-century Argentina, in hopes of preserving their cultural identity. Yet the people in this colony ended up having to call on the British government for help and, conversely, when World War I came, Welshmen from Argentina volunteered to go fight for Britain.[308] Eventually, however, the descendants of the Welsh in Argentina began to speak Spanish and were culturally absorbed as Argentines.[309]

The Welsh in the United States have likewise been absorbed into the general American population over time, though the early Welsh immigrants remained separate in language and largely endogamous in marriage in those places where there were sufficient concentrations to make this possible.[310] Early Welsh settlements in Pennsylvania left a legacy of place names from Wales, including Bryn Mawr, Haverford, Radnor, and Merion.[311] Since Wales was the first nation in the world with more than half of its population working in non-agricultural pursuits, it is hardly surprising that Welsh immigrants to the United States went heavily into mining and into steel mills, though many also became farmers, often in hills and valleys resembling those in Wales. When a mine fire in Pennsylvania in 1869 killed more than a hundred miners, at least two-thirds of them were Welsh.[312] Among the famous Americans of Welsh ancestry were Thomas Jefferson, Jefferson Davis, Charles Evans Hughes, and the legendary labor leader, John L. Lewis—the "L." standing for the historic Welsh name Llewellyn—whose union was in the traditional Welsh occupation of mining.

In Australia as well, mining was a principal occupation of the Welsh. The discovery of copper in the colony of South Australia in the 1840s led to the first significant Welsh immigration, which tripled the local Welsh population from 300 to 900 by 1851. Many of these early immigrants spoke Welsh, rather than English, and some gave Welsh names to the streets in the neighborhoods where they lived. More discoveries of copper in South Australia and, later, gold in the colony of Victoria, increased the Welsh population in Australia several-fold. Although there were fewer than 400 Welsh living in Victoria in 1851, there were more than 6,000 a decade later. By 1865, there were at least 21 Welsh chapels—as distinguished from Anglican churches— in Victoria. One of the major coal-mining regions of Australia not only became a magnet for Welsh miners but was also named New South Wales, a colony and later a state with various local Welsh place names as well. In the colony of Queensland to the north, Welsh coal mining communities sprang up and with them Welsh religious institutions using the Welsh language.

Outside these concentrations in mining communities, however, the Welsh were culturally absorbed into the predominantly English population of Australia. However, as late as 1886, half the Welsh population still spoke Welsh, though this declined rapidly among the younger generation born in Australia, and a much reduced immigration from Wales meant that there was little reinforcement of the Welsh culture from overseas. Attempts of Welsh activists to promote colonies that would keep their culture alive failed in the nineteenth century and ethnic revivals under the "multicultural" banner in the late twentieth century were too little and too late to stop the cultural and biological absorption of the Welsh into the general Australian population.[313]

The traditional breakdown of the peoples of the British Isles into English, Scots, Irish, and Welsh does not capture all the cultural divisions among them, nor necessarily the sharpest cultural divisions. Britons of the same nominal ethnicity have often differed greatly according to their regional backgrounds within England or within Scotland, for example. Thus there were large cultural differences between the highland Scots and the lowland Scots overseas as there was at home, or between each of these and the Scots who settled in Ulster County, Ireland.

Most of the Scots who immigrated to colonial America did so as indentured servants, whose passage was paid by Americans, for whom they would later work free for years in repayment.[314] Highland Scots who immigrated to North America settled primarily in North Carolina but predominated in different regions of that state from those in which the Ulster Scots were concentrated.[315] Language differences long kept the highland Scots separate from other Scots and from the American population in general, for highland Scots still spoke Gaelic in nineteenth-century America[316]—and in parts of the region in which they settled, Gaelic still had not died out completely, even in the late twentieth century.[317] The highland Scots who immigrated to Australia in the early nineteenth century likewise spoke Gaelic and required translators, as well as being largely illiterate and unskilled.[318] While the subsidized emigration schemes which took them to Australia were criticized in the highlands for having taken the cream of the local working population, in Australia the criticism was that these highlanders were the dregs of the Scottish immigration.[319] Given the differences between the highlanders and the lowlanders at that juncture, there was no necessary inconsistency between these two claims.

Most of the lowland Scots came from urban, industrial, and commercial areas of Scotland and went to similar areas in Australia.[320] Even those lowlanders who worked in agriculture came from a background of agriculture in Scotland that was advanced for its time.[321] But many of the Scottish shepherds in Australia were highlanders, reflecting in their new homeland one of the patterns of the old.[322] Though Australia and New Zealand attracted more than half of all Scots emigrating from the British Isles in the middle of the nineteenth century,[323] the proportion of highlanders among them declined over time, suggesting that the adverse comments about them might have had some basis, and thereafter more than 90 percent of the Scots arriving in Australia were lowlanders.[324]

Among Scots in general, however, there was a remarkable record of achievements overseas. Unlike the highland Scots or the Ulster Scots, most Scots immigrating from Scotland to the United States, for example, did not form enclaves but tended to assimilate into the general population.[325] They were noted for their industriousness[326] and many brought industrial skills still scarce in America.[327] Even in the late twentieth century, Americans of Scottish ancestry had incomes significantly above the national average.[328] Scots in general achieved promi-

nence and prosperity in America from the beginning. Nine men of
Scottish ancestry were generals under George Washington, constituting more than one-third of all his brigadiers. Nearly one-fifth of the
members of the Congress that adopted the Declaration of Independence were of Scottish extraction, as were two-thirds of the governors
of the original thirteen states.[329] Over time, more than a hundred men
of Scottish ancestry became governors of American states and 30 percent of all U.S. Supreme Court Justices from 1789 to 1882 were of
Scottish ancestry.[330]

In Australia as well, most Scots blended into the general population, rather than maintaining separate enclaves,[331] though the highlanders among them sometimes tended to remain socially and
culturally distinct longer.[332] The first Scots arriving in Australia, like
the first people of many other backgrounds, were convicts. However,
the Scots were numerically under-represented among these convicts,
though they were said to be among the worst criminals, since Scottish
courts were more reluctant to sentence any but the worst criminals to
transportation to Australia.[333] However, even in this early colonial
period, there were also distinguished Scots in the colony, including
Lachlan Macquarie and Sir Thomas Brisbane, both of whom became
governors of New South Wales.

The Scots' long traditions as fighting men were reflected in their
military careers overseas. In the British military forces in India in the
eighteenth century, one-third of the officers came from Scotland,
though in Britain itself Englishmen alone outnumbered Scots about
five-to-one in the population at that time.[334] The long military tradition
of the Scots kept them in demand as soldiers on the continent of
Europe as well. In France and in Poland, there were royal bodyguards
of Scots[335] and thousands of Scots fought in the Swedish army during
the Thirty Years War.[336] Scots also played an important role in modernizing Russia's military and naval forces.[337] A Scot attained the rank of
general in late seventeenth century Russia, and in the eighteenth century another Scot became a vice-admiral.

As early as the sixteenth century, a Scottish military man was made
governor of Kiev, and in the eighteenth century another Scot became
governor of Kronstadt, while yet another became governor of the
Ukraine.[338] There were also Scottish generals in Prussia and in the
Hapsburg Empire.[339] In the Western Hemisphere, there was a Scottish

vice-admiral in the Chilean navy in the nineteenth century[340] and Venezuela's battle for independence was aided by a Scottish officer who led aboriginal Indian troops into battle, to the sound of bagpipes, while dressed in his traditional highland regalia.[341]

As in Scotland itself, commerce and industry were fields in which Scots excelled overseas, both as workers and as entrepreneurs. These enterprises were not simply Scottish firms with overseas branches or operations. Often they were firms with no connection to Scotland, except for the Scottish ancestry of the people who founded them and ran them,[342] though many also sent back to Scotland for employees. Scottish merchant firms operated in China, India, Australia, Africa, the United States, and Canada.[343] An eighteenth-century Scotsman named Simon McTavish became known in Canada as the "uncrowned king of the fur trade."[344] Half of the board of directors of the first bank established in Canada were Scotsmen[345] and Scots were also prominent among bankers in Australia[346] and India,[347] while in Japan a Scotsman established a school of banking, whose Japanese students went on to become their country's bankers in later years.[348]

There were enough Scots in Meiji-era Japan to organize lodges in Yokohama, Kobe, and Nagasaki. Meanwhile, many ships for the Japanese navy were built in Scotland.[349] Shipbuilding was also a skill that the Scots took with them to other countries. As early as 1798, Scottish firms were constructing ships in Canada and, a year later, one of them was building the largest ship ever built in the maritime provinces up to that time. By the early nineteenth-century, a Scottish firm in Canada had the largest fleet of ships in the British Empire, employing 5,000 men on these ships and in the shipyards, as well as 15,000 men in the Canadian forests from which their timber came.[350] The first plate-iron floating drydock in Latin America was built by a Scotsman—its inventor—in 1863.[351]

In other fields as well, Scots had notable careers abroad. There were Scottish scholars teaching in French and German universities.[352] A Scot pioneered in metallurgy and machine-building in czarist Russia.[353] As businessmen, Scots ranged from peddlers to large-scale merchants and bankers, and operated from the villages of Poland to the fur-trading outposts of Canada. There were so many Scots in Holland that there was a Scottish church in Rotterdam.[354] In the seventeenth century, an estimated 30,000 Scots lived in Poland.[355] Most worked as peddlers.[356] Like most middleman minorities who have taken on the role of peddlers and shopkeepers, the Scots faced local resentment and discriminatory laws designed to restrict their economic activities, not only in Poland but in Prussia as well.[357] In Poland, political attacks on Scots linked them with the classic middleman minority, the Jews.[358] Nevertheless, some Scottish merchants in Poland became members of Polish guilds and other Scots became town councilors, aldermen and even burgomeisters.[359] The first sugar refinery in Danzig (present-day Gdansk) was built by a Scot.[360] Some members of the Scottish nobility also immigrated to Poland and became part of the Polish nobility.[361]

The history of the Ulster Scots overseas has been more mixed. Having begun their migration from Scotland to Ulster County before the cultural transformations which brought the Scottish people to the forefront of Western civilization, many Ulster Scots or "Scotch-Irish" did not fully share in that transformation. In colonial America, these Ulster Scots were more numerous than the Scots from Scotland. Among their many differences was that, when the revolutionary war broke out, the Ulster Scots overwhelmingly supported the American cause while many of the Scots from Scotland remained loyal to England—or, at least, were opposed to another rebellion, after the military debacle and painful reprisals following the abortive highland rebellion of 1745.[362] Although the Ulster Scots had neither socially nor biologically amalgamated with the indigenous Irish,[363] they became known initially as "Irish" in the United States, but they made a point of calling themselves "Scotch-Irish" in nineteenth century America, to distinguish themselves from the indigenous Irish immigrants who began arriving in large numbers at that time.

The term "Scotch-Irish" has also been applied loosely to include not only Ulster Protestants in general (some of whom were in fact English) but also many people from the turbulent borderlands between England and Scotland, who often settled in the Southern United States, interspersed with the Ulster Scots and sharing much of their ethos, having come from a similarly stormy and backward frontier region of Britain. Both came from places which, in the pre-industrial era, were "thinly settled and desperately poor"[364] the borderers from "a part of England where the civilization was least developed,"[365] in the words of later scholars. The same description would be as apt for the Appalachian region of the United States, where the same two peoples settled and amalgamated to produce one of the most enduring pockets of poverty among white Americans. Most of the white population of the American South as a whole came not only from what has been loosely called the "Celtic fringe," but also from that fringe at a particular time and a particular stage of its cultural evolution:

> . . . had the South been peopled by nineteenth-century Scots, Welshmen, and Ulstermen, the course of Southern history would doubtless have been radically different. Nineteenth-century Scottish and Scotch-Irish immigrants did in fact fit quite comfortably into northern American society. (Significantly the Irish, who retained their Celtic ways, did not.) But only a trickle of the flood of nineteenth-century immigrants came into the South; the ancestors of the vast majority of Southerners arrived in America before the Anglicization of Scotland, Wales, and Ulster had advanced very far.[366]

The fringe of British civilization from which they came was notable not only for its poverty and backwardness, but also for its lawlessness and violence. These included the disputed borderlands between England and Scotland—a region "accustomed" to "barbarity with slaughter, rape and fire"[367]—where warfare between the two countries was marked by atrocities and counter-atrocities, and was supplemented by unofficial violence from marauders, vigilantes, and others who kept this a region which "never enjoyed fifty consecutive years of quiet" until the decisive English victories of 1745.[368] By then, however, many people from this region had already immigrated to America, where the old traditions of violence survived, long after they were suppressed in Britain.[369]

A similar tradition of violence and counter-violence existed in Ulster County, Ireland, between the indigenous Irish and the colonizing settlers, who were predominantly Scottish. Law being too tenuous to rely upon in such places, people developed patterns of settling differences by personal fighting and family feuds. The Ulster Scots and borderers brought these distinctive cultural patterns to the United States in general and to the South in particular. Quite different from the Tidewater aristocracy of the South, both in their places of origins and in their respective ways of life in Britain and America, these common people of the more rural or backcountry regions were known as "crackers" and "rednecks" in Britain, even before they migrated to the American

South. The term "Hoosiers" was also a common name for them, though in the United States this name was applied particularly to those Southerners who migrated into Indiana and, eventually, to Indianans of whatever regional origins.[370] Whatever they were called, the people whose ancestors immigrated from the most turbulent regions of Britain represented what one social historian has called "some of the most disorderly inhabitants of a deeply disordered land."[371]

Given this background, it can hardly be surprising that hard drinking and the ruthless fighting called "rough and tumble," (which included biting off ears or noses and gouging out eyes) became hallmarks of the Southern backcountry way of life. Nor did it take much to get fighting started among these people, for "even in their poverty they carried themselves with a fierce and stubborn pride that warned others to treat them with respect."[372] Vigilante movements were another facet of their violent pattern, and the name "lynch law" has been traced to one of their number named William Lynch, whose followers often flogged and sometimes killed their victims.[373] These patterns continued long after Lynch's death in 1820, with most victims being white until the Reconstruction era in the South after the Civil War, when blacks became the main targets. The fighting clans of Scotland have been claimed as models for the Ku Klux Klan and "the fiery cross of old Scotland's hills" as the origin of the KKK's practice of burning crosses to intimidate blacks in the United States.[374] In short, the pattern of ruthless violence directed by Southern whites against blacks originated long before there were any racial differences involved and in fact before the people of the Southern backcountry had boarded the ships in Britain which took them to their new homes in the American South.

In the antebellum South, these backcountry people were seldom prosperous enough to own slaves, nor were the backcountry and upland regions in which they lived particularly suitable to plantation agriculture. Moreover, Ulster Scots settled both inside and outside the South. One of their earliest concentrations was in western Pennsylvania in colonial times, when it was frontier territory. There the Scotch-Irish became known as "troublesome settlers to the government and hard neighbors to the Indians."[375] This did not necessarily represent any special racial animosity toward the Indians, for people of the same origin were notorious for squatting on land to which they had no legal title, not only in America, but also in Australia and New Zealand.[376]

From western Pennsylvania, Scotch-Irish settlements spread down through the Cumberland gap into western Maryland, western Virginia, the Piedmont region of the Carolinas, and on into backcountry Georgia. In parts of this vast area, they shared the land with immigrants from Germany, but the two groups lived very different ways of life in separate communities, and seldom intermarried.[377]

When Ulster Scots settled in colonial New England, one of the complaints against them by their neighbors was a lack of cleanliness, and a visitor to a Scotch-Irish settlement in Pennsylvania in the late eighteenth century likewise described their log cabins as being "as dirty as in the north of Ireland, or even Scotland."[378] Among the Scotch-Irish, their pride "was a source of irritation to their English neighbors, who could not understand what they had to feel proud about."[379] Yet these immigrants—as unwelcome among the Quakers of eastern Pennsylvania as among the Puritans of Massachusetts or the Cavaliers of Virginia—included an elite of perhaps one or two percent who remained an elite in backcountry America. It was these elite families which produced such notable Americans of Scotch-Irish ancestry as Patrick Henry, Andrew Jackson, John Calhoun, James Polk, Zachary Taylor, Sam Houston, and others.[380] Even among these elites, however, some of the old traditions still survived. Portraits of these men match contemporary descriptions of them as "tall, lean and sinewy, with hard, angry, weatherbeaten features."[381] Among the precepts that Andrew Jackson's mother taught him were never to sue anybody for slander or for assault and battery: "Always settle them cases yourself."[382]

For centuries, sharp differences between the behavior patterns of white Southerners and white Northerners (especially New Englanders) were commented on by contemporary observers of American society and by scholars alike, in terms faithfully mirroring sharp differences seen in Britain between those from the main part of England, on the one hand, and the Irish, the Welsh, the Ulster Scots, and the "borderers" on the other—those outside the central English culture often being lumped together as "the Celtic fringe" or as "North Britons," though the Scottish highlanders tended to be separate and distinct from the others.[383] These cultural differences between American Northerners and Southerners extended from work habits to violence, cleanliness, alcohol consumption, inventiveness, food preferences, music, morals, and attitudes toward time, business, and education.[384] A distinguished historian summarized the world encountered by Frederick Law Olmsted during his celebrated travels through the antebellum South:

> The meager standard of living—the shabby dwellings, the coarse and monotonous fare, the absence of cleanliness and ordinary comforts, the dearth of newspapers and other reading matter—appalled this Yankee who had never encountered anything like this in even the humblest Northern homes.[385]

What was involved was not simply poverty but what Olmsted called "lazy poverty,"[386] based on neglect of work, education, or other means of social betterment. Alexis de Tocqueville before him had likewise commented on "ignorant and apathetic" Southerners who were poor, even on rich land, and who lived in "idle independence."[387] Both Olmsted and de Tocqueville attributed these regional differences among whites in the United States to the effects of differences between slave states and free states, but the distinctive cultural patterns of these particular Britons and their descendants were at least as striking in those regions of the South where slavery was virtually non-existent,[388] and the same differences between these same groups and most of the English in the British Isles could hardly be attributed to that cause, since slavery had long since disappeared in Britain.

Although the English who settled around the world—especially in such offshoot societies as the United States, Canada, and Australia—are often thought of as a more or less homogenous group, to whose cultural norms others had to adjust in these societies, their internal differences have been as striking as those among different groups of Scots. Like many immigrants to other places around the world, most of those Britons who first settled in the Massachusetts Bay colony came from a rather narrowly circumscribed area. Most originated within a 60-mile radius of the town of Haverhill in East Anglia—and even many of those who immigrated to Massachusetts from other parts of the British Isles had lived in East Anglia before moving to these other areas, from which they then immigrated to America.[389] The special subculture which long characterized Massachusetts, and to some extent New England in general, and which distinguished it sharply from the subculture of the American South, for example, paralleled in many ways the subculture of East Anglia.

Religiously, East Anglia was dominated by Puritans, as was the

early Massachusetts colony. The austere, rigid, and cerebral religion
of the Puritans, presented in plain churches with quietly grim ser-
mons, contrasted with both the emotionalism of the Southern religious
tradition[390] and the institutional traditions of the Catholic church. The
importance to the Puritans of individual understanding of the Bible
spurred them to promote widespread literacy and to produce, both in
East Anglia and in Massachusetts, higher rates of literacy than in the
general population and a disproportionate contribution to the intellectual elites of both Britain and colonial America. Nor was this reverence for education limited to an elite or even to those who were
educated themselves. Hundreds of families throughout New England
responded to appeals to donate either 12 shillings per family or a peck
of grain to help support the fledgling little college established near the
Charles River, early in the colony's history, by John Harvard.[391]

The intellectuality of the Puritans was a product of their religion
and the rigid morality that derived from it. The Puritan colonies of
America, like their counterparts in England, had much lower rates of
illegitimacy than among their countrymen at large.[392] The highly
moralistic and uncompromising outlook of the Puritans eventually put
them and their descendants on a collision course with the institution
of slavery and produced, among others, Harriet Beecher Stowe, who
was called by Abraham Lincoln "the little lady who started the Civil
War" because of her novel *Uncle Tom's Cabin*. Once they decided that
slavery was morally wrong, these descendants of the Puritans were
undeterred in their opposition to it by economic, political, or social
considerations. This moral rigidity had many sides, however. While it
propelled the abolitionist movement in America, it also propelled the
persecution of the Catholics in Ireland under Cromwell and his Puritan followers, as well as the witchhunts in colonial New England,
which claimed more victims than in any other part of North America.
It was not the ignorant who promoted the killing of women as witches,
but some of the most highly educated people in the country.

New England Puritans differed not only from the backcountry people of the South, but also from the Southern tidewater aristocracy, who
settled on the coastal plains of the American eastern seaboard and
who originated largely in southern and western parts of England with a
long tradition of very hierarchical societies, including, during the
early Middle Ages, slavery.[393] Dialects differed sharply between New

England and Virginia, just as they differed between the respective areas of England from which New Englanders and Virginians came. Phrases such as "I be" and "you be," as well as the use of the word "yaller" for yellow, "ax" for ask, and "fambly" for family were common in both Virginia and in those parts of southern and western England from which Virginians had emigrated. Calling hog's entrails "chittlins" and using "do' " for door and "flo' " for floor, or using "dis" and "dat" for this and that, were ways of talking that originated in this region, and which persisted longer in the United States as part of Southern dialect.[394] The era of mass education and the standardization of the English language left such expressions as marks of uneducated people in the American South and—by the late twentieth century—a pattern now christened "black English."

Virginians ate highly seasoned food, which became a hallmark of Southern cooking, along with much social interaction at meal times, while the Puritans in Massachusetts ate unseasoned food of little variety and with a minimum of light-hearted talk at the table.[395] The fervor for establishing public schools in Massachusetts found no counterpart in Virginia, where illiteracy was much higher and education was largely restricted to those wealthy enough to afford to have their own children educated at home by tutors. In Virginia, the printing press was deliberately restricted by the powers that be, to keep reading matter from the masses, while the aristocracy often had impressive libraries in their homes.[396]

Sexual mores were likewise radically different in the two places— illegitimacy being almost non-existent among the Puritans, with few brides being pregnant, while both pregnant brides and unwed mothers were far more common in Virginia.[397] Rape was a capital offense in Massachusetts, but was usually given light punishment in Virginia.[398] In both Virginia and in those parts of England from which Virginians came, it was common for male aristocrats to prey sexually on servant girls, their first victims in colonial America being white indentured servants and only later black slave girls.[399] Housing, gambling, and economic activities also differed sharply between Massachusetts and Virginia, as they differed between the two regions that Virginians and New Englanders came from in Britain.[400] The names given to children likewise differed greatly between these two groups, both in England and in America. Edward, for example, was a popular name in Virginia and in Wessex, from which many Virginians emigrated, but the first forty classes of undergraduates at Harvard College included only one student named Edward.[401] It would be nearly two centuries before Harvard admitted anyone named Patrick, though this was a common name in western Pennsylvania, where the Scotch-Irish were settled.[402]

The British Empire

With Britain's emergence as a major nation in Europe, it began to rival and to challenge Spain, France, and other European powers internationally. A variety of political, military, economic, and other factors led these European powers to pre-empt various parts of the less developed world for their own purposes, including heading off rivals' efforts to foreclose particular regions of the globe as sources of gold, raw materials, markets, or military bases. For thousands of years, imperial conquests have been launched by Asians, Africans, and indigenous peoples of the Western Hemisphere, as well as by Europeans. What was different about modern imperialism was its global sweep, with large colonial possessions being scattered thousands of miles away across oceans. This presupposed a new level of economic resources and technological development in which Europe was the leader, thereby creating a uniquely European age of overseas imperialism, spanning the globe.

Only gradually over the centuries did Britain move to the forefront of modern imperialism, ultimately establishing the largest empire the world has ever seen, encompassing one fourth of the land area of the Earth and one fourth of the human race.[403] Of the more than 11 million square miles of this empire in 1915, little more than one-tenth consisted of the British Isles themselves.[404] In addition to places where the British themselves settled in large numbers, such as North America, Australia, New Zealand, and South Africa, the British Empire stretched from Fiji islands in the South Pacific to the island of Ireland in the North Atlantic. In Asia, it encompassed the Malay peninsula, India, Burma, Ceylon, and the island colony of Hong Kong. It included vast areas of the African continent's east and west coasts, as well as Caribbean islands, British Guiana, Malta, and Gibraltar. Truly, the sun never set on the British Empire.

The human costs—and benefits—of this empire were enormous and incalculable. Slaughters and even atrocities were not lacking, nor was hypocrisy or arrogance. Although slavery no longer existed in Britain itself during the era of the empire, the British became the world's largest slaveholders in their Western Hemisphere colonies in the Caribbean. Aborigines were dealt with brutally in Australia, retaliation for the 1857 mutiny in India was both savage and humiliating, and 26,000 Boer women and children died in British concentration camps in South Africa. Racism often accompanied imperialism, but the British treatment of the Irish and the Boers suggested that a white skin did not provide immunity from the traumas accompanying conquest. Alongside this, and in no way offsetting it, but simply co-existing with it, was the spread of British technology, economic organization, law, and the English language that became a lingua franca not only within the vast British Empire but also among peoples who were never part of that empire. In short, Britain shared the moral evils of conquerors in general, but what it contributed to the empire and to the world were uniquely its own.

The first phase of British overseas expansion began in the sixteenth century in North America and the Caribbean. At that point, Britain was not yet unique. Spain established a contemporary empire that stretched continuously from San Francisco to the southern border of Argentina, as well as including the Philippines and parts of Europe. Only gradually did the British acquire an empire to rival or surpass that of Spain. By the middle of the eighteenth century, British forces drove the French out of Canada and India, but lost the American colonies to an insurrection abetted by France. Continued British expansion in the nineteenth century included both establishing a ruling structure over native populations (as in India and in much of Africa) and also largely supplanting the indigenes with a transplanted British population, as had happened in the North American colonies and was to happen again in Australia and New Zealand.

These transplanted British populations evolved into self-governing countries, whether within or outside the British Empire, while the indigenous populations long continued to be ruled by British authorities (as in India or Nigeria) or by local white settlers (as in Rhodesia or South Africa). By 1912, the British Empire had a population of more than 440 million people, of whom only 10 percent lived in the British Isles.[405] Despite its enormous size and diversity, the British Empire did not remain at its zenith for long, as history is measured. From the late Victorian age, when African territories began to be acquired, until the post–World War II era, when independence came to India in 1947 and then spread rapidly to other parts of the British Empire around the world over the next two decades, was a span of less than a century.

The military power that made imperial Britain more dominant on the world scene than any nation before or since was based on its economic pre-eminence. The British Empire followed rather than caused that economic predominance, and the empire played a remarkably small role in the British economy. Most British exports and investments did *not* go to its colonies. Europe was the principal outlet for British exports in the eighteenth century.[406] Later, the United States became the principal outlet, receiving more than half of all British exports in the early nineteenth century.[407] British overseas investments likewise tended to flow more to the advanced economies, rather than to those of the Third World. As late as 1914, the United States represented the largest single investment destination of British capital overseas, receiving more British investments than all the non-European portions of Asia or Africa, or all of Latin America. Britain's other major overseas investments were also in European offshoot societies and economies in Australia, Canada, Rhodesia, and South Africa.[408]

Both the costs and the benefits of empire extended well beyond the economic. Gibraltar gave the British military command of the entrance to the Mediterranean, and a naval base at Singapore made the British navy a power to be reckoned with in the Pacific. Britain remained the world's foremost naval power well into the twentieth century, using as a rule of thumb the formula that its navy must be equal in size to the largest two other navies combined. Thus in 1906, for example, when the German navy had 31 battleships and the French navy 29, the British navy had 61 battleships.[409] Only the later rise of the United States as a world naval power made this policy economically untenable as the American navy reached and then surpassed that of Britain during the 1920s.[410]

While Britain's overwhelming naval power and military strength made an empire possible, the incentives to create such an empire came from a variety of sources, of which economic gain was only one, and not necessarily the over-riding one. Prestige, politics, and religion were also factors. British missionaries were not only a social influence abroad but also a political force at home—a force sometimes on the side of imperial expansion and sometimes a force against abuses of the conquered peoples by colonial officials, business interests, or indigenous tyrants.[411] The greatest abuse of all—the slave trade—was ended as a direct result of the political influence of evangelical Christians in Britain, who were connected with missionary work in Africa.[412]

British imperialism, like some other imperialisms, brought to the conquered peoples both suffering and relief from suffering, new freedoms and new repressions, new opportunities and losses of old rights. Neither for the British themselves nor for those they conquered can an unambiguous net balance be totalled. In narrowly economic terms, however, the picture is much clearer. Counting the costs of conquest and administration, for example, against the profits and taxes extracted from the colonies, together with other economic pluses and minuses, Britain as a whole did not benefit economically from the colonies.[413] Individual investors might make fortunes (Cecil Rhodes being the classic example) but the British taxpayers bore the heavy costs of maintaining the empire. Military defense was an especially heavy drain, leading to the world's largest burden of military expenditures per capita on the British people.[414]

Britain's economic impact on the colonies was far greater than the colonies' impact on the British economy. It was not simply that the conqueror brought more advanced technology to the conquered lands. The conquered peoples themselves were able to use the existing land, with existing technology, more effectively because food, for example, could now be grown in fertile but militarily indefensible areas where it would have been foolhardy to plant before. Such situations had existed in medieval Scotland, as well as later in Africa,[415] in British dominions and in those of many other nations. More generally, confidence that an investment of labor and resources could claim its reward—whether at harvest time or when dividends were issued years later—has been crucial to the economic efforts which create national prosperity. The security and stability provided by British colonial governments also made possible large-scale immigrations of foreign peoples, bringing new skills, talents and energies—the Chinese immigration to Malaya, the Indians to East Africa, and the Lebanese to West Africa, for example—as well as similar internal migrations, such as those of the Marawis in India and the Ibos in Nigeria.

The British Empire spread not only British hegemony but also British technology, organization, capital, and the English language around the world. By the late twentieth century, English was spoken by more people—about one billion—than any other language in the world. Only 330 million spoke it as their native tongue (compared to 750 million who spoke Mandarin Chinese) but English was the world's leading "second language," serving as an international lingua franca among many non-English-speaking nations, as well as a means of direct communication with Britons, Americans, and other native English-speakers.[416] For peoples whose own native languages had no written literature, the English language opened vast new cultural horizons, encompassing not only the entire thought of the English-speaking world in medieval and modern times, but also much of the leading literature of the rest of the world, from ancient times to the present, available in English translations. The spread of English abroad was also paralleled by a standardization of English among the British themselves, as regional dialects began to erode at least as early as the nineteenth century,[417] a process accelerated in the twentieth century by the mass media.

The British Empire, at its zenith, required only about 120,000 soldiers and 6,000 civilians to run it.[418] In modern times, this reflected enormous technological differences between cultures, ranging from the use of firearms to modern naval bombardment. But vast disparities in military effectiveness were apparent even in Roman times, when men on both sides killed each other at closer range with bows and arrows, or even face to face with swords. In the case of the Roman conquest of Britain, and of England's later conquests within the British Isles, the differing military effectiveness of cultures was also paralleled by their very different economic effectiveness. This was evidenced not only by their initial economic disparities but also—especially in the case of Scotland and Wales—by the subsequent economic advancement of the conquered peoples. In Ireland, the mass confiscations of land and repression of economic opportunities for the Irish make the picture more ambiguous. However, even such a defender of Ireland and the Irish as Edmund Burke believed that the English conquest, for all its bitter injustices, left Ireland more prosperous.[419] If so, it would be part of a wider historic pattern, in which economic benefits to the conquered depend in no way on the goodwill of the conqueror. Much the same could be said of the British overseas empire.

The international economic role of Britain as a supplier of capital to the world market was greater than—and different from—Britain's role as an imperial power. Most British capital in the world market went *outside* the empire, and what did get invested within the empire was invested mostly in the autonomous, European-offshoot societies such as Canada and Australia.[420] Contrary to many theories of imperialism, this greatest of all empires did not revolve around an export of capital to the Third World.

The Evolution of Freedom

Britain's economic pioneering and imperial triumphs were by no means its only legacy to the world. Freedom, wherever it exists in the world today, owes much to developments in Britain. These include not only the historic evolution of a free society in the United Kingdom itself, providing political models and legal precedents for other free societies around the world, but also Britain's key role in destroying the international slave trade in the nineteenth century, and its crucial role when the survival of freedom in the world was threatened in the early and dark days of World War II.

Freedom was by no means a constant throughout British history, nor did it grow smoothly over time. In the repeated jockeying for power between kings and parliaments, between religious denominations, or between nobles and commoners, the boundaries of freedom were frequently shifting. Nevertheless, the idea of separated powers and of *rules* governing all the contenders for power became imbedded in British tradition over the centuries. The uneven, uncertain, and inconsistent evolution of the institutions and traditions of freedom in Britain followed no blueprint or elaborated doctrine. Its pattern is more discernible in retrospect than among those living through those historic centuries, preoccupied with fierce rivalries between dynasties, churches, courts contending among themselves for jurisdiction, foreign wars, and the enduring and bitter battles at home between Parliament and monarchs. Out of this apparent chaos, however, emerged institutions, traditions, and landmarks on the road to human freedom in general, as well as for the freedom of the British themselves.

The first and most famous of these landmarks was, of course Magna Carta, a political agreement which avoided armed conflict growing out of narrow and bitterly disputed interests between King John and his nobles, and whose historic significance for the rest of the people of England—and ultimately the world—may not have been at all obvious when this political compromise was adopted in 1215. King John had provoked this incipient rebellion among his nobles by heightened taxation and other extractions of money under numerous pretenses, all in hopes of being able to finance a reconquest of his lost territories in Normandy. Yet, from this dispute among a small ruling elite, came the tradition that people had established rights which even the king himself was required to respect. This meant that kings and queens of England could not be absolute monarchs, as rulers in so many other parts of the world were, and that the separation of powers became part of the basic political structure of the country.

While the kings of England retained enormous prerogatives for hundreds of years, they were increasingly confronted by Parliament, which was a powerful counterweight because of its control of taxation. Separated powers meant mutually limited powers—powers delineated in advance, as rulers and Parliaments sought to guard the boundaries of their respective prerogatives, with the net result, over the centuries, of freeing an expanding portion of the population from arbitrary edicts. The fact that Britain was an island, dependent for its military defense primarily on its navy, meant that for much of its history large standing armies were unnecessary and unknown—and were regarded with great suspicion. Since navies are not usable for domestic oppression like armies, both the government and the people were spared the dangers long inherent in standing armies.

For much of its later history, the British landed aristocracy, unlike that in some continental European countries such as Russia, was locally based, both in economic and in political power terms. This meant that the landed nobility threw its weight behind a decentralization of power, especially since these local elites would themselves exercise much of that power as justices of the peace and in other roles. By contrast, the Russian nobility derived much of its economic sustenance and political power from its role as either military or civil agents of the central government and therefore threw its weight behind czarist despotism. However locally despotic the British aristocracy might be in particular places and times, the decentralization which it promoted and its enduring opposition to large standing armies served to prevent the greater despotism possible by a centralized government.[421]

There were numerous overlapping jurisdictions in the law between religious and secular courts, and between baronial and royal jurisdictions, while many local legal traditions further fragmented the legal system of Britain. Over the centuries, however, there emerged a body of law common to the country as a whole—laws growing by the accretion of judicial precedents and known as the common law. Because the common law was not simply the creature of political power-holders, it became another of the forces for separation of powers and of rights limiting the scope of officials.

A second landmark in the evolution of English government were the series of armed struggles between Parliament and king in the seventeenth century, punctuated by the beheading of Charles I in 1649 and the flight of James II in 1688, in the face of uprisings against him and defections from his own supporters. At the heart of these events were the attempts of successive Stuart monarchs to wield more arbitrary power than Parliament was prepared to tolerate. After a decade without a king, following the overthrow and execution of Charles I, England restored the Stuart monarchy in 1660 when Charles II ascended the throne but, after his death in 1685, his son James II returned to attempts at arbitrary rule such as had doomed his grandfather. Far more important and of more enduring consequence than the changing of monarchs that followed, however, was the "bill of rights" proclaimed under the new monarchs, William and Mary, seeking to consolidate support for their newly established reign.

Law was made supreme, with the king no longer empowered to remove judges, who now became "arbiters between Crown and subject, acting on standards of law."[422] While an independent judiciary had been the ideal before, what made it revolutionary now was that it became a reality when judges' appointments could no longer be revoked, except for misconduct—and that could be done only by Parliament, which was itself removable by the electorate. This was part of a more general restructuring of government to produce greater freedom and religious toleration, as well as the rule of law. Beyond the bill of rights itself, but in the same spirit, freedom of the press from prior censorship was instituted in 1695.

All these things, which are now so much taken for granted, can be taken for granted only because the British pioneered in their development. Moreover, Britain as a nation became a stronger international force as internal, dynastic and religious strife subsided and Parliament became more willing to supply monarchs with the funds needed to build up the country's military and naval forces, now that they no longer feared royal despotism. Thus Britain was able to counterbalance the military threat that France posed to the British Isles and to the rest of Western Europe. Because Britain was an island nation, the revolutionary doctrine that people had rights which kings could not override was able to be fought out—and won—within the British Isles, without effective intervention from other monarchs on the European continent, to whom such doctrines were an obvious threat, even though both Charles II and James II had sought such intervention, in order to try to save their throne and their royal prerogatives. The triumph of this revolutionary concept of political freedom and the emergence of Britain as a great power on the world stage marked, as a distinguished British historian put it, "a turning point in the history of our country and of the world."[423]

The repetition of the same phrase, "bill of rights," a century later, to describe the first ten amendments to the Constitution of the United States, was one of the first emanations of these principles beyond the shores of the British Isles. It would not be the last, however, as the ideas of political freedom and the rights of citizens spread to other European nations and their offshoot societies overseas, and to other civilizations. Even where these ideas did not triumph or endure, they were ideas difficult to extinguish and sometimes they modified at least the appearances, and in some respects the practices, of authoritarian governments.

As British parliamentary government became "the mother of parliaments" in other countries, so the British legal system became a model for other countries, thereby promoting freedom for other peoples and other countries. While British law spread around the world directly with the development of the British Empire, the concepts it introduced and the traditions it nurtured continued long after many colonies became independent nations. This was especially so in transplanted British societies like Australia, New Zealand, and Canada. However, even in an outwardly different political and legal system in the United

States, the same underlying principles of limited government, separation of powers, and an independent judiciary were at the heart of the American constitution.

British political and legal principles sometimes left an enduring influence, even in some former British colonies with non-Western populations and non-Western traditions of government. British legal principles and precedents continued to be cited in the courts of independent India, and an independent Sri Lanka for a time continued to permit its legal decisions to be appealed to the privy council in London. Not all former British colonies established or preserved British governmental structures or principles, or the freedom based on them. But the line of demarcation between those that did and those that did not largely coincided with the line between free people and those living under various forms of despotism.

Freedom must be distinguished from democracy, with which it is often confused. The British people had many rights that were lacking in much of Europe, and in most of the rest of the world, long before they acquired the franchise with which to control the government. Few of the Members of Parliament were elected by popular vote prior to the Reform Act of 1832. Yet freedom of speech, separation of powers, the right to a jury trial, and the other hallmarks of a free society existed in Britain for generations before then.

Perhaps an even more remarkable contribution of Britain to the growth of freedom in the world was its leading role in the destruction of the international slave trade, and then of slavery itself. The magnitude of this achievement is hard to appreciate without first recognizing that slavery was a worldwide institution, entrenched on every inhabited continent, subjugating people of every color, language, and religion, and going back thousands of years. Moreover, the effort to stamp out slave trading, and later the institution of slavery itself, encountered widespread resistance and evasions in many regions of the world, producing a bitter struggle that lasted for more than a century. The dogged persistence of the British in that struggle was a key factor in the ultimate destruction of slavery around the world.

Not all British leaders or colonial officials shared the ideals or the fervor of the anti-slavery movement, but the political pressures generated by that movement remained powerful and unrelenting throughout the nineteenth century, and could not be ignored by any British government of any party during that era. It would be hard to find anywhere in history a record of any other country going to such efforts, for so long, in a cause from which it could gain so little and lose so much. When the British anti-slavery movement began in the late eighteenth century, Britain was itself the leading slave-trading nation in the world, and its slave plantations in the British West Indies and elsewhere were prospering and growing, producing powerful vested interests in London—interests which were nevertheless crushed by the swelling moral revolt against the institution of slavery.

One of the many ironies of history was that this leading slave-trading nation became the leading destroyer of the slave trade and, eventually, of slavery itself. Another irony was that the strong vested interests which initially fought off the anti-slavery movement for twenty years in Parliament only succeeded in making that movement's ultimate triumph more sweeping than even its advocates could have hoped at the outset of the struggle. The protracted nature of that struggle led to ever-wider public awareness of the issues and ever-growing public outrage against all aspects of slavery—ultimately sweeping the anti-slavery movement beyond its own original goal of abolishing the slave trade to seeking the abolition of slavery itself throughout the British Empire and then throughout the world.

Organized opposition to slavery arose in eighteenth-century England among the Quakers, who began to require their members to free their own slaves. Evangelical members of the Anglican church transformed anti-slavery sentiment into a political movement, with William Wilberforce and Henry Thornton leading the parliamentary battle for the end of the slave trade. Beaten badly in Parliament at the outset, the anti-slavery forces continued the fight until Parliament finally voted overwhelmingly to ban the international slave trade in 1808. By then, ever-widening opposition to slavery led to petitions from all parts of the country arriving in London with hundreds of thousands of signatures from people of the humblest ranks to those of the titled nobility. This was unprecedented in an era before mass communications or mass transportation.

Banning slavery throughout the British Empire was more than simply a matter of enacting laws. Since slaves were legally property, their owners had to be compensated for their emancipation, and that cost the British government £20 million[424]—a huge sum in the nineteenth century, when the pound sterling was of far greater value than today.

Even this was not the full cost of the anti-slavery crusade, however, for the British attack on slavery was not limited to banning it for Britons, but sought to stop other nations from engaging in the slave trade as well. Through political influence, economic bribes, and military threats, Britain was able to gain the acquiescence of many—though not all—nations to its boarding of their vessels on the high seas to search for slaves. Where slaves were found, they were freed and the vessels confiscated. Powerful nations such as France would not submit to British pressure and slave-traders of various nationalities began to fly the French flag, with or without French permission, to avoid being boarded by the British. However, after the anti-slavery movement spread to France itself, the French then followed the British in abolishing slavery and in using their navy to patrol the seas in search of slave-carrying ships. After the American civil war, the U. S. Navy also joined the anti-slave patrols in the Atlantic. Eventually, the anti-slavery crusade took root in the moral consciousness of European civilization as a whole, even in despotic countries such as czarist Russia, which stamped out the slave trade in Central Asia.

The world dominance of Great Britain enabled it to impose its anti-slavery edicts on many other sovereign nations. Even while fighting a major war against Napoleon, Britain kept some of its navy on patrol off the African coast to intercept slave ships.[425] Nor did it always confine itself to naval actions near Africa. In 1849, the British navy struck at Brazil's slave ships in Brazilian waters:

> In 1849 and 1850 . . . the British government took drastic action against the slave merchants in Brazilian territorial waters in complete disregard of Brazilian sovereignty, with the intention of wresting a commitment from the Brazilian government to pass an effective anti-slave-trade-law and see to its enforcement. Thoroughly humiliated by British incursions into the harbors of the Empire and their seizure and destruction of Brazilian slave ships even within Brazilian territorial waters, faced with threats to the legal shipping of the Empire, with military conflict, and even a blockade of Brazilian ports, the government of the Empire was compelled in July 1850 to accede to British demands in exchange for a promise to suspend the naval attacks.[426]

Similar naval efforts at intercepting the slave trade from East Africa were carried on by the British for decades. The Arab and Indian slave traders in the Indian Ocean, the Red Sea and the Persian Gulf responded like their European counterparts in the Atlantic by using smaller, sleeker craft, designed to outrun or evade naval vessels. Moreover, Middle Eastern slave traders using smaller vessels were often able to sail in coastal waters too shallow for British warships. Although the East African slave trade had been surpassed by that of West Africa, it was by no means negligible. Well over a million human beings were shipped out of Africa as slaves in the nineteenth century from ports on the Indian Ocean or the Red Sea.[427] British naval vessels, scattered over vast expanses of open water, could capture only a small fraction of the ships carrying slaves—often hidden among ordinary merchandise, rather than constituting the main cargo, as in the Atlantic—but the British navy could impose risks and costs on slave traders, at sea and in ports, the cumulative effect of which was to reduce the traffic.

In the Atlantic slave trade as well, the reduction in the number of slaves shipped from Africa to the Western Hemisphere was slight in the early decades of the nineteenth century, but unrelenting efforts at interception on the high seas over the years eventually destroyed the Atlantic slave trade by about 1860. By this time, the slave trade across the Sahara was also drastically reduced,[428] partly as a result of a ban by the Ottoman Empire in 1857, under pressure from Britain.[429] Gradually, grudging and piecemeal concessions by the Ottoman Empire reduced the importation of slaves from Africa, though much smuggling of black slaves continued and the importation of white slaves from the Caucasus region continued to flourish.[430] At one point, the British threatened to send warships into the Mediterranean to inspect Turkish ships, and punish those found to be carrying slaves, if the Ottoman Empire did not do a better job of policing the slave trade itself.[431] Aggressive British actions elsewhere in the world meant that this was not an idle threat.

Resistance in the Islamic countries was formidable, sometimes expressed in armed uprisings against both the Ottoman Empire and the British,[432] but more often was expressed in widespread evasions of the ban on slave trading. Banning the institution of slavery itself long remained only a distant hope in much of Africa and the Middle East, even after it was a reality in the Western Hemisphere. Before the end of the nineteenth century, slavery was abolished throughout the Western Hemisphere, and the spread of European colonies and spheres of influence in Africa in the late nineteenth century meant that slavery was coming under increasing pressure there as well.

Slavery retreated before the advance of British power in Africa and Asia, as it was later to retreat before the advance of French and German power in Africa, before the advance of Dutch power in the East Indies and the advance of Russian power in Central Asia. Yet the impetus for the abolition of slavery was a peculiarity of Western civilization, though some non-Western nations eventually began to move against slavery as a means of maintaining their national standing in the eyes of the world—which is to say, primarily the Western world.

In a later era, Britain again played a key role in the defense of freedom when totalitarian governments sprang up between the two World Wars of the twentieth century and many, even in democratic countries, called these aggressive, nationalistic and racist dictatorships "the wave of the future." That prediction seemed especially ominous when the early aggressions of Germany, Italy, and Japan in the 1930s and early 1940s succeeded time and again. After Nazi armies rampaged through Europe in the early years of the Second World War, winning an unbroken series of swift and stunning victories, climaxed by the fall of France in just six weeks of fighting, Britain faced the seemingly invincible forces of Nazi Germany alone. Few expected her to survive.[433] Prime Minister Winston Churchill put the grim situation to his people and to the world:

> The whole fury and might of the enemy must very soon be turned on us. Hitler knows that he will have to break us in this Island or lose the war. If we can stand up to him, all Europe may be free and the life of the world may move forward into broad, sunlit uplands. But if we fail, then the whole world, including the United States, including all that we have known and cared for, will sink into the abyss of a new Dark Age made more sinister, and perhaps more protracted, by the lights of perverted science. Let us therefore brace ourselves to our duties, and so bear ourselves that, if the British Empire and its Commonwealth last for a thousand years, men will still say, "This was their finest hour."[434]

As Churchill predicted, the full might and fury of the Nazis were turned on Britain. The dreaded massive bombing of the *Luftwaffe*, which had terrorized other nations into surrender, failed to break the British. Hitler was stopped for the first time. Britain, though lacking the military forces to launch a major counter-attack, nevertheless stalled the Nazi timetable of conquest, thus buying time, not only for itself but also for an almost completely disarmed United States to begin preparing itself militarily for the ordeal ahead. Many nations, forces, and events contributed to the final victory over Germany and Japan. But what made it all possible was that Britain withstood the fire and blast of war and refused to surrender, even when the situation looked hopeless.

It was indeed their finest hour. Freedom survives in the world today because of it.

SUMMARY AND IMPLICATIONS

The history of the British people, like the history of other peoples around the world, illustrates the enormous importance of human capital, whether in the form of specific skills, general education, or traditions and laws that facilitate both economic development and the development of free institutions. The many centuries that it took for the British to rise from cultural and economic backwardness to the forefront of world civilization in technology and political dominance suggests something of the difficulty of acquiring the necessary human capital. The vital role played in this process by numerous other peoples who came to the British Isles—whether as conquerors, immigrants, or refugees—also suggests how important cultural diffusion is. The Romans, the Normans, the Jews, the Lombards, and the Huguenots all contributed in important ways at different historical junctures to what would ultimately become a British achievement.

The geography of the British Isles also played an important role, not in determining what people would do, but in determining the boundaries of what was possible. The simple fact that Britain is an island nation and that water transport is vastly cheaper than land transport, and was especially so in the era before railroads, meant that the British could transport heavy raw materials like coal to different parts of the United Kingdom much more cheaply and rapidly than was possible within nations with large interiors such as Germany or the United States, both of which had to wait for the era of railroads to challenge the British in industrialization. The fact that the key raw materials of the industrial age—iron ore and coal—were located very near each other and also near navigable waterways in Britain again gave the British decisive early advantages over countries like Germany and the United States, as well as permanent advantages over regions of the world where such natural resources do not exist at all and cannot be imported at any feasible economic cost. Significantly, Japan—one of the few countries that was later able to rise to the industrial forefront without such natural resources—is an island like Britain and no part of Japan is more than 70 miles from the sea,[435] so imported raw materials could be brought in economically, as would be virtually impossible in the Balkans or in much of sub-Saharan Africa, for example, due to more formidable geographical barriers in these places.

Geographical advantages and cultural imports have permitted more to be accomplished within the British Isles than in many other parts of the world but, ultimately, it was the British themselves who had to accomplish it. That they did so has had enormous consequences, not only for the inhabitants of the United Kingdom, or even for past and present members of the British Empire or Commonwealths, but for the entire world. The highly varying degrees to which different segments of the British population acquired the necessary human capital demonstrates that the opportunity alone is not sufficient for economic or other accomplishments. Nor was it simply a matter of what the existing society permitted to different groups, for those same groups showed similar economic and social patterns when transplanted to other societies in North America or in Australia and New Zealand.

British law and its traditions of impartiality made London a magnet for the capital of the world, enabling Britain to industrialize with other people's capital, as well as its own. In a later era, the British colony of Hong Kong would similarly attract capital from around the world by the dependability and impartiality of its laws, while many poverty-stricken countries were unable to obtain much-needed capital because of their undependable laws and confiscatory policies toward foreign investors.

British law was of course more than an economic asset. Its separation of powers and rights of citizens against the government were the foundation of the freedom of the British themselves. The revolutions of the seventeenth century, including the beheading of King Charles I in 1649 and the uprisings in 1688 that led James II to flee to France, made the separation of powers even more dramatically vindicated and an indelible a part of the British constitution. While many other countries copied British systems of law and government, those that succeeded in creating similarly free governments were largely those that came from the same tradition—the United States, Canada, Australia, New Zealand—for the historical experiences that were distilled into powerful traditions were essential to the functioning of the legal and political institutions themselves. While these institutions could be copied by anyone, the history and traditions behind them could not be synthesized, and it was these intangibles that made the tangible institutions and structures work.

CHAPTER 3

THE AFRICANS

In understanding Black Africa, geography is more important than history.

Fernand Braudel[1]

In a strictly geographical sense, all the peoples on the continent of Africa are Africans—from the whites of South Africa to the Arabs of the Mediterranean states—but the term has in practice come to refer primarily to the indigenous peoples of Africa below the Sahara, to black Africans. The basis for this focus is not simply racial but historic, cultural, and geographic as well. As with the British, the Slavs, and others, the influence of geography in Africa has not been simply in its effects primarily on *things*—natural resources or economic prosperity, for example—but on *people*. More specifically, the effect of geography in making cultural interactions more difficult has been particularly striking as between the peoples of sub-Saharan Africa and the outside world, as well as among themselves.

To their north is a desert more vast than the continental United States and to the east, west, and south are the Indian, Atlantic, and Antarctic oceans. Moreover, the smooth coastline of sub-Saharan Africa has offered few harbors which ocean-going ships could enter and in many places the shallow coastal waterways have meant that large ships could not get near the shores. Ironically, for centuries much of the world's international trade was carried in ships that sailed past West Africa on their way between Europe and Asia around the southern tip of the continent. Seldom did they stop. Partly this was a result of wind and ocean currents that made return trips between

99

Europe and sub-Saharan Africa difficult or not economically feasible in the era of wind-driven ships, at least until far greater knowledge of those currents and of alternative routes developed.[2] Relatively little of Africa's trade entered international commerce.[3]

In the era before the modern transportation revolution of railroads, automobiles, and planes—which is to say, throughout most of human history—the geographical barriers surrounding tropical Africa have been formidable, though not absolutely impenetrable. The consequences have been not only economic but cultural. As the eminent French historian Fernand Braudel put it, "external influence filtered only very slowly, drop by drop, into the vast African continent South of the Sahara."[4] The geographic barriers to economic and cultural exchanges within various regions of sub-Saharan Africa have been formidable as well. The most striking of these barriers has been a dearth of navigable rivers or streams, though the land itself also presents difficult terrain in many places in the form of escarpments and rift valleys.

The net effect has been that the peoples of sub-Saharan Africa have historically been insulated not only from the peoples and cultures of the outside world but also from one another. Among the cultural consequences has been a linguistic fragmentation of tropical Africa, which has made African languages one third of all the languages of the world,[5] even though African peoples are only about 10 percent of the world's population. This linguistic fragmentation has been only one aspect of cultural fragmentation in general, including tribalism and many religious differences. In addition, a substantial portion of peoples of African ancestry today—60 million—live in the Western Hemisphere,[6] where they have absorbed the languages and cultures of Europeans. The imprint of Islamic civilization is also visible over large areas of sub-Saharan Africa, with the northern regions of some contemporary African states such as Nigeria, Sudan, and Tanzania being Islamic and the southern part Christian or traditional in religion, with both non-African religions reflecting the influences of past conquerors.

Black Africans became conquered peoples in two very different senses in different parts of the world—by territorial conquests and by massive enslavement. The conquerors and enslavers included other Africans, Arabs, and Europeans. Like so much of the history of Africa, these tragic events have been heavily influenced by the geography of the continent.

AFRICA

In much of sub-Saharan Africa, a combination of geographic features has had unfavorable—if not devastating—consequences for economic and cultural development, and tragic consequences for the vulnerability of black Africans to outside conquerors.

The Natural Environment

One of the remarkable facts about the African continent is that, despite being much larger than the continent of Europe, its coastline is shorter than the European coastline—indeed, shorter than the coastline of any other continent,[7] even though Africa is second only to Asia in size. This anomaly reflects Africa's lack of the numerous coastal indentations which form natural harbors in Europe, providing places where ships can dock, sheltered from the rough waters of the open seas, thereby enabling European countries to become maritime nations early in their history. In addition to a dearth of harbors, parts of sub-Saharan Africa have shallow coastal waters, so that maritime trade has often had to be conducted by the costly method of having ships anchor off-shore, with their cargoes being unloaded onto smaller vessels which could then make their way to land through these shallow waters.

Africans have generally not been seafaring peoples, except in the Mediterranean, or in parts of East Africa where these geographic constraints have not been as severe. Much of Africa, and especially sub-Saharan Africa, has developed without the benefits of a large maritime trade and the consequent stimulus of economic and cultural interchanges on a large scale with various and disparate peoples. While there has been for centuries some trade between sub-Saharan Africa and Europe, or with the peoples of North Africa and the Middle East, international trade has generally played a relatively smaller part in the total trade of Africa, as compared to other continents, not only because of a dearth of harbors, but also because of a dearth of navigable rivers reaching into the interior of the continent from the sea. River mouths opening into the sea have been blocked by sandbars in some places and in other places the few good harbors have been connected to hinterlands that were not very productive, and so have had little to offer in trade. Thin coastal plains—averaging only 20 miles in width and often backed by steep escarpments—have likewise provided little basis for large-scale international trade, even where other conditions might permit it.[8]

Low and irregular rainfall over many parts of Africa fill rivers and streams to a navigable depth only intermittently[9]—and even when filled, many rivers and streams are navigable only by smaller boats or barges, not ocean-going vessels.[10] Where the volume of water is sufficient for navigation by sizeable vessels, the many rapids and waterfalls of Africa still impede international trade. The Zaire River, for example, is 2,900 miles long and has a volume of water second only to that of the Amazon, but its rapids and waterfalls near the sea prevent ocean-going ships from reaching inland.[11] Thus, the role played by other great rivers of the world in facilitating the development of ports that became great cities, contributing to the economic and cultural development of the surrounding lands and peoples, was denied the Zaire by the intractable facts of geography. Nor is the Zaire unique among Africa's rivers. No river in sub-Saharan Africa reaches from the open sea to deep into the interior.[12] On the Mediterranean coast only the Nile reaches far inland. Significantly, the Nile spawned the most famous of the civilizations developed on the African continent, as well as the two largest cities on the continent, Cairo and Alexandria.

Except for the Nile, Africa's rivers that are even seasonally navigable tend to be concentrated in equatorial West Africa,[13] which has produced larger and more advanced societies than in many other tropical regions of the continent. In short, the peoples of Africa, like the peoples of Europe and Asia, tended to develop urban centers and larger cultural universes around navigable waterways. There have simply been far fewer of them in Africa, which has been and remains the world's least urbanized continent.[14] Among the relatively few things which have had sufficiently concentrated value in a relatively small physical size, so as to be able to repay the high costs of transport from Africa, have historically been gold, ivory, and slaves. All three became major exports. The coast of what is now Nigeria became known as "the slave coast," just as the coast of neighboring Ghana to the west was called "the gold coast" and that west of Ghana was (and still is) called "the ivory coast."

One indicator of differences in access to waterways is that, while more than a third of Europe's land mass consists of islands and peninsulas, only 2 percent of Africa's land mass consists of islands and peninsulas.[15] Such disparities in access to waterways are accentuated when the navigability of these waterways is also taken into account. Even the Niger River—the heart of a great river system in West Africa, draining an area nearly twice the size of Texas[16]—is not navigable everywhere by large vessels, and is not navigable at all in some places because of rapids.[17] At the height of the rainy season, the Niger may become "a 20-mile wide moving lake"[18] but, during the dry season, the average depth of the Niger can in places fall below 4 meters.[19] Despite its serious limitations, the Niger compares favorably with other African rivers with even more serious limitations. The Niger has been characterized as "the easiest to navigate in all of tropical Africa."[20] Navigating the Niger's chief tributary, the Benue River, for example, has been more problematical. Because of seasonal rainfall patterns, the upper Benue has been navigable only two months of the year, leading to hectic and complicated shipping patterns:

> If they let the craft stay up the Benue a day too long, the vessels will be stuck on sandbars for ten months! Yet if through caution or misinformation they withdraw the fleet too soon, much valuable merchandise is left behind and can only be evacuated by land at much greater cost . . . The first boats to go in are the commercial canoes, then follow the larger craft, and finally, when there is sufficient water at Lokoja, the largest power-craft and their barges sail up the river as fast as possible. Towards the end of the short season, the large craft have to come out first because of the fall in the level of the water; the medium-sized craft follow, and the small canoes may continue for some time evacuating small quantities of produce.[21]

Drastic changes in water levels are common in other West African rivers and streams.[22] The Senegal River has been characterized as "precariously navigable"—and only during some months, at that.[23] Like the Niger, the Senegal is not only subject to large seasonal changes in water flow but also contains rocks and rapids.[24] In East Africa, such rivers as the Zambezi are navigable only for relatively short stretches.[25] One reason for the drastic seasonal changes in water levels in African rivers is that tropical Africa is one of the few large regions of the world without a single mountain range to collect snow, whose later melting would supplement rainfall in maintaining the flow of streams and rivers. Rivers in tropical Africa are wholly dependent on rainfall and that rainfall is itself highly undependable, not only from one season to another but also from one year to the next.[26]

The term "navigable" can of course mean many things. In some of the rivers of Angola, for example, it means navigable by boats requiring no more than 8 feet of water,[27] and in parts of West Africa during the dry season, even the Niger will carry barges weighing no more than 8 tons.[28] By contrast, ships weighing 10,000 tons can go hundreds of miles up the Yangtze River in China, and smaller vessels another thousand miles beyond that.[29] Aircraft carriers can go up the Hudson River and dock at a pier in mid-Manhattan. Navigable rivers in Africa seldom mean anything approaching that. Even the Nile was unable to handle the largest vessels in Roman times.[30] Moreover, because so much of tropical Africa consists of high plateaus—almost the entire continent is more than 1,000 feet above sea-level and half the continent is more than 2,500 feet above sea-level[31]—African rivers must plunge greater vertical distances to reach the sea, making them less navigable en route. While the Amazon River falls only about 20 feet during its last 500 miles to the sea,[32] the Zaire River drops about a thousand feet in 250 miles as it approaches the sea.[33] As a geographer has put it, the African continent is "cursed with a mesa form which converts nearly every river into a plunging torrent."[34]

However impenetrable much of the interior of sub-Saharan Africa may have been to large, ocean-going ships, the continent's coastal waters have been plied by smaller boats, which could and did go inland as well, being unloaded and carried around waterfalls. Shipments from ocean-going vessels could also be loaded onto smaller craft for transportation into the interior on rivers. Local water-borne traffic between inland locations was likewise possible by carrying boats and their cargoes around rapids and waterfalls. Sometimes these boats and cargoes were carried from one river to another, thereby expanding the reach of commerce. For example, an overland route requiring 25 days of porterage on land connected the Niger and the Senegal rivers in centuries past.[35] Moreover, even rivers beset with cascades and waterfalls may have navigable stretches that add up to considerable distances—hundreds of miles on the Senegal and more than 1,500 on the Zaire—even though these are not continuous distances.[36] Thus the various regions of Africa were not hermetically sealed off from one another or from the outside world, but both the volume and the variety of trade, as well as the distances involved, were nevertheless severely curtailed, in comparison with more geographically fortunate regions of the world, where heavy and bulky cargoes of coal, ores, and grain could be shipped long distances in continuous river and ocean voyages.

A late twentieth-century comparison of the transportation costs of grain in several Asian and African nations found that these transport costs were a higher proportion of the total price paid for grain by consumers in Africa.[37] Moreover, such statistics do not capture the effect of transport costs on grain that was never shipped in the first place, precisely because higher shipping costs would have made it prohibitively expensive. Contemporary transport costs also cannot capture the handicaps created by even higher transport costs in Africa before many of the transportation advances from the rest of the world were introduced in the nineteenth and early twentieth centuries, and before Africa harbors could be dredged by modern European equipment and Western railroads built.

While it is true, as an historian has said, that "a considerable portion of West Africa" was part of "a hydrographic system that was ultimately connected to the Atlantic,"[38] the limitations of that system are a part of the story that cannot be omitted without serious distortion. Moreover, the distances between the interior hinterlands and the open seas are greater in Africa than in Europe, for example, while the means of covering those distances are much more limited by geography in Africa. In Europe, no part of the continent outside of Russia is more than 500 miles from the sea,[39] but a substantial part of tropical Africa is more than 500 miles from the sea and a portion is more than 1,000 miles from the sea.[40] Only Asia has a larger interior area remote from the sea,[41] though Asia has more navigable rivers connecting its interior with the coast.

The geographical positions of African rivers must also be taken into account. Although the Niger River originates just 200 miles from the Atlantic Ocean, it circles far inland before eventually turning back toward the sea, and covers 2,600 miles before actually reaching the ocean.[42] In general, the tenuous connection of the African interior with the sea has been one of the major geographical barriers to the economic, cultural, and political development of the continent south of the Sahara.

Land transportation in large regions of sub-Saharan Africa has also been made more difficult because of the prevalence of the tsetse fly, which has carried a fatal sickness that has affected animals as well as human beings and made the use of pack animals and draft animals impracticable in many places. Denied this aid to land transportation, Africans often carried bundles on their heads in colorful caravans that were reflections of the bleak alternatives left to them without the help of either the waterways or the animal power available to other peoples on other continents. Expensive transportation provided by human beings limited what could be carried, how far it could be carried, and how fast. In addition to the physical limitations, there were narrower limits imposed by economics, as to what items contained enough value in a relatively small space to repay the costs of this expensive method of transport.

The lack of animals' muscle power in tropical Africa has been felt not only in transportation but also in farming. A dearth of draft animals in farming often meant not only a loss of muscle power but also a dearth of fertilizer. The latter has been especially important in those parts of the continent where soils have been very much in need of fertilizer, because their low nutrient content and proneness to erosion meant that their fertility was easily exhausted by cultivation.[43] Rainfall patterns in parts of Africa—long dry spells followed by torrential downpours—increase erosion, since dry, baked soil is more easily washed away.[44] Moreover, these torrential tropical downpours tend to leach the nutrients from the soil in Africa, as in many other tropical regions. Finally, the tropics provide a disease environment in which many more deadly diseases may flourish than in temperate zones, or in mountainous tropical regions that have more temperate climates because of their heights. For example, 90 percent of all deaths from malaria in the world occur in sub-Saharan Africa.[45]

Even a listing of individual geographical disadvantages in Africa may understate the handicap they represent in combination. For example, the problem of poor water transportation, while serious in itself, is still more serious in combination with poor land transportation across much difficult terrain without the aid of pack animals. The highly variable rainfall patterns become more serious in view of where the rain falls. A geographical study of Africa found plenty of water available "where it cannot be used" and a scarcity "where it is most needed."[46]

Not all parts of sub-Saharan Africa has suffered all these disabilities simultaneously. However, the fragile fertility in some regions of tropical Africa has meant that a given territory would not permanently feed people at a given location, and this in turn meant that those people had to move on every few years to find new land that would feed them, while the land they left behind recovered its fertility. Therefore whole societies had to be mobile, foregoing the opportunities to build territorially-based communities with permanent structures, such as other Africans built in more geographically favored parts of the continent, and which were common in Europe, Asia, and the Western Hemisphere.[47]

The provincialism of isolated peoples has not been peculiar to Africa. What has been peculiar to Africa are the geographic barriers to mobility that have pervaded vast areas below the Sahara. Waterways extend the boundaries of cultural interchange, but in much of sub-Saharan Africa they did not extend those cultural boundaries very far. Like other places relatively isolated from broader cultural developments—the Scottish highlands, parts of the Balkans, or the South Sea islands, for example—much of sub-Saharan Africa tended to lag behind the technological, organizational, and economic progress in other parts of the world. A lack of literacy throughout most of sub-Saharan Africa further limited both internal development and the stimulus of contacts with distant times and places via the written word. While similar retardation afflicted particular parts of Europe or Asia, or isolated island communities around the world, in Africa such cultural isolation characterized wide areas and many peoples.

The degree of these cultural handicaps has varied in different parts of the continent, and has changed over time. Railroads, motor transport and airplanes have all added to transportation possibilities, and electronic communication media from cheap radios to television have penetrated cultural isolation, but all this has happened within a recent, minute fraction of human history, long after great cultural differences had developed among peoples with geographically restricted cultures and between them and others with more ample access to wider cultural worlds. Moreover, even in modern times, the sharp

changes in altitude of the African landscape continued to make both
roads and railroads difficult to build. The rail line from Djibouti to
Addis Abbaba, for example, rises more than 2,000 feet in its first 60
miles and more than 4,600 feet in its last 180 miles.[48]

Given the multiple and formidable geographical obstacles to its economic and cultural development, Africa's poverty is hardly surprising.
This poverty, over much of sub-Saharan Africa, is shown in many ways.
Lower incomes per capita are an obvious indicator, though the com-
plexities of international exchange rates make these statistics questionable as measures of relative standards of living. However, when the
monetary value of output per capita in Nigeria is less than 2 percent of
that in the United States—and in Tanzania less than 1 percent[49]—that
clearly cannot all be due to exchange rates. A more meaningful picture
of differences in living standards is that average life expectancies are
typically more than 70 years in Europe, Australia, the United States,
Canada, and Japan, while average life expectancies in sub-Saharan
Africa tend to be in the 50s or even the 40s.[50] Moreover, even these life
expectancies in Africa have been achieved only with the help of medical and public health measures originating elsewhere in the world.

Within this general picture of lagging economic development in
much of Africa, there have been historic and continuing variations in
economic development and political organization among the various
regions of the continent. One of the more fortunate regions of sub-
Saharan Africa, from various perspectives, has been equatorial West
Africa—what is today Nigeria, Ghana and their neighboring states.
This region has some of the continent's more fertile soil, ample rainfall, and the Niger river system.[51] Here some of the larger African
kingdoms arose. However, even in this relatively more favored region
of Africa, the states and even empires that arose were often small by
world standards. The Oyo empire, in what is today Nigeria, covered an
estimated 150,000 square kilometers, which is smaller than the American state of Colorado. The Songhay empire, which included the rich
river valleys of the central and western Sudan, was about the size of
France, which is to say, smaller than Texas. Yet these were huge states
by African standards, since most Africans lived in polities only a fraction as large, with national populations no larger than the populations
of cities or even towns in the rest of the world.[52]

In Africa, as in other parts of the world, those peoples who were more fortunate often used their advantages to subjugate others. In West Africa, this subjugation took the form both of conquest and of enslavement of fellow Africans. Across the Sahara, in North Africa, more favorable geographic conditions, including harbors on the Mediterranean, also led to larger and more advanced societies. These too used their advantages to subjugate and enslave sub-Saharan Africans. In East Africa, some of the more geographically favored areas included harbors,[53] such as the large natural harbor on the off-shore island of Zanzibar and such mainland ports as Mombasa and Kilwa. All three became major centers for the trading and shipment of slaves, usually captured from less fortunate inland tribes.[54] Here the enslavers were typically either Arabs or people of mixed Arab and African ancestry and culture, known as Swahilis.[55]

Slavery

Slavery was not unique to Africa or Africans, but was in fact common on every inhabited continent for thousands of years.[56] As recently as the eighteenth century, it existed in Eastern Europe,[57] and it continued to exist in the Middle East after the Second World War.[58] What was unusual about Africa was the magnitude of the trade in human beings within recent centuries.

Within Africa itself, slaves were used for a wide variety of tasks and under a wide variety of social arrangements. The classic plantation slavery of the Western Hemisphere was much less common in sub-Saharan Africa and some of the forms of slavery shaded off into paternalistic incorporation of slaves into extended kinship with the slaveowning family, leading some to question whether this should be classified as slavery. However, such paternalistic arrangements were at one end of a spectrum that included brutal subjugation and even using slaves as human sacrifices.[59] In some parts of Africa, such as Egypt, the Sudan, and Zanzibar, Africans were in fact plantation slaves on a large scale.[60] Even where they were not plantation slaves, however, they often nevertheless lived separately from the free population, rather than in the kinds of paternalistic domestic living arrangements that existed elsewhere.[61] In these other non-domestic occupations, mortality rates could be very high, as in Tanganyika and Zaire.[62] The proportions of slaves in the general population varied,

ranging from a minority to a majority, even in a given region, such as
the Sudan or Nigeria.[63] Most African slaves remained in Africa—
indeed, those captured in the Sudan remained in the Sudan and those
captures in Nigeria remained in Nigeria[64]—but the numbers exported
were still enormous.

In the middle of the sixteenth century, the total number of slaves
exported from Africa was between 10,000 and 20,000 annually. Two
centuries later, the number peaked at about 100,000 annually. Origins
and destinations of slaves also changed dramatically. The bulk of the
mid-sixteenth century slaves were exported from the northern savanna
and the Horn of Africa, but some time after the middle of the seventeenth century, the west coast of Africa became the principal supplier
of slaves, a position it was to hold for another hundred years, as the
European demand for slaves in the Western Hemisphere overtook the
demand for slaves in the Islamic countries of the Middle East and
North Africa.[65]

The magnitude of the slave exports from Africa is particularly striking in view of the relatively thin population of the continent then, as
now. The population of West Africa, where most of the Western Hemisphere slaves originated, has been estimated as about 11 million people at the beginning of the sixteenth century, increasing to about 20
million by the beginning of the nineteenth century.[66] In some parts of
Africa, such as the region of Angola and the Congo, enslavement was
on a scale that exceeded the natural increase of population and
resulted in depopulations of villages.[67] In addition, the massive movements of captured people overland entailed a spread of disease.
Cholera and smallpox, for example, followed the routes of the slave
trade in East Africa.[68] Markets for food and other provisions for the
slave trade also grew up along its routes.[69]

The Arabs took more women than men, partly to fill the harems of
the Ottoman Empire and other Islamic lands, so that the societies left
in the African savanna tended to have an excess of men and children.
The Atlantic slave trade took more men than women, using slaves
principally for plantation labor, so that the West African societies from
which slaves were taken had an excess of women and children.[70] In
both places the resulting sex imbalance in African societies led to a
revision of traditional sex roles, including an increase of polygyny in
West Africa.[71] In both areas, slaves were mostly young adults, so that

the slave populations were atypical of the general African population, nearly one-half of which consisted of children.[72]

By the time the Europeans discovered the Western Hemisphere at the end of the fifteenth century, Moslem merchants already dominated the slave trade in West Africa, as they did in East Africa and North Africa. The Islamic *jihads* of the eighteenth and nineteenth centuries created new Moslem states in West Africa, which in turn promoted enslavement on a larger scale.[73] Altogether, between 1650 and 1850, at least 5 million slaves were shipped from West Africa alone.[74]

Inland tribes such as the Ibo were regularly raided by their more powerful coastal neighbors and the captives led away to be sold as slaves.[75] European merchants who came to buy slaves in West Africa were confined by rulers in these countries to a few coastal ports, where Africans could bring slaves and trade as a cartel, in order to get higher prices.[76] Hundreds of miles farther south, in the Portuguese colony of Angola, hundreds of thousands of Africans likewise carried out the initial captures, enslavement and slave-trading processes, funneling the slaves into the major marketplaces, where the Portuguese took charge of them and shipped them off to Brazil.[77] Most of the slaves shipped across the Atlantic were purchased, rather than captured, by Europeans.[78] Arabs, however, captured their own slaves and penetrated far deeper into Africa than Europeans dared venture, before the era of modern medicine provided the latter with some protection against the fatal tropical diseases for which they lacked biological resistance.

Over the centuries, untold millions of human beings from sub-Saharan Africa were transported in captivity to other parts of the world. No exact statistics exist covering all sources and all destinations, and scholarly estimates vary. However, over the centuries, somewhere in the neighborhood of 11 million people were shipped across the Atlantic as slaves, and another 14 million African slaves were sent to the Islamic nations of the Middle East and North Africa.[79] On both routes, many died in transit.[80] Moreover, these 25 million people were not the only African victims of slavery, for Africa itself used large numbers of slaves in many agricultural, domestic, military, and even commercial and governmental enterprises.[81] The sum total of all the human beings who fell victim to the institution of slavery will never be known, even for Africa, much less for the world in general.

The ending of the slave trade was one of many European policies imposed upon Africa by the conquerors. This did not mean the immediate freeing of existing slaves. Simply stoping the trading of slaves was itself a monumental undertaking, lasting for at least a century. As for the freeing of existing slaves, resistance and evasion by Africans, and especially by Arabs, made this a much more protracted process in Africa and the Middle East than in the Western Hemisphere. The very phrases used in these different parts of the world reflect their very different histories. While "emancipation" was usually a specific event at a specific time in the countries of the Western Hemisphere, the "decline of slavery" was a much longer and more uneven process in Africa,[82] where slaves were still widely held in the early decades of the twentieth century.

In some Islamic countries in Africa and the Middle East, slavery lasted even longer. Saudi Arabia, Mauritania, and the Sudan continued to hold slaves on past the middle of the twentieth century.[83] Mauritania officially abolished slavery in 1980, though its own government admitted that the practice continued nevertheless.[84] Indeed, Mauritanian government officials themselves have been implicated and, more than a decade later, 30,000 black Africans were still being held as slaves in Mauritania, often under brutal conditions.[85] On a smaller scale, slavery persisted in some other African countries on the eve of the twenty-first century. In one of the backwaters of Ghana, under local customs, some offenses required restitution in the form of turning over a virgin from the offending family to be a sex slave. Estimates of the number of girls involved run into the thousands.[86] Commercial exploitation of young slaves also had not died out completely as a new millennium approached. "Trading in children is a common practice in both Benin and Nigeria," the *New York Times* reported in August, 1997.[87]

Economic History

Because written records were unknown throughout most of precolonial black Africa,[88] much of its history is lost, except as preserved in oral traditions, in the writings of Arabs or Europeans, or in the researches and surmises of archaeologists and anthropologists. Nevertheless, enough is known to dispel some common misconceptions about Africa.

The peoples of Africa were not simply hunters and gatherers of the

spontaneous produce of nature. Agriculture existed for centuries before
the Europeans came. So did animal husbandry,[89] in areas where the
tsetse fly did not make it impossible. Iron, gold, and salt were likewise
produced in Africa many centuries before the white man came[90] and, in
the late Middle Ages, Africa became Europe's principal source of
gold.[91] Cloth and clothing were manufactured in Africa more than a
thousand years before European colonization in the nineteenth century
and, while Africa later imported European cloth, it also exported its
own cloth to Europe.[92] Nor did the economy remain stagnant or unaf-
fected by new options presented through outside contacts with Europe,
Asia or the Middle East. Many crops now regarded as "traditional" in
Africa originated in Europe, Asia, or the Western Hemisphere—
including cocoa, peanuts, and tobacco.[93] Most of the rice grown in West
Africa today was indigenous to Asia.[94]

Both local and long-distance trade existed in pre-colonial Africa,
though within severe constraints imposed by geography. Caravans
were one adaptation to these constraints, providing mobile marketplaces covering long distances, though at a slow pace that could take
months for a round trip.[95] International trade extended to the Arab
states, to Europe, and to India. Nevertheless, Africa's general level of
development and standard of living were well below those of Europe.
However, the relationships of Africans to Europeans did not remain
static but changed very substantially over the centuries.

In the early centuries of European explorations along the coasts of
tropical West Africa, the balance of power was by no means so decisively on the side of the Europeans as it would become in later centuries. A fifteenth century stand-off between a Portuguese warship and
African coastal boats with fighting men was indicative. The weapons of
the Portuguese ship were not particularly effective against either the
more maneuverable African boats or against the African coast, while
the Africans were unable to board the high-hulled Portuguese ship.
The two sides ended up trading peacefully, as many other Europeans
and Africans of this era did. European firearms at this point were still
primitive, inaccurate, and slow-firing, giving them no substantial
advantages over bows and arrows or spears.

Freebooting European marauders raided African coastal settlements for booty and captured people to enslave, but the larger European governments saw such activity as impediments to trade and

sought to suppress it. Moreover, the Africans themselves were often able to fight off marauders, so that peaceful trade became the rule between Europeans and the peoples of the African coast during this era.[96] This trade was controlled and regulated by African rulers, who were able to suspend it or terminate it, whenever it suited their purposes. Not surprisingly, European traders often exchanged gifts with those who ruled in Africa, in order to remain on good terms and continue trading.[97] This trade was not necessarily in products not available in Africa. Senegambia, for example, imported approximately 150 tons of steel annually from Europe, but steel of comparable quality was being produced in Africa, though its cost in Senegambia was high because it had to be transported over land, while steel arrived from Europe by water. Even when military action was taken by Europeans in Africa during this era, it was often with the help of African allies. When the Portuguese fought without such allies, they were more than once defeated and massacred.[98]

Slaves were among the main commodities traded during this era, which preceded the era of European territorial conquests in sub-Saharan Africa. This trade was, like other trade, largely under the firm control of African rulers and it too was suspended whenever this suited the interests of those rulers. By the time, centuries later, when the balance of power swung decisively against the Africans, the vast Atlantic slave trade no longer existed. The slave trade with the Western Hemisphere had been virtually annihilated before the European "scramble for Africa" began in the 1880s and slavery itself was banned by all Western Hemisphere nations by 1888, when Brazil became the last of these nations to emancipate slaves.

Several factors influenced the belated efforts of European imperialist powers to conquer Africa, centuries after they had conquered the Western Hemisphere. Perhaps most decisive difference between the two conquests was the simple fact that disease was an enormously powerful ally of the Europeans in their conquests of the American Indians, who died in great numbers from the spread of diseases from Europe, while disease was an enormously powerful ally of the Africans in resisting European incursions. With the passing centuries, however, the use of quinine and other medical advances enabled Europeans to live in— and therefore to conquer—tropical regions. Meanwhile, the progress of European weaponry, especially the use of rifling in gun barrels to increase accuracy, turned the balance of military power decisively against those with spears or bows and arrows. At the same time, the industrial revolution created vastly increased amounts of wealth, from which European governments could easily obtain the resources required for expensive campaigns of imperial expansion, while the absence of such developments in much of the rest of the world made for a huge disparity in power that promoted European imperialism.

The readiness with which the African continent succumbed to European colonial powers was one measure of this disparity. Even a small European country like Belgium—a pawn in Europe's power politics—could carve out a huge portion of central Africa as its empire, calling it "The Belgian Congo." Portugal, a country both small and relatively backward by European standards, had an even larger colonial empire in Africa. Major European powers like Britain and France took over African territory several times their own size. Not all this was achieved through sheer military power on the battlefield. On the contrary, both the conquerors and the conquered tended to minimize their losses by agreeing to some form of indirect rule, in which local authorities continued in their traditional roles (or in strengthened versions of those roles under European hegemony) while the imperial power made policy through them and influenced or controlled who could act as local authorities. However, such abrogations of African sovereignty were not agreed to merely by persuasion, bribery, or trickery. An obvious and enormous military disparity provided the context for such agreements.

On those occasions when the military strength of the Europeans was directly confronted, the results were often disastrous for the Africans. When an outnumbered group of British troops defeated Ashanti warriors in 1873, inflicting far more casualties than they suffered, it was a pattern that was to be repeated elsewhere on the continent over the years.[99] At the historic battle of Omdurman, near Khartoum, in 1898, 20,000 British-led troops easily defeated 60,000 Sudanese, slaughtering many thousands and losing only a few hundred of their own soldiers.[100] Smaller punitive expeditions similarly applied the Europeans' military superiority to secure African compliance. Not only European governments but even private companies or groups of white settlers were able to seize control in various parts of Africa, primarily through the technological superiority of their weapons. Private groups of Arabs likewise set up their own little fiefdoms in parts of sub-Saharan Africa.

Here and there Africans won historic battles but ultimately the weight of technology, wealth, and organization were all against them, and ultimately they succumbed.

In particular places, such as early twentieth century Tanganyika, the fighting might be fierce for years, but such fighting often represented the all-out efforts of Africans against a minor portion of the manpower and firepower available to the Europeans. Where Europeans were not prepared to make larger commitments of men and resources to African colonization, a *modus vivendi* might be reached with the more formidable African forces, such as the Masai in East Africa, as a prudent alternative to warfare. But the terms of such agreements, as they evolved over the years, extended European control, even if not always to total subjugation.[101]

In one way or another, virtually the entire continent of Africa was conquered by various European powers, in part because such conquest used up relatively little of these nations' total military or economic resources,[102] rather than because of any great value of these African possessions. All sorts of special interests in Europe—missionaries, businessmen, politicians or the military—had their own reasons to urge the creation and expansion of colonialism in Africa, but officials responsible for the public treasury were often opposed,[103] viewing the matter in terms of financial costs and gains. In special cases—such as the Congo or South Africa, with their valuable mineral resources—the conquest might repay its costs, but these were exceptions rather than the rule. In a later era, when the costs of maintaining European rule became higher, whether in financial, military, or political terms, vast areas of Africa were abandoned as rapidly as they had once been conquered. Almost all the countries on this huge continent achieved independence within a span of two decades, beginning around the middle of the twentieth century.

While pre-colonial Africa had its own economic skills, institutions, and social patterns, the coming of European civilization nevertheless had a profound impact, especially in sub-Saharan Africa, where Europeans often introduced the plow, literacy, wheeled vehicles, and other fundamental advances—along with much suffering associated with conquest and continuing subjugation. The mere imposition of law and order—the cessation of inter-tribal warfare as the colonial powers established their hegemony over the contending Africans—had profound economic implications, as it once had in Roman Britain or later in Scotland. For example, land once too militarily vulnerable to cultivate could now be farmed. Thus, although whites seized vast amounts of land in Rhodesia, Africans there cultivated more of their own land than they had before the European conquests.[104] European medicine, railroads, schools, and numerous commercial products also transformed Africa's economies and cultures.

Europe's economic impact on Africa was far greater than Africa's economic effect on Europe. Contrary to various economic theories of imperialism, Africa was not a major outlet for European investment or exports. In the early twentieth century, Britain's investments in Canada alone were larger than its investments in Africa and India put together[105]—and more British money went to the United States than to Canada.[106] France and Germany were likewise reluctant to sink much of their money into Africa.[107] Commercial trade with Africa was similarly trivial for the economies of the European imperial powers. On the eve of the First World War, Germany exported more than five times as much to a small country like Belgium than to its own colonial empire,[108] which was larger than Germany itself. France likewise exported ten times as much to Belgium as to all its vast holdings in Africa. Out of Germany's total exports to the world, less than one percent went to its colonies in Africa.[109]

Africa was somewhat more significant to Europe as a source of imports, though most of these imports to Europe from Africa came from a relatively few places, such as the South African gold mines and diamond fields, or West Africa's cocoa and palm oil regions. Over all, Britain received less than 7 percent of its imports from Africa—less than from any other continent, including thinly populated Australia.[110] Nor were African colonies usually important sources of profit to European investors, or of revenue to European governments. German colonies, for example, in the years leading up to World War I, consistently absorbed expenditures greatly exceeding the revenues raised within the colonies, with taxpayers in Germany having to make up the difference. In the private economy, of 19 firms owning sisal plantations in German colonies, only 8 paid dividends. Only 4 out of 22 firms with cocoa plantations paid dividends, as did only 8 out of 58 rubber plantations and only 3 out of 48 diamond mining companies.[111]

Viewed from Africa, however, the situation looked quite different.

While trade with Africa was a small part of the total international trade of the European colonial powers, trade with these powers was a substantial proportion of the total international trade of the African colonies.[112] Moreover, African exports and imports grew substantially during the colonial era. In German East Africa, for example, exports of peanuts, rubber, cocoa, coffee and sisal all grew several-fold in the relatively brief period from 1905 to 1913.[113] Similarly dramatic increases in exports from British, French, and Belgian colonies in Africa occurred between 1938 and 1958.[114] Correspondingly, Africa had rising imports, as well as more consumption of locally produced goods, both raising the living standards of Africans. Real consumption in the Belgian Congo, for example, rose 77 percent in less than a decade, between 1950 and 1958.[115] In addition, the European impact on colonial Africa included creation of virtually the whole modern industrial and commercial sectors of many African countries.

Europeans also introduced new crops and new farming techniques,[116] as well as creating the modern infrastructure of roads, harbor facilities, rail lines, telegraphs, motor transport, and the like.[117] One small indication of what this meant economically is that a single railroad box-car could carry as much freight as 300 human beings—the usual method of transport in much of Africa—and could cover in two days a distance that would take a caravan two months.[118]

In addition to the economic changes directly attributable to the European conquerors, the consolidation of vast regions of Africa under a new law and order encouraged large-scale immigration of entrepreneurial groups from India and Lebanon, and these Indians and Lebanese created new retail and even international trade networks in East and West Africa, respectively.[119] So dominant did the Indians become over vast regions of East Africa that the rupee became the prevailing currency in much of that region.[120] However, just as Indians and Lebanese settled in Africa mostly after European imperial rule was established there, so many of them departed, or were forced out, after colonial rule ended. In the meantime, however, they added greatly to the economic development of the African continent.

These benefits were by no means without high costs. In addition to deaths from military action during the initial conquests, and often later suppressions of uprisings, there were numerous abuses, injustices, and even atrocities committed against Africans by the con-

querors. Forced labor was one of the most widespread and most deeply
resented of the chronic abuses to which conquered Africans were subjected. The conditions of this forced labor, like everything else, varied
greatly from colony to colony and from time to time. Even among contract laborers, however, conditions could be dire. In the Portuguese
colony of Angola, during the closing decades of the nineteenth century, no contract laborer who went to the offshore island of Saõ Tomé
was ever known to have returned alive.[121] After an uprising of the
Herero people in German Southwest Africa in 1904 had begun with a
massacre of 123 Europeans, a German general ordered his soldiers to
kill every Herero, armed or unarmed, whether men, women, or children. An estimated 60,000 out of the 80,000 Herero were in fact killed
before the general was recalled to Berlin.[122]

Not all the conquests in sub-Saharan Africa were by Europeans or by
nation-states. The great imbalance of power created by firearms
enabled free-lance adventurers, whether Arab or European, to move
into the more isolated or backwards regions of the continent and carve
out small empires for themselves, whether to seize and farm the land
like the Boers of southern Africa or to collect tribute and slaves, as
Arabs and Swahilis did farther north. These free-lance conquests ante-
dated the larger imperialism of European nation-states which swal-
lowed them up, along with African states and communities, in the late
nineteenth and early twentieth centuries. The most dramatic confrontation between these free-lance empires and the new imperialism of
European nation-states were the two Boer wars in which Britain
imposed its rule on the existing independent republics that had been
established by white settlers of predominantly Dutch ancestry, but who
were no longer connected with the government of the Netherlands.

The impact of European conquerors on Africa, for good and evil,
was relatively brief as history is measured—about three generations,
as compared to the centuries in which the Romans ruled Britain or
imperial China ruled parts of southeast Asia or the Moors ruled Spain.
Just as the 1880s saw the beginning of the European "scramble for
Africa," so the 1950s saw the beginning of their massive withdrawal.
This withdrawal began in the northern tier of Moslem states in the
1950s, when Libya, Morocco, and Tunisia became independent, then
spread rapidly southward over the next two decades as Nigeria, Tanzania, Uganda, the Congo, Kenya, and other black nations achieved

their independence.[123] Much as the withdrawal of Roman rule from Britain led to widespread retrogressions, so in many parts of Africa the departure of the European rulers was followed by technological break-downs, failing economies, and political chaos.

African governments by the dozens were toppled by military coups in the post-independence era. The swift disappearance of newly attained democracy, as brutal dictatorships took over, led to the cyni-cal phrase: "One man, one vote—one time." The elaborately frag-mented peoples of Africa turned upon one another, sometimes with massive bloodbaths. Approximately 30,000 Ibos were slaughtered by Moslem mobs in Nigeria, 200,000 Hutus were slaughtered by the Tut-sis in Burundi, and Idi Amin's regime slaughtered 300,000 people in Uganda.[124] A continent once virtually self-sufficient in food,[125] Africa became a massive importer of food as its own production faltered and in some places declined absolutely, in the face of rising population.[126] It was not uncommon for national output as a whole to decline absolutely for years in various African nations. In Equatorial Guinea, for example, the growth rate was negative for the decades of the 1970s and 1980s, averaging nearly minus 4 percent per annum for the 1980s and minus 9 percent for the 1970s.[127] In Burundi the annual "growth" rate of national output was minus 6 percent in 1994 and minus 18 per-cent in 1995, while in Rwanda it ranged from minus 3.2 percent in 1992 to minus 50 percent in 1994.[128]

After the soaring rhetoric and optimistic expectations at the begin-ning of independence were followed by bitter disappointments and painful retrogressions that reached into virtually every aspect of African life, the immediate political response was not so much a re-evaluation of the assumptions and policies which had led to such dis-astrous results, but instead a widespread blaming of the departed imperialists, or racial minorities such as the Indians, or even the United States, which has had relatively little role in African history, for good or ill.

AFRICAN NATIONS

Over the centuries, African nations rose and fell, like nations else-where around the world, the strong conquering the weak and either subjugating or enslaving those unable to resist. The Zulus, for example, invaded and conquered much of southern Africa in the nineteenth century, before the British arrived in 1879 to confront them and fight for control of the land. The first battle between them was won by the Zulus, leaving this scene of carnage on the battlefield:

> Two British drummer boys were hung up by their chins on butchers' hooks, their stomachs cut open like sheep. Most of the white men lay on their backs with their hands clenched, their faces contorted in agony.
>
> Almost all of the more than 1,300 dead men had been disemboweled—turned on their backs, then slashed open with a spear from sternum to groin. their intestines had spilled out onto the ground where the Zulus' bare feet had smashed them, spreading a stinking ooze across the plain. A few men had been scalped, and some had been mutilated, their genitals cut off and stuffed into their mouths, or their lower jaw chopped off and taken away as bearded trophies of victory.[129]

Although the British ultimately prevailed over the Zulus—taking few prisoners—less than a generation later they had to fight two brutal wars for control of South Africa against their fellow-Europeans, the Boers, a mixture of Dutch and other settlers who had landed in South Africa before them. In the second Boer war 26,000 Boer women and children perished in British concentration camps.[130] Such were the grim realities of imperialism in Africa, whether the imperialists were black or white. The centuries-old conquest of the agricultural Hutu by the cattle-herding Tutsis left an even larger and longer-lasting legacy of carnage among these two African peoples. After Rwanda and Burundi became independent nations in the second half of the twentieth century—the former under the Hutus and the latter under the Tutsis—in each country the dominant group proceeded to massacre the other, setting off a cycle of slaughter, revenge, and mass refugee flight, whose end was still not in sight as the century neared its end.

Nigeria

An estimated one out of every five Africans is a Nigerian. Nigeria has the largest black population of any nation on earth (followed by Ethiopia and the United States), and is the tenth most populous nation in the world, with upwards of 80 million people.[131] Like many African countries, Nigeria is composed of a variety of peoples with differing languages and religions, and as a nation is itself a creation of the colonial era. Its very name was suggested by a British journalist.[132]

The region of tropical west Africa that is now called Nigeria had a long and full history before the Europeans came. Iron was smelted in what is now Nigeria five centuries before Christ.[133] Large, complex, indigenous political systems also arose in this region of West Africa.[134] Towns and villages were common in this area,[135] and about half the population lived in these urban communities before the beginning of the twentieth century.[136]

In the nineteenth century, Nigeria was a British sphere of influence and, in the twentieth century, a British colony until independence was achieved in 1960. Britain became involved in Nigeria in stages, through a long series of *ad hoc* decisions in response to local and international events. Attempting to protect and advance a variety of British interests in the region, without incurring the costs of administering a colony, the British found themselves drawn deeper and deeper into political involvements and military actions. Britain's historic decision to ban the international slave trade in the early nineteenth century entailed a large and long-run political and military commitment in West Africa, the source of most transatlantic slave shipments. Missionary, business, and other interests also promoted British involvement in the region. Nigeria was never a major British economic asset, however, nor a particularly desirable post for British colonial officials. Many of these officials in fact sought re-assignment elsewhere at opportune moments.[137]

Britain's attempt to maintain a low-cost presence in the region led to a policy of governing through existing authorities, disturbing indigenous institutions, culture, and social systems as little as possible. Ironically, however, the very presence of the British undermined their attempt to maintain the status quo. The need for Nigerian clerks and other subordinates to help man the colonial administration required creating a new class of African people with education in the English language, with Westernized concepts, and with experience in Westernized ways of doing things. Moreover, different ethnic groups among the Africans had different degrees of receptivity to the new ways of doing things and responded differently to new opportunities to get ahead, leading to changed economic and social statuses among these groups, compared to what their relative positions had been before the British arrived. Existing military power relationships among the tribes no longer mattered, once the British had control of them all, and would not permit them to fight. Moreover, it was now safe for people from one part of Nigeria to travel and even to settle in regions that were once enemy territory. Finally, the ease with which British power prevailed militarily created not only a respect but also a mystique about things European and modern. However limited the intentions and purposes of the British colonial officials, their presence was far-reaching, and ultimately revolutionary, in its effects.

One group of Europeans whose intentions and goals were more sweeping than those of the colonial officials were the Christian missionaries. These missionaries often preceded the colonial officials in Africa, and missionary lobbies in London were in fact an important influence on British government decisions to intervene in Africa, often despite the resistance of treasury and colonial officials, who understood the bleak economic prospects there. Missionaries were seeking not only religious conversions in Africa but also radical changes in the African way of life—not only the abolition of slavery but also changed sexual mores, literacy, cleanliness, and numerous other features of Western civilization. British missionaries were at work in the region that was to become Nigeria well before the British government took over that region. Eventually, the number of missionaries in Nigeria ran into the hundreds, the number of churches into the thousands and the African members of these churches into the hundreds of thousands.[138]

Until 1898, all Western education in Nigeria was Christian missionary education—and that remained substantially true as late as 1942,[139] though the rise of an educated class of Nigerians led to growing demands that the colonial government itself do more for education. Because education in Nigeria was essentially Christian, European-centered education, it was not welcome in the Moslem northern region of the country, where more than half the population lived. Missionary education was therefore concentrated in the southern regions, leading to large and lasting disparities in the educational levels of different tribes of Nigerians, with historic consequences for the economic, social, and political future of the country. Even within the southern regions, some groups were more receptive than others. Most receptive were the Ibos, a poorer, more fragmented group, once heavily raided by slave hunters, and living in a less fertile part of Nigeria. To the Ibos, Western education was a rare opportunity to be seized.

The largest of the Nigerian groups, the Hausa-Fulani tribes from the Moslem northern region, constituted 28 percent of the population of the country around the middle of the twentieth century. The next largest group—about 18 percent of the population—were the Ibos. The Yorubas from the southwestern region of the country were very similar in size (17 percent of the population) but very different in history, economics and culture,[140] and also had the highest per capita income.[141] There were and are innumerable other groups, living either in their own geographic enclaves or scattered through regions in which other tribes have been dominant. However, the term "tribe," while used in Nigeria as elsewhere, is misleading insofar as it suggests isolated bands of people living in the wild. The major tribes of Nigeria each includes millions of people, urban as well as rural, scattered over territories as large as whole nations in Europe.

As the Nigerian economy began to be gradually transformed from a subsistence economy to a money economy under the British, exports such as peanuts, palm products and other agricultural produce increased sharply. After the turn of the century, peanut exports more than tripled over the next 20 years, while palm product exports rose more than four-fold. Cocoa exports by 1939 were more than five times what they were just 20 years earlier.[142] While Nigeria remained a predominantly rural, subsistence agricultural economy,[143] urban centers grew over the years. Most were in the western (Yoruba) region, where Ibadan had 175,000 inhabitants in 1911, more than 238,000 in 1921, and over 387,000 by 1931. Kano, an ancient commercial city in the Moslem northern region, had about 97,000 people in 1931, while not a single city in the eastern (Ibo) region had as many as 20,000 people at that time. However, by 1953 there were 5 eastern cities with more than 40,000 people—four of these cities now being larger than any city in the north except Kano. In part, this reflected the growing prosperity of the Ibos, though many Ibos were enjoying that prosperity in other parts of the country as well. At about the same mid-century mark, per capita income in the western region was twice that in the northern region, with eastern region incomes being in between.[144]

Partly these economic differences reflected differences in education in the various regions, as well as the greater initial prosperity of the Yorubas. Education remained rare throughout the colonial history of Nigeria—and very unevenly distributed. Western education in Roman letters was achieved by only 8.5 percent of all Nigerians as late as 1953, while literacy in Arab script was achieved by 5.4 percent, concentrated in the Moslem northern regions.[145] Western education, and specifically English-language education, was crucial for economic advancement in the government and in the modern industrial and commercial sectors run by the British. Here the disparities between regions was extreme.

As of 1912, for example, there were fewer than a thousand students in elementary school in northern Nigeria, where more than half the population lived, and more than 35,000 in the rest of the country. By 1926, there were approximately 5,200 primary school students in the north—and more than 138,000 in the other regions. While the growth in Western education continued in all regions, the disparities also continued. By 1957, when there were approximately 185,000 elementary school pupils receiving Western education in the northern regions, there were 2.3 million in the other regions, whose combined populations were not as large. Similar patterns of disparity existed—and persisted—in secondary education and in higher education. As late as 1937, there were fewer than a hundred secondary school students receiving Western education in the northern region and more than 4,200 in the other regions. Twenty years later, there were approximately 3,600 secondary school pupils in the north and more than 28,000 elsewhere.[146]

In higher education, the disparities were even greater. As late as 1951, out of the 16 million people in the northern region, only one had a full university degree—and he was a convert to Christianity.[147] Meanwhile, virtually all the Nigerian students in institutions of higher education, whether overseas or at home, were southern Nigerians.[148] By the academic year 1959–60, on the eve of independence, northern Nigerians were just 9 percent of the students at the University of Ibadan. Among the much larger number of Nigerian students studying abroad in foreign institutions of higher learning, only 2 percent were Hausa-Fulani as late as 1966.[149]

These vast educational disparities were of course reflected in occupational disparities. Out of 160 physicians in Nigeria in the early

1950s, 76 were Yorubas, 49 were Ibos and only one was Hausa-Fulani.[150] In the army, three-fourths of the riflemen were Hausa-Fulani, while four-fifths of the officers were southerners. As late as 1965, one half of the officer corps was specifically Ibo.[151] Even within the northern regional government, southern Nigerians outnumbered northern Nigerians in some occupations requiring medical or techni-cal skills.[152] At lower levels as well, Ibos predominated in clerical and semi-skilled jobs in the postal service, banks, and the railway—in northern Nigeria[153]—and were also prominent as traders, artisans, merchants and factory workers there.[154]

As regards the Ibos at least, none of this reflected any initial advan-tages over the northerners. Not only were the Ibos a poorer group from a less fertile region of Nigeria,[155] those who migrated to the northern region were treated as outsiders and forced to live in separate residen-tial areas, and to send their children to separate schools, by order of the local authorities.[156] Fear of the impact of foreign ideas and ways on the traditional Moslem societies of northern Nigeria led to this resis-tance to Nigerian migrants, just as it produced a ban on Christian mis-sionary work there.

The growing classes of educated and semi-educated Nigerians of whatever ethnic origins, though still only a minority of the population, were to play an important role in the country's history. By the early 1920s, there were nearly 30,000 Nigerians engaged in modern elite or sub-elite occupations, mostly clerks, teachers, or artisans, but includ-ing also more than a hundred clergymen, and a dozen or so doctors, lawyers, and civil servants. By the early 1950s, there were 35,000 Nigerian teachers alone, 27,000 clerks, 32,000 artisans and from a hundred to several hundred Nigerian managers, clergy, civil servants, doctors and lawyers.[157]

These newly created elites and sub-elites of Nigeria were histori-cally both the promoters and destroyers of British colonial rule. The newly emerging Nigerians—educated or semi-educated[158]—opposed traditional African values and patterns, which they saw as backward, and thus initially favored the spread of Western influence as a counter-weight and as a harbinger of progress.[159] Yet growing resentment of white racism and other negative features of colonialism later led the same class of people to take the lead in seeking independence.[160] This was not all mere inconsistency or opportunism. There had first to be created a nation of Nigeria for there to be an *independent* nation of Nigeria, and the emerging black Westernized elite saw the colonial power as the force needed to weld the many disparate peoples of the region into a viable body politic. The building of a railway by the British, for example, was welcomed by educated Africans as a step in nation-building.[161]

Ties between the colonial officials and traditional African rulers willing to serve them alienated the emerging educated Africans, who had a very untraditional vision of the country's future.[162] The growth of local political institutions modelled on Western democracy and the development of trade unions, especially during the 1940s, provided both the forum and the training ground for a new, Westernized Nigerian political leadership. Eventually, this black leadership pressured and negotiated independence for Nigeria, beginning in 1960.

As in much of the rest of Africa, independence in Nigeria marked the onset of internal power struggles among the disparate peoples lumped together as a nation artificially created by the colonial power. Even before independence arrived, different tribes and regions had very different reactions to the impending event. Ibos took the lead in advocating independence, urgently soon, with a strong national government.[163] The Yoruba formed their own separate movement for independence, leaving more room for regional autonomy and with more of a role for tribal solidarity.[164] The more fundamental split, however, was between the southern Nigerians as a whole and the northern Nigerians, who saw that immediate independence would mean immediate domination of the north itself by southerners, who already predominated in many branches of both the public and private sectors of the north, and whose far larger educated classes would ensure such domination in the future. Under British indirect rule, the traditional leaders and authorities in the northern region had more control of the region's way of life and its future than they could expect in a southern-dominated independent Nigeria.

The problem was not simply that there were differences of opinion, but that there were no established and mutually respected traditions for airing those differences with restraint and accommodation. Vitriolic polemics in the press and in the political arena became the norm. Epithets like "fascist" and "imperialist stooge" became common currency, along with unbridled expressions of tribal chauvinism.[165] A

northern political leader said to southerners: "We despise each other."
He said "we call each other ignorant" because one group had Western
education and culture while the other derived its education and culture from the East. He added: "To tell you the plain truth, the common
people of the North put more confidence in the white man than in
either their black Southern brothers or the educated Northerners."[166]

This was not mere hyperbole, as later events showed. Dates set for
Nigerian independence in the 1950s came and went without independence, not because the British would not grant it, but because Nigerians could not agree among themselves as to when and in what
constitutional form independence should come. After a date and a
constitution were finally agreed to, policies of "Nigerianization" of
government jobs currently held by Europeans were proclaimed. In the
northern region the policy was more specifically "Northernization,"
with emphasis on expelling southern Nigerians from these jobs, far
more than expelling European expatriates.[167]

Even the first census after independence became embroiled in
political controversy among tribes and regions, and was nullified amid
charges of fraud.[168] Riots, plots, and coups also marked the first
decade of independence. In January 1966, Nigerian Prime Minister
Balewa was assassinated in the course of a military coup. All these
political events had strong ethnic impact in a country where no single
group constituted even a third of the population, and where major geographic regions were the domains of different tribes or ethnic groups.
That the assassinated Prime Minister was from the Moslem northern
region, and most leaders of the coup were Ibo military officers from the
Christian south, proved to be of fateful significance in the way the military government's acts were perceived, resisted, and then openly
rebelled against.

In June 1966, mobs in northern cities attacked the Ibos living in
their midst, killing hundreds of them, amid widespread destruction of
property. This was only a faint foretaste of the larger tragedy ahead. In
July, a counter-coup by Moslem military officers from the north drove
the Ibo-dominated regime from power and killed its leader. In September, new and more bloody riots broke out against Ibos in the north:

> Northern soldiers chased Ibo troops from their barracks and
> murdered scores with bayonets. Screaming Moslem mobs

descended on the Ibo quarters of every northern city, killing their victims with clubs, poison arrows and shotguns. Tens of thousands of Ibos were murdered in the systematic massacres that followed.[169]

In addition to an estimated 30,000 deaths, there were more than a million Ibo refugees who fled the region to join their fellow Ibos in the southeast. This in turn led to the fateful decision of the Ibos to withdraw from Nigeria, where they no longer felt safe, and to form their own independent state, which they called Biafra. The civil war set off by the secession of May 1967 raged for more than two years. Only four African nations recognized Biafra. Both Communist and Western-bloc nations alike backed the government of oil-rich Nigeria, which was well-supplied with modern weaponry to use against the rebel forces. Nigerian government troops cut off Biafra from access to the sea—and therefore from food and military supplies. Ibos began starving to death at a rate of a thousand a day.[170]

More than a million people died in Biafra, from the fighting, starvation, and disease. In addition, three million Ibos became refugees.[171] When Biafra surrendered and again became part of Nigeria in 1970, the institutions and economy of the region were devastated, and many feared obliteration of the Ibo culture or even genocide against the Ibo people by the victorious forces.

However, in contrast to the mass slaughters in such other African nations as Burundi or Uganda, and in contrast to its own bloody precedents, Nigeria took the path of reconciliation. Industry in the war zone was rehabilitated. So were Ibo political and military personnel, including some officials of the former Biafran government. In 1982, even the exiled leader of Biafra—now a millionaire businessman living in the Ivory Coast—was granted a pardon. Ibos again became a prosperous element in the Nigerian society, holding important positions in both the public and private sectors.[172]

Military rule in Nigeria gave way to civilian government—and to reorganized political regions, designed to break up the ethnic blocs whose conflicts had plunged the country into civil war. Much of the new Nigerian government structure was modelled after that of the United States, rather than that of Britain.[173]

The turbulent history of post-independence Nigeria has been

plagued by four major and interdependent problems: (1) ethnic or tribal animosities; (2) desperate political struggles to gain control of the government at all costs; (3) widespread corruption, and (4) economic breakdowns. Because no ethnic group trusts another to rule over it, elections and even censuses bring all-out efforts to prevail by any means necessary, including force and fraud. High voter turnout, which some equate with a healthy democracy, has been in Nigeria (and in some other countries) an indication instead of a fever pitch of political polarization. So too have been the drastic differences in voting support for candidates of different ethnic background from one region to another. Even in the 1979 election, held after a new constitution designed to mitigate ethnic politics, each of 5 presidential candidates received an absolute majority of the votes in at least one state—and less than 5 percent of the vote in another state or states.[174]

Control of the government has been desperately important, not only to avoid being oppressed by rival tribes, but also because the massive role of government in the economy has made politics the pre-eminent route to prosperity, as well as power—whether for individuals, tribes, or regions. As of 1964, governments at the federal, regional, and local levels employed more than half of the wage-earners in the country.[175] Government also allocated large sums to the various regions—which is also to say, to the various tribes. In 1961, for example, the northern region, containing more than half the population of Nigeria, paid only 9 percent of the personal income taxes, while it received 45 percent of the money allocated to the various regions by the federal government. At the same time, the western region paid 64 percent of all personal income taxes and received less than one fourth of the funds allocated by the federal government to the various regions.[176] In tribal terms, the Yoruba were subsidizing the Hausa-Fulani and other northern groups. Government employment also paid far more than the private marketplace, as well as providing opportunities for additional income through corruption. A scholar specializing in the study of Nigeria summarized the situation:

> Legislators, ministers, and high-ranking civil servants could expect to earn from seven to thirty times the pay of an ordinary government laborer, even without considering their car allowances, housing subsidies, and other emoluments. And

such official earnings were trivial relative to what could be amassed through favoritism to private business concerns and diversion of public funds into private accounts.[177]

The fortunes to be made through favoritism by government officials were based on the government's role as massive dispenser of largesse and tight controller of economic activities. These included the awarding of loans, contracts, bank credit, positions on public boards and corporations, military commissions, and trade licenses. Moreover, the men whose decisions would determine such things were often from humble backgrounds, if not grinding poverty, and were now not only affluent themselves but were also able to help family members—but only so long as they stayed in office.[178] To lose office was not to return to something of comparable prestige and earnings in the private sector but to be devastated, both personally and in career terms.

The extraordinary corruption of Nigeria, as well as the ruthless repression of opponents, were products of these circumstances. The utter loss of public confidence in politicians facilitated the military coups of 1966, 1979, and 1983. Investigations after those coups revealed an astonishing scale of corruption among the deposed political leadership, with misappropriations of funds exceeding more than $30 million by just one state governor—enough to pay more than three quarters of the arrears in salaries of civil servants who had not been paid for months. The corruption of the electoral process was no less dramatic. A Yoruba governor, defeated through vote fraud, was later found by a court to have won in fact by a million votes.[179]

As an oil-exporting nation, Nigeria prospered during the era of high oil prices in the 1970s. Oil provided between 60 and 80 percent of federal and state government revenues, and the largesse this made possible kept many groups reasonably contented. Both public consumption and private investment grew rapidly during the decade of the 1970s. However, a drop in oil prices on the world market, beginning in the early 1980s, caused drastic economic and social dislocations in Nigeria.

By 1986, the value of oil exports was only about one-fifth what it had been just 6 years earlier.[180] In only three years, from 1985 to 1988, the value of the Nigerian currency fell to one-fifth its former level. The federal government laid off 50,000 workers, while the state governments and the private sector also had large-scale lay-offs.[181] Foreign workers, attracted to Nigeria from other African countries during boom times, were deeply resented during hard times—and were brutally expelled en masse, largely to Ghana.[182] During the worst period of the early 1980s, Nigeria had a declining national output for four consecutive years.[183] However, the new military government imposed austerity, including a reduction in subsidies to the state-owned airlines and public utilities, and began selling state-owned businesses. By 1988 there was a rising national output, in real terms, even allowing for inflation.[184] This growth in real output continued on into the 1990s, while the runaway inflation was reduced to just under 29 percent per year.[185]

Attempts were made to de-politicize the country's ethnic groups and foster democratic government. In 1979, a northern Moslem was elected president, with an Ibo as his running mate.[186] He was reelected in 1982—and then deposed by another military coup at the end of 1983. This new military regime was long-lived. As of 1997, it was still promising elections in 1998, though it permitted only a few political parties to form—not including those with serious possibilities of winning.[187]

The many difficulties encountered during Nigeria's first generation after independence were not altogether surprising, much less unique, and were certainly not worse than what happened in ancient Britain after the Romans withdrew. Nigeria has remained one nation, despite threatened secessions of the northern region and an actual attempt at secession by the eastern region. Clearly Nigeria learned some lessons from its economic, social, and political problems, and attempted to apply those lessons in new constitutions and new policies. The more fundamental problem for Nigeria—and other countries—is whether one nation can copy the institutions of another nation and culture without the historical evolution of traditions that made those institutions viable. Standards of honesty are particularly difficult to synthesize. A 1997 international survey ranked Nigeria the most corrupt nation in the world.[188]

Tanzania

Tanzania, on the tropical east coast of Africa, is about three times the size of Italy but has only about half as many people. The population per square mile in Tanzania is very similar to that of the United States. The country is composed of two formerly separate political entities, located respectively on the continental mainland (Tanganyika) and on the off-shore island of Zanzibar. The country's name derives from the combination of these two names,

Geographically, Tanzania's most famous feature is Mount Kilimanjaro. It also shares Lake Victoria with Uganda to the north, and in the south it shares Lake Tanganyika with Mali and Mozambique. Both bodies of water are among the ten largest lakes in the world, Lake Victoria being larger than Lake Michigan and Lake Tanganyika being larger than Lake Erie. Like much of Africa, Tanzania suffers from low and unpredictable rainfall, with only about half the country receiving 30 or more inches of rain annually.[189] The region has been plagued historically by recurring droughts, has poor soil and few permanent rivers, as distinguished from shallow streams that appear and disappear according to seasonal rainfall.[190]

The tsetse fly infests more than half the mainland,[191] making cattle and draft animals impracticable in the infected regions. Soil and topography vary greatly, with population density varying correspondingly, concentrating in those regions with relatively fertile land and sufficient rainfall. More than 90 percent of the population remained rural in the late twentieth century and Tanzania remained one of the poorest countries on the world's poorest continent.[192] In 1995, the World Bank ranked Tanzania 172nd in income among 174 nations.[193]

The region of East Africa now known as Tanzania has long had populations highly fragmented into tribal groups. Post-independence Tanzania remained fragmented into more than a hundred ethnic groups, no one of whom exceeded 13 percent of the population and the five largest of whom, put together, added up to only about one fourth of the country's population.[194] Relations among its ethnic groups have not been as central a problem in Tanzania as in Nigeria, though some tribes took advantage of educational opportunities more so than others and have been correspondingly better represented in higher level occupations, with corresponding resentments by others.[195] The various tribes speak different languages and, historically, some tribes enslaved others.[196]

In the centuries before European colonization, the coastal regions of East Africa had little contact with interior regions of the continent, as compared to its contact with the island of Zanzibar, or even with Persian Gulf peoples. This reflected the vast differences in cost between transport over water and transport over land.[197] There was trade inland but it was short-distance trade.[198] The economic ties of coastal East Africa were largely with the Arab countries or with Zanzibar, which was also controlled by Arabs. From the flourishing trade center of Zanzibar, whose leading trade items were ivory and African slaves, the Arabs began to conquer parts of coastal East Africa. Their principal targets were trading settlements such as Kilwa, which they took in 1784, the island of Pemba (1822) and the port of Mombasa, captured in 1837. Among the peoples of Zanzibar, in addition to the African population and Arab overlords, there were numerous commercial people from India, as well as foreign traders from Germany, Britain and the United States. In commerce, however, the Indians were pre-eminent and by 1861 they controlled three-quarters of the immovable property on the island.[199] As early as the eighteenth century. Indians also dominated the river trade on the mainland.[200]

Foreign influences on coastal East Africa included European imperialism, as well as the imperialism of the Arabs and the commercial dominance of the Indians. As far back as the late fifteenth century, the Portuguese visited the region. Less than a decade later, the Portuguese sacked the cities of Mombasa and Kilwa, and shortly thereafter claimed control of the coastal region. This control was neither complete nor unchallenged, however. After nearly two centuries, punctuated by the rebellions, invasions, and intrigues of various factions, the Portuguese were eventually forced out by the Arabs.[201] There was, of course, no nation of Tanganyika or Tanzania at this point. But political units in the region were growing larger and including more heterogeneous populations, though not to as great a degree as in West Africa.[202]

The interior tribes of East Africa, like isolated cultures elsewhere in the world, tended to lag behind the development of more cosmopolitan areas such as the coastal regions. Still, such outside artifacts as firearms eventually reached the interior, changing both the hunting of animals and power relationships among the tribes. Firearms meant a more widespread hunting of elephants and a need for smaller tribes to seek protection in alliances with chiefs of larger tribes that had guns. The net result was a growth of tribal empires in the era preceding European conquest of the area.[203]

Germany seized Tanganyika in the 1880s, but fierce and bloody resistance continued on into the early years of the twentieth century.[204] In the last of these rebellions, 26,000 Africans were killed according to official German figures—which do not include those who died of hunger and disease resulting from the devastations and disruptions of all-out warfare.[205] German rule in Tanganyika lasted until World War I, when a British naval blockade and military invasion brought control of the colony to the United Kingdom.

The economic and cultural impact of Germans on Tanganyika was considerable, despite the relatively short historical era of their rule, which was only about one generation. Dar es Salaam, the principal port and later capital, developed into an important town under the Germans.[206] Germans introduced new capital, new crops, and modern transportation. They also brutally oppressed the Africans with taxes and forced labor,[207] quite aside from the carnage of warfare resulting from resistance to their rule. Perhaps the most enduring cultural legacy of German rule was the rendering of Swahili into Latin letters by Germans and their spreading of this language as a unifying lingua franca through the polyglot regions of East Africa.[208] Colonialism also promoted disunity, however, by dividing the Masai tribe, for example, between British and German colonies in East Africa.[209]

Germans also penetrated the island of Zanzibar, though not as military conquerors and not as pervasively as the Indians did. There were German traders established in Zanzibar as early as the middle of the nineteenth century, and by 1870 Germans conducted almost one-third of the commerce on the island.[210] The Arabs remained the official rulers, though less and less so in substance as the British extended their influence, and eventually control. In 1890, an agreement between Britain and Germany recognized a British protectorate over Zanzibar.

German and British colonial rule was also a major factor in the Indians' contribution to the economic development of Zanzibar and the East African mainland. Indians came in greater numbers, penetrated deeper into continental Africa, and settled more permanently under colonial rule and protection.[211] Indians became the dominant commercial people throughout East Africa in general.[212] The British, as the colonial rulers of India, often brought Indians to their African territories,[213] but the Germans also encouraged Indians to immigrate to Tanganyika during their rule there.[214]

One of the major forms of trade in Tanganyika and Zanzibar was the trade in human beings—slaves. Missionary-explorer David Livingstone reported in the early 1860s that 19,000 slaves from Nyasaland were sent to Zanzibar alone.[215] As elsewhere in East Africa, the Arabs were the leading slave-traders. The British struggle against the slave trade continued for generations, encountering both African and Arab opposition.[216] The task of ending the very institution of slavery itself was especially formidable in Arab-dominated regions, such as Zanzibar.[217] It was not until 1922 that slavery was finally stamped out in Tanganyika, after the British were firmly in control.[218]

When the Germans were expelled after World War I, Indians acquired most of the real estate in Dar es Salaam.[219] For the country as a whole, Indians held an estimated 50 to 60 percent of the import-export trade, 80 percent of sisal production, 80 percent of transport service and 90 percent of all town property, as well as hundreds of small general stores, mostly in rural areas. The majority were Gujarati Indians,[220] an important commercial group in India itself.

The way of life of the interior tribes on the East African mainland was especially disrupted. While they benefitted from agricultural innovations, many local crafts succumbed to cheaper or better mass-produced goods from India, and most of the cattle in most parts of the country were wiped out by the disease rinderpest, which particularly weakened the cattle-herding Masai. The devastations of African populations caused by colonial warfare created vacant areas where thick bush grew unchecked, creating conditions for more wild game and more tsetse flies, which now infested an even larger area than before.[221]

Colonial demands for porters, in an area with a dearth of water or animal transport, were enormous and oppressive in East Africa, as they were in other parts of the continent, whether under British, French, or German rule. The Germans conscripted tens of thousands of porters in East Africa and the British 200,000. Death rates were high among the porters—sometimes as high as 20 to 25 percent.[222]

Economic growth in export products was substantial and sustained, under both German and British colonial rule. Exports from Tanganyika increased more than ten-fold between 1883 and 1913.[223] Between 1913 (under German rule) and 1938 (under British rule) the value of exports from the colony of Tanganyika more than doubled.[224] Sisal exports increased nearly five-fold, coffee more than ten-fold and peanuts became an important export.[225] These were by no means all a result of European-owned or European-directed enterprises. As of 1933, more than half the coffee produced in the country was grown by Africans, who owned a total of six million coffee bushes. Cotton production in Tanganyika was carried out almost exclusively by small African farmers living in the vicinity of Lake Victoria.[226]

Although Africans were showing themselves capable of taking initiative and responsibility in producing for the market, two world events—the Great Depression and the Second World War—promoted more use of force by the colonial authorities. As world prices fell during the Great Depression, the poll tax imposed on Africans remained the same in money terms, which is to say, it increased in real terms. To ensure the payment of this tax, the colonial official pressured African farmers into growing larger export crops, even at the expense of food. Thus Africans had to depend on government famine relief when local food crops were disappointing.

Further government control was promoted by World War II and especially by the world shortage of rubber, after the loss of British and American rubber-producing areas in Asia to the Japanese. To produce crops deemed "strategic" in the war effort and to feed the workers growing these crops, the colonial government took an active role in the economy. Among other things, this meant a greatly increased conscription of African labor—from less than a thousand workers in 1941 to more than 30,000 by 1944.[227] This exercise in government planning became a precedent for more such experiments in the post-war years. Again, the Africans were given little or no choice, as a succession of agricultural plans came down from the government—and often failed in practice.[228]

Over the years, along with economic and social benefits, the colonial government created many grievances. As elsewhere, it also created a new Westernized class among the indigenous population, a group of educated and semi-educated people with a vision of the future for their country that was unlike either the traditional past or the colonial present. Not incidentally, it was to be a future in which these Westernized elite would rise to the top. The campaign for independence in Tanganyika was led by a Western-educated, former school teacher, Julius K. Nyerere. Nyerere's Tanganyika African National Union (TANU) mobilized discontent and ambition, first among the Westernized, educated, and semi-educated Africans.[229] Despite the colonial government's resistance and repression, TANU achieved its principal goal. Tanganyika became independent in 1961. Its union with Zanzibar three years later created the new nation of Tanzania. Tanzania still bears the cultural imprint of colonial rule. Swahili, its official language, was spread under German auspices and its capital city—Dar es Salaam—was built by Arabs and has an Arabic name.[230]

As President of Tanzania, Julius Nyerere became known internationally for his lofty goals and humanitarian statements that caused him to be called "the conscience of Africa." At home, he tried to impose his vision of an egalitarian, socialist society by authoritarian methods. By government edict, a majority of Tanzania's population was grouped into villages, whether they wanted to be or not.[231] As with so many other communal agricultural schemes in various nations and eras, those in Tanzania led to people's doing as little work as possible on the communal crop and as much as possible on their own individual plots.[232] Tanzania's output per worker declined over a period of a decade and the country went from being an exporter of maize to being an importer. Hundreds of nationalized firms went bankrupt.[233] The railroad from Tanzania to Zambia broke down so often that the Africans who ran it were replaced by Chinese, at virtually all levels. Once-prosperous Zanzibar suffered the economic decline of the rest of Tanzania and was often without electricity.[234] All this occurred in a country that received more foreign aid per capita than any other—and which had large unpaid loans extended for years at zero interest.[235]

On the political front, Nyerere jailed thousands of political prisoners—more than South Africa, at one point in the 1970s[236]—and many were tortured, according to Amnesty International.[237] Nyerere was repeatedly unopposed in "elections" which he won by majorities attained elsewhere only in Communist countries. He also helped overthrow three other African governments, including the Amin regime in Uganda, which Nyerere replaced with his own puppet rulers—the latter being replaced in turn and jailed by Nyerere when the Tanzanian leader disapproved of their performance.[238] Yet his unassuming lifestyle and personality, and his idealistic statements made him an enormous favorite of Western intellectuals.[239] What the 17 million Tanzanians thought of Nyerere could not be known, for Tanzania was a one-party state with a government-controlled press and a society honey-combed with party cells that made the free expression of opinion dangerous.

The economic debacle in Tanzania reached virtually every kind of activity, agricultural or industrial, domestic or foreign. Cotton production, which was 79,000 tons in the mid-1960s, fell to about 50,000 tons by the early 1980s. Over a period of a decade, cashew production fell by more than 50 percent and sisal production by nearly 60 percent. The industrial sector, by the 1980s, was operating at from 10 to 30 percent of capacity. The total output of the country was declining and inflation averaged 35 percent per year. Perhaps most decisive of all, the Nyerere regime in Tanzania finally began to lose its credibility with international lending and donor organizations, which had subsidized its policies in the past.[240] From 1980 to 1985, per capita real income in Tanzania fell by 12 percent.[241]

The resignation of Julius Nyerere as President of Tanzania in late 1985 and the inauguration of Ali Hassan Mwinyi as the new president marked a policy change as well as a change of personalities. A modest degree of relaxation of government control in the economy began to produce signs of economic recovery, including the first rise in per capita real income in nearly a decade.[242] These changing policies also produced internal dissension within the ruling party, still headed by Nyerere after relinquishing the presidency. However, by 1990, Tanzania had achieved four consecutive years of growth in real national output and enacted a new constitution, permitting multi-party elections.[243] Clearly, some of the lessons of the mistakes of the immediate post-independence era had been learned and at least the beginnings of important changes made.

In 1995, Ali Hassan Mwinyi was succeeded as president by Benjamin Mkapa, whose cabinet has been characterized as "distinguished by youth, competence, and the absence of old faces."[244] Many of Tanzania's old problems remained, however, including pervasive corruption that extends even into the courtrooms. Lawyers have been quoted in the Tanzanian press as saying that "any judgment can be bought" and that an attorney does not need a knowledge of law books in court "if his pockets are full."[245] Well-known public figures have been assassinated, apparently by professional killers.[246] President Mkapa ran on an anti-corruption platform in 1995 and an anti-corruption commission report led to the resignation of the minister of tourism.[247] Yet how far such a deep-seated practice as official corruption, common in Africa, can be brought under control is problematical. Nevertheless, the new economic policies continued to produce economic growth in real per capita terms in the 1990s. Despite the worst drought in 40 years, in a country where most of the output is agricultural, the total value of that output continued to rise in 1995.[248] In this case at least, the devastations of nature have not had nearly the bad effects that the devastations of man produced in the first decades after independence.

Ghana

The West African nation of Ghana is slightly smaller in size than Great Britain or the American state of Oregon. The population of Ghana, however, is less than one-third that of Britain and the literacy rate in Ghana was only 30 percent in 1980, rising to 60 percent by 1990.[249] Known as the Gold Coast during more than a century of British colonial rule, Ghana reverted to its traditional name when it became an independent nation in 1957.

Geographically, nature provided no harbors in which ships could anchor and unload, sheltered from the heavy surf in that region of West Africa. As elsewhere, large vessels had to anchor off-shore and be unloaded piecemeal into canoes and small boats[250]—obviously adding to shipping costs and delays in transit, and generally impeding economic progress by limiting what goods had sufficient value to repay such additional transport costs. River traffic was also severely limited in distance by numerous rapids[251] and in volume by the shallowness of the water, which restricted the size of boats.[252] In view of this, it is hardly surprising that most of the major towns developed along the coast, from trading centers that were more easily accessible by coastwise boats than in the interior.[253] Ghana has been well-endowed with natural resources,[254] but not with the natural means of transporting them or of tying its peoples together culturally or politically, and connecting them with larger cultural developments elsewhere.

Culturally, Ghana's people are fragmented into about 100 ethnic or linguistic groups, many numbering less than 10,000 persons, and none constituting more than 15 percent of the total population.[255] They are also divided religiously among Christians, Moslems, and followers of various indigenous African religions. As in other parts of Africa, there was a history of stronger tribes in the region conquering weaker tribes or conducting raids against them to obtain slaves. The Ashanti tribe was the leading conquering and enslaving force.

The Ashanti, based in the western uplands of the region, began to dominate surrounding tribes as early as the seventeenth century, and continued their military expansion on into the second half of the nineteenth century, when they came into armed collision with the British. Like the British in a later era, the Ashanti conquerors followed a policy of indirect rule in a growing Ashanti Confederation.[256] Meanwhile, isolated European trading settlements were being established along the coast, attracted principally by the trade in gold that gave the region its name. The Portuguese arrived as early as 1471 and built their first fort in 1482. However, during the seventeenth and eighteenth centuries, the Dutch, British, Danes and Swedes also established coastal trading settlements—and also found it necessary to fortify them militarily. Soon the Europeans were fighting among themselves along the coast while Africans fought among themselves inland.

In the Gold Coast, as in other parts of the world, the British government was reluctant to take on the costs of a colonial venture that could easily be more trouble than it was worth. Where private groups of Britons wanted to try it, as in the Gold Coast, the government would authorize, sanction, and to a limited extent oversee the operation, while the private company supplied the money, the manpower, and even the fighting forces. As elsewhere, however, these kinds of low-budget imperialism acquired a life of their own in Africa. The very disunity among indigenous peoples that made them vulnerable to such incursions also threatened the stability of any modus vivendi worked out by the British with local authorities, in a fluid situation complicated by contending tribes, sporadic military incidents, and major outbreaks of tribal warfare. Eventually, as elsewhere, the British government found itself drawn into these wars, especially when the Ashanti began making attacks on coastal tribes with whom the British had agreements and alliances. Moreover, the British ban on the slave trade in 1808 had serious—and negative—economic consequences on the economy of the Gold Coast, and brought the British more and more into conflict with Africans whose economies depended on the slave trade. Eventually, in the Gold Coast as elsewhere, the British government took over the colonies from private groups.

The Ashanti invaded the coastal regions repeatedly in the early nineteenth century, disrupting trade and forcing the local European outposts to recognize Ashanti claims in these regions. The British government took control in 1821 and in 1826 defeated a new Ashanti invasion, with the help of African coastal tribes. A new treaty in 1831 saw the beginning of a long period of peace and expanding trade in the area.[257] The last Ashanti invasion took place in 1873. A force of fewer than 3,000 British troops, supported by African auxiliaries, defeated the Ashanti, invaded their homelands and burned their capital. Though the Ashanti were great warriors, that alone was not enough to prevail against modern weapons. Later uprisings by the Ashanti led the British to annex their whole territory.[258]

Over a period of generations, the Gold Coast thus became a British colony, in bits and pieces, with varying degrees of direct and indirect rule. By the early twentieth century, the British had consolidated the colony and their own position in it. Under British rule, progress was made against some of the Gold Coast's many debilitating and deadly tropical diseases, and the country's exports increased greatly. Deaths from Malaria were substantially reduced and yellow fever was almost completely eliminated. Among animal diseases, rinderpest was brought under control.[259] In the economy, the total value of exports from the Gold Coast or Ghana increased more than four-fold from 1907 to 1928 and almost ten-fold from 1928 to 1959.[260] Cocoa, introduced in 1879, became the prime export product, constituting a substantial fraction of the country's total output and accounting for a substantial fraction of its employment and often a majority of its export earnings.[261] The Gold Coast became—and remained—the world's leading producer of cocoa. Gold and manganese production, and exports and imports in general, were largely in British hands, while local commerce was in the hands of Lebanese and Indian businessmen. Cocoa production, however, was in the hands of Africans.

The British built railroads, beginning in 1898, connecting some of the commercial centers with each other, and developed modern transportation and communications links with the outside world. The country's main seaport is a man-made harbor built under the British and opened in 1928.[262] Among the human infrastructure developed under the British was a small but growing educated class, products of missionary schools established in the nineteenth century. As far back as

1881, missionaries set up more than a hundred schools in the Gold Coast, teaching about 5,000 students.[263]

Christian missionaries became an important influence in the Gold Coast, beginning in the coastal areas and then spreading through the southern part of the country. Penetration of the northern areas was more difficult because of transportation problems, and because of the existing presence of Islam there. Thus, as the missionaries established churches, schools, hospitals, and clinics, the impact of these Western influences varied regionally, accentuating cultural differences among the tribes of the Gold Coast. Another factor accentuating internal differences among the African population was the colonial government's need for clerks and other subordinates, recruited locally, but to some extent Westernized by their new roles.

As elsewhere, it was precisely this Westernized minority, a product of European church and state, that provided the impetus for the movement toward independence. As elsewhere, the leaders who came to the fore in the decolonization era were those best able to mobilize politically the grievances and resentments of the populace, and it was such leadership that then took on the very different task of creating a viable country and of meeting the high expectations which they had built up.

As in much of Africa, the emerging indigenous elites were heavily concentrated in clerical and school-teaching occupations, and disproportionately government-employed. By the 1940s there were more than 3,000 African civil servants and more than 3,000 African teachers in the Gold Coast, but fewer than 1,500 merchants and fewer than 1,400 cocoa dealers,[264] even though cocoa was the country's leading product.[265] However, there was also a significant private-economy contribution to the new Westernized African elite in Ghana, largely through the effect of cocoa. This crop was introduced into the Gold Coast by Africans and remained largely an African product, produced by numerous small indigenous peasants.[266]

As of the 1920s, the Gold Coast members of the National Congress of British West Africa, an independence movement, included a substantial representation of merchants (even though lawyers predominated),[267] in contrast with their much smaller role in other African countries. But spearheading the drive for independence was a man much more typical of the African leadership of that era: Kwame Nkrumah, a Western-educated political activist, who had no substantial background in anything else. His special appeal was to the young and the semi-educated,[268] and his political style has been characterized as "ritualistic" or mystical in an ideological, or cult-of-personality sense.[269] His imprisonment for sedition under the colonial government gave him an added appeal to his constituency. As a result of the electoral success of his party in the 1951 elections, Nkrumah was invited from prison to head up the government that would lead Ghana into independence.

Kwame Nkrumah had sweeping ideological goals—sweeping not only within Ghana but also a sweeping Pan-Africanism, with which he hoped to form a trans-national black African unified super-state. Under Nkrumah, power was centralized in the national government as against regional and local bodies. It was centralized in the executive, which subordinated the legislative and judicial branches. Ultimately, power was concentrated in Nkrumah himself, who banned opposition parties, had political adversaries imprisoned without charges for years under preventive detention, and replaced the professional elite in the civil and military services with his own hand-picked men.

Beginning its independence with more human and natural resources than most other black African nations, a higher per capita income,[270] and large foreign reserves, Ghana experienced an almost immediate economic decline in the post-colonial era. By 1965, Ghana's foreign reserves of nearly half a billion dollars in 1958 had turned into a foreign debt of a billion dollars.[271] Nkrumah's economic policies were ambitious, if not effective. He built many "prestige" projects, including a $16 million hall for one meeting of the Organization of African Unity,[272] and a national airline, even though 15 international carriers were flying into Ghana.[273] In 1966, while Nkrumah was en route to China, a military coup ended his regime in Ghana. He went into exile in Guinea, whose president Sékou Touré gave him the honorific title, "co-president."

The new government in Ghana had its own problems and excesses. Scores of Mercedes automobiles were flown in for the new rulers at a cost of more than $100,000 each, plus shipping. Half the foreign exchange received by the government's cocoa marketing agency was unaccounted for. The country's leading export, cocoa, suffered from government controls. The tonnage of cocoa beans and cocoa butter exported both declined sharply between 1966 and 1969, the former by 40 percent in just 3 years and the latter by more than half over the same period. Exports of manganese and bauxite also fell.[274] Stores became bare, transportation broke down. Ghanaians began fleeing to the Ivory Coast and Liberia.[275] From an economy that had been growing during the 1950s there was now a slight *reduction* in real output per person for the decade of the 1960s and a steeper reduction of 2.65 percent per annum between 1970 and 1982.[276] Over this latter period, Ghana's foreign debt rose from less than one-fourth of its annual output to more than a third *more* than its total output.[277]

A second coup in 1978, led by a young air force lieutenant named Jerry Rawlings, replaced the existing military government and began executing its leaders for corruption—including the former head of state, who was accused of banking $100 million of ill-gotten gains in foreign countries.[278] A year later, Rawlings returned power to civilian hands. But the country's economic woes continued. Its national debt rose, it fell years behind schedule in repaying its loans, and inflation exceeded 100 percent per annum.[279] Roads and trucks both fell into such disrepair that the cocoa crop could not be moved to the ports to be exported, and began piling up in government warehouses.[280] At the end of 1981, Lieutenant Rawlings again seized power, and soldiers began looting the shops in the capital of Accra. Civilians also looted, with police looking on.[281]

Rawlings' policies had a strong idealistic and populist flavor, including price controls that—among other things—made it uneconomic to produce cocoa, the country's most important crop. Exchange rates fixed by the government made it uneconomic for foreign industrial firms to continue operating in Ghana, causing drastic cutbacks in employment and earnings.[282] The country's total output declined absolutely, at an average rate of 4 percent per year, during the early 1980s and investment fell by one-third.[283] Ghana's per capita income, which had been more than double that of Nigeria in 1965, was less than half that of Nigeria by 1985.[284] Food shortages developed, the number of doctors declined, as did life expectancy.[285] Rawlings, however, remained popular in Ghana—an economic failure, but a political success. In 1983, however, he made a fundamental change in Ghana's economic policies, following recommendations of the World Bank. The government began to free up the market in various ways. It ended most price controls, devalued the currency internationally, and laid off 50,000 civil servants from a bloated bureaucracy that had increased in size nearly ten-fold between 1972 and 1982. Government-owned businesses were put up for sale.[286]

The response of the economy was dramatic. Ghana's economic growth rate from 1983 to 1988 averaged 6 percent per annum. Once-bare store shelves began to fill up with consumer goods. Streets began to be clogged with imported cars. Reversing years of government policy of keeping cocoa prices to the farmers artificially low, the government tripled the price paid to the producers. Over the next 5 years, cocoa production rose by 20 percent and the smuggling of cocoa to neighboring countries declined. Ghana's economic turn-around was not only a major contrast to its past under Nkrumah and later statist regimes, but was also in sharp contrast to continued economic deterioration in much of sub-Saharan Africa, where per-capita output actually declined 5 percent in 1987.[287] As Ghana's real national output continued to grow into the 1990s under freer economic policies, freer political policies were also allowed. There was a lifting of the ban on political party activity, a new constitution was approved by popular referendum,[288] and military coup leader Jerry Rawlings was elected president in 1996. More generally, there was at least a hope now that Ghana might have a more promising future in the new twenty-first century looming on the horizon.

Ivory Coast

The Republic of the Ivory Coast is a nation of more than 14 million people,[289] spread out over an area larger than France. Like many other African nations, the Ivory Coast is a creation of European colonialism and its national borders divide many ethnic groups, whose brothers live in adjoining nations. This external fragmentation is matched by internal fragmentation. There are 60 ethnic groups in the country, no one of which constitutes more than 15 percent of the population, while more than one-fourth of the population originated outside the Ivory Coast, primarily elsewhere in West Africa. There are numerous indigenous languages, roughly corresponding to the numerous ethnic groups, but French is the official language of what is officially the *République de Côte d'Ivoire*, as it is the language of education, politics, and the urban economy.[290] This too is a legacy of colonialism.

European commercial contacts preceded the colonial era by centuries. There was trade in gold, pepper, slaves, and the ivory which gave the region its name, though the decimation of the elephant population ended the ivory trade in the early eighteenth century. The first known French contact with the Ivory Coast dates back to the fifteenth century and the first French settlements to the seventeenth century. Isolated missionaries, traders, and explorers—operating under agreements with local African authorities—were quite different from French colonial rule, which began to be imposed in the late nineteenth century. Like other colonial powers, the French brought both progress and oppression. Schools were built, the economy modernized, fatal epidemic diseases banished by medical science—and the people were often subjected to direct forced labor or to taxation that forced them to work for whites in order to get money, often to the serious detriment of the native crops with which they fed themselves. Conscription for forced labor was more than an economic loss or a disruption of normal life. Thousands died from the rigors of this forced labor.[291] French colonial officials were under pressure to see that the colonies did not become an excessive burden on France's treasury, and some resorted to the use of whippings, hostages, and even executions to extract taxes from the Africans. Force was also used to change the indigenous agricultural system, to introduce cocoa as a cash crop in the Ivory Coast, for example.[292]

The Ivory Coast was part of a larger colonial empire called French West Africa, and this in turn was part of France's worldwide imperial domains, which included French Equatorial Africa, Algeria, Indo-China, Martinique and French Guiana. The French conquest of the Ivory Coast, like European conquests in much of the rest of Africa, began in the last two decades of the nineteenth century. All of French West Africa combined was about 9 times the size of France itself but, as late as 1920, its total population was only 12 million people. Much of the Ivory Coast consisted of largely uninhabited forests.[293] Even in the late twentieth century, there remained considerable amounts of unused land, as well as other lands allowed to lie fallow for long periods.[294]

Like many other parts of Africa, the Ivory Coast has lacked sheltered harbors and navigable rivers. Its jungles extended down to the water's edge. Large ocean-going vessels could not find suitable places to anchor on the coast and even small craft found the rivers dangerous or impassable, except for modest stretches that were navigable. Large

seasonal rainfall variations still complicate river travel, with rivers
going from dry beds to swollen torrents at different times of the year. In
the modern era, railroads and canals have provided more dependable
travel and shipping conditions, and harbors have been improved.[295]
Before the Europeans came, the people of the region lived in small
tribal groups and their main contact with the outside world was through
long-distance traders. Geographical handicaps, in addition to a dearth
of navigable waterways, included dense jungle covering the southern
half of the country.[296] One of the few outside influences was that of the
Islamic world, whose traders and conquerors spread the Moslem religion into the northern regions of the country. This too left an enduring
legacy. In the late twentieth century, the religion of one fourth of the
population of the country was Islam, making Moslems twice as numerous as Christians, with most of the remainder being followers of native
religions, often with Moslem or Christian admixtures.[297]

The post-independence history of the Ivory Coast diverged considerably from that of other African nations during its first two decades. But
this divergence was the deliberate choice of one leader—and was, in
that sense, very much like the authoritarianism common elsewhere in
post-independence Africa. Félix Houphouët-Boigny was an early political leader in French West Africa, with a movement centered in the
Ivory Coast and articulating the grievances of his fellow Africans
against French colonial policies. Even so, he was seeking amelioration
under colonial rule, not independence. Houphouët-Boigny was the
French-educated son of an African chief. Born in 1905, he became a
physician, a wealthy planter, and a public health official before entering politics in 1944. He spent a dozen years in France, beginning in
1946, first as the Ivory Coast's representative in parliament and then as
the first African to hold a cabinet position in a European government.[298]

The cultural assimilation and acceptance of the small group of educated Africans as "black Frenchmen" operated to mute anti-colonial-
ism and to co-opt its potential indigenous leaders. But the fall of
France in World War II and the rise of the Nazi puppet government in
Vichy undermined the legitimacy of French rule, while the racist and
exploitative policies the Vichy government followed in the African
colonies under Nazi auspices provoked resistance and sabotage. The
African solidarity this promoted was one of the ingredients in the postwar movement toward independence.[299]

After the war, Houphouët-Boigny won great popularity in 1946 for his role in bringing to an end the hated system of forced labor. New civil and political rights followed piecemeal over the years. In 1960, the Ivory Coast became an independent republic within the international French community, with Houphouët-Boigny as its first president.

The post-independence policies of the Ivory Coast differed sharply from those of most other African nations in a number of ways. It avoided executions or coups, and long resisted the widespread policy of building "showcase" industries that could not pay for themselves. It also imposed few restrictions on the transfer of foreign capital or profits and did not succumb to the political temptation to drive out foreigners in order to turn their jobs over to Africans. There were more Frenchmen in the Ivory Coast in the 1980s than there were at the time of independence twenty years earlier, and they filled many important positions in government and the economy. This produced resentments among newly educated Africans seeking careers and urging political "Africanization."[300] The Ivory Coast also made use of technical experts from Taiwan and improved seeds from Brazil, India, and the Philippines.[301] During the 1980s, the World Bank estimated that foreigners held four-fifths of all jobs in the Ivory Coast requiring a college degree.[302]

As of the time of independence, the Ivory Coast was one of the poorest nations in Africa—and in the world. However, despite an initially low level of economic development, poor soils, and few natural resource advantages, the Ivory Coast became one of the few African nations whose economy grew faster after independence than under imperialist rule. The Ivory Coast achieved one of the highest sustained growth rates of any black African nation without major petroleum deposits—and, in fact, one of the highest growth rates in the world.[303] As of the time of independence in 1960, real per capita income in the Ivory Coast was slightly less than in neighboring Ghana, but its per capita income grew at more than 4 percent per year for the decade of the 1960s, compared to less than 2 percent for the decade of the 1950s under French rule. By 1982, real income per capita in the Ivory Coast was 50 percent higher than it was in 1960 and was now also 65 percent greater than in Ghana.[304] The Ivory Coast also remained one of the few countries in Africa that could feed itself.[305]

These policies produced a prosperous peasantry and frustrated Westernized intellectuals,[306] in contrast to the reverse in other African states. In the first quarter of a century after independence, agricultural output in the Ivory Coast doubled and private consumption, exports, and gross domestic product all increased three- or four-fold, while the initially very small manufacturing sector increased five-fold.[307] In little more than a quarter of a century, the country's per capita income rose ten-fold, becoming the highest in any black African nation without petroleum deposits.[308] Among the consequences of these policies was that the Ivory Coast often had balanced budgets and avoided international balance-of-payments problems that plagued other Third World countries.[309]

Although the Ivory Coast had its economic and social problems, including corruption, these did not compare with the chaos, starvation, or mass killings in some other African nations. But its relative success brought neither the country nor its president the kind of attention or acclaim lavished on others, such as Tanzania's Nyerere or Ghana's Nkrumah. Houphouët-Boigny embraced few of the fashionable ideas, from Pan-Africanism to socialism. He was also one of the very few African leaders ever to have run a business enterprise.

Other political office-holders in black Africa, whether at the top or elsewhere in the political and bureaucratic pyramid, tended to come disproportionately from a white-collar or professional background, including school teaching. Former clerks alone accounted for one-fifth or more of the members of the legislatures of Ghana, Senegal, Guinea, and Tanzania, two-fifths or more of the legislatures of Niger, Mali and Upper Volta, and four-fifths in the former Belgian Congo.[310] In the Ivory Coast as well, at the time of independence in 1960, the previous skills of about 40 percent of the members of the National Assembly and the cabinet were either clerical or educational, and two-thirds had worked for the government.[311] But, because of the great role of the head of state in African nations, the fact that the president had a different background apparently accounted for the very different policy approach of the Ivory Coast, and for the very different economic, social, and political consequences.

Houphouët-Boigny's policies not only contrasted with those of Nkrumah in Ghana, the two leaders made a famous bet as to which approach would prove to be more successful. Although Ghana was the more prosperous country at the time and was more richly endowed with natural resources, the subsequent reversal of their respective

economic standings was a dramatic demonstration of the effects of the
two approaches. Even as regards the social position of the poor, one of
the prime talking points of Ghana's more left-wing policies, the Ivory
Coast's policies bore fruit. Although income was less equally distributed in the Ivory Coast than in Ghana, people in the bottom 20 percent
of the income distribution in the Ivory Coast had twice the real income
of people in the bottom 20 percent in Ghana. Indeed, the bottom 20
percent in the Ivory Coast averaged higher real incomes than a majority of the population of Ghana.[312] Partly this was because real income
was rising in the Ivory Coast and falling absolutely in Ghana. Also it
must be noted that even the top 20 percent in the Ivory Coast—"the
rich" by African standards—were making quite modest incomes by
the standards of Western Europe or the United States.

That this impressive record was due to the policies the country followed, rather than to natural resources or other advantages, was
painfully demonstrated in the late 1970s and in the 1980s, after the
Ivory Coast succumbed to the political temptations which had so badly
affected the economies of other African nations. Instead of continuing
its policies of concentrating government expenditures on creating
infrastructure and letting the private marketplace produce goods and
services, the country's new policies, beginning in the late 1970s,
shifted government investment into manufacturing and other state-
owned enterprises. Favorable prices for the Ivory Coast's largely agricultural exports brought in the money required to finance such
ventures. Moreover, the country's good economic reputation internationally enabled it to borrow abroad. However, such transient good fortune provided no basis for an enduring policy. When the prices of such
exports as coffee and cocoa fell in 1978 and the "oil shock" world
recession struck in 1980, a whole era in the economic history of the
Ivory Coast came to an end. Between 1975 and 1980, the country's
external debt rose by 400 percent. By 1990, the cost of servicing its
international debts absorbed 39 percent of the its export earnings,
compared to just 7 percent twenty years earlier.[313]

Even during its earlier good years, when observers spoke of the
Ivory Coast's economic "miracle," it was not a completely free-market
economy. Even then, its ventures into the kinds of state regulation
engaged in more widely by other African nations had not had good
results. For example, the availability of "soft" foreign aid loans for

centralized government planning of rice production led the Ivory Coast into policies that produced a glut of heavily subsidized rice that taxed the storage capacity of the government, cost the national budget far more than originally planned, and led to consumer prices far above those at which rice was available on the world market.[314]

Beginning in the early 1980s, the country's national income declined absolutely while population continued to grow. The long period of one-party and one-man rule likewise ultimately began to take its toll on the Ivory Coast in corruption, in economic problems, and in political repression. In 1992, the capitol city of Abidjan had its worst riots since independence, with political opposition leaders being imprisoned.[315]

After the death of Houphouët-Boigny in December 1993, he was succeeded constitutionally, on an interim basis, by former National Assembly leader Henri Konan Bédie. Bédie's chief rival for the presidency, prime minister Alasane Dramane Ouattara, resigned upon Bédie's accession to the presidency. This and a long period of national mourning, during which political activity was muted, contributed to a smooth transition. Privatization, begun in the last years of Houphët-Boigny, continued under the new regime and this helped turn the economy around.[316] After years of declining national output, the Ivory Coast's real Gross Domestic Product began to grow again, first by a modest 1.8 percent in 1994 and then by a robust 7 percent the following year.[317] After serving as interim president for nearly two years, Bédie was elected in his own right in October 1995, with an overwhelming victory at the polls. However, this presidential victory, winning 96 percent of the vote, was tarnished by the fact that two opposition leaders were barred from running and opposition rallies were forbidden.[318] Moreover, despite favorable economic and political trends, the new president began jailing journalists for even mildly critical writings. Earlier, in May 1995, Bédie's government arrested 11 army officers on suspicion of plotting a military coup, though no specifics were made public. Amnesty International has charged the Ivory Coast with jailing more than 200 people for their political opposition.[319]

By and large, where the Ivory Coast followed its own pragmatic policies in the first decades after independence, it was successful both economically and politically, at least in the sense of avoiding the traumatic problems of other tropical African nations. But, where it followed policies more like those other of African countries, it suffered many of the same consequences.

THE AFRICAN DIASPORA

There have been relatively few African immigrants to other continents, compared to the vast millions transported as slaves to the Islamic countries or to the Western Hemisphere. The story of the African diaspora is thus largely the story of those slaves and their descendants. By the middle of the twentieth century, however, there were also small but historically important groups of African expatriates in Europe and America who returned to Africa to assume leadership of the struggle for independence, and then leadership of the newly independent African states. Even aside from African emigrants and expatriates, however, the African diaspora is not co-extensive with all African slaves and their descendants. The numbers of people enslaved within Africa itself exceeded the numbers exported. History has largely forgotten them.

The Islamic Countries

Although the Islamic countries of the Middle East and North Africa imported more slaves from sub-Saharan Africa than did the European off-shoot nations of the Western Hemisphere,[320] there are in these Moslem countries today no such large, discrete and self-conscious groups of black African descent as the 60 million Negroes currently living in the Western Hemisphere.[321] Among the reasons for this anomaly were the higher mortality rates of slaves in transit to North Africa and the Middle East, their greater vulnerability to the diseases of that region, and a very low rate of reproduction.

Because the slaves were brought from long distances, often from isolated villages, they might lack biological resistance to the diseases encountered along the overland slave trade routes or at their final destinations. Although manumission was widespread in Islamic lands, the beneficiaries of this were often military slaves and others in higher occupations, where the slaves were more apt to be white rather than black.[322] In general, black slaves were used in more menial and laborious tasks, and it was these slaves who were most likely to live and die as slaves, with their children being born into slavery. They had few children, however, for both marriage and casual sex among slaves was suppressed.[323] Moreover, the death rate among those few children was so high that they rarely lived to adulthood.[324]

The widespread use of eunuchs in the harems of the Islamic countries further reduced the ability of the African slave population to reproduce itself. In the tenth century, the court of the caliph of Baghdad reportedly included 7,000 black eunuchs and 4,000 white eunuchs.[325] With the passing centuries, as European nations grew militarily stronger and become better able to resist the Islamic nations, European slaves became scarcer in the Islamic lands to which they had once been sent in great numbers. Their importation was drastically reduced in the early decades of the nineteenth century, when czarist Russia conquered the Caucasus, from which European slaves were being shipped to the Ottoman Empire.[326] However, as late as the 1850s, orders against the traffic in white slaves from Russian-controlled Georgia and Circassia were being issued by the Ottoman government.[327] By the end of the nineteenth century, white slaves had virtually disappeared, except in Arabia, while black slavery was not abolished in most Islamic countries until the period between the two World Wars of the twentieth century[328] and still existed in Mauritania and the Sudan at the end of the twentieth century.[329]

The horrors of the Atlantic voyage in packed and suffocating slave ships, together with exposure to new diseases from Europeans and other African tribes, as well as the general dangers of the Atlantic crossing in that era, took a toll in lives amounting to about 10 percent of all slaves shipped to the Western Hemisphere in British vessels in the eighteenth century—the British being the leading slave traders of that era. However, the death toll among slaves imported by the Islamic countries, many of these slaves being forced to walk across the vast, burning sands of the Sahara, was twice as high.[330] Thousands of human skeletons were strewn along one Saharan slave route alone—mostly the skeletons of young women and girls. These skeletons tended to cluster in the vicinity of wells, suggesting the last desperate efforts to reach water.[331] Slaves who could not keep up with the caravans, often because their feet had swollen from walking across the hot sands, were abandoned in the desert[332] to die a lingering death from heat, thirst and hunger. In 1849, a letter from an Ottoman official referred to 1,600 black slaves dying of thirst on their way to Libya.[333] On another route, it was said that someone unfamiliar with the desert might almost be able to find his way just by following the trail of skeletons of people and camels.[334]

Widespread loss of life began with the initial slave raids. As late as 1886, an Austrian who was an apologist for slavery nevertheless reported "Negro villages are burned, all the men killed, and their women and children are taken on months-long, terrible marches."[335] The march from slave-gathering areas, like the region around Lake Chad, across the Sahara Desert to the Mediterranean Sea took about three months and often only the strongest survived.[336] Other slave routes to Islamic countries were over water, but this meant risking interception by the British Navy, and that in turn often meant that slaves were thrown overboard to drown rather than being allowed to remain on board to be discovered as incriminating evidence. The trans-Saharan caravan route was the most deadly, however. It has been estimated that, for every slave to reach Cairo alive, ten died on the way.[337] Nor was Cairo exceptional. Missionary explorer David Livingstone, among others, estimated that several slaves were captured for every one that reached the Mediterranean alive.[338]

Women were particularly vulnerable[339]—and were more in demand than men. They brought higher prices in the Islamic countries, where they were widely used as domestic servants or as concubines. Ethiopian women sold for higher prices than Negro women, and white women from the Caucasus brought the highest prices of all.[340] A special danger to men and boys was castration, to produce the eunuchs widely used in Islamic countries for work in the harems. Because the operation was forbidden under Islamic law, it was usually performed early—and often crudely—before reaching areas under the effective control of the Ottoman Empire. An estimated ninety percent of the men or boys died from the operation, though some groups of slave traders were sufficiently skilled to have much lower mortality rates.[341] Eunuchs brought far higher prices than other slaves.[342]

Dead and dying slaves were a common sight in the wake of a slave caravan. David Livingstone said that the "common incidents" of the slave trade that he had seen were "so nauseous that I always strive to drive them from memory." For example: "One woman, who was unable to carry both her load and young child, had the child taken from her and saw its brains dashed out on a stone."[343] It was not only the Christian missionary Livingstone who was shocked by the brutality of Arab slave raiders and traders. So was Mohammed Ali, the ruler of Egypt, who was a battle-hardened military commander.[344]

The prime destination of the African slave trade to the Islamic world was Istanbul, capital of the Ottoman Empire, where the largest and busiest slave market flourished.[345] There women were paraded, examined, questioned, and bid on in a public display often witnessed by visiting foreigners, until it was finally closed down in 1847 and the slave trade in Istanbul moved underground.[346] In other Islamic countries, however, the slave markets remained open and public, both to natives and foreigners. In 1868, a British captain witnessed the scene at a slave market in Zanzibar: "Rows of girls from the age of twelve and upwards are exposed to the examination of throngs of Arab slave-dealers and subjected to inexpressible indignities by the brutal dealers."[347] This market functioned until 1873, when two British cruisers appeared off shore, followed by an ultimatum from Britain that the Zanzibar slave trade must cease or the island would face a full naval blockade.[348] This was part of a wider crackdown on the seaborne slave trade in 1873, which caused the trade to become localized, rather than to disappear entirely.[349]

The treatment of slaves in transit by slave traders often differed from the treatment of slaves at their destinations, but this varied according to both the geographical destinations and the occupational destinations of the slaves. A domestic slave in Istanbul might receive much milder treatment than a plantation slave in East Africa. Although slaves in the Islamic world performed a wide variety of work—pearl divers in the Persian Gulf,[350] seamen in the Indian Ocean and Red Sea,[351] agricultural laborers in Ethiopia[352] or Zanzibar[353]— domestic service was much more common in the Islamic world than in the Western Hemisphere and plantation labor was much rarer.

Wealthier men in the Ottoman Empire often had harems with hundreds of women and substantial numbers of eunuchs to work there. In the Sultan's palaces, black eunuchs worked in the women's quarters while white eunuchs worked in his court.[354] Both sets of eunuchs included leaders who achieved a certain prosperity and influence, or even wealth and power, but of course they perpetuated neither their race nor their culture. Eunuchs were sometimes trusted with high military or civilian posts, on grounds that they had no incentive to try to establish a rival dynasty, nor were they likely to be corrupted from their duties by the seductions of women.

While the treatment of slaves by their ultimate purchasers, as distinguished from the slave traders who brought them to market, has been considered generally milder in the Islamic world than in the Western Hemisphere plantation societies, the evidence is much sketchier, for there was no organized anti-slavery movement in the Moslem countries, as there was in Britain, the United States and elsewhere in Western civilization, to serve as a source of information on abuses of slaves. There was no market in these countries for literature such as the novel *Uncle Tom's Cabin*, or for the autobiographies of Frederick Douglass and other former slaves. There was in general very little writing about slavery in the Islamic world, where slavery was simply not an issue.[355]

Plantation slavery in the Western Hemisphere was not surrounded by walls, and so could be observed by outsiders, many of them critical of the institution of slavery itself and alive to its abuses. What happened behind the walls of Ottoman Empire homes and palaces is much less known. Still less can anyone know today what was in the minds and hearts of those slaves—how they felt about being a degraded people in a foreign land, how a eunuch felt about being deprived of a normal family life, how a concubine felt about being made available (without regard to her own feelings) to her owners or to whomever her owner might give, lend, or sell her. What is known is that there was an extremely low reproduction rate among the Africans enslaved in the Moslem countries. Black women who had children sired by slave-owners were sometimes freed but the magnitude and effect of this phenomenon were not such as to leave a major black population in the region. The story of the African diaspora today is thus largely the story of the descendants of Africans in the Western Hemisphere.

The Western Hemisphere

More Africans than Europeans were transported to the Western Hemisphere in the first four centuries after Columbus. As of 1820, there had been nearly half again as many Africans as Europeans transported to the Spanish colonies of Latin America, nearly six times as many Africans as Europeans transported to Brazil, and about eight times as many Africans as Europeans transported to the West Indian colonies of Britain, France, Holland, and Denmark. The United States was an exception, but even here the white majority who migrated to the New World outnumbered the blacks transported involuntarily by less than 20 percent.[356]

For the Western Hemisphere as a whole, about four times as many Africans as Europeans arrived in the period up to 1820.[357] However, because of the far higher mortality rates among the slaves—whose numbers could be maintained in most of the hemisphere only by continuing large-scale importations—migration statistics did not match the statistics on the respective resident black and white populations as of a given time. Thus, the resident white population in the United States in 1820 outnumbered the resident black population by more than four to one. In most of the rest of the Western hemisphere, people of African ancestry still outnumbered people of European ancestry, though not by as wide a margin as among those transported.[358] Over time, rising European immigration and a declining slave trade from Africa changed the demographic picture dramatically. By 1835, the resident white population of the Americas was more than double that of the resident black population.[359]

The formal banning of the international slave trade by Great Britain in 1808 did not immediately end the shipment of slaves across the Atlantic. Indeed, it was 1831 before the number of Europeans coming to the Western Hemisphere in a given year exceeded the number of Africans. From that point on, however, the number of slaves transported drifted slowly downward and then dropped precipitously in the 1850s. Conversely, the number of European immigrants rose dramatically, exceeding the Africans by nearly one-fifth in the 1830s, by four-fifths in the 1840s, and then by nearly twenty-fold in the 1850s.[360]

The European and African populations differed not only racially and in being free and unfree, respectively, but also culturally in at least two different senses. In addition to the differences between cultures brought over from Europe and those brought over from Africa, these cultures differed in their survivability in the New World. Particular cultural groups from Europe tended to cluster together in highly localized communities throughout the Western Hemisphere,[361] while Africans on a given plantation were often from culturally diverse areas of Africa and were forced by circumstances, as well as by the whites in charge, to acquire the language of the country in which they now found themselves. Because there were some common denominators among the cultures of West Africa,[362] where most of the slaves in the Western Hemisphere originated, the cultural contrast between the situation of blacks and whites in the New World cannot be carried to extremes, but it was a contrast nonetheless. In some cases, a mixture of slaves speaking different languages and from different cultural backgrounds was deliberately chosen by slaveowners, as a strategy to reduce solidarity and the risk of conspiracies among the slaves.

Slavery in the Western Hemisphere was largely plantation slavery, involving the routine drudgery of growing and harvesting a single crop, such as sugar in the tropics or cotton in the southern United States. Other crops were grown and other tasks had to be performed besides those of the plantation field hands, but the routine, unskilled labor of the field was the primary task of Africans in the New World. Thus they entered Western civilization at the bottom, acquiring only the rudiments of that culture, such as the spoken language and familiarity with the simplest technology. To varying degrees they lost the culture they brought over from Africa, without acquiring the full range of European culture. The most extreme examples of this pattern were the blacks in the United States.

From as early as the seventeenth century, most Negroes in the American colonies were born on American soil.[363] This was the only plantation society in the Western Hemisphere in which the African population consistently maintained its numbers without continual, large-scale importations of slaves from Africa, and in which this population grew by natural increase.[364] By contrast, Brazil over the centuries imported six times as many slaves as the United States, even though the U.S. had a larger resident slave population than Brazil—36 percent of all the slaves in the Western Hemisphere, as compared to 31 percent for Brazil. Even such Caribbean islands as Haiti, Jamaica, and Cuba each imported more slaves than the United States.[365] The net result was that more of the African culture survived in other slave societies, where that culture was continually replenished by new arrivals. African languages, for example, were still being spoken in Brazil at least as late as the end of the eighteenth century.[366] The influence of African music survived throughout the Western Hemisphere,[367] even in the United States, where American Negroes evolved new musical forms from it that became a central part of American popular music in general.

The exceptional nature of the American experience is related in part, and perhaps principally, to the geographical distance of the United States from Africa, which made the U.S. the farthest removed of all the plantation slave societies in the Western Hemisphere. It was much easier for Brazil to transport new slaves from Africa than for the United States to do so, the U.S. being so much farther from the source of supply. A slave in the United States in the mid-nineteenth century cost thirty times what he cost on the coast of Africa.[368] American slave-owners were very reluctant to lose this kind of investment—so much so that they often hired Irish immigrants to do work considered too dangerous for slaves.[369] Likewise, infant mortality rates among slaves in the antebellum South were a fraction of what they were in the West Indies,[370] much less what they were in countries closer to Africa.

In the Caribbean and in Brazil, it was considered to be cheaper to buy new slaves from Africa than to raise local slaves from infancy to working age.[371] This approach meant, among other things, importing more men than women, working slaves harder, even if this reduced their lifespan, and paying less attention to the needs of pregnant women or newborn babies. The much higher mortality rates among slaves in the Caribbean and Latin America reflected these patterns.[372] Brazilian slaves had a declining life span and Jamaica's slave population had a rate of natural *decrease* ranging from 1.5 percent to 3.7 percent annually during the eighteenth century.[373] Although much has been made of the fact that Latin slave societies tended to have laws more protective of the slave as a human being than the laws of Anglo-American societies,[374] laws were largely ineffective against slave owners throughout the Western Hemisphere.[375] Even the death of a slave from over-work or from brutal whippings was likely to go unpunished.

The more fundamental differences in the treatment of slaves were between those societies which could readily and economically replenish their supply from Africa and those which could not. The society least able to do this—the United States—better preserved the lives of existing slaves and paid more attention to pregnant slave women and their newborn babies. Only after the British ban on the international slave trade in 1808 made replacements from Africa less available did the slave population of Barbados begin to reproduce itself, and that of Jamaica began to approach that condition only in the waning years of slavery there.[376]

The general demographic make-up of different societies in the Western Hemisphere was likewise reflected in their racial policies. Where the African-ancestry population (slave and free) vastly outnumbered the European-ancestry population, whether in Latin America or in British colonies like Jamaica, the legal and social gap between slaves and free blacks tended to be widened, and elaborate racial gradations among "free persons of color" were recognized and different rights assigned to each—all with the effect of fragmenting the African-ancestry population in a divide-and-conquer pattern. Where the Europeans were clearly powerful enough to suppress all the African-ancestry population—as in Canada and in the American South—then a sharp black-white dichotomy was maintained in law and practice. In turn, this meant that internal color differences among the African-ancestry populations of the Western Hemisphere tended to make a greater social difference to the Negroes themselves in Latin America and the Caribbean than in the United States.

One consequence of these regional differences in the treatment of different segments of the African-ancestry populations were differences in racial solidarity among these geographic regions. For example, it was much more common for "free persons of color" to own slaves in Latin America and the Caribbean than in the United States. The prime exception in the U.S. was New Orleans—a former Latin American colony acquired in the Louisiana Purchase of 1803—where there was a large class of Negroes owning slaves.[377] One-third of the free colored families in New Orleans owned slaves and 3,000 "free persons of color" joined the Confederate army during the Civil War.[378] Charleston, South Carolina, another exception, had many slave-owning "free persons of color" from the British West Indies and Santo Domingo.[379] Elsewhere in the United States, where blacks owned other blacks as slaves, it was often only nominal ownership of members of their own family, given the high legal costs of obtaining freedom papers. Some whites, especially Quakers, also held nominal slaves for similar reasons, while those technically in bondage in fact lived the lives of free persons.

Demography affected the development of Africans in the Western

Hemisphere in other ways. Where a rough cross-section of European society was transplanted to the Western Hemisphere—both men and women, with widely varying skills and spread over a wide range of social and economic levels—there it was possible to confine Africans and their descendants to a narrow range of low-level occupations and roles. This was essentially the situation in the United States. But, where a predominantly male group of conquerors and settlers took control of a Western Hemisphere colony, then many more occupations, including those of skilled artisans, had to be filled by non-whites, and sexual liaisons developed with women of both African and aboriginal ancestry, leading to whole classes of mixed-ancestry people, both free and enslaved. This was the situation in much of Latin America and in the Caribbean colonies of various European nations.

The proportion of the African ancestry population that was free varied greatly from society to society in the Western Hemisphere. In Jamaica, for example, less than one-tenth of the Negroes were free in the eighteenth century and this proportion grew to only 11 percent on the eve of emancipation in 1834.[380] In Barbados, the slaves outnumbered the free Negroes even more so.[381] Yet, in the Spanish colonies, it became common for the free persons of color to outnumber the slaves—in Argentina, Mexico, Peru, and Puerto Rico, for example, and for Spanish America as a whole,[382] though not in Cuba until the late nineteenth century.[383] However, in much of Spanish America, slavery itself was not a large-scale institution, nor Negroes a significant proportion of the population. In the Portuguese colony of Brazil, where slavery was indeed a major institution, the free colored outnumbered slaves in some provinces, but not all.[384] In the French colony of Martinique, slaves outnumbered free persons of color but, in another French colony, Santo Domingo, it was just the reverse.[385]

While freedom and slavery are a stark dichotomy, in many Western Hemisphere societies there were in fact important gradations of freedom on a continuum between these polar extremes. The plantation field hand, working under the direct threat of the lash, was at one end of this continuum. Domestic slaves in general, and urban slaves in particular, had some respite from the worst oppressions of slavery, as well as opportunities to become familiar with European culture at a somewhat higher level. They could, for example, hear the language of the country as spoken by a higher class of people, rather than as spo-

ken by semi-literate white overseers. Some domestic slaves could sur-
reptitiously learn to read and write, though literacy was expressly forbidden to slaves in Western Hemisphere societies. Urban slaves, on
their own, often found employers to work for, giving part of their pay to
their owners in exchange for the privilege of living virtually as free
persons.[386] Finally, the "free person of color" was not fully free, being
subjected to many petty and sometimes humiliating legal requirements which did not apply to whites.

While slave populations in the Western Hemisphere were often
more male than female, especially on the sugar plantations in the tropics, the "free persons of color" were more female than male throughout
the hemisphere.[387] This reflected a tendency of women to be set free
more readily than men, often after bearing a child by a slave owner or
overseer. Thus "free persons of color" tended to differ from the
enslaved African population, not only in legal status but also in skin
color, cultural exposure, and sex ratios.

Plantation field hands were the least likely to be freed or to escape
successfully. House servants, urban slaves, or skilled artisans among
the slaves, were more likely to be able to earn money or the gratitude of
whites, or to form personal ties across racial lines—all of which could
be useful in ultimately gaining freedom. Moreover, existing slaves of
mixed ancestry were more likely to be given such coveted jobs. Some of
the more privileged ones were sometimes only nominally in bondage.
Blanche K. Bruce, who was later to become the first Negro Senator in
the Reconstruction era, was in childhood tutored alongside his white
master's son—or *other* son, according to those who suspected that his
master was also his father.[388] Nominal slaves were not uncommon, nor
was it uncommon for them to be mulattos. In antebellum Savannah, for
example, two of the churches in the free Negro community were headed
by ministers who were among the most prosperous members of that
community, even though they were, legally speaking, slaves.[389]

The extent to which the "free persons of color" were of mixed
ancestry varied from society to society—but it tended always to be
greater than the extent to which slaves were of mixed ancestry. In the
United States, 37 percent of the free Negroes were officially classified
as mulattos, compared to only 8 percent among the slaves.[390] This did
not mean that all other Negroes were of unmixed African ancestry, for
the term "mulatto" was often used narrowly in the United States to

mean half-white or more, omitting many other people of mixed African and European ancestries. But, whatever the term "mulatto" meant in different countries, it applied far more often to the free Negroes than to those in bondage. In Brazil, for example, the great majority of free Negroes were mulattos and the great majority of the slaves were black.[391] More than half of the "free persons of color" in Barbados and Surinam were also mulattos.[392] Mulattos commonly had a higher official status in slave societies of the Western Hemisphere, except in the United States,[393] where the black-white dichotomy was what mattered in law and practice, though even in the United States there were informal advantages for mulattos.[394]

Some "free persons of color" prospered and, especially in Latin America, passed into the white population, but most did neither. Nevertheless, however modest the achievements of most free Negroes, they had a very sizeable head start over enslaved blacks in literacy, acculturation, and experience as free people responsible for managing their own lives. In addition, they were more likely to have skills, money, or connections, even if on a modest scale. Education and acculturation in general spread very unevenly among American Negroes—first reaching the house servants and later the field hands, first the free and then the slaves, first the mulattos and then the blacks. These large historic social disparities within the African-origin population of the United States were reflected in the fact that some American Negroes graduated from college before slavery was abolished, while Negroes in the United States as a whole averaged no more than a sixth-grade education as late as 1940.[395] In the middle of the twentieth century, most of the Negro professionals in Washington, D.C. were by all indications descendants of the antebellum "free persons of color"[396]—a group that was never more than 14 percent of the American Negro population.[397]

Social, economic and cultural disparities within the African ancestry population of the Western Hemisphere were also reflected in a social separation that took generations, or even centuries, to erode. In Peru, as early as the seventeenth century, locally born Negroes worshipped separately from African-born Negroes, and then even the locally born separated again into mulatto and black congregations.[398] Throughout the era of slavery, free mulattos in the Western Hemisphere tended to distance themselves socially from blacks, both slave and free.

Although such openly-acknowledged color-consciousness was not as common in the African-ancestry population of the United States as in South America and the Caribbean, nevertheless the elite among American Negroes tended to remain, for generations after emancipation, a distinctly lighter-complexioned and socially exclusive group.[399]

In nineteenth-century Philadelphia, for example, 85 percent of mulatto men married mulatto women and 93 percent of black men married black women. Moreover, even when mulatto women married black men, these were usually black men in the top occupations among people of African ancestry.[400] Conversely, when black women married mulatto men—as fewer than 3 percent of black women did— these mulatto men were more often from the bottom occupational categories. Both patterns reflected the superior social status accorded to lighter-skinned people within the Negro community. More than skin color differences were involved, however. Crime rates were higher and housing poorer in the black neighborhoods than in the mulatto neighborhoods and a smaller percentage of black children attended schools than was the case among mulatto children.[401] A larger proportion of mulattos worked in higher-level occupations and averaged larger amounts of wealth.[402]

Philadelphia was not unique in any of these respects. In antebellum Savannah, for example, the most prosperous individuals among the free persons of color were mulattos and these tended to marry other mulattos, rather than the darker members of the free Negro population. Marriages between slave and free Negroes were more common in Savannah than marriages between mulattos and blacks.[403] For generations to come, all across the country, north and south, the elite of the American Negro community tended to be lighter in complexion than the masses—and to be very self-conscious, and sometimes snobbish, about that fact.[404] They, as well as whites, often attributed their success to Caucasian genes, rather than to historical circumstances and cultural opportunities.[405] Underlying these social phenomena was an economically very consequential transfer of valuable human capital, varying according to prior social and biological relationships with the white population, from which this human capital came.

In New Orleans during the Reconstruction era after the Civil War, 91 percent of Negro politicians were mulattos, in some cases more accurately described as quadroons or octoroons—people with only one fourth or one eighth African ancestry.[406] When light-skinned and dark-skinned Negro soldiers were separated for mental testing in one of the U.S. Army camps during the First World War, the darker Negroes turned out to have higher rates of illiteracy and the lighter-skinned Negroes to score higher on mental tests.[407] Nor was this an isolated result. A comprehensive survey of mental test results among American Negroes found that those of visibly mixed ancestry tended to score higher than those of apparently unmixed African ancestry.[408] This correlation between skin color and other social qualities was not merely a "perception" or an arbitrary "stereotype," but a fact. That this fact may be explained historically by one group's earlier and better access to higher levels of European culture, rather than by genetics, did not prevent it from being a fact nevertheless. Very real behavioral differences, as well as snobbery and vanity, underlay a tendency of the more fortunate and lighter-skinned segment of the African-ancestry population to separate itself from the black masses.

Such differences within the African-ancestry population were not limited to the United States, nor had such differences disappeared entirely by the late twentieth century. In Brazil, as late as 1980, blacks and browns were almost as residentially segregated from one another in Brazilian cities as blacks were from whites—and more so than browns from whites.[409] While the degree of urban residential segregation in general was not as great in Brazil as in the contemporary United States, the historic differences within the African-ancestry population of Brazil were similar and similarly persistent, not only as regards residential patterns but also as regards marriage patterns.[410]

As with other groups around the world, historic head starts have had enduring consequences. Long after general emancipation erased the legal distinction between "free persons of color" and the masses of blacks, their respective descendants continued to show large gaps in achievement. For example, it would be 1900 before the Negro population of the United States as a whole reached the level of literacy achieved by the "free persons of color" in 1850, and it was 1940 before American Negroes as a group would be as urbanized as the "free persons of color" were in the middle of the nineteenth century.

The Aftermath of Slavery

After enduring for thousands of years on every inhabited continent, the institution of slavery was obliterated throughout the Western Hemisphere in a period of little more than half a century. Brazil was the last nation in the hemisphere to abolish slavery in 1888, a quarter of a century after Abraham Lincoln's Emancipation Proclamation in the United States and just over half a century after slavery was abolished in the British colonies. Remarkable as the abolition of slavery was, its social consequences were not so readily abolished, and in fact endured for generations.

While the Civil War ended the legal distinction between slave and free people of African ancestry in the United States, it did not end these internal social divisions. Color stratification, in fact, tended to become more rigid,[411] now that vast numbers of newly emancipated blacks demographically swamped the "free persons of color," who were determined not to be swamped socially as well. New Orleans, with its Caribbean cultural heritage, was and remained the most extreme example of internal social stratification by color, but internal social exclusiveness based on skin color also remained important among Negroes in Chicago at least as late as the 1940s and in Washington, D.C., even after World War II.[412]

Both conservative apologists and radical critics of Western civilization have attempted to make the case that the institution of slavery made an important contribution to the economic and cultural development of the West. It has been claimed, for example, that the slavery of ancient times made possible the classical culture of Greece and Rome. However, it would be extremely difficult to sustain such a case for the slavery of the past five centuries, for which evidence is more abundant.

No nation in the Western Hemisphere, and perhaps no nation anywhere in history, so prodigally consumed so many millions of slaves as Brazil. Yet, when Brazil became the last nation in the hemisphere to abolish the institution of slavery in 1888, it was still an economically underdeveloped country. Its later industrial and commercial development was largely the work of European immigrants, who accomplished a more general and enduring transformation of the Brazilian economy within two generations than had occurred during centuries of slavery.

The most economically developed parts of Brazil—indeed, the industrial heartland of all Latin America—are precisely those areas in the southern regions of the country settled by immigrants from Germany, Italy, and Japan.[413] Even in the late twentieth century, the less developed northeastern region of Brazil continued to have a non-white majority, while the more developed and more prosperous regions continued to have a white majority.[414] Similarly in the United States, the regions where slavery was most heavily concentrated tended to be the most economically backward regions, whose white populations seldom had as high incomes as in states where slavery had never been a major institution. In Europe, it was the nations in the western region of the continent, where slavery was abolished first, that led the continent and the world into the modern industrial age.

Racial oppression was another legacy of Western society and of slavery. The Islamic countries were never as racist as the Western world, though they became more racist than before, after their large-scale importation of African slaves.[415] Among Western Hemisphere nations, racial oppression was at its worst in the United States, especially in the former slave states of the South. Lynchings of Negroes peaked at 161 per year in 1892 in the United States,[416] while this phenomenon remained unknown in Latin America and the Caribbean.[417]

Brazil, in particular, has long been noted for more relaxed race relations than the United States and, despite later revisions of Brazil's image as a country completely free of racism, it clearly has had far less racial oppression than the United States. This makes all the more striking the fact that Brazil has had larger black-white disparities in education than the United States, and Brazilians of African descent showed less upward mobility than Americans of African descent.[418] As of 1976, the average income of mulattos in Brazil was approximately half of white income and that of blacks barely more than one-third.[419] By contrast, the Negro or African-American average income in the United States was more than half that of white Americans decades earlier.[420] As of the same year, 1976, black men in the United States were earning three-fifths of the income of white men, while black women were earning 91 percent of the income of white women.[421] Clearly this was the opposite of what would be expected on the assumption that racial discrimination is the crucial factor in economic progress. However, this apparent anomaly is much more readily understandable in terms of "human capital" differences between the African-origin populations of the two countries. American Negroes, being predominantly native-born even in colonial times, became the most culturally Europeanized of all African-origin populations in the world—and the most prosperous. The contrast between blacks in Haiti and those in the United States makes the same point even more sharply. Haitian blacks, having been independent of whites for more than two centuries, should be the most prosperous in the hemisphere and American blacks the poorest, if racial oppression accounts for poverty, but in fact their respective economic positions are directly the reverse—again suggesting that human capital has a greater effect than racial oppression.

The advantages of those Africans who acquired European cultures are demonstrable in many other ways as well. Even during the era of slavery, blacks who returned to Africa from Brazil were more in demand than Africans reared in the indigenous culture, and their descendants continued to be prominent among the African elite in Nigeria, for example.[422] American Negroes who settled in Liberia in the early nineteenth century maintained an ascendancy and even a despotic rule over indigenous Africans for more than a century, until overthrown in a coup in 1980.[423] Among indigenous Africans in Africa, those more in contact with Europeans, whether in ports, capital cities, or missionary schools, advanced economically much more rapidly than their compatriots in the remote countryside—not only during the period of European colonialism, but also long afterward, in the era of independence. Most of the leaders of newly independent African nations were men educated in Europe or the United States and thoroughly Westernized. Even when they promoted Pan-Africanism, for example, they were promoting a kind of thinking found in Europe (like Pan-Slavism or Pan-Germanism) but wholly foreign to the indigenous cultures of Africa, with their heavy emphasis on community, family, and tribal ties.

Because Africans in the Western Hemisphere diaspora were introduced to European culture through the institution of slavery, it is difficult to disentangle the effects of slavery from the effects of European culture itself. Most Africans enslaved in the Western Hemisphere were introduced only to the lowest levels of European culture—only what they needed to know to function as plantation field hands.

Indeed, laws and practices throughout the hemisphere attempted to prevent their acquiring such rudiments of Western civilization as the ability to read and write, much less such higher values as concepts of human freedom and dignity. Nevertheless, by one means or another, Africans in the Western Hemisphere began the long and slow ascent toward the higher levels of European culture on their own.

By the middle of the nineteenth century, most "free persons of color" in the United States could read and write and, half a century after emancipation, so could more than half the entire Negro population of the country. This has been called "an accomplishment seldom witnessed in human history."[424] The peoples of Yugoslavia, for example, achieved 52 percent literacy only in the 1920s and four-fifths of Albanians were still illiterate at that time.[425] India near the end of the twentieth century had yet to reach the level of literacy achieved by black Americans at its beginning.

Although continuing black-white differences in income, occupations, and other social indicators have been widely attributed to racial discrimination, the experience of black immigrants from the Caribbean in the same society undermines this explanation. As of 1990, the median household incomes of immigrants from Jamaica, Barbados, Trinidad and Tobago all equalled or exceeded that of Americans in general.[426] Selective migration may well have led to an atypical sample of the people of these societies living in the United States. However, the point here is not to compare the blacks of the Caribbean with blacks in the United States, but to compare the theory that racial differences in income are due to discrimination with factual data.

SUMMARY AND IMPLICATIONS

At the heart of the history of modern Africa, and of much of the Third World, has been an enormous disparity in wealth, technology, and resulting power, between the imperial nations of Europe and the peoples of the colonized regions. The magnitude of this disparity enabled various European nations to overcome even desperate struggles of Africans to remain independent by exerting a relatively minor portion of their total resources, acquiring vast areas of Africa that were, in most cases, of minor economic significance in the Europeans' over-all scheme of things. As a scholarly study of wars over the past three centuries has noted, "the casualties and costs of one year of a colonial war were often less than those of one month of a European war."[427]

Africa was, of course, of great importance to Africans, and sometimes to particular European colonial officials, missionaries, and business interests involved there. But to Europeans in Europe it was simply another part of their world empire, and to government officials, especially in Britain, a major concern was that it not become a nuisance or a drain on the treasury. The British policy of "indirect rule" through local native authorities and indigenous institutions—modified to suit colonial purposes—was one result of the desire to minimize expenditure for a given amount of control. In most cases, with such exceptions as the "white highlands" of Kenya or the white-settler societies in Rhodesia and South Africa, there was no thought of establishing a transplanted European society in African countries, as in North America or Australia. But, while indirect rule was a mere expedient to Europeans, it profoundly affected the institutions, society, and futures of the colonized peoples. Often traditional native authorities with limited powers, and with traditional checks against those powers, became little autocrats when backed by the seemingly invincible force of the imperialist nation.

Whites on the scene could be even bigger autocrats. Moreover, low-budget imperialism required the nipping in the bud of ideas, individuals, and movements which might, if unchecked, later necessitate the costly use of troops and war materiel to maintain control. Another expedient of low-cost imperial control was the mystique of the white man,[428] over and beyond what spontaneous racism would produce. While effective for many years, the mystique of the white man was also vulnerable to any major revelation of his human frailties and shortcomings.

The house-of-cards nature of European imperialism in Africa became apparent with the rapid spread of independence in the 1960s. Few of these African nations had to wage the kind of desperate warfare for independence waged by George Washington or Simón Bólivar to achieve independence in the Western Hemisphere. When low-cost suppression failed in Africa, imprisoned African leaders were, in more than one country, simply released from custody and installed at the head of independent states by imperialist governments which, in most cases, did not find the matter worth major warfare.

In those exceptional cases where independence came only after bitter, bloody, and protracted struggles—in Kenya, Algeria, or Rhodesia-Zimbabwe, for example—the key resistance to independence came from European settler communities in Africa, rather than from economic interests within the imperial nations themselves. This is part of a larger pattern of especially bitter relations between indigenous peoples and foreign settlers who refuse to be dislodged from what is also the land of their birth—or to accept rule by the conquered indigenes, with whom they share a history of mutual distrust and hostility. Ulster county in Ireland and Israel's West Bank are other examples, showing that neither large economic interests nor color differences are essential to this phenomenon.

Although Africans have had patterns common to other conquered peoples, they have also been distinctive in some ways. Unlike either the American colonies or Britain under the Roman empire, African countries were in most cases neither replicas of the imperial society nor truly integrated into its legal system or social traditions. Though many newly independent African nations imitated the outward forms of Western democratic societies, the relatively brief period of Western rule could hardly have replicated the centuries of tradition which made democratic institutions viable in Europe and in European offshoot societies overseas. Few of these democratic institutions survived for long after independence in Africa.

The economic achievements of Europe were likewise not readily transferable to Africa, partly because of the severe geographical and climatic handicaps which long retarded economic, cultural, and political development in many parts of the continent. Moreover, the relatively brief history of Africa's exposure to European culture made widespread economic replication of European economic progress no more likely than replication of European democracy. Nevertheless, to some extent European culture did have an effect on Africans. This limited transfer of culture took place in many ways, ranging from unconscious influence to formal study. However, despite an obvious desire in many newly independent African nations to imitate the West, by building industrial manufacturing plants, for example, little of the science, technology, or organizational management skills of the Western world were transferred to Africans.

Although many Africans destined to become leaders of their countries spent years, and in some cases decades, living and studying in

Europe or the United States, what they brought back from the West were not the practical or scientific knowledge and skills behind the wealth and power of the West, but rather the social theories and moral speculations of European and American intellectuals. Much of the painful history of the first quarter of a century of African independence was a history of African leaders, without the practical knowledge or experience of either Africa or the West, attempting sweeping social experiments on their own people, based on the untested theories of Western intellectuals.

The results were often catastrophic. The entire period of a quarter of a century, beginning in 1965, averaged *negative* growth in output per capita in Uganda, Tanzania, Chad, Zambia, Ghana, Senegal, Madagascar, Zaire, Niger, Benin, and the Central African Republic.[429] This meant that many Africans were poorer after a generation of independence than they had been under imperialist rule. After economic debacles, social tragedies, political repressions, and often brutality and bloodshed, some of these countries and their leaders began to change course in the 1980s, freeing up their economies from statist controls and thus tapping the initiative and energies of their own people, leading to economic upturns in economically devastated countries like Nigeria and Ghana. By 1997, perhaps a dozen African countries were growing at 5 percent per year or better.[430]

These upturns suggest that a belated appreciation of pragmatism was beginning to replace the initial fascination with grandiose visions and soaring rhetoric that marked the beginning of the era of independence in Africa. Nevertheless, even in the last decade of the twentieth century, economic growth in Africa as a whole lagged behind that of many other countries in percentage terms, as well as absolutely. However, Africa was not unique in this. The degree of freedom has been found to be correlated with the rate of economic growth for nations in general.[431] For most of Africa, freedom for the people remained an aspiration, three decades after national independence was achieved. What African nations now had, however, that they did not have at the time of independence, was first-hand experience of what kinds of policies produced what kinds of results. Much of this experience was bitter—but an enlightening and potentially valuable heritage as well. As a study of this era concluded, "30 years of experience should not be dismissed lightly."[432]

CHAPTER 4

THE SLAVS

In eastern Europe, successions of regimes have been trying for a thousand years and more to impose a viable political hegemony on the scores of ethnic and national groups in the area, invariably in vain.

Forrest McDonald[1]

The Slavs of Eastern Europe have been both conquerors and conquered. Indeed, they were once part of a chain reaction of conquests in medieval Europe, as successive invaders from Central Asia drove portions of the Slavic population before them out of the Ukrainian steppes into the Balkans and into what is today East Central Europe, where the Slavs in turn forced the Celtic and Germanic populations farther west. In the later Middle Ages, Germanic invaders drove the Slavs back east of the Oder River.[2] To the south, Slavic invaders in the Balkans drove the Vlachs before them and forced them up into the hills and mountains of the region. At various periods of history the Slavs have also lived as conquered people under the Mongols, the Germans, the Bulgars, the Ottoman Turks, the Habsburg Empire, and—not least—under the rule of other branches of the Slavic peoples. Russian hegemony extended over Poles and Ukrainians, for example, as well as over non-Slavic peoples in the Caucasus, Central Asia, and the Baltic.

Nations that were once great empires—Poland, Bohemia, Hungary— later found themselves subjugated by countries that had been nothing by comparison with themselves: Austria, Prussia, and Russia.[3] Galling reversals of fortune such as these added the bitterness of history and the

174

outrage of lost glory to contemporary grievances among the peoples of Eastern Europe in general and among the Slavs in particular. The melange of fragmented peoples which made up the Habsburg Empire, as well as the Russian Empire and the Ottoman Empire, added intergroup frictions to national longings for re-unification with compatriots living under some other conqueror's heel. All of this combined to make Eastern Europe, during much of its history, a powder keg of ethnic violence, political assassinations, and mass uprisings brutally suppressed by autocratic powers—not to mention the national and international armies that have battled across this region time and again, devastating the land and its people.

Like the other peoples of Eastern Europe and the Balkans, Slavs have historically lagged behind the peoples of Western Europe in technology, economic well-being, education, and other indices of development. This lag in economic and cultural development partly reflected great geographical differences between the two regions of the continent. Partly also it reflected the enduring effects of the Roman legacy in Western Europe and its absence in Eastern Europe.

GEOGRAPHIC INFLUENCES

Among the geographic advantages of Western Europe lacking in Eastern Europe has been ready access to the oceans of the world. While no point in Western Europe is more than 350 kilometers from the sea, there are parts of Eastern Europe more than a 1,000 kilometers from the sea.[4] The warming influence of the Gulf stream, which moderates the winters in Western Europe, making them much milder than at corresponding latitudes in Asia or North America, is felt less and less to the east, where the continental climate is more bitterly cold in winter and the rivers are frozen for longer periods of time than the rivers of Western Europe.[5] The Baltic Sea is likewise frozen for months at a time.[6] In the Balkans, the mild, subtropical air of the Mediterranean is blocked off by mountain ranges from reaching much of Eastern and Southeastern Europe, including the hinterlands of the Dalmatian coast. Because of the isolating effect of coastal mountains along the Adriatic shore, winter temperatures inland in Sarajevo may be nearly 50 degrees colder than on the coast, little more than 100 miles away.[7] Many of the rivers of Eastern Europe flow into lakes or inland seas, rather than out into the open waters of the oceans, with their international trade routes, so that the benefits of low-cost access by water to the markets of the world—and the ideas of the world—have historically been far less available in the eastern part of the continent. In the rugged lands of the Balkans, largely lacking navigable rivers and cut off from access to the coast by mountains that come down close to the shore, it has been estimated that in Ottoman times the cost of shipping wheat overland just 100 kilometers exceeded the value of the wheat itself.[8]

The painful economic implications of such high transport costs extended well beyond wheat to commerce and industry in general, and also help explain the cultural insularity which long plagued the region. While Western European nations became the center of trade networks that reached all parts of the world, much of Eastern Europe, and especially the Balkans, remained regions of "self-sufficiency"[9]— which is to say, isolation, backwardness, and poverty. What foreign trade they had was based on supplying raw materials such as wool, grain, and lumber to Western European nations, from whom they bought manufactured goods.[10] Climate and soil are also less favorable in the Balkans, which lacks the more consistent rainfall and more fertile soils of northwestern Europe.[11] The fact that land capable of supporting human life often occurs in isolated patches in mountain valleys has meant that Balkan settlements have often developed in isolation from one another, as well as from the outside world.

For Russia, the colder winter climate of Eastern Europe, compared to Western Europe, means that, although the country has an abundance of rivers, those rivers are not abundantly available for use the year around, nor are the northern seaports, which are likewise frozen a substantial part of the year. Russia's warmer southern ports on the Black Sea have had to connect to the outside world through the narrow straits of the Bosporus and the Dardanelles, controlled by the Turks and by the Byzantines before them. Only after an 1829 treaty were Russian ships allowed through these straits, thus making large-scale grain shipments from Russia economically feasible.[12] The difference that this made is indicated by the fact that Russian grain could then undersell Croatian grain on the Dalmatian coast, since the Russian grain was shipped at low cost by water and the Croatian grain by land,[13] even though the latter was shipped for shorter distances.

While many of the Slavic lands lack the natural resource abundance of Western Europe, Russia's rich deposits of coal, oil and other resources make it one of the most fortunate countries of the world in that regard.[14] However, only relatively recently in its history have Russia's human resources allowed it to realize much of the potential of its natural resources for, as late as the end of the nineteenth century, the vast majority of Russians were still illiterate. As in other regions of the world, physical resources alone have meant little when the complementary human capital was missing.

CULTURAL DEVELOPMENT

Cultural cross-currents have been as powerful and varied in Slavic Eastern Europe as the stormy military and political history of the region. After the Magyars invaded the Hungarian plain from the east during the Middle Ages, a wedge was driven between the Slavs of the Balkans and those farther north, leading to cultural cleavages which developed among the Slavic peoples over the centuries.[15] However, even before this cultural divide was created, the Slavs had never been united politically. They lived as tribal peoples with no national government for centuries. As with many other groups, the focus of their loyalty has often been much more local and not always ethnic.[16] Such bitterly opposed peoples as the Serbs and the Croats, for example, are both Slavs, as are Czechs and Poles, Russians and Ukrainians, all of whose histories have been marked by strife with one another. Culturally, however, what has been most striking about the Slavs are their differences from peoples of Western Europe.

East–West Differences

Western civilization—the civilization of the Roman world and its cultural successors—came centuries later to the Slavs than to the French, the Germans, or the English. Christianity became the official religion of the Roman Empire in the fourth century, but the fact that the Slavs were still pagans in post-Roman times had great secular, as well as religious, significance, when the Catholic Church and the Latin language it used were a culturally unifying force in politically fragmented Europe, and the principal source for learning on the continent. What education and scholarship survived the collapse of Rome in the west were largely the education and scholarship of the church, so that educated people throughout Western Europe literally spoke the same language. An educated Frenchman understood the language of German intellectual writings or German universities as well as a German, for that language was Latin across wide regions of Europe. However, it was centuries later before the Slavs became part of this cultural universe. Moreover, their own cultural universe had no such rich literature as that of Western Europe. Indeed, it had no literature at all until written versions of Slavic languages were developed by scholars from other countries.

While much of Eastern Europe and the Balkans have often been described as "backward," either historically or today, these regions have in fact been like most of the rest of the world in their economic level and political development. They have been considered backward by comparison with the highly atypical development of a relative handful of Western European nations and their overseas offshoots, such as the United States or Australia.

The cultural fault lines in Europe between the heirs of the Roman and Byzantine empires, on the one hand, and those who remained outside this cultural orbit until much later in history, is just one of the sources of the differences in economic, social, and political developments in the various parts of Europe. Nor have these differences been small. At the beginning of the nineteenth century, per capita real income in Eastern Europe was only half of what it was in Great Britain and, after Britain's industrial take-off, only about a third as much by 1860.[17] As late as the twentieth century, real per capita incomes in parts of the Balkans were barely one-fourth of that in industrialized Western Europe.[18] Such economic and other disparities go back for centuries.[19]

One of the most common—and most unsubstantiated—explanations of poverty has been "overpopulation" but, at least as far back as the Middle Ages, population densities in Eastern Europe have been much lower than in Western Europe, whether measured by the ratio of people to land or people to arable land.[20] Travelers in Eastern Europe in medieval times often commented on the vast amount of land lying unused. In Eastern Europe, as in Spain after its reconquest from the Moors, "there was land for the asking."[21] In both cases, there was poverty rather than the prosperity implied by the theory that "overpopulation" causes poverty.

When the Slavs first moved into Eastern Europe in early medieval times, they practiced primitive slash-and-burn agriculture but, by the seventh century, they had largely changed to plowing.[22] Nevertheless, Eastern European agricultural practices for centuries continued to lag behind those in Western Europe, both because the growing scarcity of farm land in Western Europe forced farmers there to try improved methods of cultivation and because Western Europe inherited Greek and Roman legal principles of private property in land, while Eastern Europe lacked this cultural legacy and developed such principles only belatedly. Where Slavs followed practices more like those of Western Europe, they achieved results very similar to those in Western Europe. This tended to happen in areas culturally under German influence, such as Bohemia and western Poland, both parts of Germanic empires.[23]

In the Balkans, where Christianity had existed, at least in the cities, during Roman times, the mass invasions of this region by Slavs during the Middle Ages brought the destruction of cities, the replacement of Christianity by paganism, and the replacement of a sophisticated urban life by a primitive rural existence.[24] More generally, cultural differences between Eastern and Western Europeans were part of a larger and more enduring cultural gulf between those regions and peoples which had never been part of the Roman Empire, or its Byzantine offshoot and successor, and those that were heirs of the cultural traditions established by Rome and Byzantium.

This cultural divide was more salient than the strictly geographical divide, as indicated by the fact that pagan enclaves in early medieval Western Europe, such as Scotland and Denmark, likewise lagged economically and technologically behind those areas where Christianity was a token of a larger Roman cultural heritage and paganism an index of a lack of this heritage.[25] For example, although coins had been minted by the Romans, nevertheless there was no minting of coins in medieval Europe east of the Rhine before the tenth century A.D., just as the Scots and the Danes minted no coins at that time. Coinage spread eastward along with Christianity and other features of Western European civilization—the minting of coins in Eastern Europe first taking place in Poland in the late tenth century and in Hungary in the early eleventh century.[26] Even after the Russian government began minting its own coins, as late as the seventeenth century merchants in Russia rejected their country's kopeks in favor of higher-quality coins from such countries as Germany, Holland, or Sweden.[27] Printing presses appeared in many German and Italian communities during the fifteenth century, but it was the seventeenth century before such presses made their first appearances in Eastern Europe and the Balkans—significantly, first in those parts of these regions culturally dominated by Germans.[28] Even the building of artificial fish ponds began first in Western Europe and then moved, with a lag, eastward.[29]

The military technology developed during the Middle Ages— armored cavalry, stirrups, crossbows, castles and siege machines— followed the same pattern of spreading from Christian to pagan Europe, the latter being primarily Eastern Europe, but also including Celtic and Scandinavian pagan enclaves and other lands more recently turned Christian.[30] Paved streets, which existed in Italian cities in the twelfth century and in the larger towns of Western Europe by the fifteenth century, appeared later in Eastern European cities and towns.[31] Calico printing, which originated in Egypt, likewise spread from Western Europe to Eastern Europe.[32] Textiles were imported into Eastern Europe from the west because the quality of Eastern European textiles was inferior.[33] Among Jews, as among Christians, the Haskalah or enlightenment movement began in Western Europe and then moved east.[34]

Cities in East Central Europe tended to be much smaller than cities in Western Europe. Historically, Eastern Europe tended to be a supplier of raw materials such as grains, wood, and hides to Western Europe, from which it purchased manufactured goods. One sign of this relationship was that trade routes in East Central Europe tended to run from east to west, and it was along these routes that the major fairs of the region were held.[35] With disease-control as well, Eastern and Southern Europe continued to lag behind the nations of the northwestern corner of the continent. Smallpox, for example, continued to ravage the peoples of Eastern Europe and the Balkans, long after vaccination had brought it under control elsewhere in Europe.[36]

Similar patterns appeared with railroad-building. While railroads spread rapidly across Western Europe in the first half of the nineteenth century, they tended to spread later, more slowly, and on a smaller scale in Eastern Europe, and especially so in the Balkans. As late as 1860, there was not a mile of railroad track south of the Sava and the Danube.[37] It was 1878 when the first railroad reached Serbia[38] and there were still relatively few railways in much of the Balkans, even on the eve of the First World War.[39] Later in the twentieth century, the automobile spread from Western Europe to Eastern Europe, as so many other technological advances had for centuries.[40]

Not only was physical infrastructure lacking in much of Eastern Europe and the Balkans, so too was such economic infrastructure as a money economy with financial, commercial, and industrial enterprises.[41] Power looms replaced hand looms in the weaving of cotton in Western Europe by the mid-nineteenth century, while hand looms continued to be used in Eastern Europe.[42] Fairs continued to be important institutions in Eastern Europe, after they were superseded in Western Europe by permanent stores and sophisticated distribution methods. Cloth and leather production continued as domestic activities in the east after they were organized in factories in the west.[43] As many cities in Western and Central Europe grew several-fold in size during the nineteenth century, even towns remained rare in the Balkans, and there was no large city in southeastern Europe other than Constantinople.[44]

Even these striking disparities do not fully capture the lagging economic and technological development of the Slavic population, who were even less urbanized than the region in which they lived. Even though Slavs were the predominant population in medieval Eastern Europe, the towns and cities of that region had predominantly German, Jewish, and other non-Slavic populations.[45] Similarly in the Balkans, where the Slavs were also the predominant population, the larger the town in that region, the more likely it was to be Turkish.[46] Slavs were primarily peasants in the countryside, living close to a subsistence level, and having little margin for experimentation to discover better ways of working or living, or for keeping up with developments elsewhere. As late as the end of the nineteenth century, peasants in Serbia were said to be ignorant of places just ten or fifteen miles away.[47] In the Austrian Empire in 1900, the illiteracy rate among Polish adults was 40 percent, among Serbo-Croatians 75 percent, and among Ruthenians 77 percent—compared to only 6 percent among Germans in the same empire.[48]

Such patterns were not limited to Slavs, however, but were common among the peoples of Eastern Europe and the Balkans in general. More than three-quarters of the Romanians, for example, were still illiterate as late as 1899 and, on the eve of the First World War, half the Romanian children of school age were receiving no schooling.[49] Not only was Romania a predominantly agricultural country, with four-fifths of its population living in rural areas as late as 1930,[50] Romanians were even less urbanized than the various minorities who made up nearly 29 percent of the country's population. In many of the towns and cities of Romania, it was the Romanians who were not only a minority of the population[51] but were often also employed in subordinate roles as servants and unskilled laborers, while Germans, Jews, or others filled the higher-level occupations. In the Romanian province of Bukovina, for example, only a third of the urban population was Romanian in 1930, while fewer than a third of the urban population of Bessarabia and just 35 percent of the urban population of Transylvania was Romanian.[52] In short, the same regional features which held back the Slavs held back the Romanians and other non-Slavs, except for those like the Germans and the Jews, whose more advanced cultures originated elsewhere.

For the peoples of Eastern Europe, isolation from the advances of Western civilization meant not only a loss of potential economic, medical, and other benefits but also, and more fundamentally, an absence of the whole mindset characteristic of modern commercial and industrial societies. A story about a Ruthenian man who was asked what he would charge to shingle a roof is illustrative:

> He was dismayed at the idea of undertaking such a contract, and refused to make any estimate. A Jew was then given the contract, and he came to the same man and offered him a fixed sum, which was accepted, for shingles and shingling, making of course his own profit on the business.[53]

Here the Jewish contractor played a role familiar to middleman minorities around the world, serving as a cultural intermediary to get things done that were mutually beneficial to parties who were prevented by cultural barriers from making the same transaction directly themselves. Often such middlemen are blamed for "exploitation" but the more fundamental problem is that the other potential transactors are in different cultural universes.

In language and literature as well, the Slavs of Eastern Europe and the Balkans lagged behind the peoples of Western Europe. Although the languages and the literature of the Greeks and Romans went back thousands of years, and were known to educated people in Western Europe, the Slavic languages had no writings at all until the Middle Ages, when written versions of these languages were first created—by others—either by adaptations of the Latin alphabet or by creation of a Cyrillic alphabet based upon the Greek language.[54] Only then could the small literate class in Eastern Europe and the Balkans begin to create a Slavic literature, though even they often chose to write in Latin or in one of the vernacular languages of Western Europe, especially when writing on serious subjects.

While the rendering of Slavic languages into a written version began as early as the ninth century, it was the sixteenth century before Polish was rendered into Latin letters. Moreover, while some Slavic languages were rendered in Latin letters, others such as Russian were rendered into the Cyrillic script used in the Byzantine Empire. Modern Serbo-Croatian differs in its Serbian version from its Croatian version primarily by the fact that the former is written in Latin letters and the latter in Cyrillic script.[55] More than a rendering of sounds into writing was necessary, however, for Slavic languages—like other European vernaculars of the early Middle Ages—lacked the ability to express as complex and sophisticated ideas as such classical languages as Latin or Greek.[56] These classical languages had ancient philosophical texts and other advanced intellectual writings of a sort dealt with by an educated elite, while the vernacular languages were the languages of peasants, shepherds, and others whose lives were more narrowly circumscribed in terms of their cultural exposures.

Even after the Slavic languages acquired written versions, the writings in these languages were at first not merely meager in quantity but also very limited in the subjects covered. Even Czech nationalists wrote in German when publishing patriotic or anti-German tracts. Nationalistic promoters of the Czech language in the eighteenth century published primarily children's stories, light romantic novels, or material translated from German or other languages.[57] This was because the masses were the only real market for writings in the Czech language, since educated Czechs were used to reading more sophisticated material in German, Latin, or other languages that had a large and serious world literature. When the Ukrainian and Byelorussian languages were first used in plays, the point was to provide dialogue for comic characters or to make fun of these languages.[58] Moreover, the fact that most Russians, Serbs, and Bulgarians were Greek Orthodox and wrote in the Cyrillic script, while most Poles, Bohemians, and Croatians were Roman Catholic and wrote in Latin letters, created more cultural cleavages among the Slavs, as well as making it more difficult for those unfamiliar with Latin letters to follow cultural, economic, and political developments in Western Europe.

Cultural Transfers

Over the centuries, much of the advancement of agriculture in Eastern Europe was due to the movement of better methods of cultivation from Western Europe. These included improved plows, the horse collar, and new systems of crop rotation.[59] Sometimes this movement of agricultural advances was accompanied by a movement of people from Western Europe, mostly Germans, who were welcomed by Polish, Hungarian, and other Eastern and Central European landed nobility for the greater prosperity they would bring to the region. In order to attract them, these migrants were often given concessions on land, taxes and tithes, and local laws and practices were held in abeyance so that villages and towns were allowed to rule themselves according to German law.[60] In Silesia alone, there were 200 villages under German law at the end of the thirteenth century and 1,200 by the middle of the fourteenth century, when there were also 120 towns under German law.[61]

This law not only spread through urban communities in Eastern Europe, it spread to people who were not German, but who settled in these communities. Still, for much of medieval Eastern Europe, urbanization and cultural Germanization occurred together, just as urbanization and Anglicization went together in medieval Ireland, Scotland, and Wales.[62] Prior to the year 1312, the official records of the city of Cracow were kept in German—and the transition, at that point, was to Latin. Only decades later did Poles become a majority of the population in Cracow.[63] The number of Germans settling east of the Elbe-Saale line in the twelfth century alone has been estimated as 200,000,[64] at a time when populations in general were much smaller than today, so that this number of Germans settling in Eastern Europe meant far more than a similar transplantation of people would mean in modern times. Altogether, by the mid seventeenth century, an estimated one million Germans had moved into Eastern Europe.[65]

German cultural penetration of Eastern Europe was aided in some cases by the imposition of German agricultural practices on local peasants by the ruling Polish authorities.[66] The towns of medieval East Central Europe were cultural enclaves of foreigners—again, mostly Germans, but with many Jews as well and, in the Balkans, Greeks and Armenians, joined in later centuries by Turks.[67] There were "Latin quarters" where Frenchmen lived in two leading Hungarian towns and there were predominantly German mining communities in the Balkans.[68] It was not simply that foreigners congregated in towns. Most of the inhabitants of those towns were foreign, some of the towns being created by foreign settlers, but with the Slavs in any case being an overwhelmingly agricultural people with little or no urban background and few urban skills. Even where there were some native-born merchants in East Central Europe, they were usually no match for more experienced merchants who came from Western Europe and other places with a long history of commerce.[69] In Croatia and Transylvania, most of the towns founded during the Middle Ages were founded by Germans, while such port cities as Dubrovnik developed under Italian cultural influences, even when their populations were Slavic, and Sarajevo owed much of its development to the Ottoman Turks.[70]

Most of the Germans who migrated went to live under Slavic or Magyar rulers[71] though, in some cases, German knights and nobles conquered Slavic regions and subjugated the people living in them. In other cases, local nobles invited in German knights who served under them—and over the Slavic masses.[72] However, some lands passed back and forth between German and Slavic control, as in the case of Brandenburg, for example.[73] Through one process or another, the culturally German regions of Central and Eastern Europe expanded during medieval times. Even such classically German cities as Berlin and Lubeck only became German in the Middle Ages,[74] while much of the land to the east of what is modern Germany also felt the cultural impact of Germans. It was German priests, for example, who converted the Czechs to Christianity.[75]

The German role in Eastern Europe left as one legacy German words in the Slavic languages of the region. The word for fief, for example, in both the Czech and Polish languages, is based on the German word for fief, and words taken from German appear in the language of Hungary for such military things as helmet, armor, and castle.[76] The Polish words for last, pound, and ballast also derive from the corresponding German words.[77] The German language influenced the syntax, as well as the vocabulary, of the Czech language[78] and one of the dialects of Serbo-Croatian contains numerous German (and Hungarian) words.[79] German cultural influence was also shown when the rulers of the medieval Slavic peoples of Mecklenburg began to give their children German names.[80]

Many of the first teachers in Poland, Bohemia, and Hungary came from Western Europe.[81] The first university in Eastern Europe, the University of Prague, was founded in 1348 with a predominantly German faculty. Resentment of this German predominance by native Czech scholars led to preferential treatment for Czechs, which in turn led to an exodus of Germans, which then led to a closing down of the university for years.[82] Thus was enacted a drama repeated in many other parts of the world over many centuries—a transfer of cultural capital hindered or aborted by the politics of resentment. The importance of this cultural capital is indicated by the fact that it was not those parts of Eastern Europe most abundantly supplied with natural resources which became the most economically prosperous regions, but rather those with the most abundant contacts with Western Europe—Bohemia, for example,[83] rather than Russia. Romania, despite its rich soil, had low crop yields because its agricultural practices lagged behind those of Western Europe.[84]

EAST CENTRAL EUROPE

Over the centuries, the political boundaries between the nations of Eastern Europe and the Balkans have shifted greatly—including the disappearance and reappearance of whole countries such as Poland and Ukraine. The very definition of East Central Europe has reflected the turmoil which so often marked the unsettled history of that region. Some have defined it geographically as lands lying west of Russia and east of Germany or, more precisely, as lands bounded by particular rivers, mountains, and seas.[85] Others have defined it linguistically as the region bounded by peoples speaking the German, Italian, and Russian languages.[86] Such a variety of other definitions have come and gone that it has been claimed that the region has been defined at one time or other to include virtually every part of Europe except the Iberian peninsula.[87] Yet the central core of the region can be considered as being the lands comprising today Poland, Hungary, Romania, the Czech Republic, Slovakia, and the Balkan countries. Since the early Middle Ages, Slavs have been demographically predominant among the varied peoples of this region.

The shifting political boundaries which reflect the military conflicts that have plagued the region over the centuries (both world wars of the twentieth century having started in East Central Europe) are also reflected in the multiple names that many of the prominent cities in Eastern Central Europe have had—Gdańsk having also been Danzig, Kaliningrad having also been Königsberg, Bratislava having also been Pressburg, and so on.[88] Mosques converted to churches likewise show the shifting fortunes of conquest and reconquest in the Balkans.[89] In medieval and early modern times, the Slavs of East Central Europe were caught in the crossfire between the rival empires of the Ottomans and the Habsburgs, as they would again be caught between rival big-power blocs throughout most of the twentieth century.

Although Slavs have been the predominant population in East Central Europe for centuries, such groups as the Jews and the Armenians lived in parts of Eastern Europe before the Slavs, who are often thought of as indigenous to the region.[90] At the end of the nineteenth century, for example, there were nearly 2 million Germans in Hungary and more than 3 million in Poland, in addition to more than 2 million Turks in East Central Europe as a whole, and nearly 7.5 million Jews in Eastern Europe, including Russia. However, these non-Slavs were outnumbered by Poles alone, who were 15 million people scattered through Austria, Germany, and Russia.[91] Still, the non-Slavs were not a negligible element and the various Slavs were also scattered as minorities in other Slavic and non-Slavic countries. These ethnic cross-currents have been accompanied by religious cross-currents, with Catholic, Protestant, Orthodox, and Moslem clashes, as well as major heresies such as the Hussite movement among the Czechs in the fifteenth century. Overlaying all this were numerous dynastic struggles and struggles between kings and their own powerful nobles. Few regions of the world have had such fragmented peoples and cultures or such intractable conflicts.

The interpenetration of cultures was often bitterly contested. Those who felt superior did not want their superiority diluted by inferior cultures and those who resented the more fortunate economic and social conditions of others sought to band together to seek their own privileges. Thus some German guilds in Eastern Europe barred Slavs from membership and other legislation prescribed expulsion for any member who married a Slav. As for the Slavs, their anti-German views were manifested in many ways. Such verbal descriptions of Germans as "this crafty and deceitful race" were symptoms of a hostility expressed also in a pogrom against Germans in fourteenth-century Cracow and by a barring of any German, "cleric or lay," from holding a position in a Polish hospital founded in the fourteenth century. An Augustinian house founded among the Czechs in the same century likewise required that anyone admitted must be "born from two Czech-speaking parents."[92]

Whatever the economic and social benefits from cross-cultural interactions, they left sore feelings that could be—and were—exploited politically, not only in the Middle Ages but on into the twentieth century as well. In Prague, for example, the struggle between Czechs and Germans persisted, whether it was ruled by the Austro-Hungarian empire or in an independent Czechoslovakia and its successor states during World War II, as well as in the postwar era. The cultural Germanization of educated Czechs was such that, as far back as the eighteenth century, a movement to *revive* the Czech language as a literary language and a language of the stage was launched, with great difficulty.[93] Despite the eventual success of this movement, and its laying the foundations for later and more ambitious Czech nationalism, even for much of the nineteenth century it was said to be "unheard of for any army officer to speak in Czech."[94] For more than two centuries, the government of Prague was in the hands of German-speaking officials, until Czechs achieved a majority on the city council in the early 1860s and then gained control of local government in general by the 1880s. One symbolic milestone came in 1892 when the city's street signs, which had been written in both German and Czech, now became exclusively Czech.[95]

The cultural clash between the two groups during this era largely revolved around language. German had long been the language of the most prosperous and influential residents of Prague, so that even Czechs and Jews who aspired to rise economically and socially not only learned the German language but also became absorbed into local German cultural life. German was the language of the city's educated classes, the language in which business was conducted, as well as the language of the higher ranks of the military and the clergy—regardless of whether the individuals involved were of German ancestry or not.[96]

By the nineteenth century, culture rather than ancestry was the defining social characteristic and Germans in Prague took pride in being cosmopolitan Bohemians and part of the Habsburg Empire, rather than being narrowly ethnic Germans.[97] It was the Czechs who began to promote ethnic or nationalistic group identity, led by a newly arising Czech intelligentsia, as so much nationalism in other countries around the world has been led by newly arising intelligentsias.[98] In addition to producing a literature in the Czech language, these intellectuals—often the "well-educated but underemployed" sons of Czech artisans and other city dwellers of modest prosperity—began to make ethnic appeals, in order to build a following among the masses.[99] While the Germans continued for some years to favor a Bohemian identity for all, rather than specifically ethnic identities, eventually the rise of Czech nationalism provoked in response a countervailing German ethnic consciousness.[100]

In the aftermath of this ethnic polarization, Germans and Czechs began to separate more and more into their own social organizations, and the political agitation of the Czechs produced mass violence against German and Jewish businesses in Prague and other Bohemian cities.[101] Meanwhile, aspiring Czechs sought government positions, both in politics and in the state bureaucracy, while Germans and Jews continued to dominate commerce and industry. After the formation of Czechoslovakia after the First World War, the government began preferential treatment of Czechs over other ethnic groups.[102] It was a classic pattern, followed by other aspiring groups of various races in other countries around the world. The politicized Balkanization of the Austro-Hungarian empire in general reached a climax at the end of the First World War, when the empire surrendered to the allies and its army fragmented into ethnic components.[103]

Subjugation

Like other culturally fragmented, economically backward, and politically disunited peoples around the world, the Slavs of East Central Europe were subjugated in many ways—as serfs owned by their own or foreign nobles, as slaves sold in the slave markets of Europe and the Middle East, and as peoples conquered by the Ottoman, Habsburg, and other empires. Such fates appeared in succession or in combinations over a period of centuries.

Most of the Slavs of medieval Europe were for centuries either peasants or animal herders—predominantly the former in the plains and a mixture of the two in the uplands.[104] Initially, when the invading Slavs settled down to agriculture in the sixth and seventh centuries, serfdom was unknown. But, in an era when organized national governments had not yet developed in the region, peasants often sought the protection of militarily powerful nobles for physical safety in a chaotic and violent age. Over a period of time, this dependence degenerated into serfdom in much (but not all) of East Central Europe. Serfdom entailed not merely subservience but also a loss of the right to move. Serfs who sought to flee were often tortured when captured, sometimes by having their hair set on fire and their noses split.[105]

Below the serfs on the social scale were the slaves, the main differences between them being that serfs belonged to the land, and were supposed to be sold only jointly with the land, rather than as personal property that could be sold separately anywhere at any time. Moreover, serfs had certain rights, though the fact that most of these rights were enforceable only in courts set up by noble landowners made those rights somewhat tenuous when it came to disputes with those landowners themselves. Slaves, however, lacked even these precarious protections and could be bought, sold, bartered, or even killed by their owners.[106] Sometimes people were enslaved locally for crimes or for debt, and some poverty-stricken peasants sold their children into slavery in order to survive when the family could not feed itself. The institution of slavery was common within East Central Europe, and foreign marauders and conquering armies also carried off Slavs into bondage in other lands, including Spain, Germany, Egypt and Syria.[107]

An international study of slavery described the Dalmatian coast as "one of the most continuously productive sources of slaves in human history," drawing not only from the largely Slavic population of that region but also from Slavic and other peoples from farther east in the Caucasus and the Balkans.[108] Centuries before the first African was carried in bondage to the Western Hemisphere, Slavs were being enslaved on a massive scale—Russians by the hundreds of thousands being enslaved by Turkish raiders[109] and Slavs along the Dalmatian coast being enslaved by other Europeans for at least six centuries,[110] while various groups of Slavs sold one another into bondage, as well as competing with Iranians, Turks, and others to enslave before being enslaved.[111] Slavs were so widely sold into bondage that the very word for slave was derived from the word for Slav in a number of Western European languages, as well as in Arabic.[112] Behind this history lay a set of geographical factors:

> Like other long-lasting slave export areas, the Dinaric high-
> lands had certain environmental features that fostered
> poverty, population pressure, political fragmentation and
> conflict: A coastal ridge rises like a wall from the sea. Fur-
> ther inland other ridges form folds parallel to the Adriatic.
> They effectively separate the inhabited regions into long nar-
> row valley called "*polya*", each isolated from the other by
> barren mountain chains, where pasture is scant, communica-
> tion difficult. The few rivers that pierce the walls are unnavi-
> gable. The narrow gorges they cut could not until recently be
> used by wheeled vehicles. . . . Because of the complexity of
> the mountain environment, however, natural disasters were
> usually local, sometimes confined to a single valley. This
> resulted in an intense competition for resources, most often
> expressed through banditry and feud.[113]

While the geography of this area differed in various ways from that of Africa, the net effects of that geography on the people were quite similar in producing a cultural and political disunity that made both peoples vulnerable and prey to outsiders. As in the case of Africa, those who did the capturing of people were not usually the same as those who engaged in the trading of slaves. In both regions, as well as in other parts of the world, warriors, brigands, and pirates initially captured the people, while ordinary merchants then included slaves among the merchandise that they sold. Thus much of the slave trade of medieval Europe was carried on by Jews, though many of the slave trading centers were in such Christian strongholds as Venice and Dubrovnik,[114] just as merchant peoples such as the overseas Chinese in Southeast Asia or the Yao in central Africa also included their fellow human beings among the merchandise they sold. Nor was this practice at all controversial at the time.

Within East Central Europe itself, local noblemen found that serf-dom was more profitable than slavery, which accordingly began dying out in the later middle ages.[115] As for people being enslaved by out-siders, the consolidation of strong territorial states in the late medieval and early modern era was a key factor in the decline of such enslave-ment in Eastern Europe, as in other parts of the world. The rise of the Muscovite state meant that anyone attempting to enslave Russians now faced a national army, and the rise of other territorial states in Eastern Europe likewise surrounded their peoples with military power too formidable for marauders to confront. The difficulties of establish-ing such large nation-states in the rugged uplands of the Balkans left the peoples of this area vulnerable longer. However, the establishment of states in this region, and of empires ruling over this region, ended its role as a major source of slaves. By the time Western Europeans established colonies across the Atlantic and sought to have much of the work there done by slaves, Africa was one of the few remaining viable sources.

The conquests of the Ottoman Empire in medieval southeastern Europe brought many Slavs under the dominion of the Turks, whose exactions included a regular levy of male children, who were taken away as slaves to be converted to Islam and trained for military posts in the corps of the Janissaries or in various civil positions as func-tionaries of the Ottoman government. Between 15,000 and 20,000 children were taken away from their parents during the 30-year reign of Sultan Mohammed the Conqueror in the fifteenth century,[116] for example, and the practice did not die out until the latter part of the seventeenth century, by which time approximately 200,000 boys had been taken from their families in this way. Not all these children were Slavs, since this human levy applied to conquered Christians in gen-eral but, in practice, many of these children were Slavs and relatively few were Greeks or Armenians.[117]

Ottoman rule in the Balkans lasted five centuries and left a lasting imprint on the subsequent history of the region. To varying degrees and for varying lengths of time, it removed many Europeans from the cultural development of the rest of Europe, at a crucial time in the evolution of the continent. Like all non-Moslem conquered peoples in the Ottoman Empire, the Slavs were explicitly assigned a lower posi-tion in the laws and policies of the empire. Moreover, even within the

Christian community recognized officially by the Ottoman authorities, the Slavs were assigned to be part of the Greek Orthodox structure, making them subordinate in both religious and secular matters to the Greeks. However, conditions following the Ottoman conquests were usually better than the conditions on the eve of that conquest for the vast majority of the peoples of southeastern Europe.[118]

For all its harsh and unequal laws, the Ottoman Empire did establish the rule of law in an area previously devastated and disorganized by warfare and among people previously living under the arbitrary caprices of their own nobles. With these nobles forced to flee in the wake of Ottoman conquest, and with Ottoman laws making the lot of the peasant less onerous—serfdom no longer existed under the Ottomans, for example—there was initially no substantial popular resistance to being ruled from Istanbul. Only in the later centuries of the empire, when control from the top was weakened and subordinate officials in Istanbul and in the provinces gained more power and became more corrupt and overbearing toward the people under them, did resistance to Ottoman rule begin to become serious among the Slavs and among the other peoples of southeastern Europe.

Although southeastern Europe was racked for centuries by wars between various Christian European rulers and the Ottoman Empire, the division was by no means always neatly split along either religious or ethnic lines. When Sultan Bayezid I fought against the Hungarians and Wallachians in the fourteenth century, for example, his troops included Serbs.[119] Moreover, the vassals of the Ottoman Empire usually included Christian princes, who were expected to fight alongside the Ottoman Turks and often did so in practice.

Initially, the Ottoman Empire was one of the more tolerant states toward those with different religions—certainly more tolerant than contemporary medieval Europe was toward Jews or toward Christians with heterodox views. Despite Islamic laws putting Moslems on a higher plane, forcing non-Moslem subjects to pay higher taxes and to submit to numerous other restrictions, serious and petty,[120] there was far more tolerance of near-equality in practice in the early centuries of the expanding empire than in the later centuries of the empire's decline and decay. Moreover, purely ethnic differences meant much less than religious differences.

Part of this tolerance reflected the reality that a majority of the subjects of the empire were not Moslems in the early centuries. Only after the later conquests of the sixteenth century did the Ottoman Empire have a Moslem majority and it was then that intolerance toward non-Moslems developed.[121] More than demographic changes were involved, however. In its earlier, expanding, and all-conquering era, the Ottoman Empire was confident in its mission to spread Islam, its superiority as a culture, and its military invincibility. European armies and coalitions failed time and again to stop the advance of the Ottoman forces toward the heart of the continent. Even when the Ottoman army was turned back from the gates of Vienna in 1532, it was because the impending arrival of winter made a continuation of the siege impractical, rather than because the European forces opposing them were too formidable.

In later centuries, however, the relative strengths of the Ottoman Empire and its European rivals shifted. The rise of the Habsburg Empire as a power in Central Europe and of the Russian Empire in Eastern Europe brought formidable new adversaries to the fore, and the rise of Venice as a naval power and the later rise of Western Europe as a force to be reckoned with as well, marked the relative decline of the Ottoman Empire as a military power. Its sense of cultural superiority was also undermined by the economic, social, and intellectual advances of early modern Western Europe. Long disdainful of European civilization,[122] whose more backward regions it encountered in Eastern Europe and the Balkans, the Ottoman Empire made no real effort to stay abreast of developments in Western Europe and was consequently surprised and shocked when the Western Europeans eventually overtook them in both cultural and military terms.

Having routed European armies on the battlefields for centuries, the Ottomans now began to suffer crushing defeats at their hands, seeing more advanced weaponry than they could match, and watching European naval and military forces striking at Ottoman territory, while European subject populations revolted against Ottoman rule. It was in this atmosphere of defeat, danger, and disillusionment that the Ottomans turned against their own Christian subjects, whom they now resented as potential traitors. To the Christians, the breakdown of law and order within the empire, and in particular the depredations of corrupt Ottoman officials and uncontrollable troops—sent out to the provinces precisely because they were considered dangerous in the capital—destroyed whatever loyalty was left among the conquered peoples and eventually provoked armed resistance, the climax of which was the Serbian war for independence in the early nineteenth century. Thus the Ottoman Empire, whose early rise was marked by a crushing military victory against the Serbs at Kossovo in the late fourteenth century,[123] now saw its declining era marked by the successful revolt of the Serbs.

For the Serbs, as for other Slavic peoples living for centuries under Ottoman rule, that subjugation entailed cultural isolation from developments in the rest of Europe, while the religious compartmentalization imposed by Ottoman authorities isolated them from the dominant Moslem culture, except for those who converted to Islam. Moreover, the cultural subordination of the Slavs to the Greeks within the Orthodox community, to which they were assigned by the Ottomans, likewise inhibited the development of a distinctively Slavic culture in the Balkans.

A striking exception, however, was the vassal city-state of Dubrovnik on the Adriatic coast, which the Ottomans allowed to run its own affairs in exchange for annual tribute. As a port city open to the trade and ideas of the west, Dubrovnik was influenced by Italian culture but also became a center for the development of the culture of the Southern Slavs. Classics of Western European culture were translated into the languages of the Slavs, and original literary works began to be written in the Slavic languages in Dubrovnik, in contrast to the largely oral folk culture of Slavs living under direct Ottoman rule. Architects and painters also flourished in Dubrovnik, though their work too remained largely unknown among the Slavs of the interior. In this way, Dubrovnik and other cities and towns along the Dalmatian coast were outposts of Western European culture and at the same time were places where a higher Slavic culture—as distinguished from a folk culture—could develop, much as in other parts of East Central Europe in closer touch with Western Europe were able to participate in the general cultural advances of the continent over the centuries.[124]

The other great empire in which the Slavs of East Central Europe lived as conquered peoples was the Habsburg Empire. Here the relationships of the various Slavic peoples to the ruling powers was much more complicated than that of a simple conquered-and-conqueror relationship. Because the Habsburg Empire was an agglomeration of lands with a variety of histories involving prior conquests, there were sometimes layers of overlords, such as the Hungarians over the Croats, all now subject to the Germanic rulers of the empire. These rulers might mitigate or aggravate the situations of those at the bottom, depending upon the changing political relationships between the ruling powers and the intermediate nobility. In turn, this meant that the Croats, for example, might at a given time have more loyalty to the ruling Habsburgs than to the Hungarians directly over them. Thus Croatian nationalism, directed against the Hungarians' attempts at cultural magyrization, was not seen initially as a threat to the empire and received qualified support from the Habsburgs.[125] This was only one of many cross-currents among the various ethnic groups, estates, and nationalities comprising the Habsburg Empire, where there were power struggles and cultural clashes between Germans and Slovaks,[126] Serbs and Hungarians,[127] and among others.

Within these cross-currents, however, what is clear is that intellectuals took the lead in promoting nationalism in both cultural and political terms. Whether among the Czechs, the Serbs, the Croats, or other groups, it was the intelligentsia, including students and lawyers, who promoted group identity, in opposition to cultural absorption by either the Germanic or Magyar culture, while the peasant masses were slow to respond to calls for heightened ethnic or national identity.[128] But, although the Habsburg Empire was riven by internal struggles, it held together until dismembered by the Western powers after the First World War.

The Emergence of Slavic Nations

Unlike the emergence of some peoples from tribal societies to national states through internal consolidations, whether peaceful or bloody, the emergence of modern Slavic states has been largely through armed struggles against foreign conquerors. The uprisings of the Serbs against the Ottoman Empire and the Russians' driving back of Mongol conquerors, before conquering them in turn, have been part of a pattern of the emergence of Slavic peoples into nation-states of their own. Poland has likewise played the role of both conqueror and conquered, including its obliteration as an independent state for more than a century following the carving up of its territory by Russia, Prussia, and Austria in 1795. The collapse and dismemberment of the

Habsburg and Ottoman empires in the wake of the First World War freed more Slavic peoples to form more nation-states—for the first time in the case of Czechoslovakia and Yugoslavia, and as an historic resurrection in the case of Poland.

Poland

The Poland that emerged at the end of the First World War had very different borders from the Poland which existed in the thirteenth to fifteenth centuries, much less the expansive Poland that once included Lithuania and Ukraine in the sixteenth century, when the Polish commonwealth was one of the dominant powers on the European continent. The country's dismemberment at the end of the eighteenth century resulted in Russia's acquiring 62 percent of Poland's land and 45 percent of its people, with Prussia taking 20 percent of the land and 23 percent of the people, while Austria took 18 percent of the land and 32 percent of the people.[129] This partition of Poland meant not only the Poles' loss of political independence but also that Polish producers and their markets were now often separated by national boundaries, and the varying policies of the three conquering nations led to very different roles for the Poles in the differing larger economies of which they were now a part. Railroads, for example, connected the Polish regions of Russia, Prussia, and Austria, not with each other, but with other regions of the respective empires of which they were now part.

Although Poland had been, and remained well into the twentieth century, a predominantly agricultural country, such industrial development as took place there in the eighteenth and nineteenth centuries, using imported Western European technology and then Western European investment, made the Polish regions of the Russian Empire the most industrially advanced part of the czarist realm.[130] The real wages of industrial workers in these Polish regions were accordingly higher than the real wages of industrial workers in Russia as a whole, though lower than the real wages of such workers in Western Europe.[131] This was in keeping with the intermediary role of the Polish provinces as conduits for Western technology moving eastward into the less developed Russian Empire.

In Prussia, however, the role of the Polish regions was quite different. Prussia—and especially the united Germany which succeeded it—was a nation with earlier access to Western European technology. Here the Poles played a very different role, as suppliers of agricultural produce and raw materials for German industry, as well as supplying both agricultural laborers and a work force for parts of German industry. But, although Poles tended to be "backward" parts of the German economy, as contrasted with "advanced" parts of the Russian economy, the absolute standard of living of Poles under German hegemony was higher than that of Poles living under either Russian or Austrian rule,[132] simply because the Germans had a more advanced economy than those of their neighbors to the east and south. Poles in Germany were not simply passive recipients of a higher standard of living, however. They were better educated and harder-working than fellow Poles living in Russia or in the Austro-Hungarian Empire. Their agriculture was better organized, increasingly used machinery, and had higher yields than farms in the Polish regions of Russia.[133] It was the Poles from Prussia who constituted most of the skilled workers among Polish immigrants to the United States.[134]

In the Austro-Hungarian Empire, the Austrian and the Czech regions were in the forefront of Western technology and industry, while the Poles in Galicia supplied agricultural products and other raw materials. Moreover, poverty was rampant in this province. The estimated per capita food consumption in Galicia in the late nineteenth century was only half that in Europe as a whole.[135] Yet, in this empire, there were fewer restrictions on the Polish language and culture than in Russia or Prussia, so that Galicia became a cultural center for Poles in the late nineteenth century, with an influence radiating into the Polish communities of neighboring countries.[136] Moreover, stringent restrictions on the Polish language and culture in Russia and Prussia were not always effective and were not supinely accepted by the Poles. For example, a crackdown by the czarist secret police in 1882–1883 uncovered a hundred clandestine Polish schools.[137] At the same time, Lithuanian and Ukrainian nationalism were developing, destroying the political and cultural ties they had once had with the Poles in an earlier era, when they were all part of the Polish commonwealth, so that the re-establishment of that commonwealth was no longer even a goal among these peoples living under Russian rule, who were now seeking an independent Lithuania, an independent Ukraine, and an independent Poland.

Despite a variety of political movements and unsuccessful insurrections among the Poles, and a variety of changing responses by the conquering nations, as the nineteenth century neared its end there was little indication that an independent Poland was going to be reconstituted in the foreseeable future. On the other hand, there was little indication of Polish satisfaction with their existing situation. During the era of mass emigration from 1870 to 1914, there was heavy emigration of Poles from the Polish regions of Russia, Prussia and Galicia—more than a million people from each of these regions.[138] However, economic progress continued, largely through the importation of the technology of Western Europe. Electricity, for example, came into wider use and Warsaw and several other Polish cities had their own power plants. Between 1894 and 1904, electric streetcars began to run in Warsaw, Lemberg, and Cracow, and telephones and automobiles began to appear, at least among the prosperous.[139]

During the course of the First World War, Germany and Austria invaded Russia, and the territory they conquered included the Polish regions of that country, giving these powers control of all of historic Poland. However, at the end of the war, the victory of the Western Allies and the weakness of the new Communist government in Moscow left the West with the question of how to dispose of the lands of the defeated powers. Their decision was to recreate Poland.

When Poland was reconstituted as an independent nation, it was composed of regions that had developed economically as parts of the very different economies of Russia, Germany, and the Austro-Hungarian Empire, and had of course reached very different levels of development. Railroad networks, for example, were far more developed in the Polish regions of Germany than in the Polish regions of Russia,[140] simply because Germany was a more economically developed country. More important, the Poles in the western region of Poland, having been part of the German economy, were a more economically developed people:

> In the ex-Prussian western regions both the peasantry and the bourgeoisie were economically enterprising. In the southern and eastern regions, the peasantry was generally more primitive, and the Polish middle class was heavily composed of members of the professions and bureaucrats,

allowing the specifically *economic* bourgeoisie to remain predominantly Jewish. Even the landscape reflected these differences; in the ex-German areas frequent small towns which were loci of agricultural marketing and processing industries and collieries and foundries dotted the countryside, while in much of the rest of Poland the endless vista of fields, forests, and villages interspersed with an occasional city, which functioned mainly as an administrative and garrison center, prevailed.[141]

During the war that preceded its independence and which made that independence possible, Poland had suffered major economic and social losses in the battles that raged across its territory under different flags. These losses included the destruction of more than 40 percent of its bridges, 63 percent of its railroad stations, and 48 percent of the rolling stock. In addition, 450,000 Poles were killed in the war, fighting in the armies of the various contending powers.[142] More fundamental than even these large losses, which could be made up over time, was the fact that Poland was still not a major industrial nation. As late as the 1930s, only 30 percent of its population was urban.[143]

Czechoslovakia

Although Czechoslovakia, like Poland, was created by the victorious Western powers from the territories of the nations defeated in the First World War, Czechoslovakia did not represent the re-creation of a state that had once existed, but the synthesizing of a new state from ethnically and economically disparate elements. The medieval kingdom of Bohemia, the Czech heartland, was reconstituted as a province of Czechoslovakia but the Slovaks were only with some difficulty persuaded to add Slovakia to it, and smaller territories once part of Poland and Hungary were added to round out Czechoslovakia economically. Nearly half the population of the country lived in Bohemia, which was also the most economically and culturally advanced part of Czechoslovakia. The illiteracy rate in Bohemia was only 2 percent in 1921, compared to 50 percent in the province of Ruthenia.[144] This was symptomatic of other large disparities among the peoples and regions of Czechoslovakia, where only about two thirds of the population was

either Czech or Slovak.[145] Ethnic strife was to plague the history of
Czechoslovakia between the two World Wars and lead ultimately to its
breakup into a Czech Republic and an independent Slovakia in the
last decade of the twentieth century.

As a nation emerging after the First World War, Czechoslovakia was
more fortunate than Poland or some other parts of East Central
Europe, for it had sustained little damage from the war that led to its
independence. Moreover, Czechoslovakia was the most economically
prosperous of the states to emerge from the dismemberment of the
Austro-Hungarian Empire and produced half the steel and pig iron in
all of East Central Europe.[146] However, four-fifths of the population
was still rural.[147] In the Slovak capital of Bratislava, Slovaks were still
only a minority, with most of the other inhabitants being either Germans or Hungarians.[148] Much of the country's industrial development
was in the western province of Bohemia, and a substantial proportion
of it was in the hands of the Sudeten German minority there, the
largest German population outside Germany and Austria.[149]

Creation of the Czechoslovakian state did not put an end to the
internal ethnic strife between Czechs and Germans, which had
become sharper in the preceding century. Rather, the new state
became only a new arena for that strife, which led to even greater
tragedies for both Czechs and Germans. Like other newly independent
peoples, the Czechs after the First World War used their new-found
power to discriminate against their own minorities. In addition to preferential hiring of Czechs in the civil service,[150] the government was
also instrumental in transferring capital from German and German-
Jewish banks to Czech banks and in breaking up German-owned large
estates to be made into smaller farms, for the benefit of the Czech
peasantry.[151]

The more fundamental and intractable problem, however, was that
the Germans in Bohemia did not want to be a part of the new Czech
state in the first place, and asserted that the "right of self-determination of nations" which had created Czechoslovakia should apply to
them as well. The interspersed German and Czech areas of the
Bohemian borderlands made a separate German territory not feasible.
More important, from the standpoint of maintaining militarily defensible borders, Germans were concentrated near the mountainous border
areas and their secession would have eliminated the new country's

geographical defenses. Violent German protests against the denial of
their claims to self-determination led to the Czech army's opening fire
and killing more than fifty Germans.[152] The internal ethnic strife in the
new country during the 1920s was later exacerbated by the rise of the
Nazis to power in neighboring Germany during the 1930s, leading to a
strident Nazi movement among the embittered Germans of Czechoslovakia. All this culminated in the Munich crisis of 1938, in which
Czechoslovakia was dismembered under threat of invasion from Germany. Czechoslovakia's western, predominantly German Sudeten
region, was annexed by Hitler. Six months later, Germany took control
of all of Czechoslovakia, which remained under their control for the
next six years, a traumatic period of many atrocities committed against
Czechs and Slovaks, and preferential treatment given to Germans,
many of whom responded with loyalty to the Nazi cause.

A bitter backlash followed after the Second World War ended. Both
unofficial violence and official discrimination were instituted against
Germans per se, and only those who could offer proof of their loyalty to
the Czechoslovakian cause were allowed to retain their citizenship.[153]
Ultimately, more than 3 million Germans were expelled from Czechoslovakia at the end of the war, leaving behind a German population
less than one-tenth of what it had been in 1930. The fact that more
than 18,000 Germans of demonstrated loyalty to Czechoslovakia also
chose to leave on their own[154] also spoke volumes about the ethnic
polarization in the country. Nor were these Germans readily replaced.
Half a century later, there were still deserted towns and farmhouses in
the Sudetenland from which the Germans had been expelled.[155]

The fact that the Soviet army had driven the Nazis out of Czechoslovakia did not mean liberation but incorporation into the Soviet bloc of
Eastern European nations that did not regain independence until the
last decade of the twentieth century. For Czechoslovakia, it was more
than half a century since it had been a free nation.

While the mass expulsions of Germans from Czechoslovakia was one
of the largest expulsions of a given ethnic group after World War II, this
was not a unique phenomenon of the times nor were Germans the only
transferees. The population transfers in East Central Europe between
1944 and 1948 included 31 million people,[156] transferred voluntarily or
involuntarily for a variety of reasons. The widespread and large-scale
readjustments of borders between various countries of the region was

accompanied by efforts to produce greater ethnic homogeneity within the new borders. To some extent, this effort succeeded. Thus Romania, whose population was 72 percent Romanian in 1930, had an 88 percent Romanian population by 1977. Poland, whose population was 69 percent Polish in 1931, had a 97 percent Polish population in 1991.[157] Czechoslovakia, however, despite its mass expulsions of Germans, had the proportion of Czechs in its population rise only modestly, from 51 percent to 54 percent, while the Slovaks rose from 16 percent to 31 percent.[158] Hungary achieved a more than 99.5 percent Hungarian population by 1990 but this represented a relatively small rise in a population that was 92 percent in 1930.[159] Most of this ethnic homogeneity in Hungary was a result of massive losses of territory to surrounding nations in the peace treaties following the First World War.

Yugoslavia

Yugoslavia was a very different story. It never achieved anything approaching ethnic homogeneity. While nearly three-fourths of the population spoke Serbo-Croatian in 1921, these included such separate and antagonistic groups as the Muslims, Croatians, and Serbs, whose racial and linguistic affinities did not prevent much mutual hostility and friction. In addition, there were numerous smaller minorities, including the Slovenes (less than 9 percent), the Germans (4 percent), and the Magyars and Albanians (less than 4 percent each).[160] More important than the number and size of Yugoslavia's ethnic groups was their hostility to one another, exacerbated by the ruling Serbs' heavy-handed treatment of them all.[161] The country's political parties, with the exception of the Communists, represented their own respective ethnic groups or geographical regions, and therefore had every incentive to aggravate intergroup and interregional frictions.[162] Having been assembled from remnants of Ottoman, Germanic, Hungarian, and Italian cultural regions, with various systems of government and even technologies, Yugoslavia was left with such anomalies as four different systems of banking, railroads, and currency when it became an independent state in 1918.[163] Serfdom still existed in Macedonia and Bosnia-Herzegovina, until it was abolished by the new government in early 1919.[164]

In addition to being a socially and politically fragmented country,

Yugoslavia was a very poor country. The historic poverty of the Balkans was worsened by devastating losses of life and property during the First World War, in which the percentage of the Serbian population killed was more than twice as high as the percentage of the French population and three times as high as the percentage of the British population killed in the war. Between the war itself and a typhus epidemic that raged through Serbia, death claimed one-tenth of the entire Serbian population, one-fourth of their cattle, one-third of their horses, and one-half of their pigs, sheep, and goats. This traumatic experience left the Serbs not only much worse off economically, but also with a bitter sense of entitlement to both power and restitution from the resources of the new Yugoslavian state—which is to say, at the expense of the other ethnic groups who had been spared such devastation and who were in some cases formerly part of the defeated enemy states or empires.[165]

As in much of Eastern Europe, economic development in Yugoslavia owed much to imported technology, capital, and managerial expertise from Western Europe. An iron-and-steel mill was built in Yugoslavia by the German industrial giant, Krupp, while the French built a copper refinery, and the British a lead and zinc plant. The more advanced parts of Eastern Europe also contributed. Entire textile factories, including skilled workers, were imported from Czechoslovakia and Poland.[166]

In the last decade of the twentieth century, Yugoslavia's existence ended as it began, in an embittered atmosphere among its peoples, whose antagonisms went back for centuries. The country's travails during the Second World War, in which the Croats collaborated with the Nazi invaders, while the Serbs fought guerilla warfare against them, did not nothing to unify the people. Only under the iron dictatorship of the postwar Communist government headed by Josip Broz Tito was an imposed unity maintained, and in the post-Communist era the country came apart in a civil war marked by some of the world's worst atrocities since the days of the Nazis.

Achievements

Despite high illiteracy rates in some countries, regions, or ethnic groups in East Central Europe between the two World Wars—52 percent illiteracy in Yugoslavia and 80 percent in Albania[167]—some of the leading figures in the world in mathematics, science, and the arts came out of this region, whose leading universities maintained high intellectual standards, even when more basic education for the masses was neglected. These individuals of world stature included Polish mathematicians, Hungarian mathematicians and scientists (John von Neumann, Edward Teller, and Leo Szilard, for example), Czech and Polish linguists, Romanian and Yugoslav sculptors, and Hungarian composers such as Béla Bartók, not to mention prominent German and Jewish figures from the region, such as Franz Kafka and Rainier Maria Rilke.[168] However, many institutions of higher education in the region also turned out what has been aptly characterized as "an economically superfluous and politically dysfunctional academic proletariat," for their students tended toward specialization in the softer fields, rather than in the science and technology in which the region lagged behind Western Europe.[169] In Eastern Europe, as elsewhere around the world, such soft-subject intellectuals have been major sources of intergroup polarization and political instability.

RUSSIAN EMPIRES

Two Russian-dominated multinational empires succeeded one another on the same territory—the first being called candidly the Russian Empire and the second The Soviet Union. Geographically, Russia is in some ways like the rest of Eastern Europe, but its natural resource endowment is far richer. Like some other Slavic lands, Russia has vast plains—indeed the largest area of level land in the world[170]—and the Ural Mountains which mark the boundary between Europe and Asia are modest in height, like the mountains of the rest of Eastern Europe.

The sheer physical size of the Russian Empire and of the Soviet Union that succeeded it has had enormous consequences. The largest country in the world, the Soviet Union was more than twice the size of the United States and larger than the entire continent of South America. The European portion of the Union of Soviet Socialist Republics constituted more than half of all Europe, even though it was only one quarter of the total land area of the U.S.S.R. Such vast regions encompassed a wide variety of geographic and climatic environments and great natural resources, but the distances involved created high transportation costs, especially since most of these resources, including waterways, were in the Asian portion of the country, while most of the population was in the European portion.[171] A 1977 study, for example, showed that 90 percent of the energy resources of the Soviet Union were east of the Urals while nearly 80 percent of the country's energy requirement were in the European part of the U.S.S.R.[172]

While there are many rivers in Russia, containing altogether one-tenth of the total river flow in the world, the practical economic value of these rivers is limited, and the largest are by no means the most economically important. Many Russian rivers flow northward into the Arctic Ocean or flow elsewhere into inland seas, rather than serving as outlets to the great ocean trade routes of the world. More than three-fifths of their drainage is into the Arctic Ocean.[173] Russia's most famous river, the Volga, is by no means its largest—the Yeninsey and the Lena each carries more than twice as much water—but the Volga's importance derives from the fact that it flows through regions of Russia containing three-quarters of the country's population and four-fifths of its industry and farmland. It is the longest river in Europe. Not surprisingly, the Volga has carried more shipping tonnage than any other Russian river or any river in the former Soviet Union. Russian rivers are often frozen for months each winter, reducing their economic significance still further. Even the role of the Volga is reduced by the fact that it typically freezes before December in the vicinity of Moscow and remains frozen until mid-April. At its southern end, the Volga flows into an inland sea—the Caspian Sea—like so many other Russian rivers.

In natural resources, Russia stands out among the nations of Eastern Europe and of the world. In addition to having the world's largest reserves of iron ore and one-fifth of all the forested land in the world, the manganese deposits of the Soviet Union have been estimated to exceed those of every other nation except South Africa,[174] and its actual manganese production in 1980 exceeded that of any other nation by at least double.[175] The Soviet Union also led all nations in oil production for many years, producing from 10 to 20 percent of total world output.[176] It has also had one-third of the world's natural gas reserves[177] and was for many years the world's leading producer of nickel.[178] The U.S.S.R. was self-sufficient in virtually all natural resources and exported substantial amounts of gold and diamonds. As of 1978, the U.S.S. R. supplied nearly half of the industrial diamonds in the world.[179] Yet all this natural abundance did not translate into a high standard of living for the Russian people or for the other peoples of the Russian Empire, the Soviet Union, or the Commonwealth of Independent States which succeeded them.

Partly this reflected the high costs of extraction and transportation in a vast country without a network of waterways connecting the resources with the population centers. The enormously costly Trans-Siberian Railroad was built in hopes of making up for the lack of nat-ural transportation routes between the resources in Asiatic Russia and the industry and population centers of European Russia. For much of the country's history, there was also a lack of human capital among a largely illiterate population. As late as 1897, only 21 percent of the population of the Russian Empire was literate.[180] But, even after edu-cation spread and an abundance of scientists and engineers were trained during the Communist era, the government's emphasis on mili-tary uses of its resources kept living standards low. However, the de-emphasis of the military in the post-Soviet era did not prevent the continued—and sometimes worsening—poverty in the region, a fact which highlighted the political and legal obstacles to economic devel-opment, which may well have played a major role all along in the country's backwardness under czars, commissars, and then democrati-cally elected governments.

Conquests and Cultures

Like many nations, Russia has been both conqueror and conquered. For more than two centuries—from the mid-thirteenth century to the latter part of the fifteenth century—an area now known as Russia was part of the vast empire of the Golden Horde of Genghis Khan, an empire stretching from China to deep inside Eastern Europe and southward into the Middle East. However, the Mongols did not occupy and directly administer the Russian lands, as the Romans did ancient Britain. Rather, the Golden Horde exacted tribute from a Russian gov-ernmental structure left largely intact, though always subordinated to Mongol overlords, who were able to dictate policy and to choose princely rulers from among the Russians.

There was no Russia before the Mongol invasion and, though the conquerors did not attempt to create such an entity—indeed they played off the various local powers against each other—the net effect of the shifting military and political alliances over the centuries was that the grand duchy of Muscovy grew stronger. Eventually, the Muscovite state became powerful enough to challenge its overlords on the battlefield and thereafter to choose its own rulers independently, as well as to cease paying tribute. Then Muscovy began its own expansion in all directions, creating the Russian Empire under the Muscovite rulers, the czars. At its zenith, the Russian Empire extended continuously from Europe across Asia and across the Bering Straits into North America, until the sale of Alaska to the United States in 1867.

While Russia was the dominant nation in this empire, it was at the same time one of the most backward countries in Europe, lagging far behind Western Europe in economic, technological, and commercial development, as well having the lowest rate of literacy on the continent in the early twentieth century.[181] In earlier centuries, no one was more painfully aware of Russia's backwardness, or more determined to do something about it, than czar Peter the Great, who reigned from 1682 to 1725, and who made extraordinary efforts to learn about the technology of the west by going there in person—and in disguise as a workman. However, Peter's methods of introducing Western ways to Russia were not Western at all, but traditionally autocratic. Russian businessmen were ordered to Moscow and told to produce woolen cloth for the state at cost, with profits being allowed on other sales if they succeeded—and with punishment in prospect for them if they did not.[182] Peter had industries built, and the city of St. Petersburg built, not where geography or economics would dictate, but where he chose. As an economic historian put it:

> Few more inhospitable sites in European Russia could have been found to establish a major economic and political center than the damp, cold, swampy St. Petersburg. The Urals were an area rich in iron deposits and timber for fuel, although distant from the most important domestic markets and even farther from the few ports through which Russia's high grade of iron could be exported. The cost of Russian iron thus was made prohibitive by transport costs and the proliferation of intermediaries.[183]

While Peter the Great's attempts to bring Russia out of its backwardness focussed on transferring the technology of Western European to his empire, India was at that point also more advanced than Russia in both industry and agriculture, so that its products and people were also in demand in the czarist empire. Orders from Moscow in the 1620s instructed local officials in the province of Astrakhan to allow eastern merchants to go up the Volga and trade, leading to the development of a colony of sojourners from India who played a major role in the commercial development of that region. Indeed, Indian merchants and money-lenders in the city of Astrakhan were more financially formidable than their more numerous Russian counterparts.[184]

Despite Peter the Great's many efforts to advance and Westernize Russia in the early eighteenth century, much of the modern industrial development of Russia began only in the late nineteenth century, covering the last decades of the czarist era that ended in 1917. How much the strains engendered by this modernizing effort contributed to the coming of the revolution which toppled that regime is an open question.

Not only were the vast majority of the Russian people illiterate peasants, many of these peasants lived both as subjects of an autocratic government and also as serfs to particular landowners until 1861. Most of the other large subject peoples were no better off, though many had very different lifestyles, such as the nomadic peoples of Central Asia. The lives and labor of the Russian masses were cheap to their rulers. The city of St. Petersburg was built largely with forced labor.[185] Peter the Great tested Western and traditional methods of warfare in a staged battle, in which 20 men lost their lives.[186] Between the nobility and the peasantry there was little middle class.[187] Businessmen were regarded not so much as assets to the country but as prey for government—both the official treasury and individual corrupt officials.

The social milieu in czarist Russia was one in which the nobility looked down with contempt on business and businessmen. With a vast and illiterate peasantry, a class of nobles who contributed little to commercial and industrial development, and an intelligentsia hostile to capitalism,[188] it can hardly be surprising that Russia had to rely heavily on foreigners to modernize its economy.

Foreigners

At the end of the seventeenth century, Peter the Great scoured Europe for scientists, craftsmen, and productive talent of all kinds, to be brought to Russia to try to develop the economic and military strength of the empire. The first industries in Russia were founded by foreigners in the seventeenth century. The skilled labor used in these early industries, like their management, came from abroad.[189] A whole colony of foreign craftsmen existed in St. Petersburg in the eighteenth century and in the Ukraine in the early nineteenth century,[190] in addition to shopkeepers and money-lenders from India, who operated in the province of Astrakhan.[191] Armenian immigrants accounted for 40 percent of all exports and 53 percent of all imports through Astrakhan in the mid-eighteenth century. Of 250 cotton cloth factories there at that time, 209 were owned by Armenians, who also owned 32 out of 38 silk-weaving enterprises.[192]

From an early period, much of the economic and cultural development of Russia and its empire was a result of the importation of foreign knowledge and skills. Much of the Kremlin itself was built by an Italian architect. The Bering Sea, between Siberia and Alaska, was discovered by a Danish sea captain employed by the Russian government. Foreigners played a pioneering role in metallurgy, machine construction, and even government service in czarist Russia.[193] These foreigners included both sojourners and permanent settlers, individual entrepreneurs and whole groups, such as the German farmers who settled in colonies on the Volga and the Black Sea in the eighteenth century. The czars themselves were of predominantly German ancestry. Catherine the Great was a German princess before marrying the Russian prince who became Czar Peter III, whom she succeeded to the throne. Many of her male descendants later married women of German ancestry, creating a predominantly German line of czars. This was only part of a larger picture of a general cultural westernization of the Russian upper classes, which included their speaking French and being familiar with the literature, manners, and social thought of Western Europe.[194] Such cosmopolitanism, however, further widened the cultural gap between the Russian elites and masses.

Because of the huge size and large population of the Russian empire, even modest economic progress in particular sectors could translate into vast quantities of output in absolute terms. Thus, by the early eighteenth century, Russia had the largest output of pig iron in Europe,[195] though it lagged far behind Western Europe in the efficiency with which that iron was produced.[196] In the middle of the nineteenth century, Russia produced more yarn than Germany.[197] Nevertheless, as Russia advanced economically, the key roles in that advancement were played by foreign entrepreneurs and, to a considerable but lesser extent, by foreign capital. The first woolen mill in Russia was erected by the Dutch. The mining and processing of both iron and copper in Russia owed their beginnings to German and Dutch mining engineers.[198] The oil fields of the Caucasus were developed by the English and the Swedes.[199]

The greatest era of industrialization in czarist Russia began in the 1890s and continued until the First World War. Even this late in Russian history, foreigners remained a dominant factor, supplemented by the work of domestic minorities, such as the Jews, the Baltic Germans, and educated Poles. From 1885 to 1913, the annual growth rate of Russian industrial production averaged nearly 6 percent.[200] For the period from 1860 to 1913, Russia's industrial growth rate exceeded that of Britain, France or Germany, and was comparable to that of the United States.[201] However, the *level* of industrialization at which it started and ended was not as high as in Western Europe or the United States. Nevertheless, it was an impressive performance, and the 1913 level of output would not be reached again under the Communists during the next decade.[202]

Most Russian international trade had historically been carried in foreign ships and that remained so during the era of industrialization under the czars. Only 3 percent of Russian international shipping was in Russian vessels.[203] In petroleum, nearly three-quarters of all invested capital in Russia was British capital.[204] By 1899, at least 60 percent of all coal in Russia was produced by foreign companies.[205] Nearly all electrical streetcars were Belgian.[206] On the eve of the First World War, approximately one-third of the sugar mills in the country belonged to Jews, and these mills produced just over half the refined sugar in Russia.[207] At about the same time, the second, fourth, and fifth largest producers of agricultural machinery in Russia were all British firms—the number one producer of such machinery in Russia being an American firm, International Harvester.[208] The electrical construction industry in Russia was dominated by German firms, though a French subsidiary of Westinghouse was also significant.[209]

The pattern, as well as magnitude, of foreign economic activity in Russia provides clues to the sources of Russian economic backwardness. The foreigners specialized in providing what the Russians most lacked—technical and scientific skills, efficient and honest management and, to a secondary extent, capital. Russian managers were notorious for their inefficiency and corruption. A French observer in 1904 referred to "the extraordinary waste—to be polite—that reigns among Russian administrators."[210] Even after trained Russians began to emerge over the years into increasingly responsible positions, foreign firms were careful not to use Russian accountants.[211] This business corruption mirrored a pervasive corruption in the czarist government,[212] which was by no means stamped out under the Communists[213] or in the post-Soviet era.[214]

The scientific and technological superiority of foreign firms was based largely on their copying in Russia the latest advances already in use in Western Europe.[215] While much capital flowed in from Western Europe, there was also much capital raised within Russia itself, which had its wealthy classes, even though the masses of Russians were very poor. Lack of capital was not the source of Russian backwardness. Lack of entrepreneurship and technology were the crucial problems. Once sound and reliable management could be found, and Western technology applied, large amounts of capital could be raised from Russians, as well as from Western European investors. While the foreign-owned firms were new to Russia, they were not untried pioneers but usually affiliates, subsidiaries, or offshoots of firms with well-established reputations and long years of experience in Western Europe or the United States. It was the reliability of the managements that made the raising of vast amounts of capital possible, from both inside and outside Russia.

The proportion of foreign capital in major Russian industries was just under one-half in 1900, up from one-fourth in 1890,[216] even though the industries themselves were largely created by foreign entrepreneurs. In short, even at the height of foreign domination of Russian industry, most of the capital was Russian, and very little of it was supplied by the czarist government. What was lacking in Russia was not capital but the ability to use capital. That is what the foreigners provided.

Seldom were the foreign-owned firms in Russia wholly-owned subsidiaries established with the foreign firm's existing capital. Russian capital and some Russian directors or managers were more common, though the foreign management usually retained controlling interest, even if this was less than 50 percent. The foreigners tended to handle what they were best at doing—internal management of the firm and assessments of technological and market possibilities. The Russian members often proved to be very useful in external relations, especially with corrupt government officials and with shrewd and scheming Russian elements with which the firm had commercial contacts.[217] Foreign managers unfamiliar with Russian ways often met disaster in such external dealings.[218]

The managing of Russian labor was another large and growing problem for foreign entrepreneurs. The difficulty was not simply that the Russian workers were unskilled and unable to handle advanced Western equipment effectively, though these were factors that made the apparently "cheap" Russian labor costly in practice. Russian workers, often unused to the routine and rhythm of industrial life, tended to be transient or prone to absenteeism—in a word, unreliable.

These problems were at their worst at the beginning and in industries whose inherent work demands could not tolerate such behavior. When the steel industry was established in southern Russia, for example, almost all the steel workers were imported.[219] However, the enormous costs of attracting workers from Western Europe, with wages high enough to compensate them for moving and for the dreary life in Russia, led to attempts to train and retain Russian workers instead, wherever possible. Foreign workers were therefore a short-run expedient in the initial stages. Nevertheless, the resort to such expedients was indicative of another element of historic Russian economic backwardness.

It was also difficult to get Russians to work well with foreigners. While work skills and experience would come to the Russian workers with the passing years, their hostility to foreigners would in many cases also grow, fanned by the rising radical movements that would culminate in the revolutions of 1917. In the short run, the resentments of the Russian workers toward foreigners sped up the Russification of the work force, in order to reduce a source of internal friction. These frictions were by no means incidental matters. In 1900, for example, rioting Russian workers burned the dwellings and belongings of 60

Belgian workers at a glass factory, causing them to flee back to Belgium.[220] A report of a French firm in Russia in 1907 declared:

> One must remember that the mass of workers has been heavily indoctrinated in these last years and their nationalism has been over-excited. The consecutive assassinations of several plant managers have shown this all too clearly.[221]

In short, the same bitter resentments directed at more productive and more prosperous domestic minorities, such as the Germans and the Jews, extended to foreigners as well. Ironically, hostility to foreign "exploitation" was rising just as the return on foreign investments was declining sharply, as a result of growing competition created by the inflow of more foreign businesses. Initially very high rates of return— 17.5 percent in 1895—dropped under 10 percent by 1898, under 5 percent in 1900 and under 3 percent by 1906.[222] The prices of steel products—crucial to industrialization—also dropped sharply during this period, as Russia became self-sufficient in this basic industry, due to the hated foreigners in their midst.[223]

The large role of foreigners in Russian economic development did not end with the czarist regime. Only a few years after seizing power— years marked by numerous economic setbacks and catastrophes—the Communists too turned to the West for management, engineering, and technical personnel, as well as for equipment and capital. Much effort and time were required merely to restore the economy to where it had been under the czars. As of 1920, Russian production of cast iron was less than 3 percent of what it was in 1913—and was in fact less than it had been in 1718 under Peter the Great.[224] Similarly, Soviet production in the early 1920s was well below that of czarist times in platinum, agricultural implements, steam locomotives, heavy electrical equipment, tar, ammonia, and dyes, among other products.[225] Although czarist Russia had such entrepreneurial pioneers of early aviation as Igor Sikorsky and Alexander P. de Seversky, both moved to the United States after the Bolshevik revolution and contributed in a major way to the development of the American aircraft industry, while the Soviets became dependent on foreigners for the design and production of their own aircraft—military and civilian—and remained so a decade after the revolution.[226]

A massive inflow of foreign management, engineering, and technical personnel and capital restored vast areas of the Soviet economy. For example, although Russia under the czars had been the world's largest producer and exporter of oil, by 1921 Russia's oil drilling was less than one percent of what it had been at the turn of the century.[227] An American company then began drilling oil wells in the Caucasus during the 1920s, while the Japanese were developing oil production for the Soviets in the Far East, on Sakhalin Island. Oil refineries were built by British, German and American companies. The production of crude oil almost tripled from 1923 to 1928, as foreigners not only restored the industry but also introduced more advanced technology.[228]

Much the same story unfolded in other sectors of the Soviet economy. The average monthly output of coal under Soviet management jumped immediately by more than 50 percent under American management, and the output of sawmills jumped by 75 percent.[229] Such well-known German firms as Krupp and I.G. Farben also played major roles, as did such American firms as Ford, DuPont, RCA, and International Harvester, but many other countries were involved as well. Ball bearings came from Sweden and Italy, plastics and aircraft from France, turbines and other electrical industry technology from Britain.[230]

This influx of foreign personnel, equipment and capital did not end with the restoration of the Soviet economy in the 1920s. Much of Stalin's "building of socialism" in the early Five-Year Plans was in fact done by capitalists from Europe and America. As late as 1936, the Soviets reported about 6,800 foreign specialists at work in heavy industry alone—about one-fourth of them American engineers.[231] The largest project in Stalin's first five-year plan was a steel mill designed by American engineers and based on a steel mill in Gary, Indiana.[232] Soviet iron and steel construction in general, during the period from 1928 through 1932, was of American design, built under the supervision of American (and some German) engineers, using equipment from the United States and Germany.[233] Until 1930, the Soviet automobile industry produced only a Fiat truck from czarist times. The first new automobile factory under the Communist regime was built by the Ford Motor Company in the early 1930s,[234] and was modeled after Ford's famous River Rouge plant.[235] When the Soviets built the largest tractor plant in Europe, it was manufactured in the United States and later assembled in the U.S.S.R. under the supervision of American engineers.[236]

W. Averell Harriman reported to the U.S. Department of State in

1944 that Stalin had said in a conversation that "about two-thirds of all the large industrial enterprises in the Soviet Union had been built with United States help or technical assistance."[237] Nevertheless, the dramatic restoration and advancement of the Soviet economy was seen by many, including many in the western democracies, as a vindication of socialist planning in general and the Communist economic system in particular.

Indigenous Nationalities

The czarist Russian Empire and its successor, the Soviet Union, were both very racially and ethnically heterogeneous societies. The country's census has listed more than a hundred nationalities, more than 20 of them groups with foreign homelands.[238] The census of 1897, for example, showed the Russians to be just 45 percent of the population of the czarist empire and the last census of the Soviet Union in 1989 showed that Russians were not quite 51 percent of the population of the U.S.S.R.[239] This was not a country with a numerically preponderant "majority" and a fringe of "minorities." It was a collection of distinct nationalities, many numerically predominant within their own respective borders, and having distinct languages, histories, and cultures—as well as numerous smaller minorities within the borders of the member republics, some of these sub-minorities also having separate languages and cultures. Neither the Russian Empire nor the Soviet Union was simply a multi-ethnic society, such as those created by immigration in the Western Hemisphere or in parts of Southeast Asia. Lenin called the czarist empire a "prison of nations," though that term would later apply equally to the regime which he created.

Unlike other conquering European powers which created empires overseas among militarily weaker peoples, Russia found vulnerable peoples and nations on its own land borders, especially to the south and east, but also to the west. Russia accordingly expanded militarily across contiguous nations on the immense Eurasian land mass to create the largest country on Earth. Those conquered or annexed included not only whole nations, such as Armenia and the Ukraine (the latter larger than France), but also nomadic tribal peoples spread over vast reaches of land in Central Asia. There were more Moslems in the Soviet Union than in Egypt, and more Turks than in Turkey.[240]

The relationships of the Russians to the various conquered peoples of the Russian Empire and of the Soviet Union ranged across the whole spectrum of relationships found between conquerors and conquered elsewhere. In the Asian regions of the Russian Empire and of the Soviet Union, Russians brought a more advanced technology than the indigenous peoples were used to and settled in the cities, while the indigenes predominated in the surrounding countrysides.[241] In the Baltic, however, it was the conquered people who were more advanced, and who maintained a higher standard of living than in Russia, on through to the end of the Soviet Union. The differences in technological, economic, and other advancement or backwardness were not simply a contrast between European and non-European peoples, however, for the Slavic Byelorussians likewise remained an agricultural people whose cities were inhabited largely by non-Byelorussians on into the 1920s, and it was the middle of the twentieth century before Byelorussians became a majority of the urban population in Byelorussia.[242] One sign of the wide range of cultural development among the peoples of the Soviet Union was that the literacy rate in 1922 ranged from less than 4 percent in Tajikistan to more than 80 percent in Latvia and Estonia.[243]

In general, Russians played a role among the peoples of Central Asia much like the role of Western Europeans in Eastern Europe or like European imperial powers in much of the non-industrialized colonial world. That is, the Russians brought the technology, the organization and the industrial and commercial way of life of western civilization to these regions, if not always to the peoples of these regions, since the modern sectors of these societies were often Russian enclaves. In some respects, however, there were also important cultural changes brought to the peoples themselves. Some of these conquered peoples had no written language of their own, so that written versions of their existing languages had to be created by outsiders—more than forty written languages being created between the two World Wars[244]—as had happened with Eastern Europeans centuries earlier.

As in other parts of Europe in earlier times, the replacement of local dialects with a standard national language was a major transformation in itself, spread over many years. In the Soviet Union, the linguistic history of the innumerable national and ethnic groups was complicated by the fact that the creation of standardized and written versions of their languages and local dialects was often proceeding simultaneously with attempts to get more of them to speak Russian, so as to participate in the modernization of the economy and society. In a vast, polyglot supranational state, the Russian language was seen as a *lingua franca* that was especially needed to unify these sprawling domains and bring their economies up to a level that would enable the Soviet Union as a whole to be militarily viable in competition with more advanced nations in the rest of Europe. A further complicating factor was that education of any sort, in any language, was only developing in many parts of the Soviet Union, where just 40 percent of the whole population could read and write in 1926, with literacy rates being in the single digits in Siberia and Central Asia.[245]

Asian peoples long remained a predominantly pastoral or agricultural population in the countrysides, under both the czars and the Communists, while Russians and other Europeans settled in the cities to run both the modern economy and the political system.[246] However, inter-ethnic relations were never a simple dichotomy of Russian conquerors and indigenous subjects, even within a given nation, in either czarist or Communist times. Because of the historic role of Germans, Jews, and other bearers of cultures deriving from Western Europe, the indigenes—both European and Asian—often found themselves playing economic and political roles subordinate to those of others besides the Russians. Thus nineteenth-century Latvians who migrated to the cities of their country found Germans predominant in urban economic and cultural life, as Lithuanians found Poles predominant, and as others found themselves economically or culturally subordinate to Jews, Armenians or other more advanced groups, in addition to being politically subordinate to Russians.[247]

One consequence of this multi-ethnic subordination was that the resentments of the subordinate groups and nations were not directed simply toward the Russians, but toward other groups as well, such as the Armenians in Georgia.[248] Therefore even eventual freedom from Russian control, after the end of the Soviet Union in 1990, did not lead to a subsiding of nationalistic frictions but instead unleashed other inter-ethnic violence and warfare within the newly independent nations.

One indicator of the "foreign" domination of indigenes, in both czarist and Communist times, was that the various subordinate nationalities long remained only a minority of the population in the cities of their own respective nations—again, a pattern reminiscent of Eastern Europeans as a whole in previous centuries. Latvians, for example, were just 24 percent of the population of their capital city, Riga, in 1871.[249] As late as 1897, only 28 percent of the people living in Ukrainian cities were Ukrainians and only 33 percent of the people living in the cities of Georgia were Georgians.[250] Even in 1918, 97 percent of the people living in the cities of Byelorussia were *not* Byelorussians.[251]

Policies toward the various indigenous nationalities did not remain uniform over space or time, either in the czarist empire or in the Soviet Union. A crucial question in both eras was whether, or to what degree, to try to assimilate these conquered peoples to the Russian culture. Where the indigenous culture was already similar, as among fellow-Slavs in the Ukraine or Byelorussia, assimilation seemed to be a more attractive option than among groups with more radically different cultures, such as the peoples of Central Asia. Thus, although the Orthodox Church enjoyed government support in European Russia under the czars, Catherine the Great promoted the spread of Islam among the Central Asians, wanting them to become more religious and considering that conversion to Christianity seemed less likely than spreading a religion which already had a foothold among them. Such decisions, however, varied over time as well as space, especially with a change of czars or even a change of mind during the reign of a given czar. Similarly during the Soviet era, V. I. Lenin's more accommodating policies toward the non-Russian peoples gave way to a much more traditional colonial subordination of the non-Russian nationalities under Josef Stalin—ironically, himself a non-Russian.

Although the official ideology of the Soviet era proclaimed the equality of all the various peoples of the U.S.S.R., and some serious gestures were made toward cultural autonomy and toward bringing non-Europeans into the industrialization process, the results were often meager. As of 1932, there was not a single engineer or technician among the 50,000 or more Tatars working in the Donets basin[252]—and, half a century later, Central Asians could still be characterized as largely unskilled members of the labor force.[253] As in other similar situations, the costly expedient of moving outsiders in, to supply the skills and aptitudes missing locally, was increasingly resorted to in the Soviet Union after attempts to create local, industrially-trained workers and educated elites proved to be too slow or too costly.[254]

Those Russians who settled or sojourned in other Soviet republics were not simply a random sample of the Russian people. They tended to be much more educated than the general population of the Russian republic, as well as much more educated than the populations of the republics to which they went.[255] They represented a large transfer of human capital, as well as a projection of Moscow's power and control. Nor were all of these—or other—Russians necessarily descendants of people who were part of the Russian population in earlier generations. An estimated 4 million people of non-Russian ancestry chose to identify themselves as "Russians" in the 1979 census and, presumably, in their careers and lives.[256] This too is part of a common part in other empires, of subject peoples re-defining themselves as members of the ruling group.

Both cultural and political autonomy for the non-Russian nationalities began to be cut back under Stalin, in the interest of economic efficiency and political control. With the passage of time, and especially with the onset of industrialization in the late 1920s and early 1930s, the formal equality of all the Soviet nationalities and cultures was eroded by the growing reality of Russian domination. Study of the Russian language became compulsory in all non-Russian schools.[257] The Cyrillic alphabet of the Russians was imposed on many nationalities that had traditionally used Latin or Arabic writing.[258] Soviet historians began to "rehabilitate" Russian conquests of the other nationalities that had occurred during the czarist era, while the patriotic heroes, ballads, and literature of other peoples were downplayed or even suppressed.[259] Nor were these by any means the worst examples of national repression. Terror was an instrument of state policy on nationalist issues, as on other issues.

Thousands of people were killed in the Baltic republics. Byelorussians during the 1980s discovered mass graves of people killed during Stalin's purges of the 1930s. During the Second World War, there were mass deportations of whole peoples to the hinterlands—the Volga Germans and the Tatars—for actual or suspected disloyalty, and millions were killed in an artificially produced famine in the Ukraine during the 1930s. Systematic campaigns of destruction of elites in newly conquered territories in Eastern Europe began during the Second World War, when the Soviets massacred more than 14,000 Polish officers in the Katyn forest and elsewhere.[260] Those arrested and deported from

Poland ran into the hundreds of thousands, perhaps more than a million. Even in the small Baltic nations, the people deported ran into the hundreds of thousands—again, concentrating on elites with the potential for resistance.[261] There was also a resurgence of officially promoted anti-Semitism in the U.S.S.R.,[262] though conducted under the guise of attacks on "homeless cosmopolitans" and other euphemisms.

The death of Stalin 1953 brought an end to some of the worst discriminations and oppressions against the non-Russian nationalities, and also brought some substantive concessions to their cultural autonomy and to the career ambitions of rising indigenous elites. The Presidium of the Central Committee of the Communist Party in Moscow announced in 1953 that someone native to each republic, "and not a Russian sent from Moscow" should hold the position of First Secretary of the Communist Party in the individual republics. Local shake-ups in fact brought more indigenous people into the political power structures in the republics.[263] There were particularly striking changes in the Ukraine, where no Ukrainian had ever been head of the Communist Party prior to 1953 but where, from 1955 to 1972, more than nine-tenths all politburo members were Ukrainian.[264] Some of the nationalities deported *en masse* during the Second World War were allowed to return to their former homelands.[265]

While some of these changes were substantive, others were largely cosmetic. The nominally highest official of each republic—the First Secretary of the Communist Party—now tended to be a member of the nationality of that republic, while the Second Secretary was usually a Russian. Despite the greater visibility of the First Secretary, the Second Secretary represented party policy-making, as distinguished from the administrative functions of the First Secretary, who was in effect subordinate.[266] First Secretaries generally spent their careers in their own respective republics, while Second Secretaries were transferred around the Soviet Union as representatives of Moscow. Although First Secretaries tended to have greater longevity in office at a given location, it was they who were usually sacrificed in purges when things went wrong.[267]

This policy was one which evolved over time. However, the general direction of evolution was toward the pattern that became almost universal in the late 1970s—national First Secretaries and Russian Second Secretaries. For the entire period from 1954 through 1976, local nationalities supplied 69 percent of the First Secretaries of the various republics, while Russians supplied 61 percent of the Second Secretaries.[268] Moreover, non-Russian Second Secretaries were not necessarily indigenous. In 1976, there was only one indigenous Second Secretary in the entire Soviet Union.[269]

In the Soviet government in Moscow as well, the representation of the various nationalities tended to vary with whether the position was one of real power or merely one of symbolic visibility. The various peoples of the Soviet Union were well-represented in the Supreme Soviet, a parliamentary body which was far from supreme in a totalitarian state. Non-Slavic peoples were in fact over-represented in the Supreme Soviet, holding 40 percent of the seats, though they were only 26 percent of the population. But the Presidium of the Supreme Soviet and the Council of Ministers were almost invariably chaired by a Slav, and the same was true of economic planning agencies and security forces.[270] The Central Committee of the Communist Party, the Politburo, and the Secretariat, were all overwhelmingly Slavic.[271] In 1973, all Secretaries of the Central Committee of the Communist Party of the Soviet Union were Russians.[272] Earlier, during the Khrushchev era, efforts were begun to bring non-Russians into leadership positions in Moscow but, by the early 1980s, Russian dominance among party leaders returned to the levels characteristic of the late Stalinist era. As of 1980, Slavs held all but three of the top 150 posts in the Central Committee of the Communist Party.[273]

In the military, among the generals appointed in the three decades between 1940 and 1970, an estimated 91 percent were Slavs.[274] As of 1982, more than 80 percent of all Soviet commissioned officers were Russians and well over 90 percent were Slavs.[275] Among sergeants, more than half were Ukrainians.[276] Nor did this general pattern change during the Gorbachev era, when the Soviet General Staff was 98 percent Slavic—85 percent Russian, 10 percent Ukrainian, and 3 percent Byelorussian.[277] Heads of Soviet enterprises and projects outside Russia were often Russian as well. So were many heads of the secret police, the KGB, in the Soviet republics. Russians living in other republics often played an important role in the local Communist Party, though non-Slavs did not usually play an important role in the Communist Party of republics other than their own.[278]

The general pattern of population distribution during the Soviet era was that Russians spread out into other Soviet republics but the peoples of these republics tended to remain concentrated in their respective homelands. As of 1959, Russians were one-fifth of the population of the Ukraine, one-fourth the population of Kirghizia, nearly one-third of the population of Latvia and just over 40 percent of the population of Kazakhstan.[279] In the capital of Kazakhstan in Central Asia—much closer to China or India than to Moscow—70 percent of the population was Russian.[280] The Russian language was likewise spreading. The proportion of non-Russians using Russian as a first or second language rose from 48 percent in 1970 to 62 percent by 1979.[281] But only 3 percent of Russians spoke a second language. They did not have to. Even those living in other nations seldom attempted to learn the national language. Of the tens of millions of Russians living in Central Asia, for example, fewer than 10 percent spoke a Central Asian language, and Russian students at a technological institute in Estonia during the Soviet era were openly "proud" to declare that they knew not one word of Estonian.[282]

Meanwhile, some Soviet nationalities were even more geographically concentrated in the U.S.S.R.'s last census in 1989 than they had been in 1926,[283] before the Stalinist transformation of the economy and society began, causing a reduced concentration of many nationalities during the period leading up to World War II.[284] A postwar reconcentration, however, left some nationalities even more concentrated by 1989 than they were at the time of the 1897 census in the czarist empire.[285] While 47 percent of Armenians lived in Armenia in 1926, 67 percent of them lived there in 1989. While 83 percent of the Turkmen lived in Turkmenistan in 1926, 93 percent lived there in 1989. These instances represented unusually large increases in concentration, however. More typically, there was a shift of a few percentage points toward greater or lesser concentration.[286] However, the mere persistence of nationalities living in their own republics—more than 90 percent in the three Baltic states—was quite a contrast to the official ideology of one "Soviet people." These nationalities were not dispersed in any way comparable to the dispersal of "minorities" in multi-ethnic societies such as the United States.

During the last decade of the Soviet Union, rising indigenous leaders and rising nationalism in the Soviet republics led, among other things, to various preferential policies—notably in employment and university admissions—for the predominant nationality in each republic.[287] This provided an incentive not only for individuals living outside their republic to relocate to the official homeland, where they would receive preferential treatment, but also for the offspring of mixed marriages to choose their homeland identity for official purposes. The decade of the 1980s also saw an exodus of Russians from many republics, partly in response to the preferential policies for indigenous peoples and partly in response to the local nationalism which in some cases took an ominously anti-Russian turn.

More than location was involved in nationalist identity, which was also cultural. As of 1979, 99 percent of Turkmenians spoke their own mother tongue, as did about three-quarters of the Byelorussians, four-fifths of the Ukrainians, and more than 90 percent of the Armenians, Lithuanians, Georgians, Kazakhs and Uzbeks, among others. These proportions remained virtually unchanged at the 1979 Census, as compared to the Census of 20 years earlier, and still remained very similar in the last Soviet census of 1989.[288] Despite assimilationist pressures, these regional and language differences remained strong, and in some cases became accentuated.[289]

As the future of a unified Soviet Union came into question during the last years of the Gorbachev era, the fate of the large Russian minorities in other republics became a concern both to the leaders of those republics and to the Russians themselves. A 1991 poll showed that there was no non-Russian republic in which even one third of the Russians living there considered themselves citizens of that republic. More than one fourth of the Russians in non-Russian republics considered a mass exodus of Russians from their republic to be either "likely" or "very likely" in all but one of the ten republics surveyed, and a majority of the Russians thought a mass exodus probable in three republics.[290] Concern about such an exodus was especially acute in the Central Asian republics, where much of the technical and managerial expertise was in the hands of Russians.

Ukrainians

The very name "Ukraine" means "borderland." Much of the history of this vast region of the czarist empire and the Soviet Union has been shaped by that geographic fact. Neighboring states have fought over and annexed portions of the Ukraine for centuries. Scandinavians, Poles, Lithuanians, Austrians, Turks, and of course Russians, have ruled portions—or all—of the Ukraine in various eras. Ukrainians have been a conquered people for most of their history. At the same time, they have been part of the great Slavic majority which was culturally and politically dominant in both czarist and Soviet times. Czars referred to the Ukrainians as "little Russians," in contrast to the expression "great Russians," used to describe the central people of the empire. With independence, "the Ukraine"—the borderland—became simply "Ukraine," since it was now no one's borderland any more. Both terms will be used here, as appropriate to the times being discussed.

In physical size, Ukraine is larger than any nation in Western Europe. Only three Western European nations—Britain, France, and West Germany—exceeded its population of about 52 million in 1990, of whom 72 percent were Ukrainian and 22 percent were Russian. Ukraine is also rich in natural resources and long served as a major food supplier to Russia and the rest of its empire. At the end of the Soviet era, the Ukraine supplied one-fourth of the grain in the U.S.S.R., as well as one-fourth of the beef, one-third of the vegetables, and half of the granulated sugar.[291] Within the Soviet Union, only Russia had a larger population.[292]

A united Ukrainian nation has been the exception rather than the rule in history—and an independent, united Ukraine, rare and fleeting. Kievan Russia, inhabited by the ancestors of today's Ukrainians, Russians, and Byelorussians, existed from the ninth to the eleventh century. Portions of the Ukraine began to break away, some as independent principalities, and others annexed as parts of neighboring states. Kievan Russia was then over-run in the thirteenth century by the Mongol hordes, led by the descendants of Genghis Khan. Kiev, the capitol of today's Ukraine, was razed by the Mongols in 1240 A.D. A century later the Lithuanians conquered the Ukraine and began its history as a land fought over by Eastern European powers. The Ukraine was reunited in 1569, but under Polish rule.

The Ukrainians' most famous fighters for independence from foreigners were the legendary Cossacks—bands of outlaws, adventurers, or guerrillas, who arose in the fifteenth century in response to Polish domination. The Ukrainians' attempts at independence failed, as did their attempts to ally themselves first with Russia against Poland, and then with Poland against Russia. Instead, Russia and Poland divided the Ukraine between themselves, early in the eighteenth century. Cossack uprisings continued in each part of the Ukraine, with such severity that the Poles had to call in Russian military assistance on three occasions. The Cossacks were finally crushed in the Russian Ukraine in the latter half of the eighteenth century and then Poland itself was partitioned, with its share of the Ukraine going to Russia, except for Galicia, which was annexed by Austria.[293]

Russian attempts to assimilate the Ukrainians and destroy their separate culture began early. In 1720, the czar forbad the publication of any books in the Ukraine, except for religious books—and these had to be in the Russian language. In 1804, teaching in the Ukrainian language was forbidden.[294] Although the landed nobility of the Ukraine tended to accept cultural assimilation, the masses retained their folk culture and, during the nineteenth century, literary, historical, and general intellectual expressions of Ukrainian culture arose.[295] Members of the Ukrainian nationalist group were arrested by the czarist authorities and their leader sentenced to 10 years of penal service in central Asia. New bans on publications in the Ukrainian language, and on the importation of Ukrainian writings from abroad, were issued. Meanwhile, outside the Russian Empire, in Galicia, the Ukrainian language and culture were permitted greater scope by the Austrian authorities.[296]

Early in the twentieth century, an easing of czarist oppression following the 1905 uprisings in the Russian Empire allowed Ukrainian nationalism to surface again, with Ukrainian delegations to the Duma (or parliament) demanding greater cultural freedom. Far from acceding to these demands, the czarist government during World War I began a systematic destruction of the freer Ukrainian culture in Galicia, when their troops occupied it briefly.[297] After the czar was overthrown in 1917, a Ukrainian People's Republic was declared, autonomous but affiliated with Russia. This was not acceptable to the Soviet authorities in Moscow. Although the Communists had received only 10 percent of the votes cast in the Ukraine, a so-called "All-Ukrainian Congress" was called—consisting almost entirely of Russians, about three-quarters of whom were Bolsheviks—which proclaimed a Soviet Ukrainian government and called on Moscow's assistance.

In response to this appeal, Russian troops invaded the Ukraine in January 1918 to impose a Communist government under the control of Moscow. They were driven out by the forces of the Central Powers, led by Germany, and the resulting treaty of Brest-Litovsk imposed as one condition the recognition of Ukrainian independence by the Soviet Union. However, the later defeat of the Central Powers by the Western allies led to abrogation of the treaty of Brest-Litovsk, and a resumption of Soviet military operations in the Ukraine. A confused civil war reigned there until 1919, when the Soviet Union and Poland partitioned the Ukraine between them. Twenty years later, the USSR took over the Polish area of the Ukraine, as Nazi Germany and the USSR partitioned Poland as a whole at the beginning of the Second World War.

During the early years of Soviet rule in the Ukraine, Lenin attempted to pacify Ukrainian nationalism with concessions on language and culture. But the Communist officials on the scene in the Ukraine—few of whom were Ukrainian—were much less conciliatory than Lenin. Only after direct pressure from Moscow in the mid-1920s did the Communist rulers in the Ukraine allow more Ukrainian participation in the party and government, and more use of the Ukrainian language. This led to a kind of Ukrainian renaissance—which then went too far for Moscow. In 1930, under Stalin, the first major purge trials began in the Ukraine, a foretaste of what was to happen later in other parts of the Soviet Union. Of 259 Ukrainian writers who published in 1930, only 36 were still publishing in 1938. Of 115 Ukrainian Communist Party Central Committee members elected in 1934, only 3 remained in 1938.[298]

Even these purges were overshadowed by the massive famine that struck the Ukraine during the early 1930s, as Stalin's collectivization of agriculture disrupted production and produced both passive and armed resistance among the Ukrainian peasants. But the crucial factors in creating the famine were (1) the ruthless extraction of agricultural produce by the Soviet government, even when it left the peasants without food—or in some cases, even without seed for the next year's crop, and (2) the sealing off of the Ukraine's borders with Russia, where far more food was available. Although the great famine of 1930–1933 had devastating impact across broad areas of the U.S.S.R., killing millions of people, the Ukraine was the hardest hit of all. Most of the deaths occurred in the Ukraine and in the regions of the North Caucasus where Ukrainians were concentrated.[299]

The desperation of hunger in the Ukraine drove the starving peasants to eat dogs, cats, rats, weeds, earthworms, and some even human
corpses. Others defied armed Soviet troops to get at food, individually
or in groups, often paying with their lives. Death by starvation was so
widespread among the peasants that carts came daily to pick up
corpses from the streets, the homes, and the countryside. In some
places the carts came twice a day. There was no way to bury all these
bodies individually, so mass graves became commonplace. Altogether,
an estimated 5 million people died in the Ukraine during the famine.[300]

Much more was involved in this famine than simply economic inefficiency or political indifference. The thoroughness and ruthlessness
of the campaign of terror which accompanied the famine, and the
widespread and often deadly purges of Ukrainian authorities and
intellectuals which followed the famine, clearly indicated a policy to
crush national resistance of all sorts in the Ukraine, once and for all.
The massive sufferings, horrors, and atrocities accompanying the
famine-creating policies then provided an excuse for the purges that
followed, as local officials were made scapegoats for these disasters,
even though it was often the purged Communists of the Ukraine who
had from the outset warned Moscow that the food collection quotas
imposed on Ukrainian agriculture simply could not be met, not even
by starving the peasants. Despite the deaths of millions and searches
and seizures of even minute quantities of food, the original collection
goals were in fact never met. But another goal of greater importance to
Moscow was achieved: the crushing of opposition in the Ukraine and
the consolidation of Soviet power there.

The calculated nature of Soviet policy was indicated by the fact that
the worst starvation occurred in the food-growing areas, which were
the centers of peasant opposition to collectivization of agriculture and
also strongholds of Ukrainian nationalism. City-dwellers in the
Ukraine suffered malnutrition but not starvation on the same scale as
in the countryside—and extraordinary efforts were made to keep the
peasants out of the cities, just as extraordinary efforts were made to
keep Ukrainians from going to Russia to get food. Indeed, foreign
offers of famine relief were refused by the Soviet government, which
flatly denied that there was any famine in the Ukraine. One Soviet official at the time summed up the situation in a conversation with a fel-
low-Communist:

A ruthless struggle is going on between the peasantry and
our regime. It's a struggle to the death. This year was a test of
our strength and their endurance. It took a famine to show
them who is master here. It has cost millions of lives, but the
collective farm system is here to stay. We've won the war.[301]

Over the years, through all the stark and dramatic events and
changing policies in the Ukraine, a slow erosion of the Ukrainian language proceeded. In 1936, schools conducted in the Ukrainian language served 86 percent of all the students in the Ukraine. By 1973,
that figure had fallen to 60 percent. Forty percent of the schools were
conducted in the Russian language, twice as high as the proportion of
Russians in the population of the Ukraine. A similar trend appeared in
the publication of scientific writings in the Ukraine. In 1946, the
majority of scientific publications in the Ukraine were still being published in the Ukrainian language but, just 4 years later, more were
being published in Russian than in Ukrainian and, by 1975, there
were more than four times as many Ukrainian scientific journals published in the Russian language as in the language of the Ukraine.[302]

Ukrainian resistance took many forms, from informal cultural
groups to non-violent underground organizations working for secession. An estimated 40 percent of the political prisoners in Soviet labor
camps were Ukrainians, and they were prominent in organizing
protests and insurrections there. Still, Ukrainian resistance tended to
be confined to intellectuals, rather than the working class.[303] Even
after Ukraine became a sovereign nation, there were virtually the same
number of Ukrainian school children being taught in Russian as in
Ukrainian.[304]

During the Soviet era, Ukrainian culture was allowed more scope
during the tenure in office of Petro Shelest, who in 1965 became First
Secretary of the Communist Party of the Ukraine. In an apparent
attempt to calm and co-opt Ukrainian nationalists, Shelest permitted
more freedom of expression. For example, one Ukrainian writer was
permitted to keep his job, even after publishing in the West a book critical of Russian treatment of Ukrainians. Shelest's removal in 1972 and
the official denunciation of him for "local nationalism" and "national
narrow-mindedness"[305] signalled the limits of what the Soviet leadership in Moscow was prepared to tolerate. Demonstrations, firings, and

arrests among Ukrainian nationalists all increased.[306] Among the charges against the deposed Shelest was that his view of history was faulty in failing to see the czars' conquest of the Ukraine as ultimately beneficial.[307] The political nature of these cultural issues was indicated, among other things, by the fact that some Ukrainian cultural expressions were permitted in Moscow and Leningrad that were not permitted in the Ukraine itself.[308] There was no danger of igniting Ukrainian nationalism among the Russians.

When the Ukraine proclaimed its independence on August 24, 1991, it marked the end of centuries of subjugation to foreigners in general and Russians in particular. Its independence was perhaps a greater shock to the Russians than the independence of any of the other former Soviet republics, partly because of historic, racial, and cultural ties between Ukrainians and Russians. Even as a sovereign state, however, Ukraine had a cultural life that was in many ways essentially Russian.[309]

Central Asians

The peoples most different from the dominant Slavs of the Russian Empire and the Soviet Union have been the peoples of Central Asia. These differences have been racial, religious, linguistic, demographic, geographic, and historic.

The vast reaches of Central Asia exceed in size all of Western Europe, but the Turkic, historically nomadic, and predominantly Moslem peoples of Central Asia are much more thinly spread over arid lands unable to support the population densities of Europe. Altogether, however, the population of Central Asia has been quite large— 49 million people in 1989 or about one-sixth of the total population of the Soviet Union.[310] These 49 million people included about 33 million indigenous Central Asians,[311] with the remainder being primarily Russians and others who migrated in large numbers into Central Asia over the years, as well as Germans, Tatars, and others forcibly relocated there during the Second World War, in order to forestall their collaboration with the invading German-led Axis armies. One measure of the demographic impact of Russian colonization is that Kazakhs fell from 91 percent of the population of Khazakhstan in the middle of the nineteenth century to 57 percent in 1926 and to a low of 29 percent in

1962, before rebounding to about 40 percent by 1989, on the eve of the dissolution of the Soviet Union. In some years, under both the czars and the Communists, the Kazakh population declined absolutely,[312] as Russians took over some of their best land and imposed policies disrupting the indigenous way of life.

Once of enormous importance in centuries past, when the Silk Road went through Central Asia to connect Europe and China in trade, or when Genghis Khan created the world's greatest land empire in the heart of the Eurasian land mass, this region became in later centuries an economic, military, and political backwater. The discovery of sea routes between Europe and Asia made the Silk Road no longer the prime trade route, since waterborne transport was so much cheaper than land transport, even when the water routes went around the African continent on the way to India and China, before the Suez Canal was built. Suez and industrialization then left Central Asia on the periphery of world developments.

Militarily, the progress of gunpowder weapons in general and cannons in particular put an end to centuries of dominance by warriors charging on horseback, such as those who came out of Central Asia in vast hordes to conquer and strike terror among the peoples of the Far East, the Middle East, and Eastern Europe. Once conquerors of China and overlords of Russia, the peoples of Central Asia were ultimately reduced to becoming the conquered subjects first of the Chinese and then of the Russians. By the nineteenth century, czarist Russia controlled Central Asia and in the 1920s the Communists under Stalin began to carve it up into the separate republics of Kazakhstan, Turmenistan, Uzbekistan, Tajikistan, and Kyrgyzstan. Despite sweeping changes imposed on Central Asia from Moscow under the Communists, there was no great knowledge or understanding of the indigenous peoples of Central Asia. Lenin had never set foot in any of this vast region.[313]

Under both the czars and the Communists, Russians moved into Central Asia, disrupting the traditional way of life there, as well as assuming political control. The herds of animals on which so many nomadic Central Asians depended found less and less area in which to graze, as Russians took over land and reorganized the economy. The American Civil War, cutting off cotton supplies to Europe, led to a great expansion and improvement of cotton cultivation in Central Asia, which remained the major producer of cotton for the Russian

Empire and then for the Soviet Union, on into the late twentieth century.[314] This and other agricultural ventures in Central Asia had serious environmental side effects, however. By 1990, the shrinking of the Aral Sea, due to the demands of various crops for water, caused its surface to shrink to little more than half its previous size and its volume of water to much less than half.[315]

If czarist conquest was disruptive to the traditional societies of Central Asia, Communist rule was traumatic. The civil war period following the Bolshevik revolution took a heavy toll among both people and animals in Central Asia. In the brief period between 1917 and 1920, the number of livestock in Central Asia was cut in half.[316] As for people, the famine of 1921–22 is estimated to have taken almost a million lives among Kazakhs alone.[317] Collectivization under Stalin, beginning in the late 1920s, was likewise catastrophic for man and beast alike.

Collectivization in Central Asia meant forcing nomadic peoples into fixed settlements, which was often fatal to herd animals that required huge grazing areas. The number of sheep and goats declined from more than 27 million in 1929 to less than 3 million by 1934. Over the same span, the number of horses fell from more than 4 million to less than a quarter of a million. Among human beings, the number of Kazakhs declined by nearly 900,000 from 1926 to 1939—some killed resisting collectivization, some succumbing to famine, and others fleeing to China or Afghanistan.[318] Kazakhs were the hardest hit, with most of their deaths being due to starvation or to famine-related diseases.[319]

Like many other colonized regions around the world, the Central Asian republics were artificial creations of the conquerors, following ethnic and linguistic lines only very roughly, and these republics contained many ethnic minority enclaves. Thus there were substantial numbers of Uzbeks in Turkestan and Kazakhs in Uzbekistan, for example, with Kazakhs in fact constituting at one time a majority of the population in the area surrounding the Uzbek capital of Tashkent.[320] As in other parts of the colonized world, this was not due solely to arbitrary boundaries drawn by the conquering powers, though these boundaries in Central Asia as elsewhere encompassed larger aggregations of people than had coalesced politically or culturally before. In addition, enclaves of both large and small Central Asian groups were scattered throughout the region and large numbers of Slavs—mostly Russians—also moved into Central Asia.

Education, urbanization, and industrialization were major goals of
the Soviet government. However, dramatic increases in all of these over
the years in Central Asia did not produce equally dramatic increases in
education, urbanization, or industrialization for Central Asians themselves. Modernization of the region was led by Slavs who relocated
there in large numbers. The most extreme case was Kazakhstan, where
Russians came to outnumber Kazakhs from the 1960s through most of
the 1980s.[321] By 1989, however, a higher birthrate among Kazakhs and
an out-migration of Russians restored the Kazakhs as the most numerous group in Kazakhstan, though only 39.7 percent of the population,
compared to 37.8 percent who were Russians.[322] One sign of Russian
domination of the region was that, while 63 percent of Kazakhs understood the Russian language, not quite one percent of the Russians in
Kazahkstan understood the Kazakh language.[323] In none of the Central
Asian republics were the indigenous people a majority of the urban
population, even though they were all a majority in the non-urban
areas.

The economic, as well as political, subordination of Central Asian
was a pattern going all the way back to czarist times. Nearly four fifths
of the lowest-skilled industrial workers in Turkmenistan in 1914 were
Uzbeks, while more than four fifths of the mechanized workers were
Russians. In the late 1920s and early 1930s, only 7 percent of the
workers in large-scale industries in Uzbekistan were indigenous.
About a decade later, on the eve of the Nazi invasion of the U.S.S.R.,
indigenous workers had risen to 23 percent of the workers in large-
scale industry in Uzbekistan.[324] Yet, even in the 1970s, Uzbeks
remained a distinct minority among the employees of various chemi-
cal, textile, machinery, and tractor manufacturing plants in Uzbekistan. As late as 1979, less than one-third of the people working on
construction of a subway in Tashkent were indigenous.[325] Only 10 percent of the pilots at Tashkent airport were Asian, and—except for
stewards, stewardesses or workers in freight transport—only 14 percent of the air and ground personnel there were Central Asians.[326]

Most Central Asians in the Soviet Union's armed forces were
assigned to construction units. Even when they were in units that handled advanced technology, Central Asians tended to do the less technical work in those units. Racial discrimination and racial epithets
toward Central Asian soldiers were not uncommon. Extremely few of

these soldiers ever became officers or re-enlisted.[327] For many Central Asians, their military duties were distinctly un-military, and did not involve being armed or receiving training in the use of arms. However, Central Asians were a majority of the troops in the internal security forces, used to maintain order within the Soviet Union, and included guards in prisons and at *Gulag* forced labor camps. In such roles, Central Asians had a rare opportunity to boss and bully Russians who were prisoners. They were noted for their cruelty in these roles.[328]

Although a majority of the people with middle-class jobs in Kazakhstan were of Russian, Ukrainian, or other ethnic origin, Kazakhs were half of the white collar administrative personnel in the last years of the Soviet Union. However, they remained a small minority of the blue collar workers, whether skilled (3 percent) or unskilled (11 percent).[329] The Kazakhs thus followed a common pattern among newly educated members of lagging societies in seeking upward mobility via government bureaucracies.

Despite a large Slavic presence in Soviet Central Asia, intermarriages there were overwhelmingly marriages of Slavs with members of other Slavic groups and marriages of Central Asians with members of other Central Asian groups. In a period of more than a quarter of a century, only 49 marriages involved a Kazakh woman and a Russian man,[330] even though there were millions of Russians and millions of Kazakhs in Central Asia. Even among themselves, the Central Asians were not given to intermarriage. Most Uzbeks (86 percent) married other Uzbeks. Most Kazakhs (94 percent) married other Kazakhs. Endogamy among the smaller Central Asian peoples ranged from 77 percent among the Tadzhiks to 91 percent among the Turkmen and 95 percent among the Kirghiz.[331] Less than 2 percent of the children born to Uzbek women had fathers who were not Uzbek.[332]

Despite the distinctiveness of each Central Asian group, the social and cultural affinities among them have been demonstrated in many ways. When a Soviet Central Asian lived outside his own republic, it was usually in another Central Asian republic,[333] just as marriage outside a given Central Asian nationality was usually marriage with another Central Asian of a different nationality.[334] This cultural affinity among Central Asians has been demonstrated internationally as well. Central Asian troops in the Soviet army in Afghanistan in the 1970s fraternized with the local Afghans, who were racially and culturally very similar. The Soviet government then replaced Central Asian soldiers with European troops.[335] This reflected a long history of Russian distrust of Central Asians in the military, going back to czarist times. Despite an 1874 decree of "universal" military conscription, Central Asians were not in fact drafted until the desperate days of 1916—and their conscription then provoked an armed rebellion in Central Asia.[336]

Higher birthrates in the Central Asian republics have meant lower average ages in the population and more children. In the predominantly Slavic republics of the Soviet Union—Russia, the Ukraine, and Byelorussia—children under 10 years of age were an estimated 14 to 15 percent of the total population, and there were similar proportions in the Baltic republics. But, in the Central Asian republics, children under 10 were from 22 to 30 percent of the population. Nearly two-thirds of all Russian families contained only two or three persons, while more than half of all Uzbek families contained six or more.[337]

In many ways, the relationship of the Slavs to the Central Asians was like the relationship of many European peoples to non-European Third World peoples—and like the relationship of Western Europeans to Eastern Europeans in earlier centuries. The Slavs in general and the Russians in particular dominated the economic, political, and intellectual life of Soviet Central Asia and led that region into modern urbanization and industrialization. They were the cultural conduits through which the ideas, the products, the technology, and the practices of European civilization reached Central Asia. It was the czars who stamped out slavery in Central Asia, impoverishing the Turkmen who lived by slave-raids, leading to alcoholism and opium use among men whose chief preoccupation was now taken from them.[338]

How well Central Asians fared under the Soviets depends on whether the relevant comparison is with Russians, with their own past, or with similar peoples outside the U.S.S.R. in Turkey, Iran or Afghanistan, for example. Per capita income in Central Asia ranged from 47 percent of that in the Soviet Union as a whole in Tadzhikistan to 74 percent in Kazakhstan in 1980. External comparisons seem more favorable. As of the middle of the twentieth century, death rates appeared to be far lower in all of the Central Asian republics than in Iran.[339] Doctors were far more available to the Soviet Central Asians, even in rural areas.[340] The proportion of the population who were students in higher education was several times as large among Central

Asians as among the people of Iran.[341] From almost complete illiteracy before 1917, the indigenous people were by 1958 one-third of all students receiving higher education in Uzbekistan.[342] Uzbeks far outdistanced Afghans in economic growth, medical services, or education.[343] The Soviet government provided tours of Central Asia for neighboring Middle Eastern peoples.[344] As with various other conquered peoples, the Central Asians gained economically, medically, and educationally from their association with a more technologically advanced society— but at a price.

Successor States to the Soviet Union

Three small republics clustered together on the Baltic Sea—Lithuania, Latvia, and Estonia—have populations that are individually not as large as the population of New York City and collectively not as large as that of Tokyo. Yet these three little nations began the process of secession which ultimately dismembered the largest nation on earth. The formal decision to dissolve the Soviet Union was made by the presidents of the three Slavic republics—Russia, Ukraine, and Byelorussia— without the participation of the dozen other republics or of Mikhail Gorbachev, president of the union that now disappeared under him.

The era of the Russian empires ended on December 31, 1991, when the Soviet Union was dissolved. Thereafter, Russians were rulers only of Russia, and 25 million Russians became expatriates in other nations formerly controlled from Moscow. The Commonwealth of Independent States, which superseded the Union of Soviet Socialist Republics on January 1, 1992, contained most of the nations formerly in the U.S.S.R., but their relationships to one another and to Russia were now quite different. To no one was the difference more apparent or more painful than to the expatriate Russians, now transformed into subordinate minorities in countries they once dominated.

Even before the dissolution of the Soviet Union, Slavs in Central Asia had begun leaving, in response to growing nativism and preferential treatment of the indigenous population in employment and university admissions. This exodus was on a scale that led to vacancies in skilled jobs that could not be filled by the Central Asian population, despite rising skill levels among the indigenous peoples.[345] A quarter of a million Russians left Kazakhstan in 1992 alone.[346]

The varying degrees of economic prosperity among the Soviet republics seems also to have had little correlation with their desire to break away from the U.S.S.R. Latvia, Estonia, and Lithuania were the most prosperous of the Soviet republics, yet these Baltic nations were the first to declare their independence, even in the face of both economic and military reprisals. Moreover, unlike most other Soviet republics, the Baltic states refused to join the U.S.S.R.'s successor, the Commonwealth of Independent States. Conversely, the Central Asian republics, which remained among the poorer nations of the U.S.S.R. throughout its existence, were also among the least anxious to become independent, and Gorbachev in fact found one of his staunchest allies in the vain effort to preserve the Soviet Union in Nursultan Nazabaev, president of Kazakhstan.[347] Part of the reason for this pattern may be that the more prosperous republics, including Russia, were consuming less than they produced and were, in effect, subsidizing the poorer republics like those in Central Asia, which were consuming more than they produced.[348]

Economic ties among countries that had been Soviet republics continued to varying degrees, not only among those who became members of the Commonwealth of Independent States, but also among the others, including the Baltic republics whose secession had begun the disintegration of the U.S.S.R. The Russian ruble, for example, continued to be used as currency, until Russia's runaway inflation and subsequent central bank issuance of a new ruble, with arbitrary limits on convertibility of the old into the new, led various former Soviet republics to begin issuing their own national currencies. However, the regional specialization in production within the Soviet Union, and transportation networks adapted to that specialization, continued to affect trading patterns among the former Soviet republics, even as they began the process of seeking additional trading partners. Nevertheless the process of transition, not only from being a single economic unit, but also from the discredited Communist system under which all had operated to others with which they were unfamiliar, led to significant declines in living standards among the former Soviet republics as they groped toward their respective new arrangements.[349]

SLAVIC EMIGRATION

The transatlantic mass migration of Slavs began much later than that of Western Europeans. Because immigration across the Atlantic tended to follow trade routes during the age of sail, regions without large-scale trade with the New World sent few immigrants. With the advent of transatlantic steamships, however, all-passenger voyages became economically feasible, which in turn freed immigration from its dependence on trade routes. This provided the peoples of Eastern Europe, the Balkans, and Mediterranean Europe with the same access to the New World already enjoyed by Western Europeans. Between 1880 and 1914, more than four million people emigrated from Eastern Europe to the Western Hemisphere, 90 percent of them to North America. Nearly two million of these emigrants were Jews, but Slavic emigrants included more than a million Poles and hundreds of thousands of Russians and Ukrainians, among others.[350]

During the era of mass migration from Eastern Europe, wages were several times as high in the United States as in the Slavic homelands, and the Canadian government was actively recruiting immigrants with the lure of free homesteads on the western prairies, where most of the Eastern European immigrants to Canada settled.[351] The United States became the principal destination of Slavic overseas migrations, as of European overseas migrations in general. However, there were Slavic communities in such widely scattered countries as Brazil and Australia, as well as closer to home in France, Germany, and Britain. There were Poles, Czechs and Croatians among the people attracted to Australia during the mid-nineteenth century gold rush there.[352] During the 1920s, emigrants from Yugoslavia worked primarily as miners in France, Belgium, and Holland.[353] During the twenty years between the two World Wars, more than 2 million emigrants of Polish nationality left their homelands and about 900,000 returned. France was the largest single recipient, with more than 622,000 Poles, of whom nearly a third returned. So did more than 90 percent of the approximately 475,00 who went to Germany, long a destination of seasonal migrations of Poles for agricultural work. But, of the approximately 272,000 Poles who went to the United States during the same period, fewer than 12,000 returned.[354]

Overseas migration was of course not the only kind of migration, in

Eastern Europe or elsewhere. At the beginning of the twentieth century at least one-fourth of the entire adult male population of Eastern Europe had lived or worked somewhere other than where they were born. Movement across the Atlantic was therefore an extension of a tradition of migrations that already existed before trans-oceanic travel became feasible. Seasonal migrations of Poles for agricultural labor was much more common in Europe than in the United States, where only about one-fifth of Polish immigrants worked in agriculture, compared to Germany or Latvia, where the overwhelming majority did.[355] Immigration to South America was also significant—and varied significantly in its occupational makeup. As of the early 1940s, there were more than 110,00 Poles in Argentina and between 115,000 and 150,000 in Brazil.[356] For the entire period from 1927 to 1938, only 10 percent of Polish immigrants to Brazil worked in agriculture, compared to 62 percent of those who went to Argentina.[357]

Mass refugee flights have been a major part of the emigration from Eastern Europe. On the eve of the Second World War, the Polish community in France numbered nearly half a million people, fewer than 10 percent of whom had been born in France.[358] During the war itself, millions of people from Eastern Europe were sent to Germany to work as slave laborers—three and a half million Poles alone by the time the war ended.[359] In the postwar era, more than two and a half million people fled from Communist East Germany before the Berlin Wall was built to stop them. That was 15 percent of the total population of the country.[360]

While Western European countries regained their independence at the end of the war, much of Eastern Europe became satellite nations with puppet governments installed and controlled by the Soviet Union. Contrasting living standards, as well as differences between democratic and Communist societies, led to mass emigrations out of these countries. In the five years marking the end of World War II and the immediate postwar period, more than 20 million people fled westward from Eastern Europe.[361] Not all these people were Slavs by any means. This number does not include those who died en route or those refugees who fled from one part of Eastern Europe to another. It also does not include 1.5 million Poles deported to the Soviet Union.[362]

During a century of emigration from Eastern Europe, beginning in the latter part of the nineteenth century, the fate of Slavic emigrants in the countries to which they went reflected the levels of skills and capabilities they had achieved—or failed to achieve—in Eastern Europe. Among the emigrants from Russian-held Poland during the decade from 1893 to 1903, 42 percent were landless peasants and another 14 percent were agricultural laborers. Moreover, the agriculture they practiced was a backward agriculture.[363] By contrast, those Poles from the part of dismembered Poland annexed by Prussia came from an area with a more prosperous agriculture and also had some industrial and artisan skills, such as those common among Germans.[364] Among Polish immigrants to the United States during the era of mass immigration, only about one in sixteen had a trade, though they were noted for their ability to save from meager earnings, even when that required them to live on "stale bread and sausage."[365] Yet, of those Polish immigrants who did have artisan skills, most came from Prussia.[366]

As for the professions, these occupations were so rare that there were more Polish domestics than professionals in most of the countries to which they immigrated in substantial numbers from 1927 to 1938— neither figure, however, reaching 10 percent during that time.[367] The Australian census of 1933 showed that the great majority of Croatians working there were in unskilled manual occupations.[368] The majority of Czechs in Australia at the same time were also unskilled workers and agricultural laborers.[369] Even the post–World War II immigrants from the Ukraine were mostly unskilled and semi-skilled.[370]

None of these patterns has been fixed in stone, however, even for the historically brief period of a century of mass overseas migration from Eastern Europe. During more than six decades of substantial Czech emigration, the occupations of the emigrants changed from predominantly agricultural to predominantly skilled labor.[371] A study of Carpatho-Rusyn males in Minneapolis showed that, while 55 percent of those in the first generation were unskilled, this fell to just under 10 percent for the second generation and to 3 percent for the third generation.[372] Eastern European immigrants to the United States as a group had, by 1980, higher earnings than other white Americans, and also had more years of schooling.

In part this reflected their being more urbanized and slightly older. Nevertheless, this also represented dramatic changes over the generations. While just 22 percent of men from Eastern Europe who were born from 1905 to 1914 reached professional, technical, or managerial occupations, nearly 45 percent of those born between 1935 to 1944 did so. Thirty percent of all Eastern European men of all ages, living in the United States, were in managerial and professional specialties in 1980, ranging from 20 percent among Slovaks to 48 percent among Russians. Among women, 25 percent were in these occupations, ranging from 18 percent among Slovaks to 37 percent among Russians.[373] These indicators of dramatic increases in human capital among Americans of Slavic ancestry reflect not only their taking advantage of the opportunities available in the United States but also, to some extent, reflect advances of Slavs and Slavic nations in general.

SUMMARY AND IMPLICATIONS

The history of the Slavs, like the history of the British, illustrates the enormous importance of human capital—and especially of the transfer of human capital. From primitive beginnings as an illiterate, tribal people in medieval Eastern Europe, Slavs achieved not only literacy but also a world-class literature and advanced into the modern industrial and commercial world economy, with the aid of numerous cultural transfers from Western Europe and the United States. Not only the physical embodiments of Western European civilization, such as plows, coins, and printing presses moved eastward, so did knowledge, alphabets, and ideas.

For centuries Germans were especially prominent among the many non-Slavic peoples whose industrial and commercial roles within Slavic Eastern Europe and the Balkans were crucial to the modernization of these regions. Not only did such outsiders create much of the industrial and commercial sectors of the economies of many Slavic nations, they helped create within the Slavs themselves industrial and commercial experience, skills, and aptitudes, such as developed among the Poles of Prussia and the Czechs of Bohemia. While one result of this historic role was a general prestige of things German among the Slavs,[374] another result was resentment against the Germans that erupted sporadically into violence, from the riots in Cracow in 1312 to the riots in Bohemia in the nineteenth century and the slaughters and mass expulsions of ethnic German civilians from Eastern Europe and the Balkans at the end of World War II. Such ambivalent reactions to those supplying more advanced human capital has not been confined to Slavs by any means, but was also part of the reaction

to the British in India, Jews in Spain, Indians in East Africa, overseas
Chinese in Southeast Asia, and many other groups in a variety of other
countries. Nor was Slav hostility to more economically advanced
groups in their midst confined to Germans. Eastern Europe also
became one of the most virulent centers of anti-Semitism in the modern
world.

With the passing of centuries, Slavs eventually began to produce,
within their own people, individuals of worldwide stature in mathematics, the sciences, and the arts. Indeed, individuals of recognized
genius began to appear among the Slavs—the great Russian novelists
of the nineteenth century, for example—long before the masses had
achieved literacy, or the countries had achieved industrial or commercial competence, much less political freedom or even stable governments in some cases. The human infrastructure of democratic and
economically advanced nations—the collective achievements, economic experience, and evolved traditions necessary for general economic and political advancement—remained lacking in Eastern
Europe and the Balkans, long after individual geniuses had arisen
among the Slavs in a number of fields. The mass production of university graduates was no substitute for this more fundamental kind of
human capital growing out of experience. On the contrary, large numbers of people with degrees, but without skills, added to the bureau-
cratization and political instability of the Slavic lands of Europe.

In many cases, the political institutions of modern Eastern European nations were borrowed from Western European nations—the
constitution of Czechoslovakia, for example, being like that of
Britain[375]—but what could not be borrowed were the history and traditions that made those institutions work. In the ethnically fragmented
and embittered world of East Central Europe as it emerged after the
First World War, the parliamentary institutions that the nations of the
region began with often proved to be unworkable. In nations with pro-
liferations of small and often ethnically-based political parties, ruling
coalitions of these parties rose and fell with sometimes tragi-comic
frequency, making stability of laws and policies virtually impossible to
achieve. In economies so poor that access to the public treasury was
by far the most promising road to wealth, politics was often a desperate
struggle for office that turned into an extremist war of each against all.
In countries with no traditions of free government or the self-restraints

necessary for such governments, the virulence of the press was matched by political violence in the streets and, in the case of Yugoslavia, exchanges of gunshots during parliamentary debate, with a party leader being killed in parliament itself during one of these exchanges.[376]

As parliamentary government thus discredited itself in much of East Central Europe between the two World Wars, such governments succumbed to coups d'etat and authoritarian rule in Poland, Hungary, Yugoslavia, Romania, and Bulgaria.[377] In the Russian Empire, the life of free parliamentary government was even shorter, lasting less than one year in between centuries of authoritarian rule under the czars and then Communist totalitarianism that dominated the country for nearly three-quarters of a century afterward. Indeed, the strongest challenge to the democratic traditions of Western Europe and its off- shoot societies in the Western Hemisphere and Australasia came gov- ernmentally from the Soviet Union and its ideological allies around the world, though the central theory of that ideological challenge, Marxism, was another import to Eastern Europe from the West.

Even under ruthless totalitarian governments, the Soviet Union was plagued by the same kind of ethnic fragmentation and nationalism that created such havoc in the rest of Eastern Europe and in the Balkans. Whole regions defected from the U.S.S.R. at various times—immedi- ately after the revolutions of 1917, during World War II, and in the waning years of the Soviet government in the last decade of the twenti- eth century. Only the forcible military intervention of the Red Army restored the defecting territories in the first two instances.

Loyalty to the state varied greatly among the nationalities, both in czarist times and in Soviet times. Some small tribal groups absorbed into the Russian Empire readily accepted the higher cultural level of the conquerors. Other small immigrant and refugee groups who sought sanctuary in Russia from China, the Ottoman Empire, or Iran likewise became—and remained—loyal members of the host society, even when they retained their own cultural distinctiveness.[378] However, other Soviet nationalities resisted in innumerable ways, from non- cooperation to armed rebellion, despite the heavy penalties for such resistance.

The degree to which Russian hegemony was accepted was not always, or even generally, along lines of racial or cultural affinity.

Ukrainians are racially and linguistically much closer to the Russians than are the Armenians, but the latter seemed to accept the Russian-dominated government more readily, perhaps because grim historical experience left them few viable alternatives. Nor was the loyalty of a given group always the same over time. Germans, who fought loyally for Russia against German invaders in the First World War, collaborated with the Nazis during the Second World War. However, the racially very different Tatars also collaborated with the Nazis against the Soviets. The impact of Soviet policies—notably collectivization—seems more highly correlated with the responses of the various Soviet nationalities than their degree of racial or cultural similarity.

An historical assessment of the net impact of conquest is no easier in the case of the Russian Empire and the Soviet Union than elsewhere in the world. Sheer pacification has been an enormous benefit wherever and whenever it has occurred, whether in the Scottish highlands or in parts of Africa, and so it was in the Russian empires, under both czars and Communists. A distinguished scholar—and one by no means pro-Russian or pro-Soviet—has stated: "Azerbaijan was in a state of feudal anarchy when the Russians moved in, bringing with them a peace and order that Transcaucasia had not known for centuries."[379]

For some parts of the czarist empire, and later of the Soviet Union, the classic patterns of Western imperialism emerged: material progress accompanied by political and psychic oppression, the extraction of minerals and agricultural raw materials and the installation of modern industrial technology, largely run by Europeans. Central Asia was the clearest example of this. However, some other parts of the U.S.S.R. were more economically and culturally advanced than the conquerors—and remained so. Income per capita in Estonia and Latvia, for example, was about one-third higher than in Russia[380] during the Soviet era. However, even in the poorer Central Asian republics, it would be hard to argue, as some theories of imperialism do, that their peoples were "exploited" and that this explains the greater prosperity of the imperialist nation, since net transfers of wealth were toward the Central Asian republics.

The whole range of imperialist relations with conquered peoples existed within the Union of Soviet Socialist Republics. Though both the czarist and the Communist empires were very much like those of other European powers in many respects, the Soviet Union was unique in that its empire expanded in the post–World War II era, while the empires of other European nations declined and virtually disappeared, as colonies around the world gained independence. During the same era, Soviet influence and control of other nations grew, not only in the contiguous Eastern European bloc and Afghanistan, but also in overseas affiliates such as Cuba and Ethiopia. In racial or ethnic terms, Russian domination extended not only throughout the Soviet Union, where Russians were a bare majority, but also to the entire Warsaw Pact bloc, where they were little more than one-third of the population, and to the worldwide Soviet bloc, in which Russians were less than one-fourth of the population.[381] Beginning in the late 1980s, however, Russian hegemony rapidly eroded and then vanished in Eastern Europe, and began to be challenged even within the Soviet Union itself, foreshadowing a disintegration characteristic of other European empires.

In this broader historical perspective, the question is not so much why the U.S.S.R. collapsed, but why it lasted so long after Western imperialism had faded elsewhere. Stronger government control, ruthless purges, and mass slaughters had much to do with the differences. So too did a carefully fostered image of being anti-imperialist, an image widely accepted, and often repeated, among Western intellectuals, thus exempting the Soviet Union from many of the criticisms and pressures generated against the imperialism of Western European countries or the United States. In its domestic policies as well, the Soviet Union benefitted from the protective efforts of a large and prominent segment of Western intellectuals to ignore or deny its failures. The man-made famine in the Ukraine during the 1930s, for example, was ignored, down-played, or denied outright by such prominent Western intellectuals as George Bernard Shaw and the *New York Times*' Pulitzer-Prizewinning columnist Walter Duranty,[382] even though the facts that finally came out during the last days of the Soviet Union under Gorbachev showed that even more people were killed in that famine than the millions estimated in Robert Conquest's chilling and monumental study, *Harvest of Sorrow*. As Alexandr Solzhnitsyn put it, "the whole atrocity of communism could never be accommodated by the Western journalistic mind."[383]

Just as Russia drew upon Western civilization for its own development over the centuries, so it became the conduit through which the fruits of European economic and technological development reached Central Asia and other less economically developed areas. Both economically and in terms of the cultural level of its masses, Russia was backward by European standards, but it was advanced by the standards of many non-European societies. In the nineteenth century, Russian-manufactured products found a rapidly growing demand in Central Asia, even though these same products could not compete in either price or quality in the markets of Western Europe or North America.[384] The vast changes produced by the diffusion of European technical and cultural advances were testimony to the huge disparities in productive capabilities among various national and ethnic groups at the same point in time. The political response to those disparities was often resentment, whether it was the resentment of Russians toward the foreigners developing their country, or to more advanced domestic minorities like the Jews and the Germans, or the later resentment of less developed Central Asians toward the Russians.

As in many other parts of the world, there has been a continuous conflict between the economic benefits and the political turmoil created by the utilization of other people's knowledge and skills. When conquest has been the mode of cultural diffusion, resentments have been especially bitter, and especially long-lasting. The official ideology that race did not matter under Communism, that all were one "Soviet people," was ultimately exposed as a bitter mockery when the easing of central government control in the late 1980s released lethal inter-ethnic violence in Soviet Georgia, in Azerbaijan, and in Central Asia.[385] Many lives were lost in these inter-ethnic clashes,[386] which required the deployment of thousands of Soviet troops to maintain control. The final irony was that racial, ethnic, and nationality clashes—all regarded as passing anachronisms by Marxist theory, and as having been abolished by Soviet practice—not only persisted, but themselves played a major role in abolishing the Soviet Union.

The cultural history of the Slavs of Eastern Europe during the twentieth century cannot be separated from the history of the Communist system which reigned for nearly three quarters of a century in the Soviet Union and for more than four decades of Soviet hegemony over the satellite nations of Eastern Europe. The political and economic consequences of the Communist system included the priorities which that system enabled its rulers to impose on vast millions living under their rule. Thus the Russian leaders' goals—from becoming a global nuclear superpower to the technological feats of space travel to producing top Olympic athletes—could be achieved in spite of whatever costs this imposed on the Eastern European people's living standards or their freedom.

In the decades leading up to the collapse of the Soviet bloc in Eastern Europe, this region became the only one in the industrialized world in which infant mortality rose and adult lifespan declined.[387] It was also a region whose environmental degradation exceeded anything seen in industrial nations outside the Communist bloc.

Despite the greater freedom made possible by the collapse of Communist dictatorships in Eastern Europe, the degree to which such freedom emerged varied, largely according to whether particular republics had had experience with freedom before. Czechoslovakia, for example, resumed its democratic form of government from the interwar years but Yugoslavia not only failed to create the democratic institutions it had never had, it degenerated into ethnic civil war, with hideous atrocities unparalleled since the days of the Nazis. This suggests that an important part of a country's human capital is political as well as economic, and includes the experiences and traditions necessary to make the formal institutions of free government viable. The history of the collapse of democratic government in East Central Europe between the two World Wars, as well as the collapse of such governments in the second half of the twentieth century in Africa and other places where such free governments had never existed before, reinforces the conclusion that political human capital is among the intangibles without which the tangibles do not work. Certainly the vast, rich natural resources of Russia and the scientific and technological capabilities to use them make it virtually impossible to explain the poverty of the country without recognizing the great importance of the intangible framework of dependable law, without which a market economy cannot produce the prosperity that it produces in those other countries where this framework can be taken for granted.

The independence achieved or re-established in the last decade of the twentieth century by the nations of the former Soviet bloc in Eastern Europe opened new prospects of cultural, economic, and political developments in those nations and for the Slavic peoples as a whole.

Perhaps nothing so captures the uneven achievements of the Slavs as the fact that the first human being to orbit the earth was a Slav, Yuri Gagarin, and the fact that one of the most momentous breakups of a major world power in the twentieth century was that of the Soviet Union.

CHAPTER 5

WESTERN HEMISPHERE INDIANS

The American continents existed geologically, much as we now know them, before the first human crossed over from the Eurasian mainland. If the Americas only became an environment with that migration, they also became a very different environment with the arrival of Columbus and the Spaniards. But if the New World was a different environment for the Europeans than it had been for the Indians, it was also a different environment for the European invaders than their homelands of Spain or England.

Edward Whiting Fox[1]

The various indigenous peoples of the Western Hemisphere have been no more alike in their economic, cultural, military, or other achievements than the various peoples of Europe, Asia, or Africa have been. Some Indians bartered but others used money, kept accounts, and had sophisticated trading networks. Although some Indian tribes lived in tents, much like the nomads of the Middle East or Central Asia, others created buildings, monuments, and cities. When the Spanish *conquistadores* entered the Aztec capital of Tenochtitlán in 1519, they found a city larger than Seville, from which many of the Spaniards had come.

There were multi-storied dwellings built by some of the Indians in the American southwest, centuries before the Europeans arrived. One four-tiered complex covered such a large area that it remained the largest apartment complex in North America until the nineteenth century.[2] Stone masonry was also highly developed by the Maya, the Incas, and the Aztecs, among many other skills, both urban and agricultural. The maize that existed in the Western Hemisphere when the Europeans arrived was already a highly domesticated variety, so much so that it could no longer propagate itself in the wild, but had to be planted and tended by human beings.[3] Since the Western Hemisphere includes two continents—each larger than Europe—it could hardly be expected that its peoples would be any less heterogeneous than the peoples of other regions of the world. Thus, while some of the indigenous peoples of the hemisphere—the Maya, Aztecs and Incas, for example—had developed a complex urban civilization before the Europeans arrived, others in the Amazon jungle continued to live a primitive existence, even in the late twentieth century.

Systems of government also varied enormously among the indigenous peoples of the hemisphere. At one extreme was the vast Incan empire, ruled by an hereditary nobility, from whom a supreme ruler was chosen and endowed with god-like attributes, so much so that merely looking him in the eye was a crime punishable by death. At the other end of the spectrum were many of the Indian tribes of North America in which chiefs were chosen ad hoc for particular purposes and wielded only such influence as other members of the tribe chose to accord them. In between were the governing systems of the Maya, in which rulers had great powers, but each over only limited geographical areas.

While there were many impressive technological and intellectual achievements in the Western Hemisphere before the Europeans arrived, there were also things lacking in this hemisphere that were common elsewhere. Iron and steel were not produced by the Western Hemisphere Indians, even though it had been produced in Europe, Asia, and Africa for centuries before Columbus landed in the Americas. Indeed, iron and steel were important factors in the success of the European incursion, playing a major role in the weapons and armor which facilitated the Spaniards' conquests in Central and South America and which, in North America, created on the Indians' part an eagerness to trade with the initially small and vulnerable European settlements on the coastal fringes of colonial America, because these settlements supplied iron and steel products that rapidly replaced existing kitchen utensils, knives and other products made of various other materials among the Indians.

The most striking lack in the Western Hemisphere before the arrival of Europeans was the wheel, often considered one of the landmarks on the road to the development of civilization. However, this lack was not simply an intellectual lack, for the Maya had wheels on the toys they made for their children,[4] though not in practical adult uses. What was lacking was not the concept but the complementary factor that made the wheel so important in Europe and Asia—namely, animals capable of pulling wheeled vehicles. There were no horses, oxen, or other animals capable of pulling or carrying heavy loads in either North or South America before the Europeans arrived.

The other major factor lacking in most Western Hemisphere societies in pre-Columbian times was writing. Only the Maya in Central America had a fully developed system of writing and most of the Indians of North America had not even rudimentary written versions of their languages. Thus, while the knowledge of the Europeans was more readily cumulative over time and more readily disseminated as of a given time, most of the indigenous peoples of the Western Hemisphere had to depend upon substitute methods of preserving and disseminating what they knew, such as personal memory and group traditions and songs—substitutes largely reduced to subordinate roles in other parts of the world after writing became available (and after such related systems of knowledge preservation as maps and numbering systems became available).

THE GEOGRAPHICAL SETTING

While, in narrowly physical terms, the lands and waters of the Western Hemisphere were the same for the indigenous peoples as they would later be for the transplanted populations from Europe, the complete absence of horses, oxen, cattle, and sheep in the Western Hemisphere before the arrival of the Europeans was momentous in its implications for food supply in general, agriculture in particular, and above all for the size of the cultural universe available to any given Indian tribe, nation, or civilization. Horses and camels made the Silk Road a highway stretching thousands of miles across the Eurasian land mass to connect China with Europe, but nothing comparable was possible in the Western Hemisphere to connect the Iroquois on the Atlantic seaboard of North America with the Aztecs of Central America. Italians could acquire spaghetti from China but the Iroquois could acquire nothing from the Aztecs, or even be aware of their existence.

Agriculture in the Western Hemisphere was inherently limited to what could be accomplished without animal muscle power to carry or to pull loads or to plow the land, as well as to supply manure to maintain the fertility of farms. Land transport in general was obviously severely limited in the loads and the distances that were possible without animals. Even the navigable waterways were limited in their capacities to move cargo by the absence of pack animals and draft animals to transport these cargoes when they reached land. Indian canoes plied the inland and coastal waterways of the hemisphere long before the white man arrived, but larger vessels with greater cargo capacity would have exceeded the severe physical and economic limits of a land without the kinds of animals needed to make larger cargoes economically viable. Llamas were available as pack animals in limited regions of South America and dogs were used by Eskimos and by some North American plains Indians to pull loads, but these animals did not compare with horses or oxen in what they could transport.

As in much of sub-Saharan Africa, not only were loads and distances limited physically in the Western Hemisphere by an absence of the needed animals, the particular kinds of things that would be economically feasible to trade at considerable distances were even more limited economically to those things whose concentrated value could repay high transport costs, often involving human porters. Tons of grain, for example, could be shipped for hundreds of miles in Europe but not in the Western Hemisphere before the Europeans arrived and brought pack animals and draft animals. Even in those regions of the Western Hemisphere that had networks of waterways comparable to those in Western Europe, limitations on land transport limited cargoes transported by water. Moreover, limitations on the scope and range of trade were also limitations on the scope and range of cultural interchanges.

Specific geographic barriers—the Amazon jungle, the Rocky Mountains, or the vast desert in what is today the southwestern United States—were of course major barriers to large-scale cultural interactions in pre-Columbian times, but the absence of animals for transport was a more general barrier to long-range cultural interactions throughout the Americas. While these barriers were not as severe as the geographic barriers in parts of sub-Saharan Africa, they were more formidable than those in much of Europe and Asia.

The absence of herd animals like sheep and cattle, as well as the absence of load-bearing or load-pulling animals like horses and oxen, had another consequence—an absence of the many diseases carried by such animals and often acquired by human beings living in close proximity with these animals. While, in one sense, the absence of such diseases was of course a benefit, their absence also meant an absence of biological resistance to many potentially devastating diseases such as smallpox. So long as such diseases did not exist in the Western Hemisphere, the Indians' lack of biological resistance to them was of no consequence. But, once people from Europe began arriving with these diseases, the consequences were momentous, not only for those indigenous populations stricken and devastated by these diseases at the time, but also for the historic transfer of North and South America from the indigenous peoples to the European invaders. The most invincible of these invaders proved to be not the Europeans themselves but the invisible carriers of their diseases, whose existence neither they nor the Indians suspected.

The fact that the Eurasian land mass stretches predominantly east and west, while the Western Hemisphere land masses stretch predominantly north and south, means that advances in agriculture and animal husbandry could spread more readily over far more vast distances in the Old World than in the New. Plants and animals are more similar in the same latitudes, while more drastic climate changes accompany north-south movement. Thus rice cultivation could spread across Asia to Europe and ultimately to North America, but bananas could not spread from Central America to Canada. Nor could many of the animals adapted to the tropics survive in the colder climates to the north or south, so that knowledge of how to hunt or domesticate these animals was similarly restricted in how far it would be applicable, even if such knowledge could be transmitted over long distances. Moreover, the northern temperate zone and the southern temperate zone of the Western Hemisphere were too far apart to make any sharing of knowledge between them feasible in pre-Columbian times. In short, climate, like other aspects of geography, limited the size of the cultural universes of the indigenous peoples of the Western Hemisphere.

The geographical environment of the Western Hemisphere itself changed with the European conquest. Vast herds of new animals were transplanted from Europe, along with the invisible transplanting of a whole new disease environment and a whole new technology from Europe. These transplantations changed the lives of the indigenous peoples, as well as allowing the European settlers to bring much of their cultural world to the Americas. Mounted Indian warriors with herds of cattle became a "traditional" way of life on the western plains of the United States, for example, while the gauchos who herded cattle for Spanish landowners on the Argentina pampas were often part or full-blooded Indians as well.

Such physical features of the Western Hemisphere as natural harbors and rivers reaching deep inland from the sea now became far more important economically after the arrival of white invaders and settlers in ships developed in Europe, but better adapted to exploit New World conditions than were the canoes of the Indians. Those parts of the Western Hemisphere most highly developed by the Europeans were not the same as those that had been most highly developed by the indigenous peoples. Whereas the most advanced Indian civilizations developed in Central America and in the Andes Mountains, the most advanced regions developed by Europeans were those regions whose geography was most like that of Western Europe— places with natural harbors and broad coastal plains, criss-crossed by rivers deep enough to carry large ships and, eventually, places with the mineral deposits needed to build an industrial society.

Only in the narrowest physical sense was the geographic setting of the Western Hemisphere the same for the indigenous peoples and for the Europeans. The flora, the fauna, and the disease environments were changed radically, and the natural features of the land and the waters acquired a much wider range of possibilities as a result of this, as well as because of the new technology brought from Europe. Moreover, the technology that the Europeans brought to the Western Hemisphere was not simply the technology of Europe. Because of the geography of the Eurasian land mass, Europeans were able to bring to bear in the Western Hemisphere the cultural features of lands extending far beyond Europe, but incorporated into their civilization. Europeans were able to cross the Atlantic Ocean in the first place because they could steer with rudders invited in China, calculate their position on the open sea through trigonometry invented in Egypt, using numbers created in India. The knowledge they had accumulated from around the world was preserved in letters invented by the Romans and written on paper invented in China. The military power they brought with them increasingly depended on weapons using gunpowder, also invented in Asia. The cultural confrontation in the Western Hemisphere was, in effect, a one-sided struggle between cultures acquired from vast regions of the earth against cultures from much more narrowly circumscribed regions of the New World. Never have the advantages of a wider cultural universe been more dramatically or more devastatingly demonstrated than in the conquests that followed.

CONQUESTS AND CULTURES

When the Europeans arrived in the Western Hemisphere, these invaders behaved, by and large, as conquerors have behaved all over the world for thousands of years—which is to say, brutally, greedily, and with arrogance toward the conquered peoples. Indeed, that is very much the way that Indian conquerors behaved toward other Indians, long before Columbus' ships first appeared on the horizon. However, Europeans' discovery of the Western Hemisphere[5] was not only a watershed in the history of the indigenous peoples of the New World, it was one of the most momentous events in the history of the human race, for this discovery meant that each half of the planet now became aware of the other half's existence and began a massive interchange of material things and cultures, as well as a massive movement of people across the Atlantic.

Nothing would ever be the same again, in either half of the world. Foods never seen before would become crucial to the diets of people thousands of miles away—the potato in Ireland, for example—and commercial crops never grown before, such as rubber in Malaya and cocoa in Nigeria, would become mainstays of national economies. Sweet potatoes would become a defense against famine in China, which ended up producing more of this Western Hemisphere vegetable than the rest of the world put together.[6] Transfers in the other direction were also of major and transforming importance. In a hemisphere that had never seen horses before, many Indians on the American plains would become skilled horsemen, hunting and fighting mounted and using firearms. For the first time in history, millions of people would migrate across an ocean, by choice from Europe and by force from Africa, and whole new disease environments would intermingle, with devastating impact on the native peoples of North and South America. The introduction of liquor was likewise devastating and even longer lasting in its effects than the new diseases, to which the surviving remnants of the original Indian population eventually acquired biological resistance.

While the disease transfer was not all one way—an epidemic of syphilis broke out in Europe after the return of Columbus' ships from the Western Hemisphere—still the Europeans were not nearly as affected by the diseases of the Indians as the latter were by the diseases from Europe. In the tropical regions of the New World, however, both the Europeans and the Indians proved to be vulnerable to yellow fever from Africa.[7] In one way or another, and to varying degrees from place to place, American Indians would be incorporated over the centuries into a very different set of cultures from Europe. Both the natural and the man-made catastrophes they suffered undermined faith in their existing traditions and leaders, who were largely unable to ward off these new catastrophes. After a smallpox epidemic in the early eighteenth century killed nearly half the Cherokees, medicine men were repudiated and the Cherokees began to regard European doctors as more knowledgeable.[8] Earlier Indians survivors of a devastating epidemic in the vicinity of the European settlement at Roanoke interpreted their plight religiously, as evidence that the God of the Europeans was more powerful than the Indian gods.[9]

In short, the indigenous population of the hemisphere was deprived not only of land and freedom, they were, to varying degrees, deprived also of the underlying foundation of cultural traditions on which any society is based. In parts of the Western Hemisphere, they would be largely absorbed biologically as well. In the United States, very few American Indians were of unmixed ancestry by the late twentieth century and, in much of Hispanic America, mestizoes generally outnumbered pure-blooded Indians and, in some places, outnumbered people of pure-blooded European ancestry as well.

Since most of the peoples of the Western Hemisphere lacked any system of writing before the Europeans came, their pre-Columbian history—like the history of early Anglo-Saxon England and the early history of the Slavs, sub-Saharan Africans, and other non-literate peoples around the world—can only be sketchily pieced together from archaeological and other clues. The very population of the hemisphere before the first white men arrived remains a matter of conjecture and controversy. One scholar estimated the pre-Columbian population of the hemisphere as low as 8.4 million, while another estimate put it at from 90 million to 112 million.[10] What is clearer is that the population density varied, being greater in South America than in North America, greater along the coasts than in the interior, and greater on the Pacific coast than on the Atlantic coast.[11] As in other parts of the world, population densities tended to be greatest where there was more highly developed agriculture, as in the Aztec and Inca empires, and sparsest where hunting and gathering societies predominated.[12] Hunter-gatherers in what is today Mexico were looked down upon as barbarians by the more sophisticated Indian civilizations of the region,[13] as more advanced societies have disdained, conquered, enslaved, or exterminated hunter-gatherers in other parts of the world.

The indigenous population of the Western Hemisphere declined catastrophically after the diseases of Europe struck peoples with little or no biological resistance to these disease. By the end of the nineteenth century, the Indian population of the United States was between a third and a fourth of what it is estimated to have been when the first white men arrived.[14] The devastation was even worse in other parts of the Western Hemisphere. Despite differing estimates today of the absolute size of the population of Mexico when the Spaniards arrived in the sixteenth century, there is broad agreement on the drastic shrinkage of that population in the century after 1520—a decline from 22 million Indians to just 2 million.[15] The indigenous population of Peru likewise declined by approximately 90 percent after the Spanish conquest there.[16] The twentieth-century American Indian population of Brazil was less than 5 percent of its estimated level when Europeans arrived.[17] In the Caribbean, the indigenous population was virtually annihilated.[18]

The horrendous impact of new diseases may have had at least as much to do with the Indians' losing control of the hemisphere to Europeans as the military encounters between the two, in which the technological advantage generally lay with the invaders. While it has not been uncommon in history for a smaller military force from a more developed society to prevail over a numerically superior force from a society less technologically or organizationally advanced—the Roman invaders of Britain or the European invaders of Africa, for example— nevertheless the numerical disparity in the Western Hemisphere was extreme. Whether the lowest or the highest estimate of the population of the Western Hemisphere in pre-Columbian times is closer to the facts, there were still millions of Indians, and probably tens of millions. Yet the entire European population of the Western Hemisphere had not yet reached one million as late as the middle of the seventeenth century, more than 150 years after Columbus arrived.[19] By that time, the Spaniards alone had established an empire that stretched from San Francisco Bay to the River Platte in Argentina.

Comparisons of the size of the Indian and European populations as of the early generations after Columbus can be misleading, however, in so far as such comparisons suggest that there was a simple race war for possession of the hemisphere. Neither the Indians nor the whites were united, so that both alliances and battles took place across racial lines. Many Indians allied themselves with the newcomers in warfare against other Indians, for revenge against erstwhile Indian conquerors and oppressors, or to share in the spoils of war, or to gain other advantages.[20] Similarly, the Europeans fought among themselves for a variety of reasons and had Indian allies against fellow-Europeans. The British and French, for example, clashed repeatedly in battle in North America, as they did around the world, and both had Indian allies in these battles. In addition, there were simple European-versus-European battles, as there were Indian-versus-Indian battles. The Dutch sent a naval squadron to attack the British settlement in Virginia and the British government under Cromwell sent expeditionary forces to colonial America to force the surrender of royalist governments in various British colonies on the North American continent and in the Caribbean. In South America, rival contingents of Spaniards fought among themselves over the spoils of the Incan empire—and, when much of this treasure was shipped off to Spain, British privateers waited on the high seas to intercept it. In short, colonial-era rivalries and alliances were not based on race but on expediency. In 1701, a letter written by a British colonial official spoke of the Iroquois Indians to the west as "the only barrier" against the French forces, including the Indian allies of the French.[21]

As late as the first few decades of the newly created United States, major military battles between whites and Indians remained rare in this part of the hemisphere, certainly as compared to the hundreds of battles per decade that would later occur in the United States after the middle of the nineteenth century,[22] when a now vastly larger white population sought far more land and had both the numbers and the military equipment to take it. Even during this later era, however, much of the land transfer from Indians to whites in the United States was through what might be called semi-conquest, as the American government paid millions of dollars to Indians for their land, but only about half of what that land would bring in the market.[23]

Many of the conquests of the Western Hemisphere were not like the conquests of modern Europe, where one organized state attacks another militarily and, after defeating it on the battlefield, takes over its territory and its sovereignty over the people living there. Many of the early European conquests in the Western Hemisphere were a series of uncoordinated campaigns by fighting units operating under the general auspices of the governments of Spain or Portugal, but by no means always under the effective direction or control of rulers or officials on the other side of the Atlantic. Given the slowness of communications in the era of wind-driven ships, news of what was being done in the name of Spain or Portugal often reached the Iberian peninsula long after it was a fait accompli. Even Spanish viceroys in the Western Hemisphere could lose control of the situation some distance away, as both Cortés in Mexico and Pizzaro in Peru ignored the orders of their Spanish superiors in the New World.

The British colonies in North America were likewise settled and expanded in piecemeal and often uncoordinated ways, typically by land purchase rather than military conquest, in early colonial times. However, even in a given colony such as Pennsylvania, the treaties made with the Indians by the Quaker leadership in Philadelphia were often ignored by the Scotch-Irish settlers on the western frontiers, who tended to settle on whatever land they found desirable, without worrying about whether it was inside or outside some line drawn on a map in Philadelphia. Given the Scotch-Irish tradition of occupying land they had not bought—whether in Britain, America, or Australia—this could hardly be surprising.

Long after a growing population and an improving weapons technology put the Europeans clearly in the ascendancy throughout the hemi-

sphere, there were still large frontier regions where Indians maintained their independence and their ability to fight. In eighteenth-
century Argentina, for example, Spanish frontier settlements were
often subjected to Indian raids, during which captives would be taken
away by the Indians, often to be either ransomed later or to be retained
as slaves, including concubines, for the Indians preferred capturing
women and killing men, while children would be raised as members of
the tribe. It was very common for Indian tribes to have Spanish captives. Nor were the numbers involved negligible. During a long Spanish military campaign against the Indians in Argentina, more than 600
captives were freed. Their average period of captivity was nearly nine
years. Much more common was the practice of paying ransom to get
back individual Spaniards who had been carried off. Some Spanish
men also escaped but women were less likely to do so and, in fact,
some women who were ransomed later returned to the Indian communities voluntarily, for their status in Spanish society was now
degraded, since they were considered to have been dishonored by
being concubines of Indians.[24] The capture of whites and their reten-
tion among the Indians was not a phenomenon limited to Argentina, by
any means. A mid-eighteenth century report on the aftermath of
Indian raids on European frontier settlements in western Pennsylvania
stated: "The Indian villages are full of prisoners of every age and
sex."[25] White women captured by the Iroquois likewise often chose to
remain with them, because the white settler society from which they
came also considered them ruined.[26]

The importance of the discovery of the Western Hemisphere by
Europeans continued to be enormous, long after the age of discovery
itself. In addition to the new foods, medicinal herbs, and tobacco
received from the Americas, Europe developed a massive trade with
the colonies, and later independent nations, of the New World. Centuries-old patterns of trade in Europe were disrupted, and in some
cases destroyed, by a shift in the directions of commerce. The relative
importance of the Levant as a supply center for international trade
from the Middle East and the Far East declined as the Americas
replaced both international and internal European supply sources for
a variety of products.

Eventually, massive shipments of wheat from Argentina and the
United States provided the daily bread of increasing numbers of Euro-

peans and deprived many European wheat-growing peasants of their livelihoods. Sugar went from being a luxury of a few in Europe to being an item of mass consumption, supplied by the plantations of the Western Hemisphere. Cotton from the New World likewise reached the masses in Europe, making clothing more affordable than woolen garments had been. Nor was this a small contribution. In pre-industrial Europe, where ordinary people spent more than half their income for food, clothing was something purchased only a few times in a lifetime, markets in second-hand clothing flourished,[27] and hospitals had to guard against having clothes stolen from corpses by people desperate for something to wear.[28] In these circumstances, cotton from the New World was a major contribution to the European standard of living.

Gold and silver from the Western Hemisphere arrived in Europe in amounts vast enough to raise price levels across the continent—and to enable Europe to finance its chronic trade deficits with Asia, which at that time had little or no demand for European products, while Europeans imported silk, tea, and other Asian goods. In a period of about a century and a half, beginning in the early sixteenth century, 185,000 kilograms of gold were shipped to Spain from the Western Hemisphere, increasing the total amount of gold in Europe by about one-fifth. Even more vast amounts of silver flowed to Spain—more than 7 million pounds during the same period, tripling the supply of silver in Europe.[29] The "golden age of Spain" in the sixteenth century owed much to the gold and silver that poured in from Spanish colonies in the Western Hemisphere.

Spain's decline in the next century, as the supplies of these precious metals declined, revealed its own lack of internal economic development. Its lack of skilled labor and its cultural disdain for either labor or commerce[30]—both historically supplied largely by Jews and by Moorish Christians, before both were expelled in the late fifteenth and early sixteenth century—left Spain without the human capital to make its financial capital from the New World anything more than an historically transient source of spending by individuals and government. By the mid-seventeenth century, with imports vastly exceeding exports, silver could become scarce in Spain in a matter of weeks after the arrival of ships laden with silver from its American colonies.[31] Among the Spaniards themselves, gold was said to pour down on Spain like rain on a roof, flowing on away immediately.[32]

More than a material impact was made by the New World on the old. A mental revolution was set in motion as well. After centuries of looking back with reverence to the superior achievements of the Roman Empire, and to both the secular and religious authorities of ancient times, Europeans began to comment widely on the fact that these ancients never knew of the existence of half the world and so could not be such infallible guides.[33] This undermining of ancient authority was one of the Western Hemisphere's inadvertent contributions to the changing of the mental universe of Europeans, a change also brought on by the rise of science and of scientific discoveries as dramatic as geographic discoveries. Europeans now began to look forward, rather than backward, and progress became a major theme of European thought and action, for better or worse. Yet, despite the great long-run contribution of the Western Hemisphere to both the material and the immaterial development of Europe, which now seems so clear in retrospect, this does not necessarily mean that the New World immediately preoccupied Europeans proportionately at the time of its discovery and colonization. In France, for example, more than twice as many books printed between 1480 and 1700 dealt with the Ottoman Empire as dealt with the Western Hemisphere.[34]

For the Indians of North and South America, the cultural impact of the Europeans was also enormous, in at least two very different ways. In addition to what was learned directly from the Europeans, the Indians were forced to adapt to conquests which deprived them of the land and resources necessary for their previous ways of life, which could not always be resumed in the new environments to which they retreated, even when they were able to retain their own social traditions and governing practices. Moreover, just as the discovery of a vast and unsuspected hemisphere undermined Europeans' faith in their ancient forebears and their traditions, so the stunning series of military setbacks suffered by the Indians in that hemisphere undermined confidence in *their* leaders, traditions, and cultures. One consequence was a receptivity of many Indians to Christian missionaries, who brought with them the secular, as well as the religious, offerings of European culture. Thus, by the end of the seventeenth century, little more than isolated pockets of purely indigenous religions survived in the vast domains of the Spanish Empire in the Americas.[35] However, some or much of the traditional content of these religions might survive under the outward forms of Christianity, as other syncretistic religions emerged in other regions of the world where conquerors brought a different religion, such as in the Balkans under Ottoman rule or India under a series of invaders.

Ironically, the enslavement of the indigenous Indians by the invading peoples was facilitated where there was a sufficiently advanced Indian culture to support large concentrations of people in a relatively compact region, such as in areas once ruled by the Aztecs or the Incas.[36] Enslaving less advanced tribes of hunters and gatherers, spread thinly over the vast areas required for their subsistence, was much less feasible, either militarily or economically. Other organized Indian nations, with many warriors, were also not likely candidates for enslavement. To some extent, there was a selling of Indian captives by other Indians in North America.[37] However, by and large, the Europeans found it expedient to take land from the Indians and to get the labor to work that land either from Europe or from Africa.

No one knows when the Indians themselves first came to the Western Hemisphere, but archaeological evidence suggests that they did not originate in the Americas. Unlike other parts of the world, North and South America contain no skeletal remains of earlier forms of human beings or their ancestors,[38] suggesting that people had already reached their present stage of physical development before the Indians settled in the hemisphere. Hundreds of different languages were spoken by the Indians and, while these can be grouped into families of similar languages, they are not related to other languages in Europe, Africa, or Asia—except for Eskimo being spoken on both the Asian and the North American sides of the Bering Straits. It is here that the Indian peoples are thought to have entered the Western Hemisphere from Asia in prehistoric times.

Europeans from the Iberian peninsula were the earliest explorers, conquerors, and colonizers of the Western Hemisphere. A decade after Columbus' first landing in the Western Hemisphere in 1492, brazilwood was being shipped to Portugal from the country that would later be named for that wood. That same year, 1502, a Spanish expedition of 30 ships with 2,500 men landed in Santo Domingo.[39] In the early sixteenth century, Spanish explorers spread into Central and South America. From the isthmus of Panama, Balboa first saw the ocean he named Pacific in 1513. Six years later, Cortés began his conquest of

Mexico and in 1530, Pizzaro launched his expedition from Panama southward to conquer the Incan empire. The Dutch, then a major naval power and engaged in a long war with Spain, followed next, and then the English—a rising power at the time but not yet at their zenith—followed in the wake of the Dutch. Meanwhile, the French set up island colonies in the Caribbean and settlements on the North American mainland, extending from what is today Canada on down through the vast reaches of the Mississippi Valley to New Orleans.

This order in time and in power among the European imperial nations in the Western Hemisphere roughly reflected their worldwide positions. The Spaniards were the premier imperial nation, not only in power but also in experience in projecting that power overseas and establishing dominion over less advanced overseas populations, having conquered the Canary Islands years before Columbus set sail. Britain was simply not in Spain's league as of the time the Western Hemisphere was discovered. Spain was consolidating its victories over the Aztecs and the Incas while England was annexing Wales. In addition to their imperial possessions in the Americas and in Europe, the Spaniards were in the Philippines before the British were in India, Ceylon, Malaysia, or other Asian regions of what would later become the British Empire.

Europe itself had only recently repelled the incursions of non-European powers, with Columbus' first voyage being launched the same year that the Spaniards' centuries-long struggle to reconquer their own land from the ruling Moors achieved final victory in Granada. Russians only ceased paying tribute to Mongol overlords during the same century and the Ottoman Empire was still advancing up through the Balkans toward Central Europe. As imperialists, Western Europeans were unique only in being able to project their naval and military power across the oceans of the world. The Ottoman Empire and the Russian Empire were great powers among their contemporaries, but primarily on land.

While the gold and silver of the Spanish colonies poured into Europe, so in massive amounts did the animal hides and furs of North America, from the British, French and Dutch, who acquired them in trade with the Indians. The Portuguese established the sugar plantations in Brazil that would change the diets of Europe and change the history of the Western Hemisphere, as sugar plantations spread rapidly into the British, French, Spanish, and Dutch islands of the Caribbean, all using vast numbers of slaves from Africa.

Before the middle of the seventeenth century, Dutch forces had seized Brazil from the Portuguese, as they had seized Portuguese possessions on the coast of Africa, and established Dutch colonies in North America, the most notable being New Amsterdam, later to be renamed New York after the British seized it from the Dutch.[40] The British were, however, latecomers compared to the Iberians. It was a century after Cortés conquered the Aztecs that the British founded a colony in Massachusetts in 1630. The French founded Quebec in 1608 and Montreal in 1642. Their trade and territorial expansions brought them into conflict with the British, particularly those based in New York, but also including the British in settlements up and down the eastern seaboard of what would later become the United States.

CENTRAL AND SOUTH AMERICA

Central America was the scene of the earliest civilizations of the Western Hemisphere, notably that of the Olmecs, and what has been called "the New World's most brilliant civilization,"[41] that of the Maya. The largest empire, however, was in South America, that of the Incas. By and large, all these civilizations were more advanced than those of the Indians of North America and far more advanced than those found in the Caribbean, although more primitive tribes also existed in the jungles of South America. What was particularly remarkable about the civilizations of Central America was that they are among the few examples of such advanced societies developing in tropical rain forests. The Incan civilization also developed within tropical latitudes, but at largely higher altitudes, so that it did not have to contend with tropical climate and tropical diseases.

The Maya

The ancient Maya civilization was one of the great civilizations of the Western Hemisphere and the only one with a fully developed written language. It also had a well-developed numbering system (arguably better than the contemporary Roman numerals in use in Europe), a calendar, elaborate art work, knowledge of astronomy, and urban developments with massive buildings and monuments. One labyrinthine Mayan palace, for example, was roughly 300 feet long and 240 feet wide. Although the Maya, like the other indigenous peoples of the hemisphere, had no metal tools, they had a volcanic glass called obsidian, which was used for cutting, as were stone tools. What is considered the classical period of Mayan civilization extended from the middle of the third century, A.D., to the beginning of the tenth century. In other words, it had its rise and fall before the first European arrived on the scene. Yet the Maya culture was not completely obliterated, even by the Spanish conquest in the sixteenth century, and there were still six million Maya in the late twentieth century, one of whom won a Nobel Prize.[42]

The site of Mayan civilization was the Yucatan Peninsula and the adjoining mainland.[43] Here the soil, the waterways, and the climate varied considerably, ranging from deserts to rain forests, from tropical lowlands to cool, volcanic highlands, and from seashores to deep interior hinterlands. Rainfall ranges from less than 40 inches annually in much of the northern Yucatan peninsula to more than 100 inches annually in some of the southern highlands.[44] The northern portion of the peninsula has been characterized as virtually a solid limestone rock, covered with soil that tends to be thin physically in some places and not very fertile, even where it is deeper. Because water drains so readily through the limestone, rivers are rare in this region and irrigation impractical. Therefore in northern and central Yucatan, water for farming comes almost entirely from rain. To the south, where there is thicker soil, there are rivers and lakes. Altitude also increases toward the south, at a rate of about 20 centimeters (8 inches) per kilometer.[45]

Early Mayan agriculture developed within these geographical and climatic limits by allowing land to lie fallow for a number of years in between plantings. To the south, the land lay fallow from four to seven years, and in the north from eight to twenty years. Before replanting, the land was burned, so that nutrients from the burned vegetation would fertilize the soil. As in the rest of the Western Hemisphere, there were no draft animals to provide manure for fertilization. Under these circumstances, vastly more land was required to support a given population than the land actually under cultivation at any given time.[46]

The highly varied flora and fauna in the various regions of Mayan civilization, and the varying climatic and geographical conditions, provided the basis for trade in the differing products of the respective regions, with accompanying cultural interactions over wide areas. The earliest Mayan urban communities of the classical era arose in locations commanding the lowland trade routes.[47] Even after this era had passed, more than 60 percent of the Maya population lived along the major trade routes, making their living from a combination of agriculture, fishing, salt gathering, and commerce. So developed was trade that coastal communities did not have to be able to feed themselves from the agriculture in their immediate vicinity, but obtained food, textiles, and other products from the interior hinterlands.[48] Like other great civilizations, that of the Maya borrowed heavily from those who went before and from contemporaries. Its language contained loan words from other languages and its calendar apparently came from the older Olmec civilization, while aspects of the culture of the later Toltec civilization eventually amalgamated with the culture of the Maya.[49]

With all its intellectual and material accomplishments, Mayan civilization could hardly be considered humanitarian. One of its central priorities was war and one of its chief priorities in war was the capture, torture, and slaughter of enemy soldiers and leaders. As a scholar specializing in the history of the Maya put it, "the highest goal of these lineage-proud dynasts was to capture the ruler of a rival city-state in battle, to torture and humiliate him (sometimes for years), and then to subject him to decapitation following a ball game which the prisoner was always destined to lose." While atrocities have occurred around the world, this was a society in which such behavior was not simply accepted, but systematized and celebrated. Mayan art and writing featured scenes of captured enemies cut open while alive or being tortured and pleading with their captors, their leaders being debased by Mayan leaders, and Mayan warriors wearing coats decorated with the shrunken heads of their victims.[50] Human sacrifice was a feature of Mayan culture, as it was among the Aztecs and Incas. Those sacrificed included not only captured enemies but also adults and children killed to be buried with Mayan leaders, presumably to provide someone to look after their needs in the next world. Nor were enemy victims simply incidental casualties of war. Some military actions were undertaken precisely in order to obtain captives to kill in celebration of the accession of a new ruler.[51]

The extent of the Mayan culture was at no time the same as the extent of any Mayan political entity. There were always numerous rulers over different regions where Mayan culture prevailed.[52] Among the various regions, some were paramount at one period and others at other periods. One region which long remained dominant during the classical Mayan era was that centered on the urban community of Tikal.[53] Although Mayan civilization had buildings, monuments, and other characteristics of urban settings, these communities did not reach the size and density of later Aztec or Incan cities, or the size and density of leading cities in contemporary Europe—at least in their urban cores. However, including the surrounding area, an estimated 92,000 people lived in an around Tikal. Some other Mayan urban centers also had populations in the tens of thousands. Highland communities were smaller and less important, both politically and economically, than those in the lowlands that were the heart and origin of Mayan civilization.[54]

Somewhere around the ninth century, for reasons that remain unclear and the subject of controversy among archaeologists,[55] Mayan civilization began to decline. Throughout the southern lowlands, building and carving activities declined substantially, along with a decline in ceramics and other manufactured products. Hundreds of sites were abandoned. Populations in the great urban centers of the Mayan lowlands declined and some communities were abandoned.[56] Judging by the depictions of rulers in Mayan art, this era of decline saw also the decline of the god-like individual ruler, who now shared power with a ruling elite.[57] Although leading lowland communities declined or disappeared during this era, there was an offsetting rise in population and prosperity in the Yucatan peninsula.[58]

By the time the Spaniards arrived on the scene, centuries later, the great centers of Mayan civilization were already ruins, some overgrown by jungle,[59] though much of the intangible culture still survived. However, long before the Spanish invasion, indigenous invaders brought a new infusion of peoples and cultures to the Mayan regions.[60] The earliest known contact between the Maya and the Spaniards occurred in 1511, when several survivors of a Spanish shipwreck were captured by the Maya, became human sacrifices and their bodies were eaten at a feast. Other survivors of the same shipwreck were deemed too thin for a feast and were kept for a later holiday that was approaching, by which time they might be fattened up. In the meantime, they escaped.[61]

Six years later, a contingent of Spanish warriors from Cuba, searching for people to enslave on the Central American mainland, encountered the Maya, with whom they fought a battle in which the Spaniards suffered heavy losses, including numerous wounds to their leader, who died after his return to Cuba. Two years later, the Spaniards returned with four ships and 200 men for vengeance. Again, the Maya attacked, killing one and wounding 50, including the leader of the second expedition, who returned to Cuba in frustration.

The next expedition into Mayan territory, in 1519, was more formidable and was commanded by Hernán Cortés, conqueror of the people known as the Mexica and future conqueror of the Aztecs. He led an armada of eleven ships with 500 men. The Spaniards came ashore, destroyed idols in the local temples and erected a cross in one of them. In the course of their expedition through the Mayan region, Cortés was given a young orphaned girl named Marina, who spoke two of the languages of the region, and who became his translator as well as his concubine,[62] facilitating his making of alliances with various indigenous peoples who seized opportunities to attack and plunder their traditional enemies. Thus Cortés eventually came to command an army vastly larger than the Spanish contingent with which he landed.

After Cortés conquered the Aztec capital in 1521, he dispatched one of his officers on an expedition into Mayan territory. Spanish priest Bartolomé de Las Casas described these conquests: "He advanced killing, ravaging, burning, robbing and destroying all the country where he came." The atrocities being reported by de Las Casas were not, however, matters of glorification, as such things were among the Maya, but part of his years-long moral indictments of the Spanish treatment of the peoples of the Western Hemisphere. Eventually his reports and the reports of other Spanish priests raised sufficient concern in Spain to lead to admonitions, reforms, and occasionally punishments of the guilty in Spanish America, though these were seldom sufficient to prevent continuing brutalities and oppressions.

Although the Spanish *conquistadores* inflicted crushing defeats and spread mass terror among Mayan communities in the 1520s, this did not bring the entire Mayan region under their control, for there was no single government controlling all the Maya and never had been. This meant, on the one hand, that united Mayan resistance to the Spaniards did not develop but, on the other hand, it also meant that no Spanish victory, no matter how decisive, would bring all the Maya under their control. It was very much like the medieval English conquests in Ireland in that respect. In Central America, more than 20 years elapsed between the first brutal conquests of the Maya in 1523 described by de Las Casas and the Spaniards' final subjugation of the Yucatan peninsula in 1846. Even so, another Mayan nation, the Itza, held out for more than another century and a half.[63]

The Spanish conquests in Yucatan subjected the Maya to economic exactions, religious impositions and social subordination—a fate that befell other Indians elsewhere in the hemisphere. The Maya had to pay tribute to individual local Spanish overlords, much as under feudalism in Europe, and tithes to the Catholic church, as well as being subjected to a certain amount of forced labor and forcible relocation to communities in which religious or secular leaders could more readily control them and attempt to convert them to the Christian religion and Hispanic culture. Millions were forcibly relocated in the years 1550 to 1563. In addition to various officially sanctioned means of exploiting the Maya, Spaniards in power on the scene were also able to enrich themselves, and their families and friends, by extra-legal oppressions and chicanery practiced against the Indians, in violation of the rules of the Spanish state and the Catholic church.

Throughout "New Spain"—encompassing what is now Mexico and much of Central America, as well as the southwestern United States— Spanish conquerors established a variety of overlapping and often conflicting political and economic institutions. One of the most important of these was the *encomienda*, sometimes likened to a feudal fief, except that it was not a property held in perpetuity but usually a trust granted by the Spanish authorities for a specified number of generations—sometimes just for one generation—supposedly as rewards to the conquering warriors, but often as rewards for being relatives and friends of Spanish colonial officials. As under feudalism, people as well as land were part of the *encomienda*, and their tribute in money, in kind, or in labor was what supported the ruling overlords individually, as well as the colonial government in general. Many Indian communities changed hands, often more than once.[64] Among the duties of the holder of an *encomienda* was converting the Indians to Christianity and limiting how much tribute could be collected from them or how they could be treated. The carrying out of these official policies varied, however, according to the individuals and the circumstances. Some

Indians were in fact worked to death and others were sold as slaves to islands in the Caribbean.[65]

Some of these violations were more or less open secrets, typically things which the Spanish crown was reluctant to attempt to suppress or punish, at least until much later, when its effective power was greater or when some benefit would accrue to the Spanish government itself as a result of cracking down. The primary relief from the abuses of the conquerors came not from the government in Spain but from escape to parts of the region not yet under effective Spanish control. This occurred on such a scale as to cause the Spaniards to launch sporadic military operations to recapture escapees by the thousands and return them to the particular jurisdictions and overlords from which they had escaped.[66] There were also widespread Indian rebellions.[67]

One of the devastating impacts of European conquests among the Maya, as among other indigenous peoples throughout the Western Hemisphere was a massive spread of new diseases, causing deaths on such a scale as to drastically reduce the total population and undermine military resistance by the Indians. The Yucatec Maya, for example, numbered perhaps as many as 800,000 people at the time of the Spanish conquest but this number fell to about 233,000 by 1550 and to 163,000 by 1601. Afterwards, population size stabilized and, before the middle of the seventeenth century, began an increase. It is not clear how much of the population decline represented the effects of disease alone and how much migrations and escapes from Spanish rule. However, it is known that communities along the trade routes were especially hard hit by contagious diseases that spread as traders moved along such routes, leading to actual depopulations in some communities.[68] In addition to the European diseases introduced by the Spaniards, tropical yellow fever from Africa was also spread as a result of the introduction of African slaves into the region. Yellow fever wreaked havoc among both the Spaniards and the Maya, and continued to be a problem in Yucatan on into the twentieth century.[69]

Unlike the ancient Roman conquest of Britain or some of the European conquests in Africa, the Spanish conquest of the Maya did not bring major technological or organizational advances. While horses and mules were introduced, facilitating trade, that trade was carried on almost exclusively by the Maya.[70] Mayan agriculture and Mayan weaving of cloth—two of the major economic activities of the region—

remained much as they had been before the Spaniards came and the Spaniards themselves seldom engaged in either of these activities. What changed most fundamentally was not the nature of economic activity but the amount extracted from the producers and the elite to whom it was transferred. The old ruling Maya elite became a subordinate elite under the Spaniards, who now became the real power, gradually reducing the various classes among the indigenous population as a whole to the role of peasants and their religion and culture to things openly disdained. As a result of continuing inflows of people from Spain and from Africa, and the biological amalgamations that produced mestizos and mulattoes, as well as the cultural Hispanicization of the Maya and other Indians, people of both Mayan ancestry and Mayan culture eventually became a minority in their own land.[71] Biologically, however, Indians as a whole continued to be a majority of the population in most of Yucatan in the late eighteenth century. The Spaniards were about 8 percent of the total population, outnumbered by people of partial or full African ancestry, who were 12 percent of the population. These people of African ancestry tended to be part of the Hispanic culture.[72]

What the Spanish conquerors created in the regions where Mayan civilization had once prevailed was not a colony in the strict classical sense of a society consisting largely of transplanted members of the conquering race, as in British North America. Nor was it either feudalism or capitalism. While the relationship between local Spanish overlords and the Indians subject to their command and demands was feudalistic in one sense, it never attempted to produce the self-sufficient domains which feudalism at least attempted to create, for the Maya continued to produce for an interdependent market economy, as they had before the Spanish came, with the Spanish overlords simply extracting tribute and services. The economy created by the Spaniards was by no means classic capitalism, for there were government-imposed economic controls and monopolies, as well as prohibitions against trade with foreign countries. Moreover, the Spanish elite did not depend for its wealth on the making of profit from the economy so much as in using the government to gain privileges that translated into economic gain, whether from direct extractions from the Indians or from privileges in the acquisition of land or monopolies. The small Spanish community, and the still smaller Spanish elite, facilitated interlocking political, economic, religious, family, and social institutions—which in turn facilitated the kinds of corruption and abuses that flourished in colonial Latin America and continued to do so long after the colonial era was over.

The Aztecs

The peoples called generically Aztecs by the Spaniards who arrived in the Valley of Mexico in the early sixteenth century were an amalgamation of various peoples, known collectively among the indigenous people themselves as the Mexica. The Mexica had moved repeatedly over a period of more than two hundred years—from the early twelfth century to the mid-fourteenth century—before finally settling down in the Valley of Mexico. They were not strictly nomadic, however, for they stopped for varying numbers of years at various sites, practicing agriculture as well as hunting and fishing, before moving on. Often old people were abandoned to their fate as the Mexica resumed their treks to new locations.[73] As in the rest of the hemisphere, there were no wheeled vehicles or draft animals that could carry those who could not make the journey on foot through the rugged mountainous terrain.

What is called the Valley of Mexico is in fact a mountain basin, covering 25,000 square miles of fertile land. Despite being in the tropics, the climate is not tropical because of its altitude of 7,000 feet, which produces mild days and cool nights. Here an earlier civilization had arisen, that of the Toltec empire. The Mexica may have been one of the outlying vassal peoples of the Toltecs and, like some other such peoples, may have begun migrating in the wake of the collapse of that empire after barbarian attacks. The Mexica themselves have been characterized as "semi-civilized," as of the time of their movement toward the site where they were later to develop their own civilization.[74] When they finally settled down in the Valley of Mexico in the twelfth century, there were already villages and even cities there, established by a variety of other peoples, in a situation characterized as "a scene of almost Balkan complexity and flux" with fleeting and shifting alliances, marked by betrayals.[75] The newly arriving Mexica "found themselves surrounded by innumerable peoples, of whom none showed goodwill toward them."[76] In this precarious natural and human situation, the Mexica submitted as vassals to one of the stronger groups in the area, the Culhua, who permitted them to settle in a barren region where their chances of survival seemed slim.

As vassals, the Mexica joined the Culhua in a successful war against one of the many other peoples in the region. But the military prowess shown by the Mexica during these battles alarmed their masters, who planned to annihilate them as a potential rival or menace. When these plans were betrayed to the Mexica, they moved once more, out into an island in a nearby lagoon. Here, eventually, they established their capital city of Tenochtitlán, destined ultimately to become the capital of the Aztec empire. However, the Mexica or Aztecs were to pass through many vicissitudes before that happened.

There were natural advantages and disadvantages of the location of the settlement of Tenochtitlán. Being in a lagoon, it had the advantage of freeing the Aztecs from the danger of surprise attacks, since they could see any attackers before they could arrive across the water. Enclosing local inlets and canals, much like Venice, Tenochtitlán also had the great economic advantage of water transport, especially important in a region of the world without pack animals, draft animals or wheeled vehicles, where the alternative means of transporting goods and resources was by the much more costly method of human porterage. Both plants and animals were plentiful to supply food, but the Aztecs were entirely dependent upon the surrounding peoples for their supplies of both wood and stone.[77] However, they were able to trade their marine products to acquire the wood and stone they needed.

Over time, the Aztecs developed economically, culturally, politically, and militarily. Long required to pay tribute to the powerful Tepanecs, they reacted to increased exactions by forming an alliance with another tributary people to rebel against their powerful overlords. The death of the Tepanecs' wily ruler, Tezozómoc, and the rise of the great Aztec leader, Montezuma, set the stage for a dramatic confrontation between the two peoples. Tezozómoc's son and successor was far less subtle and provoked more enemies, leading ultimately to a war that led to his own death and the downfall of the Tepanec domination of the Aztecs and others. For many of these other subject peoples, however, the ascendancy of the Aztecs meant that they had simply changed masters, as the Aztecs now began to demand and receive tribute on an ever larger scale.

The Aztec empire was a confederation of city-states that was only about a century old when the Spaniards encountered it in the sixteenth century. While the city-state of Tenochtitlán dominated this confederation, the Aztecs ruled through existing authorities among the various subject people, rather than by appointing their own viceroys over them. There was no imperial standing army, but military expeditions could be organized from the male population for punitive expeditions against those who disobeyed or rebelled. The effectiveness of such methods of indirect rule tended to vary with the distance from the center of the empire, with outlying regions being more likely to disobey or rebel. Although the areas over which the Aztecs exerted varying degrees of control extended beyond the Valley of Mexico and eventually stretched from the Gulf of Mexico to the Pacific, there were also independent peoples living within that amorphous orbit, as well as subject peoples of varying degrees of submission. One of the first tasks of a new Aztec ruler was often to lead military expeditions to re-assert the authority of the empire over nominally subject peoples.

Internally, the Aztecs developed a politically complex society, with great urban centers, many technical advances and a fierce military tradition. They also built aqueducts, canals, drawbridges, and agricultural terraces, as well as building huge and elaborate stone monuments in their cities. Like other Western Hemisphere cultures, the Aztecs did not have a written language, but they came close to having one in their pictographs depicting their history and their way of life. Among the many skills used in Tenochtitlán were those of the conquered peoples, such as the Mixtecs, who were renowned as craftsmen who produced gold ornaments used by Aztec nobles.[78] Hérnan Cortés, leader of the first Spanish *conquistadores* to encounter the Aztecs, described an Aztec nobleman's two-story home in which he was a guest as being "as good as the best in Spain," both for its stonework and its woodwork.[79]

The Aztec rise to ascendancy over other peoples and to technological and cultural ascendancy was accompanied by the development of an increasingly hierarchical society internally. The ruler's disposition of huge amounts of tribute pouring in from the subject peoples enhanced his power over his own people, to whom this tribute was distributed as largess. Eventually, the ruler's role developed to such god-like dimensions that merely to look him directly in the eye was an offense punishable by death.[80] The royal succession was not hereditary, but noble leaders chose each new ruler from among the royal princes, on the basis of perceived fitness for the role. These noble classes, including priests, were set apart from the masses by laws which restricted the wearing of cotton clothing and jewels, as well as the eating of particular sumptuous foods and the drinking of cocoa, to this class—with violations of these taboos also being punishable by death. At the bottom of the hierarchy were the slaves, typically used as domestic servants or as substitutes for pack animals. Slavery was not hereditary, but was sufficiently widespread that slave traders were among the most prosperous people in the Aztec empire, and there was even a specialized occupation of bathing slaves so that they would be made suitable to be human sacrifices.[81]

Above all, the Aztec empire was one in which military prowess was emphasized and glorified. For an Aztec warrior, one of the great prizes of war were the captured enemy warriors who were led back to the capital to be sacrificed by having their hearts cut out of their living bodies on a high altar, while Aztec civilians and foreign emissaries watched, as streams of blood poured down the steps of the pyramid from this mass carnage. Rulers and dignitaries from the surrounding peoples—both subjects and independent peoples—were not merely invited but compelled to attend, a decline of the invitation being punishable by death.[82]

The number of people sacrificed on the altars of the various pyramids has been a matter of dispute among scholars, but the competing estimates are in the tens of thousands.[83] The particular Aztec warrior who had captured an enemy was not only allowed the honor of cutting his heart out, but was also awarded an arm or thigh to take home and cook for a ceremonial meal for his family. The purpose of this was not to provide food, but to fulfill cultural and religious purposes, just as the purpose of the public sacrifice was to propitiate the gods and to inure the Aztec people in general to blood and carnage.[84]

For the conquered peoples, their ordeal began immediately after conquest. When the Aztecs conquered the Mixtecs, their ruler was killed and his family enslaved. Then their chiefs who submitted to Aztec rule had to attend a victory banquet at which the Aztecs boasted of their feats and hurled humiliating insults at the vanquished. Thereafter, tribute in kind and in labor had to be paid to the Aztecs. This tribute sometimes included children to be sacrificed on the altars.

Many conquered peoples were reduced to being serfs tied to land controlled by their Aztec overlords. An even worse fate could await conquered areas that later rebelled, which could lead to a wholesale slaughter of the population.[85] Wanton brutality was not the whole story, however. The Aztecs, like such other conquerors as the Mongols, used terror as a weapon to demoralize their enemies and keep the subjugated peoples in line. Aztec leaders were often shrewdly scheming politicians, both in dealing with external peoples or with various rivals and allies within the empire.[86]

Meanwhile, as of the beginning of the sixteenth century, the Spaniards had established permanent colonies in the Caribbean, on the islands of Hispaniola and Cuba, and many Spanish explorers were beginning to survey the mainland of North and South America. Among these were Amerigo Vespucci, from whom the name "America" was derived, and Nunez de Balboa, who was the first European to see the ocean whose peaceful appearance so contrasted with the Atlantic that he named it the Pacific Ocean. Some early Spanish expeditions were able to establish friendly relations with the Indians on the mainland, exchanging glass beads—which were a novelty to the Indians—for gold. Other expeditions, however, ran into trouble. Spaniards who landed on the Yucatan peninsula in 1517 to get water were attacked by Mayans and barely made it back to the ship, after losing dozens of men and having their captain killed. For the Aztecs, however, the fateful landing was that of Hernán Cortés in 1519, commanding 500 soldiers and 100 sailors.[87]

By this time, the Aztecs were ruled by Montezuma II, grandson of the founder of the empire. He had been receiving reports of strange men from the sea, long before he actually saw the Spaniards, and was puzzled and troubled as to what this might mean, particularly in view of Aztec concerns with signs and portents. Meanwhile, Cortés and his men landed on the Yucatan peninsula, avoiding the area where the previous Spanish expedition had encountered Mayans two years earlier. Still, they too became embattled with local Indians. This time, however, the Spaniards won decisively, using their horses, firearms, and military tactics—all of which were at this point unknown to the native people. In a token of submission, the Indian chiefs gave the Spaniards food, clothing, gold, and young women, one of whom became not only the consort of Cortés and bore him a son, but also became a confidante and learned Spanish, making her invaluable as a translator.[88] As Cortés' expedition had contacts with other groups of Indians, he heard of Montezuma II and expressed a wish to meet him. Although Montezuma was far more powerful than the other Indians who had attacked the Spaniards, he decided not to oppose them immediately but to meet with them and find out more. He sent gifts to the Spaniards, including a gold disk described as being "as large as a cartwheel" and a silver disk of the same size, the two apparently representing the sun and the moon, respectively.[89]

Shortly after meeting with emissaries from Montezuma, Cortés received orders from the governor of Cuba to return there. But, having heard of the fabulous wealth of the Aztecs, and having seen the gold and silver presents, Cortés not only disobeyed his orders but also burned the ship, to eliminate any thoughts of returning among the men under his command. The expedition proceeded on toward the Aztec capital of Tenochtitlán, winning a devastating victory over another Indian people on the way—a victory reported back to Montezuma by spies. The Spaniards' military superiority derived from their horses— the first the Indians had ever seen—their armor that was impervious to Indian weapons, and their cannon, all coordinated by highly developed military tactics, which emphasized group maneuvers rather than individual fighting feats, such as those of the Indians. At this point in history, Spanish troops were among the finest fighting forces in Europe and their equipment among the best. They repeatedly defeated much larger numbers of Indians.[90]

News of the Spaniards' military prowess attracted other Indians who allied themselves with them, whether to share in the spoils or to avenge the oppressions their people had suffered from the Aztecs. On their way toward the Aztec capital, the Spaniards encountered the Cholollans, allies of the Aztecs who were pressured by Montezuma's emissaries to invite the Spaniards into their city and then to ambush them. However, an informer betrayed this plot to the Spaniards, who turned the tables and struck first, killing the Cholollan leaders who stood out in the city square to greet them, as part of the ambush plot. When word of this turn of events reached Montezuma, he became even less willing to risk his army on an open battlefield against the Spaniards, hoping instead to be able to fight in more favorable terrain within the island city of Tenochtitlán. Later, when the Spaniards arrived, he welcomed Cortés into the capital city and exchanged gifts with him, both men making friendly overtures and waiting for an opportunity to strike. By now, Cortés had with him not only 500 Spaniards but also 2,000 to 3,000 Indian warriors. However, these forces were now inside an island city of at least a quarter of a million inhabitants, the capital of an empire with even more military forces available elsewhere.

In this highly dangerous situation, the Spaniards exhibited one of the characteristics that was to be a key to their successes throughout the hemisphere—audacity in the face of danger. After two weeks as guests in Tenochtitlán, Cortés and his most trusted captains sought an audience with Montezuma, under a pretext. Once inside the imperial compound, they then seized the ruler of the Aztecs as a hostage. Now he walked across the plaza to the quarters of the Spaniards, both pretending that this was just a friendly visit. However, as the months passed with Montezuma still in captivity, it became transparent to all that he had become a captive and a puppet of the Spaniards. Eventually he openly declared himself a vassal of King Charles V of Spain.

Meanwhile, the Spanish governor of Cuba, whom Cortés had disobeyed, dispatched a new contingent of Spanish troops with orders to arrest the mutinous leader. Again displaying great audacity, Cortés went out to ambush the leader of this contingent, and then persuaded these new troops to join him and his men in the city of Tenochtitlán. The arrival of Spanish reinforcements sufficiently alarmed the Aztecs that they now began to assemble troops for an assault on the foreigners' quarters. However, Montezuma was made to climb atop a parapet and dissuade the troops from any action. By now, however, Montezuma had lost the respect of other Aztec leaders, who considered it a warrior leader's duty to die rather than betray his country to save his own life. Another monarch was chosen, Montezuma's brother who had advocated fighting the Spaniards from the outset. However, he lived less than three months, dying of smallpox that was sweeping through Mexico as a result of the Europeans' presence.[91]

In this highly volatile situation, the Spaniards precipitated a crisis that cost many of them their lives, by their contempt for the Aztec religion and their insistence on trying to install the symbols of Christianity in Aztec places of worship. When the Aztecs gathered to celebrate one of their religious occasions, the Spaniard entered the temple courtyard and proceeded to attack the religious leaders:

Then they surrounded those who danced, whereupon they
went among the drums. Then they struck the arms of one who
beat the drums; they severed both his hands, and afterwards
and afterward struck his neck, so that his head flew off,
rolling far away. Then they pierced them all with iron lances,
and they struck each with iron swords. Of some they slashed
open the back, and then the entrails gushed out. Of some
they split the head; they hacked their heads to pieces . . . [92]

While such savagery was not uncommon when the Aztecs conquered other peoples and destroyed their religious idols, it was deeply
shocking to be on the receiving end—shocking not only in human
terms, but also in religious terms, to a people to whom religion was as
important, and held with as much intolerant bigotry, as among the
Spaniards. The sacrilege and the carnage marked a point of no return
in relations between the invaders and the Aztecs, a point beyond
which all polite or devious pretenses were dropped and open warfare
became inevitable. Another armed assault on the Spanish stronghold
was launched and this time Montezuma's words failed to stop it. He
died in the battle than followed, though it is not clear whether he was
killed by Aztecs or by Spaniards.

Desperate fighting ensued, in which the Spaniards gained the upper
hand for the moment, setting fire to the sacred temple of the Aztecs
and sending idols hurtling down its steps, to the horror of the populace. However, Cortés knew that he and his men would have to try to
escape under cover of night. An alarm was given by women who spot-
ted them and another carnage followed, with the Aztecs gaining the
upper hand this time and the Spaniards and their Indian allies desperately fleeing across the existing bridges and over a floating bridge
which they had constructed. Many of the Spaniards were so laden with
gold that they could not escape. However, the Aztec's emphasis on
capturing prisoners for sacrifice and collecting booty—especially
exotic Spanish weapons in this case—allowed Cortés and many of his
Spanish troops and Indian allies to escape in the night.[93]

Had there been a simple race war for the Western Hemisphere at
that time, the position of the Spaniards would have been hopeless, for
they had not only lost many men and horses, but also their firearms.
Yet they were not only sheltered by Indians opposed to the Aztecs, but

were also able to line up more Indian allies in the months that followed. Meanwhile, news of the Aztecs' great hoards of gold and silver
attracted more Spanish adventurers by the shiploads. Within a year,
Cortés was able to lead another and more powerful army of Spaniards
and Indians in another assault on the Aztec capital. On his way back,
he encountered both resistance and collaboration—as well as circum-
spect neutrality—from different Indian communities along the way,
depending upon those communities' prior relations with the Aztecs.[94]

The new army marching on Tenochtitlán included 900 Spaniards
and thousands of Indians. After a siege that left the population inside
the city starving and racked by disease, the invaders stormed in.
Again there was desperate fighting, with the tide of battle shifting back
and forth. Finally, the Spaniards received the surrender of the military
commander with respect, but they were unable to prevent their Indian
allies from taking vengeance against the Aztecs with a wholesale
slaughter of the city's population, dining later on the limbs of those
they had killed, as so many of their people had been eaten by the
Aztecs. So great was the carnage that the stench of the rotting bodies
made Cortés sick. The hunger that had prevailed in the besieged city
was evidenced by trees stripped of their bark for food and by roots that
had been dug up to be eaten. Thus ended the empire of the Aztecs.[95]

The Incas

In pre-Columbian times, the Inca empire was one of the largest
empires in the world, and possibly the largest of all. At its zenith, this
empire stretched more than two thousand miles from north to south,
spreading over most or all of what is today Peru, Ecuador, Chile and
Bolivia, much of Colombia, and parts of Argentina, and Venezuela. In
climatic terms, it reached from just north of the Equator to nearly the
35th parallel of southern latitude, well into the temperate zone. The
heart of the empire was in the tropics, but thousands of feet above sea
level, so that it suffered neither the enervating tropical heat nor the
debilitating tropical diseases which plague other societies at the same
latitudes. The climate and the crops, such as potatoes and other
tubers, as well as maize, meant that large quantities of food could be
stored—again, unlike food in much of the tropics elsewhere—and
these large stores of food in turn provided the basis for a large army

that could spread over vast areas and yet be fed from widely scattered storehouses.

The geographic setting of the Inca empire was highly varied in temperature, rainfall, and other natural characteristics. Because of the great vertical distances in the mountainous terrain, temperatures ranged from tropical at the lowest elevations to too cold for many crops to grow at the highest elevations. What this meant was that there was great variation in the plants and animals which thrived at different elevations, within a relatively small area as the crow flies. This also meant that there were very different ways of life among various peoples who were farmers, fisherman, pastoralists and other specialists adapted to very different environments, which were not very far from one another in the horizontal plane, however separated they might be vertically. Because the water in the region derived ultimately from the westward-flowing winds from the Atlantic Ocean, there was far more rainfall on the eastern jungles and uplands than in the Andean Mountains, which intercepted enough of the remaining moisture in the air to leave the narrow Pacific coastal lands very arid.[96]

Although we speak loosely of the people of that empire as Incas, more strictly the Inca was the title of the ruler and more generally of the nobility, approximately 40,000 people who ruled the millions of others in the empire.[97] These others included conquered peoples of various ethnic, cultural, and linguistic backgrounds, and of varying degrees of loyalty and reliability as far as the empire was concerned. Like their Ottoman contemporaries, the Inca rulers often relocated large numbers of people, in order to populate recently conquered territories with politically reliable groups and disperse others to reduce the danger of insurrections.[98] The imperial race were the Quechua-speaking people who lived in the Andean mountains at the heart of the Inca empire and who spread their hegemony outward and downward to lower elevations, to peoples with very different ways of life.

Such natural and human variety in relative proximity fostered trade and other interactions, including conquest. As in other parts of the world, the mountain people—the Incas—were particularly well-adapted for fighting. But they were much more than just warriors. Culturally, the Incas were among the most advanced of the indigenous peoples of the Western Hemisphere. They built in stone—both cities and monuments—and had a system of accounting, using multicolored strings with knots, in a system somewhat similar to the abacus in China. Their great buildings included houses with halls 200 yard long and 50–60 yards wide, where great festivals were held indoors during bad weather.[99]

The highway system connecting the vast Incan empire was tens of thousands of miles long and has been considered one of the best all-weather highways built before the appearance of the automobile.[100] The hilly and mountainous terrain along the west coast of South America where the Incas reigned contained relatively little flat arable land, and so required terraced agriculture to retain the precious water. Canals and other devices were also used to control the flow and use of water. As in other parts of the world, terraces and canals required large-scale organization of people and these in turn required a power capable of controlling and directing such large numbers of people. The degree of individualism possible among the plains Indians of North America, for example, was incompatible with survival in a setting where coping with the natural environment required large-scale projects. Inca society was very hierarchical within itself, quite aside from its dominance over the subjugated peoples of the empire, some of whom were used as human sacrifices in their religious rituals.

Like most of the Indian nations of the Western Hemisphere, the Incas had no written language, so that much of what is known about their history before the Spanish conquests has had to be reconstructed from archaeological evidence. Although there was a written version of the Spanish language, most of the early *conquistadores* were illiterate, including their leader Francisco Pizzaro,[101] so that there were few, if any, contemporary written accounts of the Incas, even as they existed at the moment of their first contact with the European world, and verbal accounts of earlier times often conflicted, as verbal accounts tend to do elsewhere. However, because the Incas built so much in stone and created many objects of metal, including gold and silver, the surviving ruins and artifacts preserve a major part of the past, while such modern techniques as carbon-dating permit time sequences to be reconstructed.

What the Incas lacked, in addition to writing, was the wheel and the arch. They used logs as rollers to move large stones but not wheels on an axis, which would have been of less use than elsewhere in the world, because of the mountainous terrain and the absence of strong animals like horses or oxen. Either llamas or human porters were used to carry loads. Despite a lack of arches, the Incas were able to construct doorways and a variety of bridges, including suspension bridges.[102]

Despite the vast extension of the Incan empire and the ancient culture of the region, neither the empire nor the state from which it sprang were very long-lived in historical terms. The Incan state lasted not quite a century and the empire little more than 50 years. In addition to uprisings among the conquered peoples, there were internal struggles for power among the Incas themselves, growing in part from a lack of clear rules of succession. However, the empire was still growing to some extent, and prior conquests were still being consolidated, when Europeans first appeared on the scene in the sixteenth century. These Europeans consisted of about 260 Spaniards, about one-fourth of them mounted warriors and the rest foot soldiers.[103] Amazingly, they were able to conquer the Incan empire with its thousands of soldiers and millions of people. A remarkable confluence of circumstances led to this result. Perhaps the most remarkable of these circumstances was that the Spaniards had the audacity to make the attempt and the ruthlessness and imagination to carry it out, aided by major blunders by the rulers of the Inca people.

A bloody and devastating civil war between rival claimants for the imperial throne of the Incas was going on when the Spaniards began their expeditions down the Pacific coast of South America in the early sixteenth century, where they stopped to raid, loot, and carry off women, as well as capturing others destined to be their servants and to learn enough Spanish to act as interpreters. Stories of their depredations reached both Incan rivals—the brothers Atahaulpa and Huascar, sons of the recently deceased emperor—as well as others among the peoples of the Inca empire. This provoked much speculation about the nature of these bearded men who lived in "a house in the sea" and rode strange new creatures, horses. Some wondered if they might be something supernatural and the fulfillment of prophecies in the Incan religion. Messages were exchanged between the Spaniards and the warring factions of Incas, both the Indians and the Europeans trying to feel their way through an uncertain situation.

Meanwhile, battles between the rival Incan military forces of Huascar and Atahaulpa raged on, while various political machinations were afoot. Huascar had himself declared emperor in the Incan capital of

Cuzco, but Atahaulpa's army from Quito, Ecuador, marched relent-
lessly southward toward the capital, eventually capturing Huascar and
instituting a mass slaughter of the Inca nobles there, accompanied by
hideous atrocities against the population in general.[104] But, soon after
Atahualpa vanquished his rival for control of the empire, the
Spaniards also followed the roads into Cuzco.

The first blunder of the new Inca ruler was to under-estimate the
fighting ability of the Spaniards, by preferring to believe the disdainful
accounts of their early battles in the lowlands by some of his advisors,
rather than the eye-witness testimony of those who had actually fought
the Spaniards.[105] Flush from his own recent military victories,
Atahualpa may have been reluctant to believe that the new bearded
men he had heard of were anything that he could not handle, especially since they were a small fighting force and he was not among
those who believed them to be supernatural.

In addition to word of the activities of the Spaniards in the lowland
outskirts of the empire, word reached the emperor of devastating diseases striking and destroying the peoples of that region. Vast numbers
of people were dying in Quito, for example. These diseases spread not
simply from direct contact with the Europeans, for once diffused into
the indigenous population, the diseases travelled wherever those people travelled, whether trading, fishing or otherwise. Therefore, as the
Europeans advanced militarily, they often encountered populations
already weakened or devastated by their diseases. So it was in the
heartland of the Incas. Unknown to anyone at the time, those who
brought news of the new diseases also inadvertently brought the diseases as well. So did the Incan armies recalled from the stricken
areas. People were dying of European diseases in the Incan capital
before the first white man was ever seen there.[106]

Meanwhile, the Spaniards, having gained victories over the lowland
peoples and having looted them, proceeded on up toward the highland
heart of the Inca empire, whose treasures of gold they had heard so
much about. Increasingly impressed by the obviously advanced civilization they saw around them—and then terrified by the size of the
army they saw—they invited the Inca emperor to join them for dinner
and to have them pay homage to him, as they sought desperately for a
way to get out of the predicament in which they now found themselves.
The second and critical blunder of Atahualpa, perhaps based on his

first—the under-estimation of the Spaniards—was to agree to meet with Pizzaro and his men at their encampment.

Following carefully laid plans, concealed Spaniards ambushed and captured Atahualpa, using their cannons and horses to spread confusion and terror among the large but lightly armed body of troops accompanying the Inca. Indians by the thousands were slaughtered within a matter of hours.[107] Precisely because the Incan empire was very hierarchical and well-organized, the capture of its ruler gave the Spaniards enormous leverage over the whole realm. But first, they used the captured emperor to extract vast sums of gold and silver as ransom. The gold received as his ransom has been estimated as being worth more than $6 million in late twentieth-century dollars.[108] Nevertheless, Atahualpa was not released and eventually the Spaniards had him killed. Meanwhile, his rival Huascar was killed by Atahualpa's followers. Finally, the general in charge of Atahualpa's army was persuaded by the honeyed words of a Spanish emissary that the Inca wanted to see him and so went to the Spaniard's encampment, where he too was captured and, in due course, killed.

With much of the top leadership of both Indian factions now dead—killed by one another or by the Spaniards—the latter were now in a better position to proceed on to the capital at Cuzco. On their way, they passed a battlefield strewn with thousands or corpses of Indians killed in the civil war. Despite the huge numerical preponderance of the remaining Incas, the Spanish soldiers enjoyed great technological superiority. It was not their guns—which were still cumbersome, slow-firing, and not very accurate at this point—but their armor, their swords, and their horses which enabled them to take on vastly greater Incan military forces and win.[109] Horses, for example, not only permitted devastating cavalry charges but also often nullified the enemies' lookouts, since horses could often travel faster than word could be passed from the lookouts to warn their leaders and comrades of the Spaniards' approach. Moreover, the *conquistadores* were full-time, seasoned warriors, while much of the Incan army consisted of people who were farmers or who worked at other non-military tasks ordinarily, and who were then mobilized on particular occasions for military duty. Finally, uprisings against the Incan empire by many of the subjugated peoples added to the confusion and uncertainty of the situation.

In these circumstances, the Spaniards entered the Incan capital of

Cuzco, welcomed as liberators by its long-suffering inhabitants—a misconception initially encouraged by the Spaniards themselves. Time, however, would later reveal the bitter reality of the situation. The Spaniards who entered Cuzco, ostensibly as liberators, and who set up a puppet Inca emperor, soon revealed themselves as the real power. The looting of the territory, the forced labor of the Indian men, and the sexual exploitation of the Indian women became widespread. From Cuzco the reconquest of the disintegrating Incan empire by the Spaniards began, aided by large numbers of Incan troops led by the new ruler, Manco Inca.[110] Despite fierce resistance by many of the Indian tribes, the Spanish military superiority proved repeatedly to be decisive against even the bravest and most desperate resistance. In some cases, Indian tribes who had suffered under Atahaulpa's army from Quito now helped the Spaniards and the Incas from Cuzco.[111]

Meanwhile, back in Cuzco itself, the Spanish were on relatively good behavior pending the arrival of new reinforcements of Spaniards from Spanish colonies farther north. Numerous shiploads of Spaniards then arrived, seeking the fabled riches of Peru. Many were given custody of thousands of Indians, whose tribute and labor in the mines made the Spaniards rich. Even some Spaniards who had been peasants or artisans now became part of a wealthy ruling class, to whom such things as trade and manual labor were deemed socially unacceptable.[112] As Peru was transformed into a Spanish colony, a new capital was built along the coast, making it more accessible by ship to other Spanish colonies and to Spain, and ending the need for slow and costly porterage of supplies up into the mountainous region around Cuzco. The new colonial capital ultimately became modern Peru's capital, Lima.

After the Quitan army that had come south with Atahualpa was forced back to its homeland and crushed there by the Spaniards and the military forces of the Inca, the Spanish empire was now secure enough for its exploitation to proceed in disregard of the Indians, including the Inca and the Incan nobility who had collaborated with them. It was said that "no woman who was good-looking was safe to her husband." But, although the Spaniards had many native girls as mistresses, they seldom married them, waiting for women from Spain to arrive, now that the conquered land was secure. The arrogance of the Spaniards eventually reached the point where the Inca's own sister was raped and then his wife was taken away by one of the Pizzaros. The Inca's protests caused him to be imprisoned, then humiliated both privately and publicly. He escaped from Cuzco and went into the mountains, from which he conducted armed resistance to the Spaniards for years, and roused widespread rebellions among the Indians.[113]

Various groups of Indians for a thousand miles around arose in rebellion against the Spaniards. The battles, skirmishes, and guerilla actions raged on for years, with brutalities and atrocities being common on both sides. However, some of the Indians once subjugated by the Incas fought on the side of the Spaniards or helped them with information or supplies. Nor were the Spaniards always united. The arrival of large new contingents of Spanish troops changed the balance of power in favor of the newcomers, who were anxious to claim riches and power such as their predecessors had already acquired. Moreover, the newcomers had been sent by royal command, after the king of Spain had become disgusted with reports of the disgraceful behavior of Pizzaro's men in Peru. A civil war then ensued among the Spaniards, during which Gonzalo Pizzaro had 340 Spaniards executed and then ended up being executed himself when the royal forces triumphed.[114]

Although the triumph of the royalist faction brought royal decrees seeking better treatment of the Indians, the kings of Spain vacillated between humanitarian concerns aroused by the reports of mistreatment brought to them by both clerical and lay observers from South America and a desire to continue receiving the vast amounts of gold and silver extracted from the ground and from the natives, and which was flowing into Spain in general and into the royal coffers in particular. The result was a series of weakly enforced attempts to stop the worst abuses, together with an acquiescence in the general system in which individual Spaniards had control of thousands of Indians each and did with them largely what they wished.

The appointment of Don Francisco de Toledo as Viceroy in 1568 marked an attempt at both reforming the Spaniards and converting the Indians to Christianity and to a European way of life. More than a million and a half Indians were forcibly relocated from their scattered hillside communities to towns created for the purpose of changing their way of life, both religiously and socially. Spanish clergyman sought out and destroyed Indian religious objects, including the mummies of Incan emperors, and leaders of the indigenous religions were caught and flogged. Dictionaries were created for the Quecha language. These attempts to remake the Indians in the image of the Spaniards met resistance, evasion, flight, and even armed uprisings in which Christian churches were destroyed and their symbols smashed.[115]

In the end, the Spaniards prevailed, at least in the sense of having political control of the country and effective control of most of the indigenous population, many of whom were worked mercilessly in the silver mines and elsewhere to enrich individual Spaniards and the Spanish government, both in Spain and in the colonies. The Incan empire was destroyed as thoroughly as the Roman Empire had been destroyed. Moreover, the preservation of some parts of Roman culture by a relatively few educated men—mostly clergy—in medieval Europe allowed at least a thin strain of continuity. Because the Incan culture had no written language, even this much preservation was not possible. The complex culture of the Incans could not be sustained in the socially fragmented world of the post-conquest Indians. One sign of this were the large terraced lands which were subsequently abandoned, even though the stone-faced terraces themselves remained as ruins on into the twentieth-century. These terraces were part of a way of life no longer feasible without the cultural continuity and political hegemony on which it depended.

NORTH AMERICA

The numerous Indian tribes, nations, and confederations spread across the vast North American continent differed not only among themselves, but differed in general from the Aztecs and the Incas. By and large, the Indians of North America did not have as hierarchical or as despotic governments as those of the Aztecs and Incas, or the governments of contemporary Europeans. Indeed, questions have been raised as to whether the ways in which many North American Indians organized their collective activities should be called government at all, for chiefs might be chosen for particular purposes, such as conducting a hunt or a war, without the individuals chosen having any permanent power to dictate to their people or perhaps even to remain in authority beyond the duration of the activity for which they were chosen. Relationships among North American Indian tribes and nations seldom involved such grinding oppression as that imposed on those conquered by the Aztecs or Incas. Nevertheless, the stronger tribes or nations collected tribute from the weaker, as was common around the world and, in confederacies such as those of the Iroquois, some tribes played subordinate roles while others took the lead. This does not imply that harmonious, or even humane, relationships always existed among North American Indians, for archaeological evidence exists of both torture and cannibalism in the pre-Columbian era.[116] Cherokees enslaved other Indians and, after the European settlers arrived, sold some of them to the whites, as they would later buy and sell African slaves, or return runaway slaves to whites for the rewards.[117]

North American Indians also tended not to be not nearly as urbanized as the Aztecs or the Incas, nor to have such large concentrations of wealth as attracted the *conquistadores*. Nor were there such large concentrations of people. The entire Cherokee nation in 1690 consisted of about 20,000 people, even though the Cherokees were one of the largest tribes east of the Mississippi.[118] There were more Maya than this in and around Tikal alone and more Aztecs than this in their capital city of Tenochtitlán. Perhaps most important of all, the relationship between the Indians and the early European settlers tended to be very different from what they were in Latin America. During the colonial era, and to some extent beyond, the story of British, French, Dutch, and Swedish settlement and expansion on the North American mainland was quite different from that of the Spanish and Portuguese conquests in the rest of the hemisphere. As a leading authority on North American Indian history put it:

> Loose talk of the "conquest" of the Indians has obscured the
> fact that Indians relinquished much jurisdictional territory
> by negotiated voluntary cession appearing in the form of the
> sale of property.[119]

Not only was much land acquired this way during the colonial era, so was much land acquired after the colonies became the United States of America. This is not to say that no chicanery or force was ever involved,[120] but simply that this was not a classic conquest, as exemplified by the Spanish or Portuguese conquests, or by the conquests of nations in Europe. The difference between the way the Iberians acquired land during the colonial era and the way the British,

French, Dutch and Swedes acquired land reflected in part differences in the relative strength of Europeans and Indians in the different regions of the hemisphere. In turn, this reflected differences in the initial settlers from different parts of Europe and differing natural conditions in North America.

Because the Indians of the Atlantic seaboard, where the British, French, Dutch, and Swedes initially settled, had no such immense concentrations of wealth as those of the more advanced Aztec or Incan empires, there was nothing to attract shiploads of fighting men in search of booty. The earliest attractions of North America were the rich fishing banks off Newfoundland and the availability of animal hides and furs on a vast scale no longer seen in Europe. Fishing vessels from Britain, France, Spain, and Portugal plied the waters,[121] but the furs were best obtained by trading with the Indians. Thus a series of trading posts began to appear on shores and along rivers such as the Hudson and the St. Lawrence, which reached far into the interior and were deep enough for ocean-going ships. Quebec alone shipped 30,000 pelts to Europe in 1630.[122] The Dutch, the paramount maritime nation of the time, preferred outposts and settlements on islands, which were more defensible against attack. For them, Manhattan was an ideal site on a navigable waterway that extended hundreds of miles inland, so it was here that they established the settlement they called New Amsterdam. Farther upriver they established Fort Orange as a trading post, where the city of Albany is located today.[123] Other European powers—principally France and Britain—likewise began establishing outposts and settlements along the eastern seaboard. Their chief rivalry was among themselves, rather than with the Indians, who were anxious to trade with the newcomers for products of European industry, ranging from cooking utensils to firearms.

Unlike the troops of the *conquistadores*, the earliest European settlers on the eastern seaboard of North America included women and children, and the total numbers of people in these settlement were often too small to be regarded as a threat by the surrounding Indian nations. In the mid-seventeenth century, for example, the entire French population of New France consisted of only 300 people, scattered in four tiny settlements along the St. Lawrence River, and the population of New Sweden never reached 400.[124] Even some larger settlements had very precarious beginnings, such as the Virginia settlement along the James River, which began with 6,000 people and declined over years of hardship and hunger to a population of 1,200.[125] With the passage of time, however, larger and more formidable Europeans settlements appeared, both from the growth of some existing settlements and by the establishment of new colonies. New France had a population of more than 3,000 people by 1663 and nearly 11,000 by 1685.[126] Over the decades from 1630 to 1660, approximately 20,000 Puritans came to North America. By mid-century, there were 10,000 Europeans in Newfoundland (two-thirds of them Irish Catholics) and New Amsterdam also had 10,000 people when the British seized it from the Dutch in 1664.[127] Even these later populations may seem small, but they must be compared to the contemporary populations of individual Indian tribes in North America, especially since these tribes were by no means united in opposition to white settlers.

Meanwhile, the spread of European diseases decimated the Indians with whom they were in contact, accentuating the shift in the local population balance and in the corresponding military balance of power—a balance which affected their relations and negotiations, even when there were no actual clashes in battle. Moreover, the smaller Indian populations remaining after epidemics of European diseases required less land, so that tribes were able to trade this land—much of it already cultivated—to the European settlers, to whom such land was more valuable than a wilderness that they would have had to clear and cultivate from scratch. The decimation of tribes living near Europeans by disease also affected their balance of power with other tribes living farther away and therefore less subject to epidemics of European diseases. Thus, while a staggering 90 percent of the Wampanoag tribe in New England died of European diseases, these diseases had no such impact on the Micmac tribe of hunters and gatherers, who had less contact with whites, and who now began raiding the stricken Wampanoag communities, which also found themselves forced to cede land to the Narragansett tribe.[128]

Where the opportunities presented themselves, some white settlers not only took Indian land but also captured Indians individually or in groups for sale as slaves, many being traded to the Spaniards or to the West Indies. Such depredations in New England provoked much hostility toward Europeans in parts of the region, years before the Pilgrims landed and established a settlement at Plymouth in 1620.

Having heard of the Indian hostility before landing, the Pilgrims approached them in a belligerent posture, provoking more hostility. Thus, although the new colonists were saved from starvation by the corn found in deserted Indian cornfields, their relationships with the Indians began shakily. However, they were able to negotiate a treaty in 1621 with some of the local Indians, though apparently under the misapprehension that they had gained peace with all the Indians.[129]

Although classic government-to-government warfare and conquest were not the norm between Indians and whites in colonial North America, fighting on the frontiers was not only common but ferocious and brutal. Where Indians captured whites, for example, they took delight in dashing white children against tree trunks or scalping or dismembering them in front of their anguished parents, among the many other sadistic tortures they practiced.[130] White settlers, in turn, wiped out whole Indian communities and offered bounties for Indian scalps.[131] Whatever the relations among white and Indian leaders, along the disputed frontiers bitter hatred and unbridled savagery were mutual.

Alongside these bitter and implacable hatreds and hostilities between some whites and Indians, there developed trading relationships and military alliances between other whites and other Indians. British colonial officials and, later, American leaders often took a paternalistic view of the Indians, as did missionaries, but these were views seldom shared by pioneers confronting Indians on the frontier. Thus, while Quaker leaders in Philadelphia viewed the Indians benignly, honored treaties with them and gave them gifts, the Scotch-Irish settlers on the western Pennsylvania frontier fought the Indians as mercilessly as the Indians fought them. Farther north, Dartmouth College provided financial aid for Indian students to attend but Lord Jeffrey Amherst, for whom another college would later be named, not only fought the Indians militarily but even tried deliberately to spread smallpox among them.[132] Relationships and policies between whites and Indians had neither consistency among people nor consistency over time, on either side. Nevertheless, there were some general patterns.

While the white settlers' military strength grew with the growth of the European population and the decline in the populations of the surrounding Indian tribes, what the Europeans had from the beginning, and increasingly over time, were new products desired by the Indians.

Woolen cloth and cloth garments were major items from Europe traded by the new arrivals to their Indian neighbors, as were firearms and ammunition. Food was initially a major item desired by the settlers, until they learned from the Indians how to grow maize (corn) and other crops in an environment that was new to them. As time went on, the settlers became self-sufficient in the basic necessities, while the massive trade in the hides, and especially the furs, of animals in general and beavers in particular continued to grow as an international trade of major dimensions between North America and Europe, with the European settlers acting as middlemen, conveying European products to the Indians and furs to Europe.

Even before Europeans began to settle in colonial North America, the fur trade was an international trade with many centuries of history behind it. Russians were prominent among the supplier of furs and some of the furs acquired from the Indians of North America were sent by the Dutch to Russia, where people highly skilled in preparing furs could work on them and then return them to the Netherlands for the finishing touches. The discovery of vast regions in North America where fur-bearing animals—particularly beavers—still abounded, gave an enormous impetus to this market. As a result, fur hats became such a fashion among the affluent in Europe that the wearing of caps declined until it became a sign of being a member of the lower classes.[133]

The Indians and the European settlers were not only trading partners during the colonial era, they were often also military allies—the Mohawks with the Dutch, the Hurons with the French, and later the entire Iroquois confederacy with the British. Thus Indians were drawn into the world-wide power struggles of the European imperial nations, as these struggles were fought out in North America. This included a series of wars between the French and the British, as well as the American war of independence—in both of which the Indians fought largely on the losing side, costing them dearly in land ceded as part of their surrender, as well as in immediate casualties and lasting ill-will. European settlers, however, were usually not drawn into local wars among the Indians, except as suppliers of firearms to one side or the other or as power brokers.

In addition to economic and military ties between the colonists and the Indians in their vicinity, there were cultural changes induced among the Indians as a result of their relations with the Europeans.

Some Indians became Christians, for example, thereby creating schisms within tribes. More generally, the economic and military functions within Indian communities changed as a result of a growing reliance on trade with European settlers for the basic means of livelihood and reliance on European firearms and ammunition for hunting and for fighting wars with rival tribes. Many Indians changed their way of life, sometimes abandoning crafts which produced goods that were now more easily obtained in trade with the white settlers. Thus the Indians in contact with whites became more dependent on whites over time, while the white settlers became less and less dependent on the Indians, after learning from them how to grow the crops indigenous to North America, learning the landscape, and learning indigenous languages. A crucial factor in their changing relationship was writing (including map-making), which allowed any information given to the transplanted Europeans to be spread rapidly among them and to be made a permanent cultural possession by being committed to the printed page. The Indians, lacking writing, could lose valuable traditional skills permanently if just one generation failed to continue them. In short, the Indians lost some of their skills while the European settlers kept theirs, added what they had learned from the Indians, and continued to receive new technological and other knowledge from Europe. All this contributed to a changing balance of power over time, increasingly favoring the European settlers.

The various indigenous peoples fought among themselves for access to European trading posts, where beaver furs could be traded for goods from across the Atlantic. Among these goods, perhaps the most fateful were guns and liquor. Those Indians immediately in contact with Europeans fought off other Indians trying to reach them, so that most of the furs traded to Europeans came from Indians who had not themselves trapped the animals, but who had acquired their pelts in trade from other Indians farther away, in exchange for European goods supplied by the Indian middlemen, who made a profit on both exchanges. Thus the Cree Indians on the shores of Hudson's Bay became middlemen in the fur trade and the Iroquois, who dominated the region between the Alleghanies and the Great Lakes, cut off the Ottawas and the Hurons from Quebec and Montreal. In order to get around the Iroquois, the French ventured farther west.[134]

More than trade alone was involved. Because access to Europeans meant access to European firearms this caused a shift in the military balance of power among Indians. The Cree Indians, for example, acquired more than 10,000 firearms from the Hudson Bay Company between 1670 and 1689, not counting the additional firearms they were getting in trade with the French.[135] Those Indians in direct contact with white settlements could acquire enough firearms to shift the military balance of power against rival tribes and nations, whom they accordingly barred from having the same direct contact. Thus the Ojibwa not only acquired guns but strove to drive the Sioux and the Fox tribes away from the Great Lakes, where they too might have acquired guns. These guns could of course also be used against the white settlers, and often were, but a limiting factor for the Indians was that they needed the settlers not only to supply firearms but also to repair them and to supply ammunition. In an outbreak of warfare between Indians and whites in seventeenth-century Massachusetts, for example, the Indians won more battles but the whites won the war when the Indians' ammunition began to run out.[136]

In general, warfare between whites and Indians was less common during the colonial era than warfare among the Indians, fighting with one another for access to European settlements. Indian tribes or nations, determined to break through rival tribes or nations who held them at bay from the European trading posts, launched attacks and invasions to gain the coveted access. The Hurons held annual meetings with other local Indians, warning them not to attempt to make direct contact with the French.[137] Later, the Iroquois decimated the Hurons, forcing their remnants westward, while absorbing some of the survivors into the Iroquois confederation.[138] Meanwhile, the Europeans sought better access to the Indian suppliers of pelts, without having to go through middlemen. Many of the explorations of the British and the French were for the purpose of finding water routes taking them further inland to the Indians who were the original trappers, where trades could be made without paying the middleman's profit. Isolated European traders, more noted for their courage than their scruples, often penetrated deeper into Indian territory, in search of better trading terms and bigger profits.

Here and there, organized settlements of whites in colonial North America were able to raid or invade local Indians' territory, but usually there was no need to risk such trials of arms. Moreover, the European settlers were as anxious for the furs traded by the Indians as the Indians were for European goods. Over time, however, as the beavers began to be hunted to extinction in the eastern regions of North America, the fur trade moved west to find new beaver populations. Those Indians who had abandoned their traditional means of livelihood in favor of trade with the European settlers were left in a particularly difficult position after the loss of both hunting opportunities and of their traditional artisan skills. Where there was no such economic interdependence, as in colonial Virginia where tobacco rather than fur was the great export, military hostilities between whites and Indians developed early on. While the first James River settlers readily traded copper for food, escalating corn prices led to forcible seizures of Indian corn and cornfields by the whites, initiating a series of wars in which hundreds were killed on each side. Unlike furs, which white settlers obtained in trade with the Indians, tobacco was grown by the colonists themselves. Although the original settlers were outnumbered by the Powhatan Indians by well over a hundred to one in the early seventeenth century, the rapidly growing white population of Virginia was by 1675 more than ten times the size of the Indian population.[139]

While Europeans ultimately prevailed militarily in both North and South America, this was a much more protracted process in the United States and Canada than in Latin America. Moreover, the nature of the Europeans' hegemony differed as between the Iberians, on the one hand, and the British, French, and Americans on the other. In particular, the colonies of transplanted British and French communities in North America remained a largely insular world of their own, with Europeans living in European communities and Indians living in Indian communities, however much the boundaries between the two might move over the years and however much interaction there might be in the frontier zones between the two. Seldom was there a situation such as that in Spanish America, where a European overlord class lived directly off the work of the indigenous peoples living in European-controlled territory.

The exchange of Indian land for European goods was seldom an individual transaction. That is, individual white settlers did not usually buy land from individual Indians and go live in the midst of Indian communities. Rather, officials of the colonial settler governments purchased large tracts of land from Indian tribes and then subdivided it among individual white purchasers. Indeed, all colonial governments, at one time or another, banned individual land purchases from individual Indians because of the legal and other complications this could cause.[140]

Even after the white population grew larger and more powerful in colonial North America, expansion into Indian territory seldom took the classic form of conquest of one sovereign nation by another. The drive for expansion into Indian lands was often led by free-lance adventurers, rather than by governmental military forces. Under frontier conditions, even governments on the scene had only limited control of all the people nominally under their authority. As late as 1792, Thomas Jefferson wrote in a letter:

> I hope too that your admonitions against encroachments on the Indian lands will have a beneficial effect—the U.S. finds an Indian war too serious a thing, to risk incurring one merely to gratify a few intruders with settlements which are to cost the other inhabitants of the U.S. a thousand times their value in taxes for carrying on the war they produce. I am satisfied it will ever be preferred to send armed force and make war against the intruders as being more just & less expensive.[141]

Control on the Indian side was not necessarily any more effective, in part because many North American Indians did not have the kind of governmental structures to control their own people that Europeans did. Chiefs selected to lead hunts or to lead wars had no permanent power to impose their will on the whole society. When Indian braves saw their lands invaded by whites, they could strike back and thereby unleash a war between the races, regardless of what more cautious advice might be given them by their elders. Under these circumstances of uncontrollable groups on both sides, outbreaks of frontier warfare between Europeans and Indians did not always depend on decisions made by leaders on either side. The French had a somewhat similar problem with individual entrepreneurs in the fur trade, who in effect extended the European settlements beyond bounds considered militarily defensible.[142]

In general, the expansion of the white settlers into Indian territory in North America was directed primarily toward taking over the land itself, rather than acquiring Indians as subjects of the government or as vassals of white landowners or of European ecclesiastical establishments, as happened in much of Spanish America. One consequence of this difference was that Indian and European races were much less mixed in British North America than in Spanish America, where a substantial part of the entire population was of mixed blood after three centuries of rule by the Spaniards.[143]

Because the advancing Europeans did not generally acquire sovereignty over the Indians living on the invaded territories. the Indians forced off these lands retreated to new lands, where their sovereignty remained more or less intact. Thus, a century after the United States was formed, there were still Indian nations capable of fighting the U.S. Army and of defeating Custer at the Little Big Horn. Only after the American nation spread from the Atlantic to the Pacific was federal sovereignty imposed on Indians still living in their own enclaves.

The passage of time and the consolidation of European—and then American—government power in North America did not bring lasting peace, such as might follow a conventional conquest, for now the balance of military power shifted decisively in favor of the transplanted Europeans, whose growing populations and power meant less reason to fear wars with the Indians, as well as more reason to seek additional land for those growing populations. Thus the nineteenth century saw escalating demands against the Indians and their lands in the United States, with Indian resistance leading to many new outbreaks of war, now very much along racial lines. However, even in this later period of massive European territorial expansion westward across the North American continent, Indian resistance was still not consolidated along racial lines. Rather, tribes displaced from their traditional lands by the westward movements of whites often moved west in turn themselves, invading the lands of other Indians, much in the manner of the chain-reaction conquests in medieval Europe, when invaders from Central Asia pushed the Slavs ahead of them to invade East Central Europe and the Balkans.

The semi-conquest by which the United States acquired much of its land from the Indians by sales—free and forced—rather than by direct and unambiguous conquest, as in other cases, left American Indians in an anomalous legal position. On the one hand, Indians were

American citizens subject ultimately to the sovereignty of the federal government but, on the other hand, Indian nations had treaties with the United States giving them much sovereignty within their own remaining lands and creating many legal puzzles and controversies as to whether, or to what extent, they were subject to the laws and jurisdiction of state governments.[144] Nor were all these anomalies laid to rest during the frontier era. As late as 1996, a federal appeals court had to decider whether a state government could impose its truck license fees on trucks operating on an Indian reservation[145] and the U.S. Supreme Court had to decide whether another state could apply its gambling laws on Indian reservations.[146] Other legal issues growing out of the ambiguous process of semi-conquest, and the unresolved issues of Indian sovereignty that it left, continued to find their way into the courts, more than a hundred years after the last military battles between the Indians and federal troops.

The historical patterns which emerged over the centuries in North America grew out of the geographic, demographic, and cultural circumstances of North America, rather than because the British or French were fundamentally different from the Spaniards and Portuguese in their goals. In the very different circumstances of the Caribbean, where European invaders had overwhelming military superiority over the smaller and less advanced indigenous tribes of the islands, the British, French, and Dutch conquests were much more like those of the Spanish and Portuguese, both in the Caribbean and in the rest of the Western Hemisphere. The local Indians were either exterminated or subjugated and the islands occupied by European-run plantations where African slaves produced sugar or other crops for direct export to Europe. In North America, however, the circumstances were so different as to make the European takeover a much longer and more complicated story.

The Iroquois

As with many other Indian tribes, nations, and confederacies, the name by which the Iroquois became known to the European settlers was not the name they gave themselves, but a name given them by other Indians and transformed as it passed into European languages. As often happened, it was a pejorative name—"the killer people" in the language of the Algonquin Indians, subsequently transformed by Basque speakers and then transformed again as the name passed from the Basques to the French, to emerge as "Iroquois," pronounced differently by the English and the French.[147]

The Iroquois were not a tribe but a confederation, encompassing the Mohawks, the Senecas, the Cayugas, the Oneidas, the Onondagas, and (later) the Tuscaroras. It was also known as the Five Nations and then as the Six Nations, after the Tuscaroras joined in the early eighteenth century. Spread from east to west across what is today New York State and extending over into Canada and the northern fringe of Pennsylvania, these nations shared a family of languages used by other Indian nations, including the rival confederacy of the Huron further west, the Susquehannock nation to the south and the Cherokees farther south. The Iroquois confederation gradually took shape from a coalescing of villages, and then clusters of villages, into larger and larger political units, sometime between the middle of the fifteenth century and the early decades of the sixteenth century. This alliance formed to put an end to long and ruinous warfare among the tribes who finally came together to form the confederation. In contrast to the autocratic rule of the Aztecs and the Incas, the Iroquois confederation was one based on mutual agreement for any confederation-wide action, though individual nations within the confederation might, for example, engage in war with an external enemy on its own, provided that this did not harm other member nations. In practice, however, warfare sometimes did nevertheless break out between confederation members.[148]

Among themselves, the Iroquois were known as the people of the long house, based on their distinctive dwelling places. Several nuclear families would inhabit a wooden building about 20 feet wide and more than a hundred feet long, each family in its own cubicle and sharing hearths with an adjoining family. A collection of such long houses would be surrounded by a palisade as defense against military attack. Such towns or villages might contain as many as two thousand people and the entire Iroquois confederation contained perhaps 30,000 people.[149] Located inland from the first European settlements, the Iroquois were close enough to make such contact as they needed for trading purposes, but not close enough initially to suffer the devastating epidemics of European diseases that struck other tribes adjacent to the white settlements. Nor were their lands initially in immediate peril of being taken over. Moreover, the Iroquois were strong enough for the settlers to want to make peace and alliances with them. Indeed, as the Iroquois acquired firearms, they became more formidable to other Indian nations and confederacies, particularly to the Hurons and the Mohicans, both of whom were eventually devastated by wars launched by the Iroquois.

In Iroquois society, as it existed when the white settlers first arrived, the men were hunters and warriors, while the women farmed, performed domestic chores, and made clothing from deer skins. This farming was, as elsewhere, without the benefit of draft animals, and therefore without the animal manure used to maintain fertility in other parts of the world. This meant that the Iroquois found it necessary for the Iroquois to move to new locations every few years, as the fertility declined on a given expanse of farmland. Dependence on deer skins for clothing likewise meant that a modest number of Iroquois required a vast amount of land in which to hunt the deer required to keep themselves clothed. The Mohawks, for example, with an estimated population of less than 8,000 people, controlled an area with more than 75,000 deer, of whom about a third could be culled annually without threatening the herds with extinction.[150]

As with the Iroquois confederacy, so within its constituent nations, and even down to the individual longhouses, consensus was the mode of decision-making. As villages relocated, dissenters could split off to form their own communities, thus avoiding the internal strains of more hierarchical societies. Such social arrangements, as well as dependence on large deer populations and shifting agricultural sites, all required a very large expanse of land to support what would have been a relatively modest number of people by contemporary European standards. Such a way of life was not conducive to urban civilizations, such as those of the Aztecs and Incas, or of Europeans and Asians.

Although consensus, and often unanimity, were required for group decisions among the Iroquois, with chiefs having only such authority as was accorded them by their people for the purpose at hand, relations with among the nations of the confederation were by no means always equal and relations between the confederacy and other Indians were far from harmonious. Although equals were called "brothers" among the Iroquois, the Mohawks, Senecas, and Onondagas were considered "elder brothers" to the Oneidas, Cayugas, and Tuscaroras.[151]

Warfare between the Iroquois and their enemies involved not only the carnage of battle but also sadistic tortures of captives, which might be prolonged for hours or even days, until death finally ensued. Sometimes ritualized cannibalism was also practiced. However, not all captives were tortured or eaten, by any means. It was the men of the opposing tribe who might suffer this fate, as well as enslavement, but women and children were simply taken prisoner and usually absorbed into the conquering tribe. So were many men, depending on the needs for population replacement, especially after large losses due to warfare or to epidemics. However, prisoners brought back to the victors' village could expect to be forced to run a gauntlet, in which even the women and children of the victorious tribe would beat or stab them. Women who had suffered losses of family members could revenge themselves by torturing captives, or might choose to adopt them instead, as replacements. Later, European missionaries could likewise suffer death, mutilation, or enslavement—or might succeed in winning converts to Christianity.[152]

Trade with the European settlers began to change the Iroquois way of life in various ways from the early colonial era onward. Cloth quickly became a substitute or supplement to deerskin clothing, so that even the earliest drawings of Iroquois people seldom showed them in their authentic traditional dress as it existed before contact with the European settlers and their cloth. Copper kettles from Europe were also preferred to the indigenous earthenware pots, and iron and steel cooking utensils, knives, and arrowheads were likewise preferred to their own indigenous counterparts. Above all, firearms crucially changed the balance of power between the Iroquois and other Indian nations without such ready access to the new weapons. Moreover, as the use of firearms spread, the Iroquois abandoned their wooden and leather body armor, which had been useful against arrows but not against bullets, and now opted for the greater mobility permitted by no longer carrying this additional weight.[153] Even the wampum so much identified with North American Indians began to be made with European tools and changed in character as a result.[154]

European arms and European alliances became crucial to the outcomes of wars among Indians, so that the Iroquois among others became, increasingly over time, satellites or clients of the white settlers, without the formality of conquest in most cases. At the same time, the rivalries among European powers made the Iroquois valuable allies in the power politics and repeated outbreaks of warfare among the French, English, and Dutch. Over time, the Iroquois' domain expanded and contracted with the changing fortunes of war and power politics among Indians. Alliances shifted over the years, both among Indians and between particular Indians and particular groups of European settlers. It was considered a fundamental principle of Iroquois diplomacy to regard no treaty as settling anything once and for all.[155] Later, they would discover that many white authorities took the same view, to the detriment of the Iroquois.

As firearms began to spread among rival Indian peoples, the Mohawks lost their initial military advantages around the middle of the seventeenth century. The Mohicans and the Ottawas defeated them in 1662 and they failed to defeat the Susquehannock or the Delaware Indians the following year. Their raids against the Algonquins in Massachusetts provoked retaliatory raids against Mohawk settlements that continued for a decade. The ascendancy of the British in North America, as they drove out the Dutch and battled the French, represented for the Iroquois in general and the Mohawks in particular both the loss of their Dutch allies and the strengthening of their Indian enemies by the British. However, the British and the Iroquois eventually concluded an historic alliance called the "covenant chain," which provided a framework for peaceful settlement of their differences and established, as the British saw it, a claim to vast expanses of land from New England to the Carolinas and westward to the Great Lakes, since the various Iroquois nations had raided and made claims (of varying degrees of authenticity) to sovereignty over this region, while the British saw the alliance as establishing British sovereignty over the Iroquois.[156]

The Cherokees

Like many other North American Indians, the Cherokee tribe or nation was not a unified political unit under one authority but rather a collection of autonomous local communities connected by ties of culture, kinship, and alliances. Cherokee settlements were concentrated along the geographic dividing line of the Appalachian mountain range, from which waters flowed eastward toward the Atlantic and westward toward the Mississippi. As with other North American Indians, the area used by the Cherokees as a hunting range vastly exceeded the area in which they were permanently settled.

As of the time of initial contact with the Europeans, the Cherokees were settled mostly in what is today western North Carolina and eastern Tennessee, while also occupying part of the northern fringe of what is today Georgia and the northwestern fringe of what is today South Carolina. This irregularly-shaped settlement region extended no more than 200 miles in any given direction. However, the lands over which Cherokee hunters roamed, and which they claimed as their own, extended across most of today's Tennessee and Kentucky, major parts of the Carolinas, as well as large areas in Georgia, Alabama, Virginia, and West Virginia.[157] Initially one of the largest tribes east of the Mississippi, the Cherokees numbered about 20,000 people in 1690, but their population declined to only about half that size less just 50 years later, as warfare and European diseases took their toll among them. In short, before the arrival of the Europeans, a population measured in tens of thousands occupied an area which today supports a population measured in tens of millions. Even in the seventeenth century, far more people lived on similar-sized areas in Europe or Asia.

The Cherokees held this territory on the same basis as other nations held land around the world—military force. Archaeological evidence shows that other Indians had once occupied land that the Cherokees controlled when the Europeans arrived.[158] The Cherokees had defeated in battle the Shawnee, the Creeks, the Catawba, and the Tuscarora, with their rival claims from various points of the compass. The limits of the Cherokee domain were likewise circumscribed by military force—that of the Iroquois to the north and the Chickasaw to the west.[159] Over time, however, the new military powers from Europe would acquire the land from all of these Indians, though through varying tactics.

Just when the first contact was made between Cherokees and Europeans remains a matter of conjecture, as does the question as to whether these Europeans were Spaniards moving up from Florida or the British or French moving down from their various trade and settlement areas. However, by the late seventeenth century, contact had been made between whites and Cherokees and, by the first quarter of the eighteenth century, trading relations had been established between the two. By 1716, the government of South Carolina took control of this trade.[160] The nature and extent of the trade was new, not only because of the people and the goods involved, but also because such extensive trade had not been feasible before among the Cherokees themselves before the introduction of the horse from Europe, especially among those living in rugged mountainous areas.[161]

As elsewhere in North America, large-scale trade between the Indians and the whites set in motion massive and rapid cultural, political, and demographic changes among the Cherokees. The demand for animal skins by the Europeans led to the slaughter of an estimated quarter of a million deer over a 20-year period, with an estimated 50 tons of animal skins being delivered by the Cherokees in a single year.[162] Hunting and trading on this scale entailed a neglect of other traditional activities and industries by the Indian men and reflected also a growing Cherokee demand for European cloth, clothing, metal tools, and implements, as well as guns and decorative goods. Many of these things replaced the products of various traditional crafts among the Indians. Guns, for example, replaced bows and arrows, and metal replaced stone in knives and tomahawks. The plow and the handloom replaced traditional farming and clothes-making methods. Livestock began to kept by Indians, in imitation of the whites, and fruits and vegetables from Europe (as well as watermelons from Africa and potatoes from other parts of the country) began to be grown by the Cherokees.[163]

The most radical change, however, were the devastating European diseases that struck the Cherokee, as they did other Indians throughout the Western Hemisphere. The consequences of these diseases were cultural as well as biological, undermining faith in Cherokee medicine men, whose traditional methods of treating diseases had no effect—or even a negative effect—in trying to cope with these strange new maladies. Moreover, as the Cherokees lost hunting grounds and came to depend on European clothing and European guns for hunting, a Cherokee chief stated plainly in 1745 that they were no longer capable of living independently of the English.[164]

As elsewhere in North America, growing white populations and declining Indian populations created economic conditions in which land was often traded for European goods. While the declining population of the Cherokees made some land sales an economically reasonable way of acquiring many of the European commodities that the

Indians wanted, the magnitude of the land losses went far beyond what the Indians voluntarily offered on the market and included vast areas extorted under pressure, threats, and chicanery. The magnitude of these land losses also left the Cherokees with insufficient land to support themselves in their previous way of life, in which men's role as hunters were a major source of tribal livelihood, supplemented by women's role as farmers and homemakers. Now agriculture became the primary way of feeding themselves, with hunting much reduced, both because of the smaller hunting grounds now available and became of the growing scarcity of game, after years of increased hunting to gain animal skins and furs to trade with the white settlers.

The consequences were cultural as well as economic. Many Cherokee men disdained farming as "women's work" and both males and females were unfamiliar with the European style of intensive farming with horse-drawn plows and other agricultural tools and techniques. Federal agents sent to live among the Indians tried to provide these implements and teach these techniques, but a whole way of farming that took centuries to develop in Europe could hardly be superimposed on Indian culture very quickly, even if there had been ample farm implements and many experienced farmers working as federal agents—neither of which was the case. Even those Cherokee leaders who were anxious to acquire the means of emulating the white man's way of life—and these were by no means the norm—were reduced to constant entreaties to the federal agents to get them more plows, more horses, and more of all the other things that were necessary.

The Cherokees became dependent in other ways. The money paid for the sale of their land to the federal government was partly received in a lump sum and partly in the form of annuities. In both cases, the Cherokees had to use this money not only for the increasingly difficult task of supporting their daily livelihood but also to buy implements needed for domestic or agricultural tasks, and to repay credit advanced by both federal agents and white traders to provide food and other purchases. In short, the Cherokees were drawn into a money economy with which they had had little prior experience. At crucial times during negotiations with the federal government, federal officials could threaten the Cherokees with a suspension or cut-off of the flows of this money if the Indians did not accede to demands for more land or for rights-of-way for whites to build roads through existing Indian lands.

Perhaps the most galling dependency of all was the Cherokee dependency on law enforcement by whites at various levels of government. While the Cherokee leaders' agreements were made first with the British in colonial times and then later with the federal government of the United States, neither of these distant governments could be depended upon to exert much control over local white frontiersmen. Indeed, even local governments and local law-enforcement officials on the scene had considerable trouble controlling the independent frontiersmen, even when there was the political will to do so, which was often lacking as well when it came to protecting Indians. The net result was that it was difficult to get white squatters removed from Cherokee land and virtually impossible to get whites convicted for crimes, including murder, against Cherokees. On the other hand, Cherokees who killed whites were hanged. Even on those occasions when the U.S. Army could be gotten to force white squatters off Cherokee land, the Cherokees remained a dependent people, unable to fight their own battles as in times past.

Not surprisingly, many Cherokees did not wish to take on the white man's ways or to live in a state of dependency on white government and white justice, while other Cherokees saw cultural assimilation as the best option available under the circumstances. The internal divisions thus generated among the Cherokees became sharp, bitter, and lasting—all weakening their ability to present a united front to either local whites or to the federal government. Federal agents learned how to play on these internal divisions to advance the government's agenda, as well as their own. That agenda centered on culturally assimilating the Cherokees and acquiring more of their land.

After a history as a proud, war-like people, to be reduced themselves to either child-like dependency on the federal government or to helplessness in the face of discrimination, insults, and even crimes by white settlers was too much to be accepted by many of the Cherokees. Some sought revenge in raids on white settlements, some sought economic benefits through horse thefts and others escaped through liquor. In colonial times, the Cherokees had been able to take advantage of rivalries among the various European powers contending for land and strategic advantages in North America—especially the British, the French, and the Spanish. However, this drew the Cherokees into international conflicts, including warfare. Initially allied with the British during their wars with the French, some Cherokees switched sides when British settlers in their region used the unsettled conditions of war as an occasion to invade Cherokee lands. Defeat in battle forced the Cherokees to settle on British terms. More importantly, over time the defeat of the French by the British and then the defeat of the British by the American colonists, left the Cherokees facing a far larger and more united nation alone. This situation forced internal political changes among the Cherokees themselves, both because they needed to present a more unified front and because white officials wanted to deal with leaders capable of making agreements binding on the Cherokees, or at least on a particular branch of the Cherokees. The net result was an increase in the power of chiefs and especially of chiefs sympathetic to, or compliant with, the views of whites.

While there were leaders such as George Washington and Thomas Jefferson who took a paternalistically benevolent view of the Indians, their influence on local events and practices were limited, partly by distance and partly by the nature of the federal Constitution. The frontiersmen with whom the Indians were in immediate contact—many of them Scotch-Irish, with a history of disregard of authority on both sides of the Atlantic, as well as in Australia—were able to fight the Indians on their own, without either help or sanction from local or national governments. It was this fundamental imbalance in power that was at the heart of the Indians' troubles, however complicated the situation was by other racial, political, and other considerations. Corrupt white politicians, anxious for Indian lands, and corrupt Indian chiefs, ready to enrich themselves by selling out their own people's interests, were major factors in the transfer of Indian lands at prices far below the market level. Christian missionaries with higher motives nevertheless inadvertently contributed to internal divisiveness within the Cherokee communities, making for internal strife and disunity between assimilated and traditional Indians, in the face of constant pressures toward dispossession of the land and dissolution of the Cherokee culture and community.

Much of that pressure came from the soaring growth of the American population, which was about 5 million at the beginning of the nineteenth century and more than quadrupled to 23 million by mid-century.[165] Like many other transplanted populations, the descendants of the white settlers of the eastern seaboard conceived of themselves as being just as

native-born as the Indians—and just as entitled to the use of the land
and resources of the country. Indeed, they conceived of themselves as
better able to make these lands and resources more productive through
better technology, better farming techniques, and greater willingness to
work. Indians were seen as a nuisance and an obstacle to progress. At
more mundane levels, armed frontiersmen saw Indian hunting grounds
as empty land where they could build farms, land speculators saw a
golden opportunity to make personal fortunes by taking over Indian
lands on a grander scale, while corrupt politicians saw opportunities for
both financial gains and the advancement of their political careers by
catering to the desires of their constituents. Given these attitudes and
ambitions, on the one hand, and the great imbalance of power, on the
other, there were growing and ultimately irresistible pressures to force
the Indians further west, so that whites could take control of the territory
east of the Mississippi River.

Two very different major developments of the 1820s had lasting
effects on the Cherokees. First, a Cherokee silversmith and blacksmith
named Sequoyah decided to create for his people a system of writing for
their language, just as whites had written versions of their languages. In
addition to the practical advantages of now having a written language,
the Cherokees were said to develop a new sense of pride—a pride manifested tangibly in an 1827 rebellion.[166] On the other hand, this creation
of a written Cherokee language and the accompanying sense of cultural
parity with whites also helped alienate the less assimilated Cherokees
from those more assimilated to European culture, thereby creating yet
another source of disunity within the tribe.

The other historic event of the 1820s was the election of Andrew
Jackson as president of the United States. Jackson, himself a frontiers-
man and the leader of a populist cause, did not take the patrician pater-
nalist view of Indians held by George Washington and Thomas
Jefferson before him, but instead began a massive removal program to
force the Indians—even the acculturated "civilized tribes"—to move
west of the Mississippi, so that white settlers could expand into the
vacated territory. Jackson considered it a "farce" that the federal government dealt with Indian tribes as if they were sovereign nations, dismissed as "visionary" the recognition of Indian claims to "tracts of land
on which they have neither dwelt nor made improvements, merely
because they have seen them from the mountains or passed them in the

chase."[167] Cherokees were just one of the tribes forced from their ancestral lands to make way for white settlers under the new removal laws and policies. A variety of methods were used to get Indians off the land, leaving a variety of enduring financial obligations and legal entanglements between the federal government and the various Indian tribes.

The involuntary removal of masses of human beings, in the era before the transportation revolution, was a logistical and human nightmare. The federal government had to rely on private individuals to transport tens of thousands of Indians and to feed them en route. While these contractors often profited handsomely from this operation, it was a very different story for the Indians themselves. A contemporary newspaper account described "rotten, old, and unseaworthy boats" used to transport Indians who were crammed aboard with "not the slightest regard" for "their safety, comfort, or even decency." One such steamboat sank with more than 300 Creek Indians on board. A contemporary account by a missionary described another scene of the the resettlement: A Marine officer led caravan of two thousand Creek Indians westward into sleet storms, with the Indians wearing only cotton garments and suffering 29 deaths on the way. Altogether, about half the Creek nation perished either en route to their new western homes or in the early years of struggling to survive there. Farther north, the Winnebago tribe was forced to relocate repeatedly over a period of thirty years, also suffering mortality rates estimated at 50 percent.

It was, however, the massive sufferings of the Cherokees during their removal to the west which gave rise to the historic phrase, "the trail of tears," which could apply as well to other Indians. An estimated 15,000 people—three quarters of the Cherokee tribe—were forcibly moved west. Squads of soldiers surrounded individual Cherokee farms and marched the family members from their homes to stockades where larger groups were assembled for the trip beyond the Mississippi. A contemporary missionary described the scene: "The poor captive, in a state of distressing agitation, his weeping wife almost frantic with terror, surrounded by a group of crying, terrified children, without a friend to speak a comforting word . . ." Under such conditions, the Indians could neither sell their belongings nor make preparations for the long journey ahead of them. Local whites often looted or burned the homes left behind.[168]

Between 1795 and 1838 alone, more than 419 million acres of

Indian land was acquired by the federal government, either for cash or annuities, or in exchange of other lands, usually frontier land farther west, though some Indian reservations were also created east of the Mississippi. In just one decade, from 1828 to 1838, more than 80,000 Indians were moved west of the Mississippi.[169] Here they often encountered the armed resistance of the Indians of that region, as whites would later in the century. As early as 1816, there were clashes between the tribes migrating from the east and those already living in the regions where they were being resettled. Even after the migrating Indians established settlements, these were often raided by the indigenous Indians, as would happen to whites later on. Although federal troops were available to enforce the resettlement treaties, there were not enough of them to protect the migrating Indians, who had to defend themselves. Although no longer as used to the warriors' way of life as the plains Indians, the eastern Indians were, however, better armed. In one encounter in 1853, for example, about a hundred Sac and Fox Indians held off several hundred plains Indians.[170]

Over time, the Cherokees and the other transplanted members of the "five civilized tribes" fared better economically on the western plains than did the plains Indians themselves.[171] In the late twentieth century, the Cherokees were the largest of the Indian tribes—369,035 people, according to the 1990 census, or more than fifteen times their number in the seventeenth century. Most lived in the South, their historic homeland. The median family income of Cherokees was $24,907, or about 69 percent of the median family income of whites.[172]

The Plains Indians

As the frontier pushed farther west with the rapidly growing population of the United States in the nineteenth century, the white pioneers moving westward encountered not only the Indians displaced earlier from the eastern regions of the country but also the indigenous plains Indians—the Apaches, Comanches, Navajo, Cheyenne, and other Indians made famous in "western" movies and "wild west" literature. Many of these Indians were hunters and warriors who had retained a greater political and cultural independence of the European settlers, and some in the southwest had rebelled against Spanish rule and continued to raid Mexican settlements.

Perhaps most important of all, the plains Indians had been introduced to the horse during the era when what is today the American southwest was part of Mexico and the horse brought a revolutionary transformation of life on the plains. Tribes once sedentary and agricultural became nomadic in their pursuit of the buffalo, whose hides found a ready market in the white economy and whose meat supplied the Indians with food. The horse changed hunting techniques from those of tightly controlled large hunting parties on foot to much wider ranging and smaller groups or even individuals, who could successfully attack buffalo on horseback over much wider distances. A skilled hunter could kill enough buffalo in a matter of minutes to supply his family for months. The horse also made possible the transport of much heavier loads than had been possible by human porters or by dog-drawn sleds. Accordingly, Indian tents grew larger, now that more building material and household contents could be transported.[173] These wider-ranging forays also brought tribesmen into other tribes' hunting grounds, providing more occasions for warfare.

While the horse was the most important of the animals introduced from Europe into the Western Hemisphere, cattle and sheep also became part of the economy and the culture of the plains Indians. Two centuries before white Americans moved west in massive numbers after the Civil War, cattle and sheep had become familiar to the Indians in the west, largely because the Spaniards had brought these animals to New Spain, which encompassed what is today California and the American southwest. Thus cattle were present in this region as early as the seventeenth century, even though the golden age of American cattle herding was in the last half of the nineteenth century.[174] The horse, an essential complement for cattle herding, was likewise introduced to the plains Indians in the seventeenth century. The horse diffused northward and eastward from the Spanish settlements, the northern plains Indians getting them much later, perhaps as late as the eighteenth century. Farther south, however, Spanish records show raiding Apaches carrying off hundreds of horses in 1659, Half a century later, Comanche and Ute Indians raided Apache horses.[175]

While Indians could obtain horses through trade with the Spaniards, the latter would not trade guns to the Indians. Meanwhile, the English and the French to the east of the plains Indians would trade guns. With guns diffusing southward and westward from the British and French colonial settlements in Canada and in the thirteen American colonies, the horse frontier and the gun frontier eventually met in the eighteenth century on the great plains and a new way of life began for the Indians there. The Lewis and Clark expedition was able to buy horses from Indians in 1805 and they commented on the herds of these animals that the Indians possessed at that time.[176] By the time whites began moving into the plains in large numbers in the nineteenth century, the Indians there had long been mounted warriors with firearms. As of 1860, the Blackfoot Indians had as many horses as people.[177]

The geographic setting of the western plains was quite different from that of the eastern United States. There were far fewer navigable rivers in the west and of course there was no access to the ocean from the plains, so that waterborne transportation played a much smaller economic and military role in this region than in the east. Like other climates in the interior of continents, that on the western plains was more bitterly cold in the winter and more witheringly hot in the summer than climates in coastal areas, where a large adjacent body of water moderated temperatures. While there was fertile land in some places, there were also large regions of desert, semi-desert and otherwise barren land in the west. Under these conditions, the western Indian population was more thinly spread over vast areas, which might seem to make them more vulnerable to invasion. On the other hand, the distances involved and the scarcity of navigable waterways meant that American military forces in the region often had to be supplied by difficult and expensive overland routes and, in many places, could be deployed only by foot or on horseback before the era of railroad building in the mid-nineteenth century.

Here again, however, European diseases preceded the mass movements of whites themselves into the plains. In the quarter-century preceding the Civil War, epidemics of smallpox and cholera devastated Indians in the west. Only about half of the Blackfoot Indians survived a smallpox epidemic and only 100 out of 1,600 Mandans lived through it. Half the Comanches died of cholera and other tribes were similarly afflicted.[178] While the plains Indians were weakened in numbers, there were growing numbers of Americans and the United States government was unchallenged by any other world power in its claim to all the land from the Atlantic to the Pacific between Mexico and Canada. Unlike the Indians in colonial times, the plains Indians could expect no help from alliances with contending European imperial powers, nor did Americans any longer need the Indians as allies against such powers. The advancing technology of weaponry and transport also shifted the balance of power more toward the Americans militarily. Trains, for example, could carry troops as far in a day as they could march in a month.[179] Moreover, after the Civil War, the American army had many battle-experienced commanders, of whom Sherman and Custer were the best known, to lead troops in the west.

While the odds against the plains Indians in their resistance to the westward push of whites into their territories were less favorable than in the past, the alternatives were more desperate, for now there was no other land farther west that could be offered to them, on which to resettle. They had to fight or submit where they were. Thus the stage was set for the battles that would rage for decades on the western plains until the last battle at Wounded Knee in 1890 marked the end of Indian armed resistance. It was from this era that much of the image of the American Indian and of the American pioneers emerged. The Indian chiefs whose names became famous—Geronimo, Sitting Bull, Crazy Horse—were leaders of the fierce, bloody, bitter, but ultimately unavailing resistance.

The ferocity and mercilessness of the struggle on both sides generated burning hatreds and hideous acts of revenge and counter-revenge that poisoned relations between whites and Indians for generations. After years of smoldering resentments among Indians in Minnesota over the way they were being cheated and mistreated by federal officials, in 1862 four young Sioux murdered five white settlers on a dare, initiating an outpouring of Indian violence that led to wide-ranging attacks on white farm settlements in which the men were killed and the women and children taken captive, while bands of Indians spread across the countryside, pillaging, raping, and burning. About four hundred whites were killed in a day. American military forces struck back, capturing two thousand Sioux, of whom about three hundred were sentenced to hang, on the basis of questionable evidence about their individual guilt. After reviewing the trial record, President Lincoln reduced the number to be hanged to thirty eight—over vehement protests from local whites. The Sioux as a whole, however, lost their reservation as a result of these outbreaks and were moved farther west—as were the Winnebagos, for the local pressure to be rid of all Indians was politically irresistible.[180]

In the southwest, Indian and Hispanic inhabitants of New Mexico had a long history of raids and counter-raids against one another, as well as peaceful trade in between. With the coming of the Civil War and a movement of federal troops out of the region to fight against the Confederates in the east, the Navajos stepped up their raids. However, as the rapidly growing Union army acquired more troops, new reinforcements arrived in the region and struck back at the Navajos, not only killing many of them but also destroying their crops and livestock, in order to starve them into surrender. Meanwhile, other Indian tribes such as the Pueblos and Hopis seized the opportunity to plunder the Navajos, as did local whites. After the Navajos were forced to surrender, they were then moved by the thousands to a new region, where they had inadequate land, where their flocks were raided by the Comanches and Kiowas, and where they were barely able to survive on rations issued by the federal government.[181]

In Colorado, a massive military response to Cheyenne raids on whites led to a massacre of two hundred Indians—including women, children and even infants, all of whom were scalped and their bodies mutilated. One sign of the animosity existing between the whites and Indians at this point was that these Cheyenne scalps were then exhibited on stage in a Denver theater at intermission, to the applause of the audience. Meanwhile, as the survivors of the massacres reached Indian settlements, reactions among the Cheyenne, Sioux and Arapaho led to Indian attacks on white settlements for months thereafter, the Indians burning ranches, plundering wagon trains, ripping up miles of telegraph wire, scattering cattle herds and cutting off Denver from the east. Then the Indians melted away and even massive military expeditions failed to find them in the vast, rugged and empty lands of the region. While American military forces were able to offer more security to white settlements and travel routes, their long supply lines were not only logistical handicaps but also betrayed their visible presence to Indians, who could then escape.[182]

Not all the plains Indians fought and not all the land was conquered. The federal government continued to purchase land, at prices below the market level, and some Indians negotiated whatever terms they could, living thereafter on reservations, with varying degrees of security from white encroachment. Just as the eastern Indians had hunted beavers and deer to virtual extinction, so the plains Indians hunted the buffalo to virtual extinction, using the horse and the rifle. In both cases, this left the Indians more dependent on the surrounding white society and economy in general, and on the federal government in particular.

Government Policy

The creation of the Bureau of Indian Affairs in 1834 led to a long-term commitment to social engineering experiments with the Indians, based on radically different assumptions, methods, and goals at different periods of history, but creating dependency throughout. After the Civil War, for example, the federal government found itself feeding 100,000 Indians. The net result was that "large numbers of formerly energetic and aggressive warriors became enervated and dispirited recipients of the dole."[183]

While national policies toward the Indians were formulated in Washington, often under the influence of idealistic but uninformed humanitarian movements in the east, these policies were carried out on the reservations by federal agents who were often neither idealistic nor humanitarian, but were instead political appointees, less known for their ability than for their connections and often less interested in the wellbeing of the Indians than in their own opportunities for lucrative corruption. Indeed, the prospect of living on a bleak Indian reservation was not one likely to attract able and honest men with alternatives elsewhere, though the job of federal agent there could be very attractive to men who were the opposite of able and honest.

The hostility of the white population in the west toward the Indian, and the impatience of these local whites to acquire more of the vast amounts of land required for the plains Indians' way of life, were crucial ingredients in the mixture of motives and pressures which produced the turbulent era of Indian-white armed conflict from the mid-nineteenth century to the last decade of that century. In Alaska, where there were vast expanses of unused land were readily available for white settlers without dispossessing the native Eskimos, there was no organized warfare on either side, no reservations set aside for the indigenous people, and no campaigns for treaties to transfer title to the land on which the Eskimos lived—at the same time when all these things were going on in the American west under the same national government.[184]

In Canada, the peaceful settlement of whites on the land was for a long time more like what happened in Alaska than like what happened in the rest of the United States, but only until the growing number of whites attracted to the Canadian frontier found the available land no longer sufficient for their development and when the Indians began to experience diminished opportunities for hunting game. From that point on, the history of white-Indian relations in Canada began to follow a pattern similar to that in the United States, including an armed uprising in 1885, treaties to transfer Indian lands to whites, and the creation of Indian reservations to remove the indigenous peoples as a distraction or an obstacle to the development of the country.

In the United States, easterners appalled by stories of the cheating, oppression, and violence against Indians in the west, and convinced that Indians could be educated and taught the skills needed to adjust to the kind of life lived in American society, launched programs to train them to do just that, both through government and through private humanitarian undertakings. These schemes of social engineering included getting Indians to substitute farming for the hunting that was rapidly depleting the Buffalo herds and other game, which in turn would mean that the Indian population could feed itself by agricultural produce on much less land than that required for hunting, thereby allowing "surplus" Indian land to be sold to whites and for the west to be developed economically. Only on the transfer of Indian land was there unanimity between whites in the east and the west, as well as among the humanitarians, the speculators, and the politicians. Not surprisingly, this was the only part of the grand schemes for the Indians' future that was carried out successfully.

Forcibly herding Indians onto reservations proved to be a difficult and protracted process—and keeping them there was often even more difficult, given the limitations of the land and the unfamiliarity of the whole way of life that others had designed for the Indians. This way of life was in fundamental conflict with the Indians' habits and their cultural values. Farming, for example, was regarded by many of the plains Indian men as demeaning, while hunting, raiding, and fighting were time-honored roles. Moreover, so long as buffalo herds remained a valuable economic asset and the federal government supplied rations and annuities, incentives to change were lessened.

The problem was not one of the whole white race against the whole indigenous race, for neither side was monolithic. Moreover, blacks were a significant presence in the American west, particularly as soldiers after the Civil War, as they had been a significant presence as slaves of both Indians and whites in the antebellum South.[185] Despite the bitter hostility between whites and Indians on the American frontier—both during the era when the frontier was east of the Mississippi and later when it was out on the western plains—the humanitarian movements of eastern whites, which had great effect on the general direction of both governmental and private efforts to aid and assimilate the Indians, was equally real, even if often unrealistic in its goals and methods.

The first American program for the preferential hiring of minorities began in the Bureau of Indian Affairs in the early nineteenth century, where Indians were to be preferred as employees—a preference reaffirmed over the years in successive waves of legislation, until the federal government became the principal employer of educated Indians. These were enduring patterns. As of 1940, 60 percent of the 5,000 employees of the federal Bureau of Indian Affairs were Indians and the 1980 census revealed that a higher percentage of Indians than of any other American ethnic group worked for the federal government.[186]

SUMMARY AND IMPLICATIONS

Although the story of the conquests by European invaders in the Western Hemisphere was quite different in different regions of the hemisphere, certainly in timing and detail, there were fundamental similarities in the patterns that emerged over the centuries. European diseases and European technology were crucial elements in these conquests and the subsequent disintegration of the Indians' own cultures were crucial to the fate of the indigenous peoples. Loss of the land and other resources that made their previous way of life possible was one reason for the loss of much of the indigenous culture over time. The clear superiority of European military weapons, and of European products coveted by the Indians in preference to their own, likewise undermined Indian confidence in their own traditions.

Some practical aspects of the North American Indian culture in particular were lost because these Indians were drawn into the international trading networks of the Europeans and often, as a result, abandoned some of their indigenous products and skills in favor of supplying their needs from trade with the settlers. Because what the North American Indians had to offer were largely the hides and skins of animals that were hunted to virtual extinction, these Indians later found themselves without either the foreign sources of livelihood through trade or the skills and natural resources on which they or their ancestors had relied. From the standpoint of the white settlers in North America, on the other hand, the Indians were at first often indispensable, but in later generations became expendable, and finally were regarded as simply an obstacle to expansion across the continent, after the transplanted European society became self-sufficient and self-confident in the New World.

The situation among the indigenous peoples of South America and Central America was not the same as that among the North American Indians. Demographically, in various regions of Latin America the Indians constituted the bulk of the population, centuries after the Europeans landed. In Bolivia, for example, in the middle of the twentieth century, 60 percent of the country's population consisted of Indians speaking an indigenous language. It was another quarter of a century before a majority of Bolivians spoke Spanish.[187] Mexico's population has long been predominantly mestizo—between 75 and 90 percent—with some of the remainder being full-blooded Indians.[188] Venezuela, Chile, and Paraguay have likewise had predominantly mestizo populations.[189] Indians and mestizos were each about 40 percent of the population of Ecuador during the 1980s, with the remainder being white or black.[190] In Colombia, an estimated 50 percent of the population was mestizo, 25 percent white and the remainder black, Indian or some racially mixed combinations of these.[191] In Peru, about two-fifths of the population spoke native languages as late as 1960, though half of these people also spoke Spanish.[192] In short, while what had been British North America became demographically and culturally a transplanted European society, that was by no means equally true throughout the remainder of the hemisphere. Nor were the indigenous peoples of the hemisphere absorbed into this transplanted European culture to the same degree.

These differences between the Indians of Latin America and those of British North America reflected differences between the settlement patterns of the whites in the two regions. The mass transfer of men, women, and children to British North America more thoroughly Europeanized the United States and Canada culturally, swamping the indigenous peoples, both demographically and culturally. While the Indians of Latin America were conquered militarily much earlier, more of them remained culturally indigenous to a greater extent, even when they were forced to pay tribute or otherwise submit to subjugation by a thin layer of Spanish or Portugues overlords.

Throughout the Americas, a significant portion of the indigenous population became genetically part Caucasian—and that portion tended also to be more culturally Europeanized as well. Sometimes this was because of intermarriages but, even when racial mixtures were not formalized by marriage, obviously those Indian populations in closer proximity to white populations were more likely to become both culturally and genetically amalgamated with the Europeans. As in the case of people of African ancestry in the Western Hemisphere, those Indians more culturally and genetically similar to Europeans had more opportunities to acquire European skills, beginning with language and knowledge of European ways, all of which helped them not only in dealing with the white settlers but also in acquiring leadership roles and other privileges within Indian societies.

Relations between the Conquered and the Conquerors

The often tragic history of Western Hemisphere Indians parallels the history of conquered peoples around the world, not only in terms of the suffering endured, but also in terms of the betrayals of agreements and the contempt often shown to the subjugated peoples. While the prevalence of similar patterns in other regions of the world and other periods of history does not lessen the human tragedy or the moral enormity, it does have implications as far as causation is concerned. The reasons for this history cannot be assumed to be peculiar to either or both of the races involved, or to their particular relationships to one another or their perceptions of one another, for much the same results have been found among conquerors and conquered on every continent and in every era of history.

While violations of treaties, for example, have been common in the history of European expansion into the lands of the indigenous populations of the Western Hemisphere, treaties in other parts of the world have likewise usually remained in force only so long as the set of power relationships which led to those treaties in the first place. Among the Indians themselves, treaties were by no means regarded as permanently settling the issues covered and Indian nations betrayed both whites and one another,[193] just as Europeans broke treaties among themselves and with others.[194] Treaties between France and Germany, for example, have transferred Alsace-Lorraine back and forth according to who won the most recent war. In the Western Hemisphere, however, the tide of power ran consistently against the indigenous peoples, making treaty revisions and violations consistently against the interests of the Indians. Drastic reductions of the Indian population, by both diseases and warfare, were exacerbated in their effects on the power balance by a constantly increasing European population, growing both by immigration and by natural increase, and seeking correspondingly more and more land on which to settle. In addition, the march of technology in Europe brought dramatic improvements in the kinds of weapons used by the white population in the Americas.

Slow-firing muskets and cannons were succeeded by faster-firing weapons, made more accurate by rifling in their barrels. In the Western Hemisphere, as in Europe, Asia, and Africa, this turned the tide decisively against those who fought with bows and arrows. The Indians themselves began to master firearms, as they mastered the use of horses, which had never been seen in the Western Hemisphere before Columbus. In both cases, however, Indians were using European military patterns against people who originated such patterns and who had greater access to the latest developments, as well as controlling the supply and having the skills necessary to repair the Indians' firearms and their own. In short, despite hard-won victories here and there, the Indians were in general retreating repeatedly before the advance of the European invaders. The treaties made under these circumstances were little more than lengthy truces, lasting only until the balance of power changed still more decisively in favor of the Europeans and the latter's growing population again developed more demand for territory and resources held by the Indians. For some within the transplanted European communities of the Americas, a moral dimension did enter into these military power relationships, however. Within these societies, some religious leaders, especially, became defenders of the rights of Indians and regarded treaties as moral commitments to them, rather than simply transient artifacts of *realpolitik*.

The failure of such people to prevail, or to achieve much more than peripheral concessions and a mitigation of the worst aspects of conquest, was in keeping with the fate of political agreements and proclamations around the world, whether such commitments were made to people of the same or a different race. What was unusual about the agreements between the European invaders and the indigenous peoples of the Western Hemisphere was not that they were violated or infringed, but that voices and forces within the victorious societies protested against these violations and infringements, as well as against the general treatment of the conquered peoples. In later generations and centuries, these voices would grow louder and more effective, eventually giving some of these ancient treaties more force than other treaties of the same vintage, or other laws within the general community, that had been allowed to become "dead letters" with the passage of time.

Similar moral concerns among descendants of the conquerors led, first, to nineteenth-century attempts to artificially assimilate the indigenous peoples of the Western Hemisphere into the new prevailing culture from Europe and then—a century later—to attempts to artificially preserve or resurrect the indigenous culture that was eroding on its own. In neither case was it considered sufficient to let the indigenous peoples decide for themselves, individually, how much of the old and how much of the new they wished to accept.

Nowhere is it more necessary to make a sharp distinction between historic and contemporary effects than in assessing the impact of European society and culture on the indigenous peoples of the Western Hemisphere. For the era of the conquest and of the consolidation of European hegemony in the Americas, that impact was catastrophic, not simply because of a loss of territory and sovereignty on the part of the Indians, but also because of the widespread decimation—in some places, virtual extinction—of the indigenous population by European diseases, and because the demoralizing destruction of existing cultures could not be followed in any timely way by their replacement by the cultures of Europe needed to cope with radically different conditions. Within many Indian communities, divisive new religious doctrines tore apart the social bonds embodied and affirmed in indigenous rituals and beliefs, while loss of control of the natural resources required by the traditional way of life often rendered traditional skills obsolete and the way of life based on them impossible.

The wars, atrocities, and betrayals accompanying all this provided the dramatic events by which this era would be remembered, though such afflictions have been all too common across the planet, including in the Western Hemisphere before the first white man arrived. What was unique was the biological, social, and cultural havoc. The introduction of European liquor alone was to prove to be a curse enduring for centuries among the indigenous peoples, who proved to be exceptionally susceptible to alcoholism.

All this is wholly different from saying that the present-day descendants of these indigenous peoples are worse off than if the Europeans had never come. Most of these descendants would not even exist without those invasions and conquests, for they are the descendants of the Europeans as well as descendants of the Indians, pure-blooded descendants of the latter being the exception, rather than the rule, in both North and South America. Nor can the benefits they receive from the advances of modern medicine and technology be taken for granted, for those benefits are still largely lacking over broad areas of the world, outside the cultural orbit of Western civilization. Nowhere have the Indians shared as fully in these benefits as the general population of the Americas. How much of that is due to discriminatory treatment and how much to the Indians' not having yet acquired the full range of skills common in European offshoot societies is an empirical question, whose answer may vary in different parts of the hemisphere. However, in the United States, differences between the earnings of Indian males and white males were, by the late twentieth century, due largely to demographic, language, and educational differences.[195] Over all, however, American Indians had by 1969 an income not very different from that of black Americans.[196] As late as 1989, when per capita income for the United States as a whole was $14,420, the per capita income of Indians in the United States was $8,284.[197] Median family income for American Indians was $21,619, compared to $20,209 for blacks and $35,975 for whites.[198]

The cultural consequences of the original settlement patterns of whites in colonial North America and their subsequent movement westward is reflected in the fact that few of the descendants of eastern Indians still speak their native languages, after such a long exposure to English, while many more Indians from the western United States still do. Among the Cherokees, for examples, fewer than 10,000 still spoke their native tongue in 1990, while more than 142,000 Navajos did—even though Cherokees were the most numerous tribe of American Indians with 369,035 people, while the Navajos were second with 225,298.[199]

Some of the most basic facts about Western Hemisphere Indians remain obscure or elusive. Widely varying estimates of the population of the hemisphere in 1492 are one symptom of this. However, even in the late twentieth century, the increase in the Indian population of the United States from approximately 764,000 in 1970 to approximately 1,937,000 in 1990[200] seems difficult to attribute to any plausible rate of fertility. Such a huge increase in just 20 years seems more probably a reflection of social incentives to identity oneself as Indian. Among these incentives were the growing impact of ethnic pride and cultural "identity" trends, as well as the growing availability of both government and private benefits earmarked for a variety of minority groups, including American Indians. Given that most people who identify themselves as American Indians are not full-blooded Indians, considerable flexibility in self-identification makes it difficult to separate biological increases in this population from changing self-designations in response to changing social incentives. Considering that the number of American Indians barely doubled between the census of 1890 (when it was not quite a quarter of a million) to that of 1960 (when it was just over half a million), a nearly quadrupling of its size (to almost two million) in the 30 years after 1960 seems more like a social phenomenon than a biological phenomenon.[201]

The sense of historic or inherited guilt has become a major political factor in attempts to redress the wrongs suffered by the indigenous population, particularly in North America. Special privileges and exemptions from the laws affecting other citizens have become common for Indians, both in Canada and in the United States. For example, in the late twentieth century, special hunting and fishing rights for Indians existed in an area constituting one-fourth of the entire land area of Canada, and large economic transfers and special political rights have been conferred as well.[202] However, Indian incomes averaged less than half that of Canadians in general. Most Indians in Canada did not complete high school and the mortality rates of their infants and young children was three times the national average.[203]

In the United States, as well, the indigenous people have had special rights and many government programs designed to help them, though it is not clear whether this has in fact made them better off than they would have been otherwise. As the twentieth century neared its end, approximately half of the two million Indians in the United States still lived on reservations, often in a state of dependency. At a time when North Dakota as a whole had an unemployment rate just below 2 percent, the unemployment rate among Sioux Indians on the Standing Rock reservation in North Dakota was 75 percent.[204]

The history of the Indians in the Western Hemisphere has, unfortunately, long been seen not as something important in and of itself but as raw material for proving one thesis or another. At various times in centuries past, the conquest of the Americas was seen as a triumph and vindication of Christianity or of Western civilization, even in places where the treatment of Indians was directly counter to Christian morality and barbarous by any standard. Critics of Western civilization, however, often depicted the Indian as a "noble savage" with whom degenerate civilized man could be contrasted—again, with little regard to facts to the contrary. In our own times, cultural relativism has rewritten history in yet another way, perhaps epitomized by the semantic contortions used in response to the simple traditional statement that "Columbus discovered America." The concept of discovery has become taboo, unless it is "a reciprocity of discovery" or the even more neutral word, "contact" between the two worlds.[205] Yet, plainly, Columbus discovered America in a sense in which Indians did not discover Europe—and it was an enormous event in the history of the human race, for good or ill, or both. Quibbles about the fact that some other European explorers touched the hemisphere earlier, or that the Indians knew it was here all along, trivialize this turning point in the history of the world.

Late twentieth-century attempts to see or depict the world from the viewpoint of the conquered Indians face the intractable fact that the Indians of the era of conquest left no written accounts because their languages had no written versions—except for the language of the Maya, whose written version was only belatedly begun to be deciphered by scholars.[206] Moreover, even for literate peoples, the moral and intellectual framework within which they perceived events is by no means as apparent as the events themselves, though even the bare facts may be distorted by various biases and agendas. The most that we can hope for realistically is to see the Indians honestly from our own viewpoint today.

A complement to a necessary separation of fact from fancy is a separation of causation from morality. Those things most striking and salient from a moral point of view need not have been the most influential from a causal point of view. Unleashing wars of conquest has obvious moral implications, not only to observers of that time or later, but to the conquerors themselves, who went to great trouble to attempt to justify themselves morally and religiously, often with much ingenious hypocrisy. However, the unwitting spread of diseases is morally neutral, though often far more devastating. As a noted historian has observed:

> Not even the most brutally depraved of the conquistodors was able purposely to slaughter Indians on the scale that the gentle priest unwittingly accomplished by going from his sickbed ministrations to lay his hands in blessing on his Indian converts.[207]

Similarly, the morally revolting history of discrimination and expropriation against the indigenous populations of the Western Hemisphere have often too easily been accepted as causal explanations of their generally lower socioeconomic levels in the various societies of the Americas. Yet, from a causal perspective, there was never any reason to have expected them all to have acquired the levels of Western technological skills and organizational development which took centuries to evolve in Europe. Since Eastern Europeans generally continue to lag behind Western Europeans in these respects, more than a thousand years after the Slavs first entered East Central Europe, there is little basis for attributing all economic lags of American Indians in European off-shoot societies to the biases of the majority populations of those societies. How much is in fact due to discrimination and how much to cultural lags is an empirical question, not a foregone conclusion. In the United States, for example, by the 1980s American Indian males earned incomes quite comparable to those of white males, when various language, demographic, and other factors were held constant, even though American Indian males as a whole were still earning markedly less than white males as a whole.[208]

The proportion of the Indian and mestizo populations in twentieth-century Latin America has ranged from negligible in Argentina to demographically dominant in Peru where, in 1990, Spanish-speaking mestizos were 37 percent of the population and Quecha-speaking Indians were 45 percent.[209] Full-blooded Indians have tended to be the least favored, both by nature and man. Biological resistance to European diseases came first to those who were part-European themselves, as well as being more likely to move in a social milieu where there were Europeans from whom they could acquire biological resistance and social acculturation to the transplanted European civilization of the Western Hemisphere. In addition, both whites and mestizos often disdained and discriminated against the full-blooded Indians. The highland peoples of Peru, for example—the descendants of the Incas—were at one time referred to by the mestizos as "brutes" and "savages," and were forced to step aside, sit in the back of busses, and otherwise humble themselves before those considered their social betters.[210] The thrust of Peruvian education was to get the less assimilated Indians to acquire the Spanish language in place of the native tongues which 39 percent of the native peoples still spoke as late as 1960, as well as acquiring the modes of dress and general ways of life of the culturally westernized majority.[211]

Western Hemisphere Indians can no more be summarized than Europeans or Asians or Africans can be summarized. Their cultural levels have ranged from the sophistication of the Maya, the Aztecs and the Incas centuries ago to the primitiveness of the Amazon Indians to this moment. What is clear is that their world was irretrievably shattered—biologically, militarily, socially, and politically—and that their fate would henceforth be determined by how well they evolved new ways of dealing with a radically different and ever-changing reality around them.

CHAPTER 6

AN OVERVIEW

. . . the rich and the poor countries were not con-
stantly the same ones; the wheel did turn.

Fernand Braudel

Because this chapter concludes not only this book but also a trilogy that began with *Race and Culture* and continued with *Migrations and Cultures*, it will attempt to summarize the entire study of which this is a part and to consider, against that background, the role of ideas, the role of race, and the role of cultures in the unfolding of history. First, however, we need to confront the most blatant fact that has persisted across centuries of social history—vast differences in productivity among peoples and the economic and other consequences of such differences.

DIFFERENCES IN WEALTH PRODUCTION

Huge differences in wealth-production have been the rule, not the exception, for thousands of years of recorded history—even though, as Fernand Braudel pointed out, the particular nations and peoples that were rich and those that were poor were not constantly the same. In ancient times, for example, the Greeks and the Romans were vastly more economically advanced than the Scandinavians or the Britons, while their respective positions have been reversed in recent centuries, as has the relationship between the respective economic positions of China and Japan. Nevertheless, the reality of great disparities has persisted through all these changes, much as a river persists, even though the water which constitutes it changes constantly as it flows on into the sea.

In the late nineteenth century, just three countries—Britain, Germany, and the United States—produced two-thirds of all the manufactured goods in the world.[1] By the late twentieth century, it was estimated that 17 percent of the world's population produced four-fifths of its total output.[2] Esoteric theories seeking to explain why "the world's income" is so unequally "distributed," as if there were some central pot from which wealth was being ladled out in a discriminatory manner, often ignore the plain fact that (1) real income consists of things that are produced, that (2) much of this real income or output is not distributed at all, but is consumed where it is produced, and that (3) its production is radically different from place to place and from people to people, as has been the case throughout history. Nor are these necessarily differences between racial or ethnic groups. In 1994, it was estimated that the 36 million "overseas Chinese" scattered around the world produced as much wealth as the one billion people living in China itself.[3] Among Southeast Asian nations, annual output per capita in 1996 ranged from $107 in Myanmar (Burma) to $30,860 in Singapore.[4]

Some, but not all, of the factors behind such striking contrasts in productivity can be quantified. For example, when Britain alone produced more than 40 percent of the major inventions, discoveries and innovations in the world from the mid-eighteenth century to the first quarter of the nineteenth century, this clearly was a key indicator of its economic advancement and of the cultural capital behind that advancement. The same would be true of the United States in a later era, when it alone produced more than 80 percent of the major inventions, discoveries, and innovations in the middle of the twentieth century.[5]

While it is hardly surprising that such large productivity differences are associated with similarly striking differences in income and wealth, this mundane fact deflates widespread beliefs that, among both nations and individuals, the rich are rich *because* the poor are poor—that what is involved is primarily a transfer of wealth, rather than differences in its creation.[6] Imperialism, for example, has often been depicted as a process by which one country grows rich at the expense of another. While this can and does happen in particular instances, if "exploitation" theories were as widely applicable as supposed, then the dissolution of empires should lead to rising standards of living among the formerly conquered and presumably exploited peoples. Yet history repeatedly shows the opposite happening.

When the Roman conquerors withdrew from Britain, the Britons' standard of living declined by all indications—the cruder products, crumbling infrastructure, wilderness growing back into human settlements, and people being buried in shallower graves and without coffins, for example. Later, in the last half of the twentieth century, the withdrawal of European imperialists from sub-Saharan Africa likewise left much of that region with lower per capita incomes twenty years later than they had had when living under the domination of the imperialists. It was much the same story in Central Asia, after the dissolution of the Soviet Union made it independent of the Russians for the first time in centuries—but also left it with shortages of the skills that many of the departed Russians had supplied.

Such facts are far more consistent with the economic consequences of differences in productivity, based on differences in cultural capital, than with theories of exploitation. Even economically-motivated imperialism—and economic motives have by no means been the sole motives for conquest—has not always sought to acquire existing wealth but often, especially in modern times, to acquire resources that would produce wealth with the technology of the conqueror, even if these same resources had not made their current owners wealthy. Thus gold in South Africa and oil in the Middle East brought on the conquest of people whose own developed wealth and standards of living were modest at best.

This is not to say that there has never been any direct extraction of pre-existing wealth from conquered lands and people. Clearly, the wealth of the Incas attracted Pizzaro, for example. Yet the international transfer of pre-existing wealth still does not go very far in explaining why some nations are rich and others poor today. For Spain in its imperialist heyday, wealth was transferred in vast amounts from the conquered lands of the Western Hemisphere—much of it gold and silver already found in the hands of the indigenous population and much of it these same precious metals mined by the forced labor of the conquered people. However, once the gold and silver began to run out, Spain was left as one of the poorer countries of Europe, for it had not developed its own human capital and had expelled its Jews and Moors, who had many of the skills lacking in the Spanish population.

Slavery, the ultimate in potential for exploitation, has seldom left slave-owning regions more prosperous than comparable non-slave-owning regions—whether comparing the Southern United States with the North or comparing the northern regions of Brazil, where slaves were concentrated, with Brazil's southern regions that were heavily settled by European and Japanese immigrants. In Europe, it was the western part of the continent where slavery was abolished first, and it was this region that led Europe and the world into the industrial age. In many other parts of the world, slaves were among the luxuries and displays of wealth—not its source.

While exploitation theories unite moral condemnation with causal explanations in an emotionally appealing package, in modern times for which statistical data are available, these explanations are not as consistent with the facts as are demonstrable differences in productivity among nations and peoples. What is morally reprehensible need not coincide with what is causally salient. Moreover, morally reprehensible behavior has been all too widespread among all branches of the human race, rather than being localized in those who happened to achieve greater success in conquest or in economic activities. Seldom was evil introduced into an Eden or a golden age ended by the transfer of existing wealth.

The most famous imperialism theory of all—that of Lenin—was forced into desperate expedients, in order to maintain any semblance of consistency with the facts. His book *Imperialism* lumped together as one category "America"—that is, the entire Western Hemisphere—for statistics on the destinations of the export of capital from industrial Europe. This enabled Lenin to portray the non-industrial world as an investment outlet for "surplus" capital that would otherwise cause economic problems internally for industrial capitalist nations, in accordance with Marxian theory. He said, "enormous exports of capital are bound up most closely with vast colonies."[7] However, a country-by-country breakdown of investment statistics, rather than Lenin's gross categories like "America," would make the Marxist-Leninist theory of imperialism collapse like a house of cards. In the Western Hemisphere, as elsewhere around the world, it was precisely the already more prosperous and industrialized countries that were the prime destinations of European capital investments. In the period covered by Lenin—the late nineteenth and early twentieth centuries—the United States was the largest single recipient of British, German, and Dutch capital.[8] Conversely, for much of the twentieth century, the United States has invested more in Canada than in all of Africa and Asia put together.[9] Once again, the mundane reality is that productivity creates wealth, so that trade with and investment in more productive countries is a far more important source of wealth than "exploitation" of the Third World, however that elusive term might be defined.

Striking *changes* in productivity among peoples can often be traced to transfers of cultural capital from others—from the English to the Scots, from Western Europeans to Eastern Europeans, from China to Japan in an earlier era, or from the Islamic world to Europe in medieval times. Such transfers do not represent mutually cancelling gains and losses, as transfers of material wealth do in exploitation theories, for knowledge is not diminished at its source when it spreads to others.

Each of the four broad groups covered in this volume had their ways of life changed—even revolutionized—by transfers of human capital from others. In the case of the British, it was first the Romans in ancient times and then, in later centuries, the Normans, the Lombards, the Jews, the Huguenots, the Dutch and others who brought particular skills to the British Isles that had been largely or wholly lacking there. With the Slavs, everything from the very writing of their own languages to more advanced forms of agriculture, industry, science, and medical advances were brought to them by a wide variety of peoples from other parts of Europe and from the United States. In much of sub-Saharan Africa, everything from retail commerce to international trade networks were brought by people from India and Lebanon,[10] while modern technology came largely from Europe. In the Western Hemisphere, the classic way of life associated with the North American plains Indians—hunting buffalo with rifles on horseback—was impossible before the European invaders brought the basic ingredients of that lifestyle to the New World, along with the knowledge of how to use these and other things that became part of the way of life of the native peoples throughout the hemisphere.

Much the same story of human capital transfers can be found in the previous volume—*Migrations and Cultures*—as the German immigrants created a whole array of new industries in southern Brazil, contributed to turning Argentina from an importer of wheat to one of the world's great wheat exporters, and pioneered in creating the piano industry, the optical industry, and the beer brewing industry in the United States.[11] The Italians' role as builders has left its monuments from the Kremlin to the sewer systems of Argentina, and Italians have been winemakers from California to Australia. Among the many fields in which Jews have been prominent or predominant over the centuries, none has been more striking than their role in the apparel industry, whether in medieval Spain, the Ottoman Empire, or New York's modern garment district. The dominance of the overseas Chinese in commerce and industry in Southeast Asia has been even more complete than that of the Jews in other parts of the world, while immigrants from India have had similar economic dominance from Fiji to East Africa, and Japanese immigrants have made equally striking contributions in southern Brazil.

One of the most heartening lesson of history is that poor and primitive peoples have, more than once, not only caught up with those more fortunate, but have even advanced to the forefront of human achievement. The English and the Scots are dramatic examples from the histories in this book, but much the same story was re-enacted halfway around the world, when nineteenth-century Japan began its rapid evolution from a backward nation to one of the leading economic giants of the twentieth century. While these are heartening examples of the innate potential of poor and primitive peoples, they are also sobering reminders of how long—centuries or millennia—people with the potential for greatness may nevertheless languish in poverty and backwardness. It also underscores the importance of acquiring the cultural capital needed to move forward.

CULTURAL CAPITAL

The most striking finding from this long, multi-volume excursion into the history of peoples and cultures around the world is how distinct and enduring have been the cultural patterns of particular racial or ethnic groups. However, that does not make race or ethnicity unique. All sorts of other groupings of human beings—by religion, nationality, or geographical settings, for example—show similarly sharp distinctions in everything from income to alcoholism and from fertility rates to crime rates. It is not racial or ethnic distinctions, as such, which have proven to be momentous but *cultural* distinctions, whether associated with race, with geographical origins,[12] or with other factors. The particular culture or "human capital" available to a people has often had more influence on their economic level than their existing material wealth, natural resources, or individual geniuses.

The tendency to explain intergroup differences in a given society by the way that particular society treats these groups ignores the fact that differences between groups themselves have been the rule, not the exception, in countries around the world and down through history. These groups differ in specific skills—whether in optics, winemaking, engineering, medicine, or numerous other fields—and in attitudes toward work, toward education, toward violence, and toward life. Thus people living in the same immediate surroundings, and facing the same current economic and other options, react very differently as a result of their very different cultures, which evolved in different settings in centuries past. For example, in Brazil during its pioneer era, when vast amounts of land were available without sufficient labor being available to farm it, some large landowners offered to transfer title to portions of their land to anyone willing to work the assigned acreage free for four years and to share the crop during those four years with the current owner. Few of the local Brazilian agricultural workers were willing to accept this offer and forego immediate wages in order to become landowners themselves, but people in distant Japan moved in large numbers to Brazil to acquire land in this way.[13]

Similarly, opportunities to become merchants in Wales, Ireland, and the Scottish highlands were seldom utilized by the peoples of these regions in centuries past, but outsiders came in to become successful merchants in their midst. After the peoples of these regions emigrated to the United States and became a major part of the white population of the antebellum South,[14] the merchants among them were again largely outsiders—usually Yankees and the children of Yankees, or else Jews or immigrants from England, Germany, or the Scottish lowlands.[15] Again, it was not the immediate setting and its objective opportunities, but the respective cultures brought to those settings by different groups, which played a major role in determining what occupations would be pursued by whom and with what success.

In this series of books, we have followed the story of disparate attitudes and achievements among Chinese, German, Italian, and other immigrant groups, as well as in the histories of England, Scotland, and Eastern Europe. To some extent, we have followed the same story of human capital in reverse, in the devastating aftermath of the collapse of the Roman Empire, focussing on Britain, though much the same cultural disaster struck on the continent of Europe. It was not simply that a given set of political rulers were displaced or that particular political structures were destroyed. The elaborate institutions needed for the continued transmission of a complex civilized culture from one generation to the next simply disintegrated, along with the state apparatus that had supported it, because the invaders who were capable of destroying the Roman Empire were not capable of taking it over and running it themselves or preserving its cultural achievements. They differed fundamentally in this respect from the Manchus who invaded and took over China, preserving the Chinese culture and continuing its transmission over the generations.

The destruction of the Roman Empire by invading barbarians produced one of the most catastrophic retrogressions of whole peoples ever seen. The physical deterioration of buildings, roads, drainage systems, and other physical infrastructure was accompanied by a breakdown of law and order, a political fragmenting of countries, and a decline of education. The races of people remained the same but the loss of their cultural capital reduced their living standards, which did not return to the levels achieved in Roman times until many centuries later.

In short, the importance of human capital has been confirmed in very different ways, at various periods of history, and at levels ranging from the individual to nations to whole civilizations. In the middle of the nineteenth century, John Stuart Mill pointed out the implications of the fact that nations have made apparently miraculous recoveries from the physical destruction of war. The later examples of dramatic economic recoveries by Germany and Japan after being devastated in World War II are not unique. What war destroyed, Mill said, were the physical structures and machinery which would have deteriorated over time and would have had to be replaced anyway.[16] While the speeding up of this process is by no means a negligible matter, what is crucial to Mill's argument is that the knowledge of how to build replacements is far more important than the physical things in which that knowledge is embodied at a given moment. So long as that human capital is not destroyed, the physical destruction can always be repaired or replaced.

Conversely, physical structures left perfectly intact by the Romans when they withdrew voluntarily from Britain in the fifth century A.D., in order to defend the empire from invaders on the continent, began to deteriorate over time and were not repaired or replaced for centuries, because the Britons lacked the human capital required for the maintenance, repair, and replacement of these structures. Britons at this juncture also lacked the human capital to maintain the political institutions established over most of the island by the Romans, so that the unified colonial government of Roman Britain subsequently fragmented into local tribal rule. Even after the Britons eventually could afford to use bricks again, centuries later, they had to import these bricks from Flanders, for bricks had not been produced in Britain since Roman times.[17]

In modern times as well, industrial equipment left behind in Third World colonies as Western imperial nations withdrew in the post–World War II era likewise often deteriorated to unusable condition and some countries—notably India—fractured politically into two or more countries. In many Third World nations, massive foreign aid, whether in physical or financial terms, has often failed to lead to economic development when the necessary human capital was not present, or was present only so long as foreign engineers and technicians were present. The very different economic fates of newly independent African nations like the Ivory Coast, which allowed foreigners to continue to play a major role in their economy after independence, and initially more prosperous nations like Ghana and Nigeria which did not, is further substantiation of the importance of human capital.

Vain analogies about creating a new "Marshall Plan" for Third World nations, or for domestic ethnic ghettoes within the United States, fail to see that what the Marshall Plan accomplished in postwar Europe was to allow the Europeans to use their already existing human capital to rebuild their economies. But the resources transferred by the Marshall Plan did not create that human capital. It simply aided the survival of people who already possessed the necessary skills and experience, and allowed the process to go on without the social upheavals and political disruptions that are ever-present dangers among hungry and desperate populations.

The histories of those immigrant groups who have arrived financially destitute in many countries, and then proceeded to rise to higher levels of prosperity than the native population, is further substantiation of the role of human capital. Like war-devastated nations which continue to have the human capital needed to rise from the ruins and

recover their former prosperity, these immigrant groups without material wealth nevertheless have had what was needed to create such
wealth. Jewish immigrants, for example, have arrived in many countries bringing valuable skills in clothing manufacturing, gem cutting,
retail trade, and other specialties. Perhaps more important, they
arrived with a deep-seated appreciation of the need for skills, which in
later generations would lead their descendants to acquire different
skills as physicians, attorneys, and other professionals. Much the
same story could be told of the Gujaratis and Jains from India, the
Armenians, the Lebanese, and others.

All groups trail the long shadow of their cultural history and, while
cultures are not as innate as genes, their consequences can be more
important. When cultural and genetic characteristics go together, the
very existence of differences in human capital is often denied and disparities in economic levels attributed to malign behavior by more fortunate groups. To do otherwise would be to leave oneself open to the
devastating possibility that the genetic part of the culture-and-genes
combination is responsible for the differences in human capital,
though this conclusion is by no means compelled by the evidence.
Less traumatically but still dauntingly, to acknowledge even cultural
differences in human capital would be to create for oneself an arduous
and daunting task of catching up, rather than a more emotionally satis-
fying and politically more acceptable task of denouncing other people
and attempting to make them pay for their transgressions and/or the
transgressions of their ancestors. Since no group of human beings has
been without sin, anecdotal evidence for various accusations will
never be lacking, even when these sins are less of an explanatory factor than a fatal distraction from the hard work needed to acquire the
human capital needed to turn poverty into prosperity.

A sharp distinction must be made between historic injustices and
their contemporary consequences. Higher levels of skills spread by
brutal conquests are an obvious example. A variety of artisan skills
were more common among Polish immigrants to the United States
from Prussia, where they had lived in a German culture as a result of
Prussia's conquest by Germans in earlier centuries, than among Polish
immigrants originating in their own ancestral homeland.[18] The Islamic
culture brought to medieval Spain by the Moorish conquerors likewise
galvanized Spanish Jews intellectually, with long-range effects on the

development of secular learning and scientific achievement by the Jews.[19] That the Moslem conquest had no comparable effect on the Spanish majority, just as the English conquest had no such effect on the Welsh and the Irish as on the Scots, is evidence that cultural receptivity is a variable not to be overlooked. The different cultural responses to the same foreign culture by the Ibos and the Hausa-Faulani in Nigeria, or by the Tamils and Sinhalese in colonial Ceylon, is a pattern found among different groups in many parts of the world.

Negative Human Capital

There is also what might be called negative human capital in the form of attitudes which prevent or impede the performance of economic tasks that people are otherwise quite capable of performing, both physically and intellectually. In primitive tribes of hunters and warriors, for example, the men may feel that such things as growing food or making clothing are "woman's work" to be shunned. Similarly, conquering peoples such as the Mongols or the Spaniards may consider industry and commerce as being beneath their dignity. In societies where slaves do a great deal of the work, aversions to manual or "menial" labor may develop among the free population and, later, among the free descendants of the slaves, to whom such work is a reminder of their ancestors' lowly condition.

A special kind of negative human capital has affected the higher levels of many societies—the unacceptability of industrial and commercial leaders into the top social circles, which have been open only to an aristocracy, whose careers have been those of great landowners and high government officials. The desire to see their families reach the top social levels have often led highly successful entrepreneurs to transfer their wealth into landownership and either cease being entrepreneurs themselves or educate their children for non-entrepreneurial occupations more socially acceptable in the aristocratic circles to which they aspire.[20] Such societies deprive themselves of the great industrial and commercial dynasties which can develop and persist in countries like the United States, where there are no higher levels of aristocracy to aspire to. In societies which, in effect, sterilize their own entrepreneurs, there may be not only a loss of entrepreneurship but also a loss of investment capital, as capitalists with high propensities to save and re-invest become landowners imitating the lavish spending habits of the aristocracy.[21]

In modern Western welfare states, a whole range of low-level occupations may be left to foreigners, as the native citizens come to consider living off the state less demeaning than doing such work. In some countries, such negative human capital is increased by education, so that those who have been to schools or universities now regard a wider range of occupations as being beneath them. Whether the positive human capital they receive in educational institutions is sufficient to offset this growth in negative human capital is ultimately an empirical question and depends in part on whether their education has been in fields with practical applications or in easier and more speculative subjects. The educated unemployed are a major social, economic, and political problem in many Third World nations, and the expansion of bureaucracies to absorb them, in order to avoid political unrest among the educated unemployed, creates other problems, such as increased bureaucratic red tape that impedes the work of others who do have technological skills or entrepreneurial capabilities.

Negative human capital can take other forms as well. In some parts of the world, a willingness to lend or to allow purchases on credit is discouraged by traditions which stigmatize attempts to collect interest from kinsmen, tribesmen, or fellow villagers, and which frown on any insistence on prompt repayment of the principal. Such traditions have existed at times in widely scattered parts of the world—in West Africa, the Balkans, and Melanesia, for example.[22] Thus, in centuries past, a Serb who charged interest to fellow Serb peasants was called a "Greek," a term of condemnation, based on Serbian hostility to Greek money-lenders.[23] Whatever the historical origins or evolutionary value of such traditions in promoting mutual help during times of distress, in modern times they leave such societies with the alternatives of forfeiting the benefits of credit in the everyday operations of a market economy or allowing some other racial or ethnic group from outside this local tradition to play the role of creditors and financiers. Not only are foreign money-lenders given an advantage over local money-lenders where such traditions reign, foreign merchants are likewise favored over local merchants, who are expected to treat their customers in a more familial sort of way than is expected of strangers.

Other cultural handicaps include a proneness to violence and to other socially counterproductive attitudes and behaviors. Where cultures are conceived of not as museum pieces, but as part of the working machinery of everyday life, then they are not matters of static differences to be celebrated, but matters of competing efficacy for the various purposes they serve—efficacy as judged by those individuals deciding for themselves what to retain and what to discard, in the light of their own experience. Thus cultures which may have been functional in the settings in which they evolved tend to be re-evaluated in new settings and to survive selectively in the light of the exigencies of these new settings.

National and group pride and identity have often been assumed to be positive, if not essential, factors in advancement. Yet some of the most remarkable examples of rapid advancement have come from peoples painfully aware of their own backwardness and ashamed of it. The spectacular advancement of the Scots in the eighteenth century occurred among a people aptly described as "conscious to a painful degree of their backwardness, their poverty, their lack of polish, their provinciality."[24] A century later, the same phenomenon occurred halfway around the world, as Japan emerged from its self-imposed isolation with widely expressed feelings of inferiority to the Western world, laments about its own people's "slow comprehension," and awe of Americans to the point of having their school textbooks hold up Benjamin Franklin and Abraham Lincoln as models to emulate, more so than even Japanese heroes, as well as serious proposals to make English the language of Japan.[25] Conversely, pride in ancient achievements can keep a nation or a people tied to obsolete technologies and resistant to changes needed to catch up with contemporaries. For no nation has such pride been more justified than China, whose technological and cultural achievements once led the world for centuries. Yet no country has paid a higher price in the nineteenth and twentieth centuries for its clinging to ancient ways in the face of both Western and Japanese armed aggression with modern weapons and modern methods of organization.[26]

At the very least, the widespread assumption that promoting national or group pride and identity are essential foundations for advancement is open to very serious question on the basis of historical facts. When such pride and identity reach the point of promoting cultural isolation, they may be forms of negative human capital.

Cultural Frameworks

Cultural borrowings among nations and between civilizations demonstrate the historic importance of human capital on a grander scale. At the national level, human capital includes not only particular skills and general work habits among the people, but also institutional arrangements and social and political traditions which facilitate the production of wealth. Dependable law is one of the most important of these. Governments likely to confiscate wealth are unlikely to find much wealth to confiscate in the long run. Similarly, a political system which fails to understand or respect the inherent requirements of commerce and industry can easily render commerce and industry less productive, whether by capricious taxation, suffocating regulation, or through other means.

Without these cultural frameworks, neither abundant natural resources nor the skills required to develop them are guarantees of prosperity, as the severe economic problems of post-Communist Russia demonstrate. One of the most richly endowed nations of the world, with such resources as petroleum, uranium, iron ore, gold, and manganese, for example, Russia had also by this time trained vast numbers of scientists and engineers, perfectly capable of developing those resources. All that was lacking was a legal, political, and financial system providing both the incentives and the protections required for an efficiently functioning market economy. Secure private property rights could have attracted foreign investors from around the world, were there a higher likelihood that what was invested could be retained and the profits repatriated. Yet the Russian people suffered economically from the lack of these intangibles, despite having all the tangible things associated with prosperity. Human capital must include political and legal traditions.

As just one striking example of the importance of these political and legal intangibles affecting tangible wealth, in the late twentieth century vast petroleum deposits under the Caspian Sea were estimated to be worth perhaps as much as $4 trillion, not counting the huge reserves of natural gas also found there. Yet, despite its potential for substantially raising the standards of living of the people in adjoining Azerbaijan and Georgia, little of this wealth was in fact being developed because of political and legal entanglements, including the political difficulties of trying to get a pipeline built from these landlocked countries through neighboring states with direct access to the open seas.[27]

England's emergence as the first industrial nation, both in point of time and in terms of world pre-eminence for generations thereafter, owed much to its stable government and dependable legal framework, within which both Britons and foreigners could function in a market economy. The accumulation of knowledge behind the development of commercial law in England was a major advantage in that country's emergence as the leading nation in commerce, even before it became the leading nation in the development of modern industry. A distinguished economic historian described the process in England:

> . . . it was not until the latter part of the eighteenth century that the royal courts in London had accumulated enough experience in deciding disputes over insurance, bills of exchange, ships' charters, sales contracts, partnership arrangements, patents, arbitrations, and other commercial transactions to make English courts and law seem a factor contributing positively to the development of English commerce. The English courts allowed suits by foreign merchants and acquired a reputation for treating foreign litigants with scrupulous fairness. Mercantile transactions, insurance policies, and credit instruments subject to English law seemed more secure, more calculable in their consequences, less subject to the vagaries of sovereigns and changes of heart by one party or the other—advantages reflected in the growth of the British insurance industry, of London as a world financial center, and of British trade generally, as well as in low interest rates.[28]

Such intangibles as honesty and integrity are thus major factors in economic transactions and economic development. Like most things that are important, they differ greatly from one society to another. "While it is unimaginable to do business in China without paying bribes, to offer one in Japan is the greatest faux pas,"[29] as a knowledgeable scholar and world traveler wrote in 1997. An international survey of corruption that same year found the most corrupt countries to be Nigeria, Bolivia, Colombia, Russia, Pakistan, Mexico, Indonesia, India, Venezuela and Vietnam—all countries with serious economic problems, often despite rich natural resources. Those ranked highest in honesty were mostly Western European and Western European-offshoot societies, with the addition of Singapore and Israel.[30]

Another economically important intangible, along with honesty, are political attitudes which can view businesses as either national assets or as economic prey. Both attitudes have appeared in widely disparate governments, whether democratic or despotic. The Ottoman Empire, for example, granted foreign businesses exemptions from many of the laws and practices which hindered businesses run by its own subjects. So did early republican China, as it tried to lure back some of the overseas Chinese capital and capitalists. The political temptation, however, is to think of ever more reasons why governments should take more and more money from businesses and exert more and more control over them. The presence or absence of countervailing traditions and ideologies is crucial in determining how far this will go and therefore how much benefit or detriment will result, not simply to the businesses themselves but, more importantly, to the economy as a whole.

Among the people, a spirit of cooperation enables many resources to be combined for projects ranging from neighborly maintenance of local streets to combining to form business partnerships and industrial corporations. Where such voluntary cooperation is easy to organize, many activities can go on that would be more costly if they could only be undertaken through the more cumbersome machinery of large formal organizations, such as those of government or a national church. For example, the vast numbers of private schools and colleges spontaneously established by private initiative in the United States have few counterparts in other countries around the world. Conversely, the French have long had the reputation of being reluctant or unwilling to cooperate with one another in economic or other enterprises, because of a cultural emphasis on individual glory and invidious comparisons.[31] A similar difficulty in getting voluntary cooperation has been seen as characteristic of southern Italian culture.[32]

Whatever the merits of these particular characterizations, the larger point here is that a spirit of cooperation is an economic as well as a social asset—and is part of the human capital of a society. This spirit may be particularly valuable in countries where the formal institutions of law and government are either inefficient or corrupt, thereby making economic transactions risky, except within groups whose own internal traditions of trust and cooperation enable them to carry out economic and other activities more efficiently than other members of the same society can. A classic example would be the ability of the Chinese minority in Southeast Asia to transact business among themselves without written contracts, secure in the cultural traditions that promote the fulfillment of these agreements better than the local law could. A similar set of traditions has characterized the Hasidic Jews in New York who sell jewelry on consignment from one another without the necessity for contracts and costly legal entanglements. Like other forms of capital, cooperative spirit is neither evenly nor randomly distributed among peoples or nations. Highly status-conscious societies, such as India or Sri Lanka, may have great difficulties in getting a modest level of cooperation among workers who come from various finely subdivided social groups.[33]

Cultural Borrowing

Technological and organizational borrowings between nations and civilizations also demonstrate the potency of human capital. The Japanese people, whose figurative and literal insularity have produced very little genetic change in Japan over the centuries, have nevertheless changed dramatically from a poor and technologically backward nation in the early nineteenth century to one of the economic and technological giants of the world in the twentieth century. Here it is possible to trace quite clearly the mass transfer of Western technology in textiles, railroads, shipbuilding, electricity, chemicals, telegraphy, and photography, among other industries.[34] That this happened in Japan, but not on any comparable scale elsewhere at the time, was not due to any greater wealth in Japan than among other technologically backward nations, nor to any greater natural resources, which were in fact more lacking in Japan than in many other nations, but rather to social and political attitudes that made economic development a priority approaching an obsession.

In earlier centuries, the massive scientific and technological borrowings of Western civilization as a whole from the Islamic world and from Asia likewise provided the foundation for the West's own later rise to world pre-eminence in fields in which it had once been a follower. Literacy facilitated this process in Western Europe while illiteracy retarded it in much of Eastern Europe, before written versions of Slavic languages were created by adaptations of Latin or Greek alphabets. More than simple literary accessibility was involved, however, for transfers of technological, scientific, and commercial practices from other countries lagged long after literacy had spread, and lagged in the predominant populations of Eastern Europe long after enclaves of Germans, Jews, Greeks, and others brought these advances to the region.

In Bukovina during the nineteenth century, it was the German minority that provided most of the craftsmen, while in the city of Posen, where half the population was Polish, Germans and Jews were two-thirds of the craftsmen and controlled two-thirds of the trades and land.[35] As late as 1910, there were fewer than 800 Romanian craftsmen in the Romanian region of the Habsburg Empire—and more than 5,000 craftsmen from the Jewish minority in the same region.[36] Similar patterns could be seen on the other side of the world, where the Chinese minority in nineteenth-century Thailand supplied the great bulk of various craftsmen in Bangkok.[37] The Moriscoes played a similar role as craftsmen in medieval Spain and the Huguenots in France. Where local people were unable to compete successfully with minorities in acquiring the skills needed for such relatively modest occupations, they were often still less able to acquire the higher levels of skill needed for scientific and engineering work.

Again, differences in receptivity were at least as important as accessibility. However, without accessibility, receptivity would mean little. In many isolated places, neither accessibility nor receptivity existed—and neither did economic advancement. Much of the Balkans and much of sub-Saharan Africa fit these descriptions, as have the backwaters of Southeast Asia and many small, isolated islands in the seas of the world. What these places have had in common has not been race, but the smallness and isolation of their cultural universes. The ending of that isolation and the opening up of these societies to modern influences have typically led to technological and other advances which contrast sharply with their previous conditions, however much such societies may continue to lag behind other societies which had centuries-long headstarts in both tangible and intangible development.

Geographic Influences

Geography played a major role in the development of the British, the Slavs, the Africans, and the Indians of the Western Hemisphere—especially when geography is conceived broadly, to include climate, flora, fauna, and disease environments. The industrial revolution was greatly facilitated in the British Isles by the proximity of its key ingredients—iron ore and coal deposits—at a time when land transport costs were enormous and when potential rivals like Germany had such deposits at a greater distance from one another. In the Balkans, industrialization was all but impossible at that time, given the absence of such mineral deposits and a lack of waterways capable of bringing shipments of the necessary minerals from other parts of the world without prohibitively high transport costs.

The development of large, ocean-going commerce was physically obstructed in Africa by an absence of waterways capable of carrying such ships and bringing such commerce to the interior of the continent or, in many places, even to the shores, given the shallowness of some African coastal waters and the scarcity of natural harbors. In North America there were ample waterways capable of floating large vessels from the ocean to deep inside the continent. However, before the European invasions, there were no draft animals anywhere in the hemisphere capable of handling the kinds of huge cargoes that would have made such ships economically viable. Even local trading, whether by land or by water, was limited in its volume by the absence of pack animals or draft animals, which made human porters as necessary in the Americas as in much of sub-Saharan Africa—and as limiting in terms of what kinds of goods could be transported and how far. These were not simply economic limitations of the times but cultural limitations with enduring consequences. In neither Africa nor the Western Hemisphere did the cultural universe extend as far as in Europe or Asia, both of which had ocean-going vessels that traded over thousands of miles.

Diseases were a large geographic factor shaping the history of imperialism in Africa and in the Western Hemisphere. Although Africa was known to Europeans for centuries before they discovered the Western Hemisphere, large-scale conquests were launched first in the Americas, where disease was a major ally of the Europeans, rather than in Africa, where it was a major enemy. The happenstance that Europeans

had greater biological resistance to Indian diseases than Indians had
to European diseases made the ultimate outcome of their struggles for
control of the Western Hemisphere virtually inevitable, given that diseases were even more devastating to the Indians than European
weapons were. In Africa, the situation was the reverse, for here the
indigenous diseases were devastating to Europeans, so that invasions
that were militarily possible for centuries were not in fact feasible in
practice until European medical advances allowed whites to survive in
regions where tropical diseases abounded.

In short, while man may discriminate against various minorities,
nature discriminates against whole nations and continents. Moreover,
the consequences of radically different geographic advantages and
disadvantages last long after the peoples from given regions have relocated to other parts of the world, for the cultural development of the
people themselves is affected by their geographical opportunities, and
especially by the extent to which geography has facilitated or impeded
their contacts with a wider world. This cultural development or human
capital has proved to be crucial to the economic and social advancement of the numerous groups around the world who have been discussed in this trilogy.

While such geographical influences as rich natural resources—petroleum in the Middle East or gold in South Africa, for example—have
played major roles in the economies and in the histories of particular
nations, it is also very common for countries with rich natural resources
(such as Mexico or Nigeria) to be poor countries and for countries with
very few natural resources (such as Japan or Switzerland) to have standards of living that are among the highest in the world. Similarly, it is not
uncommon for immigrants to arrive destitute in a new land and then rise
above the average income or wealth level of the population of that country. Whether with nations or with individuals and groups, it is human
capital that is crucial to the creation of wealth and higher living standards, often far more so than their initial endowment of natural or other
wealth. Immigrants who arrive without money but with occupational
skills—Jewish immigrants to the United States being a classic example—are analogous to nations without natural resources but with the
skills and entrepreneurship to import other countries' natural resources
and process them into valuable finished products, as Japan has done in
its rise to industrial pre-eminence.

Educated Intelligentsia

Human capital must not be confused with formal education, which is just one facet of it, and still less with the growth of an intelligentsia, which may be either a positive or a negative influence on economic development and political stability, depending on the particular kinds of skills they possess and the particular attitudes they take toward those with the productive capacity to advance the economic level of a country. Modern Western industry and commerce developed at a time when the intelligentsia were a small and relatively uninfluential group. However, many Third World societies in the twentieth century became independent nations led by elites based on formal education and political charisma, but with little or no experience in economic matters and a hostility toward autonomous economic institutions and toward economically productive minorities in their own countries.

The specific kinds of education received affect not only technological and economic development in a country, but also the direction of its social and political development. Education in science and technology has obvious economic benefits, but not all groups or all nations have been equally drawn to that kind of education. In Malaysia, for example, the Chinese minority received more than 400 degrees in engineering during the decade of the 1960s, while the Malay majority received just four.[38] Differences in fields and/or qualities of education have also existed between Protestants and Catholics in Ulster, caste Hindus and untouchables in India, Russians and Kazakhs in Kazakhstan, Middle Eastern versus European and American Jews in Israel, Tamils versus Sinhalese in Sri Lanka, and whites versus blacks or Hispanics in the United States.[39] Lagging groups and lagging nations tend toward the easier subjects, rather than such difficult fields as mathematics, science, engineering, and medicine. These differences affect not only their economic productivity but also their political attitudes towards those who do have the skills to make a society more productive.

Newly educated classes have been especially likely to specialize in softer subjects and to be prominent among those fostering hostility toward more advanced groups, while promoting ethnic "identity" movements, whether such movements have been mobilized against other ethnic groups, the existing authorities, or other targets. In various periods of history, the intelligentsia in general and newly educated people in particular have inflamed group against group, promoting discriminatory policies and/or physical violence in such disparate countries as Hungary,[40] India,[41] Nigeria,[42] Kazakhstan,[43] Romania,[44] Sierra Leone,[45] Sri Lanka,[46] Canada,[47] and Czechoslovakia.[48]

Whether at the level of minority activists in a given society or at the level of leaders of national revolts against external powers, promoters of nationalism have been disproportionately intellectuals—and intellectuals from a limited range of fields. "Few nationalist militants were engineers, or economists or professional administrators," as a student of nationalism said of the generation of African leaders during the transition from colonial status to that of independent nations. Kwame Nkrumah was a British-educated lawyer, Jomo Kenyatta an anthropologist, and Léopold Senghor a poet.[49] Much the same pattern could be found in other parts of the world as well. Leaders of the Basque separatist movement in Spain and of the Quebec separatist movement in Canada were also soft-subject intellectuals.[50] In the less developed eastern regions of Europe, the rising intellectual class during the years between the two World Wars likewise tended to concentrate in the softer subjects, rather than in science or technology, and to seek careers in politics and government bureaucracies, rather than in industry or commerce.[51] Much the same pattern would be apparent half a century later in Sri Lanka, which was all too typical of Asian Third World countries in having "a surplus of unemployed graduates" who had specialized in the humanities and the social sciences.[52]

Ethnic leaders who would later promote the breakup of Yugoslavia, and the atrocities that followed, in the last decade of the twentieth century, included professors in the humanities and the social sciences, as well as a novelist and a psychiatrist.[53] The mass slaughters in Kampuchea under the Khmer Rouge were likewise led principally by intellectuals, including teachers and academics.[54] Historian A.J.P. Taylor has said that the first stage of nationalism "is led by university professors" and that "the second stage comes when the pupils of the professors get out into the world."[55] Whatever the actual sequence, the intelligentsia have played a central role in promoting intergroup and international animosities and atrocities—and in trying to artificially preserve, revive, or fabricate past glories.

Newly educated and semi-educated classes have often sought positions in government bureaucracies, rather than in industry and commerce, for which their education has usually given them few skills likely to be useful in the marketplace. Moreover, the growth of the bureaucracies needed to absorb such people, in order to prevent them from becoming a political problem, is often a handicap to the development of industrial and commercial activities, while the social and political attitudes spawned by those with diplomas and degrees, but without productive skills, constitute yet another barrier to economic development. What was said of Romania's institutions of higher education between the two World Wars—that they were "numerically swollen, academically rather lax, and politically overheated," as well as "veritable incubators of surplus bureaucrats, politicians, and demagogues"[56]—could be said of such institutions in other nations in Eastern and Southeastern Europe during that era and in various nations of Asia, Africa, and Latin America in later times.

The direct economic drain of supporting an intelligentsia with little to contribute to the economy is by no means the sole or most important cost they impose on the rest of the people in such poor societies. The kinds of policies and attitudes they promote and the internal strife they generate or aggravate are often major impediments to economic advancement or political stability. The post-independence histories of many African nations, especially, have shown the tragic results of following policies diametrically the opposite of those which developed the economies of the Western world in earlier centuries or of Japan more recently. In multi-ethnic societies, confiscatory policies toward the most economically productive groups have been promoted for the short-run benefit of those seeking a way out of their own poverty at the expense of others, rather than by becoming more productive themselves. Those targeted have included the Germans and Jews in Czechoslovakia and Romania, the Chinese in Malaysia and Indonesia, and Indians and Pakistanis in Kenya and Uganda, among many others. Those losing in the long run have included the poorer and less skilled masses, who cannot replace the more productive groups they suppress or drive out of the country.

Both internally and internationally, Western intellectuals have for centuries romanticized "noble savages" in various parts of the world, peoples who supposedly lived in some sort of Eden before evil was introduced from outside by modern Western society. Facts about the carnage, oppression or brutality in such societies have been glided

over, totally ignored, or brazenly denied by those pursuing a vision—
and disseminating that vision through their writings, teachings, motion
pictures and other channels. To the extent that they are successful in
creating a "virtual reality" different from the factual realities that public policies must contend with, this causes such policies to be misdi-
rected, ineffective, or counterproductive. Sometimes a foreign Eden is
ideologically defined, such as the Soviet Union under Stalin or China
under Mao, and again a lovely "virtual reality" has for decades completely submerged facts that included the slaughter of millions.[57] In
these and other ways, an intelligentsia can make policies less
informed—indeed, misinformed—and less intelligent than otherwise.

IDEAS AND HISTORY

The importance of human capital, whether in particular skills or in
broader social institutions and attitudes, should not be confused with
the role of ideas in history, especially such organized and articulated
ideas as have formed the stock in trade of the intelligentsia. Perhaps
the most important thing to understand about history is that it was
lived under constraints very different, and generally much narrower,
than the constraints of today. The difference between having iron ore
and coal deposits close by one another and both close by the sea, as in
parts of Britain, and having them just 10 or 20 miles apart, as in parts
of Germany, was enormous in the era before railroads, when transporting vast amounts of heavy material would mean loading it into innumerable horse-drawn carts—except that the prohibitive cost of doing
this was so apparent from the outset as to cause many rich mineral
deposits to remain unused. More generally and more fundamentally,
the scope of human volition was too circumscribed to allow much of
history to be explained as simply the putting into effect of various
ideas and ideologies, however much ideas and ideologies may preoc-
cupy intellectuals of a later era.

The Idea of Freedom

The role of ideas and ideologies in history is much more difficult to
establish than is often believed. Neither freedom nor slavery, for
example, were the results of ideas or ideologies. Freedom began to

emerge where governments were too fragmented, too poorly organized, or too much in need of voluntary cooperation to prevent its emergence. That was the situation in parts of medieval Europe, where a politically fragmented continent had numerous local rulers who needed the economic resources being produced by prosperous towns and cities, in order to finance their own wars of aggrandizement or to protect themselves from others' wars of aggrandizement. In this setting, kings and nobles competed in granting townsmen and city dwellers exemptions from the heavy-handed controls of the feudal world, in order to attract and hold the commerce and industry that meant taxes and the military power which those taxes could buy.

Where a single government held firm and undisputed control over a vast area, as in China for example during the same era, no such concessions were necessary and were not given.[58] But when Europe splintered politically after the collapse of the Roman and Byzantine empires, not only did the numerous kings have to fear each other, they also had to fear their own armed nobles and the nobles had to fear one another as well. The rise of lucrative commerce and industry, especially in Western Europe, provided both local and national despots with incentives to create islands of exemption from their own despotism, in order to serve their own economic and military self-interest by attracting people with commercial and industrial skills.

European rulers at all levels were as devoted to government control of the economy as Chinese rulers were. Not only innumerable government regulations but also a farming out of similar regulatory powers to private groups such as the guilds, as well as the creation of government-sponsored private monopolies in various commodities, clearly indicate a *dirigiste* mentality among rulers in Europe as well as in Asia. However, medieval Europe's lag behind China in technological innovation was paralleled by its lag behind China in effective governmental control. This, together with smaller and much more numerous governmental units in medieval Europe,[59] permitted artisans, merchants, and other European economic agents to escape into various enclaves beyond the jurisdiction of particular authorities, where they could practice their trades and sell their merchandise under freer conditions. Moreover, the threat of losing such valuable taxpayers made more rulers willing to relax their grip on the economy. Along with economic freedom, political freedom developed, again largely as a way of attracting and keeping economically productive classes. These classes were not simply (or primarily) the wealthy, but included masses of peasants whom Eastern European rulers lured into their domains by allowing them various exemptions from local laws.

Even before that, the fragmentation of power as between kings and local nobles in Europe led to various accommodations, after their mutual attempts at subjugation or extermination had failed. Thus the Magna Carta in Britain, and a similar pact between kings and nobles in Hungary a few years later, established the principle of a division of powers and a set of rights of subordinates[60] which would, centuries later, move down the social scale to apply eventually to the common people. Where no such fragmentation of power existed, or where there was no such lucrative commerce and industry to tempt rulers to relax their despotism, there freedom remained rare. China had a flourishing commerce and industry before medieval Europe, but since the government of China had much firmer control of a much larger territory than any contemporary European government had, the Chinese government did not need to make similar concessions to the urban middle classes. In Russia, there was no sizable middle class to whom such concessions might have been made and the czars remained among the prime examples of despotic rule in Europe.

In short, freedom in our modern political sense became a peculiarly European idea after peculiarly European circumstances brought it into being. Freedom was like a social mutation whose benefits caused it to survive and develop. Whatever the combination of factors that created the settings in which freedom became possible, once it was in place it tended to be self-perpetuating. By the time a British offshoot society was established in North America, this political freedom had spawned a whole moral and political philosophy, which persisted among the transplanted Britons who created the government of the United States. But it was an ideology rooted in history rather than in purely intellectual exercises.

Slavery as well did not exist because of racial or other ideologies. For most of human history, among peoples of all races around the world, slavery existed wherever there were sufficiently vulnerable people to make their capture and enslavement profitable. In medieval Europe, that usually meant the enslavement of Europeans by other Europeans, just as in contemporary Asia the Asians typically enslaved other Asians, and in Africa or the Western Hemisphere the indigenous peoples likewise enslaved one another. The differences between the subjugated peoples and those who subjugated them were more likely to be military, geographical, and cultural, rather than racial. Indeed, this continued to be so even in a later era, when transoceanic voyages became technologically feasible and peoples from different continents had more massive interactions than ever before, whether in the form of international trade, war, or enslavement.

Africa became the prime source of internationally traded slaves—though never the sole source—when its many fragmented communities, geographically isolated from the main currents of world economic and technological development, became accessible to Europeans seeking to develop their colonies in the Western Hemisphere. Even during this era, however, those Africans living in strongly organized states with formidable military forces at their disposal were not the ones enslaved. Rather, they were the enslavers who sold their fellow Africans to the Europeans, who in most cases acquired their slaves by purchase rather than direct capture.

Although political freedom emerged much later in history than slavery, the vicissitudes of both reflect the interactions of geographical, cultural, technological, and other factors. As larger and more powerful territorial states began to emerge over the centuries, more and more people were protected by armies and navies from slave raids by marauders. Where the consolidation of modern states lagged far behind, whether in southeastern Europe or in the Pacific island of Bali, there the local peoples continued to be enslaved by outsiders, as they did also in the more vulnerable regions of Africa.

Often there were geographical reasons why the peoples of a vast area could not be readily consolidated into cohesive, modern nation-states. They might be isolated on widely scattered small islands in the Pacific, fragmented by mountainous terrain in the Balkans, or located in the interior of a continent where navigable waterways were rare and where jungles and other geographical barriers were common, as in much of sub-Saharan Africa. In short, peoples with severe geographical and other disadvantages tended to be subjugated by peoples more favorably situated. Whether that subjugation took the form of territorial conquest, enslavement, extraction of tribute, or other forms, was a matter of what was most expedient from the standpoint of those with the greater power.

Although Western Europeans had for centuries enslaved principally the peoples of Eastern Europe and the Balkans, by the time the Western Hemisphere was discovered and conquered, Africa was one of the few remaining areas of the world where massive enslavement continued to be feasible. After still more centuries, however, the ideological contradiction between the European conception of freedom and the brutal reality of their enslavement of Africans began to produce, first in Britain and later in other European and European-offshoot nations, a growing political opposition to slavery as such—the first such mass opposition to this ancient institution in the history of the world. Because this moral opposition developed within countries with overwhelming military power and worldwide imperial hegemony, slavery came under pressure all over the planet—and was eventually destroyed by Europeans, despite opposition within their own ranks, as well as opposition and evasion by virtually every non-European civilization.

The worldwide campaign against slavery in the nineteenth and twentieth centuries demonstrates that ideas can have a major role in historic events, but yet their origins need not be in the intellectual realm. Freedom did not begin as an idea but as a reality that was then treasured and analyzed by those who possessed it. Only after centuries of habituation to freedom did it become regarded as a norm, and violations of that norm seen as intolerable—among those peoples with this particular historical experience. The relationship of ideas and history has been one of reciprocal interaction, rather than one-way causation, so that no formula can substitute for an investigation of the specifics of this interaction in particular times and places. All too often, ideas—whether religious ideas in the medieval crusades or racism in the later European enslavement of Africans—have been assumed to have been autonomous causes of historical events, when in fact much more mundane factors have been apparent and much more complex interactions were at work.

At certain times and places, circumstances may give the ideas of particular groups or individuals the power to affect a fateful choice among existing options. For example, the era of the dissolution of European empires in general, and the British Empire in particular, after the Second World War was an era when socialist economic "planning" was in the ascendancy in intellectual and political circles. Thus many of the European officials dispatched to the colonies brought with them ideas of government controls and government ownership. So did many of the indigenous leaders who had been educated in European universities where such ideas were the prevailing ones. The net result was that both the last years of European colonialism and the first years of Third World independence saw the growth of bureaucracy and of state-owned enterprises in much of the non-industrial world, usually with disastrous economic consequences. By sheer accident, however, the British colony of Hong Kong received a colonial governor devoted to the idea of a market economy and hence followed diametrically opposite policies with diametrically opposite results. Hong Kong's spectacular economic growth rate—nearly 14 percent annually for a decade—made it unlikely that its subsequent governors would risk changing what had worked so well.[61] At any given juncture, particular individuals and particular ideas may have momentous consequences. It is only in the longer view of history that fundamental social conceptions must be seen as having origins in wider circumstances.

Even purely cultural developments have often originated not in the realm of ideas but as by-products of geographic, military, and political developments. The cultural division of Europe in the twentieth century reflects fault lines going back to the days of the Roman Empire, when Western Europe was for centuries part of a literate and technologically advanced Roman culture, and much of Eastern Europe was not.

Religion

Religious ideas can be particularly difficult to trace in their historic consequences. Purely secular motives can be cloaked in religious language, as can behavior antithetical to the very religion being invoked in its defense. The violence of the medieval Crusaders against fellow Christians, including the sack of Constantinople, had no basis in the doctrines of the religion they professed. Nor did the enslavement of Moslems by other Moslems, which was forbidden by the tenets of Islam. Moreover, religious divisions are by no means clear-cut in circumstances such as those of the medieval era in the Balkans, when both Christianity and Islam were so blended with local pagan superstitions and beliefs, as well as with one another, that their folk versions were said to resemble each other more than either resembled Christianity or Islam as understood by people knowledgeable about their respective doctrines.[62] Such syncretism may have facilitated formal conversions which represented no great changes of substantive beliefs, while accommodating new legal and political realities created by conquest or reconquest.

A similar syncretism developed among the conquered indigenous peoples of the Western Hemisphere.[63] In Asia as well, and independently of conquest, Christianity was spread in a form which accepted elements of local religious beliefs and customs,[64] while the religions indigenous to Asia—Buddhism and Taoism, for example, likewise mutually influenced one another and spread in popular forms which incorporated local beliefs and superstitions.[65] Even in the late twentieth century, it was said that while "Islam dominates along the Niger," nevertheless indigenous African beliefs remained, so that an African fisherman "who prays to Allah five times a day may also sacrifice a chicken to appease the river's water spirits."[66]

Religiously-motivated actions—human sacrifice to appease the gods, as among the Aztecs—may be carried on in a manner, or on a scale, that serve secular interests, such as inuring the population to carnage or terrifying surrounding peoples, whose leaders were coerced into attending these spectacles. However sincere the motives of leaders or followers of Christian Crusades or Islamic Jihads, it is also clear that the opportunities these presented for plunder, enslavement, and empire-building did not go unnoticed. Nor would it be easy to establish what proportion of those who engaged in these activities became involved for which of these reasons.

Religious leaders may have secular, political, and even military roles. Sixteenth-century Spanish bishop Juan Rodríguez de Fonseca was said to be better at arming warships than at conducting mass,[67] while Cardinal Richilieu was renowned as a political operator, and at one time even the Pope had an army and a navy. Among the Aztecs, priests led troops into battle, as the Prophet Mohammed did among the Moslems. Separating the religious from the secular influences at work in history can be difficult even for a single individual, much less for a whole society.

Often religious labels distinguish groups whose real differences are ethnic or cultural. Thus when the inhabitants of medieval Dubrovnik refused to allow anyone who was not Catholic to remain within the city's walls overnight,[68] this was not necessarily a religious distinction being imposed, so much as a social distinction between the coastal people, who were more culturally advanced, and the tribal peoples who came down from the hills and mountains to trade in the city and whose presence overnight was considered undesirable on social grounds. Similarly, the distinction between the Catholics and the Protestants in Ulster County, Ireland, is an ethnic distinction of historic and enduring importance, even to people whose religious beliefs are tenuous. Terrorists described as "Islamic fundamentalists" are often more Westernized than traditional Moslems.[69]

None of this denies that genuinely religious belief can have major historic consequences. Louis XIV's persecutions of the Huguenots, which drove many of them to leave France, to the detriment of the French economy, were by all indications expressions of pure and simple religious bigotry, designed to get the Huguenots to convert to Catholicism without driving them out of the country. It was not that the king had a hatred for the Huguenots as a people, unlike the hatred toward Jews in some countries, for Louis rejoiced at their conversions (or apparent conversions) produced by his policies and sought to mitigate some of the many excesses against them by those carrying out his policies.[70] Even here, however, the desire for internal unity as a political asset is hard to disentangle from the desire for religious conversions as such.

Religious prohibitions against usury have had major and lasting economic and social repercussions. Such prohibitions among Christians in medieval Europe enabled Jews to become prominent among the bankers and financiers of that era, since Jews were free to charge Christians interest, both under the prevailing laws and in their own religious traditions. Similarly, religious prohibitions against Moslems charging interest enabled non-Moslem money-lenders from India to achieve prominence in Iran during the same centuries.[71] While there were legalistic ways of circumventing prohibitions against usury, both in Christian and Islamic societies, social disapproval and personal conscience were inhibitions against doing so.

Religion has played other important roles in the secular development of the world. Written religions have spread literacy to non-literate societies. Some kinds of religion have also served as an intellectual training ground for the kind of systematic thinking later required in the very different worlds of science and technology. The elaborated theology of institutional religion, as distinguished from emotional or folk religion, requires analytical attempts at reconciliation of the many moral dilemmas growing out of the inherent contradictions of human life and the conflicting requirements of the particular theology. The effect of a tradition of Talmudic analysis in preparing Jews for analytical work in science, law, and other fields has been paralleled by similar intellectual traditions among scholars in Islamic and Christian religions, though perhaps not to the same degree at the level of the masses. This intellectual relationship between religion and science has been noted especially in the case of the Puritans, both in England and America:

> Even more than most people of their time, they searched constantly for clues to God's purposes in the world. It was this impulse which led so many English Puritans to study nature with the extraordinary intensity which played a central part in the birth of modern science.[72]

Because religion, like race or political ideology, is a way of organizing great numbers of people into different camps for struggles over power and wealth, determining whether the real object is that power and wealth, rather than religion, race, or ideology as such, is not always easy. However, even in an analysis of purely secular events, religion cannot be reduced to simply a philosophical patina on economic and social factors.

Science and Technology

The role of scientific and technological ideas on economic, military, and political developments has been widely acknowledged. However, it is by no means clear that their effect on economic development has always been crucial. As two scholars specializing in industrial development have noted:

> The most popular explanations of Western prosperity are focused on science and invention. But why, if science and invention are a sufficient cause of national wealth, were not China and the Islamic nations, which were the leaders in science and invention when the West turned from feudalism and entered into the modern era, the countries that escaped from poverty to riches?

Many technological advances which originated in China, often centuries before they appeared in Europe, were nevertheless developed to a higher level in European societies. Books, for example, were printed in China centuries before the Gutenberg press appeared in Europe and the compass was used by Chinese sailors before European sailors used it. Gunpowder was used in China and India before it became known to Europeans, but it was Europe which developed the firearms and cannon that doomed Asia to a subordinate role in the age of European imperialism. Even at the level of the mathematics and science behind modern technology, Europe learned much from the Islamic and Asian worlds before beginning its own ascent to world domination.[73] In short, while ideas have been historic in their consequences in science and technology, as in other realms, ideas by themselves have not been enough. The receptivity of a given culture to ideas and innovations, and the ability of that culture to take these advances and carry them further, has been crucial.

The same pattern is shown also by Japan's absorption of Western science and technology in the nineteenth century and its rise to world prominence in these same fields in the twentieth century, surpassing the West in some fields. Partly this reflects the need not only for a physical but also a human infrastructure—technicians and engineers who can apply these ideas to concrete uses and entrepreneurs who can organize the economic resources and develop enterprises capable of making the new technology economically viable. Even at the level of the ordinary worker, vast differences in education and attitudes make a given technology feasible in one culture but not in another. The mass importation of foreign workers into the industries of the Russian Empire under the czars, or into the Middle East in the twentieth century, suggest some of the differences in people which exist at all intellectual levels, as well as at all economic levels.

Where individual achievements do not require so much in the way of complementary inputs by others, there lagging minorities or whole lagging nations may produce performances of historic and worldwide significance in particular fields. Thus a backward Russia could produce internationally recognized novelists of the highest genius such as Tolstoy and Dostoyevsky, as well as world-renowned music by Tchaikovsky, Rachmaninoff, and others. In the United States, poor and poorly educated blacks could produce popular music which shaped the direction of American popular music in general and eventually influenced popular music around the world.

Sports, art, and politics—like writing and music—have produced remarkable individual achievements which have not depended on complementary inputs by others to nearly the same extent as achievements in science, technology, or the economy. It is not merely that individuals from groups or nations which lag behind in the latter fields are able to hold their own in the former. Such groups and nations often do spectacularly well in the relatively few fields in which their talents can be expressed and are therefore concentrated. The Irish in politics and a succession of ethnic minorities in various sports illustrate this pattern. What this suggests is that peoples with very different achievement levels in many fields may nevertheless have very similar inborn potential, but that the fruition of these potentials may require vast amounts of other human capital, which is far from equally distributed around the world or within a given society. Therefore much native ability that might otherwise have been spread among a number of fields, if a lagging group had the complementary prerequisites for its development in those fields, may instead be concentrated in a relatively few fields, in which such groups do not merely hold their own but excel, sometimes spectacularly.

RACE AND RACISM

Race is not simply a biological concept and it becomes less and less of a scientific term with the continuing growth of people of mixed ancestries. Race remains, however, one of the ways of collectivizing people in our minds and of organizing them for political or other activities. In some societies, race is the most important way of separating people for differential treatment, though in other societies people are treated differently according to their religion, nationality, caste, or other social characteristics. Each characteristic has its own mystique, and there is no reason to assume that the mystique of race is unique in its pervasiveness or its power, except in particular societies. In other societies, people may face oppression, humiliation, or even genocide, while being physically indistinguishable from the surrounding population. In many cases, special modes of dress, insignia, or other indicators of group membership may be imposed, precisely because there are no natural biological indicators to provide practical guidance in carrying out policies of differential treatment.

Race is a biological concept but it is a social reality. In a society where most people are blends of various races, there may nevertheless be sharp dividing lines, with people on one side of those lines being called "black," for example, and others on the other side being called "white," even if a geneticist or an anthropologist would reject this dichotomy. But, however questionable these and other designations may be from a scientific standpoint, populations with different genetic mixtures may also differ culturally, and thus be as different in various capabilities and their consequences as if they were in fact pure races and also inherited different genetic endowments in those capabilities.

Recognition of these differences in capabilities and orientations is often called "racism," as if that somehow invalidated the observations about group differences in behavior or performance, or turned it into a mere subjective perception. But to insist that such group differences be ignored, either in causal explanations or in policy formulations, is as dogmatic as the insistence that genetics must be the reason for such differences. Where "racism" is not simply a term of abuse for political purposes, its central dogma is that genetics explains intellectual, moral, and other differences among peoples—that "race is everything," as Madison Grant said in a popular book of the early twentieth century.[74] His reductionism is matched by the reductionism of those who see in racism itself the general explanation of intergroup differences. More than an analogy is involved. The actual structure of the argument is very similar in the two cases. Specifically, the argument is that, when intergroup differences remain after taking various economic and social factors into account, these remaining differences must be attributed to the favored residual factor—whether that factor is genes or racism. At the beginning of the twentieth century, the residual factor to be credited (or blamed) was race. At the end of the twentieth century, the residual factor was racism. Both factors need careful attention, not automatic acceptance—and that careful attention must begin by defining what the terms mean.

Definitions

"Racism" is a term not only used very loosely by many, but also a term for which a more precise definition is not easy to achieve. In various usages, the term applies to the ideas of (1) those who have animosity toward people of another race, (2) those who believe that people of another race are genetically inferior, (3) those who believe in discriminating against people of another race, out of sheer self-interest, and (4) those who believe that members of another racial or ethnic group are less capable, or have other undesirable traits, as of a given time, even if for non-genetic reasons. Those who believe all these things at the same time provide the clearest examples of racism. But all four notions need not go together and often do not.

What of those who believe that other races are intellectually or otherwise inferior, but who take a benevolently paternalistic attitude toward them? If such well-meaning believers in genetic inferiority are to be considered racists, even if they favor giving largess or preferential treatment toward those considered inferior, then animosity is no longer part of our definition. What about those who wish to discriminate against another race for purely selfish reasons, such as the early twentieth-century white organizers of an anti-Japanese-immigrant movement in the United States, on precisely the ground that the Japanese were such able, intelligent, and resourceful competitors that whites could not maintain their own higher living standards in open competition with them, but required the help of special legal protection?[75] Halfway around the world, a very similar argument for preferential policies favoring the majority population was made in Malaysia, where it was claimed that otherwise the Chinese minority would best the Malays in every form of open competition: "Whatever the Malays could do, the Chinese could do better and more cheaply," according to a Malay leader who defended preferential policies for Malays and who later became prime minister.[76]

In Nigeria likewise, preferences and quotas were defended on grounds that otherwise "the less well-educated people of the North will be swamped by the thrusting people of the South."[77] Similar claims for preferential treatment, on grounds that other racial or ethnic groups have superior capabilities, have been made in India, Burma, and Fiji, sometimes accompanied by fears that either physical or cul-

tural extinction threaten without such protection.[78] If acknowledgement of superior capability in racial or ethnic groups who are targeted
for discrimination is to be included as "racism," then opposite
assumptions are being encompassed by the same word.

What of those who believe that particular racial or ethnic groups are
less capable or less desirable in various respects, even if not for genetic
reasons, and even if the people who believe this have no general animosity toward those from these groups? If the term "racism" is applied
to those who have this view, even if they support programs designed to
raise the level of capability in the group considered to be lagging, then
social workers and lynch mobs are being lumped together. Nor is this a
problem only in Western countries. A tenth-century Moslem scholar
noted that Europeans grow more pale the farther north you go and also
that the "farther they are to the north the more stupid, gross, and
brutish they are."[79] Considering that this was said at a time when southern Europe was in fact far more advanced than northern Europe, where
illiteracy was widespread and conditions often primitive, can we confi-
dently reject this as an empirical generalization about correlations
among location, skin color, and cultural development at that particular
juncture in history, and say that such a conclusion is so false that it
could only be based on bias or animosity? More to the point, would this
be racism because it dealt with the social characteristics of races, even
if it did not attribute the differences to genetics? Again, this simply
illustrates the difficulty of consistently applying the term.

The tendency to dismiss all unfavorable conclusions about any
group as racism or as prejudice, stereotypes, or other manifestations of
ignorance overlooks the fact that often those with the most unfavorable
opinion of a group are those in closest contact with them, while those
with a more favorable view know them less well and often from a
greater distance. During the generations of armed conflict between
whites and American Indians, for example, those whites with the most
unfavorable view of the Indians were often those most in contact with
them on a daily basis, while those most favorably disposed toward
Indians were often those with less personal contact. When the U.S.
army massacred an encampment of Indians in Colorado, the news was
greeted with cheers in Denver but with horror in the eastern United
States, where a peace movement developed to try to bring hostilities
with the Indians to an end. However benign or paternalistic a view of

Indians was taken by George Washington, Thomas Jefferson, or Abraham Lincoln, the most unfavorable view of them was that taken by Andrew Jackson, who had fought with Indian allies, as well as against Indian enemies, before becoming president. Perhaps the most romantic view of the American Indian was that among some intellectuals in Europe who had never seen an Indian.

The point here is that adverse opinions on any group cannot be automatically waved aside as prejudices, stereotypes, or other forms of ignorance. These opinions might be mistaken for other reasons—or they might be true. Each specific case requires evidence, analysis, or agnosticism. It is sheer dogmatism to say, a priori, that adverse opinions must be wrong. Genetic differences may be neither necessary nor sufficient to account for many differences among groups, nations, or civilizations, but these differences can nevertheless be very real and very consequential.

Sometimes the issue of racism has involved not so much capability, in either intellectual or economic terms, but *desirability* in some social sense encompassing personal hygiene, congeniality, or cultural assimilation. Thus the first Chinese seen in the United States were welcomed, for they were disproportionately visiting scholars, business leaders, or others with the social graces or admired achievements that made them acceptable.[80] It was after the later masses of largely illiterate and primitively-living Chinese laborers arrived that widespread anti-Chinese hostility developed, resulting in indiscriminate legislation directed at keeping out all Chinese and discriminating against those already in the country. Since both the earlier Chinese visitors and the later Chinese immigrants were of the same race, is "racism" a consistent term to cover the attitudes of the same generation of Americans who first welcomed them and later rejected them?

Where a particular group is dedicated to hard work, thrift, and sobriety, they may have a particularly negative attitude toward another group whom they see as lacking in these respects that are important to them. Italian Americans, for example, have often taken this view of black Americans. However, when black moderate Republican Senate candidate Edward Brooke was running for election in Massachusetts in 1966, he captured more of the normally Democratic Italian vote than either the Republican governor or the Republican president, even though other black candidates in Newark and in New York City were resoundingly defeated in predominantly Italian districts.[81] Was it "racism" to repudiate certain kinds of behavior or ideology, which was seen as more prevalent in one group rather than another, even though there was no such wholesale repudiation of other individuals of the same race who were not seen as embodying such behavior or ideology? Is this then "racism" or "behaviorism"? That is, is it race or behavior and attitudes that are being condemned?

The point here is not to derive the best definition of "racism," but to see if any specific and consistent meaning is conveyed by this widely used word. If not, then the many disparate things covered by this sweeping expression must be analyzed separately in terms that convey some clear and specific meaning.

There has been so much racism in the full sense of open animosity toward particular groups, combined with dogmatic beliefs that there is a fixed ceiling to their intellectual or other development, that the term is weakened, rather than strengthened, when it is applied sweepingly to people who have neither animosity nor a claim that some invisible ceiling dooms a whole race to be hewers of wood and drawers of water. Arthur Jensen, for example, wrote in 1969 that youngsters from socially disadvantaged racial groups could be taught much more than they were in fact being taught in the public schools[82] and Charles Murray and the late Richard J. Herrnstein wrote in their controversial 1994 book, *The Bell Curve*: "It should surprise no one to see (as one does every day) blacks functioning at high levels in every intellectually challenging field."[83] Moreover, when Herrnstein and Murray argued against a welfare system that subsidizes the birth of more babies to teenage girls,[84] they were arguing against a policy whose harmfulness does not depend on genetic theories of intelligence. In fact, the damage done is even greater if these babies' intellectual potential at conception is equal to that of other babies in other social groups. If they were never capable of being more than hewers of wood and drawers of water, the damage done would have been less.

One of the reasons for not dismissing as racism every conclusion concerning the role of genes in the development of human intelligence is that such a dismissal too often becomes a substitute for a careful critique of what has been said.[85] In many fields, even incorrect theories or conclusions can contribute to a deeper understanding of a subject, if a critique of those theories and conclusions leads to a more thorough examination of what both sides believed before the controversy, while an automatic dismissal adds nothing to our understanding and may even convince some observers that nothing rational can be said against the theory, when in fact much that is rational could be said against it. If nothing else, a serious critique can demonstrate which statements on either side can and cannot stand up under scrutiny.

"Racism" as a blanket explanation of intergroup differences is not simply an over-rated explanation. It is itself a positive hindrance to a focus on the acquisition of the human capital or cultural capital needed to rise economically and socially. If there is any central theme that emerges from the histories examined in these three volumes, it is that the cultural capital of a people is crucial to their economic and social advancement, whether that people is a racial minority, a nation-state, or a whole civilization. In some cases, the factors inhibiting the development of this human capital have been geographical or historical. But they need not include self-inflicted ideologies or ideologies congenial to sympathetic outsiders, whose sympathies may prove to be more of a handicap than the hostility of others.

A more tendentious definition of racism has emerged in the late twentieth century to exempt racial minorities themselves from the charge. Racism was now said to require *power*, which minorities do not have, so that even the most anti-white, anti-Jewish, or anti-Asian statements (including those asserting a genetic basis for depravity) were automatically exempt from the charge of racism.[86] No such proviso that power was required for racism ever existed before. That this new and self-serving escape hatch remained largely unchallenged has been one index of the level of moral intimidation surrounding racial issues. One might as well add the proviso that murder requires right-handedness, so that multiple killers who are left-handed could escape murder charges. In the ordinary sense of the word, minorities of all colors have shown themselves capable of as vicious racism as anybody else, whether in or out of power. The hostility, boycotts, or violence of African-ancestry people against people from India has been common from Kenya to South Africa, as well as in Jamaica and Guyana. Such behavior differs in no essential way from the behavior labelled "racism" when it is the African-ancestry population being abused by people of European ancestry.

Racial Differences

All differences between races are not racial differences in the sense of being caused by differing genes. Indeed, all biological differences between races are not genetic. Differing incidences of malnutrition, alcohol and drug usage, cigarette smoking, and other behavior of mothers during pregnancy can lead to babies with the same genetic potential at the moment of conception entering the world at birth already differing biologically in their mental capacities. Different child-rearing practices, beginning in the crucial years of infancy, like-wise heavily influence the direction of a child's mental development—indeed, the physical development of the brain itself[37]—in ways unlikely to be undone in later years. The cultural inheritance of the surrounding social milieu adds further differentiation, not only as between races but also as between classes, nations, and civilizations.

Even among groups whose intellectual performances have been out-standing—the Jews and the Japanese, for example—they are often outstanding in different sets of mental skills. Both Jews and Japanese have generally scored above average on I.Q. tests, for example, but those parts of the tests on which the Japanese particularly excel (spa-tial intelligence) are the parts on which Jews generally do less well than on other sections, while the outstanding verbal facility of Jews is not found among the Japanese, even when tested in their own lan-guage.[88] Differences in child-rearing practices have been cited as pos-sible reasons for these differences in the internal patterns of their respective mental performance[89] but, whatever the reasons, the differ-ences in patterns are clear-cut. Because different I.Q. tests emphasize different things, Jewish I.Q.s on the Stanford-Binet test have been sig-nificantly higher than their I.Q.s on the Wechsler test.[90] Moreover, dif-ferent subgroups of Jews have differed in I.Q., Israelis of Sephardic origins in the Middle East and North Africa scoring 14 points lower than the Ashkenazic Jews of Israel who originated in Europe or Euro-pean-offshoot societies.[91]

Demographic differences influence I.Q. test scores and educational performances, as they influence economic and other variables. It has long been common for first-born children to have higher I.Q.'s than their siblings, as do children of higher birthweights, even when their sibling is an identical twin.[92] Children born to teenage girls tend to have lower I.Q.'s and more medical problems, while—at the other end of the scale—women who have children late in life have increased chances of having a baby with Downs syndrome or other mental defects.

These patterns exist across racial lines but different racial and eth- nic groups have very different proportions of their births occurring in these various demographic categories. In groups with smaller families, for example, a higher percentage of the children will be first-borns or only children, both of whom are greatly over-represented among high- I.Q. people and among famous scientists, intellectuals, and others.[93] However, even among first-borns, it matters whether they are born to a teenage mother or to a woman in her twenties or thirties. Among Amer- icans in 1980, 31 percent of all black first-born children were born to teenage mothers, compared to only 12 percent among whites.[94] In both races, children born to teenage mothers tended to have lower I.Q.s. Efforts have been made to separate out statistically how much of the black-white I.Q. score difference of 15 points is due to teenage moth- ers, to low birthweight, to a much higher incidence of premature babies among blacks, and to other factors. Unfortunately, many disadvantages go together and interact, so that such statistical exercises may or may not capture all the causal influences. What is clear is that factors caus- ing differences between races are not necessarily racial or genetic fac- tors, particularly when there are so many social and cultural differences also involved. Nevertheless, they cannot automatically be dismissed as "perceptions" or assumed to be the fault of "society."

Other groups as well have their own characteristic demographic patterns, as they have their own patterns in other respects. Mental test scores of Chinese Americans or Puerto Rican Americans likewise dif- fer not only in the respective average levels but also in the internal patterns of their strengths and weaknesses.[95] That is, Puerto Ricans with high I.Q.s tend to have the same internal pattern of strengths and weaknesses as Puerto Ricans with low I.Q.s, but at a higher level. So do high-I.Q. and low-I.Q. Chinese.

Discussions of averages should not obscure the fact that there is much overlap among individuals from groups with high and low aver- age I.Q.s. Unfortunately, the technical definition of "overlap" in the psychometric literature—the percentage of one group which scores above another group's average—does not correspond to either a com- mon sense conception or a geometrical conception of overlap.[96] The technical definition of overlap can include a much smaller proportion of either group than the word suggests in its ordinary meaning. Despite this, overlap exists not only at a given place and time, but still more so in a wider geographic and temporal perspective. During World War I, for example, black soldiers from Ohio, Illinois, New York, and Pennsylvania scored higher on mental tests than did white soldiers from Georgia, Arkansas, Kentucky, and Mississippi,[97] even though whites nationwide scored higher than blacks nationwide.

Because the average number of intelligence-test questions answered correctly gives by definition an I.Q. of 100, a white who answered a given number of questions correctly in the 1930s could receive an I.Q. score of 100, while a black who answered the same number of questions correctly in the 1950s could receive an 85. For purely comparative purposes as of a given time, I.Q. scores may be valid, but for determining larger issues of genetic potential, such renorming of I.Q. scores conceals evidence against the claims of innate and immutable genetic limitations in mental ability. However, for determining issues of racial discrimination, I.Q. test scores at a given time can be very revealing. Do Americans of different races with the same I.Q.s have substantially different earnings? As of 1989, for example, black, white, and Hispanic Americans of the same age (29) with the same I.Q. (100) all earned between $25,000 and $26,000.[98]

Attempts by environmental theorists to say that mental tests are not predictively valid, either in general or for culturally different groups, because of a cultural bias in the tests themselves, fail completely when this ultimately empirical claim is confronted with actual empirical evidence. Innumerable studies of a wide variety of mental tests in various countries show that individuals from groups with lower average scores do not perform academically or at work any better than individuals with the same low scores from groups with higher average scores.[99] In short, the test are valid for the kinds of predictions they make, even if their results have little or no relationship to the innate genetic potential of individuals or groups at the moment of conception. Clearly, performance comes many years after conception, and in these three volumes we have already noted some of the many other influences at work in the meantime.

Those who emphasize the genetic component in intellectual ability among individuals cannot simply transfer such conclusions automatically to differences between groups known to differ greatly in many

demographic, cultural, and other environmental ways.[100] Nor can it be
assumed that our current social knowledge and statistical techniques
can accurately parcel out what proportion of the differences are attributed to what. In some purely mechanical sense, this can be done, but
the validity of such techniques is itself open to question when so many
explanatory social variables are known to be correlated with one
another that spurious correlations are an ever-present danger. This
does not mean that statistical conclusions about intergroup differences
can be automatically dismissed, but it does mean that they need not be
definitive either.

Viewing racial groups over time undermines both race and racism
as explanations of social and economic differences. Whether or not the
various peoples of Europe should be considered as different races,
they all certainly differ racially from the Chinese—and the Europeans
and the Chinese have changed relative positions dramatically from the
centuries when China was far in advance of Europe, technologically
and otherwise, to the more recent centuries when their positions have
been reversed. If genetic superiority is invoked to explain their relative positions in one era, it is contradicted by the reversal of positions
in another era. Nor is the comparison between China and European
nations unique. At various times in history, the forefront of world technological development and other cultural advancement has been in
the Middle East, in southeastern Europe, in northwestern Europe and,
in some aspects, today in Japan. But all these places and their peoples
have also lagged far behind other regions and peoples at other periods
of history. Nor have there been any such changes in the racial compo-
sitions of these peoples of these regions as to explain such epoch-making rises and falls in genetic terms.

History has also dealt unkindly with the notion that "racial purity"
produces people capable of higher achievements than those of mixed
ancestry. Madison Grant's early twentieth-century best-seller, *The
Passing of the Great Race*, expressed a common belief of its time that
"the unfortunate mongrel" not only inspires distrust and contempt but
is biologically inferior as a result of cross-breeding.[101] Historical evidence, however, tells a different story. While there may not be any
absolutely pure races in the world today, some are less mixed than others. The purest of all are likely to be those found in geographically isolated places, which are typically places poorer and less technologically

or educationally advanced than others. Nomadic groups, such as the Bedouins of the Middle Eastern deserts, also eschew racial intermixture,[102] but no one has considered them among the technological or other cultural leaders of the world. None of this says anything about genetics, but it illustrates how genetic differences are so often intertwined with other differences that determining the separate effect of genes can be a difficult and hazardous undertaking. Among both the black and the indigenous populations of the Western Hemisphere, those of partially European ancestry have had major cultural advantages over the unmixed members of their respective races, as well as being genetically different.

While some cultural patterns are peculiar to particular racial groups—the Japanese, for example—other equally distinctive patterns cut across racial lines. Some of the social patterns already noted among mountain peoples in *Migrations and Cultures*[103] have been common around the world for centuries, whether the races have been European, Asian or Middle Eastern.[104] Similarly, the social patterns found among middleman minorities have been as common among the Chinese in Southeast Asia as among the Jews of Eastern Europe, the Lebanese of West Africa, or the Indians of East Africa, even though these groups are racially distinct from one another.

The role of racism as a factor in the fates of particular groups is likewise undermined by a journey through history. In particular times and places—especially during the Nazi Holocaust—racism has indeed been tragically crucial. But much of the previous history of the persecution of Jews had little to do with race and much to do with religion, as well as reflecting a general hostility to middleman minorities around the world. For many centuries, Jews could escape persecution by converting to Christianity in Europe or to Islam in the Middle East and North Africa. It was much later in history when the racial doctrine of anti-Semitism replaced the older religious doctrine of anti-Judaism. The Nazis paid no attention to the religious or non-religious backgrounds of the millions of Jews they killed, only to their ancestry.

More is involved than intellectual questions of explaining causation or political questions of assigning blame or exploiting guilt. Those wishing to see groups rise from poverty need to know what factors produce prosperity. Clearly, groups experiencing discrimination—sometimes based on race and sometimes on other characteristics—have often risen economically, not only above other groups not subject to as much discrimination, but even above the majority population of the country that is doing the discriminating. Nor have the groups which have risen from poverty to prosperity usually done so by first overcoming the racial or other antipathies directed against them by others. Rather, it has typically been *after* they have achieved economic advancement and social acculturation that the hostility against them has abated. Asian Americans are perhaps the classic examples of this process. Chinese Americans have long since ceased to be confined to their own neighborhood ghettoes and Japanese Americans not only live dispersed among the general population but have had high rates of intermarriage with the white population.

CULTURAL DIFFUSION

What makes the history of migrations much more than a history of the redistribution of bodies internationally is that it is one of the processes by which cultures have been diffused, changing the whole economic, military, and political landscape of the world. What makes the history of conquests more than simply a history of horrors is that it, too, is one of the ways by which cultural diffusion has remade the life of the human race. Fortunately, there have been other and less stressful ways by which the advances made in some parts of the world have spread to other places and other peoples. Cultural diffusion is an explanation of large disparities among peoples at a given time—and changing world leadership over time—that is more consistent with history than either genetic or exploitation theories. As already noted, genetic explanations are inconsistent with the dramatic changes in world leadership that have taken place over the centuries, among peoples whose genetic makeup has not undergone any comparable changes. Exploitation theories are inconsistent with the declining standards of living that have often followed the freeing of supposedly exploited peoples from their erstwhile conquerors.

The discoveries, inventions, and other cultural advances that go into making a great civilization seldom—if ever—all originate within the people of that civilization. "The history of civilizations, in fact, is the history of continual mutual borrowings," as Braudel put it.[105] Another distinguished student of world cultural history has identified the principal factor in historic social change as "contact with strangers possessing new and unfamiliar skills."[106] Access to such contacts has by no means been equally available to all. Geography alone presents highly disparate opportunities for cultural diffusion in different parts of the world.

The mere fact that agricultural techniques for growing particular crops can spread more readily from east to west than from north to south—since the latter involves more profound climate changes—has meant that Asian crops could spread more readily to Europe than tropical crops in the Western Hemisphere could spread to the temperate zones of either North or South America. The numerous geographical barriers of Africa, the Balkans, or Australia before the era of transoceanic travel, have meant that the indigenous peoples of these areas have had no such access to other cultures as the peoples in more fortunate parts of Europe or Asia. When the role of draft animals and pack animals is taken into account, then the entire Western Hemisphere before 1492 likewise had narrower limits to cultural diffusion than either Europe or Asia.

When the British invaders confronted the Iroquois on the east coast of North America, the British were able to draw upon technology, science, and other cultural developments from China, India, and Egypt, not to mention various other peoples from continental Europe. But the Iroquois could not draw upon the cultural developments of the Aztecs or Incas, who remained unknown to them, though located only a fraction of the distance away as China is from Britain. While the immediate confrontation was between the British settlers and the Iroquois, the cultural resources mobilized on one side represented many more cultures from many more societies around the world. It was by no means a question of the genetic or even cultural superiority of the British by themselves, as compared to the Iroquois, for the British were by no means by themselves. They had the advantage of centuries of cultural diffusion from numerous sources, scattered over thousands of miles.

Cultural Borrowing versus Cultural Resistance

Some of the most dramatic rises from backwardness to the technological and economic forefront among the nations of the world have occurred as a result of cultural borrowing. The British in medieval and early modern times, and the Japanese in the nineteenth and twentieth centuries, have been among the most dramatic examples. As a distinguished historian has put it:

> In establishing the new drapery, the English borrowed the idea from the Dutch. For casting their first iron cannon they used French gun-founders. In packing the hull of their ships with cannon, they were quick in adopting a French invention. When renewing their navy they adopted the galleon type from the Spaniards. In each case they did not show much originality but an exceptional capacity for picking up profitable ideas, perfecting others' innovations, adapting their tools and their skills to new situations.[107]

These were by no means the only fields in which the British borrowed from other cultures. Huguenot immigrants developed the clock industry in London and German immigrants created the British piano industry.[108] The Dutch drained English marshes and the Lombards built British financial institutions. The Romans built London itself and the English language evolved out of the languages of the successive, Roman, German, and Norman invaders. A similar pattern of borrowing from other cultures could be found among the Japanese in later centuries, except that foreigners brought modern technology as sojourners rather than as conquerors or settlers. Both the British and the Japanese also became noted as international travellers who observed closely what they saw around them in other countries around the world and brought many of these ideas and practices back home with them—and yet each retained their own respective, distinctive, insular societies. These dramatic rises to the economic and technological forefront contrast with equally dramatic falls from world leadership. China, the Islamic world, and Italy are among those who illustrate this pattern, each leading the world in a number of fields at one time, and yet not only relinquishing that leadership at a later period but falling further and further behind the new leaders.

Although gunpowder was known in China as early as the tenth century, and was used by the Chinese in various implements of war,[109] its development in pistols, rifles, and cannon in Europe was not paralleled by any similar development in China. Moreover, when cannons were in later centuries introduced in China, the Chinese took little interest in them, as they took little interest in most things from the "barbarians," as they considered all non-Chinese peoples. More than vanity was involved. To admit that the outside world was ahead of China in any important way would be to shake faith in the existing order, which the Chinese government of course did not wish to do. Finally, contempt for things military, which was deeply imbedded in Chinese culture, led to a fatal neglect of this field,[110] for which China paid dearly in loss of land and sovereignty by its government and massive suffering from invaders by its people.

Japan, unlike China, had never been the leading nation of the world and could harbor no such utter disdain for all other cultures. In fact, its culture borrowed heavily from that of China, centuries before it would begin to borrow from the Western world. When the Japanese lost a naval battle in 1592 against Korean ships with cannons, they then began to equip their own ships with cannon.[111] Yet China persisted in its ancient ways even in the face of military defeats by Japan in the late nineteenth century.[112] However important past achievements may be in providing a foundation for current achievements, once these past patterns have been rendered obsolete by new developments, a glorious past may be more of a handicap than a help. As historian Arnold Toynbee put it:

> Those who have succeeded once are apt, on the next occasion, to be found 'resting on their oars' . . . In the Italian *Risorgimento* the centres which have responded in the Renaissance prove ineffective, and the lead is taken by Piedmont, which has had no part in previous Italian glories. South Carolina and Virginia, leading states of the U.S.A. in the first and second quarters of the nineteenth century, have failed to make a recovery from the Civil War comparable to that of the previously undistinguished North Carolina.[113]

The Ottoman Empire, which had maintained a military superiority over European nations for centuries, was willing to adopt such European innovations as cannon, but it did not become itself a developer of this technology, which was in fact of limited usefulness at first. However, as the technological advancement of firearms in general accelerated and new military and naval tactics became necessary in order to take advantage of them, the Ottoman Empire's merely following

Europe's lead was no longer good enough because they were following with a growing lag and losing disastrously on the battlefields and in naval engagements in the meantime.[114] Again, a glorious past proved to be a handicap when time came to adjust to fundamentally different conditions in the present.

Much the same story could be told of Venice, once the greatest naval power in the Mediterranean world, when the Mediterranean world was the most advanced part of Europe. But ships that were well adapted to the calm waters of the Mediterranean, and to the prevailing tactics of ramming and boarding enemy vessels, were wholly inadequate for coping with the kinds of ships that developed in the rougher waters of the Atlantic in the era of sails and cannon, where naval battles were now fought at a distance. What was needed was not simply a knowledge of the new technology but a rethinking of naval warfare tactics and strategies from top to bottom. Here again, traditions that had brought success for centuries were not readily jettisoned. Venice, like the other great Mediterranean naval powers, never became a match for the upstart Atlantic naval powers and, in the early seventeenth century, was reduced to calling on the aid of the British and Dutch navies to defend it against the Spanish navy.[115]

Cultural resistance is both spontaneous and artificial. The desire to cling to the familiar, or to remain loyal to traditions and to the people in whom those traditions are embodied, are all readily understandable. In addition, however, concerted campaigns to resist new cultures or to retrieve ancestral cultures already abandoned have also been promoted by both political and intellectual leaders.

A Common World Culture

The emergence of the elements of a common world culture, shared by at least the educated people of every continent, offers some hope of ultimately transcending the many group differences which may seem so colorful and delightful in theory, but which have all too often been bitter and lethal in practice. To some extent, the cultures of the world have always interacted and the most efficient methods of agriculture, industry, and organization have been copied, adapted, and spread far and wide. The plow, paper, gunpowder, and the steam engine are just some of the epoch-making developments which spread from culture to culture until they became the common property of the human race. In more recent times, the underlying scientific knowledge and scientific cast of mind behind modern technology have also spread around the world. So have ideas of personal freedom and other concepts once peculiar to Western civilization, just as products, technologies and concepts of non-Western civilizations once spread to the West and helped revitalize it in medieval times.

To some extent, we may be witnessing a transition from civilizations in the plural to what Braudel has called "civilization in the singular."[116] An increasingly common cultural universe, at least among the educated members of races and nations around the world, does not guarantee easier relations among peoples or countries, especially since the more highly educated classes have so often led the way in promoting tribalism among the masses. What an increasingly common world culture offers is an opportunity for better mutual understanding. But opportunities alone are not the whole story. It is what people do with their opportunities that determines the course of history.

NOTES

PREFACE

1. Robert Higgs, *Competition and Coercion: Blacks in the American Economy 1865–1914* (Cambridge: Cambridge University Press, 1977), p. 10.
2. A. William Salomone, "Foreword," Rodomir Luža, *The Transfer of the Sudeten Germans: A Study of Czech-German Relations, 1933–1962* (New York: New York University Press, 1964), p. xi.

ACKNOWLEDGMENTS

1. Victor Purcell, *The Chinese in Southeast Asia*, second edition (Kuala Lumpur: Oxford University Press, 1980).
2. Charles A. Price, *Southern Europeans in Australia* (Canberra: Australian National University, 1979).
3. Fernand Braudel, *The Mediterranean and the Mediterranean World in the Age of Philip II*, translated by Siân Reynolds (New York: Harper & Row, 1972).
4. For example, Bernard Lewis, *The Arabs in History* (New York: Harper & Row, 1966); *idem, The Muslim Discovery of Europe* (New York: W. W. Norton, 1982); *idem, Race and Slavery in the Middle East: An Historical Inquiry* (New York: Oxford University Press, 1990); *idem, Islam and the West* (New York: Oxford University Press, 1993); *idem, Cultures in Conflict: Christians, Muslims, and Jews, in the Age of Discovery* (New York: Oxford University Press,

1995); *idem, The Middle East: A Brief History of the Last 2,000 Years* (New York: Scribner, 1995).

CHAPTER 1: CONQUESTS AND CULTURES

1. Ulrich Bonnell Phillips, *The Slave Economy of the Old South: Selected Essays in Economic and Social History*, edited by Eugene D. Genovese (Baton Rouge: Louisiana State University Press, p. 269.
2. William H. McNeill, *The Pursuit of Power: Technology, Armed Force, and Society since A.D. 1000* (Chicago: University of Chicago Press, 19884), pp. 10–11.
3. In addition to examples in Chapter 2 of this book, see the following: "Roman Houses were typically built of stone or brick, and outfitted with a heating system conveying hot air through hollow tiles located under the floor and inside the walls. Medieval towns did not approach this Roman standard." Jean W. Sedlar, *East Central Europe in the Middle Ages, 1000–1500* (Seattle: University of Washington Press, 1994), p. 111. "No European city in the early nineteenth century had a water supply as assured as that of many cities of the Roman Empire." N. J. G. Pounds, *An Historical Geography of Europe 1800–1914* (Cambridge: Cambridge University Press, 1988), p. 146. "Decay could not remove the evidences of former Roman greatness: ruined cities, broken aqueducts . . . Cities were reduced to villages, if they continued to exist at all. Some decayed, never to be revived." N. J. G. Pounds, *An Historical Geography of Europe* (Cambridge: Cambridge University Press, 1990), p. 70.
4. Jared Diamond, *Guns, Germs, and Steel: The Fates of Human Societies* (New York: W. W. Norton & Co., 1997), pp. 53–54.
5. Jean W. Sedlar, *East Central Europe in the Middle Ages, 1000–1500* (Seattle: University of Washington Press, 1994), pp. 216–217.
6. Robert Bartlett, *The Making of Europe: Conquest, Colonization and Cultural Change, 950–1350* (Princeton: Princeton University Press, 1993), pp. 86–87.
7. Jean W. Sedlar, *East Central Europe in the Middle East*, pp. 203–204.
8. See, for example, Lord Kinross, *The Ottoman Centuries: The Rise and Fall of the Turkish Empire* (New York: William Morrow and Co., 1977), pp. 74, 77, 109, 131, 187; Edward Gibbon, *The*

Decline and Fall of the Roman Empire (New York: The Modern Library, no date), Vol. III, pp. 774–775.

9. See, for example, Meirion and Susie Harries, *Soldiers of the Sun: The Rise and Fall of the Imperial Japanese Army 1868–1945* (London: William Heinemann, Ltd., 1991), Chapter 22.

10. Eric R. Wolf, *Europe and the People without History* (Berkeley: University of California Press, 1982), p. 30.

11. See, for example, Péter Gunst, "Agrarian Systems of Central and Eastern Europe," *The Origins of Backwardness in Eastern Europe: Economics and Politics from the Middle Ages until the Early Twentieth Century*, edited by Daniel Chirot (Berkeley: University of California Press, 1989), pp. 54–56.

12. Caroline Golab, *Immigrant Destinations* (Philadelphia: Temple University Press, 1977), pp. 101–104.

13. Adam Galos and Mazimierz Wajda, "Migration in the Polish Western Territories Annexed by Prussia," *Employment-Seeking Emigrations of the Poles World-Wide: XIX and XX C.*, edited by Celina Bobinska and Andrezejich Pilch (Nakladem Uniwersytetu Jagiellonskiego, 1975), pp. 66–67.

14. Myron Weiner, *Sons of the Soil: Migration and Ethnic Conflict in India* (Princeton: Princeton University Press, 1978), pp. 221–231.

15. Robert Bartlett, *The Making of Europe: Conquest, Colonization and Cultural Change, 950–1350* (Princeton: Princeton University Press, 1993), pp. 293, 303; William H. McNeill, *The Rise of Gunpowder Empires: 1450–1800* (Washington: The American Historical Association, 1989), p. 29.

16. Carlo M. Cipolla, *Guns, Sails, and Empires: Technological Innovation and the Early Phases of European Expansion, 1400–1700* (Manhattan, Kansas: Sunflower University Press, 1992), pp. 21, 28.

17. See, for example, Carlo M. Cipolla, *Guns, Sails, and Empires: Technologies and the Early Phases of European Expansion, 1400–1700* (Manhattan, Kansas: Sunflower University Press, 1992), pp. 138–143.

18. Carlo M. Cipolla, *Guns, Sails, and Empires*, p. 85.

19. William H. McNeil, *The Pursuit of Power: Technology, Armed Forces, and Society since A.D. 1000* (Chiccago: University of Chicago Press, 1984), p. 230.

20. William H. McNeill, *The Pursuit of Power: Technology, Armed Forces, and Society since A.D. 1000* (Chicago: University of Chicago Press, 1984), p. 203.

21. John Thornton, *Africa and Africans in the Making of the Atlantic World, 1400–1680* (Cambridge: Cambridge University Press, 1995), pp. 37–39.

22. Daniel Evans, "The Slave Coast of Europe," *Slavery and Abolition*, May 1985, p. 42.

23. See, for example, Daniel Evans, "Slave Coast of Europe," *Slavery and Abolition*, Vol. 6. No. 1 (May 1985), pp. 41–58; Anthony Reid, "The Decline of Slavery in Nineteenth-Century Indonesia," *Breaking the Chains: Slavery, Bondage, and Emancipation in Modern Africa and Asia*, edited by Martin A. Klein (Madison: University of Wisconsin, 1993), p. 69; Robert O. Collins, "The Nilotic Slave Trade: Past and Present," ibid., p. 148; Bruno Lasker, *Human Bondage in Southeast Asia.*, pp. 19, 57.

24. Martin A. Klein, "Introduction: Modern European Expansion and Traditional Servitude in Africa and Asia," *Breaking the Chains: Slavery, Bondage, and Emancipation in Modern Africa and Asia*, edited by Martin A. Klein (Madison: University of Wisconsin Press, 1993), p. 22.

25. Anthony Reid, "The Decline of Slavery in Nineteenth-Century Indonesia," *Breaking the Chains*, edited by Martin Klein, p. 72.

26. Martin A. Klein, "Introduction: Modern European Expansion and Traditional Servitude in Africa and Asia," ibid., pp. 22–23.

27. See, for example, Daniel E. Schroeter, "Slave Markets and Slavery in Moroccan Urban Society," *The Human Commodity*, edited by Elizabeth Savage, p. 205; Martin A. Klein, "Slavery and Emancipation in French West Africa," *Breaking the Chains: Slavery, Bondage, and Emancipation in Modern Africa and Asia* (Madison: University of Wisconsin Press, 1993), p. 177; Mohamed Mbodj, "The Abolition of Slavery in Senegal, 1820–1890: Crisis or the Rise of a New Entrepreneurial Class?" ibid, p. 199; L. H. Gann and Peter Duignan, *The Rulers of British Africa: 1870–1914* (Stanford: Stanford University Press, 1978), pp. 12, 103; Lee V. Cassanelli, "The Ending of Slavery in Italian Somalia: Liberty and the Control of Labor, 1890–1935," *The End of Slavery in Africa*, edited by Suzanne Miers and Richard Roberts (Madison: University of Wisconsin Press, 1988), pp. 308–313.

28. Jean W. Sedlar, *East Central Europe in the Middle Ages, 100–1500* (Seattle: University of Washington Press, 1994), p. 12.

29. Ibid., pp. 61–64.

30. Robert Bartlett, *The Making of Europe*, pp. 53–54.

31. Jean W. Sedlar, *East Central Europe in the Middle Ages*, pp. 107, 127–129; Bernard Lewis, *Cultures in Conflict: Christians, Muslims, and Jews in the Age of Discovery* (New York: Oxford University Press, 1995), pp. 41, 43–44.

32. Paul Robert Magocsi, *Historical Atlas of East Central Europe*, p. 66.

33. Nigel Davies, *The Incas* (Niwot: University Press of Colorado, 1995), pp. 123–124.

34. Nigel Davies, *The Aztecs: A History* (Norman: University of Oklahoma Press, 1989), p. 110.

35. " . . . genuine Arabs played only a small part in the original development of Islamic science, and most of the credit must go to Persians, Christians, and Jews; even so, the Arabic language became the main vehicle of Islamic learning and played in the East the part played by Latin in the West." Martin Plessner, "The Natural Sciences and Medicine," *The Legacy of Islam*, edited by Joseph Schacht and G. E. Bosworth (Oxford: Oxford University Press, 1974), p. 427. See also Juan Vernet, Mathematics, Astronomy, Optics," ibid., p. 466. A somewhat different perspective is found in W. Montgomery Watt, *The Influence of Islam on Medieval Europe* (Edinburgh: Edinburgh University Press, 1972), pp. 30–43.

36. Solomon Grayzel, *A History of the Jews: From the Babylon Exile to the Present 1728–1968* (Philadelphia: The Jewish Publication Society of America, 1968), p. 266.

37. Quoted in Daniel Patrick Moynihan, *Pandaemonium: Ethnicity in International Politics* (Oxford: Oxford University Press, 1993), p. 82.

38. Ibid., p. 83.

39. "The cultural gap between Greece and Lapland was of the order of three thousand years." N. J. G. Pounds, *An Historical Geography of Europe* (Cambridge: Cambridge University Press, 1990), p. 21.

CHAPTER 2: THE BRITISH

1. Luigi Barzini, *The Europeans* (New York: Simon and Schuster, 1983), p. 47.

2. James Campbell, "The End of Roman Britain," *The Anglo-Saxons*, edited by James Campbell, et al. (Ithaca: Cornell University Press, 1982), p. 13.

3. Peter Salway, "Roman Britain," *The Oxford Illustrated History of*

Britain, edited by Kenneth O. Morgan (Oxford: Oxford University Press, 1984), p. 14; Winston S. Churchill, *A History of the English-Speaking Peoples*, Vol. I: *The Birth of Britain* (New York: Bantam Books, 1974), pp. 11, 19–20; John Burke, *Roman England* (New York: W.W. Norton & Co., 1984), p. 30.

4. I. M. Stead, *Celtic Art in Britain before the Roman Conquest* (Cambridge, Massachusetts: Harvard University Press, 1985), p. 4.

5. Edward Gibbon, *The Decline and Fall of the Roman Empire*, Vol. I (New York: Modern Library, no date), p. 19.

6. John Wacher, *The Coming of Rome* (New York: Charles Scribner's Sons, 1980), pp. 12–13, 17.

7. Ibid., p. 39.

8. Peter Salway, *Roman Britain* (Oxford: Oxford University Press, 1984), pp. 15–17.

9. Barry Cunliffe, *Iron Age Communities in Britain: An Account of England, Scotland and Wales from the Seventh Century B.C. until the Roman Conquest* (London: Routledge and Kegan Paul, 1974), pp. 16, 59–60, 265–286. The areas of pre-Roman Britain tended to be concentrated on the southern coast, further indicating the source of these coins across the English Channel. I. Hodder and M. Millett, "The Human Geography of Roman Britain," *An Historical Geography of England and Wales*, second edition, edited by R. A. Dodgshon and R. A. Butlin (London: Academic Press, Ltd., 1990), p. 27.

10. Barry Cunliffe, *Iron Age Communities in Britain*, p. 307.

11. John Wacher, *The Coming of Rome*, pp. 1–7.

12. Winston Churchill, *A History of the English-Speaking Peoples*, Vol. I, p. 12.

13. John Wacher, *The Coming of Rome*, p. 6.

14. Barry Cunliffe, *Rome and Her Empire* (New York: McGraw-Hill Book Co., 1978), p. 242.

15. Edward Gibbon, *The Decline and Fall of the Roman Empire*, Vol. I, p. 3. See also Peter Salway, *Roman Britain*, p. 69.

16. Barry Cunliffe, *Rome and Her Empire*, p. 242.

17. Winston Churchill, *A History of the English-Speaking Peoples*, Vol. I, p. 17.

18. Peter Salway, *Roman Britain*, pp. 117–119.

19. Barry Cunliffe, *Rome and Her Empire*. p. 244.

20. Ibid., p. 240.

21. T. W. Potter, *Roman Britain* (Cambridge, Massachusetts: Harvard

University Press, 1983), pp. 18, 45; R. G. Collingwood, "The Latin West: Britain, Roman Germany, The Danube Lands," *The Cambridge Ancient History*, Vol. XI: *The Imperial Peace A.D. 70–192*, edited by S. A. Cook, et al. (Cambridge: Cambridge University Press, 1980), pp. 513, 518; N. J. G. Pounds, *The Culture of the English People: Iron Age to the Industrial Revolution* (Cambridge: Cambridge University Press, 1994), pp. 36, 49.

22. John Burke, *Roman England*, pp. 13, 16, 25.

23. John Wacher, *The Coming of Rome*, p. 39.

24. Ibid., p. 72.

25. Ibid., p. 76.

26. N. J. G. Pounds, *The Culture of the English People*, p. 50.

27. Ibid., pp. 53–54.

28. F. E. Halliday, *An Illustrated Cultural History of England* (New York: Crescent Books, 1967), p. 17. "The villa of Roman Britain bore little or not relationship to the Iron Age huts that had preceded it." N. J. G. Pounds, *The Culture of the English People*, p. 66.

29. F. E. Halliday, *An Illustrated Cultural History of Englnd*, pp. 19–22.

30. John Wacher, *The Coming of Rome*, p. 79.

31. Ibid., p. 101.

32. Peter Salway, *Roman Britain*, p. 154.

33. Edward Gibbon, *The Decline and Fall of the Roman Empire*, Vol. I, pp. 1–3.

34. Winston S. Churchill, *A History of the English-Speaking Peoples*, Vol. I, p. 28.

35. F. E. Halliday, *An Illustrated Cultural History of England*, p. 25. See also C. J. Arnold, *Roman Britain to Saxon England* (Bloomington: Indiana University Press, 1984), pp. 58, 66, 71.

36. The areas of Saxon settlements around the beginning of the seventh century are mapped in G. R. J. Jones, "Celts, Saxons and Scandinavians," *An Historical Geography of England & Wales*, second edition, edited by R. A. Dodgshon and R. A. Butlin, p. 47.

37. Frank Barlow, "Who Are the English?" *The English World: History, Character, and People*, edited by Robert Blake (New York: Harry N. Abrams, Inc., 1982), pp. 49–50.

38. J. N. L. Myres, *The English Settlements* (Oxford: Oxford University Press, 1986), pp. 208–211.

39. C. J. Arnold, *Roman Britain to Saxon England*, p. 161.

40. James Campbell, Eric John, and Patrick Wormald, *The Anglo-Saxons*, p. 43. See also C. J. Arnold, *Roman Britain to Saxon England*, pp. 84, 85.

41. C. J. Arnold, *Roman Britain to Saxon England*, pp. 58, 79.

42. Ibid., pp. 63, 116.

43. James Campbell, Eric John, and Patrick Wormald, *The Anglo-Saxons*, p. 19.

44. John Burke, *Roman England* (New York: W.W. Norton & Co., 1984), p. 143.

45. Winston Churchill, *A History of the English-Speaking People*, Vol. I, p. 25.

46. G. M. Trevelyan, *English Social History: A Survey of Six Centuries, Chaucer to Queen Victoria* (Penguin Books, 1986), p. 72.

47. N. J. G. Pounds, *The Culture of the English People: Iron Age to the Industrial Revolution* (Cambridge: Cambridge University Press, 1994), p. 204.

48. C. J. Arnold, *Roman Britain to Saxon England*, pp. 38, 150.

49. G. R. J. Jones, "Celts, Saxons and Scandinavians," *An Historical Geography of England & Wales*, second edition, edited by R. A. Dodgshon and R. A. Butlin, pp. 47, 48, 58–60

50. James Campbell, Eric John, and Patrick Wormald, *The Anglo-Saxons*, p. 38.

51. Frank Barlow, "Who Are the English?" *The English World*, edited by Robert Blake, pp. 51–52.

52. R. Allen Brown, *The Normans* (New York: St. Martin's Press, 1984), pp. 5, 8, 43.

53. Ibid., p. 60.

54. Ibid., pp. 49–77.

55. Christopher Hibbert, *The English: A Social History 1066–1945* (New York: W.W. Norton, 1987), p. 121.

56. Ibid., p. 9.

57. Frank Barlow, "Who Are the English?" *The English World*, edited by Robert Blake, p. 56.

58. George Holmes, "The Medieval Centuries: The Foundation of English Institutions up to the Tudors," ibid., edited by Robert Blake, p. 62.

59. G. M. Trevelyan, *English Social History*, p. 79.

60. Robin Frame, *The Political Development of the British Isles: 1100–1400* (Oxford: Oxford University Press, 1995), pp. 54–60.

61. See George Holmes, "The Foundation of English Institutions up to

the Tudors," *The English World*, edited by Robert Blake, p. 64; Nathan Rosenberg and L. E. Birdzell, Jr., *How the West Grew Rich: The Economic Transformation of the Industrial World* (New York: Basic Books, 1986), p. 76.

62. Janet L. Abu-Lughod, *Before European Hegemony: The World System A.D. 1250–1350* (New York: Oxford University Press, 1989), pp. 84–87.

63. Lewis Mumford, *Technics and Civilization* (New York: Harcourt, Brace and Co., 1934), p. 152. Flemish peasants were also welcomed for their work in building dikes and drainage ditches. Robert Bartlett, *The Making of Europe: Conquest, Colonization adn Cultural Changes 950–1150* (Princeton: Princeton University Press, 1993), p. 114.

64. W. Cunningham, *Alien Immigrants to England* (London: Frank Cass & Co., Ltd., 1969), p. 69.

65. Ibid., p. 76.

66. Ibid., pp. 77–78.

67. Ibid., pp. xiv-xv.

68. Carlo M. Cipolla, *Clocks and Culture: 1300–1700* (New York: W.W. Norton & Co., 1977), pp. 66–69.

69. W. Cunningham, *Alien Immigrants to England*, p. xiv; Warren C. Scoville, *The Persecution of Huguenots and French Economic Development: 1680–1720* (Berkeley: University of California Press, 1960), pp. 325–340.

70. Tim Unwin, "Towns and Trade," *An Historical Geography of England and Wales,* second edition, edited by R. A. Dodgshon and R. A. Butlin, pp. 134–135.

71. John R. Harris, "Movements of Technology between Britain and Europe in the Eighteenth Century," *International Technology Transfer: Europe, Japan and the USA*, edited by David J. Jeremy (Brookfield, Vermont: Edward Elgar Publishing Company, 1991), p. 10.

72. L. C. A. Knowles, *The Industrial and Commercial Revolutions in Great Britain during the Nineteenth Century*, p. 71.

73. Nathan Rosenberg and L. E. Birdzell, Jr., *How the West Grew Rich: The Economic Transformation of the Industrial World,* pp. 115–116.

74. See, for example, Barry R. Weingast and Kenneth L. Scholtz, "How Little England Beat Big France," *Hoover Digest*, 1996, No. 2, pp. 118–125.

75. R. A Dodgshon, "The Changing Evaluation of Space 1500–1914," *An Historical Geography of England and Wales*, second edition, pp. 264–268.

76. N. Thrift, "Transport and Communication 1730–1914," pp. 457–458.

77. Ibid., p. 463.

78. Ibid., p. 463.

79. Ibid., p. 464.

80. Ibid., p. 466.

81. L. C. A. Knowles, *The Industrial and Commercial Revolutions in Britain during the Nineteenth Century*, p. 143.

82. Ibid., p. 188.

83. Nick von Tunzelmann, "Coal and Steam Power," *Atlas of Industrializing Britain 1790–1914*, edited by John Langton and R. J. Morris (London: Metheun & Co., Ltd., 1986), pp. 72–74.

84. R. A. Cage, "The Condition of Scotland 1788–1960," *The Australian People: An Encyclopedia of the Nation, Its People and Their Origins* (North Ryde, N.S.W.: Angus & Robertson, 1988), p. 759.

85. Nick, von Tunzelmann, "Coal and Steam Power," *Atlas of Industrializing Britain*, edited by John Langton and R. J. Morris, p. 78.

86. L. C. A. Knowles, *The Industrial and Commercial Revolutions in Great Britain during the Nineteenth Century* (London: George Routledge & Sons, Ltd., 1926), pp. 6, 10, 18–21, 29.

87. Mark Overton, "Agriculture," *Atlas of Industrializing Britain 1790–1914*, edited by John Langton and R. J. Morris, p. 48.

88. Ibid., p. 21.

89. G. M. Trevelyan, *English Social History*, p. 409. See also Charles Kindleberger, *World Economic Primacy: 1500 to 1990* (Oxford: Oxford University Press, 1996), pp. 130–131.

90. David J. Jeremy and Darwin H. Stapleton, "Transfer between Culturally-Related Nations: The Movement of Textile and Railroad Technologies between Britain and the United States, 1780–1840," *International Technology Transfer*, edited by David J. Jeremy (Brookfield, VT: Edward Elgar Publishing Co., 1991), p. 32.

91. Takeshi Yuzawa, "The Transfer of Railway Technologies from Britain to Japan, with Special Reference to Locomotive Manufacture," ibid., p. 204.

92. John R. Harris, " Movements of Technology Between Britain and Europe in the Eighteenth Century," *International Technology Transfer*, edited by David J. Jeremy (Brookfield, VT: Edward Elgar Publishing Co., 1991), p. 13.

93. David J. Jeremy and Darwin H. Stapleton, "Transfers between Culturally-Related Nations," ibid., pp. 40–41; Simon Ville, "Shipping Industry Technologies," ibid., pp. 80, 81.

94. L. C. A. Knowles, *The Industrial and Commercial Revolutions in Great Britain during the Nineteenth Century*, p. 56.

95. Ibid., pp. 75–75.

96. Ibid., p. 76.

97. W. O. Henderson, *The Rise of German Industrial Power: 1834–1914* (Berkeley: University of California Press, 1975), p. 44; Mark Jefferson, *Peopling the Argentine Pampa*, p. 137; Winthrop R. Wright, *British-Owned Railways in Argentina*, pp. 5, 19, 23; Neena Vreeland, et al., *Area Handbook for Malaysia*, third edition (Washington, D.C.: U.S. Government Printing Office, 1977), pp. 301–302; Dharma Kumar, *The Cambridge Economic History of India*, Vol. 2 (Hyderabad: Orient Longman, Ltd., 1984), pp. 737–761; T.O. Lloyd, *The British Empire: 1558–1983* (Oxford: Oxford University Press, 1984), p. 239; Daniel R. Headrick, *The Tools of Empire: Technology and European Imperialism in the Nineteenth Century* (New York: Oxford University Press, 1981), pp. 180–191, 195.

98. L. C. A. Knowles, *The Industrial and Commercial Revolutions in Britain during the Nineteenth Century*, p. 186.

99. Ibid., pp. 187–188.

100. Ibid., p. 192.

101. Ibid., p. 144.

102. L. C. A. Knowles, *The Industrial and Commercial Revolutions in Britain during the Nineteenth Century*, p. 194.

103. Simon Ville, "Shipping Industry Technologies," *International Technology Transfer*, edited by David J. Jeremy, p. 77.

104. Ibid., p. 221.

105. Ibid., p. 224.

106. Ibid., p. 226.

107. Walter Nugent, *Crossings: The Great Transatlantic Migrations, 1870–1914* (Bloomington: Indiana University Press, 1992), p. 36.

108. B. R. Mitchell, *European Historical Statistics: 1750–1970* (New York: Columbia University Press, 1978), pp. 215, 216.

109. Ibid., p. 223.

110. Maurice Ashley, *The People of England: A Short Social and Economic History* (Baton Rouge: Louisiana State University Press, 1982), p. 140.

111. Gregory Clark, "Why Isn't the Whole World Developed? Lessons from Cotton Mills," *Journal of Economic History*, March 1987, p. 160.

112. Jack B. Pfeiffer, "Notes on the Heavy Equipment Industry. in Chile, 1800–1910," *Hispanic American Historical Review*, February 1952, p. 139.

113. Aaren L Friedberg, *The Weary Titan: Britain and the Experience of Relative Decline, 1895–1905* (Princeton: Princeton University Press, 1988), p. 34.

114. E. H. Hunt, "Wages," *Atlas of Industrializing Britain 1780–1914* (London: Methuen & Co., Ltd., 1986), pp. 60–68.

115. Richard Lawton, "Population," *Atlas of Industrial Britain 1780–1914* (London: Methuen & Co., Ltd., 1986), p. 20.

116. In *Capital*, Marx characterized the rise as "practically insignificant" but, in a public lecture, he quantified it as "*about 40 percent*" (emphasis in the original). Karl Marx, *Capital: A Critique of Political Economy* (Chicago: Charles H. Kerr & Co., 1906), Vol. I, p. 700; Karl Marx, "Wages, Price and Profit," Karl Marx and Friedrich Engels, *Selected Works* (Moscow: Foreign Languages Publishing House, 1955), Vol. I, p. 407.

117. Peter Mathias, *The First Industrial Nation: An Economic History of Britain 1700–1914*, Second Edition (New York: Methuen & Co., 1983), p. 132.

118. G. M. Trevelyan, *English Social History: A Study of Six Centuries Chaucer to Queen Victoria* (Middlesex, England: Penguin Books, 1986) pp. 243, 271–272, 315, 325, 335, 386–387, 393n, 409, 414, 419–420, 492–493.

119. R. H. Campbell, "The Scottish Improvers and the Course of Agrarian Change in the Eighteenth Century," *Comparative Aspects of Scottish and Irish Economic and Social History: 1600–1900*, edited by L. M. Cullen and T. C. Smout (Edinburgh: John Donald Publishers, Ltd., no date), p. 204.

120. William H. McNeill, *The Rise of the West: A History of the Human Community* (Chicago: University of Chicago Press, 1991), p. 679.

121. G. M. Trevelyan, *English Social History*, p. 140–141, 178–179, 335.

122. Ibid., pp. 140–141.

123. Ibid., pp. 386–393.

124. W. A. Armstrong, "The Countryside," *The Cambridge Social History of Britain: 1750–1950*, edited by F. M. L. Thompson (Cambridge: Cambridge University Press, 1993), Vol. 1, p. 87.

125. Ibid., p. 91.

126. Ibid., pp. 113–114.

127. L. C. A. Knowles, *The Industrial and Commercial Revolutions in Britain during the Nineteenth Century*, p. 57.

128. Rondo Cameron, *A Concise Economic History of the World* (New York: Oxford University Press, 1989), p. 181.

129. Aaron L. Friedberg, *The Weary Titan: Britain and the Experience of Relative Decline 1895–1905* (Princeton: Princeton University Press, 1988), p. 26.

130. Mark Casson, *The Growth of International Business* (London: George Allen & Unwin, 1983), p. 106.

131. Gregory Clark, "British Labor in Britain's Decline," Ph.D. dissertation, Harvard University, November 1985, pp. 4–12. See also Paul Johnson, *Modern Times: A History of the World from the 1920s to the 1990s* (London: Orion Books, Ltd., 1992), pp. 601–603.

132. Charles Kindleberger, *World Economic Primacy: 1500 to 1990* (Oxford: Oxford University Press, 1996), pp. 142, 146, 159.

133. A. H. Williams, *An Introduction to the History of Wales* (Cardiff: University of Wales Press Board, 1969), pp. 1–6.

134. Ibid., p. 8.

135. Ibid., p. 48.

136. Ibid., p. 54.

137. Ibid., pp. 60–61.

138. Ibid., p. 59. See also Sir John Edward Lloyd, *A History of Wales* (London: Longmans, Green and Co., Ltd., 1967), Vol. I, p. 89.

139. Wendy Davies, "Land and Power in Early Medieval Wales," *Past and Present*, November 1978, pp. 5–6.

140. John Blair, "The Anglo-Saxon Period," *The Oxford Illustrated History of Britain*, edited by Kenneth O. Morgan, pp. 57–59.

141. C. J. Arnold, *Roman Britain to Saxon England*, p. 157.

142. John Blair, "The Anglo-Saxon Period," *The Oxford Illustrated History of Britain*, edited by Kenneth O. Morgan, p. 52.

143. Bud B. Khleif, *Language, Ethnicity and Education in Wales* (The Hague: Mouton Publishers, 1980), p. 26.

144. Michael Hechter, *Internal Colonialism: The Celtic Fringe in British National Development, 1536–1966* (Berkeley: University of California Press, 1977), p. 111.

145. Wendy Davies, "Land and Power in Early Medieval Wales," *Past and Present*, November 1978, p. 7.

146. Alan Conway, "Welsh Emigration to the United States," *Perspectives in American History*, Vol. VII (1973), pp. 195–196.

147. Ibid., pp. 207–210.

148. Ibid., p. 229n.

149. Ibid., p. 194.

150. D. W. Howell and C. Baber, "Wales," *The Cambridge Social History of Britain 1750–1950*, Vol. 1, p. 319.

151. G. Humphrys, "Industrial Change: Some Lessons from South Wales," *Geography*, November 1976, pp. 246, 249.

152. Prys T. J. Morgan, "The Clouds of Witnesses: The Welsh History of Tradition," *Anatomy of Wales*, edited by R. Brinley Jones (Glamorgan, Wales: Gwerin Publications, 1972), p. 35.

153. D. W. Howell and C. Baber, "Wales," *The Cambridge Social History of Britain 1750–1850*, Vol. 1, p. 282.

154. "Divided They Stand," *The Economist*, February 2, 1985, p. 5.

155. Ibid.

156. Prys T. J. Morgan, "The Clouds of Witnesses: The Welsh History of Tradition," *Anatomy of Wales*, edited by R. Brinley Jones, pp. 32–33.

157. Michael Hecter, *Internal Colonialism: The Celtic Fringe in British National Development, 1536–1966* (Berkeley: University of California Press, 1976), p. 189.

158. Ibid., p. 168.

159. Ibid., p. 33.

160. "Divided They Stand," *The Economist*, February 2, 1985, p. 14.

161. Ibid., pp. 4, 14, 17–18.

162. Colin J. Thomas and Colin H. Williams, "Language and Nationalism in Wales: A Case Study," *Ethnic and Racial Studies*, April 1978, pp. 237–238; Bryan Hodgson, "Wales: The Lyric Land," *National Geographic*, July 1983, p. 42.

163. Colin J. Thomas and Colin H. Williams, "Language and Nationalism in Wales: A Case Study," *Ethnic and Racial Studies*, April 1978, p. 236.

164. "Divided They Stand," *The Economist*, February 2, 1985, p. 16.

165. Ibid., p. 4.

166. D. W. Dowell and C. Baber, "Wales," *The Cambridge Social History of Britain 1750–1950*, Vol. 1, pp. 305–307.

167. Ibid., p. 312.

168. "Divided They Stand," *The Economist*, February 2, 1985, pp. 4–5.

169. Ibid., p. 3.

170. Ibid., p. 8.

171. Ibid., pp. 4, 10.

172. Ibid., p. 4.

173. Ibid., pp. 12, 14.

174. Ibid., p. 8

175. Ibid., p. 5.

176. Warren Hodge, "The Welsh, on Easy Street, Turn Backs on Tories," *New York Times*, February 28, 1997, p. A4.

177. "Divided They Stand," *The Economist*, February 2, 1985, p. 6.

178. D. W. Howell and C. Baber, "Wales," *The Cambridge Social History of Britain 1750–1950*, Vol. 1, pp. 324–325, 350–351.

179. Edward Gibbon, *The Decline and Fall of the Roman Empire*, Vol. I, p. 4.

180. "The masters of the fairest and most wealthy climates of the globe turned with contempt from gloomy hills assailed by the winter tempest, from lakes concealed in a blue mist, and from cold and lonely heaths, over which the deer of the forest were chased by a troop of naked barbarians." Ibid., p. 5.

181. James G. Leyburn, *The Scotch-Irish: A Social History* (Chapel Hill: University of North Carolina Press, 1962), p. 22.

182. Ibid., p. 25.

183. Ibid., p. 18.

184. Henry Thomas Buckle, *On Scotland and the Scotch Intellect* (Chicago: The University of Chicago Press, 1970), p. 38.

185. G. M. Trevelyan, *English Social History*, pp. 168–169.

186. Robert Bartlett, *The Making of Europe: Conquests, Colonization and Cultural Change, 950–1350* (Princeton: Princeton University Press, 1993), p. 78.

187. Donald Woodward, "A Comparative Study of the Irish and Scottish Livestock Trades in the Seventeenth Centuries," *Comparative Aspects of Scottish and Irish Economic and Social History: 1600–1900*, edited by L. M. Cullen and T. C. Smout (Edinburgh: John Donald Publisher, Ltd., no date), p. 147.

188. S. G. E. Lythe and J. Butt, *An Economic History of Scotland 1100–1939* (Glasgow: Blackie and Son Ltd., 1975), p. 5.

189. Ibid., p. 4.

190. James G. Leyburn, *The Scotch-Irish*, p. 37.

191. Henry Thomas Buckle, *On Scotland and the Scotch Intellect*, p. 27n.

192. Ibid., p. 37.

193. S. G. E. Lythe and J. Butt, *An Economic History of Scotland 1100–1939*, p. 74.

194. Henry Thomas Buckle, *On Scotland and the Scotch Intellect*, p. 37.
195. Ibid., p. 44.
196. S. G. E. Lythe and J. Butt, *An Economic History of Scotland 1100–1939*, pp. 55–56.
197. Henry Thomas Buckle, *On Scotland and the Scotch Intellect*, p. 52.
198. T. C. Smout, *A History of the Scottish People, 1560–1830* (New York: Charles Scribner's Sons, 1969), pp. 24–32.
199. G. M. Trevelyan, *English Social History*, p. 463.
200. T. C. Smout, *A History of the Scottish People, 1560–1830*, p. 34.
201. James G. Leyburn, *The Scotch-Irish*, p. 13.
202. Henry Thomas Buckle, *On Scotland and the Scotch Intellect*, p. 36.
203. T. C. Smout, *A History of the Scottish People, 1560–1830*, p. 43.
204. Robin Frame, *The Political Development of the British Isles: 1100–1400* (Oxford: Oxford University Press, 1995), pp. 98, 103–104.
205. Ibid., p. 47.
206. Winston Churchill, *A History of the English-Speaking Peoples*, Vol. I, p. 223.
207. David Hackett Fischer, *Albion's Seed*, pp. 623–624.
208. Ibid., p. 626. See also Robin Frame, *The Political Development of the British Isles 1100–1400* (Oxford: Oxford University Press, 1995), pp. 14–15.
209. David Hackett Fischer, *Albion's Seed*, pp. 621–639, 650–651; Rory Fitzpatrick, *God's Frontiersmen*, pp. 67–87, 99–102, 169–188.
210. M. Perceval-Maxwell, *The Scottish Migration to Ulster in the Reign of James I* (London: Routledge and Kegan Paul, 1973), pp. 286–287.
211. James G. Leyburn, *The Scotch-Irish*, p. 13.
212. Ibid., p. 52.
213. S. G. E. Lythe and J. Butt, *An Economic History of Scotland 1100–1939*, p. 89.
214. Ibid., p. 90.
215. Henry Thomas Buckle, *On Scotland and the Scotch Intellect*, p. 151.
216. G. M. Trevelyan, *English Social History*, p. 475.
217. Bruce Lenman, *Integration, Enlightenment, and Industrialization: Scotalnd 1746–1832* (Toronto: University of Toronto Press, 1981), p. 2.
218. T. C. Smout, *A History of the Scottish People: 1560–1830*, pp.

332–351, 462–464; G. M. Trevelyan, *English Social History*, pp. 466–468; Bruce Lenman, "Scotland: From Nation to Province," *The Cambridge Historical Encyclopedia of Great Britain and Ireland*, edited by Christopher Haigh (Cambridge: Cambridge University Press, 1985), pp. 213–214. See also T. C. Smout, *A History of the Scottish People: 1830–1950* (New Haven: Yale University Press, 1986), p. 219.

219. Bruce Lenman, *Integration, Enlightenment, and Industrialization: Scotland 1746–1832*, p. 3.

220. Bruce Lenman, *Integration, Enlightenment, and Industrialization: Scotland 1746–1832*, p. 44. Most of the leading Scottish intellectuals—and others—spent most of their careers in England. "James Mill was one of the countless Scots who, having been trained at home in strict frugality and stern Puritanic principles, have fought their way to success in England." Sir Leslie Stephen, *The English Utilitarians*, Volume II: *James Mill* (New York: Augustus M. Kelley, 1968), p. 1. Educated Scots, including David Hume, sought to purge their speech of Scottish expressions. James Mill not only purged his speech of Scotticisms but also turned his back so completely on Scotland that his children grew up wholly ignorant of his past life there. See Michael St. John Packe, *The Life of John Stuart Mill* (New York: The Macmillan Company, 1954), p. 9; Alexander Bain, *James Mill: A Biography* (New York: August M. Kelly, 1967), pp. 32n, 110; John Stuart Mill, *The Earlier Letters of John Stuart Mill: 1812–1848* (Toronto: University of Toronto Press, 1963), p. 315.

221. Ned C. Landsman, *Scotland and Its First American Colony, 1683–1765* (Princeton: Princeton University Press, 1985), Chapter 3.

222. T. C. Smout, *A History of the Scottish People: 1560–1830*, p. 333.

223. G. M. Trevelyan, *English Social History*, p. 467. Gaelic also continued to be spoken in the nineteenth century by the descendants of the Highlanders who settled in North Carolina. Duane Meyer, *The Highland Scots of North Carolina, 1732–1776* (Chapel Hill: University of North Carolina Press, 1961), p. 119.

224. Olive and Sydney Checkland, *Industry and Ethos: Scotland 1832–1914* (Edinburgh: Edinburgh University Press, 1989), p. 165.

225. James G. Leyburn, *The Scotch-Irish*, p. 74.

226. Ibid., p. 76.

227. T. C., Smout, *A History of the Scottish People, 1560–1830*, p. 96. This picture of Scottish educational achievement has been challenged by R. A. Houston, *Scottish Literacy and Scottish Identity: Illiteracy and Society in Scotland and Northern England* (Cambridge: Cambridge University Press, 1985) but he has in turn been challenged by D. J. Withrington, "A Half-Educated Nation?" *Scottish Economic and Social History*, Vol. VI (1987), pp. 72–74. My own preference is to give far more weight to contemporary observers who had the facts before their eyes than to inferences drawn two centuries later from statistics with substantial inherent gaps and pitfalls, even if these statistics are handled both ingeniously and with integrity.

228. Henry Thomas Buckle, *On Scotland and the Scotch Intellect*, p. 154.

229. T. C. Smout, *A History of the Scottish People, 1560–1830*, p. 487.

230. William R. Brock, *Scotus Americanus: A Survey of the Sources for Links between Scotland and America in the Eighteenth Century* (Edinburgh: Edinburgh University Press, 1982), pp. 114–115; Esmond Wright, "Education in American Colonies," *Essays in Scotch-Irish History*, edited by E. R. R. Green (London: Routledge & Kegan Paul, 1969), pp. 40–41.

231. Bruce Lenman, *Integration, Enlightenment, and Industrialization: Scotland 1746-1832* (Toronto: University of Toronto Press, 1981), p. 91.

232. William R. Brock, *Scotus Americanus*, p. 115.

233. Ibid., pp. 119–120.

234. Kenneth Macleod, "Scots in Russia in the Seventeenth and Eighteenth Centuries," *Journal of Russian Studies*, Vol. 46 (1983), pp. 8–9.

235. One exception was the Earl of Lauderdale, who created some interesting controversy in economics, but he was hardly a figure to rank with the leading economists of his day, much less to be considered important a century later. T. C. Smout, *A History of the Scottish People, 1560–1830*, pp. 501–504.

236. Ibid., pp. 504–505. See also *Scotland in the Age of Improvement*

237. T. C. Smoout, *Scotland and the Scottish People: 1560–1830*, p. 501.

238. Ibid., 485.

239. Ibid., p. 143.

240. Ibid., pp. 452, 461–462, 466.

241. Ibid., p. 270.

242. See ibid., pp. 290–291, 333, 344. See also Bruce Lenman, *Integration, Enlightenment, and Industrialization: Scotland 1746–1832* (Toronto: University of Toronto Press, 1981), p. 44.

243. Michael Hecter, *Internal Colonialism: The Celtic Fringe in British National Development, 1536–1966* (Berkeley: University of California Press, 1976), pp. 115–116; Eric Richards, "Scotland and the Uses of the Uses of the Atlantic Empire," *Strangers within the Realm*, edited by Bernard Bailyn and Philip D. Morgan (Chapel Hill: University of North Carolina Press, 1991), pp. 85–86.

244. T. C. Smout, *A History of the Scottish People: 1560–1830*, p. 367. See also Grady McWhiney, *Cracker Culture: Celtic Ways in the Old South* (Tuscaloosa: University of Alabama Press, 1988), p. 231. G. M. Trevelyan, *English Social History: A Survey of Six Centuries* (New York: Viking Penguin, Inc., 1986), p. 451.

245. Rosalind Mitchison, "Scotland 1750–1850," *The Cambridge Social History of Britain 1750–1950*, Vol. 1, p. 177.

246. Rosalind Mitchison, "Scotland 1750–1850." *The Cambridge Social History of Britain*, Vol. 1, p. 160

247. M. J. Daunton, "Housing," *The Cambridge Social History of Britain*, Vol. 2: *People and Their Environment*, edited by F. M. L. Thompson (Cambridge: Cambridge University Press, 1993), p. 206.

248. T. C. Smout, "Scotland 1850–1950," *The Cambridge Social History of Britain 1750–1850*, Vol. 1, pp. 211–212, 217, 225, 244.

249. Michael Hecter, *Internal Colonialism: The Celtic Fringe in British National Development, 1536–1966* (Berkeley: University of California Press, 1975), p. 142n. See also Eric Richards, "Scotland and the Uses of the Atlantic Empire," *Strangers within the Realm*, edited by Bernard Bailyn and Philip D. Morgan (Chapel Hill: University of North Carolina Press, 1991), p. 86.

250. Eric Richards, "Scotland and the Uses of the Atlantic Empire," *Strangers within the Realm*, edited by Bernard Bailyn and Philip D. Morgan, p. 98.

251. T. C. Smout, "Scotland 1850–1950," *The Cambridge Social History of Britain 1750–1850*, Vol. 1, p. 278.

252. Rosalind Mitchison, "Scotland 1750–1850," *The Cambridge Social History of Great Britain 1750–1850*, Vol. 1, p. 169.

253. T. C. Smout, "Scotland 1850–1950," *The Cambridge Social History of Britain 1750–1950*, Vol. 1, pp. 274–275.

254. *Scotland in the Age of Improvement*

255. Olive and Sydney Checkland, *Industry and Ethos: Scotland 1832–1914*, 2nd edition (Edinburgh: Edinburgh University Press, 1989), p. 15.

256. Ibid., Chapter 1.

257. Ibid., p. 20.

258. Ibid., p. 22.

259. Ibid., p. 23.

260. Ibid., p. 148.

261. Ibid., p. 147.

262. This continued to be true, well into the twentieth century. "At Oxford and Cambridge the majority of students—89 percent and 70 percent respectively—were in the arts faculties; and only in London, Manchester, Leeds and Edinburgh did science dominate." Gillian Sutherland, "Education," *The Cambridge Social History of Britain 1750–1950*, edited by F. M. L. Thompson (Cambridge: Cambridge University Press, 1993), Vol. 3, p. 167.

263. Ibid., p. 149.

264. G. M. Trevelyan, *English Social History*, p. 463.

265. Malcolm Gray, "Scottish Emigration: The Social Impact of Agrarian Change in the Rural Lowlands, 1775–1875," *Perspectives in American History*, Vol. VII (1973), pp. 112–157.

266. Ibid., p. 95.

267. M. Perceval-Maxwell, *The Scottish Migraiton to Ulster in the Reign of James I* (London: Routledge & Kegan Paul, 1973), p. 111.

268. James G. Leyburn, *The Scotch-Irish*, pp. 63, 72, 76–78, 96–97.

269. John Wacher, *The Coming of Rome*, p. 6.

270. Maire and Conor Cruise O'Brien, *A Concise History of Ireland* (New York: Beckman House, 1972), p. 47.

271. Patrick J. Blessing, "Irish," *Harvard Encyclopedia of American Ethnic Groups*, edited by Stephan Thernstrom, et al., p. 525.

272. James G. Leyburn, *The Scotch-Irish*, p. 125.

273. Arthur Young, *A Tour in Ireland: 1776–1779* (Shannon: Irish University Press, 1970), Vol. II, p. 54.

274. Ibid., Vol. I, p. 83.

275. Oliver MacDonagh, "The Irish Famine Emigration to the United States," *Perspectives in American History*, Vol. X (1976), p. 366; Eugene D. Genovese, *Roll, Jordan Roll: The World the Slaves Made* (New York: Pantheon Books, 1974), pp. 524–525; Robert W. Fogel and Stanley L. Engerman, *Time on the Cross: The Economics*

of American Negro Slavery (Boston: Little, Brown and Co., 1974), p. 125.

276. Carl Wittke, *We Who Built America* (Cleveland: Case Western Reserve University Press, 1967), p. 129.

277. Oliver MacDonagh, "The Irish Famine Emigration to the United States," *Perspectives in American History*, Vol. X (1976), p. 405.

278. W. E. Vaughan and A. J. Fitzpatrick, editors, *Irish Historical Statistics* (Dublin: Royal Irish Academy, 1978), pp. 260–261.

279. Oliver MacDonagh, "The Irish Famine Emigration to the United States," *Perspectives in American History*, Vol. X (1976), pp. 402–403.

280. Carl Wittke, *We Who Built America*, p. 134; Oscar Handlin, *Boston's Immigrants* (New York: Atheneum, 1970), Chapter IV; Diane Ravitch, *The Great School Wars* (New York: Basic Books, 1974), pp. 27–28; Maldwyn Allen Jones, *American Immigration* (Chicago: University of Chicago Press, 1970), p. 130.

281. Robert E. Kennedy, Jr., *The Irish*, p. 27.

282. W. E. Vaughan and A. J. Fitzpatrick, editors, *Irish Historical Statistics*, p. 3.

283. *The World Almanac and Book of Facts, 1981* (New York: Newspaper Enterprise Association, 1981), pp. 547, 589; U.S. Bureau of the Census, *Current Population Reports*, Series P–20, No. 249, *Characteristics of the Population by Ethnic Origin: March 1972 and 1971* (Washington: U.S. Government Printing Office, 1972), p. 11.

284. Michael Hecter, *Internal Colonialism: The Celtic Fringe in British National Development, 1536–1966* (Berkeley: University of California Press, 1976), p. 196.

285. Michael Hecter, *Internal Colonialism*, p. 184.

286. Michael Hecter, *Internal Colonialism*, pp. 92–93.

287. L. M. Cullen, "Merchant Communities Overseas, the Navigation Acts and Irish and Scottish Responses," *Comparative Aspects of Scottish and Irish Economic and Social History*, edited by L. M. Cullen and T. C. Smout (Edinburgh: John Donald Publisher, Ltd., no date), p. 174.

288. L. M. Cullen and T. C. Smout, "Economic Growth in Scotland and Ireland," *Comparative Aspects of Scottish and Irish Economic and Social History*, edited by L. M. Cullen and T. C. Smout (Edinburgh: John Donald Publishers, Ltd., no date), pp. 3, 12–13.

289. "Ireland: Packed and Gone," *The Economist*, September 9, 1989, p. 58.

290. Paul Compton, "The Conflict in Northern Ireland: Demographic and Economic Considerations," *Economic Dimensions of Ethnic Conflicts: International Perspectives*, edited by S. W. R. de A. Smaarrasomghe and Reed Coughlan (London: Pinter Publishers, 1991), pp. 35–39, 41.

291. Frederick Engels, *The Condition of the Working Class in England in 1844* (London: George Allen and Unwin, Ltd., 1952), p. 79; Oscar Handlin, *Boston's Immigrants*, p. 114.

292. Andrew M. Greeley, *The Most Distressful Nation: The Taming of the American Irish* (Chicago: Quadrangle Books, 1972) pp. 129–143, 226; Patrick O'Farrell, *The Irish in Australia* (Kensington, NSW, Australia: New South Wales University Press, 1987), pp. 164–171; Lyn Hollen Lees, *Exiles of Erin: Irish Migrants in Victorian London* (Ithaca: Cornell University Press, 1979), pp. 197, 207–211.

293. *Philadelphia: Work, Space, Family, and Group Experience in the 19th Century*, edited by Theodore Hershberg (Oxford: Oxford University Press, 1981), pp. 363–365.

294. D. Fitzpatrick, "Irish Immigration 1840–1914," *The Australian People: An Encyclopedia of the Nation, Its People and Their Origin*, edited by James Jupp (North Ryde, Australia: Angus and Robertson Publishers, 1988), p. 562.

295. Ibid., p. 561.

296. P. Hamilton, "Irish Women Immigrants in the Nineteenth Century," ibid., p. 568.

297. Patrick McKenna, "Irish Migration to Argentina," *Patterns of Migration*, edited by Patrick O'Sullivan (Leicester: Leicester University Press, 1992), p. 73.

298. Ibid., pp. 73–76.

299. Ibid., pp. 77–80.

300. Ibid., p. 78.

301. Ibid., p. 80.

302. Patrick J. Blessing, "Irish," *Harvard Encyclopedia of American Ethnic Groups*, edited by Stephan Thernstrom, et al., p. 538.

303. Carl Wittke, *The Irish in America* (New York: Russell and Russell, 1970), pp. 103–113; Nathan Glazer and D.P. Moynihan, *Beyond the Melting Pot* (Cambridge, Massachusetts: M.I.T. Press, 1966), pp. 221–229.

304. P. Lee, "Irish in Australian Politics," *The Australian People*, edited by James Jupp et al., p. 589.

305. Ibid., p. 588.
306. "Welsh," *The Australian People: An Encyclopedia of the Nation, Its People and their Origins*, edited by James Jupp (North Ryde, N.S.W.: Angus Publications, 1988), p. 841.
307. Ibid., p. 840.
308. John Baur, "The Welsh in Patagonia: An Example of Nationalistic Migration," *Hispanic American Historical Review*, November 1954, pp. 468–492.
309. E. J. Wilhelm, Jr., "The Welsh in Argentina," *The Geographical Review*, January 1968, p. 137.
310. Rowland Berthoff, "Welsh," *Harvard Encyclopedia of American Ethnic Groups*, edited by Stephan Thernstrom, et al. (Cambridge, Massachusetts: Harvard University Press, 1981), pp. 1014, 1015–1016.
311. See Alan Conway, "Welsh Emigration to the United States," *Perspectives in American History*, Vol. VII (1973), pp. 180–181, 185–186.
312. Rowland Berthoff, "Welsh," *Harvard Encyclopedia of American Ethnic Groups*, edited by Stephan Thernstrom, et al. (Cambridge, Massachusetts: Harvard University Press, 1980), p. 1012.
313. Ibid., pp. 840–845.
314. Maldwyn A. Jones, "Ulster Emigration, 1783–1815," *Essays in Scotch-Irish History*, edited by E. R. R. Green (London: Routledge & Kegan Paul, 1969), p. 49.
315. Duane Meyer, *The Highland Scots of North Carolina, 1732–1776* (Chapel Hill: University of North Carolina Press, 1961), p. 118.
316. Ibid., p. 119.
317. David Hackett Fischer, *Albion's Seed*, p. 621. See also p. 818.
318. Eric Richards, "Highland and Gaelic Immigrants," *The Australian People*, edited by James Jupp (North Ryde, NSW, Australia: Angus & Robertson, 1988), pp. 765–769.
319. Eric Richards, "Australia and the Scottish Connection 1788–1914," *The Scots Abroad*, edited by R. A. Cage, p. 122.
320. M. D. Prentis, "Scots," ibid., p. 784.
321. M. D. Prentis, "Lowland Scottish Immigrants until 1860," *The Australian People*, edited by James Jupp, p. 762.
322. Eric Richards, "Highland and Gaelic Immigrants," ibid., p. 766.
323. D. Lucs, "Scottish Immigration," *The Australian People*, edited by James Jupp, p. 780.
324. Eric Richards, "Highland and Gaelic Immigrants," *The Australian People*, edited by James Jupp, p. 764.

325. Gordon Donaldson, "Scots," *Harvard Encyclopedia of American Ethnic Groups*, edited by Stephan Thernstrom, et al., p. 915.

326. Gordon Donaldson, *The Scots Overseas*, p. 104.

327. Ibid., pp. 114–116.

328. U.S. Bureau of the Census, Current Population Reports, Series P–23, no. 116 *Ancestry and Language in the United States: November 1979* (Washington: U.S. Government Printing Office, 1982), pp. 12, 13.

329. Gordon Donaldson, *The Scots Overseas*, p. 109.

330. Ibid., p. 123.

331. Eric Richards, "Australia and the Scottish Connection 1788–1914," *The Scots Abroad: Labour, Capital, Enterprise, 1750–1914*, edited by R. A, Gage (London: Croom Helm, Ltd., 1985), p, 112.

332. Eric Richards, "Highland and Gaelic Immigrants," *The Australian People*, edited by James Jupp, p. 765.

333. Eric Richards, "Australia and the Scottish Connection 1788–1914," *The Scots Abroad*, pp. 115–116.

334. G. J. Bryant, "Scots in India in the Eighteenth Century," *The Scottish Historical Review*, April 1985, p. 23.

335. Ibid., p. 69.

336. Ibid., p. 73.

337. Kenneth Macleod, "Scots in Russia in the Seventeenth and Eighteenth Centuries," *Journal of Russian Studies*, Vol. 46 (1983), p. 9–10.

338. Ibid., pp. 3, 5, 7.

339. T. H. A. Fisher, *The Scots in Germany: Being a Contribution toward the History of the Scot Abroad* (Edinburgh: John Donald Publishers, Ltd., 1902), p. 129–130.

340. Manuel A. Fernandez, "The Scots in Latin America: A Survey," *The Scots Abroad: Labour, Capital, Enterprise, 1750–1914*, edited by R.A. Cage (London: Croom Helm, 1985), p. 225.

341. Ibid., p. 226.

342. R.H. Campbell, "Scotland," *The Scots Abroad: Labour, Capital, Enterprise, 1750–1914*, edited by R. A. Cage (London: Croom Helm, 1985), p. 19.

343. Ibid., pp. 21, 22.

344. David S. McMillan, "Scottish Enterprise and Influence in Canada, 1620–1920," *The Scots Abroad*, edited by R. A. Cage, p. 57.

345. Ibid., p. 62.

346. Eric Richards, "Australia and the Scottish Connection 1788–1914," *The Scots Abroad*, edited by R. A. Cage, pp. 147–148.

347. James G. Parker, "Scottish Enterprise in India, 1750–1914," *The Scots Abroad*, edited by R. A. Cage, p. 208.

348. Olive Checkland, "The Scots in Meiji Japan," *The Scots Abroad*, edited by R. A. Cage, p. 259.

349. Ibid., pp. 267, 268.

350. David S. Macmillan, "The Neglected Aspect of the Scottish Diaspora 1650–1850: The Role of the Entrepreneurs in Promoting and Effecting Emigration," *The Diaspora of the British*, Collected Seminar Papers No. 31 (London: University of London Institute of Commonwealth Studies, 1982), pp. 28–29.

351. Manuel A. Fernandez, "The Scots in Latin America: A Survey," *The Scots Abroad*, edited by R. A. Cage, p. 243.

352. T. H. A. Fischer, *The Scots in Germany*, p. 216.

353. Robert P. Bartlett, *Human Capital: The Settlement of Foreigners in Russia 1762–1804* (Cambridge: Cambridge University Press, 1979), p. 144.

354. T. H. A. Fischer, *The Scots in Germany*, p. 32n.

355. Ibid., pp. 32–33.

356. Ibid., p. 34.

357. Ibid., pp. 35–36.

358. Ibid., pp. 38–39, 55.

359. Ibid., p. 35.

360. Ibid., p. 61.

361. Ibid., pp. 58–59.

362. Gordon Donaldson, *The Scots Overseas* (Westport, CT: Greenwood Press, 1976), pp. 108–109.

363. James G. Leyburn, *The Scotch-Irish: A Social History* (Chapel Hill: University of North Carolina Press, 1962), p. 139. In 1556, the Irish parliament passed a law forbidding marriage between the Scots and the Irish. M. Perceval-Maxwell, *The Scottish Migraiton to Ulster in the Reign of James I* (London: Routledge & Kegan Paul, 1973), p. 4. At this period, and for centuries thereafter, religious differences alone would have been enough to discourage intermarriage, quite aside from other differences. See also Esmond Wright, "Education in the American Colonies: The Impact of Scotland," *Essays in Scotch-Irish*, edited by E. R. R. Green (London: Routledge & Kegan Paul, 1969), pp. 19–20.

364. David Hackett Fischer, *Albion's Seed*, p. 445.

365. Ibid., p. 621.

366. Grady McWhiney, *Cracker Culture: Celtic Ways in the Old South* (Tuscaloosa: University of Alabama Press, 1988), pp. 55–56.

367. M. Perceval-Maxwell, *The Scottish Migration to Ulster in the Reign of James I* (London: Routledge & Kegan Paul, 1973), p. 24.

368. David Hackett Fischer, *Albion's Seed*, pp. 623–624.

369. Ibid., p. 629.

370. Grady McWhiney, *Cracker Culture: Celtic Ways in the Old South* (Tuscaloosa: University of Alabama Press, 1988), pp. xiv–xix; David Hackett Fischer, *Albion's Seed*, pp. 756–758.

371. David Hackett Fischer, *Albion's Seed*, p. 630.

372. Ibid., p. 606.

373. Ibid., pp. 766–767.

374. George Shepperson, "Scotland: The World Perspective," *The Diaspora of the British*, Collected Seminar Papers No. 31, Institute of Commonwealth Studies (London: University of London, 1982), p. 52n.

375. James G. Leyburn, *The Scotch-Irish: A Social History* (Chapel Hill: University of North Carolina Press, 1962), p. 192

376. Rory Fitzpatrick, *God's Frontiersmen: The Scots-Irish Epic* (London: Weidenfeld and Nicolson, 1989), p. 232.

377. David Hackett Fischer, *Albion's Seed*, p. 620.

378. Ibid., p. 152.

379. Ibid, p. 615.

380. Ibid, pp. 642–650. See also Rory Fitzpatrick, pp. 124–144.

381. David Hacket Fischer, *Albion's Seed*, p. 647.

382. Ibid, p. 765.

383. Ibid, pp. 605–606, 613–615, 618–621.

384. Grady McWhiney, *Cracker Culture, passim.*; David Hackett Fischer, pp. 605–782.

385. Arthur M. Schlesinger [Sr.], *Nothing Stands Still: Essays by Arthur M. Schlesinger* (Cambridge, Massachusetts: Harvard University Press, 1969), p. 125.

386. Frederick Law Olmsted, *The Cotton Kingdom* (New York: Modern Library, 1969), p. 305

387. Alexis de Tocqueville, *Democracy in America* (New York: Alfred A. Knopf, 1966), Vol. I, pp. 363–364.

388. Grady McWhiney, *Cracker Culture*, p. 149; David Hacket Fischer, *Albion's Seed*, p. 722.

389. David Hackett Fischer, *Albion's Seed*, pp. 31–34.

390. Esmond Wright, "Education in the American Colonies: The Impact of Scotland," *Essays in Scotch-Irish History* (London: Routledge & Kegan Paul, 1969), p. 25.

391. Ibid., pp. 49, 133–134.

392. Ibid., pp. 90–91.

393. Ibid., pp. 240–246.

394. Ibid., pp. 256–264. Surviving uses of the term "chitterlings" for hog entrails remained highly localized in twentieth-century England. See David Crystal, *The Cambridge Encyclopedia of the English Language* (Cambridge: Cambridge University Press, 1996), p. 319.

395. David Hackett Fisher, *Albion's Seed*, pp. 134–139, 349–354.

396. Ibid., pp. 347–348.

397. Ibid., pp. 89, 298–299.

398. Ibid, pp. 194, 304.

399. Ibid., pp. 303–304.

400. Ibid., pp. 62–68, 151–158, 264–274, 343, 365–368, 374–382; Grady McWhiney, *Cracker Culture: Celtic Ways in the Old South* (Tuscaloosa: University of Alabama Press, 1988), pp. 74, 133–135, 253–258.

401. Ibid., p. 307.

402. Ibid., p. 684.

403. William H. Harris and Judith S. Levey, editors, *The New Columbia Encyclopedia* (New York: Columbia University Press, 1975), p. 370.

404. L. C. A. Knowles, *The Industrial and Commercial Revolutions in Britain during the Nineteenth Century*, p. 328.

405. Lance E. Davis and Robert A. Huttenback, *Mammon and the Pursuit of Empire: The Political Economy of British Imperialism, 1860–1912* (Cambridge: Cambridge University Press, 1987), p. 28.

406. Peter Mathias, *The First Industrial Nation*, p. 88.

407. Maurice Ashley, *The People of England*, p. 128.

408. Peter Mathias, *The First Industrial Nation*, p. 300.

409. Aaron L. Friedberg, *The Weary Titan: Britain and the Experience of Relative Decline, 1895–1905* (Princeton: Princeton University Press, 1988), p. 153.

410. Ibid., p. 138

411. L. H. Gann and Peter Duignan, "Reflections on Imperialism and the Scramble for Africa," *Colonialism in Africa, 1870–1960*, edited by L. H. Gann and Peter Duignan, Vol. I: *The History and Politics of Colonialism, 1870–1914* (Cambridge: Cambridge University Press, 1981), pp. 119–121, Charles Pelham Groves, "Missionary and Humanitarian Aspects of Imperialism from 1870 to 1914," ibid., p. 462–496.

412. See, for example, Standish Meacham, *Henry Thornton of Clapham: 1760–1815* (Cambridge, Massachusetts: Harvard University Press, 1964), Chapters V, VI, VII.

413. Lance E. Davis and Robert A. Huttenback, *Mammon and the Pursuit of Empire*, p. 300.

414. Ibid., p. 160.

415. T. C. Smout, *A History of the Scottish People, 1560–1830*, p. 113; L. H. Gann and Peter Duignan, *Burden of Empire: An Appraisal of Western Colonialism in Africa South of the Sahara* (Stanford: Hoover Institution Press, 1967), p. 248.

416. "The New English Empire," *The Economist*, December 20, 1986, p. 127.

417. W. A. Armstrong, "The Countryside," *The Cambridge Social History of Britain 1750–1950*, Vol. 2, p. 123

418. Lance E. Davis and Robert A. Huttenback, *Mammon and the Pursuit of Empire*, p. 14.

419. Letter of May 18, 1795, *The Correspondence of Edmund Burke*, edited by R. B. McDowell (Cambridge: Cambridge University Press, 1969), Volume VIII, pp. 246–247.

420. Lance E. Davis and Robert A. Huttenback, *Mammon and the Pursuit of Empire*, p. 42.

421. David Spring, "Landed Elites Compared," *European Landed Elites in the nineteenth Century*, edited by David Spring (Baltimore: Johns Hopkins University Press, 1977), pp. 13–17.

422. G. M. Trevelyan, *The English Revolution: 1688–1689* (Oxford: Oxford University Press, 1965), p. 89.

423. Ibid., p. 10.

424. Kathleen Mary Butler, *The Economics of Emancipation: Jamaica & Barbados, 1823–1843* (Chapel Hill: University of North Carolina Press, 1995), p. xxvi.

425. Suzanne Miers, *Britain and the Ending of the Slave Trade* (New York: Africana Publishing Co., 1975), p. 9.

426. Robert Conrad, *The Destruction of Brazilian Slavery: 1850–1888* (Berkeley: University of California Press, 1972), p. 23.

427. William Gervase Clarence-Smith, "The Economics of the Indian Ocean and Red Sea Slave Trade in the 19th Century: An Overview," *The Economics of the Indian Ocean Slave Trade in the Nineteenth Century*, edited by William Gervase Clarence-Smith, pp. 1; Marina Carter and Hubert Gerbeau, "Covert Slaves and Coveted Coolies in the Early 19th Century Mascareignes," ibid., pp. 202–203.

428. A. G. Hopkins, *An Economic History of West Africa* (New York: Columbia University Press, 1973), pp. 112–113.

429. Ehud R. Toledano, *The Ottoman Slave Trade and Its Suppression: 1840–1890*, p. 136.

430. Ibid., pp. 135–141.

431. Ibid., p. 127.

432. Ibid., pp. 132–133.

433. Indeed, Churchill himself had grave doubts, expressed privately after his being invested as Prime Minister: "Thompson congratulated him and wished him well in his enormous task. As Churchill replied, tears came into his eyes: 'God alone knows how great it is. I hope that it is not too late. I am very much afraid that it is. We can only do our best.'" Robert Shepherd, *A Class Divided: Appeasement and the Road to Munich, 1938* (London: Macmillan London, Ltd., 1988), p. 294.

434. "Their Finest Hour," June 18, 1940, *Churchill Speaks: Winston S. Churchill in Peace and War, Collected Speeches, 1897–1963* (New York: Chelsea House, 1980), p. 720.

435. Edwin O. Reischauer, *The Japanese*, p. 8.

CHAPTER 3: THE AFRICANS

1. Fernand Braudel, *A History of Civilizations*, translated by Richard Mayne (New York: The Penguin Group, 1994), p. 120.

2. John Thornton, *Africa and Africans in the Making of the Atlantic World, 1400–1680* (Cambridge: Cambridge University Press, 1995), pp. 15–16.

3. Janet L. Abu-Lughod, *Before European Hegemony: The World System A.D. 1250–1350* (New York: Oxford University Press, 1989), p. 36.

4. Fernand Braudel, *A History of Civilizations*, p. 124. Likewise, a geographer said: "Enlightenment filtering in here was sadly dimmed as it spread." Ellen Churchill Semple, *Influences of Geographic Environments* (New York: Henry Holt and Co., 1947), p. 392.

5. H. J. de Blij and Peter O. Muller, *Geography: Regions and Concepts* (New York: John Wiley & Sons, Inc., 1992), p. 394.

6. Jocelyn Murray, editor, *Cultural Atlas of Africa* (New York: Facts on File Publications, 1981), p. 70.

7. Ibid., p. 10.

8. William A. Hance, *The Geography of Modern Africa* (New York: Columbia University Press, 1964), p. 4.

9. Margaret Sedeen, editor, *Great Rivers of the World* (Washington: National Geographic Society, 1984), p. 24. See also P. T. Bauer, *West African Trade: A Study of Competition, Oligopoly and Monopoly in a Changing Economy* (Cambridge: Cambridge University Press, 1954), p. 14.

10. Edward A. Alpers, *Ivory and Slaves: Changing Pattern of International Trade in East Central Africa to the Later Nineteenth Century* (Berkeley: University of California Press, 1975), p. 5.

11. Margaret Sedeen, editor, *Great Rivers of the World*, pp. 69–70; Daniel R. Headrick, *The Tools of Empire: Technology and European Imperialism in the Nineteenth Century* (New York: Oxford University Press, 1981), p. 196.

12. See, for example, the map of Africa's navigable rivers in L. Dudley Stamp, *Africa: A Study in Tropical Development* (New York: John Wiley & Sons, 1964), p. 182.

13. J. F. Ade Ajayi and Michael Crowder, editors, *Historical Atlas of Africa* (Essex: Longman Group Ltd., 1985), map facing Section 1.

14. Jocelyn Murray, editor, *Cultural Atlas of Africa*, p. 73.

15. Roy E. H. Mellor and E. Alistair Smith, *Europe: A Geographical Survey of the Continent* (New York: Columbia University Press, 1979), p. 3.

16. Georg Gerster, "River of Sorrow, River of Hope," *National Geographic*, Vol. 148, No. 2 (August 1975), p. 162.

17. R. J. Harrison Church, *West Africa: A Study of the Environment and of Man's Use of It* (London: Longman Group, Ltd., 1974), pp. 16–18.

18. Georg Gerster, "River of Sorrow, River of Hope," *National Geographic*, Vol. 148, No. 2 (August 1975), p. 154.

19. J. M. Prichard, *Landform and Landscape in Africa* (London: Edward Arnold, Ltd., 1979), p. 46.

20. Daniel R. Headrick, *The Tools of Empire: Technology and European Imperialism in the Nineteenth Century* (New York: Oxford University Press, 1981), p. 74.

21. F. J. Pedler, *Economic Geography of West Africa* (London: Longman, Green and Co., 1955), p. 118.

22. See, for example, J. M. Pritchard, *Landform and Landscape in Africa*, pp. 46–47.

23. Virginia Thompson and Richard Adloff, *French West Africa* (Stanford: Stanford University Press, 1957), p. 292.

24. Ibid., p. 21.

25. William A. Hance, *The Geography of Modern Africa*, p. 33.

26. Kathleen Baker, "The Changing Geography of West Africa," *The Changing Geography of Africa and the Middle East*, edited by Graham P. Chapman and Kathleen M. Baker (London: Routledge, 1992), p.105.

27. Ibid., p. 499.

28. Virginia Thompson and Richard Adloff, *French West Africa*, p. 305.

29. Edwin O. Reischauer and John Fairbank, *A History of East Asian Civilization*, Volume I, pp. 20–21.

30. Ellen Churchill Semple, *Influences of Geographical Environment* (New York: Henry Holt and Co., 1947), p. 260.

31. H. J. de Blij and Peter O. Mueller, *Geography: Regions and Concepts* (New York: John Wiley & Sons, Inc.), p. 399. See also J. M. Pritchard, *Landform and Landscape in Africa* (London: Edward Arnold, Ltd., 1979), p. 14.

32. H. J. de Blij, *Physical Geography of the Global Environment* (New York: John Wiley & Sons, Inc., 1993), p. 399.

33. J. M. Pritchard, *Landform and Landscape in Africa*, p. 7.

34. Ellen Churchill Semple, *Influences of Geographic Environments* (New York: Henry Holt and Co., 1947), p. 341.

35. John Thorton, *Africa and Africans in the Making of the Atlantic World, 1400–1680* (Cambridge: Cambridge University Press, 1995), p. 18.

36. Lewis H. Gann and Peter Duignan, *Africa and the World: An Introduction to the History of Sub-Saharan Africa from Antiquity to 1840* (San Francisco: Chandler Publishing Company, 1972), pp. 24, 26.

37. Eric Thorbecke, "Causes of African Development Stagnation; Policy Diagnosis and policy Recommendations for a Long-Term Development Strategy," *Whither African Economies?* edited by Jean-Claude Berthélemy (Paris: Organisation for Economic Co-Operation and Development), p. 122.

38. John Thornton, *Africa and Africans in the Making of the Atlantic World, 1400–1680*, p. 19.

39. Ray H. Whitbeck and Olive J. Thomas, *The Geographic Factor: Its Role in Life and Civilization* (Port Washington, N.Y.: Kennikat Press, 1970), p. 167.

40. L. Dudley Stamp, *Africa*, p. 5.

41. William A. Hance, *The Geography of Modern Africa*, p. 4.

42. Georg Gerster, "River of Sorrow, River of Hope," *National Geographic*, Vol. 148, No. 2 (August 1975), p. 162.

43. J. F. Ade Ajayi and Michael Crowder, editors, *Historical Atlas of Africa*, Section 2.

44. Jocelyn Murray, editor, *Cultural Atlas of Africa*, p. 13.

45. Jeffrey Sachs, "Nature, Nurture and Growth," *The Economics*, June 14, 1997, pp. 19, 22.

46. William A. Hance, *The Geography of Modern Africa* (New York: Columbia University Press, 1964), p. 15.

47. Elizabeth Colson, "African Society at the Time of the Scramble," *Colonialism in Africa 1870–1960*, Volume I: *The History and Politics of Colonialism 1870–1914*, edited by L.H. Gann and Peter Duignan (Cambridge: Cambridge University Press, 1981), p. 41.

48. William A. Hance, *The Geography of Modern Africa*, pp. 4–5.

49. Computed from *The World Almanac and Book of Facts: 1992* (New York: Pharos Book, 1991), pp. 789, 806, 815. Some of the problems with official Tanzanian statistics are discussed in Alexander H. Sarris, "Experiences and Lessons from Research in Tanzania," *Whither African Economies?* edited by Jean-Claude Berthéllemy (Paris: Organisation for Economic Co-Operation and Development, 1995), pp. 99–110.

50. H. J. de Blij and Peter O. Muller, *Geography*, pp. 589–592.

51. J. F. Ade Ajayi and Michael Crowder, editors, *Historical Atlas of Africa*, Section I.

52. John Thornton, *Africa and Africans in the Making of the Atlantic World, 1400–1680*, pp. 104–105.

53. Edward A. Alpers, *Ivory and Slaves*, pp. 2–4.

54. See, for example, A. Sheriff, "Localisation and Social Composition of the East African Slave Trade, 1858–1873," *The Economics of the Indian Ocean Slave Trade*, edited by William Gervase Clarence-Smith, pp. 133–134, 142, 144; Francois Renault, "The Structures of the Slave Trade in Central Africa in the 19th Century," ibid., pp. 146–165; Edward A. Alpers, *Ivory and Slaves*, p. 242.

55. Francois Renault, "The Structures of the Slave Trade in Central Africa in the 19th Century," ibid., p. 148; Edward A. Alpers, *Ivory and Slaves*, pp. 191–193.

56. See, for example, Thomas Sowell, *Race and Culture: A World View* (New York: Basic Books, 1994), Chapter 7.

57. Adam Smith, *An Inquiry into the Nature and Causes of the Wealth of Nations* (New York: The Modern Library, 1937), p. 365.

58. Orlando Patterson, *Slavery and Social Death*, p. 159; Murray Gordon, *Slavery in the Arab World* (New York: New Amsterdam Books, 1989), pp. x–xi; J. O. Hunwick, "Black Slaves in the Mediterranean World: Introduction to a Neglected Aspect of the African

Diaspora," *The Human Commodity*, edited by Elizabeth Savage, p. 12; Eva Hoffman and Margot Slade, "Where Labor and Life Are Cheap," *New York Times*, August 30, 1981, Section 4, p. E 7; Bernard D. Nossiter, "U.N. Gets a Report on African Slaves," *New York Times*, August 26, 1981, p. A 11.

59. David Eltis, "Europeans and the Rise and Fall of African Slavery in the Americas: An Interpretation," *American Historical Review*, December 1993, p. 1400.

60. Martin A. Klein, "The Slave Trade in the Western Sudan during the Nineteenth Century," *The Human Commodity*, edited by Elizabeth Savage, pp. 41, 48; Janet J. Ewald, "The Nile Valley System and the Red Sea Slave Trade 1820–1880," *The Economics of the Indian Ocean Slave Trade in the Nineteenth Century*, edited by William Gervase Clarence-Smith, p. 85; Murray Gordon, *Slavery in the Arab World*, pp. 50–53.

61. Martin A. Klein, "The Slave Trade in the Western Sudan during the Nineteenth Century," *The Human Commodity*, edited by Elizabeth Savage, pp. 41, 48; Beverly B. Mack, "Women and Slavery in Nineteenth-Century Hausaland," ibid, p. 102.

62. François Renault, "The Structures of the Slave Trade in Central Africa in the 19th Century," *The Economics of the Indian Ocean Slave Trade*, edited by William Gervase Clarence-Smith, pp. 156, 157.

63. Martin A. Klein, "The Slave Trade in the Western Sudan during the Nineteenth Century," *The Human Commodity*, edited by Elizabeth Savage, pp. 50, 51; E. Ann McDougall, "Salt, Saharans, and the Trans-Saharan Slave Trade: Nineteenth Century Development," ibid., p. 61; Beverly B. Mack, "Women and Slavery in Nineteenth-Century Hausaland," ibid, p. 97.

64. Martin A. Klein, "The Slave Trade in the Western Sudan during the Nineteenth Century," *The Human Commodity*, edited by Elizabeth Savage, p. 38; Beverly B. Mack, "Women and Slavery in Nineteenth-Century Hausaland," ibid., pp. 101, 104. However, slaves were often taken from their immediate locality to reduce the dangers of escape.

65. Patrick Manning, "Contours of Slavery and Social Change in Africa," *American Historical Review*, October 1983, pp. 840, 845.

66. Eric R. Wolf, *Europe and the People Without History* (Berkeley: University of California Press, 1981), p. 204.

67. Ibid., p. 849. See also Edward A. Alpers, *Ivory and Slaves*, pp. 242–243.

68. Patrick Manning, "Contours of Slavery and Social Change in Africa," *American Historical Review*, October 1983, p. 854.

69. Ibid., p. 852.

70. Ibid., p. 844.

71. Ibid., p. 847

72. Ibid., p. 839.

73. Paul E. Lovejoy and Jan S. Hogendorn, "Slave Marketing in West Africa," *The Uncommon Market: Essays in The Economic History of the Atlantic Slave Trade*, edited by Henry A. Gemery and Jan S. Hogendorn (New York: Academic Press, 1979), pp. 218, 220–221.

74. Ibid., p. 217.

75. Harold D. Nelson, et al., *Nigeria: A Country Study* (Washington: U.S. Government Printing Office, 1982), p. 16.

76. Paul E. Lovejoy and Jan S. Hogendorn, "Slave Marketing in West Africa," *The Uncommon Market*, edited by Henry A. Gemery and Jan S. Hogendorn, pp. 221–223, *passim*.

77. Joseph C. Miller, "Some Aspects of the Commercial Organization of Slaving at Luanda, Angola—1760–1830," ibid., pp. 80–81.

78. Ibid., pp, 80–81. John Thornton, *Africa and Africans in the Making of the Atlantic World, 1400–1680* (Cambridge: Cambridge University Press, 1995), pp, 43, 107–112.

79. Ralph A. Austen, "The Trans-Saharan Slave Trade: A Tentative Census," *The Uncommon Market*, edited by Henry A. Gemery and Jan S. Hogendorn, pp. 68–69.

80. See, for example, Philip D. Curtin, "Epidemiology and the Slave Trade," *Political Science Quarterly*, June 1968, pp. 190–216; Beverly B. Mack, "Women and Slavery in Nineteenth-Century Hausaland," *The Human Commodity*, edited by Elizabeth Savage, p. 97; Reginald Coupland, *The Exploitation of East Afrcia 1856–1890: The Slave Trade and the Scramble* (Evanston: Northwestern University Press, 1967), p. 148.

81. Allan G. B. Fisher and Humphrey J. Fisher, *Slavery and Muslim Society in Africa: The Institution in Saharan and Sudanic Africa and the Trans-Saharan Trade* (London: C. Hurst & Co., 1970), pp. 97–148; William Gervase Clarence-Smith, "The Economics of the Indian Ocean and Red Sea Slave Trade in the 19th Century: An Overview," *The Economics of the Indian Ocean Slave Trade in the Nineteenth Century*, edited by William Gervase Clarence-Smith, p. 14; Lewis H. Gann and Peter Duignan, *The Burden of Empire*, p. 154.

82. Patrick Manning, "Contours of Slavery and Social Change in Africa,"

American Historical Review, October 1983, pp. 854–855; T. O. Lloyd, *The British Empire, 1558–1983* (New York: Oxford University Press, 1984), p. 273.

83. Orlando Patterson, *Slavery and Social Death* (Cambridge, Mass: Harvard University Press 1982), p. 159; Murray Gordon, *Slavery in the Arab World* (New York: New Amsterdam Books, 1989), p. xi.

84. Murray Gordon, *Slavery and the Arab World*, p. x. See also Eva Hoffman and Margot Slade "Where Labor and Life are Cheap," *New York Times*, August 30, 1981, Section 4, p. E7; Bernard D. Nossiter, "U.N. Gets A Report on African Slaves," *New York Times*, August 26, 1981, p. A11.

85. Charles Jacob and Mohamed Athic, "Bought and Sold," *New York Times*, July 13, 1994, p. A19.

86. Howard R. French, "Africa's Culture War: Old Customs, New Values," *New York Times*, February 2, 1997, Section 4, p. 1.

87. "Slave Trade in Africa is Highlighted By Arrests," *New York Times*, August 10, 1997, International section, p. 5.

88. A. G. Hopkins, *An Economic History of West Africa*, p. 8; L. H. Gann and Peter Duignan, *Burden of Empire*, p. 120

89. A. G. Hopkins, *An Economic History of West Africa*, pp. 39–42.

90. Ibid., p. 44.

91. Ibid., p. 46.

92. A. G. Hopkins, *An Economic History of West Africa*, p. 48; John Thornton, *Africa and Africans in the Making of the Atlantic World, 1400–1680* (Cambridge: Cambridge University Press, 1995), p. 51.

93. Ibid., p. 30. See also Fernand Braudel, *Civilization and Capitalism: 15th–18th Century*, Vol. III: *The Perspective of the World*, translated by Siân Reynolds, (New York: Harper & Rowm, 1984). p. 441.

94. Scott R. Pearson, J. Dirck Stryker and Charles P. Humphreys, "Introduction," *Rice in West Africa: Policy and Economics*, edited by Scott R. Pearson, et al. (Stanford: Stanford University Press, 1981), p. 1n.

95. Ibid., pp. 62–63.

96. John Thornton, *Africa and Africans in the Making of the Atlantic World, 1400–1680*, pp. 37–39.

97. Ibid., pp. 66–69.

98. Ibid., p. 116.

99. L. H. Gann and Peter Duignan, *The Rulers of British Africa, 1884–1914*, (Stanford: Stanford University Press, 1977), pp. 104–105.

100. T. O. Lloyd, *The British Empire*, 1558–1983, p. 250; William Manchester, *The Last Lion: Visions of Glory 1874–1932*, Volume I (Boston: Little, Brown and Company, 1983), pp. 269, 276, 279.

101. See, for example, T. O. Ranger, "African Reactions to the Imposition of Colonial Rule in East and Central Africa," *Colonialism in Africa 1870–1900*, Volume I, edited by L. H. Gann and Peter Duignan, pp. 293–324.

102. " . . . the casualties and cost of one year of a colonial war were often less than those of one month of a European War . . ." Geoffrey Blainey, *The Cause of War* (New York: The Free Press, 1988), p. 198; T. O. Lloyd, *The British Empire, 1558–1983*, p. 259.

103. Harold D. Nelson, *Nigeria*, p. 26; Lance E. Davis and Robert A. Huttenback, *Mammon and the Pursuit of Empire: The Political Economy of British Imperialism, 1860–1912* (Cambridge: Cambridge University Press, 1987), pp. 6–7, 10, 301–303.

104. "Introduction," *Colonialism in Africa 1870–1960*, edited by Peter Duignan and L. H. Gann, Vol IV: *The Economics of Colonialism* (Cambridge: Cambridge University Press, 1975), p. 11.

105. L. H. Gann and Peter Duignan, "Reflections on Imperialism and the Scramble for Africa," *Colonialism in Africa 1870–1960*, Volume I, edited by L. H. Gann and Peter Duignan, p. 112.

106. Ibid., p. 107.

107. Ibid., p. 107.

108. L. H. Gann, "Economic Development in Germany's African Empire, 1884–1914," *Colonialism in Africa 1870–1960*, Volume IV, edited by Peter Duignan and L. H. Gann, p. 218.

109. L. H. Gann and Peter Duignan, "Reflections on Imperialism and the Scramble for Africa," *Colonialism in Africa 1870–1960*, Volume I, edited by L. H. Gann and Peter Duignan, p. 113.

110. Sir Frederick Pedler, "British Planning and Private Enterprise in Colonial Africa," *Colonialism in Africa 1870–1960*, Volume IV, edited by Peter Duignan and L. H. Gann, p. 95.

111. L. H. Gann, "Economic Development in Germany's African Empire, 1884–1914," ibid., pp. 248–249.

112. Peter Duignan and L. H. Gann, "Economic Achievements of the Colonizers: An Assessment," ibid., p. 679.

113. L. H. Gann, "Economic Development in Germany's African Empire, 1884–1914," ibid., p. 250.

114. Peter Duignan and L. H. Gann, "Economic Achievements of the Colonizers: An Assessment," ibid., p. 682.

115. Ibid., p. 684.

116. L. H. Gann and Peter Duignan, *Burden of Empire*, p. 247.

117. "Introduction," *Colonialism in Africa 1870–1960*, edited by Peter Duignan and L. H. Gann, Volume IV, pp. 10, 20–21, 24; Charles Wilson, "The Economic Role and Mainsprings of Imperialism," ibid., p. 68; Sir Frederick Pedler, "British Planning and Private Enterprise in Colonial Africa," ibid., pp. 102, 120; L. H. Gann, "Economic Development in Germany's African Empire, 1884–1914," ibid., pp. 239–240; Jan S. Hogendorn, "Economic Initiative and African Cash Farming: Pre-Colonial Origins and Early Colonial Developments," ibid., pp. 296–297; Simon E. Katzenellenbogen, "The Miner's Frontier, Transport and General Economic Development," ibid., p. 399.

118. L. H. Gann, "Economic Development in Germany's African Empire, 1884–1914," ibid., p. 239.

119. J. S. Mangat, *A History of the Asians in East Africa c. 1886 to 1945* (Oxford: Oxford University Press, 1969); Albert Hourani and Nadim Shehadi, editors, *The Lebanese in the World* (London: I. B. Tauris & Co., Ltd., 1992), Part Four.

120. J. S. Mangat, *A History of the Asians in East Africa*, p. 10.

121. Richard J. Hammond, "Some Economic Aspects of Portuguese Africa in the Nineteenth and Twentieth Centuries," *Colonialism in Africa*, edited by Peter Duignan and L. H. Gann, p. 262.

122. Robert Cornevin, "The Germans in Africa before 1918," *Colonialism in Africa 1870–1960*, Volume I, edited by L. H. Gann and Peter Duignan, p. 388.

123. Peter Duignan and L. H. Gann, "Economic Achievements of the Colonizers: An Assessment," *Colonialism in Africa 1870–1960*, Volume IV, edited by Peter Duignan and L. H. Gann, p. 694.

124. Harold D. Nelson, *Nigeria*, p. 54; David Lamb, *The Africans* (New York: Random House, 1982), pp. 12, 78.

125. David Lamb, *The Africans*, p. 21.

126. Peter Duignan, "Introduction," *Politics and Government in African States, 1960–1985*, edited by Peter Duignan and Robert H. Jackson (Stanford: Hoover Institution Press, 1986), pp. 13–14.

127. Felicité Awassi Atsimadja, "The Changing Geography of Central Africa," *The Changing Geography of Africa and the Middle East*, edited by Graham P. Chapman and Kathleen M. Baker (London: Routledge, 1992), p. 57.

128. The Economists Intelligence Unit, *Country Report: Uganda*,

Rwanda, Burundi (London: TheEconomist Intelligence Unit, 1996), pp. 19, 31.

129. Robert B. Edgerton, *Like Lions They Fought: The Zulu War and the Last Black Empire in South Africa* (New york: The Free Press, 1988), p. 3.

130. David Harrison, *The White Tribe of Africa: South Africa in Perspective* (Berkeley: University of California Press, 1981), pp. 35–40.

131. Despite many estimates placing Nigeria's population at more than 100 million, preliminary results of the November 1991 census, conducted under stringent conditions, show a population of 88.5 million. The Economist Intelligence Unit, *Nigeria: Country Report No. 3, 1992* (London: The Economist Intelligence Unit, 1992), p. 3n. Still, questions remain even about this census, taken with such extraordinary precautions as sealing the country's borders, ordering businesses to shut down for three days, and ordering people to stay home during those three days. Kenneth B. Noble, "Census in Nigeria Halts Normal Life," *New York Times*, November 29, 1991, p. A7. See also Kenneth B. Noble, "Nigeria Reveals Census' Total, 88.5 Million, and Little More," *New York Times*, March 25, 1992, p. A12; Kenneth B. Noble, "After Nigeria's Census, Skeptic Count is High," *New York Times*, June 4, 1992, p. A13.

132. Harold D. Nelson, *Nigeria*, pp. x, xiii, 84–85.

133. Ibid., p. 3.

134. A. G. Hopkins, *An Economic History of West Africa*, p. 44.

135. Ibid., pp. 19–20.

136. L. H. Gann and Peter Duignan, *Burden of Empire*, p. 156.

137. John E. Flint, "Nigeria: The Colonial Experience from 1880–1914," *Colonialism in Africa 1870–1960*, Volume I, edited by L. H. Gann and Peter Duignan, p. 221.

138. James S. Coleman, *Nigeria*, p. 94.

139. Ibid., p. 113.

140. Larry Diamond, *Class, Ethnicity and Democracy in Nigeria: The Failure of the First Republic* (Syracuse: Syracuse University Press, 1988), p. 22.

141. James Coleman, *Nigeria*, p. 66.

142. Ibid., p. 67.

143. Ibid., pp. 68–70.

144. Ibid., p. 66.

145. Ibid., p. 135.

146. Ibid., p. 134.

147. Ibid., p. 139.

148. Okwudiba Nnoli, *Ethnic Politics in Nigeria* (Enugu, Nigeria: Fourth Dimension Publishers, 1978), p. 189.

149. A. Bamisaiye, "Ethnic Politics as an Instrument of Unequal Social-Political Development in Nigeria's First Republic," *African Notes*, Volume 6, No. 2 (1970–1971), pp. 102–103.

150. James S. Coleman, *Nigeria*, p. 142.

151. Donald L. Horowitz, *Ethnic Groups in Conflict* (Berkeley: University of California Press, 1985), pp. 448, 451.

152. Northern Nigeria, *Statistical Yearbook 1965* (Kaduna: Ministry of Economic Planning, 1965), pp. 40–41.

153. Robert Nelson and Howard Wolpe, *Nigeria: Modernization and Politics of Communalism* (East Lansing: Michigan State University, 1971), p. 127.

154. Bernard Nkemdirim, "Social Change and the Genesis of Conflict in Nigeria," *Civilizations*, Vol. 25, Nos. 1–2 (1975), p. 94; Okwudiba Nnoli, *Ethnic Politics in Nigeria*, p. 64.

155. Okwudiba Nnoli, *Ethnic Politics in Nigeria*, pp. 59, 220.

156. Larry Diamond, *Class, Ethnicity and Democracy in Nigeria*, p. 26.

157. Martin Kilson, "The Emergent Elites of Black Africa, 1900 to 1960," *Colonialism in Africa 1870–1960*, Volume II: *The History and Politics of Colonialism 1914–1960*, edited by L. H. Gann and Peter Duignan (Cambridge: Cambridge University Press, 1982), p. 364.

158. John E. Flint, "Nigeria: The Colonial Experience from 1880 to 1914," *Colonialism in Africa 1870–1960*, Volume I, edited by L. H. Gann and Peter Duignan, p. 222.

159. Ibid., pp. 222n, 224.

160. James S. Coleman, *Nigeria*, Chapter 6.

161. John E. Flint, "Nigeria: The Colonial Experience from 1880 to 1914," *Colonialism in Africa 1870–1960*, Volume I, edited by L. H. Gann and Peter Duignan, p. 241.

162. Ibid., p. 245.

163. James S. Coleman, *Nigeria*, pp. 335–339.

164. Ibid., pp. 339, 344–346.

165. Ibid., pp. 341–343, 346–347; Okwudiba Nnoli, *Ethnic Politics in Nigeria*, pp. 230–233.

166. James S. Coleman, *Nigeria*, p. 360.

167. Larry Diamond, *Class, Ethnicity and Democracy in Nigeria*, p. 50.

168. Harold D. Nelson, *Nigeria*, p. 50.

169. David Lamb, *The Africans*, p. 308.

170. Ibid., p. 309.
171. Harold D. Nelson, *Nigeria*, pp. 53–60.
172. David Lamb, *The Africans*, p. 309.
173. Ibid., p. 311.
174. John A. A. Ayoade, "Ethnic Management in the 1979 Nigerian Constitution," *Canadian Review of Studies in Nationalism*, Spring 1987, p. 140.
175. Larry Diamond, *Class, Ethnicity and Democracy in Nigeria*, p. 178.
176. A. Bamisaiye, "Ethnic Politics as an Instrument of Unequal Socio-Economic Development in Nigeria's First Republic," *African Notes* (Nigeria), Vol. 6, No. 2, 1970–71, p. 99.
177. Larry Diamond, "Class, Ethnicity, and the Democratic State: Nigeria, 1950–66," *Comparative Studies in Social History*, July 1983, p. 462.
178. Ibid., pp. 462, 466.
179. Jon Kraus, "Economic Adjustment and Regime Creation in Nigeria," *Current History*, May 1989, p. 234.
180. "Nigeria: A Time of Pride and Pessimism," *The Economist*, January 7, 1989, p. 38.
181. Jon Kraus, "Economic Adjustment and Regime Creation in Nigeria," *Current History*, May 1989, pp. 233, 234, 236.
182. Steve Mufson, "African Maverick: Nigeria's Economic Ills Prod It Into Lead Role in OPEC Price Cutting," *Wall Street Journal*, March 16, 1983, pp. 1, 20.
183. "Nigeria: A Time of Pride and Pessimism," *The Economist*, January 7, 1989, p. 38.
184. The Economist Intelligence Unit, *Nigeria: Country Report No. 3, 1992*, p. 3.
185. The Economist Intelligence Unit, *Country Report: Nigeria*, 4th quarter 1996, pp. 5, 17.
186. David Lamb, *The Africans*, p. 312.
187. The Economist Intelligence Unit, *Country Report: Nigeria*, 4th quarter, 1996 (London: The Economist Intelligence Unit, 1996), pp. 10–11.
188. Barbara Crossette, "Survey Ranks Nigeria as Most Corrupt Nation," *New York Times*, August 3, 1997, International Section, p. 3.
189. Irving Kaplan, et al., *Tanzania: A Country Study* (Washington, D.C.: The American University, 1978), p. 147.
190. L. H. Gann and Peter Duignan, *The Rulers of German Africa 1884–1914* (Stanford: Stanford University Press, 1977), p. 12. See also Edward A. Alpers, *Ivory and Slaves*, p. 4.

191. Irving Kaplan, *Tanzania*, p. 193.

192. Ibid., p. 140.

193. Harvery Glickman, "Tanzania: From Disillusionment to Guarded Optimism," *Current History*, May 1997, p. 218.

194. Irving Kaplan, *Tanzania*, p. 153.

195. Ibid., pp. 158–159.

196. Robert Cornevin, "The Germans in Africa before 1918," *Colonialism in Africa 1870–1960*, Volume I, edited by L. H. Gann and Peter Duignan, pp. 407–408, 409.

197. Andrew Coulson, *Tanzania: A Political Economy* (Oxford: Oxford University Press, 1982), pp. 10–11.

198. Ibid., p. 17.

199. Ibid., p. 24.

200. Edward A. Alpers, *Ivory and Slaves*, p. 122.

201. Irving Kaplan, *Tanzania*, pp. 17–18.

202. Ibid., p. 19.

203. Andrew Coulson, *Tanzania*, pp. 17–18.

204. Robert Cornevin, "The Germans in Africa before 1918," *Colonialism in Africa 1870–1960*, Volume I, edited by L. H. Gann and Peter Duignan, pp. 405–407.

205. Irving Kaplan, *Tanzania*, p. 39.

206. Ibid., p. 37.

207. Ibid., p. 38.

208. Robert Cornevin, "The Germans in Africa before 1918," *Colonialism in Africa 1870–1960*, Volume I, edited by L. H. Gann and Peter Duignan, pp. 405, 406–407.

209. David Lamb, *The Africans*, p. 103.

210. Robert Cornevin, "The Germans in Africa before 1918," *Colonialism in Africa 1870–1960*, Volume I, edited by L. H. Gann and Peter Duignan, p. 406.

211. J. S. Mangat, *A History of Asians in East Africa, 1886–1945* (Oxford: The Clarendon Press, 1969), p. xv.

212. Ibid., pp. 7–11.

213. Ibid., pp. 27–29.

214. Ibid., pp. 30–31, 46–47.

215. L. H. Gann and Peter Duignan, *Burden of Empire*, p. 160.

216. Irving Kaplan, et al., *Tanzania*, pp. 32–33, 42.

217. Murray Gordon, *Slavery in the Arab World*, pp. 182–207; R. W. Beachey, *The Slave Trade of Eastern African*, pp. 47–48, 55, 57, 60–64.

218. Irving Kaplan, et al., *Tanzania*, p. 40.

219. Ibid., p. 45.

220. Ibid., p. 45.

221. Andrew Coulson, *Tanzania*, pp. 26–32.

222. L. H. Gann and Peter Duignan, *The Rulers of British Africa, 1870–1914*, p. 149.

223. Gerald M. Meier, "External Trade and Internal Development," *Colonialism in Africa 1870–1960*, Volume IV, edited by Peter Duignan and L. H. Gann, p. 442.

224. Andrew Coulson, *Tanzania*, p. 44.

225. Ibid., p. 56.

226. Ibid., p. 47.

227. Ibid., p. 49.

228. Ibid., pp. 50–55.

229. Irving Kaplan, *Tanzania*, p. 55.

230. Ibid., p. 150.

231. Ibid., p. 200.

232. Ibid., p. 168.

233. Thomas Sowell, *The Economics and Politics of Race: An International Perspective* (New York: William Morrow & Co., Inc., 1983), p. 240.

234. David Lamb, *The Africans*, p. 69.

235. Thomas Sowell, *The Economics and Politics of Race*, p. 240.

236. David Lamb, *The Africans*, p. 67.

237. Ken Adelman "The Great Black Hope," *Harper's Magazine*, July 1981, p. 16.

238. David Lamb, *The Africans*, p. 67.

239. Ibid., p. 65.

240. Michael F. Lofchie, "The Roots of Economic Crisis in Tanzania," *Current History*, April 1985, pp. 159–160.

241. Harvey Glickman, "Tanzania: From Disillusionment to Guarded Optimism," *Current History*, May 1997, p. 219.

242. Michael F. Lofchie, "Tanzania's Economic Recovery," *Current History*, May 1988, p. 209.

243. The Economist Intelligence Unit, *Tanzania, Mozambique: Country Report No. 2, 1991*, pp. 3, 6.

244. Harvey Glickman, "Tanzania: From Disillusionment to Guarded Optimism," *Current History*, May 1957, p. 218.

245. The Economist Intelligence Unite, *Country Report: Tanzania, Comoros*, 2nd quarter, 1997 (London: The Economist Intelligence Unit, 1997), p. 11.

246. Ibid., p. 12.

247. Ibid., p. 10.

248. See ibid., pp. 5, 17

249. *The World Almanac and Book of Facts 1989* (New York: World Almanac, 1989), p. 678; Central Intelligence Agency, *The World Factbook 1995* (Washington: Central Intelligence Agency, 1995), p. 162.

250. Irving Kaplan, et al., *Area Handbook for Ghana* (Washington: U.S. Government Printing Office, 1971), p. 34.

251. Ibid., p. 9.

252. Ibid., p. 34.

253. Ibid., p. 12.

254. David Lamb, *Africans*, pp. 284, 285.

255. Irving Kaplan, et al., *Area Handbook for Ghana*, p. 87.

256. Ibid., p. 51.

257. Ibid., pp. 56–57.

258. Ibid., pp. 58–59.

259. David E. Apter, *Ghana in Transition* (Princeton: Princeton University Press, 1972), p. 40.

260. Gerald M. Meier, "External Trade and Internal Development," *Colonialism in Africa 1870–1960*, Volume IV, edited by Peter Duignan and L. H. Gann, p. 443.

261. Irving Kaplan, et al., *Area Handbook for Ghana*, p. 291.

262. L. H. Gann and Peter Duignan, editors, *Colonialism in Africa 1870–1960*, Volume II, p. 16.

263. Martin Kilson, "The Emergent Élites of Black Africa, 1900 to 1960," *Colonialism in Africa 1870–1960*, Volume II, edited by Peter Duignan and L. H. Gann, p. 351.

264. Ibid., p. 354.

265. Irving Kaplan, et al., *Area Handbook for Ghana*, pp. 291, 300.

266. Gerald M. Meier, "External Trade and Internal Development," *Colonialism in Africa 1870–1960*, Volume VI, edited by L. H. Gann and Peter Duignan, pp. 444–445.

267. Martin Kilson, "The Emergent Élites of Black Africa, 1900 to 1960," *Colonialism in Africa 1870–1960*, Volume II, edited by L. H. Gann and Peter Duignan, p. 380.

268. Irving Kaplan, et al., *Area Handbook for Ghana*, pp. 70–71.

269. Martin Kilson, "The Emergent Élites of Black Africa, 1900 to 1960," *Colonialism in Africa 1870–1960*, Volume II, edited by L. H. Gann and Peter Duignan, p. 387.

270. Irving Kaplan, et al., *Area Handbook for Ghana*, p. 291.

271. David Lamb, *The Africans*, p. 286.

272. David Lamb, *The Africans*, p. 286.

273. Irving Kaplan, et al., *Area Handbook for Ghana*, p. 32.

274. Irving Kaplan, et al., *Area Handbook for Ghana*, p. 269.

275. David Lamb, *The Africans*, pp. 284–285.

276. Robin W. L. Alpine and James Pickett, *Agriculture, Liberalisation and Economic Growth in Ghana and Côte D'Ivoire: 1960–1990* (Paris: Development Centre for Economc Co-Operation and Development, 1993), p. 63.

277. Robin W. L. Alpine and James Pickett, *Agriculture, Liberalisation and Economic Growth in Ghana and Côte D'Ivoire: 1960–1990* (Paris: Development Centre for Economc Co-Operation and Development, 1993), pp. 14, 15.

278. David Lamb, *The Africans*, pp. 284–287.

279. Ibid., p. 288.

280. June Kronholz, "Dark Continent: Ghana's Economic Skid Illustrates Bleak Spiral of Poverty in Africa," *Wall Street Journal*, January 4, 1982, p. 21.

281. Ibid., p. 21.

282. Steve Mufson, "End of a Dream: Once the Showpiece of Black Africa, Ghana Now is Near Collapse," *Wall Street Journal*, March 28, 1983, p. 19.

283. Robin W. L. Alpine and James Pickett, *Agriculture, Liberalisation and Economic Growth in Ghana and Côte D'Ivoire: 1960–1990* (Paris: Development Centre for Economc Co-Operation and Development, 1993), p. 17.

284. Robin W. L. Alpine and James Pickett, *Agriculture, Liberalisation and Economic Growth in Ghana and Côte D'Ivoire: 1960–1990* (Paris: Development Centre for Economc Co-Operation and Development, 1993), p. 82.

285. James Brooke, "Ghana, Once 'Hopeless,' Gets at Least the Look of Success," *New York Times*, January 3, 1989, p. A8.

286. Ibid., pp. A1, A8.

287. Ibid., pp. A1, A8.

288. The Economist Intelligence Unit, *Ghana, Sierra Leone, Liberia: Country Report No. 2, 1992* (London: The Economist Intelligence Unit, 1992), pp. 3, 8; The Economist Intelligence Unit, *Country Report: Ghana, 2nd quarter 1996* (London: The Economist Intelligence Unit, 1996), p. 3.

289. The Economist Intelligence Unit, *Côte d'Ivoire: Country Report No. 2, 1992* (London: The Economist Intelligence Unit, 1996), p. 3.

290. Robert E. Handloff, editor, *Côte d'Ivoire: A Country Study*, 3rd edition (Washington: U.S. Government Printing Office, 1991), pp. xvi, 48–51.

291. Hubert Deschamps, "France in Black Africa and Madagascar between 1920 and 1945," *Colonialism in Africa*, Vol. II: *The History and Polittics of Colonialism: 1914–1960*, edtied by L. H. Gann and Peter Duignan (Cambridge: Cambridge University Press, 1982), p. 240.

292. Hubert Deschamps, "France in Black Africa and Madagascar between 1920 and 1945," *Colonialism in Africa 1870–1960*, Volume II, edited by L. H. Gann and Peter Duignan, p. 239; Michael Crowder, "The White Chiefs of Tropical Africa," *ibid.*, p. 346; T. D. Roberts, et al., *Area Handbook for Ivory Coast*, p. 18.

293. Hubert Deschamps, "France in Black Africa and Madagascar between 1920 and 1945," *Colonialism in Africa 1870–1960*, Volume II, edited by L. H. Gann and Peter Duignan, p. 226.

294. Kathleen Baker, "The Changing Geography of West Africa," *The Changing Geography of Africa and the Middle East*, edited by Graham P. Chapman and Kathleen M. Baker (London: Routledge, 1992), p. 107.

295. T. D. Roberts, et al., *Area Handbook for Ivory Coast*, pp. 30–34, *passim*.

296. Robert E. Handloff, "Introduction," *Côte d'Ivoire: A Country Study*, 3rd edition, edited by Robert E. Handloff (Washington: U.S. Government Printing Office, 1991), p. xxv; Rachel Warner, "Historical Setting," ibid., 5, 6.

297. Ibid., pp. xvi, 64.

298. David Lamb, *The Africans*, p. 213.

299. T. D. Roberts, et al., *Area Handbook for Ivory Coast*, pp. 19–20.

300. David Lamb, *The Africans*, p. 217.

301. Charles P. Humphrey and Patricia L. Rader, "Rice Policy in the Ivory Coast," *Rice in West Africa*, edited by Scott R. Pearson, et al., p. 32.

302. June Kronholz, "Stay On: France's Role in Africa, The Colonial Master Who Didn't Go Home," *Wall Street Journal*, July 22, 1981, p. 26.

303. Arnold C. Harberger, "Introduction," Michelle Riboud, *The Ivory Coast: 1960–1985* (San Francisco: International Center for Eco-

nomic Growth, 1987), p. v; David Lamb, *The Africans*, pp. 214–215.

304. Robin W. L. Alpine and James Pickett, *Agriculture, Liberalisation and Economic Growth in Ghana and Côte D'Ivoire: 1960–1990* (Paris: Development Centre for Economc Co-Operation and Development, 1993), pp. 65, 67.

305. June Kronholz, "Stay On: France's Role in Africa," *Wall Street Journal*, July 22, 1981, p. 18.

306. See, for example, Roger Thurow, "Ivory Coast Reliance on Commodities Topples It from Role-Model Pedestal," *Wall Street Journal*, May 9, 1989, p. A18; James Brooke, "Historian Tries to Fight Longtime African Ruler," *New York Times*, February 27, 1989, p. A6.

307. Michelle Riboud, *The Ivory Coast: 1960–1985*, p. 1.

308. James Brooke, "Historian Tries to Fight Longtime African Ruler," *New York Times*, February 27, 1989, p. A6.

309. Charles P. Humphrey and Patricia L. Rader, "Rice Policy in the Ivory Coast," *Rice in West Africa*, edited by Scott R. Pearson, et al., p. 15.

310. Martin Kilson, "The Emergent Élites of Black Africa, 1900–1960," *Colonialism in Africa 1870–1960*, Volume II, edited by L. H. Gann and Peter Duignan, p. 389.

311. Ibid., pp. 392, 393.

312. Robin W. L. Alpine and James Pickett, *Agriculture, Liberalisation and Economic Growth in Ghana and Côte D'Ivoire: 1960–1990*, p. 16.

313. Ibid., p. 117.

314. Charles P. Humphrey and Patricia L. Rader, "Rice Policy in the Ivory Coast," *Rice in West Africa*, edited by Scott R. Pearson, et al., pp. 33–38, 40–41, 43, 53.

315. The Economist Intelligence Unit, *Côte d'Ivoire: Country Report No. 2, 1992*, p.3.

316. Howard W. French, "Ivory Coast Markets Its Aspirations," *New York Times*, July 9, 1996, p. A4.

317. The Economist Intelligence Unit, *Côte d'Ivoire, Mali*, 3rd Quarter 1996 (London: Economist Intelligence Unit, 1996), p. 3.

318. Howard W. French, "An African Nations's Democracy Takes a Detour," *New York Times*, October 13, 1995, p. A8. See also "What's News," *Wall Street Journal*, October 24, 1995, p. A1.

319. The Economist Intelligene Unit, *Côte d'Ivoire*, 3rd quarter, 1996, p. 4.

320. Ralph A. Austen, "The Trans-Saharan Slave Trade: A Tentative Census," *The Uncommon Market: Essays in the Economic History of the Slave Trade,* edited by Henry A. Gemery and Jan S. Hogendorn (New York: Academic Press, 1979), pp. 68–69.

321. Jocelyn Murray, editor, *Cultural Atlas of Africa,* p. 70; Bernard Lewis, *Race and Slavery in the Middle East* (New York: Oxford University Press, 1990), pp. 10, 84.

322. Bernard Lewis, *Race and Slavery in the Middle East,* p. 10.

323. See ibid., pp. 10, 56, 59, 65, 74.

324. Ibid., p. 84.

325. Ibid., p. 59.

326. See *ibid.,* pp. 72, 79.

327. Ibid., pp. 79–80.

328. Ibid., pp. 79, 82.

329. Charles Jacobs and Mohamed Athic, "Bought and Sold," *New York Times,* July 13, 1994, p. A19.

330. Roger Anstey, "The Volume and Profitability of the British Slave Trade, 1761–1807," *Race and Slavery in the Western Hemisphere: Quantitative Studies,* edited by Stanley L. Engerman and Eugene Genovese (Princeton: Princeton University Press, 1975), pp. 3, 10.

331. E. W. Bovill, *The Golden Trade of the Moors* (London: Oxford University Press, 1968), pp. 245–246.

332. Ehud R. Toledano, *The Ottoman Slave Trade and Its Suppression,* p. 109.

333. Bernard Lewis, *Race and Slavery in the Middle East,* p. 73.

334. Adbullahi Mahadi, "The Aftermath of the *Jihad* in the Central Sudan as a Major Factor in the Volume of the Trans-Saharan Slave Trade in the Nineteenth Century," *The Human Commodity: Perspectives on the Trans-Saharan Slave Trade,* edited by Elizabeth Savage (London: Frank Cass & Co., Ltd., 1992), p. 125.

335. Ibid., p. 83.

336. Ehud R. Toledano, *The Ottoman Slave Trade and Its Suppression: 1840–1890,* pp. 4, 29.

337. R. W. Beachey, *The Slave Trade of Eastern Africa,* p. 128.

338. Reginald Beachey, *The Exploitation of East Africa 1856–1890: The Slave Trade and the Scramble* (Northwestern University Press, 1967), p. 140; Allan G. B. Fisher and Humphrey J. Fisher, *Slavery and Muslim Society in Africa* (London: C. Hurst & Co., 1970), p. 77; Beverly B. Mack, "Women and Slavery in Nineteenth-Century Hausaland," *The Human Commodity,* edited by Elizabeth Savage, p. 97.

339. Ibid., p. 139.

340. Ehud R. Toledano, *The Ottoman Slave Trade and Its Suppression*, pp. 64–67. See also Murray Gordon, *Slavery and the Arab World*, pp. 98–99.

341. E. W. Bovill, *The Golden Trade of the Moors*, p. 246; Murray Gordon, *Slavery and the Arab World*, pp. 95–96; J. O. Hunwick, "Black Africans in the Mediterranean World: Introduction to a Neglected Aspect of the African Diaspora," *The Human Commodity: Perspectives on the Trans-Saharan Slave Trade*, edited by Elizabeth Savage (London: Frank Cass & Co., Ltd., 1992), pp. 21–22.

342. Murray Gordon, *Slavery and the Arab World*, pp. 94–95; William Gervase Clarence-Smith, "The Economics of the Indian Ocean and Red Sea Slave Trades in the 19th Century: An Overview," *The Economics of the Indian Ocean Slave Trade in the Nineteenth Century*, edited by William Gervase Clarence-Smith, p. 6; R. W. Beachey, *The Slave Trade of Eastern Africa*, pp. 170–174.

343. Reginald Coupland, *Exploitation of East Africa*, pp. 139–140.

344. R. W. Beachey, *The Slave Trade of Eastern Africa*, p. 123.

345. Ehud R. Toledano, *The Ottoman Slave Trade and Its Suppression*, pp. 51–52.

346. Ibid., pp. 51–53.

347. R. Coupland, *East Africa and Its Invaders*, p. 143.

348. Ibid., pp. 205–213.

349. A. Sheriff, "Localisation and Social Composition of the East African Slave Trade, 1858–1873," *The Economics of the Indian Ocean Slave Trade in the Nineteenth*, edited by William Gervase Clarence-Smith, p. 133.

350. William Gervase Clarence-Smith, "The Economics of the Indian Ocean and Read Sea Slave Trades in the 19th Century," ibid., p. 8; Thomas M. Ricks, "Slaves and Slave Traders in the Persian Gulf, 18th and 19th Centuries: An Assessment," ibid., p. 64.

351. William Gervase Clarence-Smith, "The Economics of the Indian Ocean and Read Sea Slave Trades in the 19th Century," ibid., p. 8; Thomas M. Ricks, "Slaves and Slave Traders in the Persian gulf, 18th and 19th Centuries: An Assessment," ibid., p. 65.

352. Timothy Fernyhough, "Slavery and Slave Trade in Southern Ethiopia in the 19th Century," ibid., p. 106.

353. Frederick Cooper, *Plantation Slavery on the East Coast of Africa*, p. 71.

354. See, for example, Lord Kinross, *The Ottoman Centuries*, p. 146; Bernard Lewis, *Race and Slavery in the Middle East*, p. 59.

355. Bernard Lewis, *Race and Slavery in the Middle East*, p. vi.

356. David Eltis, "Free and Coerced Transatlantic Migrations: Some Comparisons," *The American Historical Review*, April 1983, p. 278.

357. Ibid., pp. 254–255.

358. Ibid., p. 278.

359. Ibid., p. 252.

360. Ibid., p. 256.

361. See, for example, David Hackett Fischer, *Albion's Seed: Four British Folkways in America* (New York: Oxford University Press, 1989), pp. 31, 236–237, 438, 606, 621–622; Robert C. Ostergren, "Prairie Bound: Migration Patterns to a Swedish Settlement on the Dakota Frontier," *Ethnicity on the Great Plains*, edited by Frederick Luebke (Lincoln: University of Nebraska Press, 1980), pp. 84–80; Moses Rischin, *The Promised City: New York's Jews, 1870–1914* (Cambridge, Massachusetts: Harvard University Press, 1962), pp. 76, 78; Dino Cinel, *From Italy to San Francisco: The Immigrant Experience* (Stanford: Stanford University Press, 1982), p. 28. Such localization of origins and destinations have not, of course, been limited to Europeans or to people settling in the Western Hemisphere. See Thomas Sowell, *Migrations and Cultures: A World View* (New York: Basic Books, 1996), pp. 4–8.

362. John Thornton, *Africa and Africans in the Making of the Atlantic World, 1400–1680*, Chapter 7.

363. Robert William Fogel and Stanley L. Engerman, *Time on the Cross: The Economics of American Negro Slavery* (Boston: Little, Brown and Company, 1974), pp. 23–24.

364. Ibid., pp. 25–26; Richard B. Sheridan, "Mortality and Medical Treatment of Slaves in the British West Indies," *Race and Slavery in the Western Hemisphere*, edited by Stanley L. Engerman and Eugene D. Genovese, p. 286.

365. Thomas Sowell, "Three Black Histories," *Essays and Data on American Ethnic Groups*, edited by Thomas Sowell and Lynn D. Collins, p. 24.

366. A. J. R. Russell-Wood, "Colonial Brazil," *Neither Slave Nor Free: The Freedom of African Descent in the Slave Societies of the New World*, edited by David W. Cohen and Jack P. Greene (Baltimore: The John Hopkins University Press, 1972), p. 127.

367. John Thornton, *Africa and Africans in the Making of the Atlantic World, 1400–1680*, pp. 223–229.

368. David Eltis, "Free and Coerced Transatlantic Migrations: Some Comparisons," *The American Historical Review*, April 1983, p. 262.

369. When Frederick Law Olmsted noticed the racial division of labor that left the Irish doing the most dangerous work on a river boat in Alabama, he was told: "The niggers are worth too much to be risked here; if the Paddies are knocked overboard, or get their backs broke, nobody loses anything!" Frederick Law Olmsted, *The Cotton Kingdom: A Traveller's Observations on Cotton and Slavery in the American Slave States* (New York: The Modern Library, 1969), p. 215. See also ibid., p. 70; U. B. Phillips, *Life and Labor in the Old South* (Boston: Little, Brown and Co., 1953), p. 186; U. B. Phillips, *American Negro Slavery*, pp. 301–302; J. C. Furnas, *The Americans:A Social History of the United States, 1857–1914* (New York: G. P. Putnam's Sons, 1969), p. 394; Daniel Boorstin, *The Americans* (New York: Random House, 1965), p. 101.

370. Ulrich B. Phillips, *American Negro Slavery: A Survey of the Supply, Employment and Control of Negro Labor as Determined by the Plantation Regime* (Baton Rouge: Louisiana State University Press, 1966), p. 62; Robert William Fogel and Stanley L. Engerman, *Time on the Cross: The Economics of American Negro Slavery* (Boston: Little, Brown and Company, 1974), p. 123.

371. Richard B. Sheridan, "Mortality and the Medical Treatment of Slaves in the British West Indies," *Race and Slavery in the Western Hemisphere*, edited by Stanley L. Engerman and Eugene D. Genovese, p. 287; Thomas Sowell, *The Economics and Politics of Race: An International Perspective* (New York: William Morrow, 1983), p. 95.

372. Thomas Sowell, *The Economics and Politics of Race*, p. 95.

373. Gwendolyn Midlo Hall, *Social Control in Plantation Societies: A Comparison of St. Domingue and Cuba* (Baltimore: Johns Hopkins Press, 1971), pp. 13–14.

374. Frederick P. Bowser, "The Free Person of Color in Mexico City and Lima: Manumission and Opportunity, 1580–1650," *Race and Slavery in the Western Hemisphere*, edited by Stanley L. Engerman and Eugene D. Genovese, p. 339; Frank Tannenbaum, *Slave and Citizen* (New York: Vintage Books, 1946), *passim*.

375. Treatment of slaves was at least as bad in Latin America as in the United States, which had no such elaborate legal protections. See, for example, Carl N. Degler, *Either Black Nor White* (New York: MacMillan Publishing Co., 1971), pp. 67–75; Gwendolyn Midlo Hall, *Social Control in Slave Plantation Societies*, pp. 15–20; Stan-

ley M. Elkins, *Slavery* (Chicago: University of Chicago Press, 1969), pp. 51n, 78; Ulrich B. Phillips, *American Negro Slavery*, p. 52; Lewis C. Gray, *History of Agriculture in the Southern United States* Vol. 2 (Washington, D.C.: Carnegie Institution of Washington, 1933), p. 519; David Lowenthal, "Race and Color in the West Indies," *Daedalus*, Spring 1967, pp. 610–611. See also David Brion David, *The Problem of Slavery in Western Culture* (Ithaca, N.Y.: Cornell University Press, 1960), Chapter 8.

376. Richard B. Sheridan, "Mortality and Medical Treatment of Slaves in the British West Indies," *Race and Slavery in the Western Hemisphere*, edited by Stanley L. Engerman and Eugene D. Genovese, p. 286.

377. Willard B. Gatewood, *Aristocrats of Color: The Black Elite, 1880–1920* (Bloomington: Indiana University Press, 1990), p. 83; Ira Berlin, Ira Berlin, *Slaves without Masters*, pp. 124, 386; David C. Rankin, "The Impact of the Civil War on the Free Colored Community of New Orleans," *Perspectives in American History*, Vol XI (1977–78), pp. 380, 385.

378. David C. Rankin, "The Impact of the Civil War on the Free Colored Community of New Orleans," *Perspectives in American History*, Vol. XI (1977–78), pp. 385, 387.

379. David Lowenthal, *West Indian Societies*, p. 46; Eugene D. Genovese, "The Slave States of North America," *Neither Slave Nor Free*, edited by David W. Cohen and Jack P. Greene, p. 270; Philip D. Morgan, "Black Life in Eighteenth-Century Charleston," *Perspectives in American History*, New Series, Vol. I (1984), p. 212. On slave-owning by free black Charlestonians in general, see Bernard E. Powers, Jr., *Black Charlestonians: A Social History, 1822–1885* (Fayetteville: University of Arkansas Press, 1994), pp. 48–50, 72. One sign of the prosperity of some "free persons of color" in Charleston was that 75 whites there rented homes from them. Ira Berlin, *Slaves Without Masters: The Free Negro in the Antebellum South* (New York: Pantheon Books, 1974), p. 344.

380. Douglas Hall, "Jamaica," *Neither Slave Nor Free*, edited by David W. Cohen and Jack P. Greene, p. 194.

381. Jerome S. Handler and Arnold A. Sio, "Barbados," ibid., p. 220.

382. Frederick P. Bower, "Colonial Spanish America," ibid., pp. 36–37.

383. Franklin W. Knight, "Cuba," ibid., p. 284.

384. Herbert S. Klein, "Nineteenth-Century Brazil," ibid., pp. 313–314.

385. Léo Elisabeth, "The French Antilles," ibid., pp. 150, 151; Gwendolyn Midlo Hall, "Saint Domingue," ibid., p. 188.

386. Richard C. Wade, *Slavery in the Cities: The South 1820–1860* (Oxford: Oxford University Press, 1964), pp. 38–54; Lewis C. Gray, *History of Agriculture in the Southern United States to 1860* (Washington: Carnegie Institution of Washington, 1933), Vol. I, pp. 566–567; Philip D. Morgan, "Black Life in Eighteenth-Century Charleston," *Perspectives in American History*, New Series, Vol. 1 (1984), pp. 187–232; John Thornton, *Africa and Africans in the Making of the Atlantic World, 1400–1680*, pp. 177–178.

387. David W. Cohen and Jack P. Greene, "Introduction," *Neither Slave Nor Free*, p. 7.

388. William B. Gatewood, *Aristocrats of Color: The Black Elite, 1880–1920* (Bloomington: Indiana University Press, 1990), p. 4.

389. Whittington B. Johnson, *Black Savannah: 1788–1864* (Fayetteville: University of Arkansas Press,1996), pp. 111, 180.

390. Thomas Sowell, "Three Black Histories," *Essays and Data on American Ethnic Groups*, edited by Thomas Sowell and Lynn D. Collins, p. 10.

391. A. J. R. Russell-Wood, "Colonial Brazil," *Neither Slave Nor Free*, edited by David W. Cohen and Jack P. Greene, p. 97.

392. H. Hoetink, "Surinam and Curaçao," ibid., p. 62; Jerome S. Handler and Arnold A. Sio, "Barbados," ibid., p. 217.

393. David W. Cohen and Jack P. Greene, "Introduction," ibid., p. 12. See also, David W. Cohen and Jack P. Greene, "Introduction," ibid., pp. 7, 12; H. Hoetink, "Surinam and Curaçao," ibid., pp. 63, 68; Douglas Hall, "Jamaica," ibid., 196.

394. See, for example, Aedele Logan Alexander, *Ambiguous Lives: Free Women of Color in Rural Georgia, 1789–1879* (Fayetteville: University of Arkansas Press, 1991), pp. 161–162, 173–175; Bernard E. Powers, *Black Charlestonians: A Social History, 1822–1885* (Fayetteville: University of Arkansas Press, 1994), pp. 37–38, 185.

395. C. G. Woodson, *The Education of the Negro Prior to 1861* (New York: Arno Press, 1968), p. 265; U.S. Bureau of the Census, *Historical Statistics of the United States: Colonial Times to 1970*, Part I, p. 381.

396. Thomas Sowell, "Three Black Histories," *Essays and Data on American Ethnic Groups*, edited by Thomas Sowell and Lynn D. Collins, p. 12.

397. Ibid.

398. Frederick P. Bower, "The Free Person of Color in Mexico City and Lima: Manumission and Opportunity, 1580–1650," *Race and*

Slavery in the Western Hemisphere, edited by Stanley L. Engerman and Eugene D. Genovese, p. 362.

399. See Willard B. Gatewood, *Aristocrats of Color, passim*; Theodore Hershberg and Henry Williams, "Mulattoes and Blacks: Intra-group Color Differences and Social Stratification in Nineteenth-Century Philadelphia," *Philadelphia: Work, Space, Family, and Group Experience in the Nineteenth Century*, edited by Theodore Hershberg (Oxford: Oxford University Press, 1981), pp. 392–394; Adele Logan Alexander, *Ambiguous Lives*, pp. 173–175, 197–200

400. Theodore Hershberg and Henry Williams, "Mulattoes and Blacks: Intra-group Color Differences and Social Stratification in Nineteenth-Century Philadelphia," *Philadelphia*, edited by Theodore Hershberg, pp. 494–495.

401. Ibid., p. 407.

402. Ibid., p. 416.

403. Whittington B. Johnson, *Black Savannah: 1788–1864* (Fayatteville: University of Arkansas Press, 1996), pp. 3, 78, 111–112, 180.

404. See, for example, William B. Gatewood, *Aristocrats of Color: The Black Elite, 1880–1920* (Bloomington: Indiana University Press, 1990), especially pp. 149–181. See also Gunnar Myrdal, *An American Dilemma: The Negro Problem and Modern Democracy* (New York: Harper & Brothers, 1944), pp. 695–700; E. Franklin Frazier, *The Negro in the United States*, revised edition (New York: The Macmillan Co., 1971), pp. 283n, 289–291; Bernard E. Powers, Jr., *Black Charlestonians*, pp. 185–186; Stephen Birmingham, *Certain People: America's Black Elite* (Boston: Little, Brown, and Co., 1977), pp. 70–71, 130–131.

405. See, for example, Edward Byron Reuter, *The Mulatto in the United States: Including a Study of the Rôle of Mixed-Blood Races Throughout the World* (Boston: Richard G. Badger, 1918), *passim*; Willard B. Gatewood, *Aristocrats of Color: The Black Elite, 1880–1920* (Bloomington: Indiana University Press, 1990), pp. 13, 20, 88, 100–101, 108, 127.

406. David C. Rankin, "The Origins of Negro Leadership in New Orleans during Reconstruction," *Southern Black Leaders of the Reconstruction*, edited by Howard N. Rabinowitz (Urbana: University of Illinois Press, 1982), pp. 162–163.

407. *Memoirs of the National Academy of Sciences*, Vol. XV: *Psychological Testing in the United States Army*, edited by Robert M. Yerkes (Washington: U.S. Government Printing Office, 1921), pp. 735–736.

408. Audrey M. Shuey, *The Testing of Negro Intelligence*, 2nd edition (New York: Social Science Press, 1966), pp. 452–466.

409. Edward R. Telles, "Residential Segregation by Skin Color in Brazil," *American Sociological Review*, Vol. 57, No. 2 (April 1992), p. 190.

410. Ibid., p. 195.

411. Theodore Hershberg and Henry Williams, "Mulattoes and Blacks: Intra-group Color Differences and Social Stratification in Nineteenth-Century Philadelphia," *Philadelphia: Work, Space, Family, and Group Experience in the 19th Century*, edited by Theodore Hershberg (Oxford: Oxford University Press, 1981) p. 394.

412. Theodore Hershberg and Henry Williams, "Mulattoes and Blacks: Intra-Group Color Differences and Social Stratification in Nineteenth-Century Philadelphia," *Philadelphia*, edited by Theodore Hershberg, pp. 392–294.

413. See, for example, Thomas Sowell, *Migrations and Cultures: A World View* (New York: Basic Books, 1995), pp. 89–92, 128–137, 156–160; Jean Roche, *La Colonisation Allemande et Le Rio Grande Do Sul* (Paris: Institut des Études de L'Amérique Latine, 1959); Teiiti Suzuki, *The Japanese Immigrant in Brazil* (Tokyo: University of Tokyo Press, 1969); Robert F. Foerster, *The Italian Emigration of Our Times* (New York: Arno Press, 1969), pp. 279–319.

414. Edward E. Telles, "Residential Segregation by Skin Color in Brazil," *American Sociological Review*, Vol. 57, No. 2 (April 1992), p. 190.

415. Bernard Lewis, *Race and Slavery in the Middle East*, Chapter 8.

416. U.S. Bureau of the Census, *Historical Statistics of the United States: Colonial Times to 1970* (Washington, D.C.: U.S. Government Printing Office, 1976), p. 422.

417. J. Halcro Ferguson, *Latin America: The Balance of Race Redressed* (London: Oxford University Press, 1961), p. 7.

418. Thomas Sowell, *The Economics and Politics of Race*, pp. 62–107.

419. Nelson do Valle, "Updating the Cost of Not Being White in Brazil," *Race, Class, and Power in Brazil* (Los Angeles: Center for Afro-American Studies, U.C.L.A., 1985), p. 45.

420. U.S. Bureau of the Census, *Current Population Reports*, Series P–23, No. 80 (Washington: Government Printing Office, no date), p. 22, 31, 45.

421. Ibid., p. 200.

422. James S. Coleman, *Nigeria*, p. 154.

423. David Lamb, *The Africans*, pp. 123–124.

424. Robert Higgs, *Competition and Coercion* (Cambridge: Cambridge University Press, 1977), p. 120.

425. Joseph Rothschild, *East Central Europe between the Two World Wars* (Seattle: University of Washington Press, 1992), pp. 276, 359.

426. Ransford W. Palmer, *Pilgrims from the Sun: West Indian Migration to America* (New York: Twayne Publishers, 1995), p. 35.

427. Geoffrey Blainey, *The Causes of War*, p. 198.

428. As two leading proponents of British imperialism put it: "The supremacy of the English rests only to a limited extent upon their own superior force . . . To a great extent our ascendancy is 'moral' resting, that is, upon character and self-confidence. To this confidence the natives bow. . . . For a century the Englishman has behaved in India as a demi-god and the majority of the inhabitants take him at his own valuation." Quoted in Aaron L. Friedberg, *The Weary Titan; Britain and the Experience of Relative Decline, 1895–1905* (Princeton: Princeton University Press), p. 226. Similarly, in colonial Virginia, the policy was never to let the indigenous people see an Englishman sick or dying. Ian K. Steele, *Warpaths: Invasions of North America* (New York: Oxford University Press, 1994), p. 39. Even decades after the colonial era was over in Africa, the mystique of the white man was still not completely gone. See Keith B. Richburg, *Out of America: A Black Man Confronts Africa* (New York: Basic Books, 1997), pp. 7, 154–155, 157–158.

429. Robin W. L. Alpine and James Pickett, *Agriculture, Liberalisation and Economic Growth in Ghana and Côte D'Ivoire: 1960–1990* (Paris: Development Centre for Economic Co-operation and Development, 1993), p. 37.

430. Jeffrey Sachs, "Nature, Nurture and Growth," *The Economist*, June 14, 1997, p. 22.

431. Gary Becker, "The Numbers Tell the Story: Economic Freedom Spurs Growth," *Business Week*, May 6, 1996, p. 20.

432. Robin W. L. Alpine and James Pickett, *Agriculture, Liberalisation and Economic Growth in Ghana and Côte D'Ivoire: 1960–1990*, p. 128.

CHAPTER 4: THE SLAVS

1. Forrest McDonald, "Cultural Continuity and the Shaping of the American South," *Geographic Perspectives in History*, edited by

Eugene D. Genovese and Leonard Hochberg (Oxford: Basil Black-well, 1989), p. 218.

2. Jean W. Sedlar, *East Central Europe in the Middle Ages, 1000–1500* (Seattle: University of Washington Press, 1994), p. 7.

3. Lonnie R. Johnson, *Central Europe: Enemies, Neighbors, Friends* (Oxford: Oxford University Press, 1996), p. 27.

4. Michel Mollat du Jourdin, *Europe and the Sea* (Oxford: Blackwell Publishers, Ltd., 1993), p. 4; E. H. Mellor and E. Alistair Smith, *Europe: A Geographical Survey of the Continent* (New York: Columbia University Press, 1979), p. 4.

5. Ibid., pp. 14–17. See also N. J. G. Pounds, *An Historical Geography of Europe, 1800–1914*, p. 444.

6. Charles Kindleberger, *World Economic Primacy: 1500 to 1990* (Oxford: Oxford University Press, 1996), p. 91.

7. George W. Hoffman, "Changes in the Agricultural Geography of Yugoslavia," *Geographical Essays on Eastern Europe* (Blooming-ton: Indiana University, 1961), p. 114.

8. John R. Lampe, "Imperial Borderlands or Capitalist Periphery? Redefining Balkan Backwardness," *The Origins of Backwardness in Eastern Europe: Economics and Politics from the Middle Ages until the Early Twentieth Century*, edited by Daniel Chirot (Berke-ley: University of California Press, 1989) p. 184.

9. N. J. G. Pounds, *An Historical Geography of Europe: 1800–1914*, p. 488.

10. Ibid., p. 15.

11. Joseph R. Lampe, "Imperial Borderlands or Capitalist Periphery? Redefining Balkan Backwardness, 1520–1914," *The Origins of Backwardness in Eastern Europe*, edited by Daniel Chirot, p. 180.

12. Peter Gunst, "Agrarian Systems of Central and Eastern Europe," *The Origins of Backwardness in Eastern Europe*, edited by Daniel Chirot, p. 72.

13. Robert A. Kann and Zdenek V. David, *The Peoples of the Eastern Habsburg Lands, 1526–1918* (Seattle: University of Washington Press, 1984), p. 270.

14. See, for example, David E. McClave, "Physical Environment and Population," *Soviet Union: A Country Study*, second edition, edited by Raymond E. Zickel (Washington: U.S. Government Printing Office, 1991), p. 112;

15. Jean W. Sedlar, *East Central Europe in the Middle Ages*, p. 9.

16. N. J. G. Pounds, *An Historical Geography of Europe: 1800–1914* (Cambridge: Cambridge University Press, 1988), p. 101.

17. Iván T. Berend and György Ränki, *The European Periphery and Industrialization 1780–1914*, translated by Éva Pálmai (Cambridge: Cambridge University Press, 1982), pp. 15, 16.

18. John R. Lampe, "Imperial Borderlands or Capitalist Periphery? Redefining Balkan Backwardness," *The Origins of Backwardness in Eastern Europe*, edited by Daniel Chirot p. 177.

19. See, for example, David F. Good, "The Economic Lag of Central and Eastern Europe: Income Estimates for the Habsburg Successor States, 1870–1914," *Journal of Economic History*, Vol. 54. No. 4 (December 1994), pp. 869–891. See also Daniel Chirot, "Causes and Consequences of Backwardness," *The Origins of Backwardness in Eastern Europe*, edited by Daniel Chirot, p. 4; John R. Lampe, "Imperial Borderlands or Capitalist Periphery? Redefining Balkan Backwardness, 1520–1914," ibid., p. 177.

20. Peter Gunst, "Agrarian Systems of Central and Eastern Europe," *The Origins of Backwardness in Eastern Europe*, pp. 53–54.

21. Robert Bartlett, *The Making of Europe: Conquest, Colonization and Cultural Change 950–1350* (Princeton: Princeton University Press, 1993), p. 126. See also Sidney Pollard, *Marginal Europe: The Contribution of the Marginal Lands Since the Middle Ages* (Oxford: Oxford University Press, 1997), pp. 146, 149.

22. Jean W. Sedlar, *East Central Europe in the Middle Ages*, p. 84.

23. Peter Gunst, "Agrarian Systems of Central and Eastern Europe," *The Origins of Backwardness in Eastern Europe*, edited by Daniel Chirot, pp. 76, 80. "Bohemia (which would not, today, be considered part of Eastern Europe if it were not for a political accident) became socially and economically almost indistinguishable from Bavaria and Austria." Daniel Chirot, "Causes and Consequences of Backwardness," ibid., p. 5.

24. Matthew Spinka, *A History of Christianity in the Balkans: A Study of the Spread of Byzantine Culture Among the Slavs* (Chicago: The American Society of Church History, 1933), pp. 7–8.

25. Robert Bartlett, *The Making of Europe*, pp. 281–282.

26. Ibid., p. 281. Just as the Britons in earlier had copied coins minted on the continent, so the Eastern Europeans began by copying coins minted in Western Europe. Ibid., p. 283.

27. Stephen Frederic Dale, *Indian Merchants and Eurasian Trade, 1600–1750* (Cambridge: Cambridge University Press, 1940), p. 83.

28. Paul Robert Magocsi, *Historical Atlas of East Central Europe*, pp. 54–55.

29. Richard C. Hoffman, "Economic Development and Aquatic Ecosystems in Medieval Europe," *American Historical Review*, Vol. 101, No. 3 (June 1996), pp. 659–660.

30. Robert Bartlett, *The Making of Europe*, pp. 60, 70–84.

31. Jean W. Sedlar, *East Central Europe in the Middle Ages, 1000–1500*, p. 116

32. Maxine Berg, *The Age of Manufactures, 1700–1820: Industry, Innovation and Work in Britain* (London: Routledge, 1994), p. 213.

33. Jean W. Sedlar, *East Central Europe in the Middle Ages, 1000–1500*, p. 351.

34. Paul Robert Magocsi, *Historical Atlas of East Central Europe*, p. 103; Lonnie R. Johnson, *Central Europe: Enemies, Neighbors, Friends* (Oxford: Oxford University Press, 1996), p. 103.

35. Paul Robert Magocsi, *Historical Atlas of East Central Europe*, pp. 34–35.

36. N. J. G. Pounds, *An Historical Geography of Europe: 1800–1914* (Cambridge: Cambridge University Press, 1988), p. 75.

37. N. J. G. Pounds, *An Historical Geography of Europe: 1800–1914*, pp. 449–458.

38. Walter Nugent, *Crossings: The Great Transatlantic Migrations, 1870–1914* (Bloomington: Indiana University Press, 1992), p. 84.

39. Paul Robert Magocsi, *Historical Atlas of East Central Europe*, p. 92.

40. Roy E. H. Mellor and E. Alistair Smith, *Europe: A Geographical Survey of the Continent* (New York: Columbia University Press, 1979), p. 92.

41. Paul Robert Magocsi, *Historical Atlas of East Central Europe*, p. 3.

42. N. J. G. Pounds, *An Historical Geography of Europe: 1800–1914*, p. 488.

43. Ibid., p. 139.

44. Ibid., pp. 131–132. In a later period, from 1870 to 1910, various Eastern European cities experienced very substantial growth—Warsaw by 150 percent, Prague and Kiev by 154 percent, and Budapest by 175 percent. Paul Robert Magocsi, *Historical Atlas of East Central Europe*, p. 96.

45. Paul Robert Magocsi, *Historical Atlas of East Central Europe*, pp. 97; Jean W. Sedlar, *East Central Europe in the Middle Ages*, pp. 402, 411–412.

46. N. J. G. Pounds, *An Historical Geography of Europe: 1800–1914*, p. 179.

47. Ibid., p. 430.

48. Carlo M. Cipolla, *Literacy and Development in the West* (New York: Penguin Books, 1969), p. 17. It was much the same story when the empire was broken down regionally. Only about 15 percent of the children in Bosnia-Herzegovina were attending schools in 1880, but 67 percent were in Dalmatia and at least 95 percent in Austria and the Czech territories. Iván T. Berend and György Ránki, *The European Periphery and Industrialization 1780–1914* (Cambridge: Cambridge University Press, 1982), p. 57.

49. Irina Livezeanu, *Cultural Politics in Greater Romania: Regionalism, Nation Building, & Ethnic Struggle, 1918–1930* (Ithaca, N.Y.: Cornell University Press, 1993), pp. 30–31.

50. Ibid., p. 9.

51. Ibid., pp. 50, 53, 90, 92, 131, 135.

52. Ibid., pp. 53, 92, 135.

53. Emily Green Balch, *Our Slavic Fellow Citizens* (New York: Arno Press, 1969), p. 61.

54. Jean W. Sedlar, *East Central Europe in the Middle Ages*, pp. 144, 435–436.

55. Jean W. Sedlar, *East Central Europe in the Middle Ages*, pp. 144–145, 435–436.

56. Ibid., p. 435.

57. Hugh LeCaine Agnew, *Origins of the Czech National Renascence*, pp. 179, 180, 181, 183, 193, 195. In the eighteenth century, Czech scholars "wrote mostly in German or Latin" while the people "read only Czech." (Ibid., p. 212.) Even scholarly studies of Czech literary history were written in Latin or German. (Ibid., p. 116.)

58. Robert J. Kaiser, *The Geography of Nationalism in Russia and the USSR* (Princeton: Princeton University Press, 1994), p. 41.

59. Jean W. Sedlar, *East Central Europe in the Middle Ages*, p. 86. See also Roy E. H. Mellor and E. Alistair Smith, *Europe*, p. 100; Robert Bartlett, *The Making of Europe*, pp. 150–151; Sidney Pollard, *Marginal Europe*, p. 156.

60. Robert Bartlett, *The Making of Europe*, pp. 117–132; Sidney Pollard, *Marginal Europe*, pp. 152–153. There were, in fact, a variety of German laws dominating different parts of East Central Europe. See Paul Robert Magocsi, *Historical Atlas of East Central Europe*, pp. 37–41.

61. Peter Gunst, "Agrarian Systems of Central and Eastern Europe," *The Origins of Backwardness in Eastern Europe*, p. 64. German law

was not the only foreign law to prevail in particular enclaves. Dutch and Flemish migrants who came to Eastern Europe to apply the drainage techniques in which they were skilled were likewise governed by Dutch and Flemish law. Sidney Pollard, *Marginal Europe: The Contribution of the Marginal Lands Since the Middle Ages* (Oxford: Clarendon Press, 1997), pp. 156–157.

62. Robert Bartlett, *The Making of Europe*, p. 181.

63. Ibid., p. 235.

64. Robert Bartlett, *The Making of Europe: Conquest, Colonization and Cultural Change, 950–1350* (Princeton: Princeton University Press, 1993), p. 144.

65. Sidney Pollard, *Marginal Europe*, p. 151.

66. Jean W. Sedlar, *East Central Europe in the Middle Ages*, p. 86.

67. Ibid., pp. 11–12.

68. Ibid., pp. 115, 127.

69. Ibid., p. 127.

70. N. J. G. Pounds, *An Historical Geography of Europe, 1800–1914*, p. 179; Peter F. Sugar, *Southeastern Europe under Ottoman Rule*, pp. 179–180.

71. Robert Bartlett, *The Making of Europe: Conquest, Colonization and Cultural Change 950–1350* (Princeton: Princeton University Press, 1993), p. 42. See also Péter Gunst, "Agrarian Systems of Central and Eastern Europe," *The Origins of Backwardness in Eastern Europe*, pp. 63–65; Jean W. Sedlar, *East Central Europe in the Middle Ages*, p. 417.

72. Robert Bartlett, *The Making of Europe*, pp.; 30–31, 82–83. See also Jean W. Sedlar, *East Central Europe in the Middle Ages*, pp. 64, 229, 408.

73. Robert Bartlett, *The Making of Europe*, p. 17.

74. Ibid., p. 112.

75. Hugh LeCaine Agnew, *Origins of the Czech National Renascence* (Pittsburgh: University of Pittsburgh Press, 1993), p. 113.

76. Robert Bartlett, *The Making of Europe*, p. 54.

77. Ibid., p. 200.

78. Hugh LeCaine Agnew, *Origins of the Czech National Renascence*, p. 52.

79. Charles A. Price, *Southern Europeans in Australia* (Canberra: Australian National University Press, 1979), p. 55.

80. Robert Bartlett, *The Making of Europe*, pp. 274–277.

81. Jean W. Sedlar, *East Central Europe in the Middle Ages, 1000–1500* (Seattle: University of Washington Press, 1994), p. 464.

82. Ibid., pp. 470–472.

83. Peter Gunst, "Agrarian Systems of Central and Eastern Europe," *The Origins of Backwardness in Eastern Europe*, edited by Daniel Chirot, pp. 69–70.

84. Joseph Rothschild, *East Central Europe between the Two World Wars*, p. 292.

85. Bela K. Kiraly, "The Five Paradoxes of East Central European Society and Warfare from the Mid-Eighteenth Century to the 1920s," *Essays on War and Society in East Central Europe, 1740–1920* (New York: Columbia University Press, 1987), p. 3. Another possible definition of its western boundaries might be Winston Churchill's description of the location of the "iron curtain" of the Soviet era, "from Stettin in the Baltic to Trieste in the Adriatic." Winston Churchill, "The Sinews of Peace," *Churchill Speaks: Winston S. Churchill in Peace and War, Collected Speeches, 1887–1963*, edited by Robert Rhodes James (London: Chelsea House, 1980), p. 881.

86. Peter F. Sugar and Donald W. Treadgold, "Foreword to the 1993 Printing," *Southeastern Europe under Ottoman Rule, 1354–1804* (Seattle: University of Washington Press, 1993), p. ix.

87. Gordon East, "The Concept and Political Status of the Shatter Zone," *Geographical Essays on Eastern Europe*, edited by Norman J. G. Pounds (Bloomington: Indiana University Press, 1961), p. 2. Defining Central Europe has presented similar conundrums. See Lonnie R. Johnson, *Central Europe*, Chapter 1.

88. See, for example, Jean W. Sedlar, *East Central Europe in the Middle Ages*, pp. 111, 114, 115, 116, 122, 123, 126, 127, 130, 132, 136, 291, 328, 329, 335, 356, 372; Peter F. Sugar, *Southeastern Europe under Ottoman Rule, 1354–1804*, pp. 335–342; Paul Robert Magocsi, *Historical Atlas of East Central Europe*, pp. xi, xii, 5, 23, 27; Trianon Stoianovich, "Cities, Capital Accumulation, and the Ottoman Command Economy, 1500–1800," *Cities and the Rise of States in Europe, A.D. 1000 to 1800*, edited by Charles Tilly and Wim P. Blockmans (Boulder, Colorado: Westview Pres, 1994), pp. 60–61; Piotr S. Wandycz, *The Lands of Partitioned Poland, 1795–1918* (Seattle: University of Washington Press, 1993), p. 195.

89. Robert Bartlett, *The Making of Europe*, p. 311.

90. Pal Robert Magocsi, *Historical Atlas of East Central Europe*, p. 107.

91. Ibid., pp. 97–98.

92. Robert Bartlett, *The Making of Europe*, pp. 228, 236–238.

93. Hugh LeCaine Agnew, *Origins of the Czech Renascence*, Chapters 2, 3. The "golden age" of Czech literature was said to be in the sixteenth and early seventeenth centuries. Robert A. Kann and Zdenek V. David, *The Peoples of the Easter Habsburg Lands, 1526–1918*, p. 479.

94. Gary B. Cohen, *The Politics of Ethnic Survival: Germans in Prague, 1861–1914* (Princeton: Princeton University Press, 1981), p. 3.

95. Gary B. Cohen, *The Politics of Ethnic Survival: Germans in Prague, 1861–194*, p. 3.

96. Ibid., pp. 20, 22–26.

97. Ibid., pp. 25–26.

98. See, for example, Chapter 6 of this volume.

99. Gary B. Cohen, *The Politics of Ethnic Survival*, pp. 26–28.

100. Ibid., Chapters 1, 2.

101. Ibid., pp. 81–82.

102. Josef Korbel, *Twentieth-Century Czechoslovakia: The Meanings of Its History* (New York: Columbia University Press, 1977), p. 116.

103. William Pfaff, *The Wrath of Nations: Civilization and the Furies of Nationalism* (New York: Simon & Schuster, 1993), p. 104.

104. Jean W. Sedlar, *East Central Europe in the Middle Ages*, pp. 84–85.

105. Ibid., pp. 90–95.

106. Jean W. Sedlar, *East Central Europe in the Middle Ages*, p. 95.

107. David Brion Davis, *Slavery and Human Progress* (New York: Oxford University Press, 1986), p. 33.

108. Ibid., p. 33.

109. Richard Hellie, *Slavery in Russia: 1450–1725* (Chicago: University of Chicago Press, 1982), p. 21.

110. Daniel Evans, "Slave Coast of Europe," *Slavery and Abolition*, Vol. 6, No. 1 (May 1985), p. 42.

111. Richard Hellie, *Slavery in Russia*, pp. 21–22.

112. Ibid., p. 41; David Brion Davis, *Slavery and Human Progress*, pp. 32–33; J. O. Hunwick, "Black Africans in the Mediterranean," *The Human Commodity: Perspectives on the Trans-Saharan Slave Trade*, edited by Elizabeth Savage (London: Frank Cass, 1992), p. 18.

113. Daniel Evans, "Slave Coast of Europe," *Slavery & Abolition*, Vol. 6, No. 1 (May 1985), p. 42.

114. Jean W. Sedlar, *East Central Europe in the Middle Ages.*, p. 352.

115. Ibid., p. 96.

116. Ibid., p. 97.

117. Peter F. Sugar, *Southeastern Europe under Ottoman Rule, 1354–1804*, p. 56.

118. Ibid., pp. 16–19.

119. Ibid., p. 22.

120. Benjamin Braude and Bernard Lewis, "Introduction," *Christians and Jews in the Ottoman Empire: The Functioning of a Plural Society*, edited by Benjamin Braude and Bernard Lewis, Volume I: *The Central Lands* (New York: Holmes & Meier, 1982), pp. 1–15, 31–32; C. E. Bosworth, "The Concept of *Dhimma* in Early Islam," ibid., pp. 41, 46–49; , Muhammad Adnan Bakhit, "The Christian Population of the Province of Damascus in the Sixteenth Century," ibid., Vol II: *The Arabic-Speaking Lands*, pp. 26–27; Moshe Macoz, Communal Conflicts in Ottoman Syria during the Reform Era: The Role of Political and Economic Factors," ibid., pp. 93–95, 97; Dominique Chevallier, "Non-Muslim Communities in Arab Cities," ibid., p. 159.

121. Peter F. Sugar, *Southeastern Europe under Ottoman Rule*, pp. 44, 65.

122. Bernard Lewis, *The Muslim Discovery of Europe* (New York: Norton, 1982), Chapter V.

123. Lord Kinross, *The Ottoman Centuries*, pp. 57–58.

124. Peter F. Sugar, *Southeastern Europe under Ottoman Rule*, pp. 178–182; Jean W. Sedlar, *East Central Europe in the Middle Ages*, pp. 454–457.

125. Robert A. Kann and Zdenek V. David, *The Peoples of the Eastern Habsburg Lands*, pp. 181–182, 265–266.

126. Ibid., pp. 155–156, 158.

127. Ibid., p. 182.

128. See, for example, ibid., pp. 201–202, 215, 245, 249, 265, 267.

129. Piotr S. Wandycz, *The Lands of Partitioned Poland, 1795–1918* (Seattle: University of Washington Press, 1993), p. 11.

130. Ibid., pp. 204–206.

131. Ibid., p. 206.

132. Ibid., p. 229.

133. Ibid., p. 229.

134. Carol Golab, *Immigrant Destinations* (Philadelphia: Temple University Press, 1977), pp. 101–104.

135. Ibid., p. 225.

136. Piotr S. Wandycz, *The Lands of Partitioned Poland*, pp. 260–261.

137. Ibid., p. 240.

138. Ibid., p. 276.

139. Ibid., p. 371.

140. Ibid., p. 275.

141. Joseph Rothschild, *East Central Europe Between the Two World Wars* (Seattle: University of Washington Press, 1992), p. 29.

142. Piotr S. Wandycz, *The Lands of Partitioned Poland*, p. 369.

143. Paul Robert Magocsi, *Historical Atlas of East Central Europe*, p. 169.

144. Joseph Rothschild, *East Central Europe between the World Wars*, p. 92.

145. Ibid., p. 89.

146. Ibid., pp. 86–87.

147. Ibid., p. 92.

148. Paul Johnson, *Modern Times*, p. 40.

149. Joseph Rothschild, *East Central Europe between the World Wars*, pp. 78, 86.

150. Radomír Luža, *The Transfer of the Sudeten Germans: A Study of Czech-German Relations, 1933–1962* (New York: New York University, 1964), p. 9. See also p. 42.

151. Ibid., pp. 9–11.

152. Ibid., p. 34.

153. Ibid., pp. 268–271.

154. Ibid., pp. 300, 327.

155. Cacilie Rohwedder, "Germans, Czechs are Hobbled by History as Europe Moves toward United Future," *Wall Street Journal*, November 25, 1996, p. A15.

156. Paul Robert Magocsi, *Historical Atlas of East Central Europe*, p. 168.

157. Ibid., pp. 131, 137.

158. Ibid., p. 133.

159. Ibid., p. 135.

160. Joseph Rothschild, *East Central Europe between the Two World Wars*, p. 203.

161. Ibid., pp. 206–208.

162. Ibid., pp. 212–213.

163. Paul Robert Magocsi, *Historical Atlas of East Central Europe*, p. 13.

164. Ibid., p. 210.

165. Ibid., pp. 206–207.

166. Ibid., p. 268.

167. Ibid., pp. 276, 359.

168. Ibid., pp. 382–296, *passim*.

169. Ibid., p. 382.
170. Archie Brown, Michael Kaser, and Gerald S. Smith, *The Cambridge Encyclopedia of Russia and the Former Soviet Union* (Cambridge: Cambridge University Press, 1994), p. 5.
171. David E. McClave, "Physical Environment and Population," *Soviet Union: A Country Study*, second edition, edited by Raymond E. Zickel (Washington: U.S. Government Printing Office, 1991), p. 101.
172. Glen E. Curtis, "Industry," ibid., p. 488.
173. Archie Brown et al., *The Cambridge Encyclopedia of Russia and the Former Soviet Union*, pp. 6–7.
174. Ibid., pp. 17–18,
175. W. A. Douglas Jackson, "Soviet Manganese Ores: Output and Export," *Soviet Natural Resources in the World Economy*, edited by Robert G. Jensen, et al., (Chicago: University of Chicago Press, 1983), p. 517.
176. American Petroleum Institute, *Basic Petroleum Data Book* (Washington: American Petroleum Institute, 1993), Table 2.
177. Jonathan P. Stern, "Soviet Natural Gas in the World Economy," *Soviet Natural Resources in the World Economy*, edited by Robert G. Jensen, et al. (Chicago: University of Chicago Press, 1983), p. 372.
178. Russell B. Adams, "Nickel and Platinum in the Soviet Union," *Soviet Natural Resources in the World Economy*, edited by Robert G. Jensen, p. 536.
179. Theodore Shabad, "The Soviet Potential in Natural Resources: An Overview," ibid., p. 269.
180. Jeffrey Brooks, *When Russia Learned to Read: Literacy and Popular Literature, 1861–1917* (Princeton: Princeton University Press, 1985), p. 4.
181. Robert J. Kaiser, *The Geography of Nationalism in Russia and the USSR*, p. 67.
182. Richard Pipes, *Russia under the Old Regime* (New York: Charles Scribner's Sons, 1974), p. 210.
183. William L. Blackwell, *The Industrialization of Russia: A Historical Perspective*, third edition (Arlington Heights, Illinois: Harlan Davidson, Inc., 1994), p. 10.
184. Stephen Frederic Dale, *Indian Merchants and Eurasian Trade, 1600–1750* (Cambridge: Cambridge University Press, 1994), pp. 81–82, 87–88, 108–127.
185. Richard Pipes, *Russia under the Old Regime* ((New York: Charles Scribner's Sons, 1974), pp. 126–127.

186. Werner Keller, *East Minus West = Zero: Russia's Debt to the Western World 862–1962*, translated by Constantine Fitzgibbon (New York: G.P. Putnam's Sons, 1962), p. 71

187. Richard Pipes, *Russia Under the Old Regime*, p. 191.

188. Alexander Gershenkron, *Economic Backwardness in Historical Perspective*, p. 60.

189. Ibid., p. 196.

190. Robert P. Bartlett, *Human Capital*, pp. 158–164.

191. Ibid., pp. 149–150.

192. Ibid., p. 151.

193. Ibid., p. 144.

194. Hugh Seton-Watson, "Russian Nationalism in Historical Perspective," *The Last Empire*, edited by Robert Conquest, p. 18.

195. Richard Pipes, *Russia Under the Old Regime*, p. 192.

196. John P. McKay, *Pioneers for Profit*, pp. 112–113, 124.

197. Richard Pipes, *Russia Under the Old Regime*, p. 192.

198. Ibid., p. 196.

199. Ibid., p. 218.

200. John P. McKay, *Pioneers for Profit*, p. 4.

201. Ibid., p. 5.

202. Werner Keller, *East Minus West = Zero*, p. 207.

203. Thomas C. Owen, "Entrepreneurship and the Structure of Enterprise in Russia, 1800–1880," *Entrepreneurship in Imperial Russia and the Soviet Union*, edited by Gregory Guroff and Fred V. Carstensen (Princeton, N.J.: Princeton University Press, 1983), p. 62.

204. John P. McKay, *Pioneers for Profit*, p. 34.

205. Ibid., p. 144.

206. Ibid., p. 35.

207. Arcadius Kahan, "Notes on Jewish Entrepreneurship in Tsarist Russia," *Entrepreneurship in Imperial Russia and the Soviet Union*, edited by Gregory Guroff and Fred V. Carstensen, p. 115.

208. Fred V. Carstensen, "Foreign Participation in Russian Economic Life: Notes on British Enterprise, 1865–1914," ibid., p. 156.

209. John P. McKay, *Pioneers for Profit*, p. 48.

210. Ibid., p. 176.

211. Ibid., p. 187.

212. Richard Pipes, *Russia under the Old Regime*, pp. 282–286.

213. See, for example, David Pryce-Jones, *The Strange Death of the Soviet Empire* (New York: Henry Holt and Co., 1995), pp. 29, 51, 52, 53, 54. 108; "Armenia," *Soviet Nationality Survey*, January

1984, p. 1; "Chechen-Ingushia," ibid., February 1984, p. 2; "Byelorussia," ibid., March 1984, p. 3; "Kirgizia," ibid., November 1984, p. 4.

214. See, for example, David Remnick, *Resurrection: The Struggle for a New Russia* (New York: Random House, 1997), pp. 107–109, 197–199, 255, 274; Peter Galuszka, "And You Think You've Got Tax Problems," *Business Week*, May 29, 1995, p. 50.

215. John P. McKay, *Pioneers for Profit*, pp. 108, 125, 381–383.

216. Ibid., p. 32.

217. Ibid., pp. 170–171.

218. Ibid., pp. 174, 177, 181.

219. Ibid., p. 255.

220. Ibid., p. 257.

221. Ibid., p. 193.

222. Ibid., p. 139.

223. Ibid., pp. 136–137.

224. Antony C. Sutton, *Western Technology and Soviet Economic Development 1917 to 1930* (Stanford: Hoover Institution Press, 1968), p. 59.

225. Ibid., pp. 105, 132, 172, 190, 218, 221.

226. Ibid., pp. 256–257; C. Gerald Fraser, "Alexander P. de Seversky Dies at 80; Early Strategic Air Power Proponent," *The New York Times*, August 26, 1974, p. 32; Alden Whitman, "Igor Sikorsky, Helicopter Pioneer, Dies," *The New York Times*, October 27, 1972, p. A1.

227. Antony C. Sutton, *Western Technology and Soviet Economic Development 1917 to 1930*, p. 17.

228. Ibid., Chapter 2.

229. Ibid., p. 49.

230. Ibid., p. 347.

231. Ibid., p. 11.

232. Ibid., p. 62.

233. Ibid., p. 79.

234. Ibid., p. 177.

235. Ibid., p. 181.

236. Ibid., p. 185.

237. Ibid., p. 3.

238. Alexandre Bennigsen, "Soviet Minority Nationalism in Historical Perspective," *The Last Empire: Nationality and the Soviet Future*, edited by Robert Conquest (Stanford: Hoover Institution Press, 1986), p. 130.

239. Robert A. Lewis, "The Mixing of Russians and Soviet Nationalities and Its Demographic Impact," *Soviet Nationality Problems*, edited by Edward Allworth (New York: Columbia University Press, 1971), pp. 126, 131; Mikhail S. Bernstam, "The Demography of Soviet Ethnic Groups in World Perspective," *The Last Empire*, edited by Robert Conquest, p. 318.

240. Alexandre Bennigsen, "Soviet Muslims in the Muslim World," *Soviet Nationalities in Strategic Perspective*, edited by S. Enders Wimbush (London: Croom Helm, 1985), p. 207.

241. Jeff Chinn and Robert Kaiser, *Russians as the New Minority: Ethnicity and Nationalism in the Soviet Successor States* (Boulder: Westview Press, 1996), pp. 213–214.

242. Ibid., pp. 133, 134, 136.

243. Gertrude E. Schroeder, "Social and Economic Aspects of the Nationality Problem," *The Last Empire*, edited by Robert Conquest, p. 295.

244. Robert J. Kaiser, *The Geography of Nationalism in Russia and the USSR* (Princeton: Princeton University Press, 1994), pp. 67, 126.

245. Ibid., p. 129.

246. Jeff Chinn and Robert Kaiser, *Russians as the New Minority*, pp. 185, 207–238; Robert J. Kaiser, *The Geography of Nationalism in Russia and the USSR*, p. 123.

247. Jeff Chinn and Robert Kaiser, *Russians as the New Minority*, pp. 53–54.

248. Robert J. Kaiser, *The Geography of Nationalism in Russia and the USSR*, p. 81.

249. Ibid., p. 65.

250. Jeff Chinn and Robert Kaiser, *Russians as the New Minority*, p. 59.

251. Ibid., pp. 134, 136.

252. Gerhard Simon, *Nationalism and Policy Toward the Nationalities int the Soviet Union*, p. 122.

253. S. Enders Wimbush, "The Soviet Muslim Borderlands," *The Last Empire*, edited by Robert Conquest, p. 222.

254. See, for example, Gerhard Simon, *Nationalism and Policy Toward the Nationalities in the Soviet Union*, pp. 25–30, 38–41, 54–61.

255. Gerhard Simon, *Nationalism and Policy Toward the Nationalities in the Soviet Union*, p. 296.

256. Mikhail Bernstam, "The Demography of Soviet Ethnic Groups in World Perspective," *The Last Empire*, edited by Robert Conquest, p. 320.

257. Dina Rome Spechler, "Russia and the Russians," *Handbook of Major Soviet Nationalities*, ed. Zev Katz, et al. (New York: The Free Press, 1975), p. 15.

258. Ibid., p. 15; Hélène Carrère d'Encausse, *Decline of an Empire*, p. 29.

259. Hélène Carrère d'Encausse, *Decline of an Empire*, pp. 34–35.

260. Bohdan Nahaylo and Victor Swoboda, *Soviet Disunion: A History of the Nationalities Problem in the U.S.S.R.* (New York: The Free Press, 1990), p. 88.

261. Alexander Sktromas, "The Baltic States," *The Last Empire*, p. 193. See also Gerhard Simon, *Nationalism and Policy Toward the Nationalities in the Soviet Union*, pp. 179–181.

262. Ibid., pp. 207–209.

263. Ibid., pp. 228–229.

264. Ibid., pp. 232, 275.

265. Ibid., pp. 243–245.

266. Hélène Carrère d'Encausse, *Decline of an Empire*, p. 154.

267. Ibid., pp. 146–155.

268. Computed from Hélène Carrère D'Encausse, *Decline of an Empire*, p. 143. See also ibid., pp. 148–151.

269. Yaroslav Bilinsky, "Politics Purge, and Dissent in the Ukraine Since the Fall of Sheles," *Nationalism and Human Rights: Processes of Modernization in the USSR*, edited by Ihor Kamenetsky (Littleton, Colorado: Libraries Unlimited, Inc., 1977), p. 170.

270. Hélène Carrère d'Encausse, *Decline of an Empire*, pp. 125, 127.

271. Ibid., p. 139.

272. Dina Rome Spechler, "Russia and the Russians," *Handbook of Major Soviet Nationalities*, ed. Zev Katz, et al., p. 13.

273. Gerhard Simon, *Nationalism and Policy Toward the Nationalities in The Soviet Union*, p. 277.

274. Hélène Carrère d'Encausse, *Decline of an Empire*, p. 162.

275. Alexander R. Alexiev and S. Enders Wimbush, *The Ethnic Factor in the Soviet Armed Forces* (Santa Monica: The Rand Corporation, 1982), p. 22.

276. Ibid., p. 20.

277. Bohdan Nahaylo and Victor Swoboda, *Soviet Disunion*, p. 336.

278. Dina Rome Spechler, "Russia and the Russians," *Handbook of Major Soviet Nationalities*, ed. Zev Katz, et al., p. 11.

279. Hélène Carrère d'Encausse, *Decline of an Empire*, p. 76.

280. Dina Rome Spechler, "Russia and the Russians," *Handbook of Major Soviet Nationalities*, ed. Zev Katz, et al., p. 11.

281. Hélène Carrère d'Encausse, *Decline of an Empire*, p. 170.

282. Richard Pipes, "Reflections on the Nationality Problems in the Soviet Union," *Ethnicity: Theory and Experience*, edited by Nathan Glazer and Daniel P. Moynihan (Cambridge, Mass.: Harvard University Press, 1975), p. 464; Jeff Chinn and Robert Kaiser, *Russians as the New Minority*, p. 103.

283. See, for example, Gerhard Simon, *Nationalism and Policy Toward the Nationalities*, pp. 376–387; The Economist Intelligence Unit, *Commonwealth of Independent States: Country Report No. 1, 1992* (London: The Economist Intelligence Unit, 1992), p. 10.

284. Robert J. Kaiser, *The Geography of Nationalism in Russia and the USSR*, p. 116.

285. Robert A. Lewis, "The Mixing of Russians and Soviet Nationalities and Its Demographic Impact," *Soviet Nationality Problems*, edited by Edward Allworth, p. 145; Edmund Brunner, Jr., *Soviet Demographic Trends and the Ethnic Composition of Draft Age Males, 1980–1995*, p. 10.

286. Jeff Chinn and Robert Kaiser, *Russians as the New Minority*, p. 80.

287. Nancy Lubin, *Labour and Nationality in Soviet Central Asia: An Uneasy Compromise* (Princeton: Princeton University Press, 1984), p. 155.

288. Hélène Carrère d'Encausse, *Decline of an Empire: The Soviet Socialist Republics in Revolt* (New York: Harper & Row, 1981), p. 168; *Soviet Union: A Country Study*, p. 807.

289. Nancy Lubin, *Labour and Nationality in Soviet Central Asia*, pp. 167–169.

290. See Donald S. Carlisle, "Uzbekistan and the Uzbeks," *Problems of Communism*, September–October 1991, p.40.

291. The Economist Intelligence Unit, *Commonwealth of Independent States: Country Report No. 1, 1992*, p. 71.

292. Roman Szporluk, "The Ukraine and Russia," *The Last Empire* edited by Robert Conquest, p. 151.

293. Bohdan Nahaylo and C. J. Peters, *The Ukrainians and Georgians* (London: Minority Rights Group Ltd., 1981), p. 5.

294. Ibid., p. 5.

295. Roman Szporluk, "The Ukraine and the Ukrainians," *Handbook of Major Soviet Nationalities*, edited by Zev Katz, et al., p. 23; Bohdan Nahaylo and C.J. Peters, *The Ukrainians and Georgians*, p. 5.

296. Bohdan Nahaylo and C.J. Peters, *The Ukrainians and Georgians*, pp. 5–6.

297. Ibid., p. 6.

298. Ibid., pp. 7–8.

299. Robert Conquest, *Harvest of Sorrow: Soviet Collectivization and the Terror-Famine* (New York: Oxford University Press, 1986), p. 302.

300. Ibid., p. 306.

301. Ibid., p. 261.

302. Bohdan Nahaylo and C. J. Peters, *The Ukrainians and Georgians*, p. 12.

303. Ibid., pp. 9, 11.

304. Jeff Chinn and Robert Kaiser, *Russians as the New Minority*, p. 155.

305. Ibid., p. 11.

306. Roman Szporluk, "The Ukraine and the Ukrainians," *Handbook of Major Soviet Nationalities*, edited by Zev Katz, et al., pp. 44–45.

307. Ibid., p. 44n.

308. Ibid., p. 28.

309. Jeff Chinn and Robert Kaiser, *Russians as the New Minority*, pp. 148, 156–157.

310. Ihor Y. Gawdiak, "Nationalities and Religions," *The Soviet Union: A Country Study*, second edition, edited by Raymond E. Zickel (Washington: U.S. Government Printing Office 1991), p. 159.

311. Calculated from Richard Pomfret, *The Economies of Central Asia* (Princeton: Princeton University Press, 1995), p. 5.

312. Anatoly M. Khazanov, "The Ethnic Problems of Contemporary Kazakhstan," *Central Asian Survey*, Vol. 14, No. 2 (1995), pp. 245–247.

313. Richard Pomfret, *The Economies of Central Asia* (Princeton: Princeton University Press, 1995), p. 21.

314. Alec Nove and J. A. Newth, *The Soviet Middle East*, p. 57.

315. See, for example, David E. McClave, "Physical Environment and Population," *Soviet Union: A Country Study*, second edition, edited by Raymond E. Zickel (Washington: U.S. Government Printing Office, 1991), pp. 115, 117.

316. Elizabeth E. Bacon, *Central Asians Under Russian Rule*, p. 117.

317. Martha Brill Olcott, *The Kazakhs*, p. xiv.

318. Elizabeth E. Bacon, *Central Asians Under Russian Rule*, pp. 118–119; Martha Brill Olcott, *The Kazakhs*, p. 183.

319. Martha Brill Olcott, *The Kazakhs*, p. 185.

320. Steven Sabol, "The Creation of Soviet Central Asia: The 1924 National Delimitation," *Central Asian Survey*, Vol. 14, No. 2 (1995), p. 235.

321. Richard Pomfret, *The Economies of Central Asia* (Princeton: Princeton University Press, 1995), p. 21.

322. Anatoly M. Khazanov, "The Ethnic Problems of Contemporary Kazakhstan," *Central Asian Survey*, Vol. 14, No. 2 (1995), p. 246.

323. Anatoly M. Khazanov, "The Ethnic Problems of Contemporary Khazakhstan," *Central Asian Survey*, Vol. 14, No. 2 (1995), p. 255.

324. Nancy Lubin, *Labour and Nationality in Soviet Central Asia*, pp. 75, 77.

325. Ibid., pp. 86, 87.

326. Nancy Lubin, *Labour and Nationality in Soviet Central Asia*, pp. 82–85.

327. S. Enders Wimbush and Alex Alexiev, *The Ethnic Factor in the Soviet Armed Forces*, pp. 15, 16, 20, 22, 36.

328. Ibid., p. 18–19.

329. Anatoly M. Khazanov, "The Ethnic Problems of Contemporary Kazakhstan," *Central Asian Survey*, Vol. 14, No. 2 (1995), p. 248.

330. Gerhard Simon, *Nationalism and Policy Toward the Nationalities in the Soviet Union*, p. 289.

331. Hélène Carrère d'Encausse *Decline of an Empire*, p. 251.

332. Donald S. Carlisle, "Uzbekistan and the Uzbeks," *Handbook of Major Soviet Nationalities*, edited by Zev Katz, et al., p. 293.

333. Edmund Brunner, Jr., *Soviet Demographic Trends and the Ethnic Composition of Draft Age Males, 1980–1995*, p. 15.

334. Hélène Carrère d'Encausse, *Decline of an Empire*, pp. 252–253. See also Robert J. Kaiser, *The Geography of Nationalism in Russia and the USSR*, p. 142.

335. S. Enders Wimbush, "Soviet Muslim Borderlands," *The Last Empire*, edited by Robert Conquest, pp. 225–226.

336. Susan L. Curran and Dmitry Ponomareff, *Managing the Ethnic Factor in the Russian and Soviet Armed Forces*, pp. 3, 8.

337. Nancy Lubin, *Labour and Nationality in Soviet Central Asia*, p. 31.

338. Elizabeth Bacon, *Central Asians under Russian Rule: A Study of Culture Change* (Ithaca, N.Y.: Cornell University Press, 1980), p. 105.

339. Alec Nove and J. A. Newth, *The Soviet Middle East* (London: George Allen & Unwin, 1967), pp. 106–107.

340. Ibid., p. 109.

341. Ibid., pp. 109–110.

342. Nancy Lubin, *Labour and Nationality in Soviet Central Asia*, p. 116.

343. Ibid., pp. 49–50.

344. Alec Nove and J. A. Newth, *The Soviet Middle East*, p. 105.

345. Jeff Chinn and Robert Kaiser, *Russians as the New Minority: Ethnicity and Nationalism in the Soviet Successor States* (Boulder: Westview Press, 1996), p. 235.

346. Anatoly M. Kazanov, "The Ethnic Problems of Kazakhstan," *Central Asian Survey*, Vol. 14, No. 2 (1995), p. 254.

347. The London Intelligence Unit, *Commonwealth of Independent States: Country Report No. 1, 1992*, p. 21.

348. Robert J. Kaiser, *The Geography of Nationalism in Russia and the U.S.S.R.*, pp. 336–337.

349. Richard Pomfret, *The Economies of Central Asia* (Princeton: Princeton University Press, 1995), pp. 142–150, 161.

350. Ewa Morawska, "East Europeans on the Move," *The Cambridge Survey of World Migration*, edited by Robin Cohen (Cambridge: Cambridge University Press, 1995), p. 97.

351. Ibid., pp. 98–99.

352. N. Smoje, "Early Croatian Settlement of Western Australia,"*The Australian People*, edited by James Jupp, p. 338; M. J. Cigler, "Czechs," ibid., p 347; L. Paszkowski, "Poles," ibid., p.736.

353. Carl-Ulrik Schierup, "Former Yugoslavia: Long Waves of International Migration," *The Cambridge Survey of World Migration*, edited by Robin Cohen, p. 285.

354. Jerzy Zubrycki, *Polish Immigrants in Britain: A Study of Adjustment* (The Hague: Martin Nijhoff, 1956), p. 26.

355. Ibid., p. 28.

356. Halina Janowska, "An Introductory Outline of the Mass Polish Emigrations, Their Directions and Problems (1870–1945)," *Employment-Seeking Emigrations of the Poles World-Wide, XIX and XX C* edited by Celina Bonska and Andrzej Pilch (Nakladem Uniwersytetu Jagiellonskiego, no date), p. 128.

357. Jerzy Zubrycki, *Polish Immigrants in Britain*, p. 28.

358. Halina Janowska, "An Introductory Outline of the Mass Polish Emigrations, Their Directions and Problems (1870–1945)," *Employment-Seeking Emigrations of the Poles World-Wide*, edited by Celina Bobinska and Adrezej, p. 129.

359. Jersy Zubrzycki, *Polish Immigrants in Britain*, p. 53.

360. David Pryce-Jones *The Strange Death of the Soviet Empire* (New York: Henry Holt and Co., 1995), p. 68.

361. Heinz Fassmann and Rainer Münz, "European East-West Migration, 1945–1992," *The Cambridge Survey of World Migration*, edited by Robin Cohen, p. 471.

362. Jerzy Zubrzycki, *Polish Immigrants in Britain*, p. 55.

363. Ibid., p. 16.

364. Ibid., pp. 19–20.

365. Carl Wittke, *We Who Built America: The Sage of the Immigrant* (Cleveland: Case Western Reserve University Press, 1967), p. 424.

366. Caroline Golab, *Immigrant Destinations* (Philadelphia: Temple University Press, 1977), pp. 101–104.

367. Jerzy Zubrycki, *Polish Immigrants in Britain*, p. 28.

368. M. M. Algaich, "Early Croatian Settlement in Australia," *The Australian People*, edited by James Jupp, p. 337.

369. M. J. Cigler, "Czechs," ibid., p. 347.

370. M. L. Lawriwsky, "Ukrainians," ibid., p. 827.

371. Karen Johnson Freeze, "Czechs," *Harvard Encyclopedia of American Ethnic Groups*, edited by Stephan Thernstrom, et al. (Cambridge, Massachusetts: Harvard University Press, 1980), p. 263.

372. Paul Robert Magocsi, "Carpatho-Rusyns," ibid., p. 203.

373. U.S. Commission on Civil Rights, *The Economic Status of Americans of Southern and Eastern European Ancestry* (Washington: U.S. Commission on Civil Rights, 1986), pp. 25–27, 31, 33, 35, 36, 37.

374. See, for example, Joseph Rothschild, *East Central Europe Between the Two World Wars*, p. 396; Robert Bartlett, *The Making of Europe*, p 277; Hugh LeCaine Agnew, *Origins of the Czech National Renascence*, p. 113.

375. Ibid., p. 93.

376. Paul Johnson, *Modern Times: A History of the World from the 1920s to the 1990s* (London: Orion Books, Ltd., 1996), p. 40.

377. Joseph Rothschild, *East Central Europe between the Two World Wars*, pp. 54–55, 152, 234, 319, 339.

378. Alexandre Bennigsen, "Soviet Minority Nationalism in Historical Perspective," *The Last Empire*, edited by Robert Conquest, p. 138.

379. Alexandre Bennigsen, "Soviet Minority Nationalism in Historical Perspective," *The Last Empire*, ed. Robert Conquest, p. 138.

380. Gertrude E. Schroeder, "Social and Economic Aspects of the Nationality Problem," ibid., p. 300.

381. Roman Szporluk, "The Ukraine and Russia," ibid., p. 152.

382. Jean François Revel, *The Flight from Truth: The Reign of Deceit in the Age of Information* (New York: Random House, 1991), pp. 244–245, 247, 250–251; Robert Conquest, *Harvest of Sorrow: Soviet Collectivization and the Famine-Terror* (New York: Oxford University Press, 1986, pp. 316, 319–321.

NOTES   55

83. Quoted in David Remnick, *Resurrection: The Struggle for A New Russia* (New York: Random House, 1997), p. 138.
384. Martha Brill Olcott, *The Kazakhs*, p. 71.
385. "Uzbek Leader Pleads for Moscow's Aid on Unrest," *The New York Times*, June 9, 1990, p. 4.
386. " . . . the death toll from ethnic violence in the Soviet Union stood at 332—more than the total for all of last year." Michael Dobbs, "Armenia in Mourning after Clashes Kill 22," *Washington Post*, May 29, 1990, p. A18. See also Esther B. Fein, "At Least 16 Killed as Protesters Battle the Police in Soviet Georgia," *The New York Times*, April 10, 1989, pp. A1, A6; Celestine Bohlen, "The Soviets and the Enmities Within," *The New York Times*, April 16, 1989, Section E, p. 1; Roman Szporluk, "The Ukraine and Russia," ibid., p. 152.
387. Nicholas Eberstadt, *The Tyranny of Numbers: Mismeasurement and Misrule* (Washington: American Enterprise Institute Press, 1995), pp. 92–101; Mark D'Anastasio, "Red Medicine," August 18, 1987, p. A1.

CHAPTER 5: WESTERN HEMISPHERE INDIANS

1. Edward Whiting Fox, *History in Geographic Perspective* (New York: W. W. Norton & Co., 1971), p. 22.
2. Michael Coe, et al., *Atlas of Ancient America* (New York: Facts on File Publications, 1986), p. 79.
3. Ibid., p. 89.
4. Robert J. Sharer, *The Ancient Maya*, fifth edition (Stanford: Stanford University Press, 1994), p. 455.
5. Despite much aversion among late twentieth-century intellectuals to continued use of the term "discovery," none of the proposed substitutes such as "contact" captures the enormous impact of this sudden revelation of half the world to the Europeans. That the indigenous peoples of the Western Hemisphere obviously knew that it was here all along does not prevent this from being a discovery, since discovery is inherently subjective. In this case, its consequences were historic for peoples on both sides of the Atlantic. Moreover, words like "contact" imply a mutuality that simply is not true. Indians did not discover Europe. Even the relatively few Indians who actually travelled to Europe were going to a place already known to them before they left home.

6. Alfred W. Crosby, *The Columbian Voyages, the Columbian Exchange, and Their Historians* (Washington: American Historical Association, 1987), p. 18.

7. Robert W. Patch, *Maya and Spaniard in Yucatan, 1648–1812* (Stanford: Stanford University Press, 1993), pp. 42–43.

8. William G. McLoughlin, *Cherokee Renascence in the New Republic* (Princeton: Princeton University Press, 1986), pp. 17–18.

9. James H. Merrell, " 'The Customes of Our Countrey': Indians and Colonists in Early America," *Strangers within the Realm: Cultural Margins of the First British Empire*, edited by Bernard Bailyn and Philip D. Morgan (Chapel Hill: University of North Carolina Press, 1991), p. 148.

10. Henry F. Dobyns, *Native American Historical Demography: A Critical Bibliography* (Bloomington: Indiana University Press, 1976), pp. 10–21; Harold E. Driver, *Indians of North America*, second edition (Chicago: University of Chicago Press, 1975, pp. 63–65. The greater plausibility of the higher estimates is argued in Francis Jennings, *The Invasion of America: Indians, Colonialism, and the Cant of Conquest* (New York: W. W. Norton, 1976), pp. 15–31.

11. Harold E. Driver, *Indians of North America*, revised edition, p. 64.

12. Colin McEvedy and Richard Jones, *Atlas of World Population History* (New York: Penguin Books, 1978), pp. 271–273.

13. Peter Gerhard, *A Guide to the Historical Geography of New Spain*, revised edition (Norman: University of Oklahoma Press, 1993), p. 5.

14. Edward H. Spicer, "American Indians," *Harvard Encyclopedia of American Ethnic Groups*, edited by Stephan Thernstrom, et al. (Cambridge, Massachusetts: Harvard University Press, 1981), p. 59.

15. Peter Gerhard, *A Guide to the Historical Geographical of New Spain*, revised edition (Norman: University of Oklahoma Press, 1993), p. 23.

16. Noble David Cook, *Demographic Collapse: Indian Peru, 1520–1620* (Cambridge: Cambridge University Press, 1981), p. 116.

17. John Hemming, *Red Gold: The Conquest of the Brazilian Indians* (London: Macmillan, Ltd., 1978), p. 492.

18. Richard B. Sheridan, "Mortality and Medical Treatment of Slaves in the British West Indies," *Race and Slavery in the Western Hemisphere: Quantitative Studies*, edited by Stanley L. Engerman and Eugene D. Genovese (Princeton: Princeton University Press, 1975), p. 285.

19. Carlo M. Cipolla, *Before the Industrial Revolution: European Soci-*

ety and Economy, 1000–1700 (New York: W. W. Norton Company, 1976), p. 239; Carlo M. Cipolla, *Guns, Sails, and Empires: Technological Innovation and the Early Phases of European Expansion, 1400–1700* (Manhattan, Kansas: Sunflower University Press, 1992), p. 134n.

20. Harold E. Driver, *Indians of North America*, 2nd edition, pp. 471–472; Carlo M. Cipolla, *Guns, Sails, and Empires*, pp. 142–143; Nigel Davies, *The Aztecs: A History* (Norman: University of Oklahoma Press, 1989), p. 271; Francis Jennings, *The Ambiguous Iroquois Empire: The Covenant Chain Confederation of Indian Tribes with English Colonies from its beginnings to the Lancaster Treaty of 1744* (New York: W. W. Norton, 1984), pp. 108, 134.

21. Francis Jennings, *The Ambiguous Iroquois Empire*, p. xvi.

22. Terry L. Anderson, *Sovereign Nations or Reservations? An Economic History of American Indians* (San Francisco: Pacific Research Institute for Public Policy, 1995), p. 70.

23. Ibid., p. 86.

24. Susan Migden Socolow, "Spanish Captives in Indian Societies: Cultural Contact Along the Argentine Frontier, 1600–1835," *Hispanic American Historical Review*, Vol. 72, No. 1 (February 1992), pp. 73–99.

25. Daniel J. Boorstin, *The Americans: The Colonial Experience* (New York: Random House, 1958), p. 56.

26. Dean R. Snow, *The Iroquois* (Oxford: Blackwell Publishers, 1996), p. 121.

27. Francis Jennings, *The Ambiguous Iroquois Empire*, p. 62.

28. Carlo M. Cipolla, *Before the Industrial Revolution*, pp. 29, 31.

29. Eric R. Wolf, *Europe and the People Without History* (Berkeley: University of California Press, 1982), pp. 137, 139.

30. Carlo M Cipolla, *Before the Industrial Revolution* pp. 250–253; Jaime Vicens Vives, "The Decline of Spain in the Seventeenth Century," *The Economic Decline of Empires*, edited by Carlo M. Cipolla (London: Methuen & Co., Ltd., 1970), pp. 121, 127, 156.

31. Jaime Vicens Vives, "The Decline of Spain in the Seventeenth Century," *The Economic Decline of Empires*, edited by Carlo M. Cipolla, p. 147.

32. Carlo M. Cipolla, *Before the Industrial Revolution*, p. 252.

33. Ibid., p. 240.

34. Ibid., p. 245.

35. William H. McNeill, *The Rise of the West*, pp. 599–600.

36. Fernand Braudel, *The Perspective of the World*, Volume III: *Capitalism and Civilization: 15th–18th Century* (New York: Harper & Row, 1984), p. 393;

37. Angie Debo, *A History of Indians of the United States* (Norman: University of Oklahoma Press, 1990), p. 73.

38. Michael Coe, et al., *Atlas of Ancient America*, p. 28.

39. D. W. Meinig, *The Shaping of America: A Geographic Perspective on 500 Years of History*, Volume I: *Atlantic America, 1492–1800* New Haven: Yale University Press, 1986), p. 9.

40. Eric R. Wolf, *Europe and the People Without History*, pp. 129–130.

41. Robert J. Sharer, *The Ancient Maya*, fifth edition, p. 61.

42. Michael D. Coe, *The Maya*, fifth edition (New York: Thames and Hudson, 1993), pp. 24, 47, 68–70, 109, 202, 212.

43. Ibid., p. 49.

44. Robert J. Sharer, *The Ancient Maya*, fifth edition, pp. 23, 28.

45. Robert W. Patch, *Maya and Spaniard in Yucatan, 1648–1812*, p. 11.

46. Ibid., pp. 14–16.

47. Robert J. Sharer, *The Ancient Maya*, fifth edition, p. 461.

48. Robert W. Patch, *Maya and Spaniard in Yucatan, 1648–1812*, pp. 18–19.

49. Michael D. Coe, *The Maya*, fifth edition, pp. 28, 40, 146.

50. See, for examples, ibid., pp. 52, 71, 104, 107, 109, 111, 163, 199; John S. Henderson, *The World of the Ancient Maya* (Ithaca, N.Y.: Cornell University Press, 1981), pp. 195; Robert J. Sharer, *The Ancient Maya*, fifth edition, pp. 403, 516, 544; "New Light on Dark History," *The Economist*, December 21, 1996, p. 57.

51. Michael D. Coe, *The Maya*, fifth edition, pp. 56, 108, 163, 171, 182

52. Robert J. Sharer, *The Ancient Maya*, fifth edition, pp. 140, 452.

53. Ibid., p. 175.

54. John S. Henderson, *The World of the Ancient Maya*, pp. 22, 148, 194, 235; Robert J. Sharer, *The Ancient Maya*, fifth edition, pp. 470–471.

55. See, for example, Lori E. Wright and Christine D. White, "Human Biology in the Classic Maya Collapse: Evidence from Paleopathology and Paleodiet," *Journal of World Prehistory*, Vol. 10, No. 2 (June 1996), pp. 147–19.

56. Jeremy A. Sabloff and Gordon R. Willey, "The Collapse of May Civilization in the Southern Lowlands: A Consideration of History and Process," *Southwestern Journal of Anthropology*, Vol. 23, No. 4 (Winter 1967), p. 314. Robert J. Sharer, *The Ancient Maya*, fifth edition, pp. 341, 342, 353.

57. Robert J. Sharer, *The Ancient Maya*, fifth edition , pp. 338–339.
58. Ibid., p. 382.
59. Ibid., pp. 3, 341.
60. Ibid., p. 406.
61. Ibid., pp. 732.
62. Ibid., pp. 734–735.
63. Ibid., pp. 738747.
64. Peter Gerhard, *A Guide to the Historical Geography of New Spain*, revised edition, p. 9.
65. See, for example, Peter Gerhard, *The Southeast Frontier of New Spain*, revised edition (Norman: University of Oklahoma Press, 1993), pp. 9–12; Peter Gerhard, *The Northern Frontier of New Spain*, revised edition (Norman: University of Oklahoma Press, 1993), pp. 9–10; Peter Gerhard, *A Guide to the Historical Geography of New Spain*, pp. 8–10.
66. Robert W. Patch, *Maya and Spaniard in Yucatan*, p. 22.
67. Peter Gerhard, *A Guide to the Historical Geography of New Spain*, p. 7.
68. Robert W. Patch, *Maya and Spaniard in Yucatan, 1648–1812* (Stanford: Stanford University Press, 1993), pp. 22–23.
69. Ibid., pp. 42–44.
70. Ibid., p. 81.
71. Ibid.
72. Ibid., pp. 233–234, 242.
73. Nigel Davies, *The Aztecs*, p. 10.
74. Ibid., pp. 7, 8, 12, 20–21.
75. Ibid., pp. 23, 78
76. Ibid., p. 28.
77. Ibid., p. 38.
78. Richard F. Townshend, *The Aztecs* (London: Thames and Hudson, 1992), pp. 184–185.
79. Ibid., p. 171.
80. Nigel Davies, *The Aztecs*, p. 210.
81. Richard F. Townsend, *The Aztecs*, p. 187.
82. Nigel Davies, *The Aztecs*, pp. 167, 190.
83. Hugh Thomas, *Conquest: Montezuma, Cortes, and the Fall of Old Mexico* (New York: Simon & Schuster, 1993), pp. 25–26.
84. Richard F. Townsend, *The Aztecs*, pp. 91–92, 100.
85. Ibid., pp. 90–91, 101.
86. Ibid.
87. Ibid., pp. 14, 15.

88. Ibid., p. 16.

89. Ibid., pp. 21–22.

90. Ibid., pp. 23–24.

91. Nigel Davies, *The Aztecs*, p. 268.

92. Ibid.

93. Ibid., p. 270.

94. Ibid., pp. 271–272.

95. Ibid., pp. 271–282; Richard F. Townsend, *The Aztecs*, pp. 35–42.

96. Michael E. Moseley, *The Incas and Their Ancestors* (New York: Thames and Hudson, 1993), p. 29.

97. Michael E. Moseley, *The Incas and Their Ancestors*, p. 9.

98. John Hemming, *The Conquest of the Incas* (New York: Harcourt and Brace Jovanovich, 1970), pp. 171; Alan Kolata, "In the Realm of the Four Quarters," *America in 1492: The World of the Indian Peoples Before the Arrival of Columbus* (New York: Alfred A. Knopf, 1993), pp, 228–230; Steve J. Stern, *Peru's Indian Peoples and the Challenge of Spanish Conquest: Huamanga to 1640* (Madison: University of Wisconsin Press), pp. 12, 13, 20.

99. John Hemming, *The Conquest of the Incas*, p. 121.

100. Michael E. Moseley, *The Incas and the Ancestors*, pp. 910.

101. John Hemming, *The Conquest of the Inca*, p. 36.

102. John Hemming, *The Conquest of the Incas*, p. 61; Michael Coe, et al., *Atlas of Ancient America*, pp. 197, 201; Nigel Davies, *The Incas*, p. 118.

103. Michael E. Moseley, *The Incas and Their Ancestors*, p. 11.

104. Nigel Davies, *The Incas* (Niwot, Colorado: University of Colorado Press, 1995), Chapter 8; Burr Cartwright Brundage, *Empire of the Inca* (Norman: University of Oklahoma Press, 1985), Chapter 13.

105. Burr Cartwright Brundage, *Empire of the Inca* (Norman: University of Oklahoma Press, 1985), p. 298.

106. Ibid., pp. 261–262.

107. John Hemming, *The Conquest of the Incas*, pp. 36–45.

108. Ibid., p. 74.

109. Ibid., pp. 110–115.

110. Ibid., p. 138.

111. Ibid., p. 140.

112. Ibid., pp. 146, 147.

113. Ibid., pp. 180–184.

114. Ibid., p. 226.

115. Ibid., pp. 417–420.

116. Dean R. Snow, *The Iroquois*, p. 38.

117. William G. McLoughlin, *Cherokee Renascence in the New Republic*, Chapter 16.

118. William G. McLoughlin, *Cherokee Renascence in the New Republic* (Princeton: Princeton University Press, 1986), p. 3

119. Francis Jennings, *The Invasion of America*, pp. 128–129.

120. See, for example, ibid., pp. 144–145.

121. Ian K. Steele, *Warpaths: Invasions of North America* (New York: Oxford University Press, 1994), p. 58.

122. Ibid., p. 68.

123. D. W. Meinig, *The Shaping of America*, Volume I: *Atlantic America, 1492–1800*, pp. 62, 119.

124. Francis Jennings, *The Ambiguous Iroquois Empire*, pp. 91, 119.

125. D. W. Meinig, *The Shaping of America*, Vol. I, p. 148.

126. Ian K. Steele, *Warpaths*, p. 75.

127. D. W. Meinig, *The Shaping of America*, Volume I: *Atlantic America, 1492–1800*, pp. 92, 97, 119.

128. Ian K. Steele, *Warpaths*, p. 84.

129. Ibid., pp. 86–87.

130. William T. Hagan, *American Indians*, third edition (Chicago: University of Chicago Press, 1993), pp. 28–29. See also Bernard W. Sheehan, *Seeds of Extinction: Jefferson Philanthropy and the American Indian* (Chapel Hill: University of North Carolina Press, 1973), pp. 185–194.

131. William T. Hagan, *American Indians*, p. 21.

132. Ian K. Steele, *Warpaths*, p. 239.

133. Eric R. Wolf, *Europe and the People Without History*, p. 158–159; Francis Jennings, *The Invasion of America*, pp. 97–98.

134. E. E. Rich, "Trade Habits and Economic Motivation among the Indians of North America," *Canadian Journal of Economics and Political Science*, Vol. 26, No. 1 (February 1960), p. 36.

135. Ian K. Steele, *Warpaths*, pp. 76–77.

136. Ibid., pp. 96–107.

137. E. E. Rich, "Trade Habits and Economic Motivation among the Indians of North America," *Canadian Journal of Economics and Political Science*, Vol. 26, No. 1 (February 1960), p. 38.

138. Eric R. Wolf, *Europe and the People Without History*, p. 170.

139. Ian K. Steele, *Warpaths*, pp. 37–49.

140. Francis Jennings, *The Invasion of America*, pp. 129–130; Dean R. Snow, *The Iroquois*, p. 154.

141. Quoted in Terry Anderson, *Sovereign Nations or Reservations?*, p. 69.

142. Ian K. Steele, *Warpaths*, p. 76.

143. C. E. Marshall, "The Birth of the Mestizo in New Spain," *Hispanic American Historical Review*, Vol. 19 (1939), pp. 161–184.

144. See, for example, William T. Hagan, *American Indians*, third edition, pp. 200–210; Fergus M. Bordewich, "Revolution in Indian Country," *American Heritage*, Vol. 47, No. 4 (July/August 1996), pp. 34–46.

145. *Cree v. Waterbury*, Ninth Circuit Court of Appeals, *Daily Appellate Report*, March 7, 1996, pp. 2583–2585.

146. *Seminole India Tribe of Florida v. Florida*, U.S. Supreme Court, *Daily Appellate Report*, March 28, 1996.

147. Dean R. Snow, *The Iroquois*, p. 2.

148. Ibid., pp. 52–62.

149. Dean R. Snow, *The Iroquois*, pp. 40–46. Ian K. Steele, *Warpaths*, p. 113.

150. Dean R. Snow, *The Iroquois*, p. 92.

151. Ibid., p. 125; Ian K. Steele, *Warpaths*, p. 117.

152. Dean R. Snow, *The Iroquois*, pp. 32, 53, 54–55, 114–116, 127

153. Francis Jennings, *The Invasion of America*, p. 166

154. Ian K. Steele, *Warpaths*, p. 89.

155. Dean R. Snow, *The Iroquois*, p. 142.

156. Ian K. Steele, *Warpaths*, pp. 113–123.

157. See Gary C. Goodwin, *Cherokees in Transition: A Study of Changing Culture and Environment Prior to 1775* (Chicago: University of Chicago Geography Department, 1977), pp. 7, 9; William G. McLoughlin, *Cherokee Renascence in the New Republic*, p. 27.

158. Gary C. Goodwin, *Cherokees in Transition*, p. 34.

159. Ibid., p. 37.

160. Ibid., pp. 82–90.

161. Ibid., p. 93.

162. Ibid., p. 98.

163. Ibid., pp. 126–128, 130–136.

164. William G. McLoughlin, *Cherokee Renascence in the New Republic*, p. 3.

165. U.S. Bureau of the Census, *Historical Statistic of the United States: Colonial Times to 1970* (Washington: Government Printing Office, 1976), p. 8.

166. William G. McLoughlin, *Cherokee Renascence in the New Republic*, pp. 350–351.

167. William T. Hagan, *American Indians*, p. 81.

168. Ibid., pp. 89–90.

169. Paul Stuart, *Nations Within a Nation: Historical Statistics of American Indians* (New York: Greenwood Press, 1987), pp. 78, 79.

170. William T. Hagan, *American Indians*, pp. 95–96.

171. Robert M. Utley, *The Indian Frontier of the American West*, p. 261.

172. U.S. Bureau of the Census, *1990 Census of Population: Characteristics of American Indians by Tribe and Language* (Washington: U.S. Government Printing Office, 1994), p. 1, 185.

173. Terry L. Anderson, *Sovereign Nations or Reservations?*, p. 14.

174. Peter Iverson, *When Indians Became Cowboys* (Norman: University of Oklahoma Press, 1994), pp. 8–9.

175. John C. Evers, *The Horse in Blackfoot Indian Culture: With Comparative Material from Other Western Tribes* (Washington: Smithsonian Institution Press, 1969), pp. 1–4.

176. John C. Ewers, *The Horse in Blackfoot Indian Culture*, pp. 6, 13–14.

177. John C. Ewers, *The Horse in Blackfoot Indian Culture*, p. 21.

178. William T. Hagan, *American Indians*, p. 105.

179. Ibid., p. 130.

180. Robert M. Utley, *The Indian Frontier of the American West: 1846–1890* (Albuquerque: University of New Mexico Press, 1984), pp. 78–81.

181. Robert M. Utley, *The Indian Frontier of the American West*, pp. 81–86.

182. Robert M. Utley, *The Indian Frontier of the American West*, pp. 93–95.

183. Steven J. Novak, "The Real Takeover of the BIA: The Preferential Hiring of Indians," *Journal of Economic History*, Vol. L, No. 3 (September 1990), p. 644.

184. Robert M. Utley, *The Indian Frontier of the American West*, p. 267.

185. Martin Binkin, *Blacks and the Military* (Washington: The Brooking Institute, 1982), p. 15; Daniel F. Littlefield, Jr., *Africans and Seminoles: From Removal to Emancipation* (Westport, CT: Greenwood Press, 1977), pp. 5–6, 200–201.

186. Steven J. Novak, "The Rela Takeover of the BIA: The Preferential Hiring of Indians," *Journal of Economic History*, Vol. L, No. 3 (September 1990), pp. 639–654.

187. Patrick Kluck, "The Society and Its Enviroment," *Bolivia: A Country Study*, edited by Rex A. Hudson and Dennis M. Hanratty (Washington: U.S. Government Printing Office, 1991), p. 65.

188. Thomas E. Weill, et al., *Area Handbook for Mexico* (Washington: U.S. Government Printing Office, 1975), pp. 88–89.

189. Iêda Siqueira Wiarda, "The Society and Its Environment," *Venezuela: A Country Study*, fourth edition, edited by Richard A. Haggerty (Washington: U.S. Government Printing Office, 1993), p. 63; Thomas E. Weill, et al., *Area Handbook for Chile* (Washington: U.S. Government Printing Office, 1969), p. 59; Patrick Kluck, "The Society and its Environment," *Paraguay: A Country Study*, second edition, edited by Dennis M. Hanratty and Sandra W. Meditz (Washington: U.S. Government Printing Office, 1990), pp. 84–85.

190. Patricia Kluck, "The Society and Its Environment," *Ecuador: A Country Study*, edited by Dennis M. Hanratty (Washington: U.S. Government Printing Office, 1991), p. 83.

191. Bruce Michael Bagley, "The Society and Its Environment," *Colombia: A Country Study*, fourth edition, edited by Dennis M. Hanratty and Sandra W. Meditz (Washington: U.S. Government Printing Office, 1990), p. 74.

192. Paul L. Doughty, "The Society and Its Environment," *Peru: A Country Study*, edited by Rex A. Hudson (Washington: U.S. Government Printing Office, 1993), p. 128

193. See, for example, Robert M. Utley, *The Indian Frontier of the American West*, pp. 43–44, 61, 112; Robert J. Sharer, *The Ancient Maya*, fifth edition, pp. 422; Dean R. Snow, *The Iroquois*, pp. 79, 142; William T. Hagan, *American Indians*, third edition, p. 28.

194. For example, King Philip II of Spain said: "The kings have been and are bound to us by treaties, but remember that they are not true to their undertakings and only keep their word when they are too poor to go to war." John Hale, *The Civilization of Europe in the Renaissance* (New York: Atheneum, 1994), p. 95. In essay number 5 of *The Federalist Papers*, John Hay noted the conquests made by the Roman of people who were supposedly their allies. Alexander Hamilton, James Madison, and John Jay, *The Federalist Papers* (New York: New American Library, 1961), p. 53.

195. Gary D. Sandefur, "Minority Group Status and the Wages of White, Black, and Indian Workers," *Social Science Research*, March 1983, pp. 44–68.

196. See, for example, Thomas Sowell, editor, *Essays and Data on American Ethnic Groups* (Washington: The Urban Institute, 1978), p. 257.

197. U.S. Department of Commerce, Bureau of the Census, *1990 Census of Population and Housing: Summary Social, Economics, and Housing Characteristics* 1990 CPHa–5–1 (Washington: U.S. Government Printing Office, 1992), p. 228; U.S. Department of Commerce, Bureau of the Census, *1990 Census of Population: Characteristics of American Indians by Tribe and Language*, p. 182.

198. U.S. Department of Commerce, Bureau of the Census, *1990 Census of Population: Characteristics of American Indians by Tribe and Language* (1990-CP–3–7), Section 1 of 2, p. 182; U.S. Bureau of the Census, *Current Population Reports*, Series P–20, No. 446 (Washington: U.S. Government Printing Office, 1991), p. 11.

199. U.S. Bureau of the Census, *1990 Census of Population: Characteristics of American Indians by Tribe and Language*, pp. 1, 19, 862, 865.

200. U.S. Department of Commerce, Bureau of the Census *of Population: 1970*, Subject Reports: *American Indians*, PC(2)–1f (Washington: U.S. Government Printing Office, 1973), p. 1; U.S. Department of Commerce, Bureau of the Census, *1990 Census of Population: Characteristics of American Indians by Tribe and Language* (1990-CP–3–7), Section 1 of 2, p. 1.

201. The 1890 census enumerated 248,253 Indians, the 1960 census 509,147 and the 1990 census 1,937,391. See Paul Stuart, *Nations with a Nation*, p. 54; U.S. Department of Commerce, Bureau of the Census, *1990 Census of Population: Characteristics of American Indians by Tribe and Language* (1990-CP–3–7), Section 1 of 2, p. 1.

202. Mel Smith, "What Government Aboriginal Policy Is Doing to Canada," *Fraser Forum*, March 1996, pp. 5–10.

203. J. S. Frideres, "The Quest for Indian Developmenmt in Canada: Contrasts and Contradictions," *The Political Economy of North American Indians*, edited by John H. Moore (Norman: University of Oklahoma Press, 1993), pp. 164–165.

204. James Brooke, "Indians' Cruel Winter of Aid Cuts and Cold," *New York Times*, January 27, 1997, pp. A1, A8.

205. Francis Jennings, *The Invasion of America*, p. 39.

206. "New Light on Dark History," *The Economist*, December 21, 1996, pp. 55–60.

207. Francis Jennings, *The Invasion of America*, p. 22.

208. Gary D. Sandefur, "Minority Group Status and the Wages of White, Black, and Indian Males," *Social Science Research*, March 1983, pp. 44–68.

209. Rex A. Hudson, "Introduction," *Peru: A Country Study*, edited by Rex A. Hudson (Washington: U.S. Government Printing Office, 1993), p. xxxi.
210. Paul L. Doughty, "The Society and Its Environment," *Peru: A Country Study*, edited by Rex A. Hudson, p. 100.
211. Paul L. Doughty, "The Society and Environment," *Peru: A Country Study*, edited by Rex A. Hudson, p. 128.

CHAPTER 6: AN OVERVIEW

1. Aaron L. Friedberg, *The Weary Titan: Britain and the Experience of Relative Decline 1895–1905* (Princeton: Princeton University Press, 1988), p. 26.
2. Tom Betthell, "Property Law 101," *Hoover Digest*, 1996, No. 2, p. 22.
3. Andrew Tanzer, "The Bamboo Network," *Forbes*, July 18, 1994, pp. 138–145.
4. "The Tigers' Fearful Symmetry," *The Economist*, July 19, 1997, p. 35.
5. Mark Casson, *The Growth of International Business* (London: Allen & Unwin, 1983), p. 106.
6. Writing of West Africa in the middle of the twentieth century, Professor Peter T. Bauer of the London School of Economics made an observation that would apply in many other places, in both industrial and non-industrial nations: "The people often exhibit a pronounced ignorance of the operation of an exchange and market economy . . . The profit margins of the European firms and of the Levantine and African intermediaries are believed to depend solely or largely on their own decisions, which are only remotely connected with such academic matters as supply and demand. Accumulated wealth is thought to have been earned solely by the impoverishment of customers or competitors. It is a widespread article of faith that the wealth of the mercantile firms has been extracted from the Africans and has in no way been created by the activities of the merchants." P. T. Bauer, *West African Trade: A Study of Competition, Oligopoly and Monopoly in a Changing Economy* (Cambridge: Cambridge University Press, 1954), p. 9. Halfway around the world, the same fallacy was popular in Thailand, where the Chinese were seen as impoverishing the country by sending part of their income back to their families in China. As British scholar Victor Purcell put it: "Those who argue that the Chinese 'drew off wealth' ignore the fact that without the Chinese there would have been no wealth to draw

off." Victor Purcell, *The Overseas Chinese in Southeast Asia*, second edition (Kuala Lumpur: Oxford University Press, 1980), p. 123.

7. V. I. Lenin, *Imperialism, the Highest Stage of Capitalism* (Peking: Foreign Languages Press, 1975), pp. 75–76.

8. Mira Wilkins, *The History of Foreign Investment in the United States to 1914* (Cambridge, Massachusetts: Harvard University Press, 1989), p. 609.

9. U.S. Bureau of the Census, *Historical Statistics of the United States: From Colonial Times to 1870* (Washington: Government Printing Office, 1975), p. 870.

10. As regards the role of people from India in East Africa, for example, see J. S. Mangat, *A History of the Asians in East Africa* (Oxford: Clarendon Press, 1969); Robert G. Gregory, *South Indians in East Africa: An Economic and Social History, 1890–1980* (Boulder, Colorado: Westview Press, 1993); Floyd Dotson and Lillian O. Dotson, *The Indian Minority of Zambia, Rhodesia, and Malawi* (New Haven: Yale University Press, 1968); Haraprasad Chattopadhyaya, *Indians in Africa: A Socio-Economic Study* (Calcutta: Bookland Pvt. Ltd., 1978); Agehananda Bharati, *The Asians in East Africa: Jayind and Uhuru* (Chicago: Nelson-Hall Co., 1972); Michael Twaddle, *Expulsion of a Minority: Essays on Ugandan Asians* (London: The Athlone Press, 1975). On the role of the Lebanese in West Africa, see for example, Albert Hourani & Nadim Shehadi, *The Lebanese in the World: A Century of Migration* (London: I. B. Tauris & Co., Ltd., 1992), Part Four; H. L. van der Laan, *The Lebanese Traders in Sierra Leone* (The Hague: Mouton & Co., 1975); Peter Bauer, *West African Trade* (Cambridge: Cambridge University Press, 1954), pp. 148–149, 160–162, 164–167.

11. Jean Roche, *La Colonisation Allemande et le Rio Grande* (Paris: Institute des Hautes Études de L'Amerique Latine, 1959), pp. 388–389; Fred C. Koch, *The Volga Germans: In Russia and the Americas, from 1763 to the Present* (University Park: Pennsylvania State University Press, 1978), p. 227; Kathleen Neils Conzen, *Immigrant Milwaukee: Accommodation and Community in a Frontier City* (Cambridge, Massachusetts: Harvard University Press, 1976), pp. 105–105; Rudolf Kinglake, *A History of the Photographic Lens* (San Diego: Academic Press, 1989), pp. 108–309; James M. KcKeown and Joan C. McKeown, *Price Guide to Antique and Classic Cameras*, seventh edition (Hover, East Sussex, U.K.: Hove Foto Books, 1989), pp. 191–202, 205.

12. See, for example, Thomas Sowell, *Migrations and Cultures: A World View* (New York: Basic Books, 1996), pp. 9–19; Thomas Sowell, *Race and Culture: A World View* (New York: Basic Books, 1994), pp. 235–246.

13. James L. Tigner, *The Okinawans in Latin America* (Washington: Pacific Science Board, National Research Council, 1954), pp. 126–128.

14. Forrest MacDonald, "Prologue," *Cracker Culture: Celtic Ways in the Old South* (Tuscaloosa:; University of Alabama Press, 1998), p. xxi.

15. Grady McWhiney, *Cracker Culture: Celtic Ways in the Old South* (Tuscaloosa: University of Alabama Press, 1988), p. 258; Frederick Law Olmsted, *The Cotton Kingdom: A Traveller's Observations on Cotton and Slavery in the American Slave States* (New York: The Modern Library, 1969), pp. 177, 186, 212, 214, 220, 423, 427.

16. John Stuart Mill, *Principles of Political Economy with Some of Their Application to Social Philosophy*, edited by W. J. Ashley (London: Longmans, Green, and Co., 1909), pp. 74–75.

17. G. M. Trevelyan, *English Social History: A Survey of Six Countries, Chaucer to Queen Victoria* (New York: Penguin Books, 1986), pp. 34, 72n.

18. Caroline Golab, *Immigrant Destinations* (Philadelphia: Temple University Press, 1977), pp. 101–104.

19. Raphael Patai, *The Jewish Mind* (New York: Charles Scribner's Sons, 1977), pp. 122–124; Jane S. Gerber, *The Jews of Spain: A History of the Sephardic Experience* (New York: The Free Press, 1992), pp. 45, 47, 61–63, 74–75, 86.

20. See, for example, Jean W. Sedlar, *East Central Europe in the Middle Ages, 1000–1500* (Seattle: University of Washington Press, 1994), pp. 124–125.

21. See, for example, Charles Kindleberger, *World Economic Primacy: 1500–1990* (Oxford: Oxford University Press, 1996), p. 102.

22. Gareth Austin, "Indigenous Credit Institutions in West Africa, c.1750–c.1960," *Local Suppliers of Credit in the Third World, 1750–1960*, edited by Gareth Austin and Kaoru Sugihara (London: St. Martin's Press, 1993), pp. 111–112; Traian Stoianovich, "The Conquering Balkan Orthodox Merchant," *Journal of Economic History*, Vol. 20, No. 2 (June 1960), p. 304.

23. Traian Stoianovich, "The Conquering Balkan Orthodox Merchant," *Journal of Economic History*, Vol. 20, No. 2 (June 1960), p. 304.

24. Eric Richards, "Scotland and the Uses of the Atlantic Empire," *Strangers within the Realm: Cultural Margins of the First British Empire*, edited by Bernard Bailyn and Philip D. Morgan (Chapel Hill: University of North Carolina Press, 1991), p. 84.

25. Yasuo Wakatsuki, "Japanese Emigration to the United States, 1866–1924," *Perspectives in American History*, Vol. XX (1979), pp. 430–434, 438.

26. Even after suffering humiliating military defeats from Japan in the 1890s, China continued training its military forces in obsolete methods and promoting them on the basis of their knowledge of ancient writings on war. Victor Purcell, *The Boxer Rebellion: A Background Study* (Cambridge: Cambridge University Press, 1963), pp. 30–31.

27. "Caspian Oil and Quicksand," *New York Times*, August 4, 1997, p. A 14.

28. Nathan Rosenberg and L. E. Birdzell, Jr., *How the West Grew Rich: The Economic Transformation of the Industrial World* (New York: Basic Books, 1986), p. 116.

29. Angelo M. Codevilla, *The Character of Nations* (New York: Basic Books, 1997), p. 42.

30. Barbara Crossette, "Survey Ranks Nigeria as Most Corrupt Nation," *New York Times*, International Section, p. 3.

31. Charles Kindleberger, *World Economic Primacy: 1500 to 1990* (Oxford: Oxford University Press, 1996), pp. 121–122.

32. Edward C. Banfield, *The Moral Basis of a Backward Society* (New York: The Free Press, 1958), pp. 7, 8, 9–10, 18–20, 31, 37, 38, 87.

33. See, for example, R. Jayaraman, "Indian Emigration to Ceylon: Some Aspects of the Historical and Social Background of the Emigrants," *Indian Economic and Social History Review*, December 1967, pp. 35352; William McGown, *And Only Man is Vile: The Tragedy of Sri Lanka* (New York: Farrar, Straus, and Giroux, 1992), pp. 287–289.

34. See, for example, *International Technology Transfer: Europe, Japan and the USA, 1700–1914*, edited by David J. Jeremy (London: Edward Elgar Publishing Ltd., 1991); G. C. Allen and Audrey G. Donnnithorne, *Western Enterprise in Far Eastern Economic Development* (London: George Allen & Unwin, Ltd., 1962), pp. 185–237; Neil Pedlar, *The Imported Pioneers: Westerners Who Helped Build Modern Japan* (New York: St. Martin's Press, 1990).

35. Robert A. Kann; Piotr S. Wandycz, *The Lands of Partitioned*

Poland: 1795–1918 (Seattle: University of Washington Press, 1993), p. 129.

36. Robert A. Kann and Zdenek V. David, *The Peoples of the Eastern Habsburg Lands, 1526–1918* (Seattle: University of Washington Press, 1984), pp. 443–444

37. Victor Purcell, *The Overseas Chinese in Southeast Asia*, second edition (Kuala Lumpur: Oxford University Press, 1980), p. 129.

38. Mohamed Suffian bin Hashim, "Problems and Issues of Higher Education Development in Malaysia," *Development of Higher Education in Southeast Asia: Problems and Issues* (Singapore: Regional Institute of Higher Education and Development, 1973), pp. 56–78.

39. Anatoly M. Kazanova, "The Ethnic Problems of Contemporary Kazakhstan," *Century Asian Survey*, Vol. 14, No. 2 (1995), p. 253; Chandra Richard de Silva, "Sinhala-Tamil Relations and Education in Sri Lanka: The University Admissions Issue—the First Phase, 1971–7," *From Independence to Statehood: Managing Ethnic Conflict in Five African and Asian States*, edited by R. B. Goldmann and A. J. Wilson (London: Frances Pinter, 1994), pp. 125–146; Suma Chitnis, "Positive Discrimination in India with Reference to Education," ibid., pp. 31–43; Sammy Smooha and Yochanan Peres, "The Dynamics of Ethnic Equality: The Case of Israel," *Studies of Israeli Society*, edited by Ernest Krausz (New Brunswick, N.J.: Transaction Books, 1980), p. 173; Paul Compton, "The Conflict in Northern Ireland: Demographic and Economic Considerations," *Economic Dimensions of Ethnic Conflicts: International Perspectives*, edited by S. W. R. de A Smarragonghe and Reed Coughlan (London: Pinter Publishers, 1991), pp. 35–39, 41; Thomas Sowell, "Ethnicity in a Changing America," *Daedalus*, Winter 1978, pp. 231–232.

40. Ezra Mendelsohn, *The Jews of East Central Europe Between the World Wars* (Bloomington: Indiana University Press, 1983), p. 99.

41. Mary Fainsod Katzenstein, *Ethnicity and Equality: The Shiv Sena Party and Preferential Policies in Bombay* (Ithaca: Cornell University Press, 1979), pp. 75–76; Myron Weiner, *Sons of the Soil: Migration and Ethnic Conflict in India* (Princeton: Princeton University Press, 1978), pp. 287–288.

42. Larry Diamond, "Class, Ethnicity, and the Democratic State: Nigeria, 1950–1966," *Comparative Studies in Social History*, July 1983, pp. 462, 473.

43. Anatoly M. Khazanov, "The Ethnic Problems of Contemporary Khazkhstan," *Central Asian Survey*, Vol. 14, No. 2 (1995), pp. 244, 257.

44. Joseph Rothschild, *East Central Europe between the Two World Wars* (Seattle: University of Washington Press, 1992), p. 293; Irina Livezeanu, *Cultural Politics in Greater Romania: Regionalism, Nation Building, & Ethnic Struggle, 1918–1930* (Ithaca: Cornell University Press, 1993), *passim*.

45. H. L. van der Laan, *The Lebanese Traders in Sierra Leone* (The Hague: Mouton & Co., 1975), p. 292.

46. Robert N. Kearney, *Communalism and Language in the Politics of Ceylon* (Durham: Duke University Press, 1967), p. 71.

47. Conrad Black, "Canada's Continuing Identity Crisis," *Foreign Affairs*, April 1995, p. 100.

48. See, for example, Gary B. Cohen, *The Politics of Ethnic Survival: Germans in Prague, 1861–1914* (Princeton: Princeton University Press, 1983), pp. 26–28, 32, 133, 236–237; Ezra Mendelsohn, *The Jews of East Central Europe between the World Wars*, p. 167; Hugh LeCaine Agnew, *Origins of the Czech Renascence* (Pittsburgh: University of Pittsburgh Press, 1993), *passim*.

49. William Pfaff, *The Wrath of Nations: Civilization and the Furies of Nationalism* (New York: Simon & Schuster, 1993), p. 156.

50. Maurice Pinard and Richard Hamilton, "The Class Base of the Quebec Independence Movement: Conjectures and Evidence," *Ethnic and Racial Studies*, January 1984, pp. 19–54.

51. Joseph Rothschild, *East Central Europe between the Two World Wars*, p. 20.

52. Chandra Richard de Silva, "Sinhala-Tamil Relations and Education in Sri Lanka: The University Admissions Issue—The First Phase, 1970–1," *From Independence to Statehood: Managing Ethnic Conflict in five African and Asian States*, edited by Robert R. Goldmann and A. Jeyaratnam Wilson (London: Frances Pinter, Ltd. 1984), p. 126.

53. Warren Zimmerman, "The Last Ambassador: A Memoir of the Collapse of Yugoslavia," *Foreign Affairs*, March/April 1995, pp. 9, 17; William Pfaff, *The Wrath of Nations*, p. 55.

54. Paul Johnson, *Modern Times: A History of the World from the 1920s to the 1990s* (London: Orion Books Ltd., 1992), pp. 654–655.

55. Quoted in William Pfaff, *The Wrath of Nations*, p. 96.

56. Joseph Rothschild, *East Central Europe between the Two World Wars*

(Seattle: University of Washington Press, 1992), p. 385. Foreign universities complained of the low quality of Romanian students' educational preparation. (Irina Livezeanu, *Cultural Politics in Greater Romania*, p. 79.) As regards the role of the Romanian universities in producing government bureaucrats, see ibid., pp. 213, 215, 218.

57. See, for example, Paul Johnson, *Modern Times: A History of the World from the 1920s to the 1990s* (London: Orion Books Ltd., 1992), pp. 275–277; Sidney Hook, *Out of Step: An Unquiet Life in the 20th Century* (New York: Harper & Row, 1987), Chapters 17, 18; Jean-François Revel, *How Democracies Perish* (New York: Harper & Row, 1983), pp. 155–156.

58. See, for example, William H. McNeill, *The Pursuit of Power: Technology, Armed Force, and Society Since A.D. 1000* (Chicago: University of Chicago Press, 1984), p. 49.

59. "A political map of Europe for the year 1400 A.D. shows a plethora of independent and semi-independent states—kingdoms, principalities and duchies abounded." Richard Bean, "War and the Birth of the National State," *Journal of Economic History*, Vol. 33, No. 1 (March 1973), p. 203.

60. Jean W. Sedlar, *East Central Europe in the Middle Ages, 1000–1500* (Seattle: University of Washington Press, 1994), p. 287.

61. Nancy deWolf Smith, "The Wisdom That Built Hong Kong's Prosperity," *Wall Street Journal*, July 1, 1997, p. A 14.

62. Peter F. Sugar, *Southeastern Europe under Ottoman Rule, 1354–1804* (Seattle: University of Washington Press, 1993), pp. 52–54.

63. Michael D. Coe, *The Maya*, fifth edition (New York: Thames and Hudson, 1993), pp. 204, 208.

64. John K. Fairbank, Edwin O. Reischauer, and Albert M. Craig, *East Asia: Tradition and Transformation*, revised edition (Cambridge, Massachusetts: Harvard University Press, 1989), pp. 249.

65. Ibid., pp. 85–86.

66. George Gerster, "River of Sorrow, River of Hope," *National Geographic*, Vol. 148, No. 2 (August 1975), p. 156.

67. Hugh Thomas, *Conquest: Montezuma, Cortés, and the Fall of Old Mexico* (New York: Simon & Schuster, 1993), p. 83.

68. Josip Roglic, "The Geographical Setting of Medieval Dubrovnik," *Geographical Essays on Eastern Europe*, edited by Norman J. G. Pounds (Bloomington: Indiana University Press, 1961), pp. 150, 155.

69. Daniel Pipes, "The Western Mind of Radical Islam," *First Things*, December 1995, pp. 18–23.

70. Warren C. Scoville, *The Persecution of Huguenots and French Economic Development: 1680–1720* (Berkeley: University of California Press, 1960).

71. Stephen Frederic Dale, *Indian Merchants and Eurasian Trade, 1600–1750* (Cambridge: Cambridge University Press, 1994), p. 74.

72. David Hackett Fischer, *Albion's Seed: Four British Folkways in America* (New York: Oxford University Press, 1989), pp. 125–126.

73. See, for example, Fernand Braudel, *A History of Civilizations*, translated by Richard Mayne (New York: The Penguin Press, 1994), p. 80; Morris Kline, *Mathematics in Western Culture* (New York: Penguin Books, 1987), pp. 30–41, 57.

74. Madison Grant, *The Passing of the Great Race: Or the Racial Basis of European History*, fourth edition (New York: Charles Scribner's Sons, 1924), p. 100.

75. Robert A. Wilson and Bill Hosokawa, *East to America: A History of the Japanese in the United States* (New York: William Morrow and Company, Inc., 1980), p. 123.

76. Mahatir bin Mohamad, *The Malay Dilemma* (Kuala Lumpur: Federal Publications, 1970) p. 25.

77. Donald L. Horowitz, *Ethnic Groups in Conflict*, p. 178.

78. Ibid., pp. 167, 171–180.

79. Quoted in Bernard Lewis, *The Muslim Discovery of Europe* (New York: W. W. Norton, 1982), p. 139.

80. Jack Chen, *The Chinese of America* (San Francisco: Harper & Row, 1980), p. 35.

81. Mark R. Levy and Michael S. Kramer, *The Ethnic Factor: How America's Minorities Decide Elections* (New York: Simon and Schuster, 1972), p. 175, 177–178.

82. Arthur R. Jensen, "How Much Can We Boost I.Q. and Scholastic Achievement?" *Harvard Educational Review*, Winter 1969, p.117.

83. Richard J. Herrnstein and Charles Murray, *The Bell Curve*, p. 278.

84. Ibid., Chapter 9.

85. This point is pursued further in my "Ethnicity and I.Q.," *The American Spectator*, February 1995, pp. 32–37.

86. See Dinesh D'souza, *The End of Racism: Principles for a Multiracial Society* (New York: Free Press, 1995), pp. 402–407.

87. Michele Block Morse, "Brain Power: New Evidence Confirms that Early Stimulation Makes a Big Difference Later On," *Parents Magazine*, Vol. 9, No. 9 (September 1994), pp. 61–62.

88. See Miles D. Storfer, *Intelligence and Giftedness: The Contribution*

of Heredity and Early Environment (San Francisco: Jossey-Bass, Inc., 1990), pp. 298, 315.

89. Ibid., pp. 300–307, 324–329.

90. Ibid., p. 319.

91. Ibid., pp. 319, 506

92. Miles D. Storfer, *Intelligence and Giftedness: The Contributions of Heredity and Early Environment* (San Francisco: Jossey-Bass Publishers, 1990), p. 13.

93. Lilliam Belmon and Francis A. Moralla, "Birth Order, Family Size, and Intelligence," *Science*, December 14, 1973, p. 1096. But see also Judith Blake, *Family Size and Achievement* (Berkeley: University of California Press, 1989), Chapter 5.

94. Ibid., p. 137.

95. John C. Loehlin, Gardner Lindzey, and J. N. Spuhler, *Race Differences in Intelligence* (San Francisco: W. H. Freeman and Co., 1975), pp. 179–181.

96. Overlap in a geometrical sense is illustrated in Richard J. Herrnstein and Charles Murray, *The Bell Curve: Intelligence and Class Structure in American Life* (The Free Press, 1994), p. 279.

97. Otto Klineberg, *Negro Intelligence and Selective Migration* (Westport, CT: Greenwood Press, 74), p. 2.

98. Richard J. Herrnstein and Charles Murray, *The Bell Curve*, p. 323.

99. Robert Klitgaard, *Choosing Elites*, pp. 104–115; Stanley Sue and Jennifer Abe, *Predictors of Academic Achievement Among Asian Students and White Students* (New York: College Entrance Examination Board, 1988), p. 1; Robert A. Gordon and Eileen E. Rudert, "Bad News Concerning I.Q. Tests," *Sociology of Education*, July 1979, p. 176; Frank L. Schmidt and John E. Hunter, "Employment Testing," *American Psychologist*, October 1981, p. 1131; Arthur R. Jensen, "Section of Minority Students in Higher Education," *University of Toledo Law Review*, Spring–Summer, 1970, pp. 440, 443; Donald A. Rock, "Motivation, Moderators, and Test Bias," ibid., pp. 536, 537; Ronald L. Flaughter, *Testing Practices, Minority Groups and Higher Education: A Review and Discussion of the Research* (Princeton: Education Testing Service, 1970), p. 11; Arthur R. Jensen, *Bias in Mental Testing* (New York: The Free Press, 1980), pp. 479–490.

100. This point was presented forcefully—all italicized—in *The Bell Curve*, but that did not prevent demagogues from claiming that its authors had said the opposite. *"That a trait is genetically transmit-*

ted in individuals does not mean that group differences in that trait are also genetic in origin." Richard J. Herrnstein and Charles Murray, *The Bell Curve*, p. 298.

101. Madison Grant, *The Passing of the Great Race: The Racial Basis of European History*, fourth edition (New York: Charles Scribner's Sons, 1924), p. xxix.

102. Ellen Churchill Semple, *Influences of Geographic Environment* (New York: Henry Holt and Co., 1947), p. 511.

103. Thomas Sowell, *Migrations and Cultures: A World View* (New York: Basic Books, 1996), pp. 9–12.

104. Ellen Churchill Semple, *Influences of Geographic Environment* (New York: Henry Holt and Co., 1911), Chapters 15, 16.

105. Fernand Braudel, *A History of Civilizations*, translated by Richard Mayne (New York: Penguin Press, 1994), p. 8.

106. William H. McNeill, *The Rise of the West*, p. xvi. See also p. xx.

107. Carlo M. Cipolla, *Guns, Sails, and Empires: Technological Innovation and the Early Phases of European Expansion, 1400–1700* (Manhattan, Kansas: Sunflower University Press, 1992), p. 87.

108. Carlo M. Cipolla, *Clocks and Culture: 1300–1700* (New York: W. W. Norton, 1978), pp. 66–69; Alfred Dolge, *Pianos and Their Makers* (Covina, CA: Covina Publishing Co., 1911), p. 168.

109. Carlo M. Cipolla, *Guns, Sails, and Empires*, p. 104.

110. Ibid., pp. 117–121.

111. Ibid., p. 124n.

112. Victor Purcell, *The Boxer Uprising: A Background Study* (Cambridge: Cambridge University Press, 1963), pp. 30–31.

113. Arnold Toynbee, *A Study of History*, abridgement of Volumes VII-X by D. C. Somervell (Oxford: Oxford University Press, 1985), p. 369.

114. Carlo M. Cipolla, *Guns, Sails, and Empires*, pp. 90–93.

115. Ibid., pp. 84–85.

116. Fernand Braudel, *A History of Civilizations*, p. 7.

INDEX

Abyssinia, 11
Acculturation (*see* Culture)
Adam, Robert, 58
Addis Abbaba, 108
Adriatic Sea, 175, 191, 195
Affirmative Action (*see* Preferential policies)
Afghanistan, 232, 234, 235, 236, 245
Africa and Africans, x, 4, 11, 13–14, 19,
    20, 40, 51, 82, 83, 84, 85, 93, 94,
    95, 97, 99–173, 191, 192, 244, 247,
    249, 250, 252, 256, 258, 263, 271,
    272, 300, 322, 328, 340, 347, 348,
    351, 355, 356, 375
  animals, 106, 142
  climate, 102, 106–107, 133, 147–148
  corruption, 130, 131, 139, 140, 145, 152
  crops, 118
  disease, 106, 110, 114, 133, 142, 147,
    153
  East Africa, x, 17, 85, 94, 101, 103,
    109, 110, 111, 116, 118, 133–136,
    156, 242, 334, 373
  economics, 112–120, 139, 141,
    144–146, 173
  geography, 99–109, 133, 140, 191, 252
  harbors, 99, 101, 140, 147, 347

  independence, 118–119, 126, 128,
    129, 137–138, 150, 171–172
  intellectuals, 138, 147, 350
  languages 100, 122, 125, 133, 135,
    140, 146
  military coups, 120, 141, 145, 152
  mountains and uplands, 11
  occupations, 109, 110, 153
  population, 38, 110, 132, 133, 136,
    138, 140, 147
  rivers, 102–104, 105, 133, 140, 147, 148
  slavery, 109–112, 153–156, 160
  soil, 107, 108, 133
  trade, 100, 102, 103, 104–105, 106,
    113–114, 117–118, 124, 131, 134,
    135, 136–137, 140, 141, 142,
    144–145, 147, 150, 151
  West Africa, 16, 85, 94, 99, 101, 103,
    104, 105, 108, 109, 110, 111, 112,
    113, 117, 118, 122, 134, 140, 143,
    146, 147–148159, 373
African diaspora, 100
  Islamic world, 110–111, 112, 153–157
  Western Hemisphere, 77, 81, 100, 110,
    111, 112, 121, 155, 157-170, 256,
    272, 319, 321, 324, 349, 361–362,

Western Hemisphere (*cont.*)
366–367, 368, 370, 371, 373
Agriculture (*see also* Animals), 20, 23, 25,
30, 40, 42, 46–47, 53, 55, 56, 61,
62, 66, 70, 85, 112, 117, 124, 138,
182, 184, 185, 190, 197, 198, 206,
218, 227, 231, 239, 240, 244, 250,
251, 252, 253, 254, 266, 271–272,
273, 274, 307, 318, 335, 375, 378
  climate, 56, 102, 265, 266
  crops, 117
  sedentary, 6
  slash-and-burn, 6, 13, 179, 266
  soil, 56–57, 252, 266
Alaska, 210, 317, 318
Albania and Albanians, 170, 203, 205
Alben, Ruth, xiii
Alcohol, 68, 77, 235, 256, 295, 308, 324,
334, 369
Alexandria, 101
Algeria, 17, 147, 172
Algonquins, 301, 304
Ali, Mohammed, 295
Amazon Indians, 328
Amazon River, 101, 104
American and Americans (*see* United
States of America)
Amherst, Lord Jeffrey, 293
Amin, Idi, 120, 138
Amnesty International, 138
Andes Mountains, 253, 282
Andhras, 7–8
Angles, 26, 28, 29, 45
Anglican Church, 46, 47, 64, 92
Anglo-Normans, 15, 30, 53
Anglo-Saxons, 29, 45, 52
Angola, 104, 110, 111, 119
Animals, 7, 35, 42, 47, 53, 65, 68, 106,
142, 190, 204, 218, 231, 232, 251,
252, 253, 254, 255, 266, 271, 274,
282, 283–284, 286, 291, 294, 295,
297, 306, 307, 313–314, 316,
316–317, 319–320, 347, 375
Antarctic Ocean, 99

Apaches, 312, 313
Appalachian Mountains, 75, 304
Arabic language, 191, 220
Arabic numerals, 16
Arabs, 16, 94,99, 100, 109, 112, 115, 119,
134, 135, 138
Aral Sea, 232
Archaeology, 26
Architecture, 25, 29, 195
Arctic Ocean, 206
Arthur, King, 46
Argentina, 38, 39, 68, 69, 70, 83, 162,
239, 253, 258, 260, 281, 328, 333,
334
Armenia and Armenians, 185, 187, 192,
210, 216, 218, 223, 224, 244, 338
Ashanti, 115, 141–142
Assimilation (*see* Culture; Racial and eth-
nic Groups)
Astrakhan, 209, 210
Atahualpa, 284–285, 287
Atlantic Ocean, 10, 11, 39, 93, 94,99,
105, 110, 111,154, 158, 238, 251,
253, 255, 257, 259, 277, 282, 291,
299, 304, 309, 314, 378
Atrocities, 5, 19, 54, 83, 118, 119, 121,
202, 245, 267, 269, 281, 288, 293,
303, 315, 316, 324, 350
Australia, 16, 40, 63, 68, 69, 70, 71, 77,
79, 82, 83, 84, 87, 90, 97, 98, 108,
171, 178, 238, 240, 259, 309, 334,
375
Australian Aborigines, 83
Austria and Austrians, 40, 155, 174, 181,
187, 188, 189, 196, 197, 198, 199,
201, 225, 226
Azerbaijan, 244, 246, 341
Aztecs, 15, 249, 250, 251–252, 257, 263,
264, 265, 267, 269, 273-282, 289,
290, 291, 301, 302, 358, 375

Balboa, Nunez de, 263
Bali, 13, 355
Balkanization, 189

Balkans, 4, 11, 13, 15, 107, 174, 175,
    176, 178, 179, 180, 181, 182, 183,
    185, 186, 187, 190, 192, 195, 204,
    238, 241, 242, 243, 163, 264, 299,
    340, 355, 356, 357, 375
Baltic republics, 220, 221, 235, 237
Baltic Sea, 175, 236
Barbados, 161, 162, 164, 170
Bartók, Béla, 205
Basil II, Emperor, 5
Basques, 301, 350
Bédie, Henri Konan, 152
Bedouins, 373
Belgium and Belgians, 39, 115, 117, 150,
    214, 238
Benin, 112, 173
Benue River, 103
Bering Straits, 208, 263
Best-Litovsk, Treaty of, 227
Bevan, Aneurin, 51
Biafra, 129
Birth rates (see Demography)
Black, Joseph, 58
Black Sea, 176, 210
Blackfoot Indians, 314
Boats (see Ships and boats)
Boers, 8, 119, 121
Bohemia and Bohemians, 174, 179, 184,
    186, 200, 201, 241
Bolívar, Simón, 171
Bolivia and Bolivians, 281, 320, 343
Bolsheviks, 214, 226
Bonaparte, Napoleon, 12, 34, 93
"Bonnie Prince Charlie," 56
Bosnia-Herzegovina, 203
Bosporus, 176
Boudicca, 24, 45
Brandenburg, 185
Bratislava, 201
Braudel, Fernand, xiii, 99, 100, 329, 379
Brazil and Brazilians, 40, 93–94, 111,
    149, 158, 160, 162, 164, 166, 167,
    168, 238, 239, 257, 264, 265, 332,
    334, 335

Britain and the British, xi, 7, 8, 10, 11, 12,
    14, 15, 17, 19, 21, 22–98, 99, 115,
    119, 120, 121, 122, 123, 129, 132,
    134, 136, 140, 141, 142, 154, 157,
    170, 172, 204, 207, 211, 215, 225,
    230, 241, 242, 258, 264, 265, 271,
    290, 291, 292, 294, 296, 297, 300,
    305, 308, 309, 313, 329, 330, 331,
    333, 336, 337, 343, 347, 352, 354,
    356
  bill of rights, 89, 90
  Britons overseas, 68–82
  freedom, 87–96
  monarchy, 55, 88
  parliament, 86, 87, 88, 90, 92
  Roman Britain 22, 24–26, 46, 117, 337
British Empire, 15, 55, 74, 82–87, 90, 93,
    96, 118, 135, 161, 167, 259, 264
Brooke, Edward, 366
Bruce, Blanche K., 163
Bryn Mawr, 70
Buckle, Henry, 58
Buddhism, 358
Bulgaria and Bulgarians, 5, 174, 184, 243
Burke, Edmund, 87
Burma, 82, 330, 363
Burns, Robert, 58
Burundi, 120, 121, 129
Business (see Economics)
Byelorussia and Byelorussians, 183, 219,
    217, 219, 220, 222, 224, 235, 236
Byzantine Empire and Byzantines, 5, 176,
    178, 179, 183

Caesar, Julius, 22, 23, 63
Cairo, 101, 155
Calhoun, John, 78
California, 313, 314
Cambridge University, 50, 61
Canada and Canadians, 40, 67, 69, 70, 74,
    79, 83, 84, 87, 90, 108, 117, 161, 238,
    254, 264, 297, 301, 318, 325, 333, 350
Canterbury Tales, 30
Carlyle, Thomas, 59

Carribbean, 17, 82, 83, 159, 160 161,
    162, 165, 167, 168, 170, 257, 258,
    264, 265, 271, 277, 300
Casas, Bartolome de las, 269, 270
Caspian Sea, 206, 341
Catawba, 4
Catherine the Great, 58, 210, 219
Caucasus, 94, 154, 155, 174, 190, 211,
    215, 227
Cayugas, 301, 302
"Celtic fringe," 68, 76, 78
Celts, 23, 24, 29, 45, 53, 68, 174, 180
Central America, 250, 251, 253, 254, 263,
    265–289, 320
Central Asia and Central Asians 3, 5, 9,
    11, 93, 95, 174, 209, 216, 217, 218,
    219, 223, 224, 226, 230–236, 244,
    246, 249, 299, 331
  education, 233
  occupations, 230, 233, 234
  population, 230–231
  religion, 230
Ceylon, 9, 11, 82, 264, 339
Chad, 155, 173
Charles I of England, 89, 98
Charles II of England, 89, 90
Charles V of Spain, 279
Charleston, 161
Chaucer, Geoffrey, 30
Cherokees, 256, 290, 301, 304–312, 324,
    325
Cheyenne, 312, 316
Chickasaw, 305
Chile, 40, 281, 320
China and the Chinese, xi, 4, 5, 6, 7, 8, 9,
    11, 16, 17, 20, 40, 85, 104, 119, 138,
    144, 191, 207, 223, 231, 232, 242,
    243, 251, 252, 283, 329, 330, 333,
    334, 335, 336, 340, 342, 343, 344,
    345, 346, 349, 351, 352, 353, 354,
    361, 363, 366, 370, 372, 373, 374
    375, 376–377
Cholollans, 278
Churchill, Winston S., 25, 54, 95, 96

Claudius, Emperor, 23
Cleanliness, 47, 52, 60, 65, 68, 78, 366
Cloth, 30, 32, 36, 40, 180, 181, 208, 210,
    294, 303, 304, 345
Clothing, 261, 294, 304, 334, 339
Coal, 32, 35–36, 38–39, 43, 47, 50, 97,
    105, 177, 215
Cocoa, 7, 39, 142, 143, 144–145, 146,
    147, 151, 255, 276
Coffee, 39, 137
Color (*see also* Intragroup differences),
    161, 162
Colombia, 281, 343
Colorado, 108, 316, 364
Columbus, Christopher, 10, 157, 249, 250,
    255, 256, 258, 263, 264, 322, 326
Comanches, 312, 313, 314, 316
Commonwealth of Independent States,
    207, 236, 237
Communists, 203, 211, 213, 218, 228,
    231, 244, 246, 247
Congo, 110, 116, 119
Conquest, 290–291
  arrogance 223, 255, 287
  brutality, 4–5, 24, 267, 276, 277, 280,
    303, 311, 365
  conquered peoples 5, 7–8, 8–9, 14, 15,
    20–21 24–25, 45, 46, 115, 118–119,
    122–123, 123–127, 135, 136,
    137–138, 142–144, 147, 148–149,
    189–196, 197–199, 207–208,
    216–217, 218–219, 220–224,
    225–230, 230–236, 255–256,
    262–263, 270–271, 271–272,
    288–289, 297, 307–308, 311,
    317–319, 321, 323, 324–325, 326
  cultural consequences, 6–9, 19
  economic imperialism, 84, 85, 86–87,
    117, 172, 237, 330–331, 332–333
Conquest, Robert, 245
Constantinople, 181, 357
Constitution of the United States, 90, 91
Corruption, 17, 130, 131, 152, 193, 194,
    212, 270, 308, 310, 317, 343–344

Cortés, Hernán, 259, 263, 265, 269, 275, 277–281

Cossacks, 225, 226

Cotton, 137, 231–232, 261, 276

"Crackers," 76

Cracow, 184, 188, 199, 241

Crazy Horse, 315

Cree, 295, 296

Creeks, 305, 329, 340

Crime and violence, 55, 63, 68, 73, 76, 78, 128–129, 139, 168, 175, 188, 189, 202, 213–214, 218, 241, 243, 246, 318, 334, 340, 349–350, 357

Crimean War, 11

Croatia and Croatians, 8, 15, 15, 177, 183, 184, 185, 196, 204, 238, 240

Cromwell, Oliver, 64, 80, 258

Crusaders, 16, 357, 358

Cuba, 159, 162, 245, 268, 269, 277, 278, 279

Cultural Relativism (*see* Culture)

Culture (*see also* Education; Geography, cultural consequences; Human Capital; Language), 6, 177–189, 243–244, 256, 306, 312, 324, 333, 334, 339–341, 342

acculturation, 56, 69, 76, 148, 196, 219, 307, 308, 309, 374

cultural capital, 334–339, 342, 344–345

cultural changes, x

cultural competition, 341

cultural differences, x, 7–8, 29

cultural diffusion, 3, 4, 7, 8–9, 15, 16, 23, 24–25, 89–90, 96, 122–123, 159, 162, 169–170, 180, 184–186, 199, 204, 208, 210, 217, 218, 235, 241, 243, 245–246, 267, 282, 294, 304, 333, 342, 345–346, 374–379

cultural enclaves, 69, 70, 72, 180, 185, 217, 232, 346

cultural evolution, 20

cultural extermination, 15, 229

cultural frameworks, 342–345

cultural isolation, 13, 52, 107, 133, 134, 176, 181, 182, 192–193, 195, 346

cultural relativism, 326

cultural receptivity, 123, 361

cultural retrogression, 3–4, 22, 25–26, 26–27, 179, 268, 335–336, 376

cultural revivals, 71, 188, 323, 350

cultural survivals, 44, 72, 81, 159–160, 177–178, 262–263, 289, 321

cultural universe, 20, 178, 251, 252, 254–255, 262, 346, 347

group "identity," 189, 196, 227, 325, 341, 349

role of culture, x

technology, 5, 32, 159

Custer, George Armstrong, 299, 315

Cuzco, 285, 286–287, 288

Cyrillic writing, 183, 184, 220

Czarist Russia, 14, 15, 93, 154, 207, 208, 209, 211, 216, 223, 225, 231, 244

Czech Republic, 187, 201

Czechoslovakia, 19, 188, 189, 197, 200–203, 242, 247, 350, 351

Czechs, 18, 177, 183, 185, 186, 187, 188, 189, 196, 200–203, 238, 240, 241

Dalmatian Coast, 175, 176, 190–191, 195

Danes, 28, 141, 179

Danube, 181

Danzig, 75, 187

Dardanelles, 176

Dar es Salaam, 135, 136, 138

Dartmouth College, 58, 293

Delaware Indians, 304

Demography, 300, 324, 327, 369–370

age, 235, 369–370

birth rates, 233, 235

life expectancy, 65

mortality rates, 39, 40–41, 55–56, 136, 153, 154–155, 158, 160, 311

sex ratios, 3

Denmark, 26, 158, 179

Denver, 316, 365

Dinaric Highlands, 191

Discrimination, 64, 170, 188, 201, 202, 233, 324, 327, 330, 348, 349–350, 351, 364, 365, 373–374

Disease, 10, 11, 40, 47, 68, 106, 110, 133, 139, 140, 142, 145, 147, 153, 204, 232, 253, 254, 256, 257, 271, 279, 281, 285, 292, 293, 301, 306, 327, 347–348

Djibouti, 108

Donets Basin, 219

Dostoyevsky, Feodor Mikhailovich, 361

Douglass, Frederick, 157

Dublin, 64

Dubrovnik, 185, 191, 358

Duranty, Walter, 245

Earhart Foundation, xiv

East Anglia, 79–80

Economics, 84, 203, 214, 220, 237, 250, 252, 266–267, 312, 357

business and industry, 31, 32, 33, 34, 36, 39, 40, 43, 46, 48, 49, 50–51, 52, 53, 62, 66, 70, 74, 129, 143, 147, 150, 170, 176, 181, 182, 185, 189, 191, 197, 19–200, 206, 209, 210–216, 219, 231, 233, 240, 241, 293, 335, 339–340, 343, 344, 347, 350–351, 353, 354

development, 25, 26 29–44, 66, 118, 124, 135, 147, 167–168, 175, 199, 210–216, 233, 274, 345, 349, 351, 357, 360

finance, 30–31, 33, 39, 43, 50, 66, 73, 84, 97–98, 151, 181, 203, 210, 212, 213, 214, 332–333, 340, 343, 359, 376

foreigners' roles, 30–31, 47, 50–51, 97–98, 118, 132, 134, 135, 149, 209, 210–216, 246, 334, 337, 340, 342, 343, 359, 361, 375

income and wealth, 4, 40–41, 61, 124, 133, 140, 151, 152, 168, 170, 178, 197, 238, 240, 244, 312, 324, 325, 327, 329–334, 348

international trade, 23, 25, 30, 31, 32–33, 39, 40, 43, 44, 55, 84, 100, 101, 102, 117–118, 117–118, 135, 136–137, 142, 176, 180, 195, 211, 237, 238, 260–261, 294, 333

wampum, 303

Ecuador, 281, 285, 320

Edict of Nantes, 31

Edinburgh, 53, 56, 58, 60

Edinburgh Review, 59

Education (*see also* Intellectuals, Literacy and illiteracy), 50, 57–58, 61, 69, 96, 123–124, 125, 128, 142–143, 147, 178, 186, 198, 205, 220, 242, 293, 318, 324, 327, 344, 361, 367

attitudes toward education, 79, 80, 81, 123–124, 133

effects, 340, 3439

quality, 61, 205, 349

specialties, 44, 61, 62, 67, 205, 349–350, 351

Egypt, 109, 156, 180, 190, 216, 253, 373

Elites, 9, 15, 24–25, 28–29, 30, 36, 41–42, 46, 47, 49, 53, 56, 72–73, 78, 80, 81, 88–89, 126, 169, 172–173, 193, 196, 209, 210, 219, 220–221, 250, 269, 270–271, 272–273, 321, 339–340, 353

Engineering, 37, 61, 62, 214–215, 219, 350, 361

England and the English, 26–44, 45, 46, 48, 50, 52, 53, 54, 61, 62, 68, 71, 75, 76, 80, 85, 88, 92, 249, 264, 335, 343, 360

English language, 28, 29–30, 46, 47, 48–49, 53, 56, 56, 57, 65, 69, 81, 83, 85, 122, 125, 301, 304, 340, 341, 376

Environment (*see* Geography)

Eskimos, 252, 263, 317, 376

Estonia and Estonians, 217, 223, 236, 237, 244, 252, 263, 317, 376

Ethnicity (*see* Racial and ethnic Groups)

Ethiopia, 108, 121, 155, 156, 245
Eurasian land mass, 216, 231, 249, 251, 254
Europe (*see also* Western civilization), xi, 3, 4, 6, 7, 10, 11, 17, 18–19, 20, 29–34, 37, 38, 39, 41, 42, 44, 47, 56, 58, 63, 66, 82, 84, 91, 95, 99, 101, 105, 107, 108, 113, 114, 116, 117, 124, 154, 158, 168, 169, 170, 171, 172–173, 249, 250, 251, 253, 254, 256, 257, 259, 260, 261, 264, 264, 278, 291, 294, 307, 313, 322, 323, 326, 327, 331, 332, 333, 336, 337, 347, 353,354, 357, 359, 361, 369, 372, 375, 378
     climate, 175, 176, 253, 281
     East Central Europe, 174, 176, 185, 186–205, 242, 299, 327
     Eastern Europe, 5, 6, 9, 11, 20, 42, 109, 174, 177–186, 192, 194, 202, 204, 205, 206, 207, 217, 219, 220, 231, 238–246, 327, 333, 335, 345, 346, 351, 357, 373
     east-west differences, 175, 176, 177–184, 327
     geography, 175–177
     population, 178
European civilization (*see* Western civilization)
European-offshoot societies, 40, 67, 90–91, 178, 324, 327, 344, 354, 356
Expulsions, 202, 238, 241, 331

Farming (*see* Agriculture)
Ferguson, Adam, 59
Fiji, 17, 82, 334, 363
Feudalism, 42
First World War, 18, 19, 49, 70, 95, 117, 135, 136, 154, 166, 181, 182, 189, 196–197, 199, 200, 201, 203, 204, 217, 220, 221, 223, 227, 238, 239, 240, 241, 243, 244, 247, 336, 350, 351, 356
Fish, 39, 291

Flanders, 30, 31
Food, 47, 65, 81, 120, 227–228, 232, 245, 255, 261, 274, 276, 277, 281–282, 294, 297, 316, 317, 339
Ford Motor Company, 215
Foreigners, 30–31, 48
Forests and woodlands, 36–37
Fox, Edward Whiting, 149
Fox Indians, 312
France and the French, 11, 12, 15, 28, 29, 30, 31, 38, 39, 40, 43, 74, 82, 83, 90, 93, 95, 98, 108, 115, 117, 118, 136, 146, 147, 148, 158, 177, 178, 185, 204, 210, 211, 215, 225, 238, 239, 258, 262, 264, 291, 294, 295, 296, 297, 298, 300, 301, 304, 305, 308, 309, 313, 322, 344, 346, 359, 376
Franklin, Benjamin, 340
"Free persons of color," 161, 162, 163, 164, 166, 167, 170
Freedom, 87–96, 173, 247, 352–357

Gaelic, 53, 54, 56, 57
Gagarin, Yuri, 248
Galicia, 198, 199, 226
Gdansk, 75, 187
Genghis Khan, 225, 231
Geography (*see also* Animals), xiii, 10–12, 20, 23, 34, 38, 97, 99–109, 133, 140, 160, 172, 175–177, 191, 205–207, 231, 251–255, 265, 266, 282, 314, 334, 347–348, 355
     climate, 102, 103–104, 133, 175, 206, 253, 265, 266, 282, 375
     continents, 38, 101, 250, 252, 253
     cultural consequences, 99, 100, 357
     deserts, 99, 252, 266, 314, 373
     disease, 10, 11, 40, 47, 68, 142
     fertility of the soil, 176, 266, 314
     islands, 41, 88, 291
     isolation, 11, 13, 45, 52, 176
     mountain versus lowland peoples, 174, 358–359, 373

Geography (*cont.*)
mountains, 44, 45, 103–104, 175, 176, 191, 192, 206, 252, 254, 283, 306
natural resources, 140, 150, 151, 176–177, 186, 205–206, 206–207, 254, 323, 335, 342, 344, 348
soil, 266
waterways, 11–12, 27, 32, 34–35, 44, 45, 97, 99–100, 101, 102–103, 104, 105–106, 134, 140, 175–176, 191, 205, 206, 207, 252, 254, 266, 274, 291, 296, 314, 343, 347, 355
George, David Lloyd, 51
Georgia (Europe) and Georgians, 154, 218, 219, 224, 246, 341
Georgia (U.S.), 78, 305
German Language, 74, 178, 183, 186
Germany and Germans, 5, 7, 15, 26, 27, 28, 30, 38, 40, 43, 44, 95, 96, 97, 117, 134, 135, 168, 174, 177, 180–189, 190, 196, 197–198, 199, 201–202, 203, 205, 210, 211, 214, 215, 218, 225, 227, 230, 238, 239, 240, 241, 242, 244, 246, 274, 117, 135, 184, 188, 202, 211, 239, 322, 330, 333, 335, 336, 338, 346, 347, 351, 352, 376
Geronimo, 315
Ghana, 101, 108, 112, 132, 140–146, 149, 150–151, 173, 337
Gibraltar, 82, 84
Gold, 102, 113, 117, 141, 206, 261, 264, 277, 278, 280, 281, 288, 331
Golden Horde, 107
Gorbachev, Mikhail, 224, 235, 237, 245
Government, 17, 27, 41, 67, 87–91, 129–132, 144, 177, 242, 243, 250, 268, 289, 298, 299, 300, 302, 304, 307, 308, 317, 319, 342, 344, 350, 351, 353, 356, 377
democracy, 91, 243
freedom, 87–96, 242–243, 247, 352–357
economic role, 33–34, 130–131, 137,

138, 139–140, 144, 145, 146, 151–152, 173, 201, 227, 272, 344, 351, 353, 356–357
law and order, 14, 17, 28, 31, 32, 33, 52, 55, 64, 67, 76, 77, 83, 88, 89–90, 97, 116, 118, 160, 164, 179, 184, 192, 193, 194, 244, 247, 299–300, 308, 311, 325, 336, 342–343, 344, 354
monarchy, 29, 32, 33, 54, 55, 276
nation-states, 12–13, 23, 192, 355
parliament, 32, 87, 89
politics, 41
power, 32, 87–90, 91, 144, 309, 353, 354, 368
sovereignty, 299–300, 304, 310, 377
state terrorism, 220–221, 227–229, 277
taxation, 31, 66, 85, 130, 137, 147
treaties, 304, 322–323
Grant, Madison, 362, 372
Great Lakes, 295, 296, 304
Greece and Greeks, 20, 167, 183, 346
Guinea, 120, 144, 150
Gulags, 16, 234
Gulf Stream, 175
Guns (*see* Weapons)

Habsburg Empire, 17, 18, 174, 189, 190, 194, 195, 196, 197
Hadrian, Emperor, 11, 52
Haiti, 159,169
Harriman, W. Averell, 215
Harvard College, 80, 82
Hastings, Battle of, 28
Hausa-Fulani, 124, 125, 126, 130, 339
Haverford, 70
Haverhill, 79
Henry VIII, 30, 46
Henry, Patrick, 78
Herrnstein, Richard J., 367
Hindus, 16, 349
History, xi, xii, xiii, 45–46, 220, 230, 326, 338, 356, 374, 379
causation, 327, 332, 338, 356, 373

ideas, 352–362
moral issues, 327, 332
Hitler, Adolf, 19, 95, 96, 202
Holocaust, 5, 373
Hong Kong, 82, 98, 357
Hopis, 316
"Hoosiers," 77
Hoover Institution, xii, xiii, xiv
Horses (see Animals)
Houphouët-Boigny, Félix, 148, 149, 150, 152
Huascar, 284–285
Hudson River, 12, 104
Huegenots, 31, 96, 333, 346, 359, 376
Human Capital (see also Cultural capital), 3–4, 20, 34, 96, 97, 168–169, 177, 241–242, 261, 331, 334–341, 342, 344–345, 349, 352, 362, 368
Hume, David, 58
Hungary and Hungarians, 15, 18, 174, 177, 179, 184, 185, 186, 187, 193, 196, 200, 201, 203, 205, 243, 350
Hunter-gatherers, 6, 112, 257, 263
Hurons, 294, 295, 296, 301, 302
Hutcheson, Francis, 59
Hutu, 4, 120, 121

Ibos, 8, 85, 111, 120, 124, 126, 127, 128–129, 339
Ideas, 352–362
Illegitimacy, 80, 81
Illiteracy (see Literacy and illiteracy)
Imperialism, 10, 13–14, 82, 83, 85, 95, 119, 134, 171, 173, 216, 244–245, 264–265, 281, 330, 358
colonization, 16, 83, 171, 263, 264, 272, 330–331
economics, 16, 173, 214, 237, 244, 332–333
indirect rule, 15, 127, 128, 141, 142, 171, 207, 275
Incas, 250, 257, 258, 281–289, 290, 291, 302, 328, 331, 375
Income and wealth (see Economics)

Independence, 17, 66, 126–127, 128, 129, 197, 200, 225, 227, 230, 237, 238, 245, 247
India and Overseas Indians, x, 6, 7–8, 16, 17, 20, 38, 40, 82, 83, 113, 117, 118, 134, 135, 136, 149, 170, 209, 210, 223, 231, 242, 253, 255, 333, 338, 343, 345, 349, 350, 363, 375
Indian Ocean, 94, 99, 156
Indians (see Western Hemisphere Indians)
Industrial Revolution, 38, 43, 67
Infrastructure, 25, 27, 34–35, 47, 50, 53, 56, 142, 151, 181, 283, 284, 336–337
Indigenous peoples, x, 11 85, 172, 187, 221–222, 223–224, 231, 249–328
Institute for Educational Affairs, xiv
Intellectuals, 49, 50, 51, 57, 59–60, 80, 173, 189, 196, 205, 209, 229, 245, 349–352, 379
Intelligence, 367–368, 369–372
patterns, 369, 370
renorming I.Q. tests, 371
test bias, 371
Intergroup differences, 8–9, 14, 16, 47, 66, 67, 78, 80–82, 97, 124, 125–126, 127, 181, 221–222, 230, 335, 344–345, 346, 349, 363, 365, 369–374
International Harvester, 211, 215
Intragroup differences, 7–8, 9, 24–25, 36, 48–49, 53–54, 60, 63, 71, 72, 72, 79, 161, 162, 163, 164–166, 167, 198, 199–200, 369
Iran and Iranians, 191, 235, 326, 243
Ireland and the Irish, 8, 16, 26, 27, 29, 30, 48, 52, 55, 62, 63–67, 68–70 71, 76, 78, 80, 82, 86–87, 172, 184, 255, 270
Iron and steel, 35, 38–39, 40, 43, 47, 48, 49, 50, 62, 70, 97, 122, 201, 204, 206, 208, 211, 213, 250, 303, 342, 352
Iroquois, 251, 252, 258, 260, 295, 296, 300–304, 375

Islam (*see* Religion)

Israel, 172, 344, 349, 369

Istanbul, 156, 193

Italy and Italians, 28, 30, 39, 95, 132, 168, 180, 186, 203, 215, 333–334, 335, 366

Ivory Coast, 101, 129, 145, 146–153, 337

Jackson, Andrew, 78, 310, 366

Jamaica, 159, 160, 161, 170, 368

James I of England, 55

James II of England, 89, 98

James VI of Scotland, 55

Japan and Japanese, 5, 8, 11, 37, 51, 62, 95, 96, 97, 108, 137, 168, 215, 329, 332, 333, 334, 335, 336, 340, 343, 345, 348, 351, 361, 363, 369, 372, 377

Jefferson, Thomas, 70, 298, 309, 310, 366

Jews, 5, 14, 15, 16, 30, 31, 75, 96, 180, 181, 182, 185, 187, 188, 189, 191, 193, 205, 211, 214, 218, 221, 242, 246, 261, 331, 333, 334, 335, 338, 339, 346, 349, 359, 360, 369
  anti-Semitism, 221, 242

Kafka, Franz, 205

Kampuchea, 16, 350

Katyn Forest, 220

Kazakhstan and Kazakhs, 223, 224, 230, 232, 233, 235, 236, 237, 249, 350

Kenya, 17, 38, 119, 171, 351, 368

Kilwa, 109, 134

Kirghizia and Kirghiz, 223, 234

Kremlin, 210, 334

Krupp, 204, 215

Ku Klux Klan, 77

Labor unions, 44, 51, 69, 70

Lake Victoria, 133, 137

Landownership, 64, 296–297, 299, 301–302, 306–307, 308, 310–311, 311–312, 316, 346

Languages, 3, 15, 24–25, 48–49, 53, 60, 65–66, 70, 72, 81, 100, 133, 146,

178, 182–184, 185–186, 198, 224, 263, 267, 278, 283, 289, 320, 321, 324–325, 327, 328, 341
  conquerors and conquered, 3, 9, 24–25, 29–30, 46, 48, 53, 198, 223, 227, 229
  elites vs. masses, 46, 48, 182, 188–189
  lingua francas, 83, 135, 218
  political issue, 49
  standardized, 81, 217
  written, 21, 182–184, 217, 251, 256–257, 275, 283, 289, 295, 310, 326, 333, 345–346

Latin, 6, 27, 28, 45, 135, 177, 178, 183, 220, 346

Latin America, 40, 74, 84, 157, 160, 161, 164, 168, 273, 290, 320, 321, 328, 351

Latvia, 217, 236, 237, 239, 244

Law and order (*see* Government)

Lebanon and Lebanese, x, 16, 85, 118, 142, 333, 338, 373

Lenin, V. I., 216, 219, 227, 231, 232

Lewis, Bernard, xiii

Lewis, John L., 70

Liberia, 145,169

Libya, 119, 155

Lincoln, Abraham, 80, 167, 315, 340, 366

Liquor (*see* Alcohol)

Literacy and illiteracy, 4, 7, 21, 27, 53, 61–62, 72, 81, 107, 163, 164, 170, 177, 181, 200, 204–205, 207, 208, 209, 217, 218, 241, 242, 283, 345, 357, 359

Lithuania and Lithuanians, 197, 198, 218, 224, 225, 236, 237

Liu, Na, xiii, xiv

Livingstone, David, 136, 155–156

Lombards, 30, 31, 96, 333, 376

London, 25, 26, 31, 32, 33, 34, 35, 55, 68, 92, 97, 123, 343, 376

Louis XIV, 359

Magna Carta, 88, 354

Magyars, 177, 185, 196, 203

Maize, 7, 281

Malaya, Malaysia, and Malays, 8, 17, 38, 82, 85, 255, 349, 363

Mali, 133, 150

Manchus, 9, 336

Mandans, 314

Manhattan, 104, 291

Mao Zedong, 352

Maori, 4–5

Marriage, 42, 69, 287
    endogamous, 70, 234
    intermarriage, 29, 78, 188, 234, 374

Martinique, 147, 162

Marx, Karl, and Marxism, 41, 243, 332

Masai, 116, 135, 136

Massachusetts, 79–80, 81, 265, 296, 304, 366

Mauritania, 112, 154

Maya, 250, 251, 265–273, 290, 326, 328

Medical Science, 58, 108, 117, 235, 236, 324

Medicinal herbs, 260

Medicine Men, 256

Mediterranean, xi, 4, 17, 20, 38, 84, 94, 99, 101, 109, 155, 175, 238, 378

Mexica, 269, 274

Mexico, 40, 162, 257, 259, 264, 270, 273, 275, 279, 313, 314, 320, 343, 348

Micmac, 292

Middle Ages, 7, 15, 53, 59, 81, 174, 177, 178, 179, 180, 183, 185, 187, 188

Middle East, xi, 3, 5, 15, 16, 17, 38, 94,95, 101, 109, 110, 111, 112, 113, 153, 190, 207, 231, 249, 260, 331, 348, 361, 369, 373

Middleman minorities, 75, 182, 373

Migrations, x, xi, 3, 7, 16–17, 39, 63, 65, 66, 67, 68, 70, 78, 85, 96, 118, 134, 145, 157–158, 160, 184–185, 199, 216, 222–223, 224, 232, 236, 238–241, 243, 255, 273, 311–312, 315, 337–338, 348, 374
    British, 67–82
    English, 37–38, 67, 68, 71, 78, 79

Irish, 68–70
    origins and destinations, 79, 158–159
    Scots, 71–78
    Slavs, 7, 238–241
    Welsh, 70–71

Migrations and Cultures, ix, xi, 329, 333, 373

Military factors, 3, 6, 9–10, 11–12, 14–15, 18–19, 23–24, 25, 26, 27–28, 30, 41, 55, 56, 64, 73–74, 82, 84–85, 88, 95–97, 112–113, 114–116, 117, 128, 129, 135, 141–142, 153, 155, 156–157, 171, 180, 187, 189, 190, 193, 194, 200, 201–202, 207, 208, 209, 210, 218, 222, 225–226, 226–227, 231, 233–234, 234–235, 243, 246, 247, 258, 259, 262, 264, 269–270, 274, 275, 276, 277, 278, 279, 280–281, 284–285, 287, 288, 292, 292, 293, 294, 296–297, 298, 299, 300, 303–304, 305, 308, 309, 311, 312, 313, 315, 316, 317, 322, 328, 348, 353, 355, 357, 358, 365, 374, 377–378

Mill, John Stuart, v, vii, 59, 336

Mining, 30, 40, 48, 70, 71, 238

Mississippi River, 290, 310, 311, 312, 319

Mixtecs, 276

Mohawks, 294, 301, 302, 304

Mohicans, 302, 304

Mombasa, 109, 134

Mongols, 5, 10, 17, 174, 196, 207, 225, 264, 277, 339

Montezuma, 11, 277, 278

Moors, 4, 10, 17, 119, 178, 261, 264, 331, 338

Moriori, 4–5

Moscow, 199, 208, 209, 220, 221, 222, 223, 226, 227, 228, 229, 230, 236

Mountains (*see* Geography)

Multiculturalism, 71

Murray, Charles, 367

Names, 81–82, 300–301
Napier, John, 59
Narragansett, 292
Navajo, 312, 316, 325
Nazis, 5, 8, 19, 95, 96, 202, 204, 227, 244, 247, 373
Netherlands and the Dutch, 10, 12, 13, 30, 31, 39, 58, 74, 119, 121, 141, 158, 180, 211, 238, 258, 264, 265, 291, 294, 304, 333, 376, 378
New England, 78, 79, 80, 81, 292, 304
New Orleans, 161, 165, 167, 264
New York City, 59, 104, 236, 291, 334, 345, 366
New York State, 265, 301, 371
New York Times, 112, 245
New Zealand, x, 4, 67, 77, 82, 83, 90, 97, 98
Niger, 103, 104, 150, 173
Niger River, 103, 105, 108, 359
Nigeria and Nigerians, 8, 83, 85, 100, 101, 108, 110, 112, 119, 120, 121–132, 145, 169, 173, 255, 337, 339, 343, 348, 350, 363
Nile River, 101, 104
Nkrumah, Kwame, 143–144, 146, 150, 350
Normans, 5, 9, 15, 28, 30, 45, 46, 53, 54, 96, 333, 376
North Africa, 15, 101, 109, 110, 111, 153, 369
North America, 80, 82, 83, 97, 171, 208, 238, 246, 250, 254, 256, 257, 258, 259, 262, 263, 324, 325, 347, 354, 373, 375
Norwegians, 28, 37
Nyerere, Julius K., 137, 138–139, 150

Occupations, 67, 68, 126, 150, 162, 182, 198, 233, 234, 238, 239, 240, 241
  domestic servants, 68, 182, 276
  managerial, 48, 212, 213, 214–215, 241
  professional, 125, 199, 241

skills, 7, 8, 20, 31, 32, 34, 37, 40, 53, 62, 96, 150, 162, 182, 198, 210, 212, 213, 219, 233, 236, 239–240, 241, 242, 261, 275, 294, 295, 297, 319–320, 323, 324, 327, 331, 333, 335, 338, 346, 348, 351, 375
Oil, 131, 151, 206, 215, 331, 342
Olmecs, 265, 267
Olmsted, Frederick Law, 79
Oneidas, 301, 302
Onondagas, 301, 302
Oranges, 39
Ottawas, 295
Ottoman Empire, 5, 8, 9, 14, 15, 17, 18, 94, 95, 110, 154, 155, 156, 157, 174, 175, 185, 187, 190, 192–193, 194–195, 196, 197, 243, 262, 264, 334, 344, 377
Oxford University, 50, 61

Pacific Ocean, 11, 84, 257, 263, 275, 282, 284, 299, 314, 355,
Page, Agnes, xiii
Pakistan, 343, 351
Pan-Africanism, 144, 150, 169
Panama, 263, 264
Pennsylvania 7, 70, 78, 82, 259, 293, 301, 371
Persian Gulf, 94, 134, 156
Peru, 162, 164, 259, 281, 287, 320, 371
Peter the Great, 208–210, 214, 288
Philadelphia, 58, 68, 165, 259, 293
Philippines, 13, 83, 149, 264
Piracy, 39–40
Pizzaro, Francisco, 259, 264, 283, 286, 331
Pizzaro, Gonzalo, 288
Plains Indians, 312–317
Poland and Poles, 7, 15, 18, 74, 174, 177, 179, 181, 184, 185–186, 187, 196, 197–200, 203, 204, 218, 220, 221, 225–226, 238, 239 240, 241, 243, 338, 346
Politics, 69–70, 91–92, 120, 123,

127–128, 130, 131, 137–138, 139–140, 143–145, 148–149, 150, 151–152, 153, 174, 188, 189, 203, 222, 230, 242–243, 247, 308, 309, 310, 314–315, 317, 325 351, 357, 373

Population, 6, 38, 42, 53, 55, 59, 61, 64, 65, 83–84, 110, 120, 124, 125, 132, 140, 146, 158, 160–161, 178, 184, 187, 200, 202–203, 206, 210, 216, 223, 225, 230–231, 236, 238, 257, 258, 259–260, 266, 267, 268, 271, 272,289 290, 291–292, 297, 299, 305, 306, 309, 312, 319, 325, 327–328

Portugal and the Portuguese, 59, 111, 113, 114, 115, 141, 162, 259, 264, 265, 291, 300

Powhatans, 316

Preferential policies, x, 186, 189, 201, 202, 223–224, 236, 319, 325–326, 364–365

Preferential Policies, ix

Price, Charles A., xiii

Pride, 77, 78, 223, 341, 377

Property rights, 46, 342

Prussia, 7, 75, 174, 196, 197, 198, 240, 241, 330

Pueblos, 316

Puerto Rico and Puerto Ricans, 162, 316

Purcell, Victor, xiii

Puritans, 78, 79–80, 81, 292, 360

Quakers, 78, 92, 161, 259, 293

Quecha, 282, 289, 328

Quito, 285, 287, 297

Race, 45, 243–244, 318–319, 334, 338, 345, 360, 362–374, 375
  and slavery, 13, 91, 354–355
  racial differences, xi, 16, 369, 370
  racial mixture, 163–164, 167, 168, 256, 272, 299, 320, 321, 324, 325, 327–328, 362, 363, 372–373

Race and Culture, ix, 329

Racial and ethnic Groups, 66, 67, 68, 71, 358–359

Racism, 83, 126, 148, 168, 171, 356, 362–368
  definitions, 364–368
  role, 363, 372, 373

Railroads, 34–35, 36, 38–39, 50, 97, 104, 107, 108, 127, 142, 180–181, 199, 200, 203, 345, 352

Rape, 5, 24, 81

Rawlings, Jerry, 145, 146

Rebellion, 17, 22, 24, 46, 56, 64, 88, 89, 134, 135, 195, 196, 199, 229, 271, 282, 288, 310, 312, 350

Red Sea, 94, 156

"Rednecks," 76

Refrigeration, 39

Religion, 16, 29, 31, 29, 56, 57, 64, 66, 85, 89, 140, 256, 262, 276, 279–280, 322, 323, 344, 356, 357–360, 373
  Christianity, 6, 9, 14, 27, 28, 46, 85, 125, 148, 177, 179, 180, 185, 192, 193, 194, 219, 263, 270, 279, 288, 295, 326, 357, 358, 359
  Catholics, 30, 56, 57, 65, 66, 69, 80, 184, 292, 349, 359
  Islam, xiii, 4, 8, 9, 14, 15, 16, 18, 100, 111, 120, 123, 124, 140, 143, 147, 148, 153–157, 168, 192, 193, 194, 195, 203, 216, 230, 333, 338, 345, 357, 358, 360
  missionaries, 116, 122, 123, 142–143, 147, 156, 170, 262–263, 270, 303, 309, 311
  Protestants, 30, 56, 57, 64, 66, 67, 75, 349, 359
  syncretism, 263, 357–358

Retrogression (*see* Culture, cultural retrogression)

Rhodesia, 7, 83, 84, 117, 171, 172

Rice, 6, 152, 253

Rivers (*see* Waterways)

Roman Empire, xi, 4, 6, 9, 14, 15, 16, 20,
    21, 22, 23, 24–26, 27, 28, 43, 45,
    52, 96, 119, 132, 167, 172, 177,
    178, 179, 182, 255, 258, 262, 289,
    333, 335–336, 336–337, 353, 357,
    376
Romania and Romanians, 181, 182,
    186,187, 203, 243, 346, 350, 351
Rubber, 7, 255
Russia and Russians (see also Soviet
    Union), 11–12, 14, 17, 24–25, 37,
    38, 39, 40, 58, 88, 175, 176, 177,
    179 186, 187, 194, 190, 192, 196,
    197, 198,199, 264, 295–241, 243,
    264, 331, 341, 342, 349, 354, 361
Russian language, 186, 218, 223, 226,
    229
Russification, 15, 213
Ruthenia and Ruthenians, 181, 182, 200
Rwanda, 120, 121

Sac Indians, 312
Sahara Desert, 11, 13, 94, 100, 106, 107,
    109, 154, 155
Saint Petersburg, 37, 58, 208, 210
Santo Domingo, 161, 162, 263
Sarajevo, 175, 185
Savannah, 163, 165
Saving, 240, 366
Saxons, 26, 28, 45
Scandinavians, 54, 225, 329
Science, 37, 67, 69, 96, 173, 205, 212,
    242, 346, 360–362, 363, 370, 375,
    379
Scotland and the Scots, 8, 11, 15, 25, 26,
    29, 41, 43, 47, 48, 52–63, 66, 67,
    68, 71–75, 76, 78, 85, 107, 117,
    179, 244, 333, 334, 335, 339, 340
    highlanders, 36, 53–54, 56, 57, 60, 62,
        71, 72, 78
    lowlanders, 56, 60, 62, 71, 72
    Ulster Scots ("Scotch-Irish"), 63, 71,
        72, 75–78, 82, 259, 293, 309
Second World War, 5, 8, 17, 19, 84, 87,

    95–96, 109, 137, 147, 148, 154,
    167, 201, 202, 204, 217, 220, 221,
    223, 227, 238, 240, 241, 243, 244,
    247, 336, 350, 356
Segregation, 126
"Self-determination of peoples," 17–19,
    201
Serfdom, 42, 189, 190, 193, 209, 277
Senecas, 301, 302
Senegal, 14, 150, 173
Sequoyah, 310
Serbia and Serbs, 8, 15, 177, 181, 183,
    184, 186, 195, 196, 203, 204, 340
Sevastopol, 12
Seville, 249
Seversky, Alexander P. de, 214
Sex, 76, 80, 81, 123, 155, 260, 277,
    287–288, 307, 339
Shawnee, 305
Shelest, Petro, 229
Shipping, 30, 39, 47, 99–100, 104, 105
Ships and boats
    boats, 103, 104, 140, 147
    canoes, 103, 140, 252, 254
    shipbuilding, 30, 39, 62, 74
    ships, 99–100, 104, 140, 147, 211,
        254, 263
    steamships, 39–40, 47
    steel ships, 39
    warships, 12, 84, 93–94, 378
    wind-driven ships, 39, 100, 238, 259,
        378
Siberia, 210, 218
Sikorsky, Igor, 214
Silver, 261, 264, 278, 281, 288, 441
Singapore, 83, 330, 344
Sinhalese, 339, 349
Sioux, 296, 315, 316, 326
Sitting Bull, 315
Slavery, 12–13, 23, 53, 77, 79, 83, 91,
    109–112, 153–164, 190–191, 192,
    276, 289, 300, 319, 331–332, 339,
    352, 355
    abolition, 80, 332, 356

characteristics of societies victimized,
        191, 355
decline, 13–14, 112
economics, 167–168
emancipation, 112, 167
enslavement, 4–5, 12, 13, 109, 110,
        133, 155, 190, 191, 192, 260, 263,
        268, 276, 303, 355–356, 357, 358
Islamic countries, 153–157
Jews, 191
mortality rates, 153, 154–155, 158, 160
nominal slaves, 161, 163
occupations, 109, 110, 153, 154, 155,
        158, 162
sex, 112, 155, 156, 260, 268
slave trade, 85, 91–95, 109–110, 112,
        122, 141, 153–156, 158, 160,
        189–190, 191, 271, 276
treatment of slaves, 63, 154, 155–156,
        157, 160
Slavic languages, 183, 345–346
Slavs, x, 7, 9, 18, 19, 174–248, 256, 327,
        333
Slovakia and Slovaks, 187, 196, 200, 201,
        202, 203, 241
Smith, Adam, 34, 58
Social mobility, 8, 14, 42, 48, 49, 58, 62,
        125, 137, 188, 240–241, 374
"Society," ix
Solzhenitsyn, Alexandr, 245
South Africa, 14, 82, 83, 84, 99, 116, 117,
        121, 138, 171, 206, 331, 348, 368
South America, 165, 205, 239, 250, 251,
        254, 256, 257, 258, 262, 263,
        265–289, 320, 324, 375
Southeast Asia, x, 5, 17, 119, 191, 216,
        242, 330, 334, 343, 345, 346
Soviet Union, 14, 19, 202, 205–241, 243,
        244–246, 247, 248, 331, 352
    First Secretaries, 221–222
    Second Secretaries, 221–222
Sowell, Mary, xiv
Spain and Spaniards, 4, 10, 12, 17, 39, 70,
        82, 119, 157, 162, 178, 190, 242,

249, 250, 258, 259, 260, 261, 262,
        263, 264, 265, 268–273, 275,
        277–281, 283, 284–289, 290–291,
        297, 299, 320, 328 331, 334, 338,
        339, 346, 350, 376, 378
Sri Lanka, 8, 91, 345, 349, 350
Stalin, Josef V., 215–216, 219, 221, 222,
        227, 231, 232, 352
Standard of living, 4, 25–26, 27, 40–41,
        47, 52, 60, 65, 66, 79, 108, 118,
        198, 207, 217, 235–236, 237, 261,
        330–331, 342, 348
Statistical disparities, 43, 124, 125, 168,
        221–222
Steam engine, 32, 36, 39, 58, 378
Steel (*see* Iron and steel)
Stereotypes
Stigler, George J., xiv
Stuarts, 56, 89
Sudan and Sudanese, 100, 109, 110, 112,
        115, 154
Suez Canal, 231
Sugar, 7, 261, 264
Susquehannock, 301, 304
Swahili, 135, 138
Swahilis, 109, 119
Sweden and Swedes, 40, 141, 180, 211, 215
Switzerland, 39, 348

Tajikistan and Tajiks, 217, 231, 234, 235
Tamils, 8, 339, 349
Tanzania, 100, 109, 116, 132–140, 150,
        173
Tatars, 219, 220, 230, 244
Tashkent, 232, 233
Tea, 39
Technology, 9–10, 32 37, 41, 44, 62, 85,
        170, 208, 233, 247, 250, 254, 324,
        346, 360–361
    backwardness, 13, 179, 205, 208, 209,
        211, 212, 334, 345, 353, 375
    diffusion, 32, 37–38, 40, 43, 67, 204,
        208, 209, 210–216, 217, 245–246,
        306, 333, 345, 361

Teller, Edward, 205

Tenochtilán, 249, 274, 275, 278, 279, 281, 290

Tepanecs, 274

Third World, 84, 87, 150, 170, 235, 333, 337, 340, 349, 350, 357

Tikal, 268, 290

Tito, Josip Broz, 204

Tokyo, 59, 236

Tocqueville, Alexis de, 79

Toltec, 267

Toynbee, Arnold, 377

Transportation costs, 11–12, 34–35, 36, 38, 39, 97, 101, 102, 103, 105, 106, 134, 140, 176, 207, 208, 231, 314, 352

Transylvania, 182, 185

Treaties (see Government, treaties)

Trilogy, xii, 329, 334, 335, 348, 368, 371

Turkey and Turks (see also Ottoman Empire), 10, 15, 176, 181, 185, 187, 190, 216, 225, 230, 235

Turkmenistan and Turkmenians, 223, 224, 231, 234, 235

Tuscaroras, 301, 302, 305

Tutsi, 4, 120, 121

Uganda, 38, 119,120, 129, 133, 173, 351

Ukraine and Ukrainians, 174, 177, 183, 186, 197, 198, 210, 216, 219, 220, 221, 222, 223, 224–230, 235, 236, 238, 244, 245

Uncle Tom's Cabin, 80, 157

Unemployment, 50, 61, 66, 350

Union of Soviet Socialist Republics (see Soviet Union)

United States of America, 7, 11, 37, 40, 43, 44, 63, 65, 67, 69, 70, 75–82, 84, 91, 96, 97, 98, 99, 108, 117, 120, 121, 129, 133, 134, 135, 151, 157, 158, 159, 160, 161, 162, 163–166, 168, 170, 173, 178, 205, 211, 212, 215, 223, 238, 239, 240, 241, 245, 252, 256, 258–259, 270,

290, 297, 298, 299–300, 310, 324, 318, 321, 324, 325, 327, 330, 332, 333, 335, 337, 338, 339, 344, 348, 349, 354, 361, 363, 365, 366, 370, 377

Bureau of Indian Affairs, 317, 319

Constitution, 90, 91

New England, 79–81

the South, 75–79, 80, 81, 160, 161, 319, 335

U.S. Army, 166, 299, 300, 308, 365

Ural Mountains, 205, 208

Urbanization, 25, 33, 47–48, 53, 55, 61, 68, 102, 122, 124, 140, 179, 180, 182, 184, 185, 200, 201, 209, 217, 218, 218–219, 233, 249–250, 266, 267, 268, 279, 288, 301, 302, 346, 353

Ute Indians, 313

Uzbekistan and Uzbeks, 231, 232, 244, 234, 235, 236

Venezuela, 281, 320, 343

Venice, 10, 27, 191, 194, 378

Violence (see Crime and violence)

Virginia and Virginians, 58, 78, 81, 82, 258, 291, 297

Volga River, 206, 209, 210

Von Neumann, John, 205

Wales and the Welsh, 8, 26, 39, 30, 44–52, 62, 67, 70–71, 72–73, 76, 78, 85, 184, 264, 335, 339

Wampanoag Indians, 292

Wampum, 303

War (see Military factors)

Washington, D.C., 164, 167, 317

Washington, George, 171, 309, 310, 365

Watches, 31

Watt, James, 43, 50

Weapons, 9–10, 112, 113, 119, 134, 194, 250, 254, 255, 277, 286, 295–296, 302, 303, 306, 312, 313, 314, 315, 317, 322, 361, 376–377, 377–378

West Indies, 160, 292
Western Civilization, xi, 3, 6, 17, 20, 27,
    28, 41, 52, 90, 95, 123, 157, 167,
    168, 170, 177, 182, 245–246, 324,
    326, 345, 351–352, 359, 379
Western Europe, 4, 6, 20, 23, 27, 42,
    175–186, 192, 194, 195, 199, 204,
    208, 210, 211, 212, 217, 218, 225,
    230, 238, 239, 241, 242, 243, 246,
    253, 264, 327, 333, 344, 345, 353,
    356
Western Hemisphere Indians, 11, 19, 77,
    107, 191, 249–328, 347–348
  Algonquins, 301, 304
  Amazon Indians, 328
  Apaches, 312, 313
  Aztecs, 15, 249, 250, 251–252, 257,
    263, 264, 265, 267, 269, 273–381,
    289, 290, 291, 301, 302, 358, 375
  Blackfoot, 314
  Catawba, 4
  Cayugas, 301, 302
  Cherokees, 256, 290, 301, 304–312,
    324, 325
  Cheynenne, 312, 316
  Chickasaw, 305
  Comanches, 312, 313, 314, 316
  Cree, 295, 296
  Creeks, 305, 329, 340
  Culhua, 274
  Delaware, 26, 158, 179
  Fox, 312
  Hopis, 316
  Hurons, 294, 295, 296, 301, 302
  Iroquois, 251, 252, 258, 260, 295,
    300–304, 375
  Mandans, 314
  Maya, 250, 251, 265–273, 290, 326,
    328
  Micmac, 292
  Mixtecs, 276
  Mohawks, 294, 301, 302, 304
  Mohicans, 302, 304
  Narragansett, 292
  Navajo, 312, 316, 325
  Olmecs, 265, 267
  Oneidas, 301, 302
  Onondagas, 301, 302
  Ottawas, 295
  Powhatans, 297
  Pueblos, 316
  Sac, 312
  Senecas, 301, 302
  Shawnee, 305
  Sioux, 296, 315, 326
  Susquehannock, 301, 304
  Tepanecs, 274
  Toltec, 267
  Tuscaroras, 301, 302, 305
  Ute, 313
  Wampanoag, 292
  Winnebagos, 311, 315
Wheel, 251, 274, 283
Wilberforce, William, 92
William the Conqueror, 89
Wilson, Woodrow, 18, 19
Winnebagos, 311, 315
Witches, 80
Wood, 36–37, 39, 274
Wool, 30, 68–69
Work, 42, 66, 79, 213, 287, 319, 366
World Bank, 133, 145, 149
World War I (*see* First World War)
World War II (*see* Second World War)
Wright, Nancy, xiv

Yorubas, 124, 125, 126, 127, 130, 131
Yucatan peninsula, 266, 268, 270, 277
Yugoslavia, 8, 18, 19, 170, 197, 203–204,
    243, 247

Zaire, 101, 104, 109, 173
Zaire River, 101, 104
Zambezi River, 103
Zambia, 138, 173
Zanzibar, 109, 133, 134, 135–136, 138,
    156
Zulus, 120–121